CW01649584

SOCIAL SECURITY LEGISLATION 2004

VOLUME IV: TAX CREDITS AND EMPLOYER-PAID SOCIAL SECURITY BENEFITS

AUSTRALIA
Law Book Co.
Sydney

CANADA and USA
Carswell
Toronto

HONG KONG
Sweet & Maxwell Asia

NEW ZEALAND
Brookers
Auckland

SINGAPORE and MALAYSIA
Sweet & Maxwell Asia
Singapore and Kuala Lumpur

SOCIAL SECURITY LEGISLATION 2004

General Editor
David Bonner, LL.B, LL.M

VOLUME IV: TAX CREDITS AND EMPLOYER-PAID SOCIAL SECURITY BENEFITS

Commentary By

Nick Wikeley, M.B. (Cantab)
Barrister, Professor of Law, University of Southampton
Deputy Social Security Commissioner, Deputy District Chairman,
Appeals Service

David W. Williams, LL.M., Ph.D., C.T.A.
Solicitor, Social Security and Child Support Commissioner,
Deputy Special Commissioner of Income Tax and
part-time Chairman of VAT and Duties Tribunal

Consultant Editor
Child Poverty Action Group

LONDON
SWEET & MAXWELL
2004

Published in 2004 by
Sweet & Maxwell Limited of
100 Avenue Road, Swiss Cottage,
London NW3 3PF
www.sweetandmaxwell.co.uk
Typeset by Servis Filmsetting Ltd, Manchester
Printed in Great Britain by MPG Books, Bodmin, Cornwall

No natural forests were destroyed to make this product.
Only farmed timber was used and re-planted.

A catalogue record for this book is
available from the British Library

ISBN 0 421 889 209

CHILD POVERTY ACTION GROUP

The Child Poverty Action Group (CPAG) is a charity, founded in 1965, which campaigns for the relief of poverty in the United Kingdom. It has a particular reputation in the field of welfare benefits law derived from its legal work, publications, training and parliamentary and policy work, and is widely recognised as the leading organisation for taking test cases on social security law.

CPAG is therefore ideally placed to act as Consultant Editor to this 4-volume work—**Social Security Legislation 2004**. CPAG is not responsible for the detail of what is contained in each volume, and the authors' views are not necessarily those of CPAG. The Consultant Editor's role is to act in an advisory capacity on the overall structure, focus and direction of the work.

For more information about CPAG, its rights and policy publications or training courses, its address is 94 White Lion Street, London, N1 9PF (telephone: 020 7837 7979—website: *www.cpag.org.uk*).

FOREWORD

As President of the Appeal Tribunals I am happy, once again, to endorse this latest edition of the Social Security Legislation. For many years now my predecessors and I have commended the valuable contribution that these volumes make to administrative decision making generally and, more specifically, the delivery of justice with which our courts and tribunals are concerned. This new edition is no exception.

Once again we have available to us a readily usable source of comprehensive information with expert commentary covering the wide range of law that comes within our jurisdiction. To live is to change and to be perfect is to have changed often, so I am glad to say that in this spirit these volumes continue to grow and develop in a way that makes them indispensable to all those who work in this jurisdiction. I know that bringing cases to our tribunals can be a daunting experience but those doing so should be reassured that our panel members have available to them such a scholarly and expert guide to the complex law and regulations that tribunals are seeking to apply to every day situations. I warmly welcome this new edition.

HH Judge Michael Harris
President of Appeal Tribunals

PREFACE

Tax Credits and Employer-Paid Social Security Benefits is Volume IV of what is now a four volume series: *Social Security Legislation 2004*. The companion volumes are Bonner, Hooker and White, *Volume I: Non Means Tested Benefits*; Wood, Poynter, Wikeley and Bonner, *Volume II: Income Support, Jobseeker's Allowance, State Pension Credit and the Social Fund*; and Rowland and White, *Volume III: Administration, Adjudication and the European Dimension*.

Each of the volumes in the series provides a legislative text, clearly showing the form and date of amendments, and commentary up to date to April 15, 2004.

The Tax Credits Act 2002, introducing Child Tax Credit (CTC) and Working Tax Credit (WTC), represented a radical shift for the benefits system. The new tax credits require appeal tribunals, advisers and other practitioners to get to grips with concepts, in many ways drawn from the income tax system, which are radically different from traditional welfare state principles. As we explained in the Preface to last year's first edition of *Volume IV*, this was the prime reason for the launch of this new book. This volume, designed in the same format as its established companion volumes, covers CTC and WTC along with statutory sick pay (SSP), statutory maternity pay (SMP), statutory paternity pay (SPP) and statutory adoption pay (SAP). The common theme for these last four benefits is that they are all employer-paid social security benefits. But note that this volume is not entitled *Tax Credits and Inland Revenue-administered Social Security Benefits*, as Child Benefit and Guardian's Allowance, now the responsibility of the Revenue, currently remain in *Volume I: Non Means Tested Benefits*.

There have, inevitably, been difficult decisions to take in terms of the scope of this volume. For the convenience of readers this volume includes not just the substantive law relating to CTC and WTC but also the various procedural regulations governing both claimants' responsibilities and the duties of the Revenue and employers in administering claims for these benefits. This volume thus includes, amongst others, the Tax Credits (Claims and Notifications) Regulations 2002, the Working Tax Credit (Payment by Employers) Regulations 2002 and the Tax Credits (Payment by the Board) Regulations 2002. We also include the text of the relevant provisions of the Social Security Act 1998, as modified by the Tax Credits (Appeals) Regulations 2002. However, the principal statutory provisions governing appeals to appeal tribunals and to the Social Security Commissioners will be found in *Volume III* in this series. We also include in this volume relevant provisions from the Income Tax (Earnings and Pensions) Act (ITEPA) 2003.

The new tax credits have yet to generate any significant case law.

However, we have taken the opportunity in this year's second edition of *Volume IV* to bring the statutory text up to date, reflecting the various amendments made by regulations to the scope of WTC and CTC (as well as ironing out some wrinkles identified by some eagle-eyed readers). We have also expanded the commentary on key provisions in the light of the experience to date in hearing tax credits appeals. In addition, given that there has been considerable public interest in the issue of overpayments of tax credits, we have included the text of Inland Revenue Codes of Practice 23 and 26 and the Revenue's leaflet WTC3.

Users of the original three volumes in this series, and their predecessors, have over the years provided valuable comments which have invariably been helpful to the editors in ensuring that the selection of legislative material for inclusion and the commentary upon it reflect the sorts of difficulties encountered in practice. In doing so, readers have thus helped to shape the content of each of the volumes in the current series. We hope that readers will maintain that tradition. Please write to the General Editor of the series, Professor David Bonner, Faculty of Law, University of Leicester, University Road, Leicester, LE1 7RH, who will pass on any comments received to the appropriate commentator.

Our gratitude also goes to the President of the Appeals Service and his staff for continuing the tradition of help and encouragement.

July, 2004

Nick Wikeley
David Williams

NOTE ON FORTHCOMING CHANGES

The Finance Bill 2004, when enacted, will make various minor alterations to the tax provisions in this volume for the tax year starting 6 April 2004, but none central to the operation of tax credits.

The National Insurance Contributions and Statutory Payments Act 2004, when enacted, will further align the administration of national insurance contributions, statutory sick pay and statutory maternity pay with the tax administration regime, especially as regards recovery of debts, inspectors' powers and penalty provisions.

The Tax Credits (Miscellaneous Amendments No 2) Regulations 2004, SI 2004/1241 (amends the Tax Credits (Claims and Notifications) Regulations 2002, regs 21 and 29A, and the Tax Credits (Payment by the Board) Regulations 2002, regulation 3 from 1 May 2004).

The Tax Credits (Residence)(Amendment) Regulations 2004, SI 2004/1243 (amends the Tax Credits (Residence) Regulations 2002, regulation 3 with effect from 1 May 2004).

The Working Tax Credit (Entitlement and Maximum Rate) (Amendment) Regulations 2004, SI 2004/1276 (amends the Working Tax Credit (Entitlement and Maximum Rate) Regulations 2002, regulation 14 with effect from 1 June 2004).

CONTENTS

PART III
STATUTORY SICK PAY

PART IV
STATUTORY MATERNITY PAY

PART V
STATUTORY PATERNITY PAY AND STATUTORY ADOPTION PAY

PART VI
INLAND REVENUE CODES OF PRACTICE AND GUIDANCE

USING THIS BOOK, USING LEGAL AUTHORITY AND FINDING OTHER SOURCES OF INFORMATION

Introduction

This book is not designed as an introduction to, or general textbook on, the law relating to social security. Inevitably some familiarity with the social security system has been assumed. This note is designed to assist readers who are not lawyers—and also those lawyers who are not familiar with this particular field of law—by identifying the sources of social security law and showing how to find them. Volume IV also deals with income tax law, and its version of this section contains additional comments about that.

Primary sources of social security law

Social security law is based on legislation, consisting of *Acts of Parliament*, which are primary legislation and are also known as statutes, and *statutory instruments*, which are secondary or delegated legislation made by ministers acting under powers conferred by primary legislation and are also known as regulations (or, occasionally, orders). Another source of the law lies in *judicial decisions*, made, in this context, principally by Social Security Commissioners who hear appeals from appeal tribunals although some decisions of the courts are also relevant. Such judicial decisions provide authoritative interpretation of the legislation. The precise mixture of the three sources differs from benefit to benefit.

The scope of this book and the status of the commentary

This book contains an up-to-date text of the principal statutes and statutory instruments relevant to the work of appeal tribunals and Commissioners. It also contains a commentary on that legislation, referring to relevant decisions of Commissioners and the courts. The commentary aims to help readers understand the legislation and its implications. The focus in decision-making, however, must remain on the actual words of the legislation as applied by the Commissioners and courts, because the commentary merely reflects the opinion of the commentator.

Finding a particular section in a statute

Statutes consist of numbered sections (sometimes grouped in Parts, which may in turn be divided into Chapters) and they often have schedules at the end.

Suppose you wanted to find section 94 of the Social Security Contributions and Benefits Act 1992. Sometimes the word "section" is abbreviated to "s."; so you could refer to the Social Security Contributions and Benefits Act 1992, s.94.

To find this provision, you can use the contents pages to find where provisions of the Social Security Contributions and Benefits Act 1992 are printed. You can also use the running heads at the top of each page; the header on the left-hand page gives the name of the Act while the header on the right-hand page gives the year and chapter number (abbreviated "c.") as well as the section dealt with on that page. The chapter number simply indicates the order in the Parliamentary year of the statute; the Social Security Contributions and Benefits Act 1992 is chapter 4, meaning that it was the fourth statute to be passed by Parliament in 1992.

After the text of the section comes a note of the AMENDMENTS made to the provision, reference to relevant DEFINITIONS, and the commentary, which appears under the heading GENERAL NOTE. Where the section is re-enacted in consolidating legislation, that is, legislation drawing together all the amendments over time in a new statute, the DERIVATION, or source, of the provision is also given so that you can see where the provision originally appeared. This can be helpful in considering any decisions of Commissioners or the courts on the earlier form of the provision.

Finding a particular regulation

Statutory instruments consist of numbered regulations (or articles where the statutory instrument is in the form of an order rather than being a set of regulations) and, like statutes, they sometimes have schedules at the end.

Suppose you wanted to find regulation 26 of the Social Security (Incapacity for Work) (General) Regulations 1995. Sometimes the word "regulation" is abbreviated to "reg."; so you could refer to the Social Security (Incapacity for Work) (General) Regulations 1995, reg.26.

To find this provision, use the contents pages to find the Social Security (Incapacity for Work) (General) Regulations 1995. Then move forward within the regulations until you find the one you want. Again the running headers at the top of each page will assist you. The header on the right-hand page gives the statutory instrument number, that is the year of publication and the number, as in SI 1995/311, indicating that these regulations were the 311th statutory instrument made by Ministers and approved by Parliament in 1995.

As with statutes, after the text of the regulation comes a note of the AMENDMENTS made to the provision, reference to relevant DEFINITIONS, and the commentary which appears under the heading GENERAL NOTE Where the regulation is re-enacted in consolidating regulations, that is, legislation drawing together all the amendments made over time in a new set of regulations, the DERIVATION or source, of the provision is also given so that you can see where the provision originally appeared. This can be helpful in considering any decisions of Commissioners or the courts on the earlier form of the provision.

Commissioners' decisions

Both reported and unreported decisions of Commissioners are important sources of guidance on the interpretation and application of legislation relating to social security benefits and their administration. Where relevant, these are binding on both decision-makers and on tribunals. The binding nature of Commissioners' decisions is discussed below. A single Commissioner hears most appeals, though the Chief Commissioner does occasionally direct that three Commissioners sitting together should hear cases of special importance. This is then known as a Tribunal of Commissioners.

Reported Decisions

About 40 to 50 decisions a year are selected to be "reported". Selection used to be a decision of the Chief Commissioner acting alone. Later he made his selection on advice from a committee of Commissioners, but, since 2002, selection of decisions to report has been the task of an Editorial committee chaired by the Chief Commissioner. Decisions are selected for reporting only if they are of general importance and command the assent of at least a majority of Commissioners. They are published in biennial bound volumes by The Stationery Office and in looseleaf form (contact Margaret Drummond, Print Solutions, Room B0202, Benton Park Road, Newcastle-upon- Tyne NE98 1YX (tel. 0191 225 5422)) and on the world wide web (*www.dwp.gov.uk/advisers/docs/commdecs/index.asp*) by the Department for Work and Pensions (replacing the DSS). They can also be accessed via the Commissioners' website (*www.osscsc.gov.uk*). These decisions are available in all tribunal venues and can be consulted in offices of the Benefits Agency, and some main libraries.

Reported decisions are renumbered with the initial letter "R" for "reported". *R(IB) 1/00* was the first decision on incapacity benefit to be reported in 2000. A decision of a Tribunal of Commissioners is often identified by adding a letter "T" in brackets after the reference, as in *R(IB) 2/99(T)*. Scottish decisions are not specifically identified as such.

Unreported Decisions

Reported decisions are selected from a greater body of decisions in the cases dealt with by the Commissioners. Those not reported are known as unreported decisions but still have precedential value. Each Commissioner's decision is given a file number in the Office of the Social Security and Child Support Commissioners, which is a unique identification number. From 1997 cases have been registered consecutively by number within a calendar year, without a separate range of numbers for each benefit. Prior to 1995, there was a separate range of numbers for each benefit. So Commissioner's decision *CU 23/1992* is the 23rd case on unemployment benefit registered in 1992. The letters "CU" indicate that the decision is that of a Commissioner (C) and that the benefit in question is unemployment benefit (U). Between 1995 and 1997, there had been a change of approach, reflecting computerisation. The system of numbering consecutively within benefits in a particular year ceased. The lettering system remained the same, but the number after the letters, as in *CU 7328/1995*, indicated that this was the 7328th case on any benefit registered since the beginning of 1995.

Scottish decisions have an "S" after the "C" (*e.g. CSI 26/98*) and, until the Welsh office of the Commissioners was closed, Welsh decisions could be identified as having a "W" after the "C".

Until the end of 2001, some 100 decisions a year were "starred" because it was considered that they raised points of significance or interest and deserved wider circulation. They did not, however, acquire any enhanced precedential status from being starred. The practice of starring was discontinued from the start of 2002. Instead decisions that Commissioners believe should have wider currency are available on the Commissioners' new website (*www.osscsc.gov.uk*). Some decisions are selected as of particular interest and highlighted for a time in the Most Recent Decisions part of the Decisions section of that website. As with "starring", however, a decision does not gain enhanced precedential status through "highlighting".

Other sources of/on Commissioners' decisions

There are a number of other sources of valuable information or commentary on Commissioners' decisions, whether reported or unreported: publications such as the *Journal of Social Security Law*, the *Journal of Social Welfare and Family Law, Legal Action, The Law Society's Gazette*, the *Disability Rights Bulletin* and CPAG's *Welfare Rights Bulletin*. A range of reported and unreported decisions and many valuable updates and comments were also available on the website maintained by Commissioner Howell (*www.hywels.clara.co.uk/commrs/decns.htm*). This website is remaining in existence for the time being (although it has not been updated since April 28, 2002), despite the advent of the Commissioners' new website referred to above. To quote Commissioner Howell, this is "in the hope that the improved arrangements on the official website . . . will prove permanent".

What does it mean to say that a case is binding?

Reference to decisions being binding means that where a similar point is raised in a later case before an adjudicating authority bound by the decision, that adjudicating authority must accept the interpretation of the law contained in the decision. So a Commissioner's decision explaining what a term in a particular regulation means, lays down the definition of that term in much the same way as if the term had been defined in the regulations themselves. The decision may also help in deciding what the same term means when it is used in a different set of regulations, provided that the term appears to have been used in a similar text.

Appeals to the Commissioners are now available only on points of law, but before April 1987 appeals were available on points of fact as well as law. Care should be taken in reading older decisions to appreciate that some were concerned with fact rather than law, though the reported decisions invariably contain points of general application. Relevant decisions of the Commissioners and the courts are explained in the commentary to the statutory provisions in this volume, together with guidance on their significant for decision-making in the tribunals. Users of the book should remember that it is the decision itself which is binding and not the explanation of it in the commentary; that is merely the opinion of the commentator.

Using Commissioners' Decisions: the hierarchy of authority:

Although the Chief Commissioner has directed that, so far as possible, reference should be made to reported decisions only, the legal position is that all decisions of Commissioners are binding on decision-makers and tribunals. Where there is a conflict, a decision of a Tribunal of Commissioners should be preferred to a decision of a single Commissioner and a reported decision should generally be preferred to an unreported decision (*R(I) 12/75(T)*), unless the unreported decision was the later decision and the Commissioner expressly decided not to follow the earlier reported decision (see the Northern Ireland decision, *R 1/00(FC)*). Decisions of Commissioners are not binding on other Commissioners. However, a single Commissioner will always follow a decision of a Tribunal of Commissioners and will generally follow a decision of another single Commissioner (*R(I) 12/ 75(T)*). A Tribunal of Commissioners will generally follow a decision of another such Tribunal but is not bound to do so (*R(U) 4/88(T)*).

There are separate Commissioners in Northern Ireland considering legislation that is often indistinguishable from the legislation in Great Britain. Decisions of Northern Ireland Commissioners are not binding in Great Britain (*R(SB) 1/90(T)*) but are persuasive. Such decisions are included in the decisions published on the website of the Great Britain Commissioners but the selection of decisions to be reported is made by the Chief Commissioner in Northern Ireland. Looseleaf publication by The Stationery Office and on the world wide web by the Department for Social Development (*http://145.229.156.3/NIComDec7899.NSF?Open Database*) is separate from the publication of Great Britain decisions. So was the publication of bound volumes by The Stationery Office until 1999. From 2000, reported Northern Ireland decisions are included in the same bound volumes as reported decisions of Commissioners in Great Britain. References to decisions of Northern Ireland Commissioners can always be distinguished from references to decisions of Commissioners in Great Britain because the former are numbered differently with the letters identifying the type of benefit always being in brackets after the numbers, as in *C12/98(IS)*, which has been reported as *R1/00(IS)*. Unreported decisions of the Northern Ireland Commissioners can be found on the Department for Social development website at http://145.229.156.3/dmaucomdec.nsf?OpenDatabase.

Using Commissioners' Decisions at Tribunals and before the Commissioners

Decision-makers and claimants are entitled to assume that tribunals and Commissioners have immediate access to reported decisions of Commissioners and they need not provide copies, although it may sometimes be helpful to do so. However, where either a decision-maker or a claimant intends to rely on an unreported decision, it will be necessary to provide a copy of the decision to the tribunal or Commissioner. A copy of

28A. Completion of enquiry into personal or trustee return **1.15**
29. Assessment where loss of tax discovered

Relief for excessive assessments

32. Double assessment **1.16**
33. Error or mistake

34. Ordinary time-limit of six years **1.17**
36. Fraudulent or negligent conduct

APPEALS AND OTHER PROCEEDINGS

Proceedings before Commissioners

54. Settling of appeals by agreement **1.18**

105. Evidence in cases of fraud and wilful default **1.19**

MISCELLANEOUS AND SUPPLEMENTAL

112. Loss, destruction or damage to assessments, returns, etc. **1.20**
114. Want of form or errors not to invalidate assessments, etc.

151. Employer's liability **1.107**

152. Period of incapacity for work **1.108**
153. Period of entitlement
154. Qualifying days

155. Limitations on entitlement **1.109**
156. Notification of incapacity for work

1. Paternity leave [*omitted*] **1.483**
2. Statutory paternity pay [*omitted*]*

$$\frac{\pounds 5{,}060}{NI} \times N2$$

the decision should also be provided to the other party before the hearing because otherwise it may be necessary for there to be an adjournment to enable that party to take advice on the significance of the decision.

Decisions of the Courts

Decisions of the superior courts in Great Britain and Northern Ireland on questions of legal principle are almost invariably followed by decision-makers, tribunals and Commissioners, even when they are not strictly binding because the relevant court was in a different part of the United Kingdom or exercised a parallel – but not superior – jurisdiction (see the note to section 14 of the Social Security Act 1998 in Part I of *Vol III: Administration, Appeals and the European Dimension.*)

Decisions of the courts on social security matters are generally included among the reports of Commissioners' decisions. So, for example, *R(I)1/00* contains Commissioner's decisions *CSI 12/98*, the decision of the Court of Session upholding the Commissioner's decision and the decision of the House of Lords in *Chief Adjudication Officer v Faulds*, reversing the decision of the Court of Session. Some of them can also be found in the various series of law reports familiar to lawyers (in particular, in the *Law Reports*, the *Weekly Law Reports*, the *All England Law Reports*, the *Industrial Cases Reports* and the *Family Law Reports*. Decisions of the House of Lords since mid-November 1996 are available on the world wide web (*http://www.parliament.uk/judicial_work/judicial_work5.cfm*). Very recent ones are available there only hours after delivery of their Lordships' opinions. Some Court of Appeal decisions can be obtained on the Court Service website (*http://www.courtservice.gov.uk/judgments/judg_home.htm*). Sweet and Maxwell's online subscription service *Westlaw* is another valuable source (*www.westlaw.co.uk/*) , as is Smith Bernal's *Casetrack* (*www.casetrack.com*) and Butterworth's *Lexis* (*www.lexis.com/*).

European Community Law

The European Community is part of the European Union. European Community Law affecting social security is covered in the third volume in this series: Rowland and White, *Social Security Legislation 2004: Vol.III. Administration, Appeals and the European Dimension.*

The European Union has two courts: the Court of Justice of the European Communities, and the Court of First Instance. Decision-makers, tribunals and Commissioners are under a duty by reason of Article 10 (ex.5) of the EC Treaty to apply decisions of the Luxembourg courts, where relevant to cases before them, in preference to other authorities binding on them.

Decisions of the Court of Justice of the European Communities come in two parts: the Opinion of the Advocate General and the decision of the Court. It is the decision of the Court which is binding. The Court is assisted by hearing the Opinion of the Advocate General before itself coming to a conclusion on the issue before it. The Court does not always follow its Advocate General. Where it does, the Opinion of the Advocate General often elaborates the arguments in greater detail than the single collegiate judgment of the Court. No dissenting judgments appear in reports from the Court of Justice.

Decisions of the Luxembourg courts are available on the world wide web at *www.curia.eu.int/*.

The European Convention on Human Rights, the Strasbourg Court and the Human Rights Act 1998

The Court of Human Rights in Strasbourg is quite separate from the Luxembourg courts and serves a different purpose: interpreting and applying the European Convention on Human Rights, which is incorporated into United Kingdom law by the Human Rights Act 1998. From October 2, 2000, public authorities, including courts, Commissioners, tribunals and decision-makers (the Secretary of State) must act in accordance with the incorporated provisions of the Convention, unless statute prevents this. They must take into account the Strasbourg case law. They are required to interpret legislation, so far as is possible to do so, to give effect to the incorporated Convention rights. Any court or tribunal may declare secondary legislation incompatible with those rights and, in certain circumstances, invalidate it. Only the higher courts can declare a provision of primary legislation to be incompatible with those rights, but no court or tribunal can invalidate primary legislation.

The work of the Court and the impact of the Human Rights Act 1998 on social security are discussed in the third volume in this series: Rowland and White, *Social Security Legislation 2004: Vol.III: Administration, Appeals and the European Dimension.*

Judgments of the Court of Human Rights are made by majority, and separate concurring or dissenting judgments are included with the decision of the majority where the Court is not unanimous.

Decisions of the Court of Human Rights are available on the world wide web at *www.echr.coe.int/*.

Official guidance on Social Security Law

The law has been translated into a more civil servant friendly format. Prior to the decision-making and appeals changes made by the Social Security Act 1998, guidance on benefits and their administration was set out in the thirteen volume *Adjudication Officers Guide (AOG)* published by The Stationery Office. This has now been replaced by a fourteen volume *Decision Makers Guide (DMG)*. This is available on the world wide web at *http://www.dwp.gov.uk/publications/dwp/dmg/index.asp*.

The coverage of the DMG is as follows:

Volume 1	Decision Makingtd and Appeals
Volume 2	International Subjects
Volume 3	Subjects Common to all Benefits
Volume 4	Jobseeker's Allowance and Income Support
Volume 5	Jobseeker's Allowance and Income Support
Volume 6	Jobseeker's Allowance and Income Support

Volume 7	Jobseeker's Allowance and Income Support
Volume 8	No longer issued
Volume 9	No longer issued
Volume 10	Benefits for Incapacity, Disability and Maternity
Volume 11	Industrial Injuries Benefits
Volume 12	Widow's Benefit and Retirement Pension
Volume 13	State Pension Credit
Volume 14	State Pension Credit

It should be noted that the DMG is not binding on tribunals and Commissioners; it is internal guidance for the use of decision-makers within the Department.

Child Benefit and Guardian's Allowance are now administered by the Inland Revenue. A range of useful material can be found on its website at www.inlandrevenue.gov.uk/practitioners/index.shtml.

Unofficial guidance on Social Security Law

There are a large number of guides. CPAG's *Welfare Benefits Handbook*, published annually each spring, is unrivalled as a practical and comprehensive introduction from the claimant's viewpoint.

TABLE OF CASES

TABLE OF SOCIAL SECURITY COMMISSIONERS' DECISIONS

TABLE OF STATUTES

TABLE OF STATUTORY INSTRUMENTS

TABLE OF EUROPEAN DIRECTIVES

TABLE OF EUROPEAN REGULATIONS

TABLE OF EUROPEAN AND INTERNATIONAL CONVENTIONS AND TREATIES

TABLE OF ABBREVIATIONS USED IN THIS SERIES

AA	Attendance Allowance
ADHD	Attention Deficit Hyperactivity Disorder
Adjudication Regulations	Social Security (Adjudication) Regulations 1986
All E.R.	All England Law Reports (Butterworths)
AO	Adjudication Officer
AOG	HMSO, *Adjudication Officers Guide*
Attendance Allowance Regulations	Social Security (Attendance Allowance) Regulations 1991
BAMS	Benefits Agency Medical Service
Blue Books	HMSO, *The Law Relation to Social Security*, Vols. 1–11
CAO	Chief Adjudication Officer
CBA 1975	Child Benefit Act 1975
CCA 2001	Capital Allowance Act 2001
CP	Carer Premium
CPAG	Child Poverty Action Group
CPR	Civil Procedure Rules
CRU	Compensation Recovery Unit
CSA 1995	Child Support Act 1995
CS(NI)O 1995	Child Support (Northern Ireland) Order 1995
CSO	Child Support Officer
CSPSSA	Child Support, Pensions and Social Security Act 2000
CTC	Child Tax Credit
Claims and Payments Regulations 1979	Social Security (Claims and Payments) Regulations 1979
Claims and Payments Regulations 1987	Social Security (Claims and Payments) Regulations 1987
C.M.L.R.	Common Market Law Reports
Commissioners Procedure Regulations	Social Security Commissioners (Procedure) Regulations 1999
Computation of Earnings Regulations 1978	Social Security Benefit (Computation of Earnings) Regulations 1978
Computation of Earnings Regulations 1996	Social Security Benefit (Computation of Earnings) Regulations 1996
DAT	Disability Appeals Tribunal

DCP	Disabled Child Premium
Decisions and Appeals Regulations 1999	Social Security and Child Support (Decision and Appeals) Regulations 1999
Dependency Regulations	Social Security Benefit (Dependency) Regulations 1977
DLA	Disability Living Allowance
DLADWAA 1991	Disability Living Allowance and Disability Allowance (Consequential Provisions) Regulations 1991
DM	Decision Maker
DMA	Decision-making and Appeals
DMG	HMSO, *Decision-Makers Guide*
DMP	Delegated Medical Practitioner
Disability Working Allowance Regulations	Disability Working Allowance (General) Regulations 1991
DPTC	Disabled Persons Tax Credit
DSS	Department of Social Security
DWA	Disability Working Allowance
E.C.R.	European Court Reports
ECHR	European Court of Human Rights
EEA	European Economic Area
E.H.R.R.	European Human Rights Reports
EMA	Education Maintenance Allowance
EMO	Examining Medical Officer
EMP	Examining Medical Practitioner
ERA	Evoked Response Audiometry
ERA 1996	Employers Rights Act 1996
ER(NI)O 1996	Employers Rights (Northern Ireland) Order 1996
Eur.L.Rev.	European Law Review
FA	Finance Act
Family Credit Regulations	Family Credit (General) Regulations 1987
FIS	Family Income Supplement
G.P.	General Practitioner
GRP	Graduated Retirement Pension
GA Regulations	Social Security (Guardian's Allowance) Regulations 1975
General Benefit Regulations	Social Security (General Benefit) Regulations 1982
HASSASSA	Health and Social Services and Social Security Adjudication Act 1983
HNCIP	(Housewives) Non-Contributory Invalidity Pension

Hospital In-Patients Regulations	Social Security (Hospital In-Patients) Regulations 1975
HPP	Higher Pensioner Premium
HRA 1998	Human Rights Act 1998
Income Support Regulations	Income Support (General) Regulations 1987
IB Regulations	Social Security (Incapacity Benefit) Regulations 1994
IBS	Irritable Bowel Syndrome
ICA	Invalid Care Allowance
ICTA	Income and Corporation Taxes Act
IIAC	Industrial Injuries Advisory Council
I.L.J.	Industrial Law Journal
IRRA	Inland Revenue Act 1890
ITEPA 2003	Income Tax (Earnings and Pensions) Act 2003
ITS	Independent Tribunal Service
IWA	Social Security (Incapacity for Work) Act 1994
IW (General) Regulations	Social Security (Incapacity for Work) (General) Regulations 1995
IW (Transitional) Regulations	Social Security (Incapacity for Work) (Transitional) Regulations 1995
Invalid Care Allowance Regulations	Social Security (Invalid Care Allowance) Regulations 1976
JSA	Jobseeker's Allowance
JSA 1995	Jobseekers Act 1995
JS(NI)O 1995	Jobseekers (Northern Ireland) Act 1995
JSA Regulations	Jobseeker's Allowance Regulations 1996
JSA (Transitional) Regulations	Jobseeker's Allowance (Transitional) Regulations 1996
J.S.W.L.	Journal of Social Welfare Law
J.S.W.F.L.	Journal of Social Welfare and Family Law
J.S.S.L.	Journal of Social Security Law
LEL	Lower Earnings Limit
MA	Maternity Allowance
MAT	Medical Appeal Tribunal
Maternity Benefit Regulations	Social Security (Maternity Benefit) Regulations 1975
Medical Evidence Regulations	Social Security (Medical Evidence) Regulations 1976
NCIP	Non-Contributory Invalidity Pension
NI	National Insurance
OPA 1973	Overseas Pensions Act 1973
OPB	One Parent Benefit

OPSSAT	Office of the President of the Social Security Appeals Tribunal
Ogus, Barendt and Wikeley	A. Ogus, E. Barendt and N. Wikeley, *The Law of Social Security* (4th ed., Butterworths, 1995)
Overlapping Benefits Regulations	Social Security (Overlapping Benefits) Regulations 1979
Overpayments Regulations	Social Security (Payments on account, Overpayments and Recovery) Regulations
PAYE	Pay as You Earn
P.D.	Practice Direction
PD	Prescribed Disease
PIE	Period of Interruption of Employment
PIW	Period of Incapacity for Work
Persons Abroad Regulations	Social Security Benefit (Persons Abroad) Regulations 1975
Persons Residing Together Regulations	Social Security Benefit (Persons Residing Together) Regulations 1977
Prescribed Diseases Regulations	Social Security (Industrial Injuries) (Prescribed Diseases) Regulations 1985
PTA	Pure Tone Audiometry
Recoupment Regulations	Social Security (Recoupment) Regulations 1990
REA	Reduced Earnings Allowance
RMO	Regional Medical Officer
RSI	Repetitive Strain Injury
SAP	Statutory Adoption Pay
SDA	Severe Disablement Allowance
SDP	Severe Disability Premium
Severe Disablement Allowance Regulations	Social Security (Severe Disablement Allowance) Regulations 1984
SMP	Statutory Maternity Pay
SPCA 2002	State Pension Credit Act 2002
SPCA(NI) 2002	State Pension Credit Act (Northern Ireland) 2002
SPP	Statutory Paternity Pay
SSA 1975	Social Security Act 1975
SSA 1980	Social Security Act 1980
SSA 1981	Social Security Act 1981
SSA 1985	Social Security Act 1985
SSA 1986	Social Security Act 1986
SSA 1988	Social Security Act 1988
SSA 1989	Social Security Act 1989
SSA 1998	Social Security Act 1998
SS (No.2) A 1980	Social Security (No.2) Act 1980

SSAA 1992	Social Security Administration Act 1992*
SSAC	Social Security Advisory Committee
SSAT	Social Security Appeal Tribunal
SSCBA 1992	Social Security Contributions and Benefits Act 1992*
SSCB(NI) 1992	Social Security Contributions and Benefits (Northern Ireland) Act 1992
SSHBA	Social Security and Housing Benefits Act 1982
SS (MP) A 1977	Social Security (Miscellaneous Provisions) Act 1977
SSP	Statutory Sick Pay
SSPA 1975	Social Security Pensions Act 1975
SSCBA 1992	Social Security Contributions and Benefits Act 1992*
SSAA 1992	Social Security Administration Act 1992*
SS(CP)A 1992	Social Security (Consequential Provisions) Act 1992
STC	Simon's Tax Cases
TC	Tax Cases
TCA 1999	Tax Credits Act 1999
TCA 2002	Tax Credits Act 2002
TCGA 1992	Taxation of Chargeable Gains Act 1992
TCTM	Tax Credits Technical Manual
TMA 1970	Taxes Management Act 1970
USI Regulations	Social Security (Unemployment, Sickness and Invalidity Benefit) Regulations 1983
VERA 1992	Vehicle Excise and Registration Act 1992
WFTC	Working Family Tax Credit
White Paper	Jobseeker's Allowance, Cm.2687 (October 1994)
Widow's Benefit and Retirement Pension Regulations	Social Security (Widow's Benefit and Retirement Pensions) Regulations 1979
Wikeley, Annotations	N. Wikeley, "Annotations to Jobseekers Act 1995 (c.18)" in *Current Law Statutes Annotated* (1995)
Wikeley, Ogus and Barendt	Wikeley, Ogus and Barendt *The Law of Social Security* (5th ed., Butterworths, 2002)
W.L.R.	Weekly Law Reports
Workmen's Compensation Acts	Workmen's Compensation Acts 1925 to 1945
WRPA 1999	Welfare Reform and Pensions Act 1999
WRP(NI)O 1999	Welfare Reform and Pensions (Northern Ireland) Order 1999
WTC	Working Tax Credit

*Where the context makes it seem more appropriate these could also be referred to as Contributions and Benefits Act 1992, Administration Act 1992

CHANGE OF NAME FROM DEPARTMENT OF SOCIAL SECURITY TO DEPARTMENT FOR WORK AND PENSIONS

The Secretaries of State for Education and Skills and for Work and Pensions Order 2002 (SI 2002/1397) makes provision for the change of name from the Department of Social Security to Department for Work and Pensions. Article 9(5) provides:

> "(5) Subject to article 12 [which makes specific amendments], any enactment or instrument passed or made before the coming into force of this Order shall have effect, so far as may be necessary for the purposes of or in consequence of the entrusting to the Secretary of State for Work and Pensions of the social security functions, as if any reference to the Secretary of State for Social Security, to the Department of Social Security or to an officer of the Secretary of State for Social Security (including any reference which is to be construed as such a reference) were a reference to the Secretary of State for Work and Pensions, to the Department for Work and Pensions or, as the case may be, to an officer of the Secretary of State for Work and Pensions."

PART I

THE INLAND REVENUE
TAX CREDITS AND SOCIAL SECURITY

Inland Revenue Regulation Act 1890

(53 & 54 Vict. c.21)

Arrangement of Selected Sections

Introduction and General Note

The Inland Revenue, as it is commonly known, is a separate major United Kingdom government department but, unlike most central government departments, it has no Secretary of State or minister at its head. Instead, under this Act, it is established with a Board of Inland Revenue comprised of Commissioners and charged under this and other legislation with the care and management of inland revenue. The TCA 1999 extended that charge to include the working families' tax credit and disabled person's tax credit. The TCA 2002 extends the remit of the Inland Revenue further by providing that WTC and CTC are in the charge of the Inland Revenue, and also transferring child benefit and guardian's allowance to it. 1.02

As part of the transfer of functions to the Inland Revenue from the former Department of Social Security, powers also have to be brought back from the devolved Northern Ireland ministries. The TCA 1999 and now the TCA 2002 therefore contain provisions to transfer functions, premises, and officers from the Northern Ireland government to the Home Civil Service and Inland Revenue. The TCA 2002, s.64 contains provisions amending the Northern Ireland Act 1998 for this purpose.

Section 1 of the Inland Revenue Regulation Act (IRRA) 1890 empowers Her Majesty to appoint individual Commissioners, who are known as Commissioners of Inland Revenue. They are separate from, but often confused with, the Commissioners for the General and the Special Purposes of Income Tax (the tax appeal Commissioners) appointed under the TMA 1970.

Two or more Commissioners of Inland Revenue may, under s.2, constitute the Board of Inland Revenue. Powers are usually given to the Board rather than individual Commissioners, and this is the pattern followed by the TCA 2002. In addition, the Board may, under s.4, appoint officers and may, under s.4A, delegate their functions to their officers. These provisions are necessary because the Inland Revenue, being a creature of statute, does not exercise any prerogative powers or have any inherent powers of delegation as does a Secretary of State.

Section 2 of the TCA 2002, repeating provisions also in the TCA 1999, adopts and adapts the IRRA 1890 to ensure that tax credits are brought fully within the statutory framework by which the Inland Revenue operates.

The other provisions repeated here are those that set the key institutional and statutory framework within which the Board of Inland Revenue and its officers work.

The government announced in March 2004 that the Inland Revenue would be merged with her Majesty's Commissioners of Customs and Excise to form a single tax authority. Details of this, which will require legislation to replace this Act, have not yet been announced.

Commissioners and Officers

Appointment of Commissioners

1.03 **1.**—(1) It shall be lawful for Her Majesty the Queen to appoint persons to be Commissioners for the collection and management of inland revenue and the Commissioners shall hold office during Her Majesty's pleasure.

(2) The Commissioners shall have all necessary powers for carrying into execution every Act of Parliament relating to Inland Revenue, and shall in the exercise of their duty be subject to the authority, discretion, and control of the Treasury, and shall obey all orders and instructions which had been or may be issued to them in that behalf by the Treasury.

Quorum of Commissioners

1.04 **2.**—The Commissioners may act by any two or more of their number, and by that number shall constitute a board of commissioners, and may do and order and direct and permit to be done throughout the United Kingdom or in any part thereof all acts, matters, and things relating to Inland Revenue:

Provided that where by any Act of Parliament or otherwise anything has been or is hereafter expressly directed or authorised to be done by one of the Commissioners, it shall be valid if done by one Commissioner.

Offices

1.05 **3.**—The Commissioners shall have their chief office in London and shall also keep offices in such other places as they deem necessary, and those offices shall be kept open on the prescribed days and during the prescribed hours.

Appointment of collectors, officers, and other persons

1.06 **4.**—(1) The Commissioners shall, unless the Treasury otherwise direct, appoint such collectors, officers, and other persons for collecting, receiving, managing, and accounting for Inland Revenue as are not required by law to be appointed by any other authority.

(2) All such appointments shall continue in force notwithstanding the death of any Commissioner, or his ceasing to hold office, and the persons holding the same shall have full power to execute the duties of their respective offices and to enforce, in the execution thereof, all laws, regulations, penalties and forfeitures relating to Inland Revenue in every part of the United Kingdom.

(3) The Commissioners may suspend, reduce, discharge, or restore as they see cause, any such collector, officer or person.

(4) Where a collector, officer, or person is authorised to receive or collect or have in his custody or possession any money arising from Inland Revenue, the Commissioners may require him to give security to their satisfaction.

Exercise of functions of Commissioners

4A.—Any function conferred by or under any enactment, including any future enactment, on the Commissioners may be exercised by any officer of the Commissioners acting under their authority: **1.07**

Provided that this section shall not apply to the making of any statutory instrument.

Obstruction of Officers

11.—If any person by himself or by any person in his employ obstructs, molests, or hinders— **1.08**

(a) an officer or any person employed in relation to Inland Revenue in the execution of his duty, or of any of the powers or authorities by law given to the officer or person; or

(b) any person acting in the aid of an officer or any person so employed;

he shall for every such offence incur a fine of level 3 of the standard scale.

Commissioners to keep accounts

13.—(1) The Commissioners shall collect and cause to be collected every part of Inland Revenue, and all money under their care and management, and shall keep distinct accounts thereof at their chief office. **1.09**

(2) There shall be set forth in such accounts the amounts respectively charged, collected, and received, and remaining in arrear of each part of Inland Revenue and of the several payments made or allowed by the Commissioners in respect of each such part and of the expenses of collection and management of the said revenue, and of all other payments and expenses made or incurred on any other account whatsoever.

Rules as to evidence in certain cases

24.—(1) All regulations, minutes, and notices purporting to be signed by a secretary or assistant secretary of the Commissioners and by their order shall, until the contrary is proved, be deemed to have been so signed and to have been made and issued by the Commissioners, and may be proved by the production of a copy thereof purporting to have been so signed. **1.10**

(2) In any proceeding the letter or instructions under which a collector or officer or person employed in relation to Inland Revenue has acted shall be sufficient evidence of any order issued by the Treasury or by the Commissioners, and mentioned or referred to therein.

(3) Evidence of a person being reputed to be or having acted as a Commissioner, or collector, or officer, or person employed in relation to inland revenue, shall, unless the contrary is proved, be sufficient evidence of his appointment or authority to act as such.

(4) Any notice or other document purporting to be issued in exercise of any function conferred on the Commissioners shall, until the contrary is proved, be deemed to be so issued.

Definitions

1.11 **39.**—In this Act, unless the context otherwise requires—
"Inland Revenue" means the revenue of the United Kingdom collected or imposed as stamp duties, taxes . . . . . and placed under the care and management of the Commissioners, and any part thereof;
"Commissioner" means Commissioner of Inland Revenue;
"Collector" means Collector of Inland Revenue;
"Officer" means Officer of Inland Revenue.

Taxes Management Act 1970

(1970 c.9)

ARRANGEMENT OF SELECTED SECTIONS

PART I

ADMINISTRATION

PART II

RETURNS OF INCOME AND GAINS

Income tax

Records

(1970 c.9)

Interpretation

118. Interpretation

INTRODUCTION AND GENERAL NOTE

1.21 The TMA 1970 was a consolidation measure, but it has been extensively and repeatedly amended since 1970. Only two sections apply directly to tax credits: s.1 (read to include tax credits) and s.54. For the express application of s.54, see Tax Credits (Appeals) Regulations 2002, reg.3. But TCA 2002 refers to several other sections. Set out below are the key sections of the TMA 1970 that apply for the purposes of the income tax assessments, alongside which tax credit calculations will be made in most cases.

In addition, the selection includes other provisions setting out the power of the Inland Revenue to investigate and deal with income tax assessments, the scope for a taxpayer to amend a self-assessment or request an amendment of an assessment, and formal sections dealing with evidence and documentation.

As s.1 indicates, this Act also deals with assessments and administration of capital gains tax and corporation tax, but all provisions relating only to those taxes have been excluded from this selection, as have provisions dealing with other taxes or past taxes.

PART I

ADMINISTRATION

Taxes under care and management of the Board

1.22 **1.**—(1) Income tax, corporation tax . . . and capital gains tax shall be under the care and management of the Commissioners of Inland Revenue (in this Act referred to as "the Board"), and the definition of "Inland Revenue" in section 39 of the Inland Revenue Regulation Act 1890 shall have effect accordingly.

(2) The Board shall appoint inspectors and collectors of taxes who shall act under the direction of the Board.

(2A) The Board may appoint a person to be an inspector or collector for general or for such specific purposes as the Board think fit.

(2B) Where in accordance with the Board's administrative practices a person is authorised to act as an inspector or collector for specific purposes, he shall be deemed to have been appointed to be an inspector or collector for those purposes.

(3) Any legal proceedings or administrative act relating to any tax begun by one inspector or collector may be continued by another inspector or, as the case may be, another collector; and any inspector or collector may act for any division or other area.

Declarations on taking office

1.23 **6.**—(1) Every person who is appointed to be—

(a) a General Commissioner or a Special Commissioner . . .

shall make a declaration in the form set out in Part I of Schedule 1 to this Act before another person holding the same office, or before a General Commissioner.

(2) Every person who is appointed to be a clerk or assistant clerk to the General Commissioners for any division, or who assists any such clerk, shall make a declaration in the form set out in Part I of Schedule 1 to this Act. A clerk or assistant clerk shall make the declaration before a General Commissioner for the division, and a person who assists any such clerk shall make the declaration before such a General Commissioner or the clerk.

(3) Every person who is appointed to be a member of the Board shall make a declaration in the form set out in Part II of Schedule 1 to this Act before another member of the Board.

(4) Every person who is appointed an inspector or collector, or who is appointed by the Board to serve in any other capacity, shall make a declaration in the form set out in Part III of Schedule 1 to this Act before such person as the Board may direct.

(5) A declaration under this section shall be made as soon as may be after first appointment to the office in question.

PART II

RETURNS OF INCOME AND GAINS

Income tax

Personal return

8.—(1) For the purpose of establishing the amounts in which a person is chargeable to income tax and capital gains tax for a year of assessment, . . . he may be required by a notice given to him by an officer of the Board— 1.24

(a) to make and deliver to the officer, on or before the day mentioned in subsection (1A) below, a return containing such information as may reasonably be required in pursuance of the notice, and

(b) to deliver with the return such accounts, statements and documents, relating to information contained in the return, as may reasonably be so required.

(1A) The day referred to in subsection (1) above is—

(a) the 31st January next following the year of assessment, or

(b) where the notice under this section is given after the 31st October next following the year, the last day of the period of three months beginning with the day on which the notice is given.

(1AA) For the purposes of subsection (1) above—

(a) the amounts in which a person is chargeable to income tax and capital gains tax are net amounts, that is to say, amounts which take into account any relief or allowance a claim for which is included in the return; and

(b) the amount payable by a person by way of income tax is the difference between the amount in which he is chargeable to income tax and the aggregate amount of any income tax deducted at source and any tax credits to which section 231 of the principal Act applies.

(1B) In the case of a person who carries on a trade, profession, or business in partnership with one or more other persons, a return under this section shall include each amount which, in any relevant statement, is stated to be equal to his share of any income, loss, tax, credit or charge for the period in respect of which the statement is made.

(1C) In subsection (1B) above "relevant statement" means a statement which, as respects the partnership, falls to be made under section 12AB of this Act for a period which includes, or includes any part of, the year of assessment or its basis period.

(2) Every return under this section shall include a declaration by the person making the return to the effect that the return is to the best of his knowledge correct and complete.

(3) A notice under this section may require different information, accounts and statements for different periods or in relation to different descriptions of source of income.

(4) Notices under this section may require different information, accounts and statements in relation to different descriptions of person.

(5) In this section and sections 8A, 9 and 12AA of this Act, any reference to income tax deducted at source is a reference to income tax deducted or treated as deducted from any income or treated as paid on any income.

Returns to include self-assessment

1.25 **9.**—(1) Subject to subsections (1A) and (2) below, every return under section 8 or 8A of this Act shall include a self-assessment, that is to say—

(a) an assessment of the amounts in which, on the basis of the information contained in the return and taking into account any relief or allowance a claim for which is included in the return, the person making the return is chargeable to income tax and capital gains tax for the year of assessment; and

(b) an assessment of the amount payable by him by way of income tax, that is to say, the difference between the amount in which he is assessedto income tax under paragraph (a) above and the aggregate amount of any income tax deducted at source and any tax credits to which section 231 of the principal Act applies

but nothing in this subsection shall enable a self-assessment to show as repayable any income tax treated as deducted or paid by virtue of sections 233(1), 246D(1), 249(4), 421(1), 547(5) of the principal Act or section 626 of ITEPA.

(1A) The tax to be assessed on a person by a self-assessment shall not include any tax which, under Chapter I or IV of Part XIV of the principal Act or under section 394(2) of ITEPA 2003, is charged on the administrator of a scheme (within the meaning of section 658A of that Act) and is assessable by the Board in accordance with that section.

(2) A person shall not be required to comply with subsection (1) above if he makes and delivers his return for a year of assessment—

(a) on or before the 30th September next following the year; or

(b) where the notice under section 8 or 8A of this Act is given after the 31st July next following the year, within the period of two months beginning with the day on which the notice is given.

(3) Where, in making and delivering a return, a person does not comply with subsection (1) above, an officer of the Board shall, if subsection (2) above applies, and may in any other case—

(a) make the assessment on his behalf on the basis of the information contained in the return; and

(b) send him a copy of the assessment so made;

and references . . . in this Act to a person's self-assessment include references to an assessment made on a person's behalf under this subsection.

(3A) An assessment under subsection (3) above is treated for the purposes of this Act as a self-assessment and as included in the return.

(4) Subject to subsection (5) below—

(a) at any time before the end of the period of nine months beginning with the day on which a person's return is delivered, an officer of the Board may by notice to that person so amend that person's self-assessment as to correct any obvious errors or mistakes in the return (whether errors of principle, arithmetical mistakes or otherwise); and

(b) at any time before the end of the period of twelve months beginning with the filing date, a person may by notice to an officer of the Board so amend his self-assessment as to give effect to any amendments to his return which he has notified to such an officer.

(5) No amendment of a self-assessment may be made under subsection (4) above at any time during the period—

(a) beginning with the day on which an officer of the Board gives notice of his intention to enquire into the return; and

(b) ending with the day on which the officer's enquiries into the return are completed.

(6) In this section and section 9A of this Act "the filing date" means the day mentioned in section 8(1A) or, as the case may be, section 8A(1A) of this Act.

Amendment of personal or trustee return by taxpayer

9ZA.—(1) A person may amend his return under section 8 or 8A of this Act by notice to an officer of the Board. 1.26

(2) An amendment may not be made more than 12 months after the filing date.

(3) In this section "the filing date" means the day mentioned in section 8(1A) or, as the case may be, section 8A(1A) of this Act.

Correction of personal or trustee return by Revenue

9ZB.—(1) An officer of the Board may amend a return under section 8 or 8A of this Act so as to correct obvious errors or omissions in the return (whether errors of principle, arithmetical mistakes or otherwise). 1.27

(2) A correction under this section is made by notice to the person whose return it is.

(3) No such correction may be made more than nine months after—

(a) the day on which the return was delivered, or

(b) if the correction is required in consequence of an amendment of the return under section 9ZA of this Act, the day on which that amendment was made.

(4) A correction under this section is of no effect if the person whose return it is gives notice rejecting the correction.

(5) Notice of rejection under subsection (4) above must be given—

(a) to the officer of the Board by whom the notice of correction was given,

(b) before the end of the period of 30 days beginning with the date of issue of the notice of correction.

Notice of enquiry

1.28 **9A.**—(1) An officer of the Boardmay enquire into a return under section 8 or 8A of this Act if he gives notice of his intention to do so ("notice of enquiry")—

(a) to the person whose return it is ("the taxpayer"),

(b) within the time allowed.

(2) The time allowed is—

(a) if the return was delivered on or before the filing date, up to the end of the period of twelve months after the filing date;

(b) if the return was delivered after the filing date, up to and including the quarter day next following the first anniversary of the day on which the return was delivered;

(c) if the return is amended under section 9ZA of this Act, up to and including the quarter day next following the first anniversary of the day on which the amendment was made.

For this purpose, the quarter days are 31st January, 30th April, 31st July and 31st October.

(3) A return which has been the subject of one notice of enquiry may not be the subject of another, except one given in consequence of an amendment (or another amendment) of the return under section 9ZA of this Act.

(4) An enquiry extends to anything contained in the return, or required to be contained in the return, including any claim or election included in the return, subject to the following limitation.

Amendment of return by taxpayer during enquiry

1.29 **9B.**—(1) This section applies if a return is amended under section 9ZA of this Act (amendment of personal or trustee return by taxpayer) at a time when an enquiry is in progress into the return.

(2) The amendment does not restrict the scope of the enquiry but may be taken into account (together with any matters arising) in the enquiry.

(3) So far as the amendment affects the amount stated in the self-assessment included in the return as the amount of tax payable, it does not take effect while the enquiry is in progress and—

(a) if the officer states in the closure notice that he has taken the amendment into account and that—
  (i) the amendment has been taken into account in formulating the amendments contained in the notice, or
  (ii) his conclusion is that the amendment is incorrect, the amendment shall not take effect;

(b) otherwise, the amendment takes effect when the closure notice is issued.

(4) For the purposes of this section the period during which an enquiry is in progress is the whole of the period—

(a) beginning with the day on which notice of enquiry is given; and
(b) ending with the day on which the enquiry is completed.

Amendment of self-assessment during enquiry to prevent loss of tax

9C.—(1) This section applies where an enquiry is in progress into a return as a result of notice of enquiry by an officer of the Board under section 9A(1) of this Act. 1.30

(2) If the officer forms the opinion—

(a) that the amount stated in the self-assessment contained in the return as the amount of tax payable is insufficient; and
(b) that unless the assessment is immediately amended there is likely to be a loss of tax to the Crown,

he may by notice to the taxpayer amend the assessment to make good the deficiency.

(3) In the case of an enquiry which under section 9A(5) of this Act is limited to matters arising from an amendment of the return, subsection (2) above only applies so far as the deficiency is attributable to the amendment.

(4) For the purposes of this section the period during which an enquiry is in progress is the whole of the period—

(a) beginning with the day on which notice of enquiry is given, and
(b) ending with the day on which the enquiry is completed.

Choice between different Cases of Schedule D

9D.—(1) Where in the case of a return under section 8 or 8A of this Act— 1.31

(a) alternative methods are allowed by the Tax Acts for bringing amounts into charge to tax,
(b) the return is made using one of those methods but could have been made using an alternative method, and
(c) an officer of the Board determines which of the alternative methods is to be used,

the officer's determination is final and conclusive, for the purposes of any enquiry into the return, as to the basis of charge to be used.

(2) For the purposes of this section the cases where the Tax Acts allow alternative methods for bringing amounts into charge to tax are where they may be brought into charge either—

(a) in computing profits chargeable to tax under Case I or II of Schedule D; or
(b) as amounts within Case III, IV or V of that Schedule.

Records

Records to be kept for purposes of returns

1.32 **12B.**—(1) Any person who may be required by a notice under section 8, 8A, or 12AA of this Act (or under any of those sections as extended by section 12 of this Act) to make and deliver a return for a year of assessment or other period shall—

(a) keep all such records as may be requisite for the purpose of enabling him to make and deliver a correct and complete return for the year or period; and
(b) preserve those records until the end of the relevant day, that is to say, the day mentioned in subsection (2) below or, where a return is required by a notice given on or before that day, whichever of that day and the following is the latest, namely—
  (i) where enquiries into the return or any amendment of the return are made by an officer of the Board, the day on which, by virtue of section 28A(1) or 28B(1) of this Act, those enquiries are treated as completed; and
  (ii) where no enquiries into the return or any amendment of the return are so made, the day on which such an officer no longer has power to make such enquiries.

(2) The day referred to in subsection (1) above is—

(a) in the case of a person carrying on a trade, profession or business alone or in partnership or a company, the fifth anniversary of the 31st January next following the year of assessment or (as the case may be) the sixth anniversary of the endof the period;
(b) in any other case, the first anniversary of 31st January next following the year of assessment or, where a return is delivered by the person concerned after that date, the quarter day next following the first anniversary of the day on which the return is delivered;

and the quarter days for the purposes of this subsection are 31st January, 30th April, 31st July and 31st October.

(2A) Any person who—

(a) is required, by such a notice as is mentioned in subsection (1) above given at any time after the end of the day mentioned in subsection (2) above, to make and deliver a return for a year of assessment or other period; and
(b) has in his possession at that time any records which may be requisite for the purpose of enabling him to make and deliver a correct and complete return for the year or period,

shall preserve those records until the end of the relevant day, that is to say, the day which, if the notice had been given on or before the day mentioned in subsection (2) above, would have been the relevant day for the purposes of subsection (1) above.

(3) In the case of a person carrying on a trade, profession or business alone or in partnership—

(a) the records required to be kept and preserved under subsection (1) or (2A) above shall include records of the following, namely—

(i) all amounts received and expended in the course of the trade, profession or business and the matters in respect of which the receipts and expenditure take place, and

(ii) in the case of a trade involving dealing in goods, all sales and purchases of goods made in the course of the trade; and

(b) the duty under that subsection shall include a duty to preserve until the end of the relevant day all supporting documents relating to such items as are mentioned in paragraph (a)(i) or (ii) above.

(4) Except in the case of records falling within subsection (4A) below, the duty under subsection (1) or (2A) above to preserve records may be discharged by the preservation of the information contained in them; and where information is so preserved a copy of any document forming part of the records shall be admissible in evidence in any proceedings before the Commissioners to the same extent as the records themselves.

(4A) The records which fall within this subsection are—

(a) any statement in writing such as is mentioned in—

(i) subsection (1) of section 234 of the principal Act (amount of qualifying distribution and tax credit); or

(ii) subsection (1) of section 352 of that Act (gross amount, tax deducted, and actual amount paid, in certain cases where payments are made under deduction of tax), which is furnishedby the company or person there mentioned, whether after the making of a request or otherwise;

(b) any certificate or other record (however described) which is required by regulations under section 566(1) of the principal Act to be given to a sub-contractor (within the meaning of Chapter IV of Part XIII of that Act) on the making of a payment to which section 559 of that Act (deductions on account of tax) applies;

(c) any such record as may be requisite for making a correct and complete claim in respect of, or otherwise requisite for making a correct and complete return so far as relating to, an amount of tax—

(i) which has been paid under the laws of a territory outside the United Kingdom, or

(ii) which would have been payable under the law of such a territory but for a relief to which section 788(5) of the principal Act (relief for promoting development and relief contemplated by double taxation arrangements) applies.

(5) Subject to subsections (5A) and (5B) below any person who fails to comply with subsection (1) or (2A) above in relation to a year of assessment or accounting period shall be liable to a penalty not exceeding £3,000.

(5A) Subsection (5) above does not apply where the records which the person fails to keep or preserve are records which might have been requisite only for the purposes of claims, elections or notices which are not included in the return.

(5B) Subsection (5) above also does not apply where—

(a) the records which the person fails to keep or preserve are records falling within paragraph (a) of subsection (4A) above; and
(b) an officer of the Boardis satisfied that any facts which he reasonably requires to be proved, and which would have been proved by the records, are proved by other documentary evidence furnishedto him.

(6) For the purposes of this section—
(a) a person engaged in the letting of property shall be treated as carrying on a trade; and
(b) "supporting documents" includes accounts, books, deeds, contracts, vouchers and receipts.

Part IV

Assessment and Claims

Completion of enquiry into personal or trustee return

1.33 **28A.**—(1) An enquiry under section 9A(1) of this Act is completed when an officer of the Boardby notice (a "closure notice") informs the taxpayer that he has completed his enquiries and states his conclusions. In this section "the taxpayer" means the person to whom notice of enquiry was given.

(2) A closure notice must either—
(a) state that in the officer's opinion no amendment of the return is required; or
(b) make the amendments of the return required to give effect to his conclusions.

(3) A closure notice takes effect when it is issued.

(4) The taxpayer may apply to the Commissioners for a direction requiring an officer of the Boardto issue a closure notice within a specified period.

(5) Any such application shall be heard and determined in the same way as an appeal.

(6) The Commissioners hearing the application shall give the direction applied for unless they are satisfied that there are reasonable grounds for not issuing a closure notice within a specified period.

Assessment where loss of tax discovered

1.34 **29.**—(1) If an officer of the Board or the Board discover, as regards any person (the taxpayer) and a year of assessment—
(a) that income which ought to have been assessed to income tax, or chargeable gains which ought to have been assessed to capital gains tax, have not been assessed, or
(b) that an assessment to tax is or has become insufficient, or
(c) that any relief which has been given is or has become excessive,

the officer or, as the case may be, the Board may, subject to subsections (2) and (3) below, make an assessment in the amount, or the further amount, which ought in his or their opinion to be charged in order to make good to the Crown the loss of tax.

(2) Where—

(a) the taxpayer has made and delivered a return under section 8 or 8A of this Act in respect of the relevant chargeable period, and

(b) the situation mentioned in subsection (1) above is attributable to an error or mistake in the return as to the basis on which his liability ought to have been computed,

the taxpayer shall not be assessed under that subsection in respect of the year of assessment there mentioned if the return was in fact made on the basis or in accordance with the practice generally prevailing at the time when it was made.

(3) Where the taxpayer has made and delivered a return under section 8 or 8A of this Act in respect of the relevant year of assessment, he shall not be assessed under subsection (1) above—

(a) in respect of the year of assessment mentioned in that subsection; and

(b) in the case of a return under section 8 or 8A, in the same capacity as that in which he made and delivered the return,

unless one of the two conditions mentioned below is fulfilled.

(4) The first condition is that the situation mentioned in subsection (1) above is attributable to fraudulent or negligent conduct on the part of the taxpayer or a person acting on his behalf.

(5) The second condition is that at the time when an officer of the Board—

(a) ceased to be entitled to give notice of his intention to enquire into the taxpayer's return under section 8 or 8A of this Act in respect of the relevant year of assessment; or

(b) informed the taxpayer that he had completed his enquiries into that return,

the officer could not have been reasonably expected, on the basis of the information made available to him before that time, to be aware of the situation mentioned in subsection (1) above.

(6) For the purposes of subsection (5) above, information is made available to an officer of the Board if—

(a) it is contained in the taxpayer's return under section 8 or 8A of this Act in respect of the relevant year of assessment (the return), or in any accounts, statements or documents accompanying the return;

(b) it is contained in any claim made as regards the relevant year of assessment by the taxpayer acting in the same capacity as that in which he made the return, or in any accounts, statements or documents accompanying any such claim;

(c) it is contained in any documents, accounts or particulars which, for the purposes of any enquiries into the return or any such claim by an officer of the Board, are produced or furnished by the taxpayer to the officer, whether in pursuance of a notice under section 19A of this Act or otherwise; or

(d) it is information the existence of which, and the relevance of which as regards the situation mentioned in subsection (1) above—

(i) could reasonably be expected to be inferred by an officer of the Board from information falling within paragraphs (a)–(c) above; or

(ii) are notified in writing by the taxpayer to an officer of the Board.

(7) In subsection (6) above—

(a) any reference to the taxpayer's return under section 8 or 8A of this Act in respect of the relevant year of assessment includes—

(i) a reference to any return of his under that section for either of the two immediately preceding year of assessment; and

(ii) where the return is under section 8 and the taxpayer carries on a trade, profession or business in partnership, a reference to any partnership return with respect to the partnership for the relevant year of assessment or either of those periods; and

(b) any reference in paragraphs (b) to (d) to the taxpayer includes a reference to a person acting on his behalf.

(8) An objection to the making of an assessment under this section on the ground that neither of the two conditions mentioned above is fulfilled shall not be made otherwise than on an appeal against the assessment.

(9) Any reference in this section to the relevant year of assessment is a reference to—

(a) in the case of the situation mentioned in paragraph (a) or (b) of subsection (1) above, the chargeable period mentioned in that subsection; and

(b) in the case of the situation mentioned in paragraph (c) of that subsection, the year of assessment in respect of which the claim was made.

(10) In this section "profits"—

(a) in relation to income tax, means income,

(b) in relation to capital gains tax, means chargeable gains, and

(c) in relation to corporation tax, means profits as computed for the purposes of that tax.

Relief for excessive assessments

Double assessment

1.35 **32.**—(1) If on a claim made to the Board it appears to their satisfaction that a person has been assessed to tax more than once for the same cause and for the same chargeable period. . ., they shall direct the whole, or such part of any assessment as appears to be an overcharge, to be vacated, and thereupon the same shall be vacated accordingly.

(2) An appeal on a claim under this section shall lie to any of the bodies of Commissioners having jurisdiction to hear an appeal against the assessment, or the later of the assessments, to which the claim relates.

Error or mistake

1.36 **33.**—(1) If a person who has paid income tax or capital gains tax under an assessment (whether a self assessment or otherwise) alleges that the assessment was excessive by reason of some error or mistake in a return, he may by notice in writing at any time not later than 5 years after the 31st January next following the year of assessment to which the return relates, make a claim to the Board for relief.

(2) On receiving the claim the Board shall inquire into the matter and shall, subject to the provisions of this section, give by way of repayment such relief . . . in respect of the error or mistake as is reasonable and just:

Provided that no relief shall be given under this section in respect of an error or mistake as to the basis on which the liability of the claimant ought to have been computed where the return was in fact made on the basis or in accordance with the practice generally prevailing at the time when the return was made.

(2A) No relief shall be given under this section in respect of—

(a) an error or mistake as to the basis on which the liability of the claimant ought to have been computed where the return was in fact made on the basis or in accordance with the practice generally prevailing at the time when it was made; or

(b) an error or mistake in a claim which is included in the return.

(3) In determining the claim the Board shall have regard to all the relevant circumstances of the case, and in particular shall consider whether the granting of relief would result in the exclusion from charge to tax of any part of the profits of the claimant, and for this purpose the Boardmay take into consideration the liability of the claimant and assessments made on him in respect of chargeable periods other than that to which the claim relates.

(4) If any appeal is brought from the decision of the Board on the claim the Special Commissioners shall hear and determine the appeal in accordance with the principles to be followed by the Board in determining claims under this section; and neither the appellant nor the Board shall be entitled to appeal under section 56A of this Act against the determination of the Special Commissioners except on a point of law arising in connection with the computation of profits.

(5) In this section, "profits"—

(a) in relation to income tax, means income; and

(b) in relation to capital gains tax, means chargeable gains; and

(c) in relation to corporation tax, means profits as computed for the purposes of that tax.

Time limits

Ordinary time-limit of six years

34.—(1) Subject to the following provisions of this Act, and to any other provisions of the Taxes Acts allowing a longer period in any particular class of case, an assessment to income tax or capital gains tax may be made at any time not later than five years after the 31st January next following the year of assessment to which it relates. 1.37

(2) An objection to the making of any assessment on the ground that the time-limit for making it has expired shall only be made on an appeal against the assessment.

Fraudulent or negligent conduct

1.38 **36.**—(1) An assessment on any person (in this section referred to as "the person in default") for the purpose of making good to the Crown a loss of income tax or capital gains tax attributable to his fraudulent or negligent conduct or the fraudulent or negligent conduct of a person acting on his behalf may be made at any time not later than 20 years after the 31st January next following the year of assessment the year of assessment to which it relates.

(2) Where the person in default carried on a trade, profession or business with one or more other persons at any time in the period for which the assessment is made, an assessment in respect of the profits or gains of the trade, profession or business for the purpose mentioned in subsection (1) above may be made not only on the person in default but also on his partner or any of his partners.

(3) If the person on whom the assessment is made so requires, in determining the amount of the tax to be charged for any chargeable period in any assessment made for the purpose mentioned in subsection (1) above, effect shall be given to any relief or allowance to which he would have been entitled for that chargeable period on a claim or application made within the time allowed by the Taxes Acts.

(3A) In subsection (3) above, "claim or application" does not include an election under section 257BA of the principal Act (elections as to transfer of married couple's allowance).

(4) Any act or omission such as is mentioned in section 98B below on the part of a grouping (as defined in that section) or member of a grouping shall be deemed for the purposes of subsection (1) above to be the act or omission of each member of the grouping.

PART V

APPEALS AND OTHER PROCEEDINGS

Proceedings before the Commissioners

Settling of appeals by agreement

1.39 **54.**—(1) Subject to the provisions of this section, where a person gives notice of appeal and, before the appeal is determined by the Commissioners, [1 the officer of the Board] and the appellant come to an agreement, whether in writing or otherwise, that the [1 . . .] decision under appeal should be treated as upheld without variation, or as varied in a particular manner or as [1set aside], the like consequences shall ensue for all purposes as would have ensued if, at the time when the agreement was come to, the Commissioners had determined the appeal and had upheld the [1. . .] decision without variation, had varied it in that manner or [1had set it aside], as the case may be.

(2) Subsection (1) of this section shall not apply where, within thirty days from the date when the agreement was come to, the appellant gives notice in writing to [1 the officer of the Board] that he desires to repudiate or resile from the agreement.

(3) Where an agreement is not in writing—

(a) the preceding provisions of this section shall not apply unless the fact that an agreement was come to, and the terms agreed, are confirmed by notice in writing given by [1 the officer of the Board] to the appellant or by the appellant to [1 the officer of the Board]; and

(b) the references in the said preceding provisions to the time when the agreement was come to shall be construed as references to the time of the giving of the said notice of confirmation.

(4) Where—

(a) a person who has given a notice of appeal notifies [1 the officer of the Board], whether orally or in writing, that he desires not to proceed with the appeal; and

(b) thirty days have elapsed since the giving of the notification without [1 the officer of the Board] giving to the appellant notice in writing indicating that he is unwilling that the appeal should be treated as withdrawn,

the preceding provisions of this section shall have effect as if, at the date of the appellant's notification, the appellant and [1 the officer of the Board] had come to an agreement, orally or in writing, as the case may be, that the [1. . .] decision under appeal should be upheld without variation.

(5) The references in this section to an agreement being come to with an appellant and the giving of notice or notification to or by an appellant include references to an agreement being come to with, and the giving of notice or notification to or by, a person acting on behalf of the appellant in relation to the appeal.

AMENDMENT

1. Tax Credits (Employer Penalty Appeals) Regulations 2003 (SI 2003/1382), reg. 9 (June 18, 2003).

GENERAL NOTE

This section is central to the way in which the Inland Revenue deals with disputed amounts of tax, and also with underpayments and penalties. It is applied to tax credits by ss.39(6) and 63(8) of the TCA 2002. For its application to tax credits penalties see the general note to s.31 of that Act. The Inland Revenue published a code of practice on the settlement of tax credit appeals, *IR168, how tax credits settlements are negotiated.* But see from March 2004 codes of Practice 23 and 27, and leaflets WTC3 and WTC4 at the end of this volume. For the application of this section to employers' appeals, see the Tax Credits (Employer Penalty Appeals) Regulations 2003 (SI 2003/1382).

PART X

PENALTIES, ETC.

Evidence in cases of fraud or wilful default

1.40 **105.**—(1) Statements made or documents produced by or on behalf of a person shall not be inadmissible in any such proceedings as are mentioned in subsection (2) below by reason only that it has been drawn to his attention that—

(a) pecuniary settlements may be accepted instead of a penalty being determined, or proceedings being instituted, in relation to any tax, and

(b) though no undertaking can be given as to whether or not the Board will accept such a settlement in the case of any particular person, it is the practice of the Board to be influenced by the fact that a person has made a full confession of any fraudulent conduct to which he had been a party and has given full facilities for investigation,

and that he was or may have been induced thereby to make the statements or produce the documents.

(2) The proceedings mentioned in subsection (1) above are—

(a) any criminal proceedings against the person in question for any form of fraudulent conduct in connection with or in relation to tax; and

(b) any proceedings against him for the recovery of any tax due from him and

(c) any proceedings for a penalty or on appeal against the determination of a penalty.

PART XI

MISCELLANEOUS AND SUPPLEMENTAL

Documents

Loss, destruction or damage to assessments, returns, etc.

1.41 **112.**—(1) Where any assessment to tax, or any duplicate of assessment to tax, or any return or other document relating to tax, has been lost or destroyed, or been so defaced or damaged as to be illegible or otherwise useless, the Commissioners, inspectors, collectors and other officers having powers in relation to tax may, notwithstanding anything in any enactment to the contrary, do all such acts and things as they might have done, and all acts and things done under or in pursuance of this section shall be as valid and effectual for all purposes as they would have been, if the assessment or duplicate of assessment had not been made, or the return or other document had not been made or furnished or required to be made or furnished.

Provided that, where any person who is charged with tax in consequence or by virtue of any act or thing done under or in pursuance of this section proves to the satisfaction of the Commissioners having jurisdiction in the case that he has already paid any tax for the same chargeable periodin respect of the subject matter and on the account in respect of and on which he is so charged, relief shall be given to the extent to which the liability of that person has been discharged by the payment so made either by abatement from the charge or by repayment, as the case may require.

(2) In this section, "the Commissioners" means, as the case may require, either the Board or the General or Special Commissioners concerned.

(3) The references in subsection (1) above to assessments to tax include references to determinations of penalties; and in its application to such determinations the proviso to that subsection shall have effect with the appropriate modifications.

Want of form or errors not to invalidate assessments, etc.

114.—(1) An assessment or determination, warrant or other proceeding which purports to be made in pursuance of any provision of the Taxes Acts shall not be quashed, or deemed to be void or voidable, for want of form, or be affected by reason of a mistake, defect or omission therein, if the same is in substance and effect in conformity with or according to the intent and meaning of the Taxes Acts, and if the person or property charged or intended to be charged or affected thereby is designated therein according to common intent and understanding. 1.42

(2) An assessment or determination shall not be impeached or affected—

(a) by reason of a mistake therein as to—

(i) the name or surname of a person liable, or

(ii) the description of any profits or property, or

(iii) the amount of the tax charged, or

(b) by reason of any variance between the notice and the assessment or determination.

Interpretation

Interpretation

118.—(1) In this Act, unless the context otherwise requires— 1.43

"Act" includes an Act of the Parliament of Northern Ireland; and "enactment" shall be construed accordingly;

"the Board" means the Commissioners of Inland Revenue;

"body of persons" means any body politic, corporate or collegiate, and any company, fraternity, fellowship and society of persons, whether corporate or not corporate;

[. . .][1]

"chargeable gain" has the same meaning as in the 1992 Act;

"chargeable period" means a year of assessment or a company's accounting period;

"collector" means any collector of taxes;

"company" has the meaning given by section 832(1) of the principal Act (with section 468 of that Act) . . .;

"the General Commissioners Regulations" means the General Commissioners (Jurisdiction and Procedure) Regulations 1994;

"incapacitated person" means any infant, person of unsound mind, lunatic, idiot or insane person;

"infant", in relation to Scotland, except in section 73 of this Act, means a person under legal disability by reason of nonage, and, in the said-section 73, means a person under the age of 18 years;

"inspector" means any inspector of taxes;

"ITEPA 2003" means the Income Tax (Earnings and Pensions) Act 2003;

"partnership return" has the meaning given by section 12AA(10A) of this Act;

"the principal Act" means the Income and Corporation Taxes Act 1988;

"the relevant trustees", in relation to a settlement, shall be construed in accordance with section 7(9) of this Act;

"return" includes any statement or declaration under the Taxes Acts;

"the Special Commissioners Regulations" means the Special Commissioners (Jurisdiction and Procedure) Regulations 1994;

"successor", in relation to a person who is required to make and deliver, or has made and delivered, a partnership return , and "predecessor" and "successor", in relation to the successor of such a person, shall be construed in accordance with section 12AA(11) of this Act;

"tax", where neither income tax nor capital gains tax nor corporation tax . . . is specified, means any of those taxes except that in sections 20, 20A, 20B, 20C and 20D it does not include development land tax;

"the Taxes Acts" means this Act and—

(a) the Tax Acts . . . ; and

(b) the Taxation of Chargeable Gains Act 1992 and all other enactments relating to capital gains tax;

"the 1992 Act" means the Taxation of Chargeable Gains Act 1992;

"trade" includes every trade, manufacture, adventure or concern in the nature of trade.

(2) For the purposes of this Act, a person shall be deemed not to have failed to do anything required to be done within a limited time if he did it within such further time, if any, as the Board or the Commissioners or officer concerned may have allowed; and where a person had a reasonable excuse for not doing anything required to be done he shall be deemed not to have failed to do it unless the excuse ceased and, after the excuse ceased, he shall be deemed not to have failed to do it if he did it without unreasonable delay after the excuse had ceased: . . .

(3) For the purposes of section 36 and Part X of this Act, an assessment made in the partnership name and the tax charged in such an assessment shall, according to the law in Scotland as well as according to the law elsewhere in the United Kingdom, be deemed to be respectively

an assessment made on the partners and tax charged on and payable by them.

(4) For the purposes of this Act, the amount of tax covered by any assessment shall not be deemed to be finally determined until that assessment can no longer be varied, whether by any Commissioners on appeal or by the order of any court.

AMENDMENT

[1] Words repealed by FA 2003, Sch.43.

Income and Corporation Taxes Act

(1988 c.1)

ARRANGEMENT OF SELECTED SECTIONS

PART I

THE CHARGE TO TAX

Income Tax

PART II

PROVISIONS RELATING TO THE SCHEDULE A CHARGE

General

PART III

GOVERNMENT SECURITIES

Income and Corporation Taxes Act

Part IV

Provisions Relating to the Scheduled Charge

Chapter 1

Supplementary Charging Provisions

1.47 55. Mines, quarries, and other concerns

Chapter 2

Income Tax: Basis of Assessment, Etc.

Cases I and II

60. Assessment on current year basis
61. Basis of assessment at commencement
62. Change of basis period
63. Basis of assessment after discontinuance
64. Case III assessments

Cases III, IV and V

65. Case IV and V assessments: general
65A. Case V income from land outside the United Kingdom: income tax

Case VI

69. Case VI assessments

Chapter 5: Computational Provisions

74. General rules as to deductions not allowable

(Part V Repealed)

(Part VI: Company Distributions: Omitted)

Part VII

General Provisions Relating to Taxation of the Income of Individuals

Chapter 3

Taxation of Income of Spouses

General Rules

282. Construction of references to husband and wife living together **1.48**
282A. Jointly held property
282B. Jointly held property: declarations

Chapter 4

Special Provisions

325. Interest on deposits with National Savings Bank **1.49**
329. Interest on damages for personal injuries
329AA. Personal injury damages in the form of periodical payments
329AB. Compensation for personal injury under statutory or other schemes

Chapter 5

Residence of Individuals

334. Commonwealth citizens and others temporarily abroad
335. Residence of persons working abroad
336. Temporary residents in the United Kingdom

(PART VIII: TAXATION OF COMPANIES: OMITTED)

PART IX

ANNUAL PAYMENTS AND INTEREST

Annual Payments

General Rule

347A. General rule
347B. Qualifying maintenance payments

(PART X: LOSS RELIEF AND GROUP RELIEF: OMITTED)

(PART XI: CLOSE COMPANIES: OMITTED)

(PART XII: SPECIAL CLASSES OF COMPANIES AND BUSINESSES: OMITTED)

(PART XIII: MISCELLANEOUS SPECIAL PROVISIONS: OMITTED)

(PART XIV: REPEALED)

PART XV

SETTLEMENTS

CHAPTER 1A

LIABILITY OF SETTLOR

Main Provisions

1.50 660A. Income arising under settlement where settlor retains an interest
660B. Payments to unmarried children of settlor
660C. Nature of charge on settlor

Supplementary provisions

660E. Application to settlements by two or more settlors
660G. Meaning of "settlement" and related expressions

CHAPTER 1B

PROVISIONS AS TO CAPITAL SUMS PAID TO SETTLOR

677. Sums paid to settlor otherwise than as income
678. Capital sums paid by body connected with settlement

PART XVI

ESTATES OF DECEASED PERSONS IN COURSE OF ADMINISTRATION

695. Limited interests in residue 1.51
696. Absolute interests in residue

(PART XVII: TAX AVOIDANCE: OMITTED)

(PART XVIII: DOUBLE TAXATION RELIEF: OMITTED)

PART XIX

SUPPLEMENTAL

Miscellaneous

817. Deductions not to be allowed in computing profits and gains 1.52
829. Application of Income Tax Acts to public departments and avoidance of exempting provisions
831. Interpretation of this Act
832. Interpretation of Tax Acts
833. Interpretation of Income Tax Acts
835. "Total income" in the Income Tax Acts

(SCHEDULES OMITTED)

INTRODUCTION AND GENERAL NOTE

Set out below are selected sections from the ICTA 1988. This Act was a consolidation Act, bringing forward with minimal changes the provisions of the Income Tax Act 1952 and subsequent amendments in annual Finance Acts. But the Income Tax Act 1952 itself consolidated the Income Tax 1918, again a consolidating measure. So some of the wording in the 1988 Act dates back to the original income tax legislation, the Income Tax Act 1803. Recently, the Inland Revenue has started a serious exercise in codifying and rewriting the whole of the law relating to income tax. ITEPA 2003, extracts from which are set out in this volume, started this process. As a result, s.19 of this Act (which contained Sch.E) 1.53

has been repealed and replaced, along with the whole of Parts V and XIV (the latter dealing with pensions) and many other sections or subsections.

The selection includes the key sections necessary to understand the operation of the income test in s.7 of the TCA 2002 and the Tax Credits (Definition and Calculation of Income) Regulations 2002. Some of the sections are directly referred to in those Regulations. Others are necessary to understand those sections.

Any selection such as this should carry a health warning. Much of the Taxes Act is irrelevant to individuals and their tax credit calculations, and is therefore excluded. But other sections are excluded by editorial choice because they are likely to be only of occasional relevance to tax credits claimants, and are unlikely to lead to disputes about tax credits awards or entitlements. By contrast, sections dealing with the taxation of, for example, disability funds, are included, as they may be relevant. Most anti-avoidance provisions are also excluded, notwithstanding that some are made expressly relevant to tax credits calculations by the Regulations. This is because they are unlikely to be relevant save by reason of an enquiry or discovery calculation, and in practice, if there is a dispute, it is likely to go to the tax appeal tribunals.

Inevitably, including some sections and excluding others does not give a complete picture of the legislation. In some cases, references will be needed to the full legislation.

As with social security law in these volumes, it is important that the reader look at the text of the legislation as it operates in the year of assessment relevant to the particular problem. That text is available both in hardback form and on the internet from the Inland Revenue. There are also popular commercial consolidations available.

The text included is the amended text of each section up to and including the amendments by ITEPA 2003.

Much of the text set out here, including all the provisions dealing with Schs A, D and F, are currently being rewritten as part of the Tax Law Rewrite programme. A draft Income Tax (Trading and Other Income) Bill has now been published by the Inland Revenue This will be subject to special parliamentary procedure, and the current plans are to have the Bill enacted with effect from April 6, 2005. The forms adopted in this Bill has been foreshadowed in the Tax Credits (Definition and Calculation of Income) Regulations.

Part I

The Charge to Tax

Income tax

The charge to income tax

1.54 **1.**—(1) Income tax is charged in accordance with the provisions of the Income Tax Acts on—

(a) all amounts which, under those Acts, are charged to tax under any of Schedules A, D and F (set out in sections 15, 18 and 20),

(b) all amounts which are charged to tax under any of the following provisions of ITEPA 2003—

(i) Part 2 (employment income)
(ii) Part 9 (pension income), and
(iii) Part 10 (social security income), and

(c) any other amounts which, under the Income Tax Acts, are charged to income tax.

(2) Where any Act enacts that income tax shall be charged for any year, income tax shall be charged for that year—

(aa) in respect of so much of an individual's total income as does not exceed £1,920, at such rate as Parliament may determine to be the starting rate for that year;

(a) in respect of any income which does not fall within paragraph (aa) above or paragraph (b) below, at such rate as Parliament may determine to be the basic rate for that year;

(b) in respect of so much of an individual's total income as exceeds £29,900 at such higher rate as Parliament may determine;

but this subsection has effect subject to any provision of the Income Tax Acts providing for income tax to be charged at a different rate in certain cases.

(2A) The amount up to which an individual's income is by virtue of subsection (2) above chargeable for any year at the starting rate shall be known as the starting rate limit.

(3) The amount up to which an individual's income is by virtue of subsection (2) above chargeable for any year at the starting rate or the basic rate shall be known as the basic rate limit . . .

(4)–(7) *omitted*

General Note

This is the main charging s. for income tax. It charges income tax on the kinds of income defined in this Act and other Income Tax Acts (that is, ITEPA and the Finance Acts imposing a charge to income tax) if, in any tax year, that year's Finance Act imposes a charge to income tax. This is therefore the key section that links the many provisions defining kinds of income for the purpose of income tax liability to the imposition of that liability in any tax year in this and all subsequent Acts imposing provisions dealing with income tax. It does not impose either capital gains tax or corporation tax. **1.55**

Fractions of a pound, and yearly assessments

2.—(1) The due proportion of income tax shall be charged for every fractional part of one pound. **1.56**

(2) Every assessment and charge to income tax shall be made for a year commencing on the 6th April and ending on the following 5th April.

Schedule A

15.—(1) The Schedule referred to as Schedule A is as follows: **1.57**

SCHEDULE A

1.—(1) Tax is charged under this Schedule on the annual profits arising from a business carried on for the exploitation, as a source of rents or other receipts, of any estate, interest or rights in or over land in the United Kingdom.

(2) To the extent that any transaction is entered into for the exploitation, as a source of rents or other receipts, of any estate, interest or rights in or over land in the United Kingdom, it is taken to be entered into in the course of such a business.

(3) All businesses and transactions carried on or entered into by a particular person or partnership, so far as they are businesses or transactions the profits of which are chargeable to tax under this Schedule, are treated for the purposes of this Schedule as, or as entered into in the course of carrying on, a single business.

There are qualifications to this rule in the case of—

(a) companies not resident in the United Kingdom (see subsection (1A) below); and

(b) insurance companies (see sections 432AA and 441B(2A)).

(4) The receipts referred to in the expression "as a source of rents or other receipts" include—

(a) payments in respect of a licence to occupy or otherwise to use land or the exercise of any other right over land, and

(b) rent charges, ground annuals and feu duties and other annual payments reserved in respect of, or charged on or issuing out of, the land.

2.—(1) This Schedule does not apply to profits arising from the occupation of land.

(2) This Schedule does not apply to—

(a) profits charged to tax under Case I of Schedule D under—

(i) section 53(1) (farming and market gardening); or

(ii) section 55 (mines, quarries and other concerns);

(b) receipts or expenses taken into account as trading receipts or expenses under section 98 (tied premises);

(c) rent charged to tax under Schedule D under—

(i) section 119 (rent, etc. payable in connection with mines, quarries and other concerns); or

(ii) section 120(1) (certain rent, etc. payable in respect of electric line wayleaves).

(3) The profits of a Schedule A business carried on by a company shall be computed without regard to items giving rise to—

credits or debits within Chapter II of Part IV of the Finance Act 1996 (loan relationships), or exchange gains or losses within Chapter II of Part II of the Finance Act 1993 (foreign exchange gains and losses); or

credits or debits within Schedule 26 to the Finance Act 2002 (derivative contracts).

This Schedule does not affect the operation of those provisions.

3.—(1) For the purposes of this Schedule a right to use a caravan or houseboat, where the use to which the caravan or houseboat may be put in pursuance of the right is confined to use at a single location in the United Kingdom, is treated as a right deriving from an estate or interest in land in the United Kingdom.

(2) In sub-paragraph (1)—

"caravan" has the meaning given by section 29(1) of the Caravan Sites and Control of Development Act 1960; and

"houseboat" means a boat or similar structure designed or adapted for use as a place of human habitation.

4.—(1) In the case of a furnished letting, any sum payable for the use of furniture shall be taken into account in computing the profits chargeable to tax under this Schedule in the same way as rent. Expenses in connection with the provision of furniture shall similarly be taken into account in the same way as expenses in connection with the premises.

(2) A furnished letting means where—

(a) a sum is payable in respect of the use of premises, and

(b) the tenant or other person entitled to the use of the premises is also entitled, in connection with that use, to the use of furniture.

(3) This paragraph does not apply if the receipts and expenses are taken into account in computing the profits of a trade consisting in, or involving, making furniture available for use in premises.

(4) In this paragraph—

(a) any reference to a sum includes the value of consideration other than money, and references to a sum being payable shall be construed accordingly; and

(b) "premises" includes a caravan or houseboat within the meaning of paragraph 3.

General Note

This is the charging section imposing income tax on profits arising from exploiting land in the United Kingdom. "Land" in this section means "land" in the lawyer's sense, not the geological sense. For the exploitation of land by way of agriculture, mining or other methods, see ICTA, s.53 (farming and market gardening on UK land forms a single trade) and s.55 (mines, etc.) below. 1.58

The section does not charge tax on capital accretions or gains from any sale or other disposal of land. This includes premiums for leases payable instead of rent. Part of the premium for a lease of under 50 years is turned into income for income tax purposes by ICTA, s.34. That section is one of those listed in Tax Credits (Definition and Calculation of Income) Regulations, reg.14, as notional income for the purposes of a tax credits calculation. Other forms of capital gain from landare not relevant to tax credits save for the limited but powerful, and seldom used, anti-avoidance provision in ICTA, s.776 (also listed in reg.14).

The main charge to income tax under this section is therefore on rents and licence payments for the use of land. This includes furnished lettings and payments by lodgers. The scope of this charge is limited in practice by the "rentaroom" scheme allowing the exclusion of payments of up to £4,250 a year to an owner–occupier of a house by someone living as a lodger in the house with him or her. See F(2)A 1992, Sch.10.

For details of the application of this section, see sections 21–24 below and the provisions relevant to Sch.D, Case I.

Schedule D

18.—(1) The Schedule referred to as Schedule D is as follows: 1.59

SCHEDULE D

Tax under this Schedule shall be charged in respect of—

(a) the annual profits or gains arising or accruing—
 (i) to any person residing in the United Kingdom from any kind of property whatever situated in the United Kingdom or elsewhere; and
 (ii) to any person residing in the United Kingdom from any trade, profession or vocation, whether carried on in the United Kingdom or elsewhere; and
 (iii) to any person, whether a Commonwealth citizen or not, although not resident in the United Kingdom from any property whatever in the United Kingdom or from any trade, profession or vocation exercised within the United Kingdom; and

(b) all interest of money, annuities and other annual profits or gains not charged under Schedule A or under ITEPA 2003 as employment income, pension income or social security income, and not specially exempted from tax.

(2) Tax under Schedule D shall be charged under the Cases set out in subsection (3) below, and subject to and in accordance with the provisions of the Tax Acts applicable to those Cases respectively.

(3) The Cases are—

Case I: tax in respect of any trade carried on in the United Kingdom or elsewhere but not contained in Schedule A;

Case II: tax in respect of any profession or vocation not contained in any other Schedule;

Case III: tax in respect of—

(a) any interest of money, whether yearly or otherwise, or any annuity or other annual payment, whether such payment is payable within or out of the United Kingdom, either as a charge on any property of the person paying the same by virtue of any deed or will or otherwise, or as a reservation out of it, or as a personal debt or obligation by virtue of any contract, or whether the same is received and payable half-yearly or at any shorter or more distant periods, but not including any payment chargeable under Schedule A; and

(b) all discounts; and

(c) income, from securities which is payable out of the public revenue of the United Kingdom or Northern Ireland;

Case IV: tax in respect of income arising from securities out of the United Kingdom;

Case V: tax in respect of income arising from possessions out of the United Kingdom not being employment income, pension income or social security income on which tax is charged under ITEPA 2003;

Case VI: tax in respect of any annual profits or gains not falling under any other Case of Schedule D and not charged by virtue of Schedule A or by virtue of ITEPA 2003 as employment income, pension income, or social security income.

(3A) *Omitted*

(3B) The references in Case IV of Schedule D to income arising from securities out of the United Kingdom, and in Case V of Schedule D to income arising from possessions out of the United Kingdom, shall be taken, in the case of relevant foreign holdings, to include references to the following—

(a) any proceeds of such a sale or other realisation of coupons for foreign dividends as is effected by a bank in the United Kingdom which pays the proceeds over or carries them into an account;

(b) any proceeds of a sale of such coupons to a dealer in coupons in the United Kingdom by a person who is not a bank or another dealer in coupons.

(3C) In this section "relevant foreign holdings" means—

(a) any securities issued by or on behalf of a government or a public or local authority in a country outside the United Kingdom; or

(b) any shares or securities issued by or on behalf of a body of persons not resident in the United Kingdom;

and "securities" here includes loan stock and similar securities.

(3D) In this section "foreign dividends" means—

(a) in relation to relevant foreign holdings falling within subsection (3C)(a) above, interest or annual payments payable out of the revenue of the government or authority in question; and

(b) in relation to relevant foreign holdings falling within subsection (3C)(b) above, any dividends, interest or annual payments payable in respect of the holdings in question.

(3E) In this section—

(a) "bank" has the meaning given by section 840A; and

(b) references to coupons include, in relation to any foreign dividends, warrants for and bills of exchange purporting to be drawn or made in payment of those dividends.

(4) The provisions of Schedule D and of subsection (2) above are without prejudice to any other provision of the Tax Acts directing tax to be charged under Schedule D or under one or other of the Cases set out in subsection (3) above, and tax directed to be so chargedshall be charged accordingly.

(5) Parts III and IV contain further provisions relating to the charge to tax under Schedule D.

General Note

1.60 The six cases of Schedule D date in their language from 1803, with surprisingly little change. The Tax Law Rewrite Project is in the process of rewriting the provisions into several heads of income tax, and these are reflected in the Tax Credits (Definition and Calculation of Income) Regulations 2002. The relevant heads are:

Trading income (including income from professions or vocations): Cases I and II

Investment income: Case III

Foreign income: Cases IV and V (these include foreign trading income and foreign investment income)

Miscellaneous income: Case VI (the "sweeper").

Like Schedule A, none of the Cases of Schedule D directly includes any capital gains or accretions. Any capital gain is taxed, if at all, to capital gains tax under the Taxation of Chargeable Gains Act 1992.

Deductions against income: general rules

Section 817 (below) sets out the general rule that no deductions are allowed against income for income tax purposes save by express statutory authority. No deductions of any kind are allowed against investment income (s.64 below). Income deductions for trading income are set out in s.74 (below) and subsequent sections of this Act. 1.61

The converse of the rule that capital gains are not charged to income tax is that capital expenditure cannot be set off against income for income tax purposes save by express provision. No capital deductions are allowed against investment income. Capital deductions are allowed against the other Cases of Sch.D only under the terms of the Capital Allowances Act 2001.

For further rules applying these charging provisions, see ss.46–74 below.

Schedule F

20.—(1) The Schedule referred to as Schedule F is as follows: 1.62

SCHEDULE F

1. Subject to section 95(1A)(a), income tax under this Schedule shall be chargeable for any year of assessment in respect of all dividends and other distributions in that year of a company resident in the United Kingdom which are not specially excluded from income tax, and for the purposes of income tax all such distributions shall be regarded as income however they fall to be dealt with in the hands of the recipient.

2. For the purposes of this Schedule and all other purposes of the Tax Acts (other than section 95(1)) of this Act and section 219(4A) of the Finance Act 1994 any such distribution in respect of which a person is entitled to a tax credit shall be treated as representing income equal to the aggregate of the amount or value of that distribution and the amount of that credit, and income tax under this Schedule shall accordingly be charged on that aggregate.

(2) Except as provided by section 171 of the Finance Act 1993 or section 219 of the Finance Act 1994 (underwriters) no distribution which is chargeable under Schedule F shall be chargeable under any other provision of the Income Tax Acts.

(3) Part VI contains further provisions relating to company distributions and tax credits.

General Note

Schedule F is the charge to income tax on payments made to their shareholders by United Kingdom companies. The charge is expressly on "dividends and other distributions" made by those companies. That phrase is extensively defined in this Act, in particular in ss.209–218. The definition is a wide one. It expressly includes all dividends, including capital dividends (s.209(2)(a)), and any other distribution out of the assets of a company whether in cash or otherwise (s.209(2)(b)). There are then extensive anti-avoidance provisions. The two main aims of these provisions are to establish a division between interest (charged to tax under Sch.D, Case III) and dividends and also between dividends and issues of shares (capital transactions). Payments of interest in ordinary course of business, and not associated with share issues, are not a dividend or other distribution by the company, but payments of interest on interest-bearing shares will usually be dividends. Some issues of shares, such as stock dividends, may be treated as dividends. 1.63

One practical importance of these provisions is that dividends must be paid with tax credits under ss.231 and following of this Act. These tax credits are nothing whatsoever to do with tax credits under the TCA 2002. A tax credit in this sense is a form of advance payment of the income tax on the dividend or distribution for the recipient, but paid by the company at the same time as the main payment. So it is a direct credit against the recipient's income tax liability for receiving the dividend or distribution. The full value of the dividend or distribution is therefore the dividend paid plus the tax credit issued at the same time. Under present rules, the tax credit is one-ninth of the dividend (or 10 per cent of the gross sum used to pay the dividend): s.231(1A) of this Act.

Dividends and distributions from foreign companies are charged to income tax under Case V (or if they are paid in respect of securities, Case IV) of Sch.D.

PART II

PROVISIONS RELATING TO THE SCHEDULE A CHARGE

General

Persons chargeable and basis of assessment

1.64 **21.**—(1) Income tax under Schedule A shall be charged on and paid by the persons receiving or entitled to the income in respect of which the tax is directed by the Income Tax Acts to be charged.

(2) Income tax under Schedule A is charged on the full amount of the profits arising in the year of assessment.

(3) This section does not apply for the purposes of corporation tax.

Computation of amount chargeable

1.65 **21A.**—(1) Except as otherwise expressly provided, the profits of a Schedule A business are computed in the same way as the profits of a trade are computed for the purposes of Case I of Schedule D.

(2) The following provisions apply in accordance with subsection (1)—

section 72 (apportionment); the provisions of Chapter V of Part IV (computational provisions relating to the Schedule D charge), except as mentioned in subsection (4) below;
section 577 (business entertainment expenses);
section 577A (expenditure involving crime);
sections 579 and 580 (redundancy payments);
section 588 (training courses for employees);
section 589A (counselling services for employees);
section 73(2) of the Finance Act 1988 (consideration for restrictive undertakings);
section 43 of the Finance Act 1989 (Schedule D: computation);
section 76 of that Act (expenses in connection with non-approved retirement benefit schemes);
sections 112 and 113 of that Act (expenditure in connection with provision of security asset or service);

sections 42 and 46(1) and (2) of the Finance Act 1998 (provisions as to computation of profits and losses).

(3) Section 74(1)(d) of this Act (disallowance of provisions for future repairs) applies in relation to a Schedule A business as if the reference to premises occupied for the purposes of the trade were to premises held for the purposes of the Schedule A business.

(4) The following provisions in Chapter V of Part IV of this Act do not apply, or are excepted from applying, in accordance with subsection (1)—

section 82 (interest paid to non-residents);

section 87 (treatment of premiums taxed as rent);

section 96 (farming and market gardening: relief for fluctuating profits); and

section 98 (tied premises: receipts and expenses treated as those of trade).

(5) Part 1 of Schedule 22 to the Finance Act 2001 (deduction for capital expenditure on remediation of contaminated land) applies in accordance with subsection (1), and the other Parts of that Schedule (further provision as to relief for remediation of contaminated land) have effect in relation to a Schedule A business in accordance with their provisions.

Application of other rules applicable to Case I of Schedule D

21B.—The following provisions apply for the purposes of Schedule A in relation to a Schedule A business as they apply for the purposes of Case I of Schedule D in relation to a trade— **1.66**

sections 103 to 106, 108, 109A and 110 (post-cessation receipts and expenses, etc.);

section 113 (effect for income tax purposes of change in the persons engaged in carrying on trade);

section 337(1) (effect of company beginning or ceasing to carry on trade);

section 401(1) (pre-trading expenditure);

section 44 of and Schedule 6 to the Finance Act 1998 (change of accounting basis).

Construction of Part II

24.—(1) In this Part, except where the context otherwise requires— **1.67**

"lease" includes an agreement for a lease, and any tenancy, but does not include a mortgage or heritable security, and "lessee", "lessor" and "letting" shall be construed accordingly;

"lessee" and "lessor" include respectively the successors in title of a lessee or a lessor;

"premises" includes any land; and

"premium" includes any like sum, whether payable to the immediate or a superior landlord or to a person connected (within the meaning of section 839) with the immediate or a superior landlord.

(2) For the purposes of this Part, any sum (other than rent) paid on or in connection with the granting of a tenancy shall be presumed to have been paid by way of premium except in so far as other sufficient consideration for the payment can be shown to have been given.

(3) Where paragraph (c) of section 38(1) applies, the premium, or an appropriate part of the premium, payable for or in connection with either lease mentioned in that paragraph may be treated as having been required under the other.

(4) References in this section to a sum shall be construed as including the value of any consideration, and references to a sum paid or payable or to the payment of a sum shall be construed accordingly.

(5) In the application of this Part to Scotland—

"assignment" means an assignation;

"intermediate landlord" means, where an occupying lessee is a sub-lessee, any person for the time being holding the interest of landlord under a sub-lease which comprises the property of which the occupying lessee is sub-lessee, but does not include the immediate landlord;

"premium" includes in particular a grassum payable to any landlord or intermediate landlord on the creation of a sub-lease; and

"reversion" means the interest of the landlord in the property subject to the lease.

(6) In Schedule A and in sections 25 to 31—

(a) references to a lease extend only to a lease conferring a right, as against the person whose interest is subject to the lease, to the possession of the premises;

(b) "rent" includes a payment by the tenant to defray the cost of work of maintenance of, or repairs to, the demised premises, not being work required by the lease to be carried out by the tenant; and

(c) "tenant's repairing lease" means a lease where the tenant is under an obligation to maintain and repair the whole or substantially the whole of the premises comprised in the lease.

(7) For the purposes of Schedule A and sections 25 to 31, a lease shall be taken to be at a full rent if the rent reserved under the lease (including an appropriate sum in respect of any premium under the lease) is sufficient, taking one year with another, to defray the cost to the lessor of fulfilling his obligations under the lease and of meeting any expenses of maintenance, repairs, insurance and management of the premises subject to the lease which fall to be borne by him.

PART III

GOVERNMENT SECURITIES

Savings certificates and tax reserve certificates

1.68 **46.**—(1) Subject to subsections (3)–(6) below, income arising from savings certificates shall not be liable to tax.

(2) Tax shall not be chargeable in respect of the interest on tax reserve certificates issued by the Treasury.

(3) Subsection (1) above does not apply to any savings certificates which are purchased by or on behalf of a person in excess of the amount

which a person is for the time being authorised to purchase under regulations made by the Treasury or, as respects Ulster Savings Certificates, by the Department of Finance and Personnel.

(4) Subsection (1) above does not apply to Ulster Savings Certificates unless—

(a) the holder is resident and ordinarily resident in Northern Ireland when the certificates are repaid; or

(b) the certificates were purchased by him and he was so resident and ordinarily resident when they were purchased.

(5) A claim under this section in respect of Ulster Savings Certificates shall be made to the Board.

(6) In this section, "savings certificates" means savings certificates issuedunder section 12 of the National Loans Act 1968 or section 7 of the National Debt Act 1958 or section 59 of the Finance Act 1920 and any war savings certificates as defined in section 9(3) of the National Debt Act 1972, together with any savings certificates issued under any corresponding enactment forming part of the law of Northern Ireland.

PART IV

PROVISIONS RELATING TO THE SCHEDULE D CHARGE

CHAPTER 1

SUPPLEMENTARY CHARGING PROVISIONS

Mines, quarries and other concerns

55.—(1) Profits arising out of land in the case of any concern specified in subsection (2) below shall be charged to tax under Case I of Schedule D. **1.69**

(2) The concerns are—

(a) mines and quarries (including gravel pits, sand pits and brickfields);

(b) ironworks, gasworks, salt springs or works, alum mines or works (not being mines falling within the preceding paragraph) and waterworks and streams of water;

(c) canals, inland navigation, docks and drains or levels;

(d) fishings;

(e) rights of markets and fairs, tolls, bridges and ferries;

(f) railways and other ways;

(g) other concerns of the like nature as any of the concerns specified in paragraphs (b)–(e) above.

CHAPTER 2

INCOME TAX: BASIS OF ASSESSMENT, ETC.

Cases I and II

Assessment on current year basis

1.70 **60.**—(1) Subject to subsection (2) below and section 63A, income tax shall be charged under Cases I and II of Schedule D on the full amount of the profits of the year of assessment.

(2) Where, in the case of a trade, profession or vocation, a basis period for the year of assessment is given by subsection (3) below or sections 61 to 63, the profits of that period shall be taken to be the profits of the year.

(3) Subject to sections 61 to 63, the basis period for a year of assessment is as follows—

(a) if the year is the first year of assessment in which there is an accounting date which falls not less than 12 months after the commencement date, the period of 12 months ending with that accounting date; and

(b) if there is a basis period for the immediately preceding year and that basis period is not given by section 61, the period of 12 months beginning immediately after the end of that basis period.

(4) In the case of a person who, if he had not died, would under the provisions of this section and sections 61 to 63A have become chargeable to income tax for any year, the tax which would have been so chargeable—

(a) shall be assessed and charged on his personal representatives; and

(b) shall be a debt due from and payable out of his estate.

(5) In this section and sections 61 to 63—

"accounting date", in relation to a year of assessment, means a date in the year to which accounts are made up or, where there are two or more such dates, the latest of those dates;

"the commencement date" and "the commencement year" mean respectively the date on which and the year of assessment in which the trade, profession or vocation is set up and commenced.

Basis of assessment at commencement

1.71 **61.**—(1) Notwithstanding anything in section 60, where the year of assessment is the commencement year, the computation of the profits chargeable to income tax under Case I or II of Schedule D shall be made on the profits arising in the year.

(2) Subject to section 63, where the year of assessment is the year next following the commencement year and—

(a) there is an accounting date in the year and the period beginning with the commencement date and ending with the accounting date is a period of less than 12 months; or

(b) the basis period for the year would, apart from this subsection, be given by section 62(2) and the period beginning with the commencement date and ending with the new date in the year is a period of less than 12 months,

the basis period for the year is the period of 12 months beginning with the commencement date.

(3) In this section, "the new date" has the same meaning as in section 62.

Change of basis period

62.—(1) Subsection (2) below applies where, in the case of a trade, profession or vocation— 1.72

(a) an accounting change, that is, a change from one accounting date ("the old date") to another ("the new date"), is made or treated as made in a year of assessment; and

(b) either section 62A applies or the year of assessment is the year next following or next but one following the commencement year.

(2) The basis period for the year of assessment is as follows—

(a) if the year is the year next following the commencement year or the relevant period is a period of less than 12 months, the period of 12 months ending with the new date in the year; and

(b) if the relevant period is a period of more than 12 months, that period;

and in this subsection the "relevant period" means the period beginning immediately after the end of the basis period for the preceding year and ending with the new date in the year.

(3) Where subsection (2) above does not apply as respects an accounting change made or treated as made in a year of assessment ("the first year"), this section and section 62A shall have effect in relation to the next following year ("the second year") as if the change had not been made or treated as made.

(4) As a consequence of subsection (3) above—

(a) an accounting change shall be treated as made in the second year if the date or, as the case may be, the latest date in that year to which accounts are made up is a date other than the date of the endof the basis period for the first year; and

(b) no such change shall be treated as made in the second year if that date is the date of the end of that period.

(5) For the purposes of this section an accounting change is made in the first year of assessment in which accounts are not made up to the old date, or accounts are made up to the new date, or both.

Basis of assessment after discontinuance

63.—Where a trade, profession or vocation is permanently discontinued in a year of assessment other than the commencement year, the basis period for the year shall be the period beginning— 1.73

(a) where the year is the year next following the commencement year, immediately after the end of the commencement year; and

(b) in any other case, immediately after the end of the basis period for the preceding year of assessment, and (in either case) ending with the date on which the trade, profession or vocation is permanently discontinued.

Cases III, IV and V

Case III Assessments

1.74 **64.**—Income tax under Case III of Schedule D shall be computed on the full amount of the income arising within the year of assessment, and shall be paid on the actual amount of that income, without any deduction.

Cases IV and V assessments: general

1.75 **65.**—(1) Subject to the provisions of this section and sections 66 and 67, income tax chargeable under Case IV or Case V of Schedule D shall be computed on the full amount of the income arising in the year preceding the year of assessment, whether the income has been or will be received in the United Kingdom or not, subject in the case of income not received in the United Kingdom—

(a) to the same deductions and allowances as if it had been so received; and

(b) to a deduction on account of any annuity or other annual payment (not being interest) payable out of the income to a person not resident in the United Kingdom.

(2) . . . income tax chargeable under Case IV or V of Schedule D on income arising from any pension shall be computed on the amount of that income subject to a deduction of one-tenth of the amount of the income.

(2A) Subject to section 65A, income tax chargeable under Case V of Schedule D on income which—

(a) arises from any business carried on for the exploitation, as a source of rents or other receipts, of any estate, interest or rights in or over any land outside the United Kingdom; and

(b) is not income immediately derived by any person from the carrying on by him of any trade, profession or vocation, either solely or in partnership,

shall be computed in accordance with the rules which are applicable under the Income Tax Acts to the computation of the profits of a Schedule A business.

(2B) The provisions of Schedule A shall apply for determining for the purposes of subsection (2A) above where income falls within paragraph (a) of that subsection as they would apply if—

(a) the land in question were in the United Kingdom, or

(b) a caravan or houseboat which is to be used at a location outside the United Kingdom were to be used at a location in the United Kingdom;

and any provision of the Income Tax Acts in pursuance of which there is deemed in certain cases to be a Schedule A business in relation to any landin the United Kingdom shall have effect, where the corresponding circumstances arise with respect to land outside the United Kingdom, as if, for the purposes of that subsection, there were deemed to be a business such as is mentioned in that paragraph.

(3) Income tax chargeable under Case IV or V of Schedule D on income which is immediately derived by a person from the carrying on by him of any trade, profession or vocation either solely or in partnership shall be computed in accordance with the rules applicable to Cases I and II of Schedule D (including sections 60 to 63A and 113); and subsection (1)(a) above shall not apply.

Nothing in this subsection shall be taken to apply sections 60 to 63 or 113 in relation to income chargeable under Case V of Schedule D but computed in accordance with this subsection.

(4) Subsections (1) to (3) and section 65A below above shall not apply to any person who makes a claim to the Board stating that he is not domiciled in the United Kingdom, or that, being a Commonwealth citizen or a citizen of the Republic of Ireland, he is not ordinarily resident in the United Kingdom.

(5) Where subsection (4) above applies the tax shall, subject to sections 66 and 67, be computed—

(a) in the case of tax chargeable under Case IV, on the full amount, so far as the same can be computed, of the sums received in the United Kingdom in the year preceding the year of assessment, without any deduction or abatement; and

(b) in the case of tax chargeable under Case V, on the full amount of the actual sums received in the United Kingdom in the year preceding the year of assessment from remittances payable in the United Kingdom, or from property imported, or from money or value arising from property not imported, or from money or value so received on credit or on account in respect of any such remittances, property, money or value brought or to be brought into the United Kingdom, without any deduction or abatement other than is allowed under the provisions of the Income Tax Acts in respect of profits charged under Case I of Schedule D.

(6) For the purposes of subsection (5) above, any income arising from securities or possessions out of the United Kingdom which is applied outside the United Kingdom by a person ordinarily resident in the United Kingdom in or towards satisfaction of—

(a) any debt for money lent to him in the United Kingdom or for interest on money so lent; or

(b) any debt for money lent to him outside the United Kingdom and received in or brought to the United Kingdom; or

(c) any debt incurred for satisfying in whole or in part a debt falling within paragraph (a) or (b) above,

shall be treated as received by him in the United Kingdom (and, for the purposes of subsection (5)(b) above, as so received from remittances payable in the United Kingdom).

(7) Where a person ordinarily resident in the United Kingdom receives in or brings to the United Kingdom money lent to him outside the United Kingdom, but the debt for that money is wholly or partly satisfied before he does so, subsection (6) above shall apply as if the money had been received in or brought to the United Kingdom before the debt was so

satisfied, except that any sums treated by virtue of that subsection as received in the United Kingdom shall be treated as so received at the time when the money so lent is actually received in or brought to the United Kingdom.

(8) Where—

(a) a person ("the borrower") is indebted for money lent to him; and

(b) income is applied by him in such a way that the money or property representing it is held by the lender on behalf of or to the account of the borrower in such circumstances as to be available to the lender for the purpose of satisfying or reducing the debt by set-off or otherwise,

that income shall be treated as applied by the borrower in or towards satisfaction of the debt if, under any arrangement between the borrower and the lender, the amount for the time being of the borrower's indebtedness to the lender, or the time at which the debt is to be repaid in whole or in part, depends in any respect directly or indirectly on the amount or value so held by the lender.

(9) For the purposes of subsections (6) to (8) above—

(a) a debt for money lent shall, to the extent to which that money is applied in or towards satisfying another debt, be deemed to be a debt incurred for satisfying that other debt, and a debt incurred for satisfying in whole or in part a debt falling within paragraph (c) of subsection (6) above shall itself be treated as falling within that paragraph; and

(b) "lender" includes, in relation to any money lent, any person for the time being entitled to repayment.

Case V income from land outside the UK: income tax

1.76 **65A.**—(1) This section applies where a person is chargeable to income tax under Case V of Schedule D in respect of income which—

(a) arises from a business carried on for the exploitation, as a source of rents or other receipts, of any estate, interest or rights in or over land outside the United Kingdom, and

(b) is not income to which section 65(3) applies (income immediately derived from carrying on a trade, profession or vocation).

(2) The provisions of Schedule A apply to determine whether income falls within subsection (1)(a) above as they would apply to determine whether the income fell within paragraph 1(1) of that Schedule if—

(a) the land in question were in the United Kingdom, or

(b) a caravan or houseboat which is to be used at a location outside the United Kingdom were to be used at a location in the United Kingdom.

(3) Any provision of the Taxes Acts which deems there to be a Schedule A business in the case of land in the United Kingdom applies where the corresponding circumstances arise with respect to land outside the United Kingdom so as to deem there to be a business within subsection (1)(a) above.

(4) All businesses and transactions carried on or entered into by a particular person or partnership, so far as they are businesses or transactions

the income from which is chargeable to tax under Case V of Schedule D in accordance with this section, are treated for the purposes of the charge to tax under Case V as, or as entered into in the course of carrying on, a single business (an "overseas property business").

(5) The income from an overseas property business shall be computed for the purposes of Case V of Schedule D in accordance with the rules applicable to the computation of the profits of a Schedule A business. Those rules apply separately in relation to—

(a) an overseas property business, and

(b) any actual Schedule A business of the person chargeable, as if each were the only Schedule A business carried on by that person.

(6) Sections 80 and 81 (expenses in connection with foreign trades and travel between trades etc.) do not apply in relation to the computation of the profits of an overseas property business.

(7) Sections 503 and 504 of this Act . . . do not apply to the profits or losses of an overseas property business.

(8) Where under this section rules expressed by reference to domestic concepts of law apply in relation to land outside the United Kingdom, they shall be interpreted so as to produce the result that most closely corresponds with the result produced for Schedule A purposes in relation to land in the United Kingdom.

Case VI

Case VI assessments

69.—Income tax under Case VI of Schedule D shall be computed on 1.77
the full amount of the profits or gains arising in the year of assessment.

CHAPTER 5

COMPUTATIONAL PROVISIONS

General rules as to deductions not allowable

74.—(1) Subject to the provisions of the Tax Acts, in computing the 1.78
amount of the profits to be charged under Case I or Case II of Schedule D, no sum shall be deducted in respect of—

(a) any disbursements or expenses, not being money wholly and exclusively laid out or expended for the purposes of the trade, profession or vocation;

(b) any disbursements or expenses of maintenance of the parties, their families or establishments, or any sums expended for any other domestic or private purposes distinct from the purposes of the trade, profession or vocation;

(c) the rent of the whole or any part of any dwelling-house or domestic offices, except any such part as is used for the purposes of the trade, profession or vocation, and where any such part is so used, the sum so deducted shall not, unless in any particular case it appears that having regard to all the circumstances some greater sum ought to be deducted, exceed two-thirds of the rent bona fide paid for that dwelling-house or those offices;

(d) any sum expended for repairs of premises occupied, or for the supply, repairs or alterations of any implements, utensils or articles employed, for the purposes of the trade, profession or vocation, beyond the sum actually expended for those purposes;

(e) any loss not connected with or arising out of the trade, profession or vocation;

(f) any capital withdrawn from, or any sum employed or intended to be employed as capital in, the trade, profession or vocation, but so that this paragraph shall not be treated as disallowing the deduction of any interest;

(g) any capital employed in improvements of premises occupied for the purposes of the trade, profession or vocation;

(h) any interest which might have been made if any such sums as aforesaid had been laid out at interest;

(j) any debts except—

(i) a bad debt proved to be such;

(ii) a debt or part of a debt released by the creditor wholly and exclusively for the purposes of his trade, profession or vocation as part of a relevant arrangement or compromise; and

(iii) a doubtful debt to the extent estimated to be bad, meaning, in the case of the bankruptcy or insolvency of the debtor, the debt except to the extent that any amount may reasonably be expected to be received on the debt;

(k) any average loss beyond the actual amount of loss after adjustment;

(l) any sum recoverable under an insurance or contract of indemnity;

(m) any annuity or other annual payment (other than interest) payable out of the profits;

(n) any interest paid to a person not resident in the United Kingdom if and so far as it is interest at more than a reasonable commercial rate;

(o) any interest in so far as the payment of that interest is or would be, otherwise than by virtue of section 375(2), either—

(i) a payment of interest to which section 369 applies, or

(ii) a payment of interest to which that section would apply but for section 373(5);

(p) any royalty or other sum paid in respect of the user of a patent;

(q) any rent, royalty or other payment which is by section 119 or 120 declared to be subject to deduction of tax under section 348 or 349 as if it were a royalty or other sum paid in respect of the user of a patent.

(2) In paragraph (j) of subsection (1) above, "relevant arrangement or compromise" means—

(a) a voluntary arrangement which has taken effect under or by virtue of the Insolvency Act 1986 or the Insolvency (Northern Ireland) Order 1989; or

(b) a compromise or arrangement which has taken effect under section 425 of the Companies Act 1985 or Article 418 of the Companies (Northern Ireland) Order 1986.

PART VII

GENERAL PROVISIONS RELATING TO TAXATION OF INCOME OF INDIVIDUALS

CHAPTER 2

TAXATION OF INCOME OF SPOUSES

General Rules

Construction of references to husband and wife living together

282.—A husband and wife shall be treated for income tax purposes as living together unless— 1.79

(a) they are separated under an order of a court of competent jurisdiction, or by deed of separation; or

(b) they are in fact separated in such circumstances that the separation is likely to be permanent.

GENERAL NOTE

This is the long-standing approach of the Inland Revenue to dealing with the question whether a married couple are living together. Note that the rule is not applied to social security income for income tax purposes under ITEPA 2003. See s.669 of that Act which applies the social security meanings to income tax for those purposes. But it is this definition, not the social security definition, that applies for tax credits purposes. See TCA 2002, s.3(5). There is no income tax definition of an "unmarried couple" and no provision dealing with same-sex couples as income tax law ignores all relationships other than that between husband and wife.

Jointly held property

282A.—(1) Subject to the following provisions of this section, income arising from property held in the names of a husband and his wife shall for the purposes of income tax be regarded as income to which they are beneficially entitled in equal shares. 1.80

(2) Subsection (1) above shall not apply to income to which neither the husband nor the wife is beneficially entitled.

(3) Subsection (1) above shall not apply to income—

(a) to which either the husband or the wife is beneficially entitled to the exclusion of the other; or

(b) to which they are beneficially entitled in unequal shares, if a declaration relating to it has effect under section 282B.

(4) Subsection (1) above shall not apply to—

(a) earned income; or

(b) income which is not earned income but to which section 111 applies.

(5) Subsection (1) above shall not apply to income to which the husbandor the wife is beneficially entitled if or to the extent that it is treated by virtue of any other provision of the Income Tax Acts as the income of the other of them or of a third party.

(6) References in this section to a husband and his wife are references to a husband and wife living together.

Jointly held property: declarations

1.81 **282B.**—(1) The declaration referred to in section 282A(3) is a declaration by both the husband and the wife of their beneficial interests in—

(a) the income to which the declaration relates; and

(b) the property from which that income arises.

(2) Subject to the following subsections, a declaration shall have effect under this section in relation to income arising on or after the date of the declaration; but a declaration made before the 6th June, 1990 shall also have effect in relation to income arising before that date.

(3) A declaration shall not have effect under this section unless notice of it is given to the inspector, in such form and manner as the Board may prescribe, within the period of 60 days beginning with the date of the declaration.

(4) A declaration shall not have effect under this section in relation to income from property if the beneficial interests of the husband and the wife in the property itself do not correspond to their beneficial interests in the income.

(5) A declaration having effect under this section shall continue to have effect unless and until the beneficial interests of the husband and wife in either the income to which it relates, or the property from which the income arises, cease to accord with the declaration.

CHAPTER 4

SPECIAL PROVISIONS

Interest on deposits with National Savings Bank

1.82 **325.**—Where the total income of an individual for the year of assessment includes, or would but for this section include, any sums paid or credited in respect of interest on deposits with the National Savings Bank, other than investment deposits, those sums shall be disregarded for all purposes of the Income Tax Acts, other than the furnishing of information, if or in so far as they do not exceed £70.

Interest on damages for personal injuries

329.—(1) The following interest shall not be regarded as income for any income tax purpose— 1.83

(a) any interest on damages in respect of personal injuries to a plaintiff or any other person, or in respect of a person's death, which is included in any sum for which judgment is given by virtue of a provision to which this paragraph applies; and

(b) any interest on damages or solatium in respect of personal injuries sustained by a pursuer or by any other person, decree for payment of which is included in any interlocutor by virtue of section 1 of the Interest on Damages (Scotland) Act 1958.

(2) The provisions to which subsection (1)(a) above applies are—

(a) section 3 of the Law Reform (Miscellaneous Provisions) Act 1934;

(b) section 17 of the Law Reform (Miscellaneous Provisions) Act (Northern Ireland) 1937;

(c) section 35A of the Supreme Court Act 1981;

(d) section 69 of the County Courts Act 1984;

(e) section 33A of the Judicature (Northern Ireland) Act 1978; and

(f) Article 45A of the County Courts (Northern Ireland) Order 1980.

(3) A payment in satisfaction of a cause of action, including a payment into court, shall not be regarded as income for any income tax purpose to the extent to which it is in respect of interest which would fall within subsection (1) above if included in a sum for which a judgment is given or if decree for payment of it were included in an interlocutor.

(4) In this section, "personal injuries" includes any disease and any impairment of a person's physical or mental condition.

Personal injury damages in the form of periodical payments

329AA.—(1) Where— 1.84

(a) an agreement is made settling a claim or action for damages for personal injury on terms whereby the damages are to consist wholly or partly of periodical payments; or

(b) a court awarding damages for personal injury makes an order incorporating such terms,

the payments shall not for the purposes of income tax be regarded as the income of any of the persons mentioned in subsection (2) below and accordingly shall be paid without any deduction under section 348(1)(b) or 349(1).

(2) The persons referred to in subsection (1) above are—

(a) the person ("A") entitled to the damages under the agreement or order;

(b) any person who, whether in pursuance of the agreement or order or otherwise, receives the payments or any of them on behalf of A;

(c) any trustee who, whether in pursuance of the agreement or order or otherwise, receives the payments or any of them on trust for the benefit of A under a trust under which A is during his lifetime the sole beneficiary.

(3) The periodical payments referred to in subsection (1) above, or any of them, may, if the agreement or order mentioned in that subsection or

a subsequent agreement so provides, consist of payments under one or more annuities purchased or provided for, or for the benefit of, A by the person by whom the payments would otherwise fall to be made.

(4) Sums paid to, or for the benefit of, A by a trustee or trustees shall not be regarded as his income for the purposes of income tax if made out of payments which by virtue of this section are not to be regarded for those purposes as income of the trustee or trustees.

(5) In this section "personal injury" includes any disease and any impairment of a person's physical or mental condition.

(6) For the purposes of this section, a claim or action for personal injury includes—

(a) such a claim or action brought by virtue of the Law Reform (Miscellaneous Provisions) Act 1934;

(b) such a claim or action brought by virtue of the Law Reform (Miscellaneous Provisions) Act (Northern Ireland) 1937;

(c) such a claim or action brought by virtue of the Damages (Scotland) Act 1976;

(d) a claim or action brought by virtue of the Fatal Accidents Act 1976;

(e) a claim or action brought by virtue of the Fatal Accidents (Northern Ireland) Order 1977.

(7) In relation to such an order as is mentioned in paragraph (b) of subsection (1) above "damages" includes an interim payment which the court, by virtue of rules of court in that behalf, orders the defendant to make to the plaintiff; and where, without such an order, the defendant agrees to make a payment on account of the damages that may be awarded against him in such an action as is mentioned in paragraph (a) of that subsection, that paragraph shall apply to the payment and the agreement as it applies to damages and to such an agreement as is there mentioned.

(8) In the application of subsection (7) above to Scotland for references to the plaintiff and the defendant there shall be substituted references to the pursuer and the defender.

Compensation for personal injury under statutory or other schemes

1.85 **329AB.**—(1) Section 329AA applies to annuity payments under an award of compensation made under the Criminal Injuries Compensation Scheme as it applies to payments of damages in that form under such an agreement or order as is mentioned in subsection (1) of that section.

(2) In subsection (1) above, "the Criminal Injuries Compensation Scheme" means—

(a) the scheme established by arrangements made under the Criminal Injuries Compensation Act 1995; or

(b) arrangements made by the Secretary of State for compensation for criminal injuries and in operation before the commencement of that scheme.

(3) If it appears to the Treasury that any other scheme or arrangement, whether established by statute or otherwise, makes provision for the making of periodical payments by way of compensation for personal injury within the meaning of section 329AA, the Treasury may by order

apply that section to those payments with such modifications as the Treasury consider necessary.

CHAPTER 5

RESIDENCE OF INDIVIDUALS

Commonwealth citizens and others temporarily abroad

334.—Every Commonwealth citizen or citizen of the Republic of Ireland— 1.86

(a) shall, if his ordinary residence has been in the United Kingdom, be assessed and charged to income tax notwithstanding that at the time the assessment or charge is made he may have left the United Kingdom, if he has so left the United Kingdom for the purpose only of occasional residence abroad; and

(b) shall be charged as a person actually residing in the United Kingdom upon the whole amount of his profits or gains, whether they arise from property in the United Kingdom or elsewhere, or from any allowance, annuity or stipend, or from any trade, profession, employment or vocation in the United Kingdom or elsewhere.

GENERAL NOTE

This section and the two following sections are included as the only express provisions in the Tax Acts dealing with the definition of "residence" and "ordinary residence". 1.87

Residence of persons working abroad

335.—(1) Where— 1.88

(a) a person works full-time in one or more of the following, that is to say, a trade, profession, vocation, office or employment; and

(b) no part of the trade, profession or vocation is carried on in the United Kingdom and all the duties of the office or employment are performed outside the United Kingdom;

the question whether he is resident in the United Kingdom shall be decided without regard to any place of abode maintained in the United Kingdom for his use.

(2) Where an office or employment is in substance one of which the duties fall in the year of assessment to be performed outside the United Kingdom there shall be treated for the purposes of this section as so performedany duties performed in the United Kingdom the performance of which is merely incidental to the performance of the other duties outside the United Kingdom.

Temporary residents in the United Kingdom

336.—(1) A person shall not be charged to income tax under a charge to which subsection (1A) applies as a person residing in the United 1.89

Kingdom, in respect of profits or gains received in respect of possessions or securities out of the United Kingdom, if—

(a) he is in the United Kingdom for some temporary purpose only and not with any view or intent of establishing his residence there; and

(b) he has not actually resided in the United Kingdom at one time or several times for a period equal in the whole to six months in any year of assessment,

but if any such person resides in the United Kingdom for such a period he shall be so chargeable for that year.

(1A) This subsection applies to—

(a) the charge under Schedule D;

(b) the charge under Part 9 of ITEPA 2003 (pension income) in respect of

(i) income to which section 573, 605, 609, 610, 611, 623, or 629 of that Act applies;

(ii) any annual payment to which section 633 of that Act applies which is made by or on behalf of a person who is outside the United Kingdom; or

(iii) income to which section 583 of that Act applies if the paying scheme (see subsection (3) of that section) is a pilots' benevolent fund (see section 587 of that Act); and

(c) the charge under Part 10 of ITEPA 2003 (social security income) in respect of benefits to which section 678 of that Act applies (foreign benefits).

(2) For the purposes of Cases I, II and III of Schedule E, a person who is in the United Kingdom for some temporary purpose only and not with the intention of establishing his residence there shall not be treated as resident in the United Kingdom if he has not in the aggregate spent at least six months in the United Kingdom in the year of assessment, but shall be treated as resident there if he has.

(3) The question whether—

(a) a person falls within subsection (1)(a) above, or

(b) for the purposes of subsection (2) above a person is in the United Kingdom for some temporary purpose only and not with the intention of establishing his residence there,

shall be decided without regard to any living accommodation available in the United Kingdom for his use.

General Note

The text set out here is that as partly amended to deal with the introduction of ITEPA 2003. Due to faulty drafting only some of the necessary changes were made. Provisions in the Finance Bill 2004 will, assuming they are enacted, make the other changes and remove the mention of Cases I, II and II in subs.(2) as these are now spent.

PART IX

ANNUAL PAYMENTS AND INTEREST

ANNUAL PAYMENTS

General rule

347A.—(1) A payment to which this section applies shall not be a charge on the income of the person liable to make it, and accordingly— **1.90**

(a) his income shall be computed without any deduction being made on account of the payment, and

(b) the payment shall not form part of the income of the person to whom it is made or of any other person.

(1A) This subsection applies to—

(a) the charge under Schedule D,

(b) the charge under Part 9 of ITEPA 2003 (pension income) in respect of—

(i) income to which section 573, 605, 609, 610, 611, 623 or 629 of that Act applies;

(ii) income to which section 583 of that Act applies if the paying scheme (see subsection (3) of that section) is a pilot's benefit fund (see section 587 of that Act), and

(c) the charge under Part 10 of ITEPA 2003 (social security income) in respect of benefits to which section 678 of that Act applies (foreign benefits).

(2) This section applies to any annual payment made by an individual which would otherwise be within the charge to tax under Case III of Schedule D except—

(a) a payment of interest;

(b) a covenanted payment to charity;

(c) a payment made for bona fide commercial reasons in connection with the individual's trade, profession or vocation; and

(d) a payment to which section 125(1) applies.

(3) This section applies to a payment made by personal representatives (within the meaning given in section 701(4)) where—

(a) the deceased would have been liable to make the payment if he had not died, and

(b) this section would have applied to the payment if he had made it.

(4) A maintenance payment arising outside the United Kingdom shall not be within the charge to tax under Case V of Schedule D if, because of this section, it would not have been within the charge of tax under Case III had it arisen in the United Kingdom; and for this purpose "maintenance payment" means a periodical payment (not being an instalment of a lump sum) which satisfies the conditions set out in paragraph (a) and (b) of section 347B(5).

(5) No deduction shall be made under section 65(1)(b) or 68(1)(b) of this Act or section 355 of ITEPA 2003 (deductions for certain payments by non-domiciled employees with foreign employers) on account of an annuity or other annual payment which would not have been within the charge to tax under Case III of Schedule D if it had arisen in the United Kingdom.

(6) References in subsection (2) above to an individual include references to a Scottish partnership in which at least one partner is an individual.

(7) In subsection (2)(b) above "a covenanted payment to charity" means a payment made under a covenant made otherwise than for consideration in money or money's worth in favour of a body of persons or trust established for charitable purposes only whereby the like annual payments (of which the payment in question is one) become payable for a period which may exceed three years and is not capable of earlier termination under any power exercisable without the consent of the persons for the time being entitled to the payments.

(8) For the purposes of subsection (7) above the bodies mentioned in section 507 shall each be treated as a body of persons established for charitable purposes only.

Qualifying maintenance payments

1.91 **347B.**—(1) Subject to subsection (1A) below in this section "qualifying maintenance payment" means a periodical payment which—

- (a) is made under an order made by a court in a Member State, or under a written agreement the proper law of which is the law of a member State or of a part of a Member State,
- (b) is made by one of the parties to a marriage (including a marriage which has been dissolved or annulled) either—
  - (i) to or for the benefit of the other party and for the maintenance of the other party, or
  - (ii) to the other party for the maintenance by the other party of any child of the family,
- (c) is due at a time when—
  - (i) the two parties are not a married couple living together, and
  - (ii) the party to whom or for whose benefit the payment is made has not remarried, and
- (d) is not a payment in respect of which relief from tax is available to the person making the payment under any provision of the Income Tax Acts other than this section.

(1A) A periodical payment is not a qualifying maintenance payment unless either of the parties to the marriage mentioned in subsection (1)(b) above was born before 6th April 1935.

(2) . . . subject to subsection (3) below, a person making a claim for the purpose shall be entitled, for a year of assessment to an income tax reduction calculated by reference to an amount equal to the aggregate amount of any qualifying maintenance payments made by him which fall due in that year.

(3) The amount by reference to which any income tax reduction is to be calculated under this section shall be limited to the amount specified in section 257A(5A) for the year.

(4) Where qualifying maintenance payments falling due in a year of assessment are made by a person who also makes other maintenance payments attracting relief for that year, subsection (3) above shall apply as if the limit imposed by it were reduced by an amount equal to the aggregate amount of those other payments.

(5) The reference in subsection (4) above to other maintenance payments attracting relief for a year is a reference to periodical payments which—

(a) are made under an order made by a court (whether in the United Kingdom or elsewhere) or under a written or oral agreement, and

(b) are made by a person—

(i) as one of the parties to a marriage (including a marriage which has been dissolved or annulled) to or for the benefit of the other party to the marriage and for the maintenance of the other party; or

(ii) to any person under 21 years of age for his own benefit, maintenance or education; or

(iii) to any person for the benefit, maintenance or education of a person under 21 years of age,

and in respect of which the person making them is entitled by virtue of section 36(3) of the Finance Act 1988 but otherwise than in accordance with section 38(2)(a) of that Act to make a deduction in computing his income for the year.

(5A) Where any person is entitled under this section for any year of assessment to an income tax reduction calculated by reference to the amount determined in accordance with subsections (2) and (3) above ("the relevant amount"), the amount of that person's liability for that year to income tax on his total income shall be the amount to which he would-have been liable apart from this section less whichever is the smaller of—

(a) the amount equal to the 10 per cent of the relevant amount; and

(b) the amount which reduces his liability to nil; and in this subsection, "the appropriate percentage" means . . . 15 per cent . . .

(5B) In determining for the purposes of subsection (5A) above the amount of income tax to which a person would be liable apart from any income tax reduction under this section, no account shall be taken of—

(a) any income tax reduction under Chapter I of Part VII;

(b) any relief by way of a reduction of liability to tax which is given in accordance with any arrangements having effect by virtue of section 788 or by way of a credit under section 790(1); or

(c) any tax at the basic rate on so much of that person's income as is income the income tax on which he is entitled to charge against any other person or to deduct, retain or satisfy out of any payment.

(6) . . .

(7) In this section—

"child of the family", in relation to the parties to a marriage, means a person under 21 years of age—

(a) who is a child of both those parties; or

(b) who (not being a person who has been boarded out with them by a public authority or voluntary organisation) has been treated by both of them as a child of their family;

"periodical payment" does not include an instalment of a lump sum.

(8) In subsection (1)(a) above, the reference to an order made by a court in the United Kingdom includes a reference to a maintenance assessment.

(9) Where—

(a) any periodical payment is made under a maintenance assessment by one of the parties to a marriage (including a marriage which has been dissolved or annulled);

(b) the other party to the marriage is, for the purposes of the Child Support Act 1991 or (as the case may be) the Child Support (Northern Ireland) Order 1991, a parent of the child or children with respect to whom the assessment has effect;

(c) the assessment was not made under section 7 of the Child Support Act 1991 (right of child in Scotland to apply for maintenance assessment; and

(d) any of the conditions mentioned in subsection (10) below is satisfied,

this section shall have effect as if the payment had been made to the other party for the maintenance by that other party of that child or (as the case may be) those children.

(10) The conditions are that—

(a) the payment is made to the Secretary of State in accordance with regulations made under section 29 of the Child Support Act 1991, by virtue of subsection (3)(a)(ii) of that section;

(b) the payment is made to the Department of Health and Social Services for Northern Ireland in accordance with regulations made under Article 29 of the Child Support (Northern Ireland) Order 1991, by virtue of paragraph (3)(a)(ii) of that Article;

(c) the payment is retained by the Secretary of State in accordance with regulations made under section 41 of that Act;

(d) the payment is retained by the Department of Health and Social Services for Northern Ireland in accordance with regulations made under Article 38 of that Order.

(11) In this section, "maintenance assessment" means a maintenance assessment made under the Child Support Act 1991 or the Child Support (Northern Ireland) Order 1991.

(12) Where any periodical payment is made to the Secretary of State or to the Department of Health and Social Services for Northern Ireland—

(a) by one of the parties to a marriage (including a marriage which has been dissolved or annulled); and

(b) under an order—

(i) made under section 106 of the Social Security Administration Act 1992 or section 101 of the Social Security Administration (Northern Ireland) Act 1992 (recovery of expenditure on benefit from person liable for maintenance) in respect of income support claimed by the other party to the marriage; or

(ii) made by virtue of section 23 of the Jobseekers Act 1995 (recovery of sums in respect of maintenance), or any corresponding enactment in Northern Ireland, in respect of an income-based jobseeker's allowance claimed by the other party to the marriage,

this section shall have effect as if the payment had been made to the other party to the marriage to or for the benefit, and for the maintenance, of that other party or (as the case may be) to that other party for the maintenance of the child or children concerned.

(13) In subsection (12) above, "income-based jobseeker's allowance" has the same meaning as in the Jobseekers Act 1995 or, for Northern Ireland, the same meaning as in any corresponding enactment in Northern Ireland.

PART XV

SETTLEMENTS

CHAPTER 1A

LIABILITY OF SETTLOR

Main provisions

Income arising under settlement where settlor retains an interest

660A.—(1) Income arising under a settlement during the life of the settlor shall be treated for all purposes of the Income Tax Acts as the income of the settlor and not as the income of any other person unless the income arises from property in which the settlor has no interest. **1.92**

(2) Subject to the following provisions of this section, a settlor shall be regarded as having an interest in property if that property or any derived property is, or will or may become, payable to or applicable for the benefit of the settlor or his spouse in any circumstances whatsoever.

(3) The reference in subsection (2) above to the spouse of the settlor does not include—

(a) a person to whom the settlor is not for the time being married but may later marry, or

(b) a spouse from whom the settlor is separated under an order of a court, or under a separation agreement or in such circumstances that the separation is likely to be permanent, or

(c) the widow or widower of the settlor.

(4) A settlor shall not be regarded as having an interest in property by virtue of subsection (2) above if and so long as none of that property, and no derived property, can become payable or applicable as mentioned in that subsection except in the event of—

(a) the bankruptcy of some person who is or may become beneficially entitled to the property or any derived property, or

(b) an assignment of or charge on the property or any derived property being made or given by some such person, or
(c) in the case of a marriage settlement, the death of both parties to the marriage and of all or any of the children of the marriage, or
(d) the death of a child of the settlor who had become beneficially entitled to the property or any derived property at an age not exceeding 25.

(5) A settlor shall not be regarded as having an interest in property by virtue of subsection (2) above if and so long as some person is alive and under the age of 25 during whose life that property, or any derived property, cannot become payable or applicable as mentioned in that subsection except in the event of that person becoming bankrupt or assigning or charging his interest in the property or any derived property.

(6) The reference in subsection (1) above to a settlement does not include an outright gift by one spouse to the other of property from which income arises, unless—

(a) the gift does not carry a right to the whole of that income, or
(b) the property given is wholly or substantially a right to income.

For this purpose, a gift is not an outright gift if it is subject to conditions, or if the property given or any derived property is or will or may become, in any circumstances whatsoever, payable to or applicable for the benefit of the donor.

(7) The reference in subsection (1) above to a settlement does not include an irrevocable allocation of pension rights by one spouse to the other in accordance with the terms of a relevant statutory scheme (within the meaning of Chapter I of Part XIV).

(8) Subsection (1) above does not apply to income arising under a settlement made by one party to a marriage by way of provisions for the other—

(a) after the dissolution or annulment of the marriage, or
(b) while they are separated under an order of a court, or under a separation agreement or in such circumstances that the separation is likely to be permanent, being income payable to or applicable for the benefit of that other party.

(9) Subsection (1) above does not apply to income consisting of—

(a) annual payments made by an individual for bona fide commercial reasons in connection with his trade, profession or vocation; or
(b) qualifying donations for the purposes of section 25 of the Finance Act 1990; or
(c) a benefit under an approved pension arrangement.

(10) In this section "derived property", in relation to any property, means income from that property or any other property directly or indirectly representing proceeds of, or of income from, that property or income therefrom.

(11) In this section "approved pension arrangement" means—

(a) an approved scheme or exempt approved scheme;
(b) a relevant statutory scheme;
(c) a retirement benefits scheme set up by a government outside the United Kingdom for the benefit, or primarily for the benefit, of its employees;

(d) a contract or scheme which is approved under Chapter III of Part XIV (retirement annuities);
(e) a personal pension scheme which is approved under Chapter IV of that Part;
(f) an annuity purchased for the purpose of giving effect to rights under a scheme falling within any of paragraphs (a) to (c) and (e) above;
(g) any pension arrangements of any description which may be prescribedby regulations made by the Secretary of State.

(12) In subsection (11) above "approved scheme", "exempt approved-scheme", "relevant statutory scheme" and "retirement benefits scheme" have the same meaning as in Chapter I of Part XIV.

Payments to unmarried minor children of settlor

660B.—(1) Income arising under a settlement which does not fall to be treated as income of the settlor under section 660A but which during the life of the settlor— **1.93**
(a) is paid to or for the benefit of an unmarried minor child of the settlor; or
(b) would otherwise be treated (apart from this section) as income of an unmarried minor child of the settlor in any year of assessment

shall be treated for all the purposes of the Income Tax Acts as the income of the settlor for that year and not as the income of any other person.

(2) Where income arising under a settlement is retained or accumulatedby the trustees, any payment whatsoever made thereafter by virtue or in consequence of the settlement, or any enactment relating thereto, to or for the benefit of an unmarried minor child of the settlor shall be deemed for the purposes of subsection (1) above to be a payment of income if or to the extent that there is available retained or cumulated income.

(3) There shall be taken to be available retained or accumulated income at any time when the aggregate amount of the income which has arisen under the settlement since it was made or entered into exceeds the aggregate amount of income so arising which has been—
(a) treated as income of the settlor; or
(b) paid (whether as income or capital) to or for the benefit of, or otherwise treated as the income of, a beneficiary other than an unmarried minor child of the settlor; or
(c) applied in defraying expenses of the trustees which were properly chargeable to income (or would have been so chargeable but for any express provisions of the trust).

(4) Where an offshore income gain (within the meaning of Chapter V of Part XVII) accrues in respect of a disposal of assets made by a trustee holding them for a person who would be absolutely entitled as against the trustee but for being a minor, the income which by virtue of section 761(1) is treated as arising by reference to that gain shall for the purposes of this section be deemed to be paid to that person.

(5) If in any year of assessment the aggregate amount of a child's relevant settlement income does not exceed £100, subsection (1) does not apply in relation to that income. A child's "relevant settlement income"

means income paid to or for the benefit of, or otherwise treated as income of, that child which apart from this subsection would be treated as income of the settlor under subsection (1).

(6) In this section—

(a) "child" includes a stepchild and an illegitimate child;

(b) "minor" means a person under the age of 18 years, and "minor child" shall be construed accordingly; and

(c) references to payments include payments in money or money's worth.

Nature of charge on settlor

1.94 **660C.**—(1) Tax chargeable by virtue of this Chapter shall be charged

(a) in the case of income falling within subsection (1A) below, as if it were income to which section 1A applies by virtue of subsection (2)(b) of that section; and

(b) in the case of any other income, under Case VI of Schedule D.

(1A) Income falls within this subsection if it is—

(a) income chargeable under Schedule F;

(b) income to which section 1A applies by virtue of its being equivalent foreign income falling within subsection (3)(b) of that section and chargeable under Case V of Schedule D;

(c) a distribution in relation to which section 233(1) applies;

(d) a qualifying distribution whose amount or value is determined in accordance with section 233(1A);

(e) a non-qualifying distribution, within the meaning of section 233(1B);

(f) income treated as arising by virtue of section 249;

(g) income treated as received by virtue of section 421(1)(a).

(2) In computing the liability to income tax of a settlor chargeable by virtue of this Chapter the same deductions and reliefs shall be allowed as would have been allowed if the income treated as his by virtue of this Chapter had been received by him.

(3) Subject to section 833(3), income which is treated by virtue of this Chapter as income of a settlor shall be deemed for the purposes of this section to be the highest part of his income.

Supplementary provisions

Application to settlements by two or more settlors

1.95 **660E.**—(1) In the case of a settlement where there is more than one settlor, this Chapter shall have effect in relation to each settlor as if he were the only settlor, as follows.

(2) In this Chapter, in relation to a settlor—

(a) references to the property comprised in a settlement include only property originating from that settlor; and

(b) references to income arising under the settlement include only income originating from that settlor.

(3) For the purposes of section 660B there shall be taken into account, in relation to the child of the settlor only—

(a) income originating from that settlor; and

(b) in a case in which section 660B(2) applies, payments which are under that provision (as adapted by subsection (4) below) to be deemed to be payments of income.

(4) In applying section 660B(2) to a settlor—

(a) the reference to income arising under the settlement includes only income originating from that settlor; and

(b) the reference to any payment made by virtue or in consequence of the settlement or any enactment relating thereto includes only a payment made out of property originating from that settlor or income originating from that settlor.

(5) References in this section to property originating from a settlor are references to—

(a) property which that settlor has provided directly or indirectly for the purposes of the settlement; and

(b) property representing that property; and

(c) so much of any property which represents both property so provided and other property as, on a just apportionment, represents the property so provided.

(6) References in this section to income originating from a settlor are references to—

(a) income from property originating from that settlor; and

(b) income provided directly or indirectly by that settlor.

(7) In subsections (5) and (6) above—

(a) references to property or income which a settlor has provided directly or indirectly include references to property or income which has been provided directly or indirectly by another person in pursuance of reciprocal arrangements with that settlor, but do not include references to property or income which that settlor has provided directly or indirectly in pursuance of reciprocal arrangements with another person; and

(b) references to property which represents other property include references to property which represents accumulated income from that other property.

Meaning of "settlement" and related expressions

660G.—(1) In this Chapter— 1.96

"settlement" includes any disposition, trust, covenant, agreement, arrangement or transfer of assets, and

"settlor", in relation to a settlement, means any person by whom the settlement was made.

(2) A person shall be deemed for the purposes of this Chapter to have made a settlement if he has made or entered into the settlement directly or indirectly, and, in particular, but without prejudice to the generality of the preceding words, if he has provided or undertaken to provide funds directly or indirectly for the purpose of the settlement, or has made with

any other person a reciprocal arrangement for that other person to make or enter into the settlement.

(3) References in this Chapter to income arising under a settlement include, subject to subsection (4) below, any income chargeable to income tax by deduction or otherwise, and any income which would have been so chargeable if it had been received in the United Kingdom by a person domiciled, resident and ordinarily resident in the United Kingdom.

(4) Where the settlor is not domiciled, or not resident, or not ordinarily resident, in the United Kingdom in a year of assessment, references in this Chapter to income arising under a settlement do not include income arising under the settlement in that year in respect of which the settlor, if he were actually entitled there to, would not be chargeable to income tax by deduction or otherwise by reason of his not being so domiciled, resident or ordinarily resident. But where such income is remitted to the United Kingdom in circumstances such that, if the settlor were actually entitled to that income when remitted, he would be chargeable to income tax by reason of his residence in the United Kingdom, it shall be treated for the purposes of this Chapter as arising under the settlement in the year in which it is remitted.

Chapter 1B

Provisions as to Capital Sums Paid to Settlor

Sums paid to settlor otherwise than as income

1.97 **677.**—(1) Any capital sum paid directly or indirectly in any year of assessment by the trustees of a settlement to which this section applies to the settlor shall—

(a) to the extent to which the amount of that sum falls within the amount of income available up to the end of that year, be treated for all the purposes of the Income Tax Acts as the income of the settlor for that year;

(b) to the extent to which the amount of that sum is not by virtue of this subsection treated as his income for that year and falls within the amount of the income available up to the end of the next following year, be treated for those purposes as the income of the settlor for the next following year;

and so on for each subsequent year up to a maximum of ten subsequent years, taking the reference in paragraph (b) to the year mentioned in paragraph (a) as a reference to that and any other year before the subsequent year in question.

(2) For the purposes of subsection (1) above, the amount of income available up to the end of any year shall, in relation to any capital sum paid as mentioned in that subsection, be taken to be the aggregate amount of income arising under the settlement in that year and any previous year which has not been distributed, less—

(a) the amount of that income taken into account under that subsection in relation to that sum in any previous year or years; and
(b) the amount of that income taken into account under that subsection in relation to any other capital sums paid to the settlor in any year before that sum was paid; and
(c) so much of any income arising under the settlement in that year and any previous year which has not been distributed as is shown to consist of income which has been treated as income of the settlor by virtue of section 671, 672, 674, 674A or 683; and
(d) any income arising under the settlement in that year and any previous year which has been treated as the income of the settlor by virtue of section 673; and
(e) any sums paid by virtue or in consequence of the settlement, to the extent that they are not allowable, by virtue of section 676, as deductions in computing the settlor's income for that year or any previous year; and
(f) any sums paid by virtue or in consequence of the settlement in that year or any previous year which have been treated as the income of the settlor by virtue of section 664(2)(b); and
(fa) any income arising under the settlement in that year or any previous year which has been treated as income of the settlor by virtue of section 660A or 660B; and
(g) any sums included in the income arising under the settlement as amounts which have been or could have been apportioned to a beneficiary as mentioned in section 681(1)(b); and
(h) an amount equal to tax at the rate applicable to trusts on—
 (i) the aggregate amount of income arising under the settlement in that year and any previous year which has not been distributed, less
 (ii) the aggregate amount of the income and sums referred to in paragraphs (c), (d), (e), (f) and (g) above.

(3) Where any amount is included in a person's income by virtue of section 421 in respect of any loan or advance, there shall be a corresponding reduction in the amount (if any) afterwards falling to be so included in respect of it by virtue of this section.

(4) Where the capital sum paid to the settlor is a sum paid by way of loan, then—
(a) if the whole of it is repaid, no part of that sum shall by virtue of subsection (1) above be treated as the settlor's income for any year of assessment after that in which the repayment occurs; and
(b) if one or more capital sums have previously been paid to him by way of loan and wholly repaid, the amount of that capital sum shall be treated as equal to its excess, if any, over so much of the sum or sums previously paid as has already fallen to be treated as his income by virtue of that subsection.

(5) Where the capital sum paid to the settlor is a sum paid by way of complete repayment of a loan, then, if an amount not less than that sum is thereafter lent by the settlor to the trustees of the settlement, no part of that sum shall by virtue of subsection (1) above be treated as his income for any year of assessment after that in which the further loan is made.

(6) Where the whole or any part of any sum is treated by virtue of this section as income of the settlor for any year, it shall be treated as income of such an amount as, after deduction of tax at the rate applicable to trusts for that year, would be equal to that sum or that part of that sum.

(7) Tax chargeable by virtue of this section shall be charged under Case VI of Schedule D; and there shall be set off against the tax charged on any amount treated by virtue of this section as income of the settlor for any year an amount equal to—

(a) tax at the rate applicable to trusts for that year on the amount so treated as his income; or

(b) so much of the amount of tax at that rate as is equal to the tax charged,

whichever is the less.

(8) In computing the liability to income tax of a settlor chargeable by virtue of this section, the same deductions and reliefs shall be allowed as would have been allowed if the amount treated as his income by virtue of this section had been received by him as income.

(9) This section applies to any settlement wherever made, and whether made before or after the passing of this Act, and in this section—

(a) "capital sum" means, subject to subsection (10) below—

(i) any sum paid by way of loan or repayment of a loan; and

(ii) any other sum paid otherwise than as income, being a sum which is not paid for full consideration in money or money's worth,

but does not include any sum which could not have become payable to the settlor except in one of the events specified in section 673(3) or, in the case of a sum paid on or after the 6th April, 1995, in one of the events specified in section 660A(4) or on the death under the age of 25 of any such person as is mentioned in section 660A(5)24; and

(b) references to sums paid to the settlor include references to sums paid to the wife or husband of the settlor or to the settlor (or the husband or wife of the settlor) jointly with another person.

(10) For the purposes of this section there shall be treated as a capital sum paid to the settlor by the trustees of the settlement any sum which—

(a) is paid by them to a third party at the settlor's direction or by virtue of the assignment by him of his right to receive it where the direction or assignment was given or made on or after 6th April 1981; or

(b) is otherwise paid or applied by them for the benefit of the settlor, and which would not apart from this subsection be treated as a capital sum paid to him.

Capital sums paid by body connected with settlement

1.98 **678.**—(1) Where—

(a) a capital sum is paid after the 5th April 1981 to the settlor in a year of assessment by any body corporate connected with the settlement in that year, and

(b) an associated payment has been or is made directly or indirectly to that body by the trustees of the settlement,

for the purposes of section 677 as having been paid to the settlor by the trustees of the settlement.

(2) A capital sum to which subsection (1) above applies shall—

(a) to the extent to which the amount of that sum falls within the total of the associated payment or payments made up to the end of the year of assessment in which it is paid, be treated as having been paid to the settlor in that year;

(b) to the extent to which the amount of that sum is not treated as paid to the settlor in that year and falls within the total of the associated payment or payments made up to the end of the next following year (less what was taken into account under this subsection in relation to that sum in the previous year), be treated as having been paid to the settlor in the next following year,

and so on for each subsequent year, taking the references in paragraph (b) to the year mentioned in paragraph (a) as references to that and any other year before the subsequent year in question.

(3) In this section "associated payment", in relation to any capital sum paid to the settlor by a body corporate, means—

(a) any capital sum paid to that body by the trustees of the settlement; and

(b) any other sum paid or asset transferred to that body by those trustees which is not paid or transferred for full consideration in money or money's worth,

being a sum paid or asset transferred in the five years ending or beginning with the date on which the capital sum is paid to the settlor.

(4) For the purposes of this section any capital sum paid by a body corporate, and any associated payment made to a body corporate, at a time when it is, within the meaning of section 416, associated with another body corporate may be treated as paid by or made to that other body corporate.

(5) In this section "capital sum" has the same meaning as in section 677; and any question whether a capital sum has been paid to the settlor by a body corporate or to a body corporate by the trustees shall be determined in the same way as any question under that section whether a capital sum has been paid to the settlor by the trustees.

(6) Subsection (1) above does not apply to any sum paid to the settlor by way of loan or repayment of a loan if—

(a) the whole of the loan is repaid within 12 months of the date on which it was made; and

(b) the period for which amounts are outstanding in respect of loans made to the settlor by that or any other body corporate connected with the settlement, or by him to that or any other such body, in any period of five years does not exceed 12 months.

Part XVI

Estates of Deceased Persons in Course of Administration

Limited interests in residue

1.99 **695.**—(1) The following provisions of this section shall have effect in relation to a person who, during the period commencing on the death of a deceased person and ending on the completion of the administration of his estate ("the administration period") or during a part of that period, has a limited interest in the residue of the estate or in a part thereof.

(2) When any sum has been paid during the administration period in respect of that limited interest, the amount of that sum shall be deemed for all tax purposes to have been paid to that person as income for the year of assessment in which that sum was paid or, in the case of a sum paidin respect of an interest that has ceased, for the last year of assessment in which it was subsisting.

(3) Where, on the completion of the administration of the estate, there is an amount which remains payable in respect of that limited interest, that amount shall be deemed for all tax purposes to have been paid to that person as income for the year of assessment in which the administration period ends or, in the case of a sum which is deemed to be paid in respect of an interest that ceased before the end of that period, for the last year of assessment in which that interest was subsisting.

(4) Any amount which is deemed to have been paid to that person as income for any year by virtue of this section shall—

(a) in the case of a United Kingdom estate, be deemed to be income of such an amount as would after deduction of income tax for that year be equal to the amount deemed to have been so paid, and to be income which has borne income tax at the applicable rate; and

(b) in the case of a foreign estate, be deemed to be income of the amount deemed to have been so paid, and shall be chargeable to income tax under Case IV of Schedule D as if it were income arising from securities in a place out of the United Kingdom.

(5) Where—

(a) a person has been charged to income tax for any year by virtue of this section in respect of an amount deemed to have been paid to him as income in respect of an interest in a foreign estate ("the deemed income"), and

(b) any part of the aggregate income of that estate for that year has borne United Kingdom income tax by deduction or otherwise ("the aggregate income"),

the tax so charged on him shall, on proof of the facts on a claim, be reduced by an amount bearing the same proportion thereto as the amount of the deemed income which has borne United Kingdom income tax, less the tax so borne, bears to the amount of the aggregate income, less the tax so borne.

(6) Where relief has been given under subsection (5) above, such part of the amount in respect of which he has been charged to income tax as

corresponds to the proportion mentioned in that subsection shall, for the purpose of computing his total income, be deemed to represent income of such an amount as would after deduction of income tax be equal to that part of the amount charged.

Absolute interests in residue

696.—(1) The following provisions of this section shall have effect in relation to a person who, during the administration period or during a part of that period, has an absolute interest in the residue of the estate of a deceased person or in a part thereof. 1.100

(2) There shall be ascertained in accordance with section 697 the amount of the residuary income of the estate for each whole year of assessment, and for each broken part of a year of assessment, during which—

(a) the administration period was current; and

(b) that person had that interest;

and the amount so ascertained in respect of any year of part of a year or, in the case of a person having an absolute interest in a part of a residue, a proportionate part of that amount, is in this Part referred to as the "residuary income" of that person for that year of assessment.

(3) When any sum has been paid during the administration period in respect of that absolute interest, that sum, except so far as it is excluded from the operation of this subsection, shall be deemed for all tax purposes to have been paid to that person as income for the year of assessment in which it was actually paid.

(3A) A payment shall be excluded from the operation of subsection (3) above to the extent (if any) that the aggregate of that sum and all the sums which—

(a) have been paid previously during the administration period in respect of that absolute interest, and

(b) fall under this section to be treated as paid to that person as income,

exceeds the aggregated income entitlement of that person for the year of assessment in which the sum is paid.

(3B) For the purposes of this section the aggregated income entitlement of that person for any year of assessment is the amount which would be the aggregate of the amounts received for that year of assessment and all previous years of assessment in respect of the interest if that person had a right in each year to receive, and had received—

(a) in the case of a United Kingdom estate, his residuary income for that year less income tax at the applicable rate for that year; and

(b) in the case of a foreign estate, his residuary income for that year.

(4) In the case of a United Kingdom estate, any amount which is deemed to have been paid to that person as income for any year by virtue of subsection (3) above shall be deemed to be income of such an amount as would, after deduction of income tax for that year, be equal to the amount deemed to have been so paid, and to be income that has borne income tax at the applicable rate.

(5) Where, on the completion of the administration of the estate, the aggregate of all the sums which, apart from this subsection—

(a) have been paid during the administration period in respect of that absolute interest, and
(b) fall under this section to be treated as paid to that persons as income,

is exceeded by the aggregated income entitlement of that person for the year of assessment in which the administration of the estate is completed, then an amount equal to the amount of the excess shall be treated for the purposes of subsections (3) to (4) above as having been actually paid, immediately before the end of the administration period, in respect of that interest.

(6) In the case of a foreign estate, any amount which is deemed to have been paid to that person as income for any year by virtue of this section shall be deemed to be income of that amount and shall be chargeable to income tax under Case IV of Schedule D as if it were income arising from securities in a place out of the United Kingdom.

(7) Where—

(a) a person has been charged to income tax for any year by virtue of this section in respect of an amount deemed to have been paid to him as income in respect of an interest in a foreign estate ("the deemed income"), and
(b) any part of the aggregate income of that estate for that year has borne United Kingdom income tax by deduction or otherwise ("the aggregate income"),

the tax so charged on him shall, on proof of the facts on a claim, be reduced by an amount bearing the same proportion thereto as the amount of the deemed income which has borne United Kingdom income tax bears to the amount of the aggregate income.

(8) For the purposes of any charge to corporation tax under this section, the residuary income of a company shall be computed in the first instance by reference to years of assessment, and the residuary income for any such year shall be apportioned between the accounting periods (if more than one) comprising that year.

Part XIX

Supplemental

Miscellaneous

Deductions not to be allowed in computing profits or gains

1.101 **817.**—(1) In arriving at the amount of profits or gains for tax purposes—

(a) no other deductions shall be made than such as are expressly enumerated in the Tax Acts; and
(b) no deduction shall be made on account of any annuity or other annual payment (not being interest) to be paid out of such profits

or gains in regard that a proportionate part of income tax is allowed to be deducted on making any such payment.

(2) In arriving at the amount of profits or gains from any property described in the Tax Acts or from any office or employment, no deduction shall be made on account of diminution of capital employed, or loss sustained, in any trade or in any profession, employment or vocation.

Application of Income Tax Acts to public departments and avoidance of exempting provisions

829.—(1) Subject to subsections (2) and (3) below, all the provisions of the Income Tax Acts relating to the assessment, charge, deduction and payment of income tax shall apply in relation to public offices and departments of the Crown. 1.102

(2) Nothing in those provisions of the Income Tax Acts shall require the payment by any such office or department of any tax which would be ultimately borne by the Crown unless it is tax which would not have been so borne but for a failure by a public office or department of the Crown to make a deduction required by virtue of subsection (1) above.

(2A) Subsections (1) and (2) above have effect in relation to Chapter 4 of Part 13 of this Act (sub-contractors in the construction industry) as if the whole of any deduction required to be made under section 559 were in all cases a deduction of income tax.

(3) Subsection (1) above shall not apply to public offices and departments of any country, state, province or colony within section 320(3)(b) or (c) and nothing in subsection (1) above shall exempt any government from taxation to which it is liable in connection with any office or department by virtue of section 25 of the Finance Act 1925 (liability in respect of trading operations of Dominion governments and others).

(4) No letters patent granted or to be granted by the Crown to any person, city, borough or town corporate of any liberty, privilege or exemption from subsidies, tolls, taxes, assessments or aids, and no statute which grants any salary, annuity or pension to any person free of any taxes, deductions or assessments, shall be construed or taken to exempt any person, city, borough or town corporate, or any inhabitant of any city, borough or town corporate, from income tax, and all non-obstantes in any such letters patent or statute made or to be made to the contrary effect shall be void.

Interpretation of this Act

831.—(1) In this Act, except so far as the context otherwise requires— 1.103

(a) "the Corporation Tax Acts" means the enactments relating to the taxation of the income and chargeable gains of companies and of company distributions (including provisions relating also to income tax); and

(b) "the Income Tax Acts" means the enactments relating to income tax, including any provisions of the Corporation Tax Acts which relate to income tax.

(2) In this Act "the Tax Acts", except so far as the context otherwise requires, means this Act and all other provisions of the Income Tax Acts and the Corporation Tax Acts.

(3) In this Act—
"ITEPA 2003" means the Income Tax (Earnings and Pensions) Act 2003;
"the Management Act" means the Taxes Management Act 1970;
"the 1968 Act" means the Capital Allowances Act 1968;
"the 1970 Act" means the Income and Corporation Taxes Act 1970;
"the 1979 Act" means the Capital Gains Tax Act 1979;
"the 1990 Act" means the Capital Allowances Act 1990; and
"the 1992 Act" means the Taxation of Chargeable Gains Act 1992.

(4) Section 1 of the Family Law Reform Act 1987, the paragraph inserted in Schedule 1 to the Interpretation Act 1978 by paragraph 73 of Schedule 2 to that Act and section 1(3) of the Law Reform (Parent and Child) (Scotland) Act 1986 (legal equality of illegitimate children), shall be disregarded in construing references in this Act to a child or to children (however expressed).

(5) This Act, so far as it relates to capital gains tax, shall be construed as one with the 1992 Act.

(6) Any reference in this Act to a section, Part or Schedule is a reference to that section, Part or Schedule of or to this Act, unless the context otherwise requires.

Interpretation of the Tax Acts

1.104 **832.**—(1) In the Tax Acts, except in so far as the context otherwise requires—
"Act" includes an Act of the Parliament of Northern Ireland and a Measure of the Northern Ireland Assembly;
"additional rate", in relation to any year of assessment for which income tax is charged, means 10 per cent or such rate as Parliament may determine;
"authorised unit trust" has the meaning given by section 468(6);
"basic rate", in relation to the charging of income tax for any year of assessment, means the rate of income tax determined in pursuance of section 1(2)(a), and any reference to the basic rate limit shall be construedin accordance with section 1(3);
"the Board" means the Commissioners of Inland Revenue;
"body of persons" means any body politic, corporate or collegiate, and any company, fraternity, fellowship and society of persons whether corporate or not corporate;
"building society" means a building society within the meaning of the Building Societies Act 1986;
"capital allowance" means any allowance under the Capital Allowances Act (including enactments which under this Act are to be treated as contained in that Act);
"the Capital Allowances Act" means the Capital Allowances Act 2001;
"chargeable gain" has the same meaning as in the 1992 Act;
"chargeable period" means an accounting period of a company or a year of assessment;
"close company" has the meaning given by sections 414 and 415;
"collector" means any collector of taxes;

"company" means, subject to subsection (2) below, any body corporate or unincorporated association but does not include a partnership, a local authority or a local authority association;
"distribution" has the meaning given by Part VI with section 418;
"farm land" means land in the United Kingdom wholly or mainly occupied for the purposes of husbandry, but excluding any dwelling or domestic offices, and excluding market garden land, and "farming" shall be construed accordingly;
"for accounting purposes" means for the purposes of accounts drawn up in accordance with generally accepted accounting practice;
"franked investment income" means income of a company resident in the United Kingdom which consists of a distribution in respect of which the company is entitled to a tax credit (and which accordingly represents income equal to the aggregate of the amount or value of the distribution and the amount of that credit);
"franked payment" shall be construed in accordance with section 238, but subject to section 247(1);
"generally accepted accounting practice" has the meaning given by section 836A;
"group income" has the meaning given by section 247(2);
"higher rate", in relation to the charging of income tax for any year of assessment, means any rate of income tax determined in pursuance of section 1(2)(b);
"industrial assurance business" means any such business carried on before the day appointed for the coming into force of section 167(4) of the Finance Act 1996 as was industrial insurance within the meaning given by section 1(2) of the Industrial Assurance Act 1923 or Article 3(1) of the Industrial Assurance (Northern Ireland) Order 1979;
"inspector" means any inspector of taxes;
"interest" means both annual or yearly interest and interest other than annual or yearly interest;
"investment LLP" and "property investment LLP" have the meaning given by section 842B;
"local authority association" has the meaning given by section 519;
"lower rate", in relation to the charging of income tax for any year of assessment, means the rate of income tax specifiedin or determined in pursuance of section 1A(1B);
"market garden land" means land in the United Kingdom occupied as a nursery or garden for the sale of the produce (other than land used for the growth of hops) and "market gardening" shall be construed accordingly;
"notice" means notice in writing or in a form authorised (in relation to the case in question) by directions under section 118 of the Finance Act 1998;
"ordinary share capital", in relation to a company, means all the issued share capital (by whatever name called) of the company, other than capital the holders of which have a right to a dividend at a fixedrate but have no other right to share in the profits of the company;
"overseas property business" has the meaning given by section 65A(4) or 70A(4);

"period of account"—

(a) in relation to a person, means any period for which the person draws up accounts, and

(b) in relation to a trade, profession vocation or other business means any period for which accounts of the business are drawn up;

"preference dividend" means a dividend payable on a preferred share or preferred stock at a fixed rate per cent. or, where a dividend is payable on a preferred share or preferred stock partly at a fixed rate per cent. and partly at a variable rate, such part of that dividend as is payable at a fixed rate per cent.;

"the rate applicable to trusts" shall be construed in accordance with section 686(1A);

"the rate of advance corporation tax" means the rate referred to in section 14(3);

"recognised clearing system" has the meaning given by section 124(6);

"Schedule A business" means any business the profits or gains of which are chargeable to income tax under Schedule A, including the business in the course of which any transaction is by virtue of paragraph 1(2) of that Schedule to be treated as entered into;

"the Schedule F ordinary rate" shall be construed in accordance with section 1B(2);

"the Schedule F trust rate" shall be construed in accordance with section 686(1A);

"the Schedule F upper rate" shall be construed in accordance with section 1B(2);

"starting rate", in relation to the charging of income tax for any year of assessment, means the rate of income tax determined in pursuance of section 1(2)(aa), and any reference to the starting rate limit shall be construed in accordance with section 1(2A);

"surplus of franked investment income" has the meaning given by section 238;

"tax credit" means a tax credit under section 231;

"trade" includes every trade, manufacture, adventure or concern in the nature of trade;

"Ulster Savings Certificates" means savings certificates issued or treated as issued under section 15 of the Exchequer and Financial Provisions Act (Northern Ireland) 1950;

"unit holder" has the meaning given by section 468(6);

"unit trust scheme" has the meaning given by section 469;

"year of assessment" means, with reference to any income tax, the year for which such tax was granted by any Act granting income tax;

"the year 1988–89" means the year of assessment beginning on 6th April 1988, and any corresponding expression in which two years are similarly mentioned means the year of assessment beginning on 6th April, in the first-mentioned of those two years;

and a source of income is within the charge to corporation tax or income tax if that tax is chargeable on the income arising from it, or would be so chargeable if there were any such income, and references to a person, or to income, being within the charge to tax, shall be similarly construed.

(2) The definition of "company" is subject to section 468, and does not apply in the following provisions of this Act, that is to say—

Chapter 1 of Part XVII;
sections 774 to 777;
section 839;
paragraph 15 of Schedule 3;

(and also does not apply where the context otherwise requires because some other definition of "company" applies).

(3) Except so far as the context otherwise requires, in the Tax Acts, and in any enactment passedafter 12th March 1970 which by any express provision is to be construed as one with the Tax Acts, the Corporation Tax Acts or the Income Tax Acts, "tax", where neither income tax nor corporation tax is specified, means either of those taxes.

(4) Subsection (3) above is without prejudice to the provisions of section 9 which apply income tax law for certain purposes of corporation tax, and accordingly the employment of "income tax" rather than "tax" in any provision of the Tax Acts is not a conclusive indication that that provision is not applied to corporation tax by that section.

(4A) Any reference in the Tax Acts to franked investment income received by a company apply to any such income received by another person on behalf of or in trust for the company, but not to any such income received by the company on behalf of or in trust for another person.

(5) In the Tax Acts any reference to a child, however expressed, shall be construed as including a reference to an adopted child. This subsection does not apply for the purposes of paragraph 10 of Schedule 30.

Interpretation of Income Tax Acts

833.—(1) In the Income Tax Acts references to profits or gains shall not include references to chargeable gains. **1.105**

(2) References in the Income Tax Acts to the retail prices index are references to the general index of retail prices (for all items) published by the Office for National Statistics; and if that index is not published for a month which is relevant for the purposes of any provision of those Acts that provision shall be construed as referring to any substituted index or index figures by that office.

(3) For the purposes of any provision of the Income Tax Acts (other than section 550 . . .) requiring income of any description to be treated as the highest part of a person's income, his income shall be calculated without regard to—

(a) any payment or other benefit charged to tax under Chapter 3 of Part 6 of ITEPA 2003 (payments and other benefits of termination of employment); or

(b) any amount included in his total income by virtue of section 547(1)(a) . . .

(4) Subject to subsections (5) and (6) below, in the Income Tax Acts "earned income" means, in relation to any individual—

(a) any payment charged to tax under ITEPA 2003 except—

(i) payments that meet the conditions in section 623 of that Act (return of surplus employee additional voluntary contributions); and
(ii) jobseeker's allowance (to which Chapter 3 of Part 10 of that Act applies);

(b) any income from any property which is attached to or forms part of the general earnings from any employment; and
(c) any income which is charged under Schedule . . . D and is immediately derived by the individual from the carrying on or exercise by him of his trade, profession or vocation, either as an individual or, in the case of a partnership, as a partner personally acting in the partnership.

(5) Without prejudice to the generality of the provisions of subsection (4) above, in the Income Tax Acts, except so far as is otherwise expressly provided, "earned income" also includes, in relation to any individual, income which is earned income by virtue of section 529.

(6) The provisions of this section are without prejudice to any other provision of the Income Tax Acts directing income to be treated as earned income.

"Total income" in the Income Tax Acts

1.106 **835.**—(1) In the Income Tax Acts "total income", in relation to any person, means the total income of that person from all sources estimated in accordance with the provisions of the Income Tax Acts.

(2) Any person who, on his own behalf or on behalf of another person, delivers a statement of the amount of his or that other person's total income shall observe the rules and directions contained in section 836.

(3) Where deductions reduce a person's total income and the order in which they are made or in which income of different descriptions is reduced thereby may affect his liability to income tax the deductions shall be made and treated as reducing income in accordance with subsections (4) and (5) below.

(4) Subject to any express provisions of the Income Tax Acts, any deductions allowable in computing a person's total income or to be made from a person's total income shall be treated as reducing income of different descriptions in the order which will result in the greatest reduction of his liability to income tax.

(5) Deductions from total income under Chapter I of Part VII shall be made after any other deductions and shall not affect the amount to be taken as a person's total income for the purposes of section 257(5), 257A(5) or 274.

(6) In estimating the total income of any person—

(a) any income which is chargeable with income tax by way of deduction at the basic rate or the lower rate in force for any year or which for the purposes of Schedule F comprises an amount amount which is equal to a tax credit calculated by reference to the tax credit fraction shall be deemed to be income of that year; and
(b) any deductions which are allowable on account of sums payable under deduction of income tax at the basic rate in force for any

year out of the property or profits of that person shall be allowed as deductions in respect of that year;

notwithstanding that the income or sums, as the case may be, accrued or will accrue in whole or in part before or after that year.

(7) Where an assessment has become final and conclusive for the purposes of income tax for any year of assessment—

(a) that assessment shall also be final and conclusive in estimating total income; and

(b) no allowance or adjustment of liability, on the ground of diminution of income or loss, shall be taken into account in estimating total income unless that allowance or adjustment has previously been made on an application under the special provisions of the Income Tax Acts relating thereto.

(8) Subsection (7) above shall apply in relation to—

(a) any relief under section 353;

(b) any relief by reason of the operation of an election for the herd basis under Schedule 5; and

(c) any allowance given effect under section 258 or 479 of the Capital Allowances Act;

as it applies in relation to allowances or adjustments on the ground of diminution of income or loss.

Social Security Contributions and Benefits Act 1992

(1992 c.4)

SECTIONS REPRODUCED

PART XI

STATUTORY SICK PAY

Employer's liability

The qualifying conditions

Limitations on entitlement, etc.

Rates of payment, etc.

1.110 157. Rates of payment
158. Recovery by employers of amounts paid by way of statutory sick pay (*repealed*)
159. Power to substitute provisions for section 158(2) (*repealed*)
159A. Power to provide for recovery by employers of sums paid by way of statutory sick pay

Miscellaneous

1.111 160. Relationship with benefits and other payments, etc.
161. Crown employment—Part XI
162. Special classes of persons
163. Interpretation of Part XI and supplementary provisions

Part XII

Statutory Maternity Pay

1.112 164. Statutory maternity pay—entitlement and liability to pay
165. The maternity pay period
166. Rate of statutory maternity pay
167. Funding of employers' liabilities in respect of statutory maternity pay
168. Relationship with benefits and other payments, etc.
169. Crown employment—Part XII
170. Special classes of persons
171. Interpretation of Part XII and supplementary provisions

Part XIIZA

Statutory Paternity Pay

1.113 171ZA. Entitlement: birth
171ZB. Entitlement: adoption
171ZC. Entitlement: general
171ZD. Liability to make payments
171ZE. Rate and period of pay
171ZF. Restrictions on contracting out
171ZG. Relationship with contractual remuneration
171ZH. Crown employment—Part XIIZA
171ZI. Special classes of person
171ZJ. Part XIIZA: supplementary
171ZK. Power to apply Part XIIZA to adoption cases not involving placement

Part XIIZB

Statutory Adoption Pay

Part XIII

General

Interpretation

Schedules

Part XI

Statutory Sick Pay

General Note

Statutory sick pay (SSP) was originally introduced in April 1983 by the Social Security and Housing Benefits Act 1982. The main primary legislation is now to be found in Pt XI, annotated here; there are also various sets of regulations, principally the SSP (General) Regulations 1982 (SI 1982/894), which are contained in Pt III of this volume. Section 151(1) of the SSCBA 1992 provides that an employer is liable to pay to an employee for any day of incapacity for work in 1.117

relation to the employee's contract of service with that employer, where the day in question is a qualifying day (see s.154) which forms part of a period of incapacity to work (see s.152) and falls within a period of entitlement as between that employer and that employee (s.153 and Sch.11). Incapacity must be duly notified to the employer, and SSP may be withheld in the event of non-existent or late notification (see s.156). Those who are self-employed (who by definition lack an employer) and those who are unemployed are excluded from entitlement to SSP. Some employees are also excluded from SSP. Section 153(3) and Sch.11 prevent the requisite period of entitlement arising as between employer and employees in various types of case (*e.g.* low earners, women at a certain stage of pregnancy, some persons affected by trade disputes).

SSP is payable at a weekly rate. The daily rate will depend on the number of qualifying days in the week (see s.157). SSP is not payable in respect of the first three qualifying days (or "waiting days") in any period of entitlement (see s.155(1)). SSP cannot be paid in kind or by the provision of board and lodging or other services or facilities (SSP (General) Regulations 1982 (SI 1982/894), reg.8). Any day of incapacity for work in relation to a contract of service which falls within a period of entitlement to SSP precludes concurrent entitlement to incapacity benefit (Sch.12, para.1). Employees reach their maximum entitlement to SSP as against any one employer in any one period of entitlement when they have been entitled in that period to 28 times the appropriate weekly rate of SSP (see s.155(4)). This is typically after 28 weeks of continuous incapacity. If the person remains incapacitated after that, he or she must look to incapacity benefit or, failing that, a means-tested benefit.

At the start of the SSP scheme in 1983, employers were able to recoup the entire amount paid from the National Insurance contributions and the PAYE tax that they were required to collect and account for to the Inland Revenue. The initial effect of SSP was thus to transfer the cost of administration from the State to the employer. The Statutory Sick Pay Act 1991 limited employers to recouping 80 per cent of the cost of SSP payments, but "small employers" were still able to claim full reimbursement. This was followed by the Statutory Sick Pay Act 1994, which abolished employers' general right to recover (some of) the costs of SSP. The special rules for reimbursing small employers were then repealed (although they remain for the purposes of SMP). Instead, in principle any employer—not just small employers—can recover the costs of SSP payments under the Percentage Threshold Scheme. However, this reimbursement is only available where the employer's expenditure on SSP exceeds 13 per cent of their gross National Insurance contributions liability—in other words, only where there is an epidemic of illness in the workforce (see further Statutory Sick Pay Threshold Order 1995 (SI 1995/512)).

In certain circumstances, where an employer does not, or because of insolvency, cannot, discharge their statutory liability to pay SSP, that liability became that of the Board of Inland Revenue (s.151(6), SSP (General) Regulations 1982 (SI 1982/894), regs 9A–9C). This liability was transferred from the Secretary of State to the Board of the Inland Revenue with effect from April 1, 1999, under the Social Security Contributions (Transfer of Functions, etc.) Act 1999, s.1(2) and Sch.2, along with those functions under SSP (General) Regulations 1982, regs 10 and 14.

The arrangements for resolving disputes about entitlement to SSP were changed with effect from April 1, 1999. Before that date, certain questions could be referred to an AO, thus opening up the usual channels of appeal to SSATs, Commissioners and ultimately the courts. Since that date the Social Security Contributions (Transfer of Functions, etc.) Act 1999 and the Statutory Sick Pay and Statutory Maternity Pay (Decisions) Regulations 1999 (SI 1999/776) have replaced the AO with an officer of the Board in Inland Revenue. Consequently, decision-making and appeals are now governed by Pt II of the 1999 Act, with the right of appeal lying to the tax appeal Commissioners. An employment tribunal has no jurisdiction under the Employment Rights Act 1996 to entertain an employee's complaint that SSP has not been paid: (per Mr Recorder Luba QC in *Taylor Gordon & Co. Ltd v Timmons* (EAT/0159/03/RN, at para.43)).

Employer's liability

Employer's liability

151.—(1) Where an employee has a day of incapacity for work in relation to his contract of service with an employer, that employer shall, if the conditions set out in sections 152 to 154 below are satisfied, be liable to make him, in accordance with the following provisions of this Part of this Act, a payment (to be known as "statutory sick pay") in respect of that day. **1.118**

(2) Any agreement shall be void to the extent that it purports—

(a) to exclude, limit or otherwise modify any provision of this Part of this Act; or

(b) to require an employee to contribute (whether directly or indirectly) towards any costs incurred by his employer under this Part of this Act.

(3) For the avoidance of doubt, any agreement between an employer and an employee authorising any deductions from statutory sick pay which the employer is liable to pay to the employee in respect of any period shall not be void by virtue of subsection (2)(a) above if the employer—

(a) is authorised by that or another agreement to make the same deductions from any contractual remuneration which he is liable to pay in respect of the same period, or

(b) would be so authorised if he were liable to pay contractual remuneration in respect of that period.

(4) For the purposes of this Part of this Act [[1]a day of incapacity for work in relation to a contract of service means a day on which] the employee concerned is, or is deemed in accordance with regulations to be, incapable by reason of some specific disease or bodily or mental disablement of doing work which he can reasonably be expected to do under that contract.

(5) In any case where an employee has more than one contract of service with the same employer the provisions of this Part of this Act shall, except in such cases as may be prescribed and subject to the following provisions of this Part of this Act, have effect as if the employer were a different employer in relation to each contract of service.

(6) Circumstances may be prescribed in which, notwithstanding the provisions of subsections (1) to (5) above, the liability to make payments of statutory sick pay is to be a liability of the [[2]Commissioners of Inland Revenue].

[[2](7) Regulations under subsection (6) above must be made with the concurrence of the Commissioners of Inland Revenue.]

AMENDMENTS

1. Social Security (Incapacity for Work) Act 1994, s.11(1) and Sch.1, para.34 (April 13, 1995).
2. Social Security Contributions (Transfer of Functions, etc.) Act 1999, s.1(1) and Sch.1, para.9 (April 1, 1999)

DEFINITIONS

"contract of service"—see s.163(1).
"employee"—*ibid.* and SSP (General) Regulations 1982, reg.16.
"employer"—see s.163(1).
"prescribed"—*ibid.*

GENERAL NOTE

Subs. (1)–(3)

1.119 The general liability on employers to pay SSP—where the qualifying conditions are fulfilled by the employee—is set out in subs.(1). Employers cannot contract out of this liability (subs.(2), but note the qualification in subs.(3)).

Subs. (4)

1.120 For the purposes of SSP, a day of incapacity for work in relation to any contract of service may arise in either of two ways. The first is where the employee is actually incapable by reason of some specific disease or bodily or mental disablement of doing work which he or she can reasonably be expected to do under that contract. On "incapable of work" and "by reason of some specific disease or bodily or mental disablement", see the annotations to SSCBA 1992, s.171B(2) in Vol.I to this series. The second, and alternative, possibility is where the employee, although not actually incapable, falls within the protection of regulations which deem a day to be one of incapacity for work. On deemed incapacity, see SSP (General) Regulations 1982 (SI 1982/894), reg.2.

Subs. (5)

1.121 This contemplates that an employee who has more than one contract of service with the same employer could get SSP in respect of each contract of service, where the eligibility conditions were satisfied with respect to each contract. This provision is modified by SSP (General) Regulations 1982 (SI 1982/894), reg.21.

Subs. (6)

1.122 See SSP (General) Regulations 1982 (SI 1982/894), regs 9A–9C and see also General Note to Pt XI of this Act, above.

The qualifying conditions

Period of incapacity for work

1.123 **152.**—(1) The first condition is that the day in question forms part of a period of incapacity for work.

(2) In this Part of this Act "period of incapacity for work" means any period of four or more consecutive days, each of which is a day of incapacity for work in relation to the contract of service in question.

(3) Any two periods of incapacity for work which are separated by a period of not more than 8 weeks shall be treated as a single period of incapacity for work.

(4) The Secretary of State may by regulations direct that a larger number of weeks specified in the regulations shall be substituted for the number of weeks for the time being specified in subsection (3) above.

(5) No day of the week shall be disregarded in calculating any period of consecutive days for the purposes of this section.

(6) A day may be a day of incapacity for work in relation to a contract of service, and so form part of a period of incapacity for work, notwithstanding that—

(a) it falls before the making of the contract or after the contract expires or is brought to an end; or

(b) it is not a day on which the employee concerned would be required by that contract to be available for work.

DEFINITIONS

"contract of service"—see s.163(1).
"employee"—*ibid.* and SSP (General) Regulations 1982, reg.16.
"period of incapacity for work"—see subs.(2).
"week"—see s.163(1).

GENERAL NOTE

Liability to pay SSP can only arise if the qualifying day which is one of incapacity for work also forms part of a period of incapacity for work (subs.(1)). A period of incapacity for work is formed by any period of four or more consecutive days of incapacity for work in relation to the contract of service in question (subs.(2)). Every day of the week counts for determining periods of consecutive days (subs.(4)). Any two periods of incapacity "link" to form a single period where they are not separated by more than eight weeks, counting the separation period from the end of the "first" period. Note that under subs.(5), a day can still be one of incapacity for work in relation to the contract of service and thus be part of a period of incapacity for work where it is not one on which the contract would require the employee to be available for work, or where it falls before the contract was made or after it expires or is otherwise brought to an end. **1.124**

Period of entitlement

153.—(1) The second condition is that the day in question falls within a period which is, as between the employee and his employer, a period of entitlement. **1.125**

(2) For the purposes of this Part of this Act a period of entitlement, as between an employee and his employer, is a period beginning with the commencement of a period of incapacity for work and ending with whichever of the following first occurs—

(a) the termination of that period of incapacity for work;

(b) the day on which the employee reaches, as against the employer concerned, his maximum entitlement to statutory sick pay (determined in accordance with section 155 below);

(c) the day on which the employee's contract of service with the employer concerned expires or is brought to an end;

(d) in the case of an employee who is, or has been, pregnant, the day immediately preceding the beginning of the disqualifying period.

(3) Schedule 11 to this Act has effect for the purpose of specifying circumstances in which a period of entitlement does not arise in relation to a particular period of incapacity for work.

(4) A period of entitlement as between an employee and an employer of his may also be, or form part of, a period of entitlement as between him and another employer of his.

(5) The Secretary of State may by regulations—

(a) specify circumstances in which, for the purpose of determining whether an employee's maximum entitlement to statutory sick pay has been reached in a period of entitlement as between him and an employer of his, days falling within a previous period of entitlement as between the employee and any person who is or has in the past been an employer of his are to be counted; and

(b) direct that in prescribed circumstances an employer shall provide a person who is about to leave his employment, or who has been employed by him in the past, with a statement in the prescribed form containing such information as may be prescribed in relation to any entitlement of the employee to statutory sick pay.

(6) Regulations may provide, in relation to prescribed cases, for a period of entitlement to end otherwise than in accordance with subsection (2) above.

(7) In a case where the employee's contract of service first takes effect on a day which falls within a period of incapacity for work, the period of entitlement begins with that day.

(8) In a case where the employee's contract of service first takes effect between two periods of incapacity for work which by virtue of section 152(3) above are treated as one, the period of entitlement begins with the first day of the second of those periods.

(9) In any case where, otherwise than by virtue of section 6(1)(b) above, an employee's earnings under a contract of service in respect of the day on which the contract takes effect do not attract a liability to pay secondary Class 1 contributions, subsections (7) and (8) above shall have effect as if for any reference to the contract first taking effect there were substituteda reference to the first day in respect of which the employee's earnings attract such a liability.

(10) Regulations shall make provision as to an employer's liability under this Part of this Act to pay statutory sick pay to an employee in any case where the employer's contract of service with that employee has been brought to an end by the employer solely, or mainly, for the purpose of avoiding liability for statutory sick pay.

(11) Subsection (2)(d) above does not apply in relation to an employee who has been pregnant if her pregnancy terminated, before the beginning of the disqualifying period, otherwise than by confinement.

(12) In this section—

"confinement" is to be construed in accordance with section 171(1) below;

"disqualifying period" means—
(a) in relation to a woman entitled to statutory maternity pay, the maternity pay period; and
(b) in relation to a woman entitled to maternity allowance, the maternity allowance period;
"maternity allowance period" has the meaning assigned to it by section 35(2) above; and
"maternity pay period" has the meaning assigned to it by section 165(1) below.

DEFINITIONS

"confinement"—see subs.(12).
"contract of service"—see s.163(1).
"disqualifying period"—see subs.(12).
"employee"—see s.163(1) and SSP (General) Regulations 1982, reg.16.
"employer"—*ibid.*
"maternity allowance"—*ibid.*
"maternity allowance period"—subs.(12).
"maternity pay period"—*ibid.*
"period of incapacity for work"—see s.163(1).
"prescribed"—see *ibid.*
"week"—see *ibid.*

GENERAL NOTE

Subss.(1) and (2)

There can be no liability to pay SSP unless the qualifying day, being one of incapacity for work forming part of a period of incapacity for work, also falls within a period of entitlement as between the employee and his employer (subs.(1)). Such a period of entitlement generally begins on the first day of a period of incapacity for work (subs.(2)), but note the modifications effected by subss.(7), (8), and (9). A period of entitlement ends with whichever of the circumstances set out in subs.(2)(a)–(d) first occurs. Note that subs. 2(d) does not apply in the circumstances set out in subs.(11). **1.126**

The position of "regular casual" workers was dealt with by the Court of Appeal in *Brown v Chief Adjudication Officer* [1997] I.R.L.R. 110. So long as such workers have worked continuously for a period of three months, or for a series of periods totalling three months in aggregate and not separated by more than eight weeks, they become entitled to the minimum periods of notice provided for by s.86 of Employment Rights Act 1996, and their contract of employment will not terminate unless it is frustrated or is terminated by their employer.

Subs.(3)

In the circumstances set out in Sch.11 below, no period of entitlement arises with respect to the particular period of incapacity for work there referred to, thus excluding certain employees from SSP in respect of that period of incapacity for work. **1.127**

Subs.(4)

An employee may have a period of entitlement with more than one employer at the same time, albeit that the length of the period with each is not coterminous. **1.128**

Subs. (5)

1.129 See SSP (General) Regulations 1982 (SI 1982/894), reg.3A.

Subs. (6)

1.130 See SSP (General) Regulations 1982 (SI 1982/894), reg.3 dealing with prisoners, pregnant women entitled neither to SMP nor to maternity allowance, and setting a maximum three-year limit on any one period of entitlement.

Subs. (10)

1.131 See SSP (General) Regulations 1982 (SI 1982/894), reg.4.

Qualifying days

1.132 **154.**—(1) The third condition is that the day in question is a qualifying day.

(2) The days which are for the purposes of this Part of this Act to be qualifying days as between an employee and an employer of his (that is to say, those days of the week on which he is required by his contract of service with that employer to be available for work or which are chosen to reflect the terms of that contract) shall be such day or days as may, subject to regulations, be agreed between the employee and his employer or, failing such agreement, determined in accordance with regulations.

(3) In any case where qualifying days are determined by agreement between an employee and his employer there shall, in each week (beginning with Sunday), be at least one qualifying day.

(4) A day which is a qualifying day as between an employee and an employer of his may also be a qualifying day as between him and another employer of his.

Definitions

"contract of service"—see s.163(1).
"employee"—*ibid.* and SSP (General) Regulations 1982, reg.16.
"employer"—see s.163(1).
"week"—*ibid.*

General Note

1.133 In order to attract SSP liability, the day of incapacity which forms part of a period of incapacity for work and falls within a period of entitlement must also be a qualifying day (subs.(1)). Under subs.(2) an employer and employee are permitted a degree of freedom to determine by agreement which days of the week will for them rank as such, although subs.(3) stipulates that such agreements must specify at least one qualifying day per week. Furthermore SSP (General) Regulations 1982 (SI 1982/894), reg.5(3) renders ineffective an agreement treating as qualifying days any day identified expressly or otherwise by reference to it being a day of incapacity for work in relation to the employee's contract of service with an employer, or by reference to a period of incapacity for work or to a period of entitlement. Where there is no agreement on qualifying days or the only agreement is one rendered ineffective by reg.5(3), qualifying days are determined in accordance with SSP (General) Regulations 1982, reg.5(2).

Limitations on entitlement

155.—(1) Statutory sick pay shall not be payable for the first three qualifying days in any period of entitlement. 1.134

(2) An employee shall not be entitled, as against any one employer, to an aggregate amount of statutory sick pay in respect of any one period of entitlement which exceeds his maximum entitlement.

(3) The maximum entitlement as against any one employer is reached on the day on which the amount to which the employee has become entitled by way of statutory sick pay during the period of entitlement in question first reaches or passes the entitlement limit.

(4) The entitlement limit is an amount equal to 28 times [[1]the weekly rate applicable in accordance with] section 157 below.

(5) Regulations may make provision for calculating the entitlement limit in any case where an employee's entitlement to statutory sick pay is calculated by reference to different weekly rates in the same period of entitlement.

AMENDMENT

1. Social Security (Incapacity for Work) Act 1994, s.8 (April 6, 1995).

DEFINITIONS

"employee"—see s.163(1) and SSP (General) Regulations 1982, reg.16.
"employer"—see s.163(1).
"period of entitlement"—*ibid.*
"qualifying day"—*ibid.*

Notification of incapacity for work

156.—(1) Regulations shall prescribe the manner in which, and the time within which, notice of any day of incapacity for work is to be given by or on behalf of an employee to his employer. 1.135

(2) An employer who would, apart from this section, be liable to pay an amount of statutory sick pay to an employee in respect of a qualifying day (the "day in question") shall be entitled to withhold payment of that amount if—

(a) the day in question is one in respect of which he has not been duly notified in accordance with regulations under subsection (1) above; or
(b) he has not been so notified in respect of any of the first three qualifying days in a period of entitlement (a "waiting day") and the day in question is the first qualifying day in that period of entitlement in respect of which the employer is not entitled to withhold payment—
 (i) by virtue of paragraph (a) above; or
 (ii) in respect of an earlier waiting day by virtue of this paragraph.

(3) Where an employer withholds any amount of statutory sick pay under this section—

(a) the period of entitlement in question shall not be affected; and

(b) for the purposes of calculating his maximum entitlement in accordance with section 155 above the employee shall not be taken to have become entitled to the amount so withheld.

Rates of payment, etc.

Rates of payment

1.136 **157.**—(1) Statutory sick pay shall be payable by an employer at the weekly rate of [2£66.15].

(2) The Secretary of State may by order—

[1(a) amend subsection (1) above so as to substitute different provision as to the weekly rate or rates of statutory sick pay; and]

(b) make such consequential amendments as appear to him to be required of any provision contained in this Part of this Act.

(3) The amount of statutory sick pay payable by any one employer in respect of any day shall be the weekly rate applicable on that day divided by the number of days which are, in the week (beginning with Sunday) in which that day falls, qualifying days as between that employer and the employee concerned.

AMENDMENTS

1. Social Security (Incapacity for Work) Act 1994, s.8 (April 6, 1995).
2. Social Security Benefits Up-rating Order 2004 (SI 2004/552), art.9 (April 6, 2004).

Recovery by employers of amounts paid by way of statutory sick pay

1.137 **158.**—[1 . . .]

AMENDMENTS

1. Statutory Sick Pay Percentage Threshold Order 1995 (SI 1995/512), reg.5(a) (April 6, 1995).

Power to substitute provisions for section 158(2)

1.138 **159.**—[1 . . .]

AMENDMENTS

1. Statutory Sick Pay Percentage Threshold Order 1995 (SI 1995/512), reg.5(a) (April 6, 1995).

[1Power to provide for recovery by employers of sums paid by way of statutory sick pay

1.139 **159A.**—(1) The Secretary of State may by order provide for the recovery by employers, in accordance with the order, of the amount (if any) by which their payments of, or liability incurred for, statutory sick pay in any period exceeds the specified percentage of the amount of their liability for contributions payments in respect of the corresponding period.

(2) An order under subsection (1) above may include provision—

(a) as to the periods by reference to which the calculation referred to above is to be made;

(b) for amounts which would otherwise be recoverable but which do not exceed the specified minimum for recovery not to be recoverable;

(c) for the rounding up or down of any fraction of a pound which would otherwise result from a calculation made in accordance with the order; and

(d) for any deduction from contributions payments made in accordance with the order to be disregarded for such purposes as may be specified,

and may repeal sections 158 and 159 above and make any amendments of other enactments which are consequential on the repeal of those sections.

(3) In this section—

"contributions payments" means payments which a person is required by or under any enactment to make in discharge of any liability of his as an employer in respect of primary or secondary Class 1 contributions; and

"specified" means specified in or determined in accordance with an order under subsection (1).

(4) The Secretary of State may by regulations make such transitional and consequential provision, and such savings, as he considers necessary or expedient for or in connection with the coming into force of any order under subsection (1) above.]

AMENDMENTS

1. Statutory Sick Pay Act 1994, s.3 (February 10, 1994).

Miscellaneous

Relationship with benefits and other payments, etc.

160.—Schedule 12 to this Act has effect with respect to the relationship between statutory sick pay and certain benefits and payments. **1.140**

Crown employment—Part XI

161.—(1) Subject to subsection (2) below, the provisions of this Part of this Act apply in relation to persons employed by or under the Crown as they apply in relation to persons employed otherwise than by or under the Crown. **1.141**

(2) The provisions of this Part of this Act do not apply in relation to persons serving as members of Her Majesty's forces, in their capacity as such.

(3) For the purposes of this section Her Majesty's forces shall be taken to consist of such establishments and organisations as may be prescribed

[1by regulations made by the Secretary of State with the concurrence of the Treasury], being establishments and organisations in which persons serve under the control of the Defence Council.

AMENDMENT

1. Social Security Contributions (Transfer of Functions, etc.) Act 1999, s.1(1) and Sch.1, para.10 (April 1, 1999)

Special classes of persons

1.142 **162.**—(1) The Secretary of State [1may with the concurrence of the Treasury] make regulations modifying this Part of this Act in such manner as he thinks proper in their application to any person who is, has been or is to be—

(a) employed on board any ship, vessel, hovercraft or aircraft;
(b) outside Great Britain at any prescribed time or in any prescribed circumstances; or
(c) in prescribed employment in connection with continental shelf operations, as defined in section 120(2) above.

(2) Regulations under subsection (1) above may in particular provide—

(a) for any provision of this Part of this Act to apply to any such person, notwithstanding that it would not otherwise apply;
(b) for any such provision not to apply to any such person, notwithstanding that it would otherwise apply;
(c) for excepting any such person from the application of any such provision where he neither is domiciled nor has a place of residence in any part of Great Britain;
(d) for the taking of evidence, for the purposes of the determination of any question arising under any such provision, in a country or territory outside Great Britain, by a British consular official or such other person as may be determined in accordance with the regulations.

AMENDMENT

1. Social Security Contributions (Transfer of Functions, etc.) Act 1999, s.1(1) and Sch.1, para.11 (April 1, 1999).

Interpretation of Part XI and supplementary provisions

1.143 **163.**—(1) In this Part of this Act—

"contract of service" (except in paragraph (a) of the definition below of "employee") includes any arrangement providing for the terms of appointment of an employee;

"employee" means a person who is—

(a) gainfully employed in Great Britain either under a contract of service or in an office (including elective office) with emoluments chargeable to income tax under Schedule E; and
(b) over the age of 16;

but subject to regulations, which may provide for cases where any such person is not to be treated as an employee for the purposes of this Part of this Act and for cases where any person who would not otherwise be an employee for those purposes is to be treated as an employee for those purposes;

"employer", in relation to an employee and a contract of service of his, means a person who under section 6 above is, or [2the condition in] subsection (1)(b) of that section would be, liable to pay secondary Class 1 contributions in relation to any earnings of the employee under the contract;

"period of entitlement" has the meaning given by section 153 above;

"period of incapacity for work" has the meaning given by section 152 above;

[1 . . .]

"prescribed" means prescribed by regulations;

"qualifying day" has the meaning given by section 154 above;

"week" means any period of seven days.

(2) For the purposes of this Part of this Act an employee's normal weekly earnings shall, subject to subsection (4) below, be taken to be the average weekly earnings which in the relevant period have been paid to him or paid for his benefit under his contract of service with the employer in question.

(3) For the purposes of subsection (2) above, the expressions "earnings" and "relevant period" shall have the meaning given to them by regulations.

(4) In such cases as may be prescribed an employee's normal weekly earnings shall be calculated in accordance with regulations.

(5) Without prejudice to any other power to make regulations under this Part of this Act, regulations may specify cases in which, for the purposes of this Part of this Act or such of its provisions as may be prescribed—

(a) two or more employers are to be treated as one;

(b) two or more contracts of service in respect of which the same person is an employee are to be treated as one.

(6) Where, in consequence of the establishment of one or more National Health Service trusts under Part I of the National Health Service and Community Care Act 1990 or the National Health Service (Scotland) Act 1978, a person's contract of employment is treated by a scheme under that Part or Act as divided so as to constitute two or more contracts, [3or where an order under paragraph 23(1) of Schedule 5A to the National Health Service Act 1977 provides that a person's contract of employment is so divided,] regulations may make provision enabling him to elect for all of those contracts to be treated as one contract for the purposes of this Part of this Act or of such provisions of this Part of this Act as may be prescribed; and any such regulations may prescribe—

(a) the conditions that must be satisfied if a person is to be entitled to make such an election;

(b) the manner in which, and the time within which, such an election is to be made;

(c) the persons to whom, and the manner in which, notice of such an election is to be given;

(d) the information which a person who makes such an election is to provide, and the persons to whom, and the time within which, he is to provide it;

(e) the time for which such an election is to have effect;
(f) which one of the person's employers under the two or more contracts is to be regarded for the purposes of statutory sick pay as his employer under the one contract;

and the powers conferred by this subsection are without prejudice to any other power to make regulations under this Part of this Act.

(7) Regulations may provide for periods of work which begin on one day and finish on the following day to be treated, for the purposes of this Part of this Act, as falling solely within one or other of those days.

AMENDMENT

1. Jobseekers Act 1995, section 41(5) and Sch.3 (April 1, 1996).
2. Social Security Act 1998, section 86 and Sch.7, para.74 (April 6, 1999).
3. Health Act 1999 (Supplementary, Consequential etc. Provisions) Order 2000 (SI 2000/90), Art.3(1) and Sch.1, para.27 (February 8, 2000).

PART XII

STATUTORY MATERNITY PAY

Statutory maternity pay—entitlement and liability to pay

1.144 **164.**—(1) Where a woman who is or has been an employee satisfies the conditions set out in this section, she shall be entitled, in accordance with the following provisions of this Part of this Act, to payments to be known as "statutory maternity pay".

(2) The conditions mentioned in subsection (1) above are—
(a) that she has been in employed earner's employment with an employer for a continuous period of at least 26 weeks ending with the week immediately preceding the 14th week before the expectedweek of confinement but has ceased to work for him, [3 . . .];
(b) that her normal weekly earnings for the period of eight weeks ending with the week immediately preceding the 14th week before the expected week of confinement are not less than the lower earnings limit in force under section 5(1)(a) above immediately before the commencement of the 14th week before the expected week of confinement; and
(c) that she has become pregnant and has reached, or been confined before reaching, the commencement of the 11th week before the expected week of confinement.

(3) The liability to make payments of statutory maternity pay to a woman is a liability of any person of whom she has been an employee as mentioned in subsection (2)(a) above.

[3(4) A woman shall be entitled to payments of statutory maternity pay only if—
(a) she gives the person who will be liable to pay it notice of the date from which she expects his liability to pay her statutory maternity pay to begin; and

(b) the notice is given at least 28 days before that date or, if that is not reasonably practicable, as soon as is reasonably practicable.]

(5) The notice shall be in writing if the person who is liable to pay the woman statutory maternity pay so requests.

(6) Any agreement shall be void to the extent that it purports—

(a) to exclude, limit or otherwise modify any provision of this Part of this Act; or

(b) to require an employee or former employee to contribute (whether directly or indirectly) towards any costs incurred by her employer or former employer under this Part of this Act.

(7) For the avoidance of doubt, any agreement between an employer and an employee authorising any deductions from statutory maternity pay which the employer is liable to pay to the employee in respect of any period shall not be void by virtue of subsection (6)(a) above if the employer—

(a) is authorised by that or another agreement to make the same deductions from any contractual remuneration which he is liable to pay in respect of the same period; or

(b) would be so authorised if he were liable to pay contractual remuneration in respect of that period.

(8) Regulations shall make provision as to a former employer's liability to pay statutory maternity pay to a woman in any case where the former employer's contract of service with her has been brought to an end by the former employer solely, or mainly, for the purpose of avoiding liability for statutory maternity pay.

(9) The Secretary of State may by regulations—

(a) specify circumstances in which, notwithstanding subsections (1) to (8) above, there is to be no liability to pay statutory maternity pay in respect of a week;

(b) specify circumstances in which, notwithstanding subsections (1) to (8) above, the liability to make payments of statutory maternity pay is to be a liability [[2]of the Commissioners of Inland Revenue];

(c) specify in what circumstances employment is to be treated as continuous for the purposes of this Part of this Act;

(d) provide that a woman is to be treated as being employed for a continuous period of at least 26 weeks where—

(i) she has been employed by the same employer for at least 26 weeks under two or more separate contracts of service; and

(ii) those contracts were not continuous;

(e) provide that any of the provisions specified in subsection (10) below shall have effect subject to prescribed modifications [[3]in such cases as may be prescribed]

[[3](ea) provide that subsection (4) above shall not have effect, or shall have effect subject to prescribed modifications, in such cases as may be prescribed;]

(f) provide for amounts earned by a woman under separate contracts of service with the same employer to be aggregated for the purposes of this Part of this Act; and

(g) provide that—

(i) the amount of a woman's earnings for any period; or

(ii) the amount of her earnings to be treated as comprised in any payment made to her or for her benefit,

shall be calculated or estimated in such manner and on such basis as may be prescribed and that for that purpose payments of a particular class or description made or falling to be made to or by a woman shall, to such extent as may be prescribed, be disregarded or, as the case may be, be deducted from the amount of her earnings.

(10) The provisions mentioned in subsection (9)(e) above are—

(a) subsection (2)(a) and (b) above; and

(b) [[4] section 166(1) and (2)], [[1] . . .] below.

[[2](11) Any regulations under subsection (9) above which are made by virtue of paragraph (b) of that subsection must be made with the concurrence of the Commissioners of Inland Revenue.]

Amendments

1. Maternity Allowance and Statutory Maternity Pay Regulations 1994 (SI 1994/1230, reg.6 (October 16, 1994).

2. Social Security Contributions (Transfer of Functions, etc.) Act 1999, s.1(1) and Sch.1, para.12 (April 1, 1999).

3. Employment Act 2002, s.20 (April 6, 2003).

4. Employment Act 2002, s.53 and Sch.7, para.6 (April 6, 2003).

Definitions

"confined"—see s.171(1).

"confinement"—see *ibid.*

"earnings"—see *ibid.* and reg.20 of the Statutory Maternity Pay (General) Regulations 1986.

"employee"—see s.171 and reg.17 of the Statutory Maternity Pay (General) Regulations 1986.

"employed earner"—see section 2.

"employer"—see section 171(1).

"modifications"—see *ibid.*

"normal weekly earnings"—see section 171(4).

"prescribed"—see section 171(1).

"week"—see *ibid.*

General Note

1.145 Statutory Maternity Pay (SMP) provides an income for employees and former employees during a period of maternity leave. In order to qualify for SMP a woman must have worked for an employer for 26 weeks continuously into the week (known as the qualifying week) preceding the 14th week before the expected date of her confinement (subs.(2)(a)). Part III of the SMP (General) Regulations 1986 (SI 1986/1960) defines the concept of continuous employment. The woman must also have been earning during the last eight weeks of her employment an amount at least equal to the lower earnings limit for contribution purposes (subs.(2)(b)). She must, moreover, have become pregnant and have reached (or given birth before reaching) the start of the 11th week before the expected week of confinement (subs.(2)(c)). The further requirement that she must actually have left that employment because of her pregnancy or confinement was repealed by the Employment Act 2002. This repeal itself effectively supersedes reg.2 of the Statutory Maternity Pay (General) (Modification and

Amendment) Regulations 2000 (SI 2000/2883), which modified the original version of subs.(2)(a) of the Act in relation to pregnant women who were dismissed or whose employment was otherwise terminated without consent.

Where a woman leaves her employment earlier than 11 weeks before the expected week of confinement she loses her entitlement to SMP (unless she has given birth), but if her employer has dismissed her solely or mainly for the purpose of avoiding the liability to pay SMP she will remain entitled. This applies even if she has been working for that employer for only a short period, so long as it is at least eight continuous weeks (see reg.3 of the SMP (General) Regulations 1986 (SI 1986/1960)). If a woman qualifies for SMP from more than one employer she is entitled to receive it from each of them (*ibid.*, reg.18).

It is a precondition of entitlement to SMP that the woman has given notice of her intention to leave by reason of pregnancy or confinement at least 28 days (21 days before the Employment Act 2002) before leaving, unless it is not reasonably practicable to do so and she gives it thereafter as soon as it is reasonably practicable to do so (subs.(4); see further SMP (General) Regulations 1986 (SI 1986/1960), reg.23). This would be so if the baby arrives unexpectedly early, but may also extend to a woman who did not know of the notice requirement and had not been put on inquiry about it. (That was the position taken by the Employment Appeal Tribunal in *Nu-Swift International Ltd. v Mallison* [1979] I.C.R. 157 in relation to maternity pay.) The notice must be in writing if the employer so requests (subs.(5)).

A woman is not entitled to SMP if at any time during the maternity pay period (on which see s.165) she is imprisoned or sentenced to imprisonment (other than suspended). SMP is lost for the remainder of the period whether or not she is imprisoned for the whole period (see reg.9 of the SMP (General) Regulations 1986 (SI 1986/1960)).

The liability to pay SMP rests with the employer (subs.(3)). In certain circumstances, where an employer does not, or because of insolvency, cannot discharge his liability to pay SMP, that liability is discharged by the Board (at least since April 1, 1999; see subs.(9)(b), SMP (General) Regulations 1986 (SI 1986/1960), reg.7 and Social Security Contributions (Transfer of Functions, etc.) Act 1999, s.1(2) and Sch.2.; the same applies to the Secretary of State's functions under SMP (General) Regulations, regs 25, 30 and 31).

SMP, therefore, like SSP, is administered by the employer whilst the Board of the Inland Revenue is responsible for the resolution of certain disputes about entitlement. Until April 1, 1999, this was achieved by enabling the reference of certain questions to an AO, thereby opening up the usual channels of appeal to SSATs, Commissioners and the courts. With effect from April 1, 1999, the Social Security Contributions (Transfer of Functions, etc.) Act 1999, and the Statutory Sick Pay and Statutory Maternity Pay (Decisions) Regulations 1999 (SI 1999/776) replaced the role of AO with that of an officer of the Board of Inland Revenue. Consequently decision-making and appeals relating to SMP are governed by Pt II of the 1999 Act, with the right of appeal lying to the tax appeal Commissioners.

The maternity pay period

165.—(1) Statutory maternity pay shall be payable, subject to the provisions of this Part of this Act, in respect of each week during a prescribed period ("the maternity pay period") of a duration not exceeding [[2]26 weeks]. 1.146

(2) Subject to subsections (3) and (7) below, the first week of the maternity pay period shall be the 11th week before the expected week of confinement.

(3) Cases may be prescribed in which the first week of the period is to be a prescribed week later than the 11th week before the expected week of confinement, but not later than [[1]the week immediately following the week in which she is confined].

(4) Statutory maternity pay shall not be payable to a woman by a person in respect of any week during any part of which she works under a contract of service with him.

(5) It is immaterial for the purposes of subsection (4) above whether the work referred to in that subsection is work under a contract of service which existed immediately before the maternity pay period or a contract of service which did not so exist.

(6) Except in such cases as may be prescribed, statutory maternity pay shall not be payable to a woman in respect of any week after she has been confined and during any part of which she works for any employer who is not liable to pay her statutory maternity pay.

(7) Regulations may provide that this section shall have effect subject to prescribed modifications in relation—

(a) to cases in which a woman has been confined before the 11th week before the expected week of confinement; and

(b) to cases in which—

(i) a woman is confined[[1] at any time after the end of the week immediately preceding the 11th week] before the expected week of confinement; and

(ii) the maternity pay period has not then commenced for her.

AMENDMENTS

1. Maternity Allowance and Statutory Maternity Pay Regulations 1994 (SI 1994/1230, reg.3 (October 16, 1994).

2. Employment Act 2002, s.18 (April 6, 2003).

DEFINITIONS

"confined"—see s.171(1).
"confinement"—*ibid.*
"employer"—*ibid.*
"maternity pay period"—*ibid.*
"modifications"—*ibid.*
"prescribed"—*ibid.*
"week"—*ibid.*

GENERAL NOTE

1.147 SMP is payable for a period of 26 weeks (18 weeks before the commencement of the Employment Act 2002 in April 2003) (subs.(1)). These begin no earlier than 11 weeks before the estimated week of confinement (subs.(2)). A woman can therefore choose when to finish work: so long as it is after the qualifying week she is entitled to SMP from the 11th week, or the week after she finishes, whichever is the later. Regulations provide for this period to be varied when the woman gives birth early (see SMP (General) Regulations 1986 (SI 1986/1960), reg.2).

A woman is not entitled to receive SMP for any week in which she works for the employer who is liable to pay her SMP (subs.(4)). Nor is she entitled if she works for another employer after her confinement (subs.(6)) unless she had worked for two or more employers up to her qualifying week, one of whom was not liable to pay her SMP, and it is now that employer for whom she is working after confinement (see reg.8 of the SMP (General) Regulations 1986 (SI 1986/1960)). But where she works for a new employer after her confinement, even if she works only briefly, she loses her entitlement for the remainder of the maternity pay period. Apparently there is no restriction on working for another employer before confinement.

[1Rate of statutory maternity pay

166.—(1) Statutory maternity pay shall be payable to a woman— 1.148

(a) at the earnings-related rate, in respect of the first six weeks in respect of which it is payable; and

(b) at whichever is the lower of the earnings-related rate and such weekly rate as may be prescribed, in respect of the remaining portion of the maternity pay period.

(2) The earnings-related rate is a weekly rate equivalent to 90 per cent of a woman's normal weekly earnings for the period of eight weeks immediately preceding the 14th week before the expected week of confinement.

(3) The weekly rate prescribed under subsection (1)(b) above must not be less than the weekly rate of statutory sick pay for the time being specifiedin section 157(1) above or, if two or more such rates are for the time being so specified, the higher or highest of those rates.]

AMENDMENT

1. Employment Act 2002, s.19 (April 6, 2003).

DEFINITIONS

"confinement"—see s.171(1).
"maternity pay period"—*ibid.*
"normal weekly earnings"—*ibid.*
"prescribed"—*ibid.*
"week—*ibid.*

GENERAL NOTE

A new s.166 was substituted by s.19 of the Employment Act 2002. This preserved the pre-existing position so far as the rate of payment for the first six weeks of the maternity pay period is concerned. During this initial period SMP is paid at the earnings-related rate of 90 per cent of the woman's average weekly earnings in the eight weeks preceding the qualifying week (subss.(1)(a) and (2)). Thereafter, SMP is paid at either the standard prescribed rate (£100 per week in 2003/04) or the earnings-related rate, whichever is the lower (subs.(1)(b)), for the balance of 20 weeks. Previously the balance of the maternity pay period was just 12 weeks, but the then lower rate was always payable, irrespective of whether the earnings-related rate was lower. However, it should be noted that the non-earnings-related-weekly rate of SMP increased from £75 a week in 2002/03 to £100 p.w. in 2003/04 (and to £102.80 p.w. in 2004/05). 1.149

There remains an important issue relating to the SMP earnings calculation and the extent to which this takes into account pay rises. As a result of the decision of the European Court of Justice in *Gillespie v Northern Health and Social Services Board* [1996] I.R.L.R. 214, the earnings calculation for SMP purposes must take into account any pay rise which is backdated into the "relevant period" (on the meaning of which see SSCBA 1992, s.171(4) and (5) and SMP (General)

Regulations 1986 (SI 1986/1960, reg.21)). The *Gillespie* decision led to a limited amendment to the relevant regulations (SMP (General) Regulations 1986, reg.21(7), inserted by the SMP (General) Amendment Regulations 1996 (SI 1996/1335)). The question remains whether a woman on maternity leave should receive the benefit of any pay rise which has been implemented after the qualifying week and before the end of paid maternity leave. Regulation 21(7), it has been argued, fails to give full effect to the ruling in *Gillespie* by limiting it to cases in which the pay increase is backdated into the relevant period. The Court of Appeal referred a series of questions on this point to the European Court of Justice in *Alabaster v Woolwich plc* [2002] E.W.C.A. Civ. 211; [2002] 1 C.M.L.R. 56; [2002] I.R.L.R. 420. On the request for a preliminary ruling, the ECJ ruled as follows:

> "Article 119 of the Treaty must be interpreted as requiring that, in so far as the pay received by the worker during her maternity leave is determined, at least in part, on the basis of the pay she earned before her maternity leave began, any pay rise awarded between the beginning of the period covered by the reference pay and the end of the maternity leave must be included in the elements of pay taken into account in calculating the amount of such pay. This requirement is not limited to cases where the pay rise is back-dated to the period covered by the reference pay."

Alabaster v Woolwich plc and Secretary of State for Social Security Case C-147/02 (2004) ECJ CELEX LEXIS 120 (March 30, 2004), para.50.

[1 Funding of employers' liabilities in respect of statutory maternity pay

1.150 **167.**—(1) Regulations shall make provision for the payment by employers of statutory maternity pay to be funded by the Commissioners of Inland Revenue to such extent as may be prescribed.

(2) Regulations under subsection (1) shall—

(a) make provision for a person who has made a payment of statutory maternity pay to be entitled, except in prescribed circumstances, to recover an amount equal to the sum of—
  (i) the aggregate of such of those payments as qualify for small employers' relief; and
  (ii) an amount equal to 92 per cent of the aggregate of such of those payments as do not so qualify; and
(b) include provision for a person who has made a payment of statutory maternity pay qualifying for small employers' relief to be entitled, except in prescribed circumstances, to recover an additional amount, determined in such manner as may be prescribed—
  (i) by reference to secondary Class 1 contributions paid in respect of statutory maternity pay;
  (ii) by reference to secondary Class 1 contributions paid in respect of statutory sick pay; or
  (iii) by reference to the aggregate of secondary Class 1 contributions paid in respect of statutory maternity pay and secondary Class 1 contributions paid in respect of statutory sick pay.

(3) For the purposes of this section a payment of statutory maternity pay which a person is liable to make to a woman qualifies for small employers' relief if, in relation to that woman's maternity pay period, the person liable to make the payment is a small employer.

(4) For the purposes of this section "small employer", in relation to a woman's maternity pay period, shall have the meaning assigned to it by regulations, and, without prejudice to the generality of the foregoing, any such regulations—

(a) may define that expression by reference to the amount of a person's contributions payments for any prescribed period; and

(b) if they do so, may in that connection make provision for the amount of those payments for that prescribed period—

(i) to be determined without regard to any deductions that may be made from them under this section or under any other enactment or instrument; and

(ii) in prescribed circumstances, to be adjusted, estimated or otherwise attributed to him by reference to their amount in any other prescribed period.

(5) Regulations under subsection (1) may, in particular, make provision—

(a) for funding in advance as well as in arrear;

(b) for funding, or the recovery of amounts due under provision made by virtue of subsection (2)(b), by means of deductions from such amounts for which employers are accountable to the Commissioners of Inland Revenue as may be prescribed, or otherwise;

(c) for the recovery by the Commissioners of Inland Revenue of any sums overpaid to employers under the regulations.

(6) Where in accordance with any provision of regulations under subsection (1) an amount has been deducted from an employer's contributions payments, the amount so deducted shall (except in such cases as may be prescribed) be treated for the purposes of any provision made by or under any enactment in relation to primary or secondary Class 1 contributions—

(a) as having been paid (on such date as may be determined in accordance with the regulations); and

(b) as having been received by the Commissioners of Inland Revenue, towards discharging the employer's liability in respect of such contributions.

(7) Regulations under this section must be made with the concurrence of the Commissioners of Inland Revenue.

(8) In this section, "contributions payments", in relation to an employer, means any payments which the employer is required, by or under any enactment, to make in discharge of any liability in respect of primary or secondary Class 1 contributions.]

AMENDMENT

1. Employment Act 2002, s.21 (April 6, 2003).

DEFINITIONS

"contributions payments"—see subs.(8).
"employer"—see s.171(1).
"maternity pay period"—*ibid.*
"prescribed"—*ibid.*

GENERAL NOTE

1.151 The new s.167, substituted by s.21 of the Employment Act 2002, is different from its predecessor in two main respects. First, it allows regulations to be made which enable employers to recover SMP from tax and other payments due to the Inland Revenue (see subs.(5)(b) and now Statutory Maternity Pay (Compensation of Employers) and Miscellaneous Amendment Regulations 1994 (SI 1994/1882), reg.6), and not just from payments of national insurance contributions, as was previously the case. Secondly, as with the tax credits regime, it provides for regulations to be made enabling employers to apply to the Inland Revenue for advance funding (*ibid.*, reg.5). Formerly employers could only deduct, in arrears, the amount of SMP payments from contributions payments due to the Revenue.

Relationship with benefits and other payments, etc.

1.152 **168.**—Schedule 13 to this Act has effect with respect to the relationship between statutory maternity pay and certain benefits and payments.

GENERAL NOTE

1.153 As a general rule, entitlement to SMP precludes any entitlement to maternity allowance, SSP or incapacity benefit for the same period. Where SMP is paid, it is treated as going towards the employer's contractual obligation (if any) to pay maternity pay for the same period. If a woman receives maternity allowance because she does not earn enough to qualify for SMP, but then receives a backdated pay increase, making her then entitled to SMP, the employer is required to meet the difference between the maternity allowance paid and the SMP due (SMP (General) Regulations 1986 (SI 1986/1960), reg.21B).

Crown employment—Part XII

1.154 **169.**—The provisions of this Part of this Act apply in relation to women employed by or under the Crown as they apply in relation to women employed otherwise than by or under the Crown.

Special classes of persons

1.155 **170.**—(1) The Secretary of State may [1 with the concurrence of the Treasury] make regulations modifying this Part of this Act in such manner as he thinks proper in their application to any person who is, has been or is to be—

(a) employed on board any ship, vessel, hovercraft or aircraft;
(b) outside Great Britain at any prescribed time or in any prescribed circumstances; or
(c) in prescribed employment in connection with continental shelf operations, as defined in section 120(2) above.

(2) Regulations under subsection (1) above may in particular provide—

(a) for any provision of this Part of this Act to apply to any such person, notwithstanding that it would not otherwise apply;
(b) for any such provision not to apply to any such person, notwithstanding that it would otherwise apply;
(c) for excepting any such person from the application of any such provision where he neither is domiciled nor has a place of residence in any part of Great Britain;

(d) for the taking of evidence, for the purposes of the determination of any question arising under any such provision, in a country or territory outside Great Britain, by a British consular official or such other person as may be determined in accordance with the regulations.

AMENDMENT

1. Social Security Contributions (Transfer of Functions, etc.) Act 1999, s.1(1) and Sch.1, para.14 (April 1, 1999).

DEFINITIONS

"Great Britain"—see s.172(a).
"prescribed"—see s.171(1).

Interpretation of Part XII and supplementary provisions

171.—(1) In this Part of this Act— **1.156**

"confinement" means—

(a) labour resulting in the issue of a living child; or
(b) labour after [[1]24 weeks] of pregnancy resulting in the issue of a child whether alive or dead;

and "confined" shall be construed accordingly; and where a woman's labour begun on one day results in the issue of a child on another day she shall be taken to be confined on the day of the issue of the childor, if labour results in the issue of twins or a greater number of children, she shall be taken to be confined on the day of the issue of the last of them;

"dismissed" is to be construed in accordance with [[3]Part X of the Employment Rights Act 1996];

"employee" means a woman who is—

(a) gainfully employed in Great Britain either under a contract of service or in an office (including elective office) with emoluments chargeable to income tax under Schedule E; and
(b) over the age of 16;

but subject to regulations [[5]made with the concurrence of the Inland Revenue] which may provide for cases where any such woman is not to be treated as an employee for the purposes of this Part of this Act and for cases where a woman who would not otherwise be an employee for those purposes is to be treated as an employee for those purposes;

"employer", in relation to a woman who is an employee, means a person who under section 6 above is, or but for [[4]the condition in] subsection (1)(b) of that section would be, liable to pay secondary Class 1 contributions in relation to any of her earnings;

"maternity pay period" has the meaning assigned to it by section 165(1) above;

"modifications" includes additions, omissions and amendments, and related expressions shall be construed accordingly;

"prescribed" means specified in or determined in accordance with regulations;

"week" means a period of seven days beginning with Sunday or such other period as may be prescribed in relation to any particular case or class of cases.

(2) Without prejudice to any other power to make regulations under this Part of this Act, regulations may specify cases in which, for the purposes of this Part of this Act or of such provisions of this Part of this Act as may be prescribed—

(a) two or more employers are to be treated as one;

(b) two or more contracts of service in respect of which the same woman is an employee are to be treated as one.

(3) Where, in consequence of the establishment of one or more National Health Service trusts under Part I of the National Health Service and Community Care Act 1990 or the National Health Service (Scotland) Act 1978, a woman's contract of employment is treated by a scheme under that Part or Act as divided so as to constitute two or more contracts, [[2]or where an order under paragraph 23(1) of Schedule 5A to the National Health Service Act 1977 provides that a woman's contract of employment is so divided,] regulations may make provision enabling her to elect for all of those contracts to be treated as one contract for the purposes of this Part of this Act or of such provisions of this Part of this Act as may be prescribed; and any such regulations may prescribe—

(a) the conditions that must be satisfied if a woman is to be entitled to make such an election;

(b) the manner in which, and the time within which, such an election is to be made;

(c) the persons to whom, and the manner in which, notice of such an election is to be given;

(d) the information which a woman who makes such an election is to provide, and the persons to whom, and the time within which, she is to provide it;

(e) the time for which such an election is to have effect;

(f) which one of the woman's employers under the two or more contracts is to be regarded for the purposes of statutory maternity pay as her employer under the one contract;

and the powers conferred by this subsection are without prejudice to any other power to make regulations under this Part of this Act.

(4) For the purposes of this Part of this Act a woman's normal weekly earnings shall, subject to subsection (6) below, be taken to be the average weekly earnings which in the relevant period have been paid to her or paid for her benefit under the contract of service with the employer in question.

(5) For the purposes of subsection (4) above "earnings" and "relevant period" shall have the meanings given to them by regulations.

(6) In such cases as may be prescribed a woman's normal weekly earnings shall be calculatedin accordance with regulations.

[[5](7) Regulations under any of subsections (2) to (6) above must be made with the concurrence of the Commissioners of Inland Revenue.]

AMENDMENTS

1. Still-Birth (Definition) Act 1992, s.2 (October 1, 1992).
2. Health Act 1999 (Supplementary, Consequential etc. Provisions) Order 2000, Art.3, Sch.1, para.27 (SI 2000/90) (February 8, 2000).
3. Employment Rights Act 1996, s.240 and Sch.1, para.51(5) (August 23, 1996).
4. Social Security Act 1998, s.86 and Sch.7, para.75 (April 6, 1999).
5. Social Security Contributions (Transfer of Functions, etc.) Act 1999, s.1(1) and Sch.1, para.15 (April 1, 1999).

[1 PART XIIZA

STATUTORY PATERNITY PAY

AMENDMENT

1. Part XIIZA was inserted by the Employment Act 2002, s.2 (December 8, 2002).

GENERAL NOTE

Part XIIZA of the SSCBA 1992 was inserted by the Employment Act 2002. **1.157** The 2002 Act followed the Employment Relations Act 1999, which itself included a number of "family friendly" employment measures (*e.g.* new rights to 13 weeks' unpaid parental leave and to unpaid time off to deal with family crises). The ordinary period of maternity leave was also increased in 1999 from 14 to 18 weeks (this period was extended to 26 weeks in April 2003 by other provisions in the Employment Act 2002), along with several other reforms designed to simplify the notoriously complex rules governing maternity leave and pay. A further review was announced in the 2000 Budget statement, which led to the publication of a Green Paper, *Work and Parents: Competitiveness and Choice* (DTI, December 2000). The Government's decisions on that review were announced at or around the time of the 2001 Budget statement, and were followed by the issue of three further consultation documents on the frameworks for maternity, paternity and adoption leave and pay. In November 2001 the DTI published a summary of responses to these various papers in the *Government's Response on Simplification of Maternity Leave, Paternity Leave and Adoption Leave.*

The Government's proposals were then brought forward in the Bill which became the Employment Act 2002. Part I of the 2002 Act dealt with statutory leave and pay. Thus, s.1 introduced a right to paternity leave in the Employment Rights Act 1996 (inserting ss.80A-80E), while s.2 inserted this Pt XIIZA into the SSCBA 1992 to make provision for statutory paternity pay (SPP). Sections 3 and 4 dealt with adoption leave and statutory adoption pay (SAP) respectively (on the latter see SSCBA 1992, Pt XIIZB). The procedural provisions relating to SPP and SAP were contained in ss.5–16 of the 2002 Act. (The 2002 Act also included measures to establish statutory minimum dismissal, disciplinary and grievance procedures and changes to employment tribunal procedures.)

The amendments made by c.1 of Pt I of the Employment Act 2002 relating to paternity and adoption, including the insertion of Pt XIIZA into the SSCBA 1992, came into force on December 8, 2002 (Employment Act 2002 (Commencement No.3 and Transitional and Saving Provisions) Order 2002, art.2(2) and Sch.1, Pt II). However, art.3 and Sch.3, para.1 of the same Order provide that Part XIIZA shall have effect only in relation to a person who satisfies the prescribed conditions of entitlement in respect of a child who is either (a) born on or after April 6, 2003 (or whose expected week of birth begins on or after that date); or (b) matched for the purposes of adoption with a person who is notified of having been matched on or after April 6, 2003 (or placed for adoption on or after that date).

SPP is payable for a two week period only (SSCBA 1992, s.171ZE(2)). Such paid paternity leave must be taken in a single block within the first eight weeks after the child's birth (SSCBA 1992, s.171ZE(3)). There are, in fact, two forms of SPP, known in the regulations (the Statutory Paternity Pay and Statutory Adoption Pay (General) Regulations 2002 (SI 2002/2822)) as SPP (birth) and SPP (adoption), although these terms do not appear in the primary legislation. The principal eligibility criteria for SPP (birth) are set out in SSCBA 1992, s.171ZA and for SPP (adoption) in s.171ZB. Entitlement to SPP (birth) arises in respect of children born on or after April 6, 2003, or whose expected week of birth begins on or after that date (SPP and SAP (General) Regulations 2002, reg.3(1)(a); see also (Employment Act 2002 (Commencement No. 3 and Transitional and Saving Provisions) Order 2002, art.3 and Sch.3). Similarly, entitlement to SPP (adoption) arises where the adoptive parent is notified of having been matched on or after April 6, 2003 or the child is placed for adoption on or after that date (SPP and SAP (General) Regulations 2002, reg.3(1)(b)). Section 171ZC contains general conditions of entitlement (*e.g.* as to giving the requisite notice to the employer). Section 171ZD places the liability to make payments of SPP on employers (the recovery mechanisms are the same as for SMP), while s.17ZE, with the associated regulations, deals with matters such as the rate and period of pay. Although paid for a shorter period than SMP, SPP is paid at the same rate as SMP. Sections 171ZF–171ZK make provision for various types of special cases and matters of interpretation, etc.

Entitlement: birth

1.158 **171ZA.**—(1) Where a person satisfies the conditions in subsection (2) below, he shall be entitled in accordance with the following provisions of this Part to payments to be known as "statutory paternity pay".

(2) The conditions are—

(a) that he satisfies prescribed conditions—
   (i) as to relationship with a newborn child; and
   (ii) as to relationship with the child's mother;

(b) that he has been in employed earner's employment with an employer for a continuous period of at least 26 weeks ending with the relevant week;

(c) that his normal weekly earnings for the period of eight weeks ending with the relevant week are not less than the lower earnings limit in force under section 5(1)(a) above at the end of the relevant week; and

(d) that he has been in employed earner's employment with the employer by reference to whom the condition in para.(b) above is satisfied for a continuous period beginning with the end of the relevant week and ending with the day on which the child is born.

(3) The references in subsection (2) above to the relevant week are to the week immediately preceding the 14th week before the expected week of the child's birth.

(4) A person's entitlement to statutory paternity pay under this section shall not be affected by the birth, or expected birth, of more than one childas a result of the same pregnancy.

(5) In this section, "newborn child" includes a child stillborn after 24 weeks of pregnancy.

DEFINITIONS

"employer"—see s.171ZJ(1)
"newborn child"—see subs.(5)
"prescribed"—see s.171ZJ(1)
"the relevant week"—see subs.(3)
"week"—see s.171ZJ(5)

GENERAL NOTE

Subs. (2)(a)

The entitlement conditions referred to in subs.(2)(a) are those prescribed in reg.4(2)(b) and (c) of the Paternity and Adoption Leave Regulations 2002 (SI 2002/2788), which are incorporated by the cross-reference in reg.4 of the SPP and SAP (General) Regulations 2002 (SI 2002/2822). These requirements are that the employee is, first, either (i) the father of the child, or (ii) married to or the partner of the child's mother, but not the child's father (reg.4(2)(b)); and, secondly, has, or expects to have (i) responsibility for the upbringing of the child (if he is the child's father); or (ii) the main responsibility (apart from any responsibility of the mother) for the upbringing of the child (if he is the mother's husband or partner but not the child's father) (reg.4(2)(c)). **1.159**

Subs. (2)(b)

On the extended meaning of continuous employment, see SPP and SAP (General) Regulations 2002, regs 33–37. **1.160**

Subs. (2)(c)

The minimum threshold requirement that the claimant's earnings are not less than the National Insurance lower earnings limit necessarily excludes those fathers on very low incomes, and typically in part-time work, from SPP. Arguably this is the group of men whose families are most at risk of social exclusion and thus most in need of support such as SPP. The problem is exacerbated by the fact that the National Insurance scheme, unlike the income tax system, does not aggregate earnings from *e.g.* two part-time jobs with different employers. (But note the special case of associated employers: see SPP and SAP (General) Regulations 2002, reg.38.) Women who do not meet the lower earnings limit requirement do not qualify for SMP (SSCBA 1992, s.164(2)(b)) but may qualify for maternity allowance (SSCBA 1992, s.35—see Vol.I of this series). There is, at present, no such alternative form of income maintenance for fathers in a similar position. This was the one aspect in relation to this part of the Employment Act 2002 which caused considerable disquiet amongst Government back-benchers during the Standing Committee debates on the Bill (Standing Committee F, January 10, 2002, cols 333–360). The minister promised members that the DWP and Department of Health were actively considering how to provide support for low-wage adoptive parents with some form of support equivalent to maternity allowance. **1.161**

Subs. (2)(b)–(d)

The entitlement conditions are modified if a person fails to meet the conditions set out in subsection (2)(b)–(d) because the child's birth occurred earlier than the **1.162**

14th week before the expected week of the birth: see SPP and SAP (General) Regulations 2002, reg 5. This modification is in exercise of the regulation-making powers under section 171ZC(3)(a).

Subs. (4)

1.163 Thus, SPP is not paid for twice as long in the case of a father of twins.

Entitlement: adoption

1.164 **171ZB.**—(1) Where a person satisfies the conditions in subsection (2) below, he shall be entitled in accordance with the following provisions of this Part to payments to be known as "statutory paternity pay".

(2) The conditions are—

(a) that he satisfies prescribed conditions—

(i) as to relationship with a child who is placed for adoption under the law of any part of the United Kingdom, and

(ii) as to relationship with a person with whom the child is so placed for adoption;

(b) that he has been in employed earner's employment with an employer for a continuous period of at least 26 weeks ending with the relevant week;

(c) that his normal weekly earnings for the period of 8 weeks ending with the relevant week are not less than the lower earnings limit in force under section 5(1)(a) at the end of the relevant week;

(d) that he has been in employed earner's employment with the employer by reference to whom the condition in paragraph (b) above is satisfied for a continuous period beginning with the end of the relevant week and ending with the day on which the child is placedfor adoption; and

(e) where he is a person with whom the child is placed for adoption, that he has elected to receive statutory paternity pay.

(3) The references in subsection (2) to the relevant week are to the week in which the adopter is notified of being matched with the child for the purposes of adoption.

(4) A person may not elect to receive statutory paternity pay if he has elected in accordance with section 171ZL below to receive statutory adoption pay.

(5) Regulations may make provision about elections for the purposes of subsection (2)(e) above.

(6) A person's entitlement to statutory paternity pay under this section shall not be affected by the placement for adoption of more than one child as part of the same arrangement.

(7) In this section, "adopter", in relation to a person who satisfies the condition under subsection (2)(a)(ii) above, means the person by reference to whom he satisfies that condition.

Definitions

"adopter"—see subs.(7)
"employer"—see s.171ZJ(1)
"normal weekly earnings"—see s.171ZJ(6)
"prescribed"—see s.171ZJ(1)

"the relevant week"—see subs.(3)
"week"—see s.171ZJ(5)

GENERAL NOTE

The conditions prescribed under subs.(2)(a) are, first, that the claimant is married to or the partner of a child's adopter (or in a case where there are two adopters, married to or the partner of the other adopter) and, secondly, has, or expects to have, the main responsibility for the upbringing of the child (apart from the responsibility of the child's adopter, or in a case where there two adopters, together with the other adopter): SPP and SAP (General) Regulations 2002 (SI 2002/2822), reg.11. Note that, unusually, reg.11 specifically includes same-sex partners. "Partner" is defined by reg.11(2) as meaning a person (excluding certain defined relatives) "who lives with the adopter and the child in an enduring family relationship", irrespective of whether the relationship between the adults is heterosexual or same-sex in nature. 1.165

Entitlement: general

171ZC.—(1) A person shall be entitled to payments of statutory paternity pay in respect of any period only if— 1.166

(a) he gives the person who will be liable to pay it notice of the date from which he expects the liability to pay him statutory paternity pay to begin; and
(b) the notice is given at least 28 days before that date or, if that is not reasonably practicable, as soon as is reasonably practicable.

(2) The notice shall be in writing if the person who is liable to pay the statutory paternity pay so requests.

(3) The Secretary of State may by regulations—

(a) provide that subsection (2)(b), (c) or (d) of section 171ZA or 171ZB above shall have effect subject to prescribed modifications in such cases as may be prescribed;
(b) provide that subsection (1) above shall not have effect, or shall have effect subject to prescribed modifications, in such cases as may be prescribed;
(c) impose requirements about evidence of entitlement;
(d) specify in what circumstances employment is to be treated as continuous for the purposes of section 171ZA or 171ZB above;
(e) provide that a person is to be treated for the purposes of section 171ZA or 171ZB above as being employed for a continuous period of at least 26 weeks where—
    (i) he has been employed by the same employer for at least 26 weeks under two or more separate contracts of service; and
    (ii) those contracts were not continuous;
(f) provide for amounts earned by a person under separate contracts of service with the same employer to be aggregated for the purposes of section 171ZA or 171ZB above;
(g) provide that—
    (i) the amount of a person's earnings for any period; or
    (ii) the amount of his earnings to be treated as comprised in any payment made to him or for his benefit,

shall be calculated or estimated for the purposes of section 171ZA or 171ZB above in such manner and on such basis as may be prescribed and that for that purpose payments of a particular class or description made or falling to be made to or by a person shall, to such extent as may be prescribed, be disregarded or, as the case may be, be deducted from the amount of his earnings.

DEFINITIONS

"employer"—see s.171ZJ(1)
"modifications"—see *ibid.*
"prescribed"—see *ibid.*
"week"—see s.171ZJ(5)

GENERAL NOTE

1.167 See further regs 6 and 7 of the SPP and SAP (General) Regulations 2002 (SI 2002/2822) on the period of payment and notice requirements for SPP (birth). The requirements relating to evidence of entitlement are in reg.9. The equivalent provisions for SPP (adoption) are in regs 12, 13 and 15.

Liability to make payments

1.168 **171ZD.**—(1) The liability to make payments of statutory paternity pay under section 171ZA or 171ZB above is a liability of any person of whom the person entitled to the payments has been an employee as mentioned in subsection (2)(b) and (d) of that section.

(2) Regulations shall make provision as to a former employer's liability to pay statutory paternity pay to a person in any case where the former employee's contract of service with him has been brought to an end by the former employer solely, or mainly, for the purpose of avoiding liability for statutory paternity pay.

(3) The Secretary of State may, with the concurrence of the Board, by regulations specify circumstances in which, notwithstanding this section, liability to make payments of statutory paternity pay is to be a liability of the Board.

DEFINITIONS

"the Board"—see s.171ZJ(1)
"employer"—see *ibid.*

GENERAL NOTE

1.169 This section, placing the liability to make payments of SPP on employers, follows the same approach as the provisions governing SMP (s.164(3) and (8)). Note that there is no liability to pay SPP in respect of any week during which the claimant either is entitled to SSP or is detained in custody (or sentenced to imprisonment): SPP and SAP (General) Regulations 2002 (SI 2002/2822), reg.18. Similarly, there is no liability to pay SPP in the week that the person entitled dies.

The rules governing the funding of SPP and employers' responsibilities in connection with SPP payments are contained in the SPP and SAP (Administration) Regulations 2002 (SI 2002/2820). The special circumstances in which the Board is liable to pay SPP under subs.(3) are set out in SPP and SAP (General) Regulations 2002, reg.43.

Rate and period of pay

171ZE.—(1) Statutory paternity pay shall be payable at such fixed or earnings-related weekly rate as may be prescribed by regulations, which may prescribe different kinds of rate for different cases. **1.170**

(2) Statutory paternity pay shall be payable in respect of—

(a) a period of two consecutive weeks within the qualifying period beginning on such date within that period as the person entitled may choose in accordance with regulations; or

(b) if regulations permit the person entitled to choose to receive statutory paternity pay in respect of—

(i) a period of a week, or

(ii) two non-consecutive periods of a week,

such week or weeks within the qualifying period as he may choose in accordance with regulations.

(3) For the purposes of subsection (2) above, the qualifying period shall be determined in accordance with regulations, which shall secure that it is a period of at least 56 days beginning—

(a) in the case of a person to whom the conditions in section 171ZA(2) above apply, with the date of the child's birth, and

(b) in the case of a person to whom the conditions in section 171ZB(2) above apply, with the date of the child's placement for adoption.

(4) Statutory paternity pay shall not be payable to a person in respect of a statutory pay week if it is not his purpose at the beginning of the week—

(a) to care for the child by reference to whom he satisfies the condition in sub-paragraph (i) of section 171ZA(2)(a) or 171ZB(2)(a) above; or

(b) to support the person by reference to whom he satisfies the condition in sub-paragraph (ii) of that provision.

(5) A person shall not be liable to pay statutory paternity pay to another in respect of a statutory pay week during any part of which the other works under a contract of service with him.

(6) It is immaterial for the purposes of subsection (5) above whether the work referred to in that subsection is work under a contract of service which existed immediately before the statutory pay week or a contract of service which did not so exist.

(7) Except in such cases as may be prescribed, statutory paternity pay shall not be payable to a person in respect of a statutory pay week during any part of which he works for any employer who is not liable to pay him statutory paternity pay.

(8) The Secretary of State may by regulations specify circumstances in which there is to be no liability to pay statutory paternity pay in respect of a statutory pay week.

(9) Where more than one child is born as a result of the same pregnancy, the reference in subsection (3)(a) to the date of the child's birth shall be read as a reference to the date of birth of the first child born as a result of the pregnancy.

(10) Where more than one child is placed for adoption as part of the same arrangement, the reference in subsection (3)(b) to the date of the

child's placement shall be read as a reference to the date of placement of the first child to be placed as part of the arrangement.

(11) In this section—

"statutory pay week", in relation to a person entitled to statutory paternity pay, means a week chosen by him as a week in respect of which statutory paternity pay shall be payable;

"week" means any period of seven days.

DEFINITIONS

"employer"—see s.171ZJ(1)
"statutory pay week"—see subsection (11)
"week"—see *ibid.*

GENERAL NOTE

1.171 The weekly rate of SPP for 2004–05 is the lesser of £102.80 and 90 per cent of normal weekly earnings (on which see SPP and SAP (General) Regulations 2002 (SI 2002/2822), reg.40): SPP and SAP (Weekly Rates) Regulations 2002 (SI 2002/2818), reg.2.

The qualifying period for SPP (birth), *i.e.* the period within which the SPP period must occur, is the period of 56 days from the date of the child's birth (SPP and SAP (General) Regulations 2002, reg.8). For SPP (adoption), the 56 days runs from the date of the child's placement for adoption: see reg.14.

Regulation 18 of the SPP and SAP (General) Regulations 2002, made under para.(8), sets out the circumstances in which there is no liability to pay SPP (where SSP is payable, or the person has died or is in legal custody).

The rules governing the time for paying SPP are set out in reg.42 of the SPP and SAP (General) Regulations 2002. SPP may be paid in the same way as ordinary remuneration but must not include payment in kind or by way of board and lodging: reg.41.

Restrictions on contracting out

1.172 **171ZF.**—(1) Any agreement shall be void to the extent that it purports—

(a) to exclude, limit or otherwise modify any provision of this Part of this Act; or

(b) to require an employee or former employee to contribute (whether directly or indirectly) towards any costs incurred by his employer or former employer under this Part of this Act.

(2) For the avoidance of doubt, any agreement between an employer and an employee authorising any deductions from statutory paternity pay which the employer is liable to pay to the employee in respect of any period shall not be void by virtue of subsection (1)(a) above if the employer—

(a) is authorised by that or another agreement to make the same deductions from any contractual remuneration which he is liable to pay in respect of the same period; or

(b) would be so authorised if he were liable to pay contractual remuneration in respect of that period.

DEFINITION

"employer"—see s.171ZJ(1)

General Note

These restrictions on contracting out follow the equivalent provisions for SSP (s.151(2)–(3)) and SMP (s.164(6)–(7)). 1.173

Relationship with contractual remuneration

171ZG.—(1) Subject to subsections (2) and (3) below, any entitlement to statutory paternity pay shall not affect any right of a person in relation to remuneration under any contract of service ("contractual remuneration"). 1.174

(2) Subject to subsection (3) below—

(a) any contractual remuneration paid to a person by an employer of his in respect of any period shall go towards discharging any liability of that employer to pay statutory paternity pay to him in respect of that period; and

(b) any statutory paternity pay paid by an employer to a person who is an employee of his in respect of any period shall go towards discharging any liability of that employer to pay contractual remuneration to him in respect of that period.

(3) Regulations may make provision as to payments which are, and those which are not, to be treated as contractual remuneration for the purposes of subsections (1) and (2) above.

Definitions

"contractual remuneration"—see subsection (1)
"employer"—see section 171ZJ(1)

General Note

This section mirrors Sch.12, para.2, the equivalent provision in relation to SSP, and Sch.13, para.3, which governs SMP to the same effect. The basic principle is that entitlement to SPP does not affect a claimant's rights to any contractual remuneration (subs.(1)), subject to the significant exception that any payment of contractual remuneration can be regarded as the discharge of SPP liability and vice versa (subs.(2)). Regulations made under subs.(3) provide that the payments to be treated as contractual remuneration are sums payable under a contract of service (a) by way of remuneration, (b) for incapacity for work due to sickness or injury, or (c) by reason of the birth or adoption of a child (SPP and SAP (General) Regulations 2002 (SI 2002/2822), reg.19). 1.175

Crown employment—Part XIIZA

171ZH.—The provisions of this Part of this Act apply in relation to persons employed by or under the Crown as they apply in relation to persons employed otherwise than by or under the Crown. 1.176

General Note

This mirrors s.169, the equivalent provision for SMP. 1.177

Special classes of person

171ZI.—(1) The Secretary of State may with the concurrence of the Treasury make regulations modifying any provision of this Part of this Act 1.178

in such manner as he thinks proper in its application to any person who is, has been or is to be—

(a) employed on board any ship, vessel, hovercraft or aircraft;

(b) outside Great Britain at any prescribed time or in any prescribed circumstances; or

(c) in prescribed employment in connection with continental shelf operations, as defined in section 120(2) above.

(2) Regulations under subsection (1) above may, in particular, provide—

(a) for any provision of this Part of this Act to apply to any such person, notwithstanding that it would not otherwise apply;

(b) for any such provision not to apply to any such person, notwithstanding that it would otherwise apply;

(c) for excepting any such person from the application of any such provision where he neither is domiciled nor has a place of residence in any part of Great Britain;

(d) for the taking of evidence, for the purposes of the determination of any question arising under any such provision, in a country or territory outside Great Britain, by a British consular official or such other person as may be determined in accordance with the regulations.

DEFINITIONS

"Great Britain"—see s.172(a)
"prescribed"—see s.171ZJ(1)

GENERAL NOTE

1.179 This enabling provision is in the same terms as s.162, which applies to SSP. See further the Statutory Paternity Pay and Statutory Adoption Pay (Persons Abroadand Mariners) Regulations 2002 (SI 2002/2821).

Part XIIZA: supplementary

1.180 **171ZJ.**—(1) In this Part of this Act—

"the Board" means the Commissioners of Inland Revenue;

"employer", in relation to a person who is an employee, means a person who under section 6 above is, or but for the condition in subsection (1)(b) of that section would be, liable to pay secondary Class 1 contributions in relation to any of the earnings of the person who is an employee;

"modifications" includes additions, omissions and amendments, and related expressions are to be read accordingly;

"prescribed" means prescribed by regulations.

(2) In this Part of this Act, "employee" means a person who is—

(a) gainfully employed in Great Britain either under a contract of service or in an office (including elective office) with emoluments chargeable to income tax under Schedule E; and

(b) over the age of 16.

(3) Regulations may provide—

(a) for cases where a person who falls within the definition in subsection (2) above is not to be treated as an employee for the purposes of this Part of this Act; and

(b) for cases where a person who would not otherwise be an employee for the purposes of this Part of this Act is to be treated as an employee for those purposes.

(4) Without prejudice to any other power to make regulations under this Part of this Act, regulations may specify cases in which, for the purposes of this Part of this Act or of such provisions of this Part of this Act as may be prescribed—

(a) two or more employers are to be treated as one;

(b) two or more contracts of service in respect of which the same person is an employee are to be treated as one.

(5) In this Part, except section 171ZE, "week" means a period of seven days beginning with Sunday or such other period as may be prescribed in relation to any particular case or class of cases.

(6) For the purposes of this Part of this Act, a person's normal weekly earnings shall, subject to subsection (8) below, be taken to be the average weekly earnings which in the relevant period have been paid to him or paid for his benefit under the contract of service with the employer in question.

(7) For the purposes of subsection (6) above, "earnings" and "relevant period" shall have the meanings given to them by regulations.

(8) In such cases as may be prescribed, a person's normal weekly earnings shall be calculated in accordance with regulations.

(9) Where—

(a) in consequence of the establishment of one or more National Health Service trusts under Part I of the National Health Service and Community Care Act 1990 (Chapter 19) or the National Health Service (Scotland) Act 1978 (Chapter 29), a person's contract of employment is treated by a scheme under that Part or Act as divided so as to constitute two or more contracts; or

(b) an order under paragraph 23(1) of Schedule 5A to the National Health Service Act 1977 (Chapter 49) provides that a person's contract of employment is so divided;

regulations may make provision enabling the person to elect for all of those contracts to be treated as one contract for the purposes of this Part of this Act or such provisions of this Part of this Act as may be prescribed.

(10) Regulations under subsection (9) above may prescribe—

(a) the conditions that must be satisfied if a person is to be entitled to make such an election;

(b) the manner in which, and the time within which, such an election is to be made;

(c) the persons to whom, and the manner in which, notice of such an election is to be given;

(d) the information which a person who makes such an election is to provide, and the persons to whom, and the time within which, he is to provide it;

(e) the time for which such an election is to have effect;

(f) which one of the person's employers under two or more contracts is to be regarded for the purposes of statutory paternity pay as his employer under the contract.

(11) The powers under subsections (9) and (10) are without prejudice to any other power to make regulations under this Part of this Act.

(12) Regulations under any of subsections (4) to (10) above must be made with the concurrence of the Board.

GENERAL NOTE

1.181 "*Earnings*": The definition and enabling power under subss.(6) and (7) should be read with reg.39 of the SPP and SAP (General) Regulations 2002 (SI 2002/2822), which defines this term.

"*Employee*": The definition under subs.(2) is modified by regulations made under subs.(3). Thus those who are treated as employed earners under the Social Security (Categorisation of Earners) Regulations 1978 (SI 1978/1689) are also treated as employees for the purpose of SPP: SPP and SAP (General) Regulations 2002, reg.32(1). Apprentices are also covered (reg.32(2)). Employed earners who do not meet the residence or presence requirements under the rules governing National Insurance contributions are excluded from the definition of employee for these purposes (reg.32(3)). Continuous employment is dealt with by regs 33–37. Employment with more than one employer (subs.(4)) is covered by reg.38.

"*National Health Service trusts*": The special position of NHS employees with more than one contract of employment (*e.g.* with different NHS trusts) is dealt with by the SPP and SAP (National Health Service Employees) Regulations 2002 (SI 2002/2819). These regulations enable such employees to elect to treat two or more such contracts as one contract of employment.

"*Normal weekly earnings*": The definition and enabling power under subss.(6) and (7) should be read with reg.40 of the SPP and SAP (General) Regulations 2002, which defines this term.

Power to apply Part XIIZA to adoption cases not involving placement

1.182 **171ZK.**—The Secretary of State may by regulations provide for this Part to have effect in relation to cases which involve adoption, but not the placement of a child for adoption under the law of any part of the United Kingdom, with such modifications as the regulations may prescribe.

DEFINITIONS

"modifications"—see s.171ZJ(1)
"United Kingdom"—see s.172(b)

GENERAL NOTE

1.183 See further the Social Security Contributions and Benefits Act 1992 (Application of Pts XIIZA and XIIZB to Adoptions from Overseas) Regulations 2003 (SI 2003/499) and the Statutory Paternity Pay (Adoption) and Statutory Adoption Pay (Adoptions from Overseas) (No.2) Regulations 2003 (SI 2003/1194).

[1 PART XIIZB

STATUTORY ADOPTION PAY

AMENDMENT

1. Part XIIZB was inserted by the Employment Act 2002, s.4 (December 8, 2002).

GENERAL NOTE

Part XIIZB of the SSCBA 1992 was inserted by the Employment Act 2002. On the background to the introduction of statutory adoption pay (SAP), see the General Note to Pt XIIZA on statutory paternity pay (SPP), introduced at the same time. The amendments made by c.1 of Pt I of the Employment Act 2002 relating to paternity and adoption, including the insertion of Pt XIIZB into the SSCBA 1992, came into force on December 8, 2002 (Employment Act 2002 (Commencement No.3 and Transitional and Saving Provisions) Order 2002, art.2(2) and Sch.1, Part 2). However, art.3 and Sch.3, para.2 of the same Order provide that Part XIIZB shall have effect only in relation to a person with whom a child is, or is expected to be placed for adoption on or after April 6, 2003. 1.184

Adoptive parents have a right under employment legislation to 26 weeks' ordinary adoption leave with the option of 26 weeks' additional adoption leave, mirroring the arrangements now in place for maternity leave. SAP is payable for 26 weeks (SSCBA 1992, s.171ZN(2)), as with SMP (but unlike the mere two weeks for SPP). The rules governing entitlement to SAP are set out in SSCBA 1992, s.171ZL: employees must have completed 26 weeks' service with their employer by the time they are matched with the child to be adopted and their earnings, on average, must be at least equal to the lower earnings limit for the purpose of National Insurance contributions. The liability to make payments of SAP is placed on employers (SSCBA 1992, s.171ZM), with the recovery arrangements being as for SMP. Provision for various types of special cases and for matters of interpretation is to be found in SSCBA 1992, ss.171ZO–171ZT.

Entitlement

171ZL.—(1) Where a person who is, or has been, an employee satisfies the conditions in subsection (2) below, he shall be entitled in accordance with the following provisions of this Part to payments to be known as "statutory adoption pay". 1.185

(2) The conditions are—

(a) that he is a person with whom a child is, or is expected to be, placed for adoption under the law of any part of the United Kingdom;

(b) that he has been in employed earner's employment with an employer for a continuous period of at least 26 weeks ending with the relevant week;

(c) that he has ceased to work for the employer;

(d) that his normal weekly earnings for the period of 8 weeks ending with the relevant week are not less than the lower earnings limit in force under section 5(1)(a) at the end of the relevant week; and

(e) that he has elected to receive statutory adoption pay.

(3) The references in subsection (2)(b) and (d) above to the relevant week are to the week in which the person is notified that he has been matched with the child for the purposes of adoption.

(4) A person may not elect to receive statutory adoption pay if—

(a) he has elected in accordance with section 171ZB above to receive statutory paternity pay, or

(b) where the child is, or is expected to be, placed for adoption with him as a member of a married couple and his spouse is a person to whom the conditions in subsection (2) above apply, his spouse has elected to receive statutory adoption pay.

(5) A person's entitlement to statutory adoption pay shall not be affectedby the placement, or expected placement, for adoption of more than one childas part of the same arrangement.

(6) A person shall be entitled to payments of statutory adoption pay only if—

(a) he gives the person who will be liable to pay it notice of the date from which he expects the liability to pay him statutory adoption pay to begin; and

(b) the notice is given at least 28 days before that date or, if that is not reasonably practicable, as soon as is reasonably practicable.

(7) The notice shall be in writing if the person who is liable to pay the statutory adoption pay so requests.

(8) The Secretary of State may by regulations—

(a) provide that subsection (2)(b), (c) or (d) above shall have effect subject to prescribed modifications in such cases as may be prescribed;

(b) provide that subsection (6) above shall not have effect, or shall have effect subject to prescribed modifications, in such cases as may be prescribed;

(c) impose requirements about evidence of entitlement;

(d) specify in what circumstances employment is to be treated as continuous for the purposes of this section;

(e) provide that a person is to be treated for the purposes of this section as being employed for a continuous period of at least 26 weeks where—

(i) he has been employed by the same employer for at least 26 weeks under two or more separate contracts of service; and

(ii) those contracts were not continuous;

(f) provide for amounts earned by a person under separate contracts of service with the same employer to be aggregated for the purposes of this section;

(g) provide that—

(i) the amount of a person's earnings for any period; or

(ii) the amount of his earnings to be treated as comprised in any payment made to him or for his benefit;

shall be calculated or estimated for the purposes of this section in such manner and on such basis as may be prescribed and that for that purpose payments of a particular class or description made or falling to be made to or by a person shall, to such extent as may be prescribed, be disregarded or, as the case may be, be deducted from the amount of his earnings;

(h) make provision about elections for statutory adoption pay.

DEFINITIONS

"employee"—see s.171ZS(2)
"employer"—see s.171ZS(1)
"modifications"—see *ibid.*
"normal weekly earnings"—see s.171ZS(6)
"prescribed"—see s.171ZS(1)
"relevant week"—see subs.(3)

"United Kingdom"—see s.172(b)
"week"—see s.171ZS(5)

General Note

This section sets out the qualifying conditions for receipt of SAP. A person is entitled to SAP if he or she meets each of five conditions (subs.(2)). First, the claimant must have an approved match with the child. Secondly, the person must be an employee who has satisfied the service qualification of continuous service with the same employer for at least 26 weeks by the week in which the approved match is made. Thirdly, the person must have actually stopped working for that employer (see also s.171ZN(3) (and (4)). Fourthly, the employee's average weekly earnings must be not less than the lower earnings limit for National Insurance contributions. Finally, the person must have elected to receive SAP, which requires that he or she provide the employer with an appropriate notification (see subs.(6) and (7); see also reg.23 of the SPP and SAP (General) Regulations 2002 (SI 2002/2822)) and evidence of entitlement (SPP and SAP (General) Regs 2002, reg.24). 1.186

SAP is available to an adoptive parent of a child newly placed for adoption, whether the child is being adopted within the United Kingdom or from overseas. There are, however, some slight differences in the provisions for SAP for domestic and overseas adoptions respectively: see further SSCBA 1992, s.171ZT. It is also important to note that entitlement to SAP arises only for children who are newly placed for adoption. It is therefore not possible to receive SAP for a step-family adoption or where the child is adopted by his or her existing foster carers.

Liability to make payments

171ZM.—(1) The liability to make payments of statutory adoption pay is a liability of any person of whom the person entitled to the payments has been an employee as mentioned in section 171ZL(2)(b) above. 1.187

(2) Regulations shall make provision as to a former employer's liability to pay statutory adoption pay to a person in any case where the former employee's contract of service with him has been brought to an end by the former employer solely, or mainly, for the purpose of avoiding liability for statutory adoption pay.

(3) The Secretary of State may, with the concurrence of the Board, by regulations specify circumstances in which, notwithstanding this section, liability to make payments of statutory adoption pay is to be a liability of the Board.

Definitions

"the Board"—see s.171ZS(1)
"employee"—see s.171ZS(2)
"employer"—see s.171ZS(1)

General Note

This section, placing the liability to make payments of SAP on employers, follows the same approach as the provisions governing SMP (s.164(3) and (8)) and SPP (s.171ZD). Note that there is no liability to pay SAP in respect of any week during which the claimant either is entitled to SSP or is detained in custody (or sentenced to imprisonment): SPP and SAP (General) Regulations 2002 (SI 1.188

2002/2822), reg.27 (but note that, unlike with SPP, there are exceptions to the latter preclusionary rule: reg.27(2)). As with SPP, however, there is no liability to pay SAP in the week that the person entitled dies.

The rules governing the funding of SAP and employers' responsibilities in connection with SAP payments are contained in the SPP and SAP (Administration) Regulations 2002 (SI 2002/2820). The special circumstances in which the Boardis liable to pay SAP under subs.(3) are set out in SPP and SAP (General) Regulations 2002, regs 43 and 44 (the latter applying solely to SAP and not SPP).

Rate and period of pay

1.189 **171ZN.**—(1) Statutory adoption pay shall be payable at such fixed or earnings-related weekly rate as the Secretary of State may prescribe by regulations, which may prescribe different kinds of rate for different cases.

(2) Statutory adoption pay shall be payable, subject to the provisions of this Part of this Act, in respect of each week during a prescribed period ("the adoption pay period") of a duration not exceeding 26 weeks.

(3) A person shall not be liable to pay statutory adoption pay to another in respect of any week during any part of which the other works under a contract of service with him.

(4) It is immaterial for the purposes of subsection (3) above whether the work referred to in that subsection is work under a contract of service which existed immediately before the adoption pay period or a contract of service which did not so exist.

(5) Except in such cases as may be prescribed, statutory adoption pay shall not be payable to a person in respect of any week during any part of which he works for any employer who is not liable to pay him statutiory adoption pay.

(6) The Secretary of State may by regulations specify circumstances in which there is to be no liability to pay statutory adoption pay in respect of a week.

(7) In subsection (2) above, "week" means any period of seven days.

(8) In subsection (3), (5) and (6) above, "week" means a period of seven days beginning with the day of the week on which the adoption pay period begins.

DEFINITIONS

"adoption pay period"—see subs.(2)
"employer"—see s.171ZS(1)
"prescribed"—see *ibid.*
"week"—see subss.(7) and (8)

GENERAL NOTE

1.190 This section provides that SAP is payable for a period of up to 26 weeks (the "adoption pay period" under subs.(2)). The rate of SAP is the same as that for SMP, namely (from April 2004) the lesser of £102.80 a week or 90 per cent of the employee's average weekly earnings: SPP and SAP (Weekly Rates) Regulations 2002 (SI 2002/2818), reg.3. More detailed rules relating to the adoption pay periodare set out in regs 21 and 22 of the SPP and SAP (General) Regulations 2002 (SI 2002/2822).

Restrictions on contracting out

171ZO.—(1) Any agreement shall be void to the extent that it purports— 1.191

(a) to exclude, limit or otherwise modify any provision of this Part of this Act; or

(b) to require an employee or former employee to contribute (whether directly or indirectly) towards any costs incurred by his employer or former employer under this Part of this Act.

(2) For the avoidance of doubt, any agreement between an employer and an employee authorising any deductions from statutory adoption pay which the employer is liable to pay to the employee in respect of any period shall not be void by virtue of subsection (1)(a) above if the employer—

(a) is authorised by that or another agreement to make the same deductions from any contractual remuneration which he is liable to pay in respect of the same period; or

(b) would be so authorised if he were liable to pay contractual remuneration in respect of that period.

DEFINITIONS

"employee"—see s.171ZS(2)
"employer"—see s.171ZS(1)

GENERAL NOTE

These restrictions on contracting out are in the same terms as the equivalent provisions for SSP (s.151(2)–(3)), SMP (s.164(6)–(7)) and SPP (s.171ZF). See also SPP and SAP (General) Regulations 2002 (SI 2002/2822), reg.30. 1.192

Relationship with benefits and other payments etc.

171ZP.—(1) Except as may be prescribed, a day which falls within the adoption pay period shall not be treated as a day of incapacity for work for the purposes of determining, for this Act, whether it forms part of a period of incapacity for work for the purposes of incapacity benefit. 1.193

(2) Regulations may provide that in prescribed circumstances a day which falls within the adoption pay period shall be treated as a day of incapacity for work for the purposes of determining entitlement to the higher rate of short-term incapacity benefit or to long-term incapacity benefit.

(3) Regulations may provide that an amount equal to a person's statutory adoption pay for a period shall be deducted from any such benefit in respect of the same period and a person shall be entitled to such benefit only if there is a balance after the deduction and, if there is such a balance, at a weekly rate equal to it.

(4) Subject to subsections (5) and (6) below, any entitlement to statutory adoption pay shall not affect any right of a person in relation to remuneration under any contract of service ("contractual remuneration").

(5) Subject to subsection (6) below—

(a) any contractual remuneration paid to a person by an employer of his in respect of a week in the adoption pay period shall go towards discharging any liability of that employer to pay statutory adoption pay to him in respect of that week; and

(b) any statutory adoption pay paid by an employer to a person who is an employee of his in respect of a week in the adoption pay period shall go towards discharging any liability of that employer to pay contractual remuneration to him in respect of that week.

(6) Regulations may make provision as to payments which are, and those which are not, to be treated as contractual remuneration for the purposes of subsections (4) and (5) above.

(7) In subsection (5) above, "week" means a period of seven days beginning with the day of the week on which the adoption pay period begins.

DEFINITIONS

"adoption pay period"—see s.171ZN(2)
"contractual remuneration"—see subs.(4)
"employee"—see s.171ZS(2)
"employer"—see s.171ZS(1)
"prescribed"—see *ibid.*
"week"—see subs.(7)

GENERAL NOTE

1.194 The basic principle is that entitlement to SAP does not affect a claimant's rights to any contractual remuneration (subs.(4)), subject to the significant exception that any payment of contractual remuneration can be regarded as the discharge of SAP liability and vice versa (subs.(5)). Regulations made under subs.(6) provide that the payments to be treated as contractual remuneration are sums payable under a contract of service (a) by way of remuneration, (b) for incapacity for work due to sickness or injury or (c) by reason of the adoption of a child (SPP and SAP (General) Regulations 2002 (SI 2002/2822), reg.28).

Crown employment—Part XIIZB

1.195 **171ZQ.**—The provisions of this Part of this Act apply in relation to persons employed by or under the Crown as they apply in relation to persons employed otherwise than by or under the Crown.

GENERAL NOTE

1.196 This mirrors s.169, the equivalent provision for SMP, and s.171ZH, which deals with SPP.

Special classes of person

1.197 **171ZR.**—(1) The Secretary of State may with the concurrence of the Treasury make regulations modifying any provision of this Part of this Act in such manner as he thinks proper in its application to any person who is, has been or is to be—

(a) employed on board any ship, vessel, hovercraft or aircraft;
(b) outside Great Britain at any prescribed time or in any prescribed circumstances; or
(c) in prescribed employment in connection with continental shelf operations, as defined in section 120(2) above.

(2) Regulations under subsection (1) above may, in particular, provide—

(a) for any provision of this Part of this Act to apply to any such person, notwithstanding that it would not otherwise apply;

(b) for any such provision not to apply to any such person, notwithstanding that it would otherwise apply;

(c) for excepting any such person from the application of any such provision where he neither is domiciled nor has a place of residence in any part of Great Britain;

(d) for the taking of evidence, for the purposes of the determination of any question arising under any such provision, in a country or territory outside Great Britain, by a British consular official or such other person as may be determined in accordance with the regulations.

DEFINITIONS

"Great Britain"—see s.172(a)
"prescribed"—see s.171ZS(1)

GENERAL NOTE

This enabling provision is in the same terms as s.162, which applies to SSP, and s.17ZI, which deals with SPP. See further the Statutory Paternity Pay and Statutory Adoption Pay (Persons Abroad and Mariners) Regulations 2002 (SI 2002/2821). **1.198**

Part XIIZB: supplementary

171ZS.—(1) In this Part of this Act— **1.199**

"adoption pay period" has the meaning given by section 171ZN(2) above;

"the Board" means the Commissioners of Inland Revenue;

"employer", in relation to a person who is an employee, means a person who under section 6 above is, or but for the condition in subsection (1)(b) of that section would be, liable to pay secondary Class 1 contributions in relation to any of the earnings of the person who is an employee;

"modifications" includes additions, omissions and amendments, and related expressions are to be read accordingly;

"prescribed" means prescribed by regulations.

(2) In this Part of this Act, "employee" means a person who is—

(a) gainfully employed in Great Britain either under a contract of service or in an office (including elective office) with emoluments chargeable to income tax under Schedule E; and

(b) over the age of 16.

(3) Regulations may provide—

(a) for cases where a person who falls within the definition in subsection (2) above is not to be treated as an employee for the purposes of this Part of this Act; and

(b) for cases where a person who would not otherwise be an employee for the purposes of this Part of this Act is to be treated as an employee for those purposes.

(4) Without prejudice to any other power to make regulations under this Part of this Act, regulations may specify cases in which, for the purposes of this Part of this Act or of such provisions of this Part of this Act as may be prescribed—

(a) two or more employers are to be treated as one;

(b) two or more contracts of service in respect of which the same person is an employee are to be treated as one.

(5) In this Part, except sections 171ZN and 171ZP, "week" means a period of seven days beginning with Sunday or such other period as may be prescribed in relation to any particular case or class of cases.

(6) For the purposes of this Part of this Act, a person's normal weekly earnings shall, subject to subsection (8) below, be taken to be the average weekly earnings which in the relevant period have been paid to him or paid for his benefit under the contract of service with the employer in question.

(7) For the purposes of subsection (6) above, "earnings" and "relevant period" shall have the meanings given to them by regulations.

(8) In such cases as may be prescribed, a person's normal weekly earnings shall be calculated in accordance with regulations.

(9) Where—

(a) in consequence of the establishment of one or more National Health Service trusts under Part II of the National Health Service and Community Care Act 1990 (Chapter 19) or the National Health Service (Scotland) Act 1978 (Chapter 29), a person's contract of employment is treated by a scheme under that Part or Act as divided so as to constitute two or more contracts; or

(b) an order under paragraph 23(1) of Schedule 5A to the National Health Service Act 1977 (c.49) provides that a person's contract of employment is so divided;

regulations may make provision enabling the person to elect for all of those contracts to be treated as one contract for the purposes of this Part of this Act or such provisions of this Part of this Act as may be prescribed.

(10) Regulations under subsection (9) above may prescribe—

(a) the conditions that must be satisfied if a person is to be entitled to make such an election;

(b) the manner in which, and the time within which, such an election is to be made;

(c) the persons to whom, and the manner in which, notice of such an election is to be given;

(d) the information which a person who makes such an election is to provide, and the persons to whom, and the time within which, he is to provide it;

(e) the time for which such an election is to have effect;

(f) which one of the person's employers under two or more contracts is to be regarded for the purposes of statutory adoption pay as his employer under the contract.

(11) The powers under subsections (9) and (10) are without prejudice to any other power to make regulations under this Part of this Act.

(12) Regulations under any of subsections (4) to (10) above must be made with the concurrence of the Board.

DEFINITIONS

"Earnings": see General Note to s.171ZJ.
"Employee": see General Note to section 171ZJ.
"National Health Service trusts": see General Note to section 171ZJ.
"Normal weekly earnings": see General Note to section 171ZJ.

Power to apply Part XIIZB to adoption cases not involving placement

171ZT.—The Secretary of State may by regulations provide for this Part to have effect in relation to cases which involve adoption, but not the placement of a child for adoption under the law of any part of the United Kingdom, with such modifications as the regulations may prescribe. **1.200**

GENERAL NOTE

See further the Social Security Contributions and Benefits Act 1992 (Application of Pts XIIZA and XIIZB to Adoptions from Overseas) Regulations 2003 (SI 2003/499) and the Statutory Paternity Pay (Adoption) and Statutory Adoption Pay (Adoptions from Overseas) (No. 2) Regulations 2003 (SI 2003/1194). **1.201**

PART XIII

GENERAL

Interpretation

Application of Act in relation to territorial waters

172.—In this Act— **1.202**
(a) any reference to Great Britain includes a reference to the territorial waters of the United Kingdom adjacent to Great Britain;
(b) any reference to the United Kingdom includes a reference to the territorial waters of the United Kingdom.

Age

173.—For the purposes of this Act a person— **1.203**
(a) is over or under a particular age if he has or, as the case may be, has not attained that age; and
(b) is between two particular ages if he has attained the first but not the second;

and in Scotland (as in England and Wales) the time at which a person attains a particular age expressed in years is the commencement of the relevant anniversary of the date of his birth.

References to Acts

174.—In this Act— **1.204**
"the 1975 Act" means the Social Security Act 1975;

"the 1986 Act" means the Social Security Act 1986;
"the Administration Act" means the Social Security Administration Act 1992;
"the Consequential Provisions Act" means the Social Security (Consequential Provisions) Act 1992;
"the Northern Ireland Contributions and Benefits Act" means the Social Security Contributions and Benefits (Northern Ireland) Act 1992;
"the Old Cases Act" means the Industrial Injuries and Diseases (Old Cases) Act 1975; and
"the Pensions Act" means the [1 Pensions Schemes Act 1993].

AMENDMENT

1. Pension Schemes Act 1993, s.190 and Sch.8, para.41 (February 7, 1994).

Section 153(3) SCHEDULE 11

CIRCUMSTANCES IN WHICH PERIODS OF ENTITLEMENT TO STATUTORY SICK PAY DO NOT ARISE

1.205 **1.** A period of entitlement does not arise in relation to a particular period of incapacity for work in any of the circumstances set out in para.2 below or in such other circumstances as may be prescribed.

[5**1A.** Regulations made under paragraph 1 must be made with the concurrence of the Treasury.]

2. The circumstances are that—

(a) at the relevant date the employee is [1 over the age of 65];
(b) [6 . . .];
(c) at the relevant date the employee's normal weekly earnings are less than the lower earnings limit then in force under section5(1)(a) above;
[2(d) in the period of 57 days ending immediately before the relevant date the employee had at least one day on which—
 (i) he was entitled to incapacity benefit (or would have been so entitled had he satisfied the contribution conditions mentioned in section 30A(2)(a) above); or
 (ii) [4 . . .]
 (iii) he was entitled to a severe disablement allowance;]
(e) [2 . . .]
(f) the employee has done no work for his employer under his contract of service;
(g) on the relevant date there is [3 . . .] a stoppage of work due to a trade dispute at the employee's place of employment;
(h) the employee is, or has been, pregnant and the relevant date falls within the disqualifying period (within the meaning of section 153(12) above).

3. In this Schedule, "relevant date" means the date on which a period of entitlement would begin in accordance with section 153 above if this Schedule did not prevent it arising.

4. [6 . . .]

5. [2 . . .]

6. For the purposes of paragraph 2(f) above, if an employee enters into a contract of service which is to take effect not more than eight weeks after the date on which a previous contract of service entered into by him with the same employer ceased to have effect, the two contracts shall be treated as one.

7. Paragraph 2(g) above does not apply in the case of an employee who proves that at no time on or before the relevant date did he have a direct interest in the trade dispute in question.

8. Paragraph 2(h) above does not apply in relation to an employee who has been pregnant if her pregnancy terminated, before the beginning of the disqualifying period, otherwise than by confinement (as defined for the purposes of statutory maternity pay in section 171(1) above).

AMENDMENTS

1. Statutory Sick Pay Act 1994, s.1 (April 6, 1994).
2. Social Security (Incapacity for Work) Act 1994, s.11(1) and Sch.1, para.43 (April 6, 1995).
3. Jobseekers Act 1995, s.41(5) and Sch.3 (October 7, 1996).
4. Social Security Act 1998, s.73 (April 6, 1999).
5. Social Security Contributions (Transfer of Functions, etc.) Act 1999, s.1(1) and Sch.1, para.20 (April 1, 1999).
6. Fixed-term Employees (Prevention of Less Favourable Treatment) Regulations 2002 (SI 2002/2034), reg.11 and Sch.2, para.1 (October 1, 2002).

DEFINITIONS

"contract of service"—see s.163(1).
"disqualifying period"—see s.153(12).
"employee"—see s.163(1) and SSP (General) Regulations 1982, reg.16.
"employer"—see s.163(1).
"period of entitlement"—see *ibid.*
"period of incapacity for work"—see s.163(1).
"prescribed"—see *ibid.*
"relevant date"—see para.(3).

GENERAL NOTE

Para.(1)

The general rule, stated here, is that no period of entitlement to SSP can arise in any of the circumstances set out in para.(2) or in such circumstances as are prescribed by regulations. The relevant regulation is reg.3 of the SSP (General) Regulations 1986 (SI 1982/894), which excludes prisoners and women entitled neither to SMP nor to maternity allowance who have reached a particular stage in their pregnancy or have been confined before reaching that stage. **1.206**

Para.(2)

This sets out the categories of persons for whom a period of entitlement does not arise for the purposes of para.(1), and so who are excluded from the scope of SSP. The "relevant date" is the date on which a period of entitlement would otherwise begin were it not for the provisions of this Schedule (para.(3)). Thus the relevant date will usually be the first day of incapacity for work in the period of incapacity for work in question (s.153(2), but note the modifying provisions in (7), (8) and (9)). Those persons who are excluded from SSP by virtue of this paragraph may be able to claim incapacity benefit or, in the case of pregnant women, SMP or maternity allowance. The particular exclusions are: **1.207**

(1) persons aged over 65 on the relevant day (sub-para.(2)(a));
(2) employees whose earnings are below the National Insurance lower earnings limit (sub-para.(2)(c));
(3) claimants whose day of incapacity links back to a recent entitlement to incapacity benefit (sub-para.(2)(d));
(4) employees who have yet to start work under the contract of service (sub-para.(2)(f), but note the linking rule in para.6);

(5) employees who are subject to a stoppage of work due to a trade dispute at their place of employment (sub-para.(2)(g), but note the exception in para.7);

(6) employees who are or have been pregnant and where the relevant date falls within the disqualifying period for persons entitled to SMP or maternity allowance (sub-para.(2)(h), but note the exception in para.8).

Para. (7)

1.208 The effect of the wording of this exception is that if the employee has at some time before the relevant date had a direct interest in the trade dispute, he or she cannot take advantage of this provision and so is caught by the exclusion in sub-para.(2)(g): see *R(SSP) 1/86*.

Section 160 SCHEDULE 12

RELATIONSHIP OF STATUTORY SICK PAY WITH BENEFITS AND OTHER PAYMENTS, ETC

The general principle

1.209 **1.**—Any day which—

(a) is a day of incapacity for work in relation to any contract of service; and

(b) falls within a period of entitlement (whether or not it is also a qualifying day);

shall not be treated for the purposes of this Act as a day of incapacity for work for the purposes of determining whether a period is [[1] . . .] [[2]a period of incapacity for work for the purposes of incapacity benefit].

Contractual remuneration

1.210 **2.**—(1) Subject to sub-paragraphs (2) and (3) below, any entitlement to statutory sick pay shall not affect any right of an employee in relation to remuneration under any contract of service ("contractual remuneration").

(2) Subject to sub-para.(3) below—

(a) any contractual remuneration paid to an employee by an employer of his in respect of a day of incapacity for work shall go towards discharging any liability of that employer to pay statutory sick pay to that employee in respect of that day; and

(b) any statutory sick pay paid by an employer to an employee of his in respect of a day of incapacity for work shall go towards discharging any liability of that employer to pay contractual remuneration to that employee in respect of that day.

(3) Regulations may make provision as to payments which are, and those which are not, to be treated as contractual remuneration for the purposes of sub-paragraph (1) or (2) above.

[[2]Incapacity benefit

1.211 **3.**—(1) This paragraph and paragraph 4 below have effect to exclude, where a period of entitlement as between an employee and an employer of his comes to an end, the provisions by virtue of which short-term incapacity benefit is not paid for the first three days.

(2) If the first day immediately following the day on which the period of entitlement came to an end—

(a) is a day of incapacity for work in relation to that employee; and

(b) is not a day in relation to which paragraph 1 above applies by reason of any entitlement as between the employee and another employer,

that day shall, except in prescribed cases, be or form part of a period of incapacity for work notwithstanding section 30C(1)(b) above (by virtue of which a period of incapacity for work must be at least 4 days long).

(3) Where each of the first two consecutive days, or the first three consecutive days, following the day on which the period of entitlement came to an end is a day to which paragraph (a) and (b) of sub-paragraph (2) above apply, that sub-paragraph has effect in relation to the second day or, as the case may be, in relation to the second and third days, as it has effect in relation to the first.

4.—(1) Where a period of entitlement as between an employee and an employer of his comes to an end, section 30A(3) above (exclusion of benefit for first three days of period) does not apply in relation to any day which—

(a) is or forms part of a period of incapacity for work (whether by virtue of paragraph 3 above or otherwise); and

(b) falls within the period of 57 days immediately following the day on which the period of entitlement came to an end.

(2) Where sub-paragraph (1) above applies in relation to a day, section 30A(3) above does not apply in relation to any later day in the same period of incapacity for work.]

[2Incapacity benefit for widows and widowers

5. Paragraph 1 above does not apply for the purpose of determining whether the conditions specified in section 40(3) or (4) or section 41(2) or (3) above are satisfied.] **1.212**

Unemployability supplement

6. Paragraph 1 above does not apply in relation to paragraph 3 of Schedule 7 to this Act and accordingly the references in paragraph 3 of that Schedule to a period of interruption of employment shall be construed as if the provisions re-enacted in this Part of this Act had not been enacted. **1.213**

AMENDMENTS

1. Jobseekers Act 1995, s.41(5) and Sch.3, para.1 (October 7, 1996)
2. Social Security (Incapacity for Work) Act 1994, s.11(1) and Sch.1, para.44 (April 13, 1995).

GENERAL NOTE

Para.(1)

No day which falls within a period of entitlement for the purposes of SSP (whether or not it is a qualifying day) can count as a day of incapacity for the purposes of establishing entitlement to incapacity benefit. **1.214**

Paras (3) and (4)

These paragraphs assist certain persons, not caught by para.(1), who have days of incapacity subsequent to the end of a period of entitlement, to qualify for incapacity benefit by not applying the normal rules, *e.g.* on waiting days. See further SSP (General) Regulations 1982 (SI 1982/894), reg.12. **1.215**

Section 168 SCHEDULE 13

RELATIONSHIP OF STATUTORY MATERNITY PAY WITH BENEFITS AND OTHER PAYMENTS, ETC.

The general principle

[2**1.** Except as may be prescribed, a day which falls within the maternity pay period shall not be treated as a day of incapacity for work for the purposes of determining, for this Act, whether it forms part of a period of incapacity for work for the purposes of incapacity benefit.] **1.216**

[1Incapacity benefit

2.—(1) Regulations may provide that in prescribed circumstances a day which falls within the maternity pay period shall be treated as a day of incapacity for work for the purpose of determining entitlement to the higher rate of short-term incapacity benefit or to long-term incapacity benefit. **1.217**

(2) Regulations may provide that an amount equal to a woman's statutory maternity pay for a period shall be deducted from any such benefit in respect of the same period and a

woman shall be entitled to such benefit only if there is a balance after the deduction and, if there is such a balance, at a weekly rate equal to it.]

Contractual remuneration

1.218 **3.**—(1) Subject to sub-paragraphs (2) and (3) below, any entitlement to statutory maternity pay shall not affect any right of a woman in relation to remuneration under any contract of service ("contractual remuneration").

(2) Subject to sub-paragraph (3) below—

(a) any contractual remuneration paid to a woman by an employer of hers in respect of a week in the maternity pay period shall go towards discharging any liability of that employer to pay statutory maternity pay to her in respect of that week; and

(b) any statutory maternity pay paid by an employer to a woman who is an employee of his in respect of a week in the maternity pay period shall go towards discharging any liability of that employer to pay contractual remuneration to her in respect of that week.

(3) Regulations may make provision as to payments which are, and those which are not, to be treated as contractual remuneration for the purposes of sub-paragraphs (1) and (2) above.

AMENDMENTS

1. Social Security (Incapacity for Work) Act 1994, s.11(1) and Sch.1, para.45(3) (April 6, 1995).
2. Jobseekers Act 1995, s.41(4) and Sch.2, para.37 (October 7, 1996).

Social Security Administration Act 1992

(1992 c.5)

SECTIONS REPRODUCED

PART I

CLAIMS FOR PAYMENTS AND GENERAL ADMINISTRATION OF BENEFIT

Statutory sick pay

1.219 14. Duties of employees, etc. in relation to statutory sick pay

Statutory maternity pay

1.220 15. Duties of women etc. in relation to statutory maternity pay

PART VII

INFORMATION

Information held by tax authorities

1.221 122. Supply of information held by tax authorities for fraud prevention and verification

122A. Supply of information by Inland Revenue for purposes of contributions

Statutory sick pay and other benefits

Statutory maternity pay and other benefits

PART I

CLAIMS FOR AND PAYMENTS AND GENERAL ADMINISTRATION OF BENEFIT

Statutory Sick Pay

Duties of employees etc. in relation to statutory sick pay

14.—(1) Any employee who claims to be entitled to statutory sick pay from his employer shall, if so required by his employer, provide such information as may reasonably be required for the purpose of determining the duration of the period of entitlement in question or whether a period of entitlement exists as between them. 1.224

(2) The Secretary of State may by regulations direct—

(a) that medical information required under subsection (1) above shall, in such cases as may be prescribed, be provided in a prescribed form;

(b) that an employee shall not be required under subsection (1) above to provide medical information in respect of such days as may be prescribed in a period of incapacity for work.

(3) Where an employee asks an employer of his to provide him with a written statement, in respect of a period before the request is made, of one or more of the following—

(a) the days within that period which the employer regards as days in respect of which he is liable to pay statutory sick pay to that employee;

(b) the reasons why the employer does not so regard the other days in that period;

(c) the employer's opinion as to the amount of statutory sick pay to which the employee is entitled in respect of each of those days,

the employer shall, to the extent to which the request was reasonable, comply with it within a reasonable time.

Statutory maternity pay

Duties of women etc. in relation to statutory maternity pay

1.225 **15.**—(1) A woman shall provide the person who is liable to pay her statutory maternity pay—

(a) with evidence as to her pregnancy and the expected date of confinement in such form and at such time as may be prescribed; and

(b) where she commences work after her confinement but within the maternity pay period, with such additional information as may be prescribed.

(2) Where a woman asks an employer or former employer of hers to provide her with a written statement, in respect of a period before the request is made, of one or more of the following—

(a) the weeks within that period which he regards as weeks in respect of which he is liable to pay statutory maternity pay to the woman;

(b) the reasons why he does not so regard the other weeks in that period; and

(c) his opinion as to the amount of statutory maternity pay to which the woman is entitled in respect of each of the weeks in respect of which he regards himself as liable to make a payment;

the employer or former employer shall, to the extent to which the request was reasonable, comply with it within a reasonable time.

PART VII

[1 INFORMATION

Information held by tax authorities

Supply of information held by tax authorities for fraud prevention and verification

1.226 **122.**—(1) This section applies to information which is held—

(a) by the Commissioners of Inland Revenue or the Commissioners of Customs and Excise; or

(b) by a person providing services to the Commissioners of Inland Revenue or the Commissioners of Customs and Excise in connection with the provision of those services.

(2) Information to which this section applies may, with the authority of the Commissioners concerned, be supplied to, or to a person providing services to, the Secretary of State or the Northern Ireland Department—

(a) for use in the prevention, detection, investigation or prosecution of offences relating to social security; or

(b) for use in checking the accuracy of information relating to benefits, contributions or national insurance numbers or to any other matter relating to social security and (where appropriate) amending or supplementing such information.

(3) Information supplied under subsection (2) above shall not be supplied by the recipient to any other person or body unless—

(a) it could be supplied to that person or body under that subsection;

(b) it is supplied for the purposes of any civil or criminal proceedings relating to the Contributions and Benefits Act, the Jobseekers Act 1995 or this Act or to any provision of Northern Ireland legislation corresponding to any of them; or

(c) it is supplied under section 122C below;

and shall not be so supplied in those circumstances without the authority of the Commissioners concerned.

(4) But where information suppliedunder subsection (2) above has been used (in accordance with paragraph (b) of that subsection) in amending or supplementing other information, it is lawful for it to be—

(a) supplied to any person or body to whom that other information could be supplied; or

(b) used for any purpose for which that other information could be used.

(5) This section does not limit the circumstances in which information may be supplied apart from this section.]

AMENDMENT

1. Social Security Administration (Fraud) Act 1997, s.1 (July 1, 1997).

[1 Supply of information by Inland Revenue for purposes of contributions

122A.—(1) This section applies to information which is held— **1.227**

(a) by the Commissioners of Inland Revenue; or

(b) by a person providing services to the Commissioners of Inland Revenue in connection with the provision of those services.

(2) Information to which this section applies may, with the authority of the Commissioners, be supplied to, or to a person providing services to, the Secretary of State or the Northern Ireland Department for use for any purpose relating to contributions.

(3) Information supplied under subsection (2) above shall not be supplied by the recipient to any other person or body unless—

(a) it could be supplied to that person or body under that subsection; or

(b) it is supplied for the purposes of any civil or criminal proceedings relating to the Contributions and Benefits Act, the Jobseekers Act 1995 or this Act or to any provision of Northern Ireland legislation corresponding to any of them,

and shall not be so supplied in those circumstances without the authority of the Commissioners.

(4) But where information supplied under subsection (2) above has been used in amending or supplementing other information, it is lawful for it to be—

(a) supplied to any person or body to whom that other information could be supplied; or

(b) used for any purpose for which that other information could be used.

(5) This section does not limit the circumstances in which information may be supplied apart from this section.]

AMENDMENT

1. Social Security Administration (Fraud) Act 1997, s.1 (July 1, 1997).

Statutory sick pay and other benefits

Disclosure by Secretary of State for purpose of determination of period of entitlement to statutory sick pay

1.228 **129.**—Where the Secretary of State considers that it is reasonable for information held by him to be disclosed to an employer, for the purpose of enabling that employer to determine the duration of a period of entitlement under Part XI of the Contributions and Benefits Act in respect of an employee, or whether such a period exists, he may disclose the information to that employer.

Duties of employers—statutory sick pay and claims for other benefits

1.229 **130.**—(1) Regulations may make provision requiring an employer, in a case falling within subsection (3) below to furnish information in connection with the making, by a person who is, or has been, an employee of that employer, of a claim for—

[1(a) short-term incapacity benefit;]

(b) a maternity allowance;

[1(c) long-term incapacity benefit;]

(d) industrial injuries benefit; [2 . . .]

(e) [2 . . .].

(2) Regulations under this section shall prescribe—

(a) the kind of information to be furnished in accordance with the regulations;

(b) the person to whom information of the prescribed kind is to be furnished; and

(c) the manner in which, and period within which, it is to be furnished.

(3) The cases are—

(a) where, by virtue of paragraph 2 of Schedule 11 to the Contributions and Benefits Act or of regulations made under paragraph 1 of that Schedule, a period of entitlement does not arise in relation to a period of incapacity for work;

(b) where a period of entitlement has come to an end but the period of incapacity for work which was running immediately before the period of entitlement came to an end continues; and

(c) where a period of entitlement has not come to an end but, on the assumption that—

(i) the period of incapacity for work in question continues to run for a prescribed period; and

(ii) there is no material change in circumstances;

the period of entitlement will have ended on or before the end of the prescribed period.

(4) Regulations—

(a) may require employers to maintain such records in connection with statutory sick pay as may be prescribed;

(b) may provide for—

(i) any person claiming to be entitled to statutory sick pay; or

(ii) any other person who is a party to proceedings arising under Part XI of the Contributions and Benefits Act;

to furnish to the Secretary of State, within a prescribed period, any information required for the determination of any question arising in connection there with; and

(c) may require employers who have made payments of statutory sick pay to furnish to the Secretary of State such documents and information, at such times, as may be prescribed.

AMENDMENTS

1. Social Security (Incapacity for Work) Act 1994, s.11(1) and Sch.1, para.49 (April 6, 1995).

2. Welfare Reform and Pensions Act 1999, s.88 and Sch.13, Pt IV (April 6, 2001).

Statutory maternity pay and other benefits

Disclosure by Secretary of State for purpose of determination of period of entitlement to statutory maternity pay

131.—Where the Secretary of State considers that it is reasonable for information held by him to be disclosed to a person liable to make payments of statutory maternity pay for the purpose of enabling that person to determine— **1.230**

(a) whether a maternity pay period exists in relation to a woman who is or has been an employee of his; and

(b) if it does, the date of its commencement and the weeks in it in respect of which he may be liable to pay statutory maternity pay,

he may disclose the information to that person.

Duties of employers—statutory maternity pay and claims for other benefits

132.—(1) Regulations may make provision requiring an employer in prescribedcircumstances to furnish information in connection with the making of a claim by a woman who is or has been his employee for— **1.231**

(a) a maternity allowance;

(b) [[1]short-term incapacity benefit;]

(c) [[1]long-term incapacity benefit under section 30A], 40 or 41 of the Contributions and Benefits Act; [[2] . . .]

(d) [2 . . .].

(2) Regulations under this section shall prescribe—

(a) the kind of information to be furnished in accordance with the regulations;

(b) the person to whom information of the prescribed kind is to be furnished; and

(c) the manner in which, and period within which, it is to be furnished.

(3) Regulations—

(a) may require employers to maintain such records in connection with statutory maternity pay as may be prescribed;

(b) may provide for—

(i) any woman claiming to be entitled to statutory maternity pay; or

(ii) any other person who is a party to proceedings arising under Part XII of the Contributions and Benefits Act,

to furnish to the Secretary of State, within a prescribed period, any information required for the determination of any question arising in connection there with; and

(c) may require persons who have made payments of statutory maternity pay to furnish to the Secretary of State such documents and information, at such time, as may be prescribed.

AMENDMENTS

1. Social Security (Incapacity for Work) Act 1994, s.11(1) and Sch.1, para.50 (April 6, 1995).

2. Welfare Reform and Pensions Act 1999, s.88 and Sch.13, Pt IV (April 6, 2001).

Social Security Act 1998

1.232 (AS AMENDED AND AS MODIFIED BY THE TAX CREDITS (APPEALS) REGULATIONS 2002 (SI 2002/2926))

Provisions added or amended by SI 2002/2926 are in italics, whilst deleted provisions are indicated by [. . .] in the relevant text.

SECTIONS REPRODUCED

1.233 12. Appeal to appeal tribunal
13. Redetermination, etc. of appeals by tribunal
14. Appeal from tribunal to Commissioner
15. Appeal from a Commissioner on point of law
16. Procedure
17. Finality of decisions
28. Correction of errors and setting aside of decisions
39. Interpretation, etc. of chapter 2

Schedule 4—Social Security Commissioners
Schedule 5—Regulations as to procedure: provision which may be made

Appeal to appeal tribunal

12.—*(1) An appeal which is to an appeal tribunal by virtue of section 63 of the Tax Credits Act 2002, including an application for a direction under section 19(9) of that Act, (a "tax credit appeal") may be brought by—* 1.234

(a) a claimant whose claim for a tax credit is the subject of the appeal;
(b) the person on whom the penalty to which the appeal relates was imposed;
(c) the person applying for the direction under section 19(9) of that Act; or
(d) such other person as may be prescribed.

(2)–(6) [. . .]

(7) Regulations may make provision as to the manner in which, and the time within which, appeals are to be brought, *and may in particular extend the time limit for giving notice of appeal specified in section 39(1) of the Tax Credits Act 2002.*

(8) In deciding *a tax credit appeal* [. . .], an appeal tribunal—

(a) [. . .]
(b) shall not take into account any circumstances not obtaining at the time when the decision appealed against was made.

(9) [. . .].

Redetermination etc. of appeals by tribunal

13.—(1) This section applies where an application is made to a person under section 14(10)(a) below for leave to appeal from a decision of an appeal tribunal. 1.235

(2) If the person considers that the decision was erroneous in point of law, he may set aside the decision and refer the case either for redetermination by the tribunal or for determination by a differently constituted tribunal.

(3) [. . .]

[[1] (4) In [. . .] section 14 below "the principal parties" means—

(a) the persons mentioned in subsection (3)(a) and (b) of that section, [. . .]
(b) [. . .].

AMENDMENT

1. Social Security Contributions (Transfer of Functions, etc.) Act 1999, Sch.7, para.26 (April 1, 1999).

Appeal from tribunal to Commissioner

14.—(1) Subject to the provisions of this section, an appeal lies to a Commissioner from any decision of an appeal tribunal [. . .] on the groundthat the decision of the tribunal was erroneous in point of law. 1.236

(2) In the case of statutory sick pay or statutory maternity pay an appeal lies under this section at the instance of any of the following—

(a) the Secretary of State;
(b) the employee concerned;

(c) the employer concerned;
(d) a trade union, where—
(i) the employee is a member of the union at the time of the appeal and was so immediately before the matter in question arose; or
(ii) the matter in question concerns the entitlement of a deceased person who was at the time of his death a member of the union; and
(e) an association of employers of which the employer is a member at the time of the appeal and was so immediately before the matter in question arose.

(3) In any other case an appeal lies under this section at the instance of any of the following—
(a) the *Board*;
(b) the claimant and such other person as may be prescribed;
(c) in any of the cases mentioned in subsection (5) below, a trade union; and
(d) [. . .].

(4) [. . .]

(5) The following are the cases in which an appeal lies at the instance of a trade union—
(a) where the claimant is a member of the union at the time of the appeal and was so immediately before the matter in question arose;
(b) where that matter in any way relates to a deceased person who was a member of the union at the time of his death;
(c) [. . .].

(6) Subsections (2), (3) and (5) above, as they apply to a trade union, apply also to any other association which exists to promote the interests and welfare of its members.

(7) If each of the principal parties to the appeal expresses the view that the decision appealed against was erroneous in point of law, the Commissioner may set aside the decision and refer the case to a tribunal with directions for its determination.

(8) Where the Commissioner holds that the decision appealed against was erroneous in point of law, he shall set it aside and—
(a) he shall have power—
(i) to give the decision which he considers the tribunal should have given, if he can do so without making fresh or further findings of fact; or
(ii) if he considers it expedient, to make such findings and to give such decision as he considers appropriate in the light of them; and
(b) in any other case he shall refer the case to a tribunal with directions for its determination.

(9) Subject to any direction of the Commissioner, a reference under subsection (7) or (8)(b) above shall be to a differently constituted tribunal.

(10) No appeal lies under this section without the leave—
(a) of the person who constituted, or was the chairman of, the tribunal when the decision was given or, in a prescribed case, the leave of such other person as may be prescribed; or
(b) subject to and in accordance with regulations, of a Commissioner.

(11) Regulations may make provision as to the manner in which, and the time within which, appeals are to be brought [. . .].

(12) Schedule 4 to this Act shall have effect with respect to the appointment, remuneration and tenure of office of Commissioners and other matters relating to them.

Appeal from a Commissioner on point of law

15.—(1) Subject to subsections (2) and (3) below, an appeal on a question of law shall lie to the appropriate court from any decision of a Commissioner. 1.237

(2) No appeal under this section shall lie from a decision except—

(a) with the leave of the Commissioner who gave the decision or, in a prescribed case, with the leave of a Commissioner selected in accordance with regulations; or

(b) if he refuses leave, with the leave of the appropriate court.

(3) An application for leave under this section in respect of a Commissioner's decision may only be made by—

(a) a person who, before the proceedings before the Commissioner were begun, was entitled to appeal to the Commissioner from the decision to which the Commissioner's decision relates;

(b) any other person who was a party to the proceedings in which the first decision mentioned in paragraph (a) above was given;

(c) any other person who is authorised by regulations to apply for leave;

and regulations may make provision with respect to the manner in which and the time within which applications must be made to a Commissioner for leave under this section and with respect to the procedure for dealing with such applications.

(4) On an application to a Commissioner for leave under this section it shall be the duty of the Commissioner to specify as the appropriate court—

(a) the Court of Appeal if it appears to him that the relevant place is in England or Wales;

(b) the Court of Session if it appears to him that the relevant place is in Scotland; and

(c) the Court of Appeal in Northern Ireland if it appears to him that the relevant place is in Northern Ireland,

except that if it appears to him, having regard to the circumstances of the case and in particular to the convenience of the persons who may be parties to the proposed appeal, that he should specify a different court mentioned in paragraphs (a) to (c) above as the appropriate court, it shall be his duty to specify that court as the appropriate court.

(5) In this section—

"the appropriate court", except in subsection (4) above, means the court specified in pursuance of that subsection;

"the relevant place", in relation to an application for leave to appeal from a decision of a Commissioner, means the premises where the person or authority whose decision was the subject of the Commissioner's decision usually exercises his or its functions.

Procedure

1.238 **16.**—(1) Regulations ("procedure regulations") may make any such provision as is specified in Schedule 5 to this Act.

(2) Procedure regulations prescribing the procedure to be followed in cases before a Commissioner shall provide that any hearing shall be in public except in so far as the Commissioner for special reasons otherwise directs.

(3) It is hereby declared—

(a) that the power to prescribe procedure includes power to make provision as to the representation of one person, at any hearing of a case, by another person whether having professional qualifications or not; [. . .]

(b) [. . .]

(4) [. . .]

(5) [. . .]

(6) If it appears to a Commissioner that a matter before him involves a question of fact of special difficulty, he may direct that in dealing with that matter he shall have the assistance of one or more experts.

In this subsection, "expert" means a person appearing to the Commissioner to have knowledge or experience which would be relevant in determining the question of fact of special difficulty.

(7) If it appears to the Chief Commissioner (or, in the case of his inability to act, to such other of the Commissioners as he may have nominatedto act for the purpose) that—

(a) an application for leave under section 14(10)(b) above; or

(b) an appeal;

falling to be heard by one of the Commissioners involves a question of law of special difficulty, he may direct that the application or appeal be dealt with, not by that Commissioner alone, but by a tribunal consisting of any three or more of the Commissioners.

If the decision of the tribunal is not unanimous, the decision of the majority shall be the decision of the tribunal; and the presiding Commissioner shall have a casting vote if the votes are equally divided.

(8) Where a direction is given under subsection (7)(a) above, section 14(10)(b) above shall have effect as if the reference to a Commissioner were a reference to such a tribunal as is mentioned in subsection (7) above.

(9) Except so far as it may be appliedin relation to England and Wales by procedure regulations, Part I of the Arbitration Act 1996 shall not apply to any proceedings under this Chapter.

Finality of decisions

1.239 **17.**—*(1) Subject to the provisions of—*

(a) sections 12 to 16 of this Act, and

(b) the Tax Credits Act 2002,

any decision made in accordance with those provisions in respect of an appeal which, by virtue of section 63 of the Tax Credits Act 2002 (or of provisions of this Act applied by regulations made under that section), is to an appeal tribunal or lies to a Commissioner, shall be final.

(2) If and to the extent that regulations so provide, any finding of fact or other determination embodied in or necessary to such a decision, or on which such a decision is based, shall be conclusive for the purposes of—

(a) further such decisions;
(b) [. . .];
(c) [. . .].

Correction of errors and setting aside of decisions

28.—(1) Regulations may make provision with respect to— 1.240

(a) the correction of accidental errors in any decision or record of a decision made under any relevant enactment; and
(b) the setting aside of any such decision in a case where it appears just to set the decision aside on the ground that—
   (i) a document relating to the proceedings in which the decision was given was not sent to, or was not received at an appropriate time by, a party to the proceedings or a party's representative or was not received at an appropriate time by the body or person who gave the decision; or
   (ii) a party to the proceedings or a party's representative was not present at a hearing related to the proceedings.

(1A) [. . .]

(2) Nothing in subsection (1) above shall be construed as derogating from any power to correct errors or set aside decisions which is exercisable apart from regulations made by virtue of that subsection.

(3) In this section "relevant enactment" means—

(a) any of sections 12 to 17 above, and
(b) any enactment contained or referred to in section 19(10), 38 or 39 of, or Schedule 2 to, the Tax Credits Act 2002.

Supplemental

Interpretation etc. of chapter 2

39.—(1) In this chapter— 1.241

"appeal tribunal" means an appeal tribunal constituted under Chapter I of this Part;

"the Board" means the Commissioners of Inland Revenue;

"claimant" means a person who makes (whether or not jointly with another) a claim for a tax credit in accordance with sections 3 and 4 of the Tax Credits Act 2002, and includes a person entitled to make such a claim on behalf of another person by virtue of regulation 17 or 18 of the Tax Credits (Claims and Notifications) Regulations 2002;

"Commissioner" [[1](except in the expression "tax appeal Commissioners)] means the Chief Social Security Commissioner or any other Social Security Commissioner, and includes a tribunal of three or more Commissioners constituted under section 16(7) above;

[. . .]
[. . .]
(2) [. . .]
(3) [. . .]

AMENDMENT

1. Social Security Contributions (Transfer of Functions, etc.) Act 1999, Sch.7, para.35 (April 1, 1999).

SCHEDULE 4

SOCIAL SECURITY COMMISSIONERS

Appointment

1.242 **1.**—(1) Her Majesty may from time to time appoint, from among persons who have a 10 year general qualification or advocates or solicitors in Scotland of at least 10 years' standing—

(a) a Chief Social Security Commissioner; and
(b) such number of other Social Security Commissioners as Her Majesty thinks fit.

(2) If the Lord Chancellor considers that, in order to facilitate the disposal of the business of Social Security Commissioners, he should make an appointment in pursuance of this sub-paragraph, he may appoint—

(a) a person who has a 10-year general qualification; or
(b) an advocate or solicitor in Scotland of at least 10 years' standing; or
(c) a member of the bar of Northern Ireland or solicitor of the Supreme Court of Northern Ireland of at least 10 years' standing,

to be a Social Security Commissioner (but to be known as a deputy Commissioner) for such periodor on such occasions as the Lord Chancellor thinks fit.

(3) In this paragraph, "10-year general qualification" shall be construed in accordance with section 71 of the Courts and Legal Services Act 1990.

Remuneration, etc.

1.243 **2.** The Lord Chancellor shall pay to a Commissioner such salary or other remuneration, and such expenses incurred in connection with the work of a Commissioner or any tribunal presided over by a Commissioner, as he may determine.

3.—(1) The Lord Chancellor or, in Scotland, the *Board* may pay to any person who attends any proceedings under section 14 of this Act such travelling and other allowances as he may determine.

(2) In this paragraph the reference to travelling and other allowances includes a reference to compensation for loss of remunerative time.

Tenure of office

1.244 **4.**—(1) Commissioners shall vacate their offices on the day on which they attain the age of 70, but subject to section 26(4) to (6) of the Judicial Pensions and Retirement Act 1993 (power to authorise continuance in office up to the age of 75).

(2) Nothing in sub-paragraph (1) above or in section 13 or 32 of the Judicial Pensions Act 1981 (which relate to pensions for Commissioners) shall apply to a person by virtue of his appointment in pursuance of paragraph 1(2) above.

5.—(1) A Commissioner may be removed from office by the Lord Chancellor on the ground of incapacity or misbehaviour.

(2) Nothing in sub-paragraph (1) above applies to a Commissioner appointed before May 23, 1980.

Delegation of functions

1.245 **6.** The Lord Chancellor may by regulations provide—

(a) for officers authorised by the Lord Chancellor or, in Scotland, by the *Board* to make any determinations which fall to be made by Commissioners;

(b) for the procedure to be followed by such officers in making such determinations;
(c) for the manner in which such determinations by such officers may be called in question.

Certificates

7. A document bearing a certificate which— 1.246
(a) is signed by a person authorised in that behalf by the *Board*; and
(b) states that the document, apart from the certificate, is a record of a decision of a Commissioner;
shall be conclusive evidence of the decision; and a certificate purporting to be so signed shall be deemed to be so signed unless the contrary is proved.

Supplemental

8. Where the Lord Chancellor proposes to exercise a power conferred on him by paragraph 1(2), 5(1) or 6 above, it shall be his duty to consult the Lord Advocate with respect to the proposal. 1.247

SCHEDULE 5

Regulations as to Procedure: Provision Which May Be Made

1. Provision prescribing the procedure to be followed in connection with— 1.248
(a) the making of decisions or determinations by [. . .], an appeal tribunal or a Commissioner; and
(b) the withdrawal of claims, applications, appeals or references falling to be decided or determined by [. . .], an appeal tribunal or a Commissioner.

2. Provision as to the striking out or reinstatement of proceedings.

3. Provision as to the form which is to be used for any document, the evidence which is to be required and the circumstances in which any official recordor certificate is to be sufficient or conclusive evidence.

4. Provision as to the time within which, or the manner in which—
(a) any evidence is to be produced; or
(b) any application, reference or appeal is to be made, *including provision extending the time limit for giving notice of appeal specified in section 39(1) of the Tax Credits Act 2002.*

5. Provision for summoning persons to attend and give evidence or produce documents and for authorising the administration of oaths to witnesses.

6. Provision with respect to the procedure to be followed on appeals to and in other proceedings before appeal tribunals.

7. Provision for authorising an appeal tribunal consisting of two or more members to proceedwith any case, with the consent of the claimant, in the absence of any member.

8. Provision for empowering an appeal tribunal to give directions for the disposal of any purported appeal which the tribunal is satisfied that it does not have jurisdiction to entertain.

9. Provision for the non-disclosure to a person of the particulars of any medical advice or medical evidence given or submitted for the purposes of a determination.

Social Security Contributions (Transfer of Functions, etc.) Act 1999

(1999 c.2)

An Act to transfer from the Secretary of State to the Commissioners of Inland Revenue or the Treasury certain functions relating to national insurance contributions, the National Insurance Fund, statutory sick pay, statutory maternity pay 1.249

or pension schemes and certain associated functions relating to benefits; to enable functions relating to any of those matters in respect of Northern Ireland to be transferred to the Secretary of State, the Commissioners of Inland Revenue or the Treasury; to make further provision, in connection with the functions transferred, as to the powers of the Commissioners of Inland Revenue, the making of decisions and appeals; to provide that rebates payable in respect of members of money purchase contracted-out pension schemes are to be payable out of the National Insurance Fund; and for connected purposes.

Arrangement of Sections

Part I

General

Transfer of functions

Exercise by Board of functions transferred to them

Part II

Decisions and Appeals

Part III

Miscellaneous and Supplemental

Part I

General

Transfer of functions

Transfer to Board of certain functions relating to contributions, etc.

1.—(1) Schedule 1 to this Act (which contains amendments transferring to the Board certain functions of the Secretary of State which have been exercised by the Contributions Agency and certain associated functions of the Secretary of State in relation to benefits, together with other amendments related to the transfer of those functions) shall have effect. 1.254

(2) The functions of the Secretary of State under the provisions of subordinate legislation specified in Schedule 2 to this Act are hereby transferred to the Board.

Definition

"Board"—see s.27.

General Note

1.255 This section introduces Schs 1 and 2 to the Act. Schedule 1 transferred to the Inland Revenue, with effect from April 1, 1999, the day-to-day operational functions previously carried out by the Contributions Agency on behalf of the Secretary of State for Social Security. Schedule 1 accordingly amended the provisions of various Acts conferring such functions on the Secretary of State in order to reflect this transfer, typically by the simple substitution of "Inland Revenue" for "Secretary of State". The principal statutes affected were the SSCBA 1992, SSAA 1992 and the Pensions Schemes Act 1993. Schedule 1 is not included in this volume as the relevant amendments have been made to SSCBA 1992 and SSAA 1992 as they appear in these volumes. Schedule 2 lists the delegated legislation in respect of which the functions of the Secretary of State for Social Security have been transferred to the Inland Revenue. For the transfer of responsibility for policy functions, see s.2 and Sch.3.

Transfer of other functions to Treasury or Board

1.256 **2.** Schedule 3 to this Act (which contains amendments transferring to the Treasury or the Board certain other functions of the Secretary of State, together with amendments related to the transfer of those functions) shall have effect.

Definition

"Board"—see s.27.

General Note

1.257 This section introduces Sch.3 to the Act which transferred, with effect from April 1, 1999, policy responsibility for NICs to the Treasury or Inland Revenue as appropriate. These functions consist mainly of the exercise of powers to make secondary legislation in relation to NICs, and the control and management of the National Insurance Fund. The division of these functions as between the Treasury and the Inland Revenue follows the same pattern as for tax matters. Thus regulation-making powers are reserved to the Treasury where they affect substantive issues such as the existence or size of a tax liability. Regulation-making powers relating to administrative matters are vested in the Board of the Inland Revenue. There is a further complication in that not all the Secretary of State's former functions in relation to NICs were suitable for wholesale transfer. Where a regulation-making power affects the operation of the contributory benefits system, it remains the responsibility of the Secretary of State (see, *e.g.* Sch.3, para.19(3)). Similarly policy responsibility (and hence the prime powers to promulgate secondary legislation) for SMP and SSP (and contracted-out pension schemes) remain with the Secretary of State for Work and Pensions. In such cases provision is made for the regulations to be made by the Inland Revenue or the Treasury with the concurrence of the Secretary of State or vice versa (*see e.g.*, Sch.3, para.2).

Exercise by Board of functions transferred to them

General functions of Board

1.258 **3.**—(1) Contributions shall be under the care and management of the Board.

(2) Subject to subsection (3) below, for the purposes of the Inland Revenue Regulation Act 1890 ("the 1890 Act") the definition of "Inland Revenue" in section 39 of that Act shall be taken to include contributions.

(3) The following provisions of the 1890 Act shall not apply in relation to contributions—

(a) section 13 (duty of Commissioners in relation to collection and the keeping of accounts), so far as relating to the keeping of accounts;

(b) sections 21 and 22 (proceedings for fines, etc.);

(c) [[1] . . .];

(d) section 32 (power to reward informers);

(e) section 34 (expenses of prosecutions); and

(f) section 35 (power to mitigate fines and stay proceedings).

(4) The reference in section 10 of the Exchequer and Audit Departments Act 1866 (gross revenues of Board and of Commissioners of Customs and Excise to be paid into Exchequer) to the gross revenues of the department of the Inland Revenue shall not be taken to include—

(a) contributions; or

(b) any sums (other than contributions) which are payable into the National Insurance Fund or the Northern Ireland National Insurance Fund.

(5) In any declaration for the purposes of section 6 of the Taxes Management Act 1970 (declarations on taking office), whether made before or after the commencement of this section, the reference to an offence relating to Inland Revenue shall be taken to include a reference to—

(a) an offence relating to contributions, statutory sick pay or statutory maternity pay; or

(b) an offence under regulations made under Part III of the Pension Schemes Act 1993 or Part III of the Pension Schemes (Northern Ireland) Act 1993.

(6) In Schedule 2 to the Social Security Contributions and Benefits Act 1992 (levy of Class 4 contributions with income tax) and Schedule 2 to the Social Security Contributions and Benefits (Northern Ireland) Act 1992, paragraph 6(2) (which is superseded by subsection (1) above) shall cease to have effect.

(7) In this section, "contributions" includes contributions under Part I of the Social Security Contributions and Benefits (Northern Ireland) Act 1992.

AMENDMENT

1. Welfare Reform and Pensions Act 1999, s.88 and Sch.13, Pt VI (April 6, 2000).

DEFINITIONS

"Board"—see s.27.
"contributions"—see subs.(7) and s.27.
"the 1890 Act"—see s.3(2).

GENERAL NOTE

This provision bought NICs within the remit of the Inland Revenue so far as care and management are concerned (subs.(1)). It also brought contributions **1.259** within the definition of "Inland Revenue" for the purposes of s.39 of the Inland Revenue Regulation Act 1890, thereby placing the Board under a duty to collect NICs (subs.(2)). This is not, however, an absolute duty; the overriding obligation to undertake the "care and management" of NICs allows the duty to collect contributions to be tempered by considerations of efficiency and cost to the Exchequer. The section makes a number of further amendments in subss.(3)–(5) to the legislation which governs the role and functions of the Inland Revenue, and the powers and duties of its officers, in order to reflect the general transfer of functions.

Recovery of contributions where income tax recovery provisions not applicable

1.260 **4.** The provisions of Schedule 4 shall have effect with respect to the recovery of—

(a) those Class 1, Class 1A, Class 1B and Class 2 contributions to which regulations under paragraph 6 of Schedule 1 to the Social Security Contributions and Benefits Act 1992 (power to combine collection of contributions with income tax) do not apply;

(b) Class 4 contributions payable by virtue of regulations under section 18 of that Act; and

(c) interest or penalties payable under regulations made under paragraph 7A or 7B of Schedule 1 to that Act.

DEFINITION

"contributions"—see s.27.

GENERAL NOTE

1.261 This section introduces Sch.4 (not included in this volume), which concerns the procedures available to enforce the collection of contributions that have not been paid on time, aligning the Inland Revenue's enforcement powers as regards unpaid NICs and tax.

Powers relating to enforcement

1.262 **5.** Schedule 5 to this Act (which relates to the enforcement powers of the Board in relation to functions transferred to them by this Act) shall have effect.

DEFINITION

"Board": s.27.

GENERAL NOTE

1.263 Schedule 5 (not included in this volume) governs the enforcement powers concerned with the functions transferred to the Inland Revenue. In particular, SSAA 1992, ss.110–121 were amended and a new s.110ZA inserted, all with a view to transferring operational responsibility for enforcement matters from the Secretary of State for Social Security to the Inland Revenue. As part of this process of alignment with tax sanctions, any failure to comply with the obligation to produce information or documents when so required is now subject to a civil rather than criminal penalty.

Disclosure of information

6. Schedule 6 to this Act (which contains amendments relating to the supply or disclosure of information) shall have effect. **1.264**

General Note

Schedule 6 (not included in this volume) was designed to enable the pre-existing flows of information to continue across the revised inter-departmental boundaries. This was essential given the close relationship between NICs (for which much responsibility is now transferred to the Inland Revenue) and the other social security functions of the former DSS. **1.265**

Use of information by Board

7.—(1) Information which is held— **1.266**

(a) by the Board; or

(b) by a person providing services to the Board, in connection with the provision of those services,

for the purposes of functions specified in any paragraph of subsection (2) below may be used for the purposes of, or for any purposes connected with, the exercise of functions specifiedin any other paragraph of that subsection, and may be supplied to any person providing services to the Board for those purposes.

(2) The functions referred to in subsection (1) above are—

(a) the functions of the Board in relation to tax;

(b) their functions in relation to contributions, statutory sick pay and statutory maternity pay; and

(c) their functions under Part III of the Pension Schemes Act 1993 or Part III of the Pension Schemes (Northern Ireland) Act 1993.

(3) In subsection (2)(b) above, "contributions" includes contributions under Part I of the Social Security Contributions and Benefits (Northern Ireland) Act 1992.

Definitions

"Board"—see s.27.
"contributions"—*ibid.*

General Note

This section enables the Inland Revenue to use data held for one of its functions (listed in subs.(2)) for the purposes of other functions (also so listed). Thus information which is held in connection with contributions may be used in relation to tax matters (subs.(2)(a) and (b)). This power mirrors that contained in SSA 1998, s.3, which permits the Secretary of State to pool data held for the purposes of functions relating to social security, child support and war pensions. However, the section does not provide for the pooling of Inland Revenue and DWP data more generally across the departmental boundary: thus, information gathered for tax purposes cannot be passed to the Secretary of State in connection with child support. **1.267**

PART II

DECISIONS AND APPEALS

Decisions by officers of Board

1.268 **8.**—(1) Subject to the provisions of this Part, it shall be for an officer of the Board—

(a) to decide whether for the purposes of Parts I to V of the Social Security Contributions and Benefits Act 1992 a person is or was an earner and, if so, the category of earners in which he is or was to be included;

(b) to decide whether a person is or was employed in employed earner's employment for the purposes of Part V of the Social Security Contributions and Benefits Act 1992 (industrial injuries);

(c) to decide whether a person is or was liable to pay contributions of any particular class and, if so, the amount that he is or was liable to pay,

(d) to decide whether a person is or was entitled to pay contributions of any particular class that he is or was not liable to pay and, if so, the amount that he is or was entitled to pay,

(e) to decide whether contributions of a particular class have been paid in respect of any period,

(f) subject to and in accordance with regulations made for the purposes of this paragraph by the Secretary of State with the concurrence of the Board, to decide any issue arising as to, or in connection with, entitlement to statutory sick pay, [4, statutory maternity pay, statutory paternity pay or statutory adoption pay],

(g) to make any other decision that falls to be made [4 under Parts XI to XIIZB of the Social Security Contributions and Benefits Act 1992 (statutory sick pay, statutory maternity pay, statutory paternity pay and statutory adoption pay)],

[4(ga) to make any decision that falls to be made under regulations under section 7 of the Employment Act 2002 (funding of employers' liabilities to make payments of statutory paternity or adoption pay),];

(h) to decide any question as to the issue and content of a notice under subsection (2) of section 121C of the Social Security Administration Act 1992 (liability of directors etc. for company's contributions);

(i) to decide any issue arising under section 27 of the Jobseekers Act 1995 (employment of long-term unemployed: deductions by employers), or under any provision of regulations under that section, as to—

(i) whether a person is or was an employee or employer of another;

(ii) whether an employer is or was entitled to make any deduction from his contributions payments in accordance with regulations under section 27 of that Act;

(iii) whether a payment falls to be made to an employer in accordance with those regulations;
(iv) the amount that falls to be so deducted or paid; or
(v) whether two or more employers are, by virtue of regulations under section 27 of that Act, to be treated as one,

[3(ia) to decide whether to give or withdraw an approval for the purposes of para.3B(1)(b) of Sch.1 to the Social Security Contributions and Benefits Act 1992,];

(j) [2 . . .];

(k) to decide whether a person is liable to a penalty under—
(i) paragraph 7A(2) or 7B(2)(h) of Schedule 1 to the Social Security Contributions and Benefits Act 1992; or
(ii) section 113(1)(a) of the Social Security Administration Act 1992;

(l) to decide the [2 . . .] penalty payable under any of the provisions mentioned in [2 paragraph (k)] above; and

(m) to decide such issues relating to contributions, other than the issues specified in paragraphs (a) to (l) above or in paragraphs 16 and 17 of Schedule 3 to the Social Security Act 1998, as may be prescribed by regulations made by the Board.

(2) Subsection (1)(c) and (e) above do not include any decision relating to Class 4 contributions other than a decision falling to be made—
(a) under subsection (1) of section 17 of the Social Security Contributions and Benefits Act 1992 as to whether by regulations under that subsection a person is or was excepted from liability for Class 4 contributions, or his liability is or was deferred; or
(b) under regulations made by virtue of subsection (3) or (4) of that section or section 18 of that Act.

(3) Subsection (1)(g) above does not include—
(a) any decision as to the making of subordinate legislation; or
(b) any decision as to whether the liability to pay statutory sick pay [4, statutory maternity pay, statutory paternity pay or statutory adoption pay] is a liability of the Board rather than the employer.

(4) [1 . . .].

AMENDMENTS

1. Welfare Reform and Pensions Act 1999, s.88 and Sch.13, Part VI (April 6, 2000).
2. Child Support, Pensions and Social Security Act 2000, ss.76(6), 85 and Sch.9, Pt VIII (July 28, 2000).
3. Child Support, Pensions and Social Security Act 2000, ss.77(5) (July 28, 2000).
4. Employment Act 2002, s.9(2) and (3) (December 8, 2002).

DEFINITIONS

"Board"—see s.27.
"contributions"—*ibid.*
"employed earner"—see SSCBA 1992, s.2(1)(a).
"employment"—see SSCBA 1992, s.122.

General Note

1.269 This section provides for officers of the Inland Revenue to take decisions on a range of specified questions in relation to SMP, SSP, NICs, employment status and related matters. The extensive list of such decisions, set out in subs.(1), covers much of the former jurisdiction of the Secretary of State for Social Security under SSAA 1992, s.17(1), with the addition of some further matters. For example, the function of making decisions as to entitlement to SMP or SSP (subs.(1)(f)) was traditionally a function of an adjudication officer (SSAA 1992, s.20(3)) but was then transferred to the Secretary of State (SSA 1998, s.8(1)(d)) before now moving to an officer of the Board. This is one of the areas in which the power to make regulations still rests with the Secretary of State (albeit with the agreement of the Board), as the policy responsibility for these benefits is retained by the DWP (see General Note to s.2). However, in terms of decision making on matters of entitlement to SSP (and, by analogy, to SMP, SPP and SAP), the Board has an "exclusive and exhaustive jurisdiction" (per Mr Recorder Luba QC in *Taylor Gordon & Co. Ltd v Timmons* (EAT/0159/03/RN, at para. 43). Thus an employment tribunal has no jurisdiction under the Employment Rights Act 1996 to entertain an employee's complaint that SSP has not been paid.

For the relevant regulation-making powers, see s.9 and for provision for variation and supersession of decisions made under s.8, see s.10. Appeals against decisions made under s.8 are heard by the General or Special Commissioners, not by appeal tribunals constituted under SSA 1998 (ss.11–13).

Regulations with respect to decisions

1.270 **9.**—(1) Subject to the provisions of this Part and of the Social Security Administration Act 1992, provision may be made by the Board by regulations as to the making by their officer of any decision under or in connection with the Social Security Contributions and Benefits Act 1992, the Social Security Administration Act 1992 or the Jobseekers Act 1995 which falls to be made by such an officer.

(2) Where it appears to an officer of the Board that a matter before him involves a question of fact requiring special expertise, he may direct that in dealing with that matter he shall have the assistance of one or more experts.

(3) In subsection (2) above "expert" means a person appearing to the officer of the Board to have knowledge or experience which would be relevant in determining the question of fact requiring special expertise.

Definitions

"Board"—see s.27.
"expert"—see subs.(3).

General Note

1.271 Subsection (1), modelled on SSA 1998, s.11, provides for the Board to make regulations governing procedural matters relating to decisions made by Inland Revenue staff under s.8.

Subsections (2) and (3) enable Inland Revenue officers to seek specialist advice before making a decision (*e.g.* as to medical evidence relevant to a claim for SSP). In the first instance SMP or SSP decisions are made by the employer, and only referred for a formal decision where the parties are unable to reach agreement. There are only about 500 referrals each year concerning SMP or SSP; most of these cases concern the linking or employment rules, with perhaps no more than 50 involving a medical issue (*per* Baroness Hollis of Heigham, Parliamentary Under-Secretary of State for Social Security, *Hansard*, H.L. Debs. Vol. 596, col. 322 (January 14, 1999)).

Decisions varying or superseding earlier decisions

10.—(1) [1 Subject to subsection (2A) below,] the Board may by regulations make provision— **1.272**

(a) for any decision of an officer of the Board under section 8 of this Act (including a decision superseding an earlier decision) to be varied either within the prescribed period or in prescribed cases or circumstances;

(b) for any such decision to be superseded, in prescribed circumstances, by a subsequent decision made by an officer of the Board; and

(c) for any such decision as confirmed or varied by the tax appeal Commissioners on appeal to be superseded, in the event of a material change of circumstances since the decision was made, by a subsequent decision made by an officer of the Board.

(2) The date as from which—

(a) any variation of a decision, or

(b) any decision superseding an earlier decision,

is to take effect shall be determined in accordance with the regulations.

[1(2A) The decisions in relation to which provision may be made by regulations under this section shall not include decisions falling within section 8(1)(ia) above.]

(3) In this section "prescribed" means prescribed by regulations under this section.

AMENDMENTS

1. Child Support, Pensions and Social Security Act 2000, s.77(6) (July 28, 2000).

DEFINITIONS

"Board": s.27.
"prescribed": subs.(3).

GENERAL NOTE

This enabling provision reflects similar powers, governing Secretary of State decisions, contained in SSA 1998, ss.9 (revision) and 10 (supersession). **1.273**

Appeals against decisions of Board

11.—(1) This section applies to any decision of an officer of the Board under section 8 of this Act or under regulations made by virtue of section **1.274**

10(1)(b) or (c) of this Act (whether as originally made or as varied under regulations made by virtue of section 10(1)(a) of this Act).

(2) In the case of a decision to which this section applies—

(a) if it relates to a person's entitlement to statutory sick pay [1, statutory maternity pay, statutory paternity pay or statutory adoption pay], the employee and employer concerned shall each have a right to appeal to the tax appeal Commissioners, and

(b) in any other case, the person in respect of whom the decision is made and such other person as may be prescribed shall have a right to appeal to the tax appeal Commissioners.

(3) In subsection (2)(b) above "prescribed" means prescribed by the Board by regulations.

(4) This section has effect subject to section 121D of the Social Security Administration Act 1992 (appeals in relation to personal liability notices).

AMENDMENT

1. Employment Act 2002, s.9(4) (December 8, 2002).

DEFINITIONS

"Board"—see s.27.
"prescribed"—see subs. (3)
"the tax appeal Commissioners"—see s.19.

GENERAL NOTE

1.275 This section provides for a right of appeal to an independent tribunal, the tax appeal Commissioners (i.e. the General or Special Commissioners for income tax; see s.19), against any Inland Revenue decision taken under s.8. Both employees and employers have a right of appeal in relation to decisions on SMP and SSP entitlement (subs.(2)(a)). Note also that subs.(2)(b) contains a broader regulation-making power to give interested parties in other decisions a right of appeal. This provision only provides for additional rights of appeal; unlike SSA 1998, s.12(2), there is no power to prescribe in regulations for cases in which there is to be no right of appeal.

Exercise of right of appeal

1.276 **12.**—(1) Any appeal against a decision must be brought by a notice of appeal in writing given within 30 days after the date on which notice of the decision was issued.

(2) The notice of appeal shall be given to the officer of the Board by whom notice of the decision was given.

(3) The notice of appeal shall specify the grounds of appeal, but on the hearing of the appeal the tax appeal Commissioners may allow the appellant to put forward any ground not specified in the notice, and take it into consideration if satisfied that the omission was not wilful or unreasonable.

(4) Subject to [1paragraph 3B(8) of Schedule 1 to the Social Security Contributions and Benefits Act 1992 (which provides for appeals under that paragraph to be heard by the Special Commissioners), to] section 121D of the Social Security Administration Act 1992 (which provides for

an appeal against a decision under that section to be heard by the Special Commissioners) and to regulations under section 46A of the Taxes Management Act 1970 (regulations about jurisdiction), any appeal under this section shall be heard by the General Commissioners, except that the appellant may elect in accordance with section 46(1) of the Taxes Management Act 1970 to bring the appeal before the Special Commissioners instead of the General Commissioners.

(5) Subsections (5A) to (5E) of section 1 of the Taxes Management Act 1970 (which relate to an election to bring proceedings before the Special Commissioners) shall have effect in relation to an election under subsection (4) above as they have effect in relation to an election under subsection (4) of that section.

AMENDMENTS

1. Child Support, Pensions and Social Security Act 2000, s.77(7) (July 28, 2000).

DEFINITIONS

"Board"—see s.27.
"the General Commissioners"—see s.19.
"the Special Commissioners"—*ibid.*
"the tax appeal Commissioners"—*ibid.*

GENERAL NOTE

This section, governing rights of appeal, is modelled on the provisions governing tax appeals (Taxes Management Act 1970, s.31) rather than those for social security matters (SSA 1998, s.12). **1.277**

Subs. (1)

This provision adopts the standard 30-day appeal deadline in s.31(1) of the Taxes Management Act 1970. **1.278**

Subs. (2)

This requirement mirrors s.31(2) of the Taxes Management Act 1970. **1.279**

Subs. (3)

This provision is modelled on s.31(5) of the Taxes Management Act 1970 and gives the appellant the opportunity to raise additional grounds before the tribunal to those specifiedin the notice of appeal. **1.280**

Subs. (4) and (5)

Subsection (4) follows s.31(4) of the Taxes Management Act 1970 in directing appeals to the lay (and locally-based) General Commissioners unless the appellant elects to go before the Special Commissioners, a national and legally qualified tribunal). Subsection (5) incorporates further provisions of the 1970 Act governing the circumstances in which an appellant's election to go to the Special Commissioners may be withdrawn by agreement with the Inland Revenue, or set aside by the General Commissioners. **1.281**

Regulations with respect to appeals

13.—(1) The Board may, by regulations made with the concurrence of the Lord Chancellor and the Lord Advocate, make provision with respect to appeals to the tax appeal Commissioners under this Part. **1.282**

(2) Regulations under subsection (1) above may, in particular—

(a) make provision with respect to any of the matters dealt with in the following provisions of the Taxes Management Act 1970—

(i) section 44 and Schedule 3 (assigning proceedings to General Commissioners);

(ii) sections 48 to 54 (appeals to the tax appeal Commissioners under the Taxes Acts); and

(iii) sections 56 and 56A (appeals from their decisions); or

(b) provide for any of those provisions of that Act to apply, with such modifications as may be specified in the regulations, in relation to an appeal to the tax appeal Commissioners under this Part.

(3) In sections 56B and 56C of the Taxes Management Act 1970 (power of Lord Chancellor to make regulations about the practice and procedure to be followed in connection with appeals to the tax appeal Commissioners under the Taxes Acts), any reference to an appeal includes a reference to an appeal to the tax appeal Commissioners under this Part.

(4) Any regulations under section 56B of the Taxes Management Act 1970 which are in force immediately before the commencement of subsection (3) above shall apply in relation to appeals to the tax appeal Commissioners under this Part, subject to any necessary modifications, as they apply in relation to appeals to those Commissioners under the Taxes Acts.

(5) In this section, "the Taxes Acts" has the same meaning as in the Taxes Management Act 1970.

DEFINITIONS

"Board"—see s.27.
"the General Commissioners"—see s.19.
"the tax appeal Commissioners"—*ibid.*
"the Taxes Acts"—see subs.(5).

GENERAL NOTE

1.283 This section enables the Inland Revenue to make regulations about the procedures to apply for appeals to the tax appeal Commissioners against decisions under s.8. Such regulations can only be made with the concurrence of the Lord Chancellor and the Lord Advocate, who are responsible for funding the tax appeal Commissioners. In general terms, most of the provisions about appeals in Pt V of the Taxes Management Act 1970 are adopted for the purposes of such appeals. However, given that there are material differences between tax and matters such as SSP and SMP, subs.(2)(b) provides for appropriate modifications to be made to these appellate procedures. This reflects the existing arrangements for appeals to the tax appeal Commissioners in relation to Class 4 NICs, under SSCBA 1992, Sch.2, para.8.

Matters arising as respects decisions

1.284 **14.**—(1) The Board may by regulations make provision as respects matters arising—

(a) pending any decision of an officer of the Board under section 8 of this Act which relates to—

(i) statutory sick pay [1, statutory maternity pay, statutory paternity pay or statutory adoption pay], or

(ii) any person's liability for contributions;

(b) pending the determination by the tax appeal Commissioners of an appeal against any such decision,

(c) out of the variation, under regulations made under section 10 of this Act or on appeal, of any such decision, or

(d) out of the making of a decision which, under regulations made under that section, supersedes an earlier decision.

(2) Regulations under this section may, in particular—

(a) make provision making a person liable to pay contributions pending the determination by the tax appeal Commissioners of an appeal against a decision of an officer of the Board; and

(b) make provision as to the repayment in prescribed circumstances of contributions paid by virtue of the regulations.

(3) Regulations under this section must be made with the concurrence of the Secretary of State in so far as they relate to statutory sick pay [1, statutory maternity pay, statutory paternity pay or statutory adoption pay].

AMENDMENTS

1. Employment Act 2002, s.9(5) (December 8, 2002).

DEFINITIONS

"Board"—see s.27.
"contributions"—*ibid.*

GENERAL NOTE

This section is modelled on SSA 1998, s.18. It vests the Board with a parallel regulation-making power to deal with matters arising before a decision is made or an appeal is heard (subss.(1)(a) and (b)), or concerning the consequences of varying or superseding a previous decision (including a variation following an appeal) (subss.(1)(c) and (d)). As such regulations may have implications for benefit rights in relation to SMP and SSP, in those instances the power can only be exercised with the agreement of the Secretary of State for Work and Pensions (subs.(3)). **1.285**

Power to make provision for period before commencement of new social security appeal provisions

15.—(1) The Secretary of State may by regulations modify any of the enactments to which this subsection applies during any period in which section 8 of this Act is in force but Chapter II of Part I of the Social Security Act 1998 (social security decisions and appeals) is not yet wholly in force. **1.286**

(2) Subsection (1) above applies to—

(a) Pt II of the Social Security Administration Act 1992 (adjudication); and

(b) the Acts amended by section 16 of, and Schedule 7 to, this Act.

General Note

1.287 This transitional provision enabled the new decision-making arrangements introduced under this Act to co-exist with the existing system for contributions, SSP, SMP and pensions schemes during the period of transition from the SSAA 1992 regime to that under the SSA 1998. The provision was needed as the SSA 1998 did not become fully operational until after the day appointed for the operational transfer under this Act (April 1, 1999).

Decisions under Pension Schemes Act 1993

1.288 **16.**—(1) The function of determining the questions referred to in subsection (1) of section 170 of the Pension Schemes Act 1993, as that section has effect before the commencement of paragraph 131 of Schedule 7 to the Social Security Act 1998, is hereby transferred to an officer of the Board.

(2) In section 170 of the Pension Schemes Act 1993 (decisions and appeals), as substituted by paragraph 131 of Schedule 7 to the Social Security Act 1998, for subsections (2) to (4) there is substituted—

"(2) It shall be for an officer of the Inland Revenue—

(a) to make any decision that falls to be made under or by virtue of Part III of this Act, other than a decision which under or by virtue of that Part falls to be made by the Secretary of State;
(b) to decide any issue arising in connection with payments under section 7 of the Social Security Act 1986 (occupational pension schemes becoming contracted-out between 1986 and 1993); and
(c) to decide any issue arising by virtue of regulations made under paragraph 15 of Schedule 3 to the Social Security (Consequential Provisions) Act 1992 (continuing in force of certain enactments repealed by the Social Security Act 1973).

(3) In the following provisions of this section a 'relevant decision' means any decision which under subsection (2) falls to be made by an officer of the Inland Revenue, other than a decision under section 53 or 54.

(4) Sections 9 and 10 of the 1998 Act (revision of decisions and decisions superseding earlier decisions) apply as if—

(a) any reference in those sections to a decision of the Secretary of State under section 8 of that Act included a reference to a relevant decision; and
(b) any other reference in those sections to the Secretary of State were, in relation to a relevant decision, a reference to an officer of the Inland Revenue.

(5) Regulations may make provision—

(a) with respect to the procedure to be adopted on any application made under section 9 or 10 of the 1998 Act by virtue of subsection (4); and
(b) generally with respect to such applications, revisions under section 9 and decisions under section 10;

but may not prevent such a revision or decision being made without such an application.

(6) Section 12 of the 1998 Act (appeal to appeal tribunal) applies as if, for the purposes of subsection (1)(b) of that section, a relevant decision were a decision of the Secretary of State falling within Schedule 3 to the 1998 Act.

(7) The following provisions of the 1998 Act (which relate to decisions and appeals)—

sections 13 to 18;
sections 25 and 26;
section 28; and
Schedules 4 and 5;

shall apply in relation to any appeal under section 12 of the 1998 Act by virtue of subs.(6) above as if any reference to the Secretary of State were a reference to an officer of the Inland Revenue."

GENERAL NOTE

This section transferred to the Inland Revenue the function of making decisions on contracting-out matters which arise mainly under Pt III of the Pensions Schemes Act 1993 (subs.(1)). This is effected by the amendments made to the Pensions Schemes Act 1993 by subs.(2). However, SSA 1998 decision-making and appeals procedures are retained for such matters, including a right of appeal on pensions matters to an appeal tribunal, whereas the normal route of appeal is to the tax appeal Commissioners. The official justification for this is that "work on contracted-out pensions is separate from other current Contributions Agency work, and is specialised and often highly technical and quite distinct from tax and contributions work" (Social Security Contributions (Transfer of Functions, Etc.) Act 1999, *Explanatory Notes*, para.190). The counter argument is that social security appeal tribunals have little practical experience in this field and that it would be better for such appeals to be heard by the Special Commissioners (*per* Lord Goodhart, *Hansard*, H.L. Vol.596, cols 325–327, January 14, 1999). **1.289**

Arrangements for discharge of decision-making functions

17.—(1) The Secretary of State may make arrangements with the Board for any of his functions under Chapter II of Part I of the Social Security Act 1998 in relation to— **1.290**

(a) a decision whether a person was (within the meaning of regulations) precluded from regular employment by responsibilities at home; or
(b) a decision whether a person is entitled to be credited with earnings or contributions in accordance with regulations made under section 22(5) of the Social Security Contributions and Benefits Act 1992;

to be discharged by the Board or by officers of the Board.

(2) No such arrangements shall affect the responsibility of the Secretary of State or the application of Chapter II of Part I of the Social Security Act 1998 in relation to any decision.

(3) Until the commencement of Chapter II of Part I of the Social Security Act 1998, the references to that chapter in subsections (1) and (2) above shall have effect as references to Part II of the Social Security Administration Act 1992.

DEFINITION

"Board"—see s.27.

GENERAL NOTE

This section enables decisions on home responsibilities protection or credits to be performed by officers of the Inland Revenue as agents for the Secretary of State **1.291** for Work and Pensions. This arrangement is appropriate as such decisions primarily impact upon entitlement to social security benefits.

Amendments relating to decisions and appeals

1.292 **18.** Schedule 7 to this Act (which contains amendments relating to decisions and appeals) shall have effect.

GENERAL NOTE

1.293 Schedule 7 provides for the detailed responsibilities of existing legislation relating to decision-making and appeals (Taxes Management Act 1970, SSCBA 1992, SSAA 1992, Pensions Schemes Act 1993, Employment Rights Act 1996 and SSA 1998).

Interpretation of Part II

1.294 **19.** In this Part—

"the General Commissioners" means the Commissioners for the general purposes of the income tax appointed under section 2 of the Taxes Management Act 1970;

"the Special Commissioners" means the Commissioners for the special purposes of the Income Tax Acts appointed under section 4 of the Taxes Management Act 1970;

"the tax appeal Commissioners" means the General Commissioners or the Special Commissioners.

GENERAL NOTE

1.295 This defines the "tax appeal Commissioners" as a generic term covering both the General Commissioners and the Special Commissioners appointed under ss.2 and 4 of the Taxes Management Act 1970 respectively. Curiously, the expression "tax appeal Commissioners" is not actually employed in the Taxes Management Act 1970 itself.

PART III

MISCELLANEOUS AND SUPPLEMENTAL

1.296 **20.–26.** [*Omitted*]

Interpretation

1.297 **27.** In this Act, unless a contrary intention appears—

"the Board" means the Commissioners of Inland Revenue;

"contributions" means contributions under Part I of the Social Security Contributions and Benefits Act 1992.

28. [*Omitted*]

GENERAL NOTE

1.298 The provisions in Pt III (with the exception of s.27) fall outside the scope of this volume and so are omitted. Section 20 provides that rebates in respect of money purchase contracted-out pension schemes should be funded from the National Insurance Fund. Sections 21 and 22 deal with the transfer of contracts and property from the former DSS to the Inland Revenue. Section 23 provides for the transfer of functions by Order in Council. Section 24 enables provision to be made for Northern Ireland by Order in Council while s.25 concerns regulation and Order making powers generally; s.26 introduces Schs 8 (savings and transitional provisions), 9 (consequential amendments) and 10 (repeals and revocations). Section 28 governs the short title, commencement and extent of the Act.

SCHEDULES

Schedule 1 [*Omitted*]

SCHEDULE 2

TRANSFER OF FUNCTIONS UNDER SUBORDINATE LEGISLATION

1.299

Number	Title	Provisions conferring functions transferred
SI 1979/591	The Social Security (Contributions) Regulations 1979	All the regulations except regs 36–39, 41, 42 and 44
SI 1982/894	The Statutory Sick Pay (General) Regulations 1982	Regulations 9A to 9C, 10 and 14
SI 1983/376	The Statutory Sick Pay (Compensation of Employers) and Miscellaneous Provisions Regulations 1983	Regulation 3 (so far as remaining in force)
SI 1986/1960	The Statutory Maternity Pay (General) Regulations 1986	Regulations 7, 25, 30 and 31
SI 1987/1115	The Personal and Occupational Pension Schemes (Incentive Payments) Regulations 1987	All the regulations (so far as remaining in force)
SI 1990/536	The Social Security (Refunds) (Repayment of Contractual Maternity Pay) Regulations 1990	Regulations 2 and 3
SI 1992/796	The State Scheme Premiums (Actuarial Tables) Regulations 1992	All the regulations
SI 1994/1882	The Statutory Maternity Pay (Compensation of Employers) and Miscellaneous Amendment Regulations 1994	Regulations 3 and 6
SI 1995/512	The Statutory Sick Pay Percentage Threshold Order 1995	Article 4
SI 1996/195	The Employer's Contributions Re-imbursement Regulations 1996	Regulations 7, 8 and 9
SI 1996/1172	The Occupational Pension Schemes (Contracting-out) Regulations 1996	All the regulations except regs 23 and 61
SI 1996/1245	The Social Security (Additional Pension) (Contributions Paid in Error) Regulations 1996	All the regulations
SI 1996/1537	The Personal and Occupational Pension Schemes (Protected Rights) Regulations 1996	All the regulations except reg.4(3)
SI 1996/1977	The Occupational Pension Schemes (Mixed Benefit Contracted-out Schemes) Regulations 1996	Regulation 3

Number	**Title**	**Provisions conferring functions transferred**
SI 1997/38	The Occupational Pension Schemes (Contracting-out) Transitional Regulations 1997	All the regulations
SI 1997/358	The Occupational and Personal Pension Schemes (Contracting-out etc: Review of Determinations) Regulations 1997	All the regulations
SI 1997/470	The Personal Pension Schemes (Appropriate Schemes) Regulations 1997	All the regulations
SI 1997/664 (c.23)	The Pensions Act 1995 (Commencement No.10) Order 1997	Articles 4 and 13
SI 1998/1397	The Occupational Pension Schemes (Contracting-out) (Amount Required for Restoring State Scheme Rights and Miscellaneous Amendment) Regulations 1998	All the regulations
SI 1998/1846	The Occupational Pension Schemes (Validation of Rule Alterations) Regulations 1998	Regulation 2

Schedules 3–10 [*Omitted*]

Tax Credits Act 2002

(2002 c.21)

ARRANGEMENT OF SECTIONS

PART I

TAX CREDITS

General

Child tax credit

Working tax credit

10. Entitlement **1.302**
11. Maximum rate
12. Childcare element

Rate

13. Rate **1.303**

Decisions

14. Initial decisions **1.304**
15. Revised decisions after notifications
16. Other revised decisions
17. Final notice
18. Decisions after final notice
19. Power to enquire
20. Decisions on discovery
21. Decisions subject to official error
22. Information, etc. requirements: supplementary
23. Notice of decisions

Payment

24. Payments **1.305**
25. Payments of working tax credit by employers
26. Liability of officers for sums paid to employers
27. Rights of employees
28. Overpayments
29. Recovery of overpayments
30. Underpayments

Penalties

31. Incorrect statements, etc. **1.306**
32. Failure to comply with requirements
33. Failure by employers to make correct payments
34. Supplementary

Fraud

35. Offence of fraud **1.307**
36. Powers in relation to documents

Interest

37. Interest **1.308**

Appeals

1.309 38. Appeals
39. Exercise of right of appeal

Supplementary

1.310 40. Annual reports
41. Annual review
42. Persons subject to immigration control
43. Polygamous marriages
44. Crown employment
45. Inalienability
46. Giving of notices by Board
47. Consequential amendments
48. Interpretation

PART II

CHILD BENEFIT AND GUARDIAN'S ALLOWANCE

Transfer of functions etc.

1.311 49. Functions transferred to Treasury
50. Functions transferred to the Board
51. Consequential amendments
52. Transfer of property, rights and liabilities (*omitted*)
53. General functions of the Board
54. Transitional provisions

Minor amendments

1.312 55. Continuing entitlement after death of child
56. Presence in United Kingdom
57. Abolition of exclusion of tax exempt persons

PART III

SUPPLEMENTARY

Information etc.

1.313 58. Administrative arrangements
59. Use and disclosure of information

Other supplementary provisions

60. Repeals 1.314
61. Commencement
62. Transitional provisions and savings
63. Tax credits appeals etc.: temporary modifications
64. Northern Ireland
65. Regulations, orders and schemes (*omitted*)
66. Parliamentary etc. control of instruments (*omitted*)
67. Interpretation
68. Financial provision (*omitted*)
69. Extent (*omitted*)
70. Short title (*omitted*)

Schedule 1—Rights of employees (*omitted*) Schedule 2—Penalties: supplementary
Schedule 3—Tax credits: consequential amendments (*omitted*)
Schedule 4—Transfer of functions: consequential amendments (*omitted*)
Schedule 5—Use and disclosure of information (*omitted*)
Schedule 6—Repeals and revocations (*omitted*)

GENERAL NOTE

Scope and scheme of the Act

The Tax Credits Bill 2001 was introduced to the House of Commons as a Treasury measure. It was subject to minimal amendment as it went through its parliamentary proceedings in the House of Commons. The Speaker ruled that it was not a Money Bill (possibly because of Pt II of the Act). It was subject to rigorous challenge in the House of Lords. The criticisms ranged from normal political confrontations about tax and social security measures to a challenge to the fundamental approach, even the title, of the Bill itself. It was at that stage also (after strong protests from the opposition parties and an apology from the minister piloting the Bill through the House) that important government technical and drafting amendments were tabled. The main focus of opposition criticism was on the issue whether tax credits counted as public expenditure or as tax uncollected. In fact, that issue did not feature in the Bill at all as it does not require legislation. The answer (after a disagreement about the right approach, recorded in the note) was published in the Red Book (the Financial Statement) published by the Treasury to accompany the Chancellor 2002 Budget (See *2002 Financial Statement*, Box C2, p. 216). It is that tax credits count as public expenditure in so far as they exceed the income tax due from the claimant, and as negative taxation in so far as they do not. Tax credits under the Tax Credits Act 1999 are classified as public expenditure. During Parliamentary debates, it was said that as a ballpark figure, 90 per cent of the amount was public expenditure and 10 per cent tax foregone. 1.315

The Tax Credits Act 2002 ("this Act") repeals and replaces the Tax Credits Act 1999 ("TCA 1999") in its entirety and carries further the reforms started by that Act. But this Act also provides a framework both to extend existing tax credits and for a further round of reform beyond the current scope of tax credits. In doing so, it also takes further the measures introduced by a separate Act, the Social Security Contributions (Transfer of Functions, etc.) Act 1999. That Act transferred certain functions from the then Department of Social Security and its Northern Ireland equivalent to the Treasury and Inland Revenue. This Act transfers further functions by similar measures from what is now the Department for Work and Pensions and its Northern Ireland equivalent, the NI Department for Social Development, to the Treasury and Inland Revenue.

This Act makes provision for the following changes:

(a) replacing several existing forms of support for children by tax and social security provisions with a *child tax credit*;

(b) replacing working families' tax credit, disabled person's tax credit and New Deal 50 plus employment credit with a new, wider *working tax credit*;

(c) replacing the current system for claims, decision making, payment, and appeals relating to tax credits with a new system;

(d) transferring the functions of administering child benefit and guardian's allowance from the DWP to the Treasury and Inland Revenue;

(e) making minor amendments to the rules about entitlement to child benefit;

(f) introducing administrative arrangements to empower co-ordination between the Inland Revenue and those providing social security benefits.

The Act is structured in three Parts. Part I (Tax credits) provides the necessary primary legislative framework to introduce the child tax credit and working tax credit. It also provides a common procedure for those tax credits. Schedules 1–3 to the Act are associated with this Part. Part II (Child benefit and guardian's allowance) makes provision for the transfer of functions concerning child benefit and guardian's allowance to the Treasury and Inland Revenue, and the associated minor amendments to entitlement. Schedule 4 is associated with this Part. Part III (Supplementary) makes additional provision for both other Parts. Schedules 5 and 6 are associated with this Part.

Tax credits

1.316 The introduction of a programme of tax credits has been a major aspect of the approach to reform of the tax and benefit systems by the Treasury since the Labour government took office in 1997. But neither the TCA 1999 nor this Act were opposed in principle on this issue by the other main political parties. The substantive policy and the detail have been criticised, but not the general approach. The main thrust of Pt I of this Act, introducing the child tax credit (CTC) and the working tax credit (WTC), is to extend the tax credits introduced by the TCA 1999 and consolidate those reforms.

Tax credits under the Tax Credits Act 1999

1.317 The TCA 1999 was inherently a transitional measure. The TCA 1999 introduced two new tax credits in place of benefits administered by the then Department of Social Security (DSS). WFTC replaced the previous benefit known as family credit. At the same time DPTC replaced disability working allowance (DWA), originally introduced in 1992. But the TCA 1999 did not attempt to change the basic structure of WFTC and DPTC from their predecessor social security benefits. Nonetheless, the fundamental linking between earnings, income tax and NICs, and WFTC was achieved and most aspects of the poverty and unemployment traps finally removed. In addition, two important changes were introduced in 1999. The levels of benefit (now tax credit) provided were increased, and additional assistance was given to claimants who incurred work related childcare expenses. The statutory authority for WFTC thus remained s.128 of the SSCBA 1992, and that for DPTC s.129 of that Act. Similarly, the detail of WFTC and DPTC remained, respectively, in the Family Credit (General) Regulations 1987 (SI 1987/1973) and Disability Working Allowance (General) Regulations 1992 (SI 1992/2887) that laid down the legislative detail for the social security benefits. Nor did the TCA 1999 attempt to change the social security rules and procedures under which the tax credits were administered. Administration was transferred to the Inland Revenue but continued to be governed by the SSAA 1992 and SSA 1998, and appeals continued to go to the social security appeal bodies. However, the most important change to date in operating tax credits as against social security benefits is that some tax credits are paid by employers to their employees with net earnings. This was part of government policy to link benefits with work ("welfare to work"). The difficulties and cost of employers operating the legislation have been the subject of criticism and lobbying by those representing employers.

Tax credits under the Tax Credits Act 2002

The introduction of the current reforms was announced by the Chancellor of the Exchequer, Gordon Brown, in his 1999 Budget and confirmed in his 2000 Budget. The detailed shape of the proposals was first announced in an Inland Revenue consultation paper published in July 2001: *New Tax Credits: Supporting families, making work pay and tackling poverty*. This received significant comment from many sources and the Inland Revenue published its *Response* in November 2001. **1.318**

Child tax credit

CTC is a means-tested social security benefit for all those responsible for children and qualifying young persons, although it is presented as a tax credit. Government policy for the support of children appears to be motivated by two interacting pressures. The first is that the Government's target is to halve child poverty by 2010 and to abolish it altogether by 2020. The second is the profound-demographic shift occurring in Britain, as in the rest of Europe, because of the reduction in the number of children being born, due to a sharp drop in the female fertility rate. The government's response is the CTC, which provides a single tax credit payable to any person who is responsible for one or more children or qualifying young persons (s.8(1)). The Act provides only minimal detail about how CTC works, but the intended figures were published in the 2002 Budget and draft regulations were published before the Bill was given royal assent. Details are set out in the note to ss.8 and 9 below. **1.319**

Support for children through the tax and social security systems was previously provided in several ways. The first and most important provision was child benefit. The second line of support for children in poorer families was by way of an addition or increase to individual means-tested benefits (or tax credits). Thirdly, and separately from the income-related benefits, contributory and other social security benefits also made provision for dependent children (e.g. the child dependency increases under SSCBA 1992, ss.80 and 85 and the child increase for carer's allowance under SSCBA 1992, s.90). There were further provisions in the Social Security (Dependency) Regulations 1977 (SI 1977/ 343). Moreover, a few individuals looking after children as their guardians can claim guardian's allowance, under SSCBA 1992, s.77. Finally, and separately again from these sources of assistance for those bringing up children, the Finance Act 2000 introduced the children's tax credit as s.257AA of the ICTA 1988, supported by Sch.13B to that Act. Despite its name, this was not a tax credit, but an income tax reduction. It only overlapped with the social security benefits in so far as the claimants of those benefits were also income tax payers.

This Act sweeps away all mention of SSCBA 1992, ss.80 and 90 (but *not* s.85, which allows for increases for retirement pensioners for an adult caring for children for whom the pensioner is receiving child credit). With them go the relevant regulations. Section 257AA of ICTA 1988 also goes. So also, by regulation, does the overlap between child benefit and CTC. Any overlap with WTC is also avoided by regulation. Further regulations remove, as from April 6, 2004, the separate tests and overlaps as regards income support and jobseeker's allowance. The childcare provisions are decoupled from CTC and are paid only as part of WTC. As a result, for the first time since before the Beveridge Report (in the social security system) and since 1920 (in the personal income tax system), there is from 2003 an integrated approach to providing state support to those responsible for children. One further series of steps remain to complete the integration:

the combination of the tax credit with child benefit. That is brought about at the administrative level in part by Pt II of this Act (see below).

Working tax credit

1.320 WTC is not a social security benefit, although it has its immediate origins in WFTC and DPTC, which were income-related social security benefits. WTC has been repackaged as a tax credit, usually payable by employers through the pay packet, and extended beyond the limits of social security provision to assist all on low pay. It continues the process of integration by absorbing not only the two social security benefits but also New Deal 50 Plus. New Deal 50 Plus was the name given to a variant of the employment credits payable under the Employment and Training Act 1973. As its name suggests, it was a new form of employment assistance brought in to encourage the older claimant back into work. It was not a social security benefit and was never within the scope of the former DSS, being run instead by the former separate Department for Education and Employment and its predecessors.

WTC is designed as a general provision for all in "qualifying remunerative work", though tantalisingly this Act does not define that central term. Rather, regulations specify that work will qualify (if paid or in the expectation of payment) if it is over 16 hours a week for those with children, those who are disadvantaged by disability, and those over 50. Anyone else over 25 will qualify if working 30 hours a week (Working Tax Credit (Entitlement and Maximum Rate) Regulations 2002 (SI 2002/2005), reg.4). Those under 25 who are not in the specific groups are excluded. The definition is designed to integrate with the national minimum wage to provide a minimum level of take-home pay for all those entitled to claim. The Inland Revenue now also has responsibility for enforcement of the national minimum wage.

Despite the integration of benefits and allowances within both WTC and CTC, the two tax credits will operate separately from the point of view of claimants. While WTC was usually paid to a family through the pay packet of the working member of the family (or one of them), CTC will usually be paid direct to the main carer for the children, preferably through a credit transfer to a bank or similar account. In practice, therefore, in the case of joint claimants, CTC will often be paid to the mother along with child benefit, while WTC may well go to the father as part of his take-home pay. Nor are the conditions of the two credits the same, so an increase of income may affect one credit more than the other, while changes such as the arrival of a new child will alter one and not the other. But in the technical sense, WTC is a true tax credit, so can result in the take-home pay of a claimant being higher than the gross pay from the employer in cases where the amount of tax credit awarded is greater than the amount of income tax and NI contributions payable.

Commencement

1.321 Section 61 (Commencement) and subsequent sections came into effect on Royal Assent (8 July 2002). Pt I (ss.1–48) is brought into effect under the Tax Credits Act 2002 (Commencement No. 1) Order 2002 (SI 2002/1727) made that day. The balance of the Act was brought in by the Tax Credits Act 2002 (Commencement No. 2) Order 2003 (SI 2003/392) (Pt II), the Tax Credits Act 2002 (Commencement No. 3 and Transitional Provisions and Savings) Order 2003 (SI 2003/938) (the abolition of the child additions and benefits under s.1(3) of the Act) and Tax Credits Act 2002 (Commencement No. 4, Transitional Provisions and Savings) Order 2003 (SI 2003/962) (the remainder).

The pattern of introduction of tax credits is as follows:

General:

July 9, 2002	regulation-making powers

For all claimants except those on income support and jobseeker's allowance:

August 1, 2002	making claims and relevant provisions
January 1, 2003	making decisions on claims
April 6, 2003	entitlements to payment of awards and abolition of child additions from all benefits save as below.

For claimants over 60 transferring to or qualifying for state pension credit:

October 1, 2003	making claims and awards.

For other claimants of income support or jobseeker's allowance:

April 6, 2004	phased introduction of CTC to all claimants.

PART I

TAX CREDITS

General

Introductory

1.—(1) This Act makes provision for— 1.322

(a) a tax credit to be known as child tax credit, and

(b) a tax credit to be known as working tax credit.

(2) In this Act references to a tax credit are to either of those tax credits and references to tax credits are to both of them.

(3) The following (which are superseded by tax credits) are abolished—

(a) children's tax credit under section 257AA of the Income and Corporation Taxes Act 1988 (Chapter 1),

(b) working families' tax credit,

(c) disabled person's tax credit,

(d) the amounts which, in relation to income support and income-based jobseeker's allowance, are prescribed as part of the applicable amount in respect of a child or young person, the family premium, the enhanced disability premium in respect of a child or young person and the disabled child premium,

(e) increases in benefits in respect of children under sections 80 and 90 of the Social Security Contributions and Benefits Act 1992 (Chapter 4) and sections 80 and 90 of the Social Security Contributions and Benefits (Northern Ireland) Act 1992 (Chapter 7), and

(f) the employment credit under the schemes under section 2(2) of the Employment and Training Act 1973 (Chapter 50) and section 1 of the Employment and Training Act (Northern Ireland) 1950 (Chapter 29 (NI)) known as "New Deal 50 Plus".

DEFINITIONS

"child tax credit"—see s.8.
"tax credit"—see subs. 2.
"working tax credit"—see s.10.

GENERAL NOTE

1.323 Section 1 is, as its title states, purely an introductory section. Strictly it adds nothing to the enacting provisions of Pt I, but it flags up the two kinds of tax credit payable under the Act and also the benefits repealed (by s.60 and Sch.6). Subsection (1) lists the two tax credits introduced by the Act, but (as with the rest of Pt I) is drafted so that other tax credits could be added to the list in the subsection, and the machinery sections of the Act (which apply to "tax credits" as defined in subs.(2)) would then apply to the new tax credits also. At the date of writing, no specific further tax credits have been suggested.

Functions of Board

1.324 **2.**—(1) Tax credits are to be under the care and management of the Board.

(2) Section 10 of the Exchequer and Audit Departments Act 1866 (c.39) (gross revenues to be paid to Exchequer) is to be construed as allowing the Board to deduct payments for or in respect of tax credits before causing the gross revenues of their department to be paid to the account mentioned in that section.

(3) For the purposes of the Inland Revenue Regulation Act 1890 (c.21) the definition of "inland revenue" in section 39 of that Act is to be taken to include tax credits.

(4) The reference in section 4(1) of that Act (appointment of collectors, officers and other persons) to collecting, receiving, managing and accounting for Inland Revenue is to be taken to include a reference to paying and managing tax credits.

(5) The duties of the Board under section 13 of that Act (Board to keep accounts) are to include a duty to set forth in the accounts mentioned in that section—

(a) the amounts of the several payments made by them of or in respect of tax credits,

(b) the amounts of the expenses of paying and managing tax credits, and

(c) the amounts received by them in respect of tax credits,

distinguishing in each case between amounts relating to child tax credit and amounts relating to working tax credit.

(6) In any declaration for the purposes of section 6 of the Taxes Management Act 1970 (Chapter 9) (declarations on taking office), whether made before or after the commencement of this section, the reference to an offence relating to Inland Revenue is to be taken to include a reference to an offence relating to a tax credit.

DEFINITIONS

"the Board"—see s.67.
"child tax credit"—see s.8.
"tax credit"—see s.1(2).
"working tax credit"—see s.10.

GENERAL NOTE

1.325 This section echoes the terms of TCA 1999, s.5. It is a series of drafting devices designed to extend the legislation under which the Board of Inland Revenue operates to cover the tax credits established by this Act. The two main Acts of Parliament under which the IRC operates are the Inland Revenue Regulation Act 1890 ("IRRA 1890") and the Taxes Management Act 1970 ("TMA 1970").

Subs. (1)

This re-enacts TCA 1999, s.5(1) and integrates tax credits into the general remit given to the Inland Revenue by TMA 1970, s.1. It is regarded as the basis under which the Inland Revenue operates general extra statutory concessions, reaches settlements to deal with disputes in cases where the law or the facts are not clear, and more generally functions as a government department free of direct ministerial control over individual decisions. It contrasts with the structure of the social security system under the SSA 1998 under which all decisions, including the individual acceptance of claims, are decisions of "the Secretary of State", and where the Secretary of State and officers have minimal discretion under, or in applying, the legislation. **1.326**

Subs. (2)

This repeats TCA 1999, s.5(2) save for a drafting change from "tax credit" to "tax credits" also found in subs.(3)–(6) and elsewhere in re-enacted provisions from the 1999 Act. It allows the Inland Revenue to deduct the total of tax credits paid out from the revenues collected before payment into the Consolidated Fund (see s.67). **1.327**

Subss. (3)–(6)

Subsection (3) repeats TCA 1999, s.5(3) so as to integrate tax credits into the IRRA 1890. The lower case reference to "Inland Revenue" is to tax collected by the Inland Revenue. Subsection (4) (following TCA 1999, s.5(4)) is the other drafting link felt necessary into the language of the 1890 Act. Subsection (5) extends the duty of the Inland Revenue under the IRRA 1890 to keep detailed accounts of the tax credits and related sums. Subsection (6) extends the secrecy declarations that must be made by all Inland Revenue officials, and by judiciary and others involved in appeals, to cover information concerning tax credits (see TCA 1999, s.5(6)). The extension is both prospective and retrospective. **1.328**

Claims

3.—(1) Entitlement to a tax credit for the whole or part of a tax year is dependent on the making of a claim for it. **1.329**

(2) Where the Board—

(a) decide under section 14 not to make an award of a tax credit on a claim, or

(b) decide under section 16 to terminate an award of a tax credit made on a claim,

(subject to any appeal) any entitlement, or subsequent entitlement, to the tax credit for any part of the same tax year is dependent on the making of a new claim.

(3) A claim for a tax credit may be made—

(a) jointly by the members of a married couple or unmarried couple both of whom are aged at least sixteen and are in the United Kingdom [(and neither of whom are members of a polygamous unit)][1]; or

[(aa) jointly by the members of a polygamous unit all of whom are aged at least sixteen and are in the United Kingdom, or][1];

(b) by a person who is aged at least sixteen and is in the United Kingdom but is not entitled to make a claim under paragraph (a) (jointly with another).

(4) Entitlement to a tax credit pursuant to a claim ceases—

(a) in the case of a joint claim, if the persons by whom it was made could no longer jointly make a joint claim; and

[(aa) in the case of a joint claim under subsection (3)(a), if a member of the married or unmarried couple becomes a member of a polygamous unit, and

(ab) in the case of a joint claim under subsection (3)(aa), if there is any change in the persons who comprise the polygamous unit, and][1]

(b) in the case of a single claim, if the person by whom it was made could no longer make a single claim.

(5) In this Part "married couple" means a man and woman who are married to each other and are neither—

(a) separated under a court order, nor

(b) separated in circumstances in which the separation is likely to be permanent.

(6) In this Part "unmarried couple" means a man and a woman who are not a married couple but are living together as husband and wife.

[(6A) In this Part, "polygamous unit" has the meaning given by regulation 2 of the Tax Credits (Polygamous Marriages) Regulations 2003.][1]

(7) Circumstances may be prescribed in which a person is to be treated for the purposes of this Part as being, or as not being, in the United Kingdom.

(8) In this Part—

"joint claim" means a claim under paragraph (a) [or (aa)][1] of subsection (3), and

"single claim" means a claim under paragraph (b) of that subsection.

AMENDMENTS

1. Modifications for the purposes of application to polygamous units by Tax Credits (Polygamous Marriages) Regulations 2003 (SI 2003/742), reg.4 (April 6, 2003).

DEFINITIONS

"award"—see s.14(1).
"the Board"—see s.67.
"claim"—see subs.(1), s.4.
"entitlement"—see s.18(1).
"joint claim"—see subs.(8).
"married couple"—see subs.(5).
"prescribed"—see s.67.
"single claim"—see subs.(8).
"tax credit"—see s.1(2).
"tax year"—see s.47.
"unmarried couple"—see subs.(8).

GENERAL NOTE

1.330 This is the first of the sections in the Act that create the necessary compromise for tax credits between the general approach of income tax administration and the general approach of social security administration. Subsection (1) adopts and adapts the requirement from SSAA 1992, s.1(1), that there can be no entitlement to a tax credit without a claim. Subsection (2) reinforces this. Subsections (3) and following set out both the main conditions for making a claim and the requirement that both (or all) those who are partners to a marriage (or equivalent) join in making the claim. Subsection (8) adopts appropriate definitions for joint and single claims. There is also a definition of "claimant" in s.9(8), which would be better placed here in subs.(8).

Subs. (1)

The standard claim form is TC600. Claims can be made on this form both in writing and electronically via the Inland Revenue's dedicated website *www.taxcredits.inlandrevenue.gov.uk*. The subsection requires a claim for each tax year. In practice a claim is needed for payment in the first year, but claimants may be treated as making claims for renewals for later years once an award has been made in the first year.

The Inland Revenue has accepted that it is appropriate in some cases to make protective claims where a claim will lead to a nil award on the then current information about income, but where a claimant may later in the tax year be entitled to tax credits. In such cases, nil awards will be made. See *Tax Adviser*, June 2003, p.13. The Inland Revenue's statistics showed that at October 2003 about 130,000 nil awards had been made.

Subs. (2)

This adopts in part a policy of SSA 1998, s.8, that a claim ceases to have effect when a decision has been made on it. A new claim is required if the Board refuses or ends a tax credit award for a tax year and for any reason the claimant wants that decision revisited. In practice, however, the Board may choose to make a "nil" award, so leaving the matter open to review if circumstances change, rather than a reclaim. **1.331**

Subs. (3)

This is the primary provision entitling a claim to be made. It imposes a series of conditions on all claimants: **1.332**

(a) if a claimant is one of a married or unmarried couple (or of a polygamous unit) then the claim can only be made in the names of both (or all) of them;
(b) the claimant or claimants must be over 16; and
(c) the claimant or claimants (and if more than one, all) must be "in the UK".

The following subsections make provisions for those conditions. But s.42 excludes those subject to immigration control from entitlement except in specified cases. The approach of requiring joint claims is also reinforced by s.4(1)(g), which enables regulations to treat a single claim as a joint claim. This has been extended by regulations under s.43 to cover polygamous units, the policy again being that all the members of a polygamous unit must be linked to the claim.

Subs. (4)

This is designed to stop the claim under subs.(3) continuing if the identity of the claimant(s) changes because an individual gains a partner, a couple breaks up, or a polygamous unit changes membership. But it deals with *entitlement* not *award*, and its inclusion at this point in this section is a little obscure. It links with the provisions on joint claims (or deemed joint claims) to withdraw *entitlement* where joint claimants are no longer *entitled to make* a joint claim, thus stopping both joint claims and claims deemed to be joint. Nonetheless its interaction with ss.17 and 18 and with a continuing *award* is not clear. It appears to suggest that **1.333** an award can continue without underlying entitlement. However, under the Tax Credits (Claims and Notifications) Regulations 2002 (SI 2002/ 2014), reg.21, notification must be given whenever a joint claim should become a single claim, or the reverse. In practice, this applies to awards as much as to entitlement.

Subss. (5), (6) and (6A)

1.334 These set out important definitions for "married couple" and "unmarried couple". They reflect another necessary compromise between tax law and social security law. Unlike the rules applying under TCA 1999, these are the income tax definitions, not the social security definitions, see ICTA s.282 (para.1.79). For a full account of the social security rules, see the notes in Vol.II of this work to SSCBA 1992, s.137. Subsection (6A) was inserted to apply the language and approach of joint claims to polygamous marriages. No provision is made for same-sex couples.

Subs. (7)

1.335 This allows jurisdictional limits to be placed on entitlement to tax credit. Again, this breaks away from social security practice (which deals with Great Britain and Northern Ireland separately) to adopt income tax practice. It is supplemented by s.42 (persons subject to immigration control) and regulations made under that section. The main regulations under this subsection are the Tax Credits (Residence) Regulations 2003 (SI 2003/642). These impose a test of "ordinary residence" on most claimants.

Claims: supplementary

1.336 **4.**—(1) Regulations may—

(a) require a claim for a tax credit to be made in a prescribed manner and within a prescribed time,

(b) provide for a claim for a tax credit made in prescribed circumstances to be treated as having been made on a prescribed date earlier or later than that on which it is made,

(c) provide that, in prescribed circumstances, a claim for a tax credit may be made for a period wholly or partly after the date on which it is made,

(d) provide that, in prescribed circumstances, an award on a claim for a tax credit may be made subject to the condition that the requirements for entitlement are satisfied at a prescribed time,

(e) provide for a claim for a tax credit to be made or proceeded with in the name of a person who has died,

(f) provide that, in prescribed circumstances, one person may act for another in making a claim for a tax credit,

(g) provide that, in prescribed circumstances, a claim for a tax credit made by one member of a married couple or an unmarried couple is to be treated as also made by the other member of the married couple or unmarried couple[1], and

(h) provide that a claim for a tax credit is to be treated as made by a person or persons in such other circumstances as may be prescribed.

(2) The Board may supply to a person who has made a claim for a tax credit (whether or not jointly with another)—

(a) any information relating to the claim, to an award made on the claim or to any change of circumstances relevant to the claim or such an award,
(b) any communication made or received relating to such an award or any such change of circumstances, and
(c) any other information which is relevant to any entitlement to tax credits pursuant to the claim or any such change of circumstances or which appeared to be so relevant at the time the information was supplied.

AMENDMENTS

1. Tax Credits (Polygamous Marriages) Regulations 2003 (SI 2003/742) amends s.4(1)(g) as follows for the purposes of polygamous marriages:

"In section 4(1)(g)—

(a) for "member of a married couple or an unmarried couple" substitute "or more members of a polygamous unit";
(b) for "of the married couple or unmarried couple" substitute "or members".

DEFINITIONS

"award"—see s.14(1).
"the Board"—see s.67.
"claim"—see s.3(1).
"entitlement"—see s.18(1).
"joint claim"—see s.3(8).
"married couple"—see s.3(5).
"prescribed"—see s.67.
"single claim"—see s.3(8).
"tax credit"—see s.1(2).
"tax year"—see s.47.
"unmarried couple"—see s.3(8).

GENERAL NOTE

Regulations for the purposes of subs.(1) are made by the Board by negative procedure: ss.65(2), 66(3). The main regulations made are the Tax Credits (Claims and Notifications) Regulations 2002 (SI 2002/2014). **1.337**

The most important point relevant to this section is that those Regulations require a claim to be made not later than three months after the date from which it can operate. For a claim to be effective from the beginning of a tax year, it must be made (that is, received by an appropriate office) before July 6 in that year. If made later than that, it will not operate for more than three months before the date on which the claim was actually made. But, unlike backdated claims for social security benefits, the three months backdating is automatic and is not dependent on grounds being shown for a "late claim". Nor is there any discretion to extent the three months' backdating of a claim in any circumstances. See reg.7 of those regulations. The only exception, under reg.8, applies to claimants claiming a disability element of WTC as part of the claim.

Subsection (2) gives the Inland Revenue power that it would otherwise not have to inform a claimant of information of which it knows that is relevant to a claim, or to an award or entitlement continuing. This will ensure that either member of a joint claiming couple can be informed of anything that the other member of the couple tells the Inland Revenue. This cuts across the privacy as between members of a couple that was respected by the Inland Revenue following the introduction of individual self-assessment for income tax.

Period of awards

1.338 **5.**—(1) Where a tax credit is claimed for a tax year by making a claim before the tax year begins, any award of the tax credit on the claim is for the whole of the tax year.

(2) An award on any other claim for a tax credit is for the period beginning with the date on which the claim is made and ending at the end of the tax year in which that date falls.

(3) Subsections (1) and (2) are subject to any decision by the Board under section 16 to terminate an award.

DEFINITIONS

"award"—see s.14(1).
"the Board"—see s.67.
"claim"—see s.3(1).
"tax credit"—see s.1(2).
"tax year"—see s.47.

GENERAL NOTE

1.339 This section applies to both CTC and WTC. It confirms the import of s.3(1), namely that a claim is for one tax year at a time, and provides that any award is for that tax year (or, if made during the year, for what is left of it). This is subject to the power in s.16 to end an award, after which a new claim must be made (s. 3(2)). Effect is given to these provisions by the Tax Credits (Claims and Notifications) Regulations 2002 (SI 2002/2014), regs 4–11. Regulations 11 and 12 of those regulations provide a mechanism whereby a reply to a notice relating to one year of claim under s.17 of this Act can be treated as a claim for the following year.

Subsection (2), on its face, prevents retrospective claims, but it must be read with regs 4 and following of the Tax Credits (Claims and Notifications) Regulations 2002. These make provision for the "date on which a claim is made". Under reg.7, the general rule is that a claim is treated as made for the purposes of this subsection up to three months before the date on which the claim is received by an appropriate office, if *entitlement* extends that far back. This, like other issues about *award* and *entitlement*, seems to conflate the making of an award with entitlement (see the note to s.6). It will only be known that a person is entitled once a final decision is made under s.17 of this Act after the end of the year, while the award operates on the basis that the person is probably entitled.

Notifications of changes of circumstances

1.340 **6.**—(1) Regulations may provide that any change of circumstances of a prescribed description which may increase the maximum rate at which a person or persons may be entitled to a tax credit is to do so only if notification of it has been given.

(2) Regulations under subsection (1) may—

(a) provide for notification of a change of circumstances given in prescribed circumstances to be treated as having been given on a prescribed date earlier or later than that on which it is given,

(b) provide that, in prescribed circumstances, a notification of a change of circumstances may be given for a period wholly or partly after the date on which it is given, and

(c) provide that, in prescribed circumstances, an amendment of an award of a tax credit in consequence of a notification of a change of circumstances may be made subject to the condition that the requirements for entitlement to the amended amount of the tax credit are satisfied at a prescribed time.

(3) Regulations may require that, where a person has or persons have claimed a tax credit, notification is to be given if there is a change of circumstances of a prescribed description which may decrease the rate at which he is or they are entitled to the tax credit or mean that he ceases or they cease to be entitled to the tax credit.

(4) Regulations under this section may—

(a) require a notification to be given in a prescribed manner and within a prescribed time,

(b) specify the person or persons by whom a notification may be, or is to be, given, and

(c) provide that, in prescribed circumstances, one person may act for another in giving a notification.

DEFINITIONS

"award"—see section 14(1).
"claim"—see s.3(1).
"entitlement"—see s.18(1).
"maximum rate"—see ss.9 and 11.
"prescribed"—see s.67.
"tax credit"—see s.1(2).

GENERAL NOTE

The Bill on which this Act was based was tabled in, and passed through, the House of Commons without a clear distinction being drawn between the measures relating to *award* of a tax credit on a claim and the later issue of *entitlement* to that credit. As a result, there is no clear progression in the sections of the Act from claims to award to entitlement. This section might from context appear to be about awards, but subs.(1) is drafted to cover only entitlement issues. The link is provided partly under subs.(2) and partly by s.15, which links changes in awards to the rate at which someone *may be* entitled to a tax credit. **1.341**

"Change of circumstances" is, of course, a familiar social security concept on which the SSA 1998 relies heavily for powers to change decisions after they are made but where they have continuing effect. There is also a general duty on claimants to report changes of circumstances of relevance to benefit awards. This section allows a similar duty to be imposed on tax credit claimants. The section is purely empowering. Regulations may be made by the Revenue by negative procedure: ss.65(2) and 66(3). The relevant regulations are the Tax Credits (Claims and Notifications) Regulations 2002 (SI 2002/2014), regs 19–29. Those regulations, however, take a substantially different approach to changes of circumstances to those operated for social security benefits.

The nature of a "change of circumstances" and the treatment adopted for making and dealing with changes of circumstance requires some further explanation because of the differences in the ways in which the rules operate compared with those for income support or jobseeker's allowance. The main differences are—

(a) not all changes of circumstances during a year will result in a change of circumstances affecting the award or entitlement;
(b) the duty to notify changes of circumstances is limited in scope and applies only to some changes;
(c) failure to notify when there is a duty to do so may make the person failing to notify liable to penalties and penalty proceedings under ss.31(1) and 32(3).

Relevant changes of circumstances

1.342 Because the income test under s.7 is applied to the tax year (or period of award) as a whole, a change in income levels during a year may be irrelevant to award or entitlement levels, and so not constitute a change of circumstances. This will be particularly so towards the end of a tax year. Further, because of the "buffer" built into the income test by s.7(3), any increase of income over the year as a whole of less than (currently) £2,500 is irrelevant in any event. Changes in capital are also immaterial, as it is only the (taxable) income from capital that affects the level of award and entitlement. For similar reasons, a change of job (with a gap of under seven days between jobs) will also not affect an award or entitlement unless either it changes the income level significantly over the year as a whole or it decreases the hours worked below 16, or—for WTC only—it increases or decreases the hours above or below 30.

The changes that are relevant are significant income changes, as noted above, and other changes that will stop entitlement or cause its overall level to be changed. This may apply differently to CTC and WTC. But not all those changes must be reported.

Changes that must be reported

1.343 There is, somewhat counter intuitively, no duty to report a change of circumstances that may decrease the rate at which a person is or may be entitled to either WTC or CTC.

There is a duty to report only the following changes of circumstance that affect or may affect entitlement, or the level of entitlement to either tax credit—

(a) when a single claimant becomes a member of a couple or joint claimants split up, so ending entitlement under section 3(4);
(b) for WTC only, when the estimated level of childcare charges decreases by more than £10 a week.

This duty is imposed by reg.21 of the Tax Credits (Claims and Notifications) Regulations 2002 (SI 2002/2014). In all other cases, changes adverse to the claimant may be reported, but otherwise will be dealt with after the year of assessment when the decision on entitlement is considered.

Changes that may be reported

1.344 Under regs 20 and 25 of the Tax Credits (Claims and Notifications) Regulations 2002, a change of circumstances that may increase an award or entitlement to either WTC or CTC will only do so if notification of the change has been given to the Inland Revenue within three months of the date when the change occurred. Later notice will be backdated not more than three months. This time limit is, however, extended under reg.26 for those claiming the disability or severe disability elements of WTC. In all other cases, notification of any change of circumstances that will or may benefit the claimant should be made within the three months' limit to prevent both loss of award and loss of entitlement.

Automatic notification?

Part II of this Act transfers responsibility for child benefit to the Inland Revenue. The decision of the Court of Appeal in *Hinchy v Secretary of State for Work and Pensions* [2003] EWCA Civ 138, [2003] All E.R. (D) 273 (Feb) (and subject to any appeal to the House of Lords) would suggest that notification to the Inland Revenue of a new child, or a child or young person ceasing to be in the responsibility of a claimant, is also notification to the Inland Revenue for the purposes of CTC. This combined approach is, it appears, the approach on which the Revenue itself is also working. **1.345**

Failure to report

Leaving aside fraudent or other cases of deliberate non-disclosure, if a change of circumstances is not reported when it happens it will be picked up directly or indirectly when the claimant replies to the Inland Revenue's final notice issued under s.17. This is because of the declaration necessary under s.17. If it is a relevant change, then the entitlement to WTC and/or CTC will be confirmed at a different rate to that of the award. This will result in an overpayment (see s.28) if the level of award is, as a result, higher than the level of entitlement. It could also result in an underpayment (see s.30), but only to the extent that the notification is regarded as in time for any part of the relevant tax year. In most cases, if the notification is more than three months after the end of the tax year then the right to an increased entitlement will have been lost. **1.346**

The Inland Revenue has announced that it will not seek penalties from a taxpayer who has a nil award following a claim and who then fails to make a mandatory notification of a change of circumstances. See *Tax Adviser*, June 2003, p.13.

Income test

7.—(1) The entitlement of a person or persons of any description to a tax credit is dependent on the relevant income— **1.347**

(a) not exceeding the amount determined in the manner prescribed for the purposes of this paragraph in relation to the tax credit and a person or persons of that description (referred to in this Part as the income threshold), or

(b) exceeding the income threshold by only so much that a determination in accordance with regulations under section 13(2) provides a rate of the tax credit in his or their case.

(2) Subsection (1) does not apply in relation to the entitlement of a person or persons to a tax credit for so long as the person, or either of the persons, is entitled to any social security benefit prescribed for the purposes of this subsection in relation to the tax credit.

(3) In this Part "the relevant income" means—

(a) if an amount is prescribed for the purposes of this paragraph and the current year income exceeds the previous year income by not more than that amount, the previous year income,

(b) if an amount is prescribed for the purposes of this paragraph and the current year income exceeds the previous year income by more than that amount, the current year income reduced by that amount,

(c) if an amount is prescribed for the purposes of this paragraph and the previous year income exceeds the current year income by not more than that amount, the previous year income,

(d) if an amount is prescribed for the purposes of this paragraph and the previous year income exceeds the current year income by more than that amount, the current year income increased by that amount, and

(e) otherwise, the current year income.

(4) In this Part "the current year income" means—

(a) in relation to persons by whom a joint claim for a tax credit is made, the aggregate income of the persons for the tax year to which the claim relates, and

(b) in relation to a person by whom a single claim for a tax credit is made, the income of the person for that tax year.

(5) In this Part "the previous year income" means—

(a) in relation to persons by whom a joint claim for a tax credit is made, the aggregate income of the persons for the tax year preceding that to which the claim relates, and

(b) in relation to a person by whom a single claim for a tax credit is made, the income of the person for that preceding tax year.

(6) Regulations may provide that, for the purposes of this Part, income of a prescribed description is to be treated as being, or as not being, income for a particular tax year.

(7) In particular, regulations may provide that income of a prescribed description of a person for the tax year immediately before the preceding tax year referred to in subsection (5) is to be treated as being income of that preceding tax year (instead of any actual income of that description of the person for that preceding tax year).

(8) Regulations may for the purposes of this Part make provision—

(a) as to what is, or is not, income, and

(b) as to the calculation of income.

(9) Regulations may provide that, for the purposes of this Part, a person is to be treated—

(a) as having income which he does not in fact have, or

(b) as not having income which he does in fact have.

(10) The Board may estimate the amount of the income of a person, or the aggregate income of persons, for any tax year for the purpose of making, amending or terminating an award of a tax credit; but such an estimate does not affect the rate at which he is, or they are, entitled to the tax credit for that or any other tax year.

AMENDMENTS

Subsection 2 is amended as it applies to polygamous units by Tax Credits (Polygamous Marriages) Regulations 2003 (SI 2003/742), reg.6.

DEFINITIONS

"award"—see s.14(1).
"the Board"—see s.67.
"claim"—see s.3(1).
"entitlement"—see s.18(1).
"joint claim"—see s.3(8).
"married couple"—see s.3(5).
"prescribed"—see s.67.

"single claim"—see s.3(8).
"tax credit"—see s.1(2).
"tax year"—see s.47.
"unmarried couple"—see s.3(8).

GENERAL NOTE

This is a framework and empowering section making provision for the imposition of an income test on all claimants for both CTC and WTC. The relevant regulations are the Tax Credits (Definition of Calculation of Income) Regulations 2002 (SI 2002/2006) and the Tax Credits (Income Thresholds and Determination of Rates) Regulations 2002 (SI 2002/2008). The powers to make regulations are Treasury powers requiring affirmative procedures. The policy behind the Act is to follow WFTC by making the benefit income-related but, unlike WFTC, there is no separate test of capital. Further, the regulations link the income test closely to income tax rules, thus breaking away from the separate social security means tests. **1.348**

Subs. (1)

This is worded to refer "a tax credit" so that different amounts may be prescribed for different tax credits. Regulation 3 of the Tax Credits (Income Thresholds and Determination of Rates) Regulations 2002 sets a threshold for WTC of £5,060, and for CTC of £13,480, with a further higher threshold for the family element only of CTC of £50,000 in reg.8 of those Regulations. **1.349**

Subs. (2)

This disapplies the income test, so allowing payment of a tax credit without reference to separate means-testing, where the prescribed benefits are in payment. The benefits are prescribed by Tax Credits (Income Thresholds and Determination of Rates) Regulations 2002, reg.4 as covering only some claimants for income support and jobseeker's allowance. In those cases, other regulations operate to stop any claim for CTC (WTC is not applicable) until April 6, 2004 in any event. **1.350**

Subs. (3)

See reg.5 of the Tax Credits (Income Thresholds and Determination of Rates) Regulations 2002. This prescribes the sum of £2,500 for paras (a) and (b) only, so paras (c) and (d) do not apply at present. See the note to that regulation. **1.351**

Subss. (6)–(9)

See the Tax Credits (Definition and Calculation of Income) Regulations 2002, as amended. **1.352**

Subs. (10)

This is a wide power to deal with awards. It allows the Inland Revenue to make, change or stop an award during the tax year on the basis of an estimate only. That estimate will be the decision made under ss.14(1), 15(1) or 16(1). Any of these decisions are subject to appeal and, on appeal, it will be for the appeal tribunal to make the estimate (subject to any settlement of the appeal under s.54 of the TMA 1970). See further the note to s.39 below. It is understood that the standard practice of the Inland Revenue is to make all initial decisions on the basis of the previous year's income using this power. Where a claim form indicates that the current year's income should be used, the Inland Revenue then makes an immediate revision under s.15. **1.353**

Child tax credit

Entitlement

1.354 **8.**—(1) The entitlement of the person or persons by whom a claim for child tax credit has been made is dependent on him, or either of them, being responsible for one or more children or qualifying young persons.

(2) Regulations may make provision for the purposes of child tax credit as to the circumstances in which a person is or is not responsible for a child or qualifying young person.

(3) For the purposes of this Part a person is a child if he has not attained the age of sixteen; but regulations may make provision for a person who has attained that age to remain a child for the purposes of this Part after attaining that age for a prescribed period or until a prescribed date.

(4) In this Part "qualifying young person" means a person, other than a child, who—

(a) has not attained such age (greater than 16) as is prescribed, and
(b) satisfies prescribed conditions.

(5) Circumstances may be prescribed in which a person is to be entitled to child tax credit for a prescribed period in respect of a child or qualifying young person who has died.

Amendments

Subsection (1) is amended as it applies to polygamous units by Tax Credits (Polygamous Marriages) Regulations 2003 (SI 2003/742), reg.7.

Definitions

"child"—see subs.(3).
"prescribed"—see s.67.
"qualifying young person"—see subs.(4).

General Note

1.355 This section sets the central tests for claiming child tax credits, namely that there be a child or young person for whom the claimant is, or joint claimants are, responsible. Subsection (1) provides that entitlement to child tax credit is dependent on these tests. It is deliberately parallel to SSCBA 1992, s.141, the section entitling claimants to child benefit for each of the children for whom a claimant is responsible. Subsection (2) makes provision for regulations defining responsibility for a child. This is covered by SSCBA 1992, s.143 and supporting regulations. Subsection (3) defines a child as someone who has not reached the age of 16, but also allows the age to be extended by regulation. Child benefit is payable for all children who have not reached 16 (SSCBA 1992, s.142(1)). Child benefit is also payable for certain children over 16, but for child tax credit purposes they are known as "qualifying young persons". Subsection (4) allows regulations to define that category. The intention is, as with child benefit, to include certain young persons over 16 but not over 19, depending on ongoing education (but not covering students undergoing higher education). The effect confirms a general policy to exclude those over 16 from being "children" for state benefit purposes, but to include them, along with students, in a separate category. This is because those over 16 can claim some benefits in their own right. See further the Child Tax Credit Regulations 2002 (SI 2002/2007).

Subs. (5)

This is a new rule which makes identical provision as that in s.54 of this Act, ensuring that both child benefit and child tax credit remain payable for a period (set by regulations at eight weeks) after the death of a child or, in the case of child tax credit, qualifying young person. 1.356

Maximum rate

9.—(1) The maximum rate at which a person or persons may be entitled to child tax credit is to be determined in the prescribed manner. 1.357

(2) The prescribed manner of determination must involve the inclusion of—

(a) an element which is to be included in the case of all persons entitled to child tax credit, and

(b) an element in respect of each child or qualifying young person for whom the person is, or either of them is or are, responsible.

(3) The element specified in paragraph (a) of subsection (2) is to be known as the family element of child tax credit and that specified in paragraph (b) of that subsection is to be known as the individual element of child tax credit.

(4) The prescribed manner of determination may involve the inclusion of such other elements as may be prescribed.

(5) The prescribed manner of determination—

(a) may include provision for the amount of the family element of child tax credit to vary according to the age of any of the children or qualifying young persons or according to any such other factors as may be prescribed,

(b) may include provision for the amount of the individual element of child tax credit to vary according to the age of the child or qualifying young person or according to any such other factors as may be prescribed, and

(c) must include provision for the amount of the individual element of child tax credit to be increased in the case of a child or qualifying young person who is disabled and to be further increased in the case of a child or qualifying young person who is severely disabled.

(6) A child or qualifying young person is disabled, or severely disabled, for the purposes of this section only if—

(a) he satisfies prescribed conditions, or

(b) prescribed conditions exist in relation to him.

(7) If, in accordance with regulations under section 8(2), more than one claimant may be entitled to child tax credit in respect of the same child or qualifying young person, the prescribed manner of determination may include provision for the amount of any element of child tax credit included in the case of any one or more of them to be less than it would be if only one claimant were so entitled.

(8) "Claimant" means—

(a) in the case of a single claim, the person who makes the claim; and

(b) in the case of a joint claim, the persons who make the claim.

AMENDMENTS

Subsection (2) is amended as it applies to polygamous units by Tax Credits (Polygamous Marriages) Regulations 2003 (SI 2003/742), reg.8.

DEFINITIONS

"child"—see s.8(3).
"child tax credit"—see s.8
"claimant"—see subs.(8).
"disabled"—see subs.(6).
"prescribed"—see s.67.
"qualifying young person"—see s.8(4).
"severely disabled"—see subs.(6).

GENERAL NOTE

1.358 This section is again a mixture of defining provisions and empowering provisions. Subsection (1) provides that the way in which entitlement to CTC is to be calculated is to be set out in regulations. The first set of regulations for this purpose are the Child Tax Credit Regulations 2002 (SI 2002/2007). Subsections (2) and (3) provide that in every case an award of CTC must involve both a "family element" for the claimant and an "individual element" for each child or young person. The amount of the individual element must be higher for children or young persons who are disabled, and higher again if they are seriously disabled, but definition of those conditions is left to regulations: subss.(5)(c) and (6). This continues in another form the disabled child premium payable under income support. The other provisions in the section are permissive.

Subs. (7)

1.359 A recurrent problem for child benefit is where more than one person has or claims to have responsibility for a child. Child benefit can only be claimed by one claimant and is indivisible (even between married parents living together). For CTC purposes, this enabling provision seems to imply that a lower amount of CTC can be paid to a claimant where there is more than one claim, thus allowing splitting of entitlement. However, no provision has been made for this in regulations: see Child Tax Credit Regulations 2002 (SI 2002/2007), reg.3.

Working tax credit

Entitlement

1.360 **10.**—(1) The entitlement of the person or persons by whom a claim for working tax credit has been made is dependent on him, or either of them, being engaged in qualifying remunerative work.

(2) Regulations may for the purposes of this Part make provision—

(a) as to what is, or is not, qualifying remunerative work, and
(b) as to the circumstances in which a person is, or is not, engaged in it.

(3) The circumstances prescribed under subsection (2)(b) may differ by reference to—

(a) the age of the person or either of the persons,
(b) whether the person, or either of the persons, is disabled,

(c) whether the person, or either of the persons, is responsible for one or more children or qualifying young persons, or

(d) any other factors.

(4) Regulations may make provision for the purposes of working tax credit as to the circumstances in which a person is or is not responsible for a child or qualifying young person.

AMENDMENTS

Subsections (1) and (3) are amended as they apply to polygamous units by Tax Credits (Polygamous Marriages) Regulations 2003 (SI 2003/742), reg.9.

DEFINITIONS

"child"—see s.8(3).
"disabled"—see s.11(7).
"engaged"—see subs.(2).
"qualifying remunerative work"—see subs.(2).
"qualifying young person"—see s.8(4).
"responsible for a child"—see subs.(4).

GENERAL NOTE

This section is the parallel to s.8, laying down the central test for claiming WTC **1.361** by single or joint claimants, and defining or providing for definition of the key terms.

Subs. (1)

This makes the central test for WTC "being engaged in qualifying remunera- **1.362** tive work". "Remunerative work" is the test used in WFTC and family credit before that (see Family Credit (General) Regulations 1987 (SI 1987/1973, reg.4). It is also used in the regulations defining entitlement to income support and jobseeker's allowance. See the notes to Income Support (General) Regulations 1987, reg.4, and Jobseeker's Allowance Regulations 1996, reg.51, in Vol.II of this work. The test of "work" has been held by Commissioners to be wider than "employment" (*R(FC) 2/90*), although the requirement that it be "remunerative"—defined as work done for payment or in expectation of payment—excludes volunteers (*R(IS) 12/92*).

Subs. (2)

This provides for further definition of what is "qualifying" work, and also when **1.363** someone is "engaged" in work. This is used to set the number of hours that must be worked in order to count for WTC purposes, but it also allows the start and finish of a period of work to be defined and intermittent work patterns to be subject to regulation.

See the WTC (Entitlement and Maximum Rate) Regulations 2002 (SI 2002/2005), reg.4.

Subs. (3)

This permits the qualifying conditions for WTC to be varied between different **1.364** claimants. Regulation 4 of the Working Tax Credit (Entitlement and Maximum Rate) Regulations 2002 provides that the minimum work level is 16 hours a week for those with children, those over 50, and those suffering disabilities (carrying forward the tests from WFTC, New Deal 50 Plus, and DPTC) but 30 hours a week for other claimants aged 25 or over. No WTC is to be payable to those aged under 25 unless one of the "16-hour" tests applies to them.

Subs. (4)

1.365 This provides that responsibility for a child or qualifying young person may be defined differently for WTC purposes to the definition under s.8 for CTC purposes. This links with s.12, the childcare element of WTC. However, the regulations have not to date adopted any distinction.

Maximum rate

1.366 **11.**—(1) The maximum rate at which a person or persons may be entitled to working tax credit is to be determined in the prescribed manner.

(2) The prescribed manner of determination must involve the inclusion of an element which is to be included in the case of all persons entitled to working tax credit.

(3) The prescribed manner of determination must also involve the inclusion of an element in respect of the person, or either or both of the persons, engaged in qualifying remunerative work—

- (a) having a physical or mental disability which puts him at a disadvantage in getting a job, and
- (b) satisfying such other conditions as may be prescribed.

(4) The element specified in subsection (2) is to be known as the basic element of working tax credit and the element specifiedin subsection (3) is to be known as the disability element of working tax credit.

(5) The prescribed manner of determination may involve the inclusion of such other elements as may be prescribed.

(6) The other elements may (in particular) include—

- (a) an element in respect of the person, or either of the persons or the two taken together, being engaged in qualifying remunerative work to an extent prescribed for the purposes of this paragraph;
- (b) an element in respect of the persons being the members of a married couple or an unmarried couple,
- (c) an element in respect of the person not being a member of a married couple or an unmarried couple but being responsible for a child or qualifying young person;
- (d) an element in respect of the person, or either or both of the persons, being severely disabled; and
- (e) an element in respect of the person, or either or both of the persons, being over a prescribed age, satisfying prescribed conditions and having been engagedin qualifying remunerative work for not longer than a prescribed period.

(7) A person has a physical or mental disability which puts him at a disadvantage in getting a job, or is severely disabled, for the purposes of this section only if—

- (a) he satisfies prescribed conditions, or
- (b) prescribed conditions exist in relation to him.

AMENDMENTS

For the purposes of applying this section to polygamous units, Tax Credits (Polygamous Marriages) Regulations 2003 (SI 2003/742), reg.10 omits subs.(6)(c) and introduces alternative wording to subss.(3) and (6).

Definitions

"child"—see s.8(3).
"married couple"—see s.3(5).
"physical or mental disability"—see subs.(7).
"prescribed"—see s.67.
"qualifying young person"—see s.8(4).
"severely disabled"—see subs.(7).
"unmarried couple"—see s.3(6).

General Note

This parallels s.9 for WTC. Subsection (1) allows the determination of WTC rates to be set by regulations, but subss.(2) and (4) require that anyone entitled to WTC must receive a basic element of credit. There must also be an additional disability element in appropriate cases (carrying forward the policy of DPTC): subss.(3) and (4). Subsection (7) sets the test for the disability element in terms reflecting the terms of award of DPTC and DWA under the previous law (SSCBA 1992, s.129). There may also be a childcare element, but this is provided for in s.12. Subsections (5) and (6) are purely permissive. Effect is given to these provisions by the WTC (Entitlement and Maximum Rate) Regulations 2002 (SI 2002/2005). **1.367**

Childcare element

12.—(1) The prescribed manner of determination of the maximum rate at which a person or persons may be entitled to working tax credit may involve the inclusion, in prescribed circumstances, of a childcare element. **1.368**

(2) A childcare element is an element in respect of a prescribed proportion of so much of any relevant childcare charges as does not exceed a prescribed amount.

(3) "Childcare charges" are charges of a prescribed description incurred in respect of childcare by the person, or either or both of the persons, by whom a claim for working tax credit is made.

(4) "Childcare", in relation to a person or persons, means care provided—

(a) for a child of a prescribed description for whom the person is responsible, or for whom either or both of the persons is or are responsible, and
(b) by a person of a prescribed description.

(5) The descriptions of persons prescribed under subsection (4)(b) may include descriptions of persons approved in accordance with a scheme made by the appropriate national authority under this subsection.

(6) "The appropriate national authority" means—

(a) in relation to care provided in England, the Secretary of State,
(b) in relation to care provided in Scotland, the Scottish Ministers,
(c) in relation to care provided in Wales, the National Assembly for Wales, and
(d) in relation to care provided in Northern Ireland, the Department of Health, Social Services and Public Safety.

(7) The provision made by a scheme under subsection (5) must involve the giving of approvals, in accordance with criteria determined by or under the scheme, by such of the following as the scheme specifies—

(a) the appropriate national authority making the scheme;
(b) one or more specified persons or bodies or persons or bodies of a specified description, and
(c) persons or bodies accredited under the scheme in accordance with criteria determined by or under it.
(8) A scheme under subsection (5) may authorise—
(a) the making of grants or loans to, and
(b) the charging of reasonable fees by, persons and bodies giving approvals.

AMENDMENTS

1. Subsections (3) and (4) are modified, as they apply to polygamous units, by Tax Credits (Polygamous Marriages) Regulations 2003 (SI 2003/742), reg.11.

DEFINITIONS

"appropriate national authority"—see subs.(6).
"child"—see s.8(3).
"childcare"—see subs.(4).
"childcare charges"—see subs.(3).
"maximum rate"—see s.11(1).
"prescribed"—see s.67.
"tax credit"—see s.1(2).

GENERAL NOTE

1.369 The childcare element was introduced to family credit in response to a successful discrimination challenge to the previous law before the European Court of Justice in *Meyers v Adjudication Officer*, Case C-116/94 [1995] All E.R. (EC) 705. Successive governments have made it more generous, and it is now given further prominence by its own section in this Act. However, the section is in form entirely permissive, even if the failure to implement it at all might invite a further challenge to the European Court. Subsections (2)–(4) provide that the element is a credit for a part of the charges incurred by a claimant for "childcare" provided for prescribed children by prescribed persons. Regulation 7 of the Tax Credits (Income Thresholds and Determination of Rates) Regulations 2002 (SI 2002/2008) specifies this proportion to be 70 per cent. The important issue here is the identity of those who may provide the childcare. Government policy is that childcare providers should be licensed or supervised. But the way in which that is to be done is a devolved matter for the separate governments of England, Scotland, Wales and Northern Ireland. This reflects the fact that both education and social welfare functions are now functions of the separate national authorities. Subsections (5)–(8) give effect to this. Responsibility for both policy and operation of the childcare registration rules is therefore outside the responsibilities of the Inland Revenue and outside the jurisdiction of the appeal tribunals.

Rate

Rate

1.370 **13.**—(1) Where, in the case of a person or persons entitled to a tax credit, the relevant income does not exceed the income threshold (or his or their entitlement arises by virtue of section 7(2)), the rate at which he is or they are entitled to the tax credit is the maximum rate for his or their case.

(2) Regulations shall make provision as to the manner of determining the rate (if any) at which a person is, or persons are, entitled to a tax credit in any other case.

(3) The manner of determination prescribed under subsection (2)—
(a) may involve the making of adjustments so as to avoid fractional amounts, and
(b) may include provision for securing that, where the rate at which a person or persons would be entitled to a tax credit would be less than a prescribed rate, there is no rate in his or their case.

DEFINITIONS

"the income threshold"—see s.7(1)(a).
"maximum rate"—see ss.9(1) and 11(1).
"prescribed"—see s.67.
"relevant income"—see s.7(3).
"tax credit"—see s.1(2).

GENERAL NOTE

This short section supplements s.7 in defining the maximum rate of WTC for a claimant, and a minimum level of payment, and provides for regulations to determine these. See the Tax Credits (Income Thresholds and Determination of Rates) Regulations 2002 (SI 2002/2008), which set out a multi-stage formula. 1.371

Decisions

Initial decisions 1.372

14.—(1) On a claim for a tax credit the Board must decide—
(a) whether to make an award of the tax credit, and
(b) if so, the rate at which to award it.

(2) Before making their decision the Board may by notice—
(a) require the person, or [either or both] [any or all][1] of the persons, by whom the claim is made to provide any information or evidence which the Board consider they may need for making their decision, or
(b) require any person of a prescribed description to provide any information or evidence of a prescribed description which the Board consider they may need for that purpose, by the date specified in the notice.

(3) The Board's power to decide the rate at which to award a tax credit includes power to decide to award it at a nil rate.

AMENDMENTS

1. Subsection (2) is modified in its application to polygamous units by Tax Credits (Polygamous Marriages) Regulations 2003 (SI 2003/742), reg.12.

DEFINITIONS

"claim"—see s.3(8).
"the Board"—see s.67.
"tax credit"—see s.1(2).

GENERAL NOTE

1.373 This section imposes a duty on the Inland Revenue to decide a claim properly made under s.3 by making an award (or not), but it sets no time limit on that decision. An award is a decision to pay the tax credit. It is not a decision on entitlement. That is made later, under s.18. This explains the section title "initial decisions" (in the first draft of the Bill it was "provisional decisions"). Section 7(10) provides that the Inland Revenue may make this decision on the basis of an estimate. A decision under subs.(1) can be appealed (s.38).

This imposes the formal duty to deal with a claim by making or refusing an award. The Revenue may use the power to estimate the income of claimants under s.7(10) rather than wait for information from an examination of the claim. Or it may make an award and examine the claim more thoroughly afterwards. A decision to award or refuse under this subsection is subject to appeal: s.38(1). However, Revenue practice is to attempt to deal with any such appeal by a settlement under the terms of s.54 of the Taxes Managements Act 1970. See Code of Practice 23 and the note to s.39 below.

Subs. (2)
This empowers the Inland Revenue to require further information before making the decision by notice (see s.45 as to the notice). Penalties attach to failure to reply to a notice or to wrong replies (ss.31 and 32). The subsection also permits information to be required from others. This has been applied by the Tax Credits (Claims and Notifications) Regulations 2002 (SI 2002/2014), regs 30–32 to employers and those providing childcare.

Inland Revenue practice appears not to be using this section and those that follow as drafted. Subsection (2) gives the Revenue powers to seek information "before making their decision". There are separate powers once an award is made. Revenue practice is to examine claims both before and during the award in the same way. Its general approach is that "we examine claims during the year so we can ensure that the payments we are making match your circumstances and income" (*Code of Practice 23, p. 3*—see at end of volume). In other words, the award is often made and then examined rather than the previous DSS practice of making full enquiries before an award is made and then making retrospective first payments. This is possible for tax credits, as they are based on a full year's claim at a time, in a way that is not possible for most social security benefits, to which individuals have entitlements on a daily or weekly basis. Rather, it follows the approach long used by the Inland Revenue under the PAYE system for taxing employment income. There are separate powers to examine an award under s.16. See further the note to that section. Examinations both before a claim is decided (under this section) and during the award (under s.16) are conducted under the procedure laid down by the Inland Revenue in Code of Practice 23, *Child Tax Credit and Working Tax Credit, Local Office Examinations,* set out in full at the end of the volume. Unlike Revenue enquiries (see s.19), there is no power to stop an examination under this section.

Subs. (3)
This allows the award of a nil rate, so awarding a tax credit without payment. This "has the effect of keeping an entitlement going even though no money is in payment or in process. It makes it easier for the claimant and it makes it easier for us" (Baroness Hollis, House of Lords Grand Committee, May 23, 2002, CWH 146). This again reflects the fact that at this stage the decision is an initial

decision only. It also means that a claimant with a nil award can ask for a review to deal with a change of circumstances rather than having to make a new claim. This gives a practical solution to a recurring problem under the SSAA 1992 and the SSA 1998 of reviews, revisions and supersessions. The adoption of this practice will, in particular, avoid some of the more awkward aspects of supersession.

Revised decisions after notifications

15.—(1) Where notification of a change of circumstances increasing the maximum rate at which a person or persons may be entitled to a tax credit is given in accordance with regulations under section 6(1), the Board must decide whether (and, if so, how) to amend the award of the tax credit made to him or them. 1.374

(2) Before making their decision the Board may by notice—

(a) require the person by whom the notification is given to provide any information or evidence which the Board consider they may need for making their decision; or

(b) require any person of a prescribed description to provide any information or evidence of a prescribed description which the Board consider they may need for that purpose,

by the date specified in the notice.

DEFINITIONS

"the Board"—see s.67.
"maximum rate"—see ss.9(1) and 11(1).
"prescribed"—see s.67.
"tax credit"—see s.1(2).

GENERAL NOTE

Section 6 makes provision for a claimant to tell the Inland Revenue of a change of circumstances that should or may increase the tax credit to be awarded. This section imposes a duty on the Inland Revenue to consider if the award made under s.14 should be amended if such a notification is given (subs.(1)). The decision, including a decision not to amend, is appealable (s.38). Subsection (2) gives the Inland Revenue the same powers to enquire as s.14(2). The same provisions about notice (s.45) and penalties (ss.31 and 32) apply. Following the comment in s.14, it may be noted that although the heading of the section refers to revision, the text of the section does not. The power in this section is to "amend". That is the term used in the TMA 1970 when either the taxpayer or the Inland Revenue changes a tax return (see ss.9ZA and 9ZB of the TMA 1970). 1.375

Examinations conducted under subs.(2) are covered by Inland Revenue Code of Practice 23, *Child Tax Credit and Working Tax Credit, Local Office Examinations,* set out at the end of this volume. Unlike Revenue enquiries (see s.19), there is no power to stop an examination under this section.

It is understood that the standard practice of the Inland Revenue is to make all initial decisions on the basis of the previous year's income using the power in s.7(10). Where a claim form indicates that the current year's income should be used, the Inland Revenue then makes an immediate revision under this section.

Other revised decisions

16.—(1) Where, at any time during the period for which an award of a tax credit is made to a person or persons, the Board have reasonable grounds for believing— 1.376

(a) that the rate at which the tax credit has been awarded to him or them for the period differs from the rate at which he is, or they are, entitled to the tax credit for the period; or

(b) that he has, or they have, ceased to be, or never been, entitled to the tax credit for the period, the Board may decide to amend or terminate the award.

(2) Where, at any time during the period for which an award of a tax credit is made to a person or persons, the Board believe—

(a) that the rate at which a tax credit has been awarded to him or them for the period may differ from the rate at which he is, or they are, entitled to it for the period, or

(b) that he or they may have ceased to be, or never been, entitled to the tax credit for the period,

the Board may give a notice under subsection (3).

(3) A notice under this subsection may—

(a) require the person, or either or both of the persons, to whom the tax credit was awarded to provide any information or evidence which the Board consider they may need for considering whether to amend or terminate the award under subsection (1); or

(b) require any person of a prescribed description to provide any information or evidence of a prescribed description which the Board consider they may need for that purpose,

by the date specified in the notice.

AMENDMENTS

Subsection (3) is modified as it appplies to polygamous units by Tax Credits (Polygamous Marriages) Regulations 2003 (SI 2003/742), reg.13.

DEFINITIONS

"the Board"—see s.67.
"tax credit"—see s.1(2).

GENERAL NOTE

1.377 The procedure laid down in this section gives the Board flexibility to alter a decision at any time because the Inland Revenue has "reasonable grounds to believe" that a change is appropriate (subs.(1)). These general terms reflect the flexibility given to the Secretary of State under the SSA 1998, and transferred to the Board by the TCA 1999. But it is clear that, unlike that under the TCA 1999, the procedure is not a mirror of the 1998 Act procedure. As noted in s.15, the drafter has deliberately avoided the revision and supersession language of both the SSAA 1992 and the SSA 1998. Despite the heading of the section, the operative power is to "amend" or "terminate" an award. Both this section and s.15 also avoid introducing the troublesome distinction between revisions and supersessions under the SSA 1998.

The Board has power to give notice if it "believes" that the award of a tax credit may be wrong (subs.(2)). As might be expected, this is wider than the power to amend or terminate. The notice may require information or evidence from claimants and others, as defined in regulations (subs.(3)). Current regulations empower the Inland Revenue to seek information from employers and childcare providers (see note to s.14). Penalties attach to the failure to respond or to a false response (ss.31 and 32).

As noted under s.14 above, the Revenue follow a common practice for examining claims both before awards are made and of awards once made. See the Inland Revenue Code of Practice 23, *Child Tax Credit and Working Tax Credit, Local Office Examinations,* set out at the end of this volume. In practice, the Revenue uses the power to undertake an examination during the period of award where previous practice would more often have been to make enquiries before the award was made. The result is that more adjustments to awards are made than occurs with other benefits. This is also partly because an award of a tax credit if for a whole year, and depends on the income and circumstances of the whole year. Previously, an award of working families' tax credit was for 26 weeks, and was based mainly on past income and circumstances. Unlike Revenue enquiries (see s.19), there is no power to stop an examination under this section.

Final notice

17.—(1) Where a tax credit has been awarded for the whole or part of a tax year— **1.378**

(a) for awards made on single claims, the Board must give a notice relating to the tax year to the person to whom the tax credit was awarded, and

(b) for awards made on joint claims, the Board must give such a notice to the persons to whom the tax credit was awarded (with separate copies of the notice for each of them if the Board consider appropriate).

(2) The notice must either—

(a) require that the person or persons must, by the date specified for the purposes of this subsection, declare that the relevant circumstances were as specified or state any respects in which they were not, or

(b) inform the person or persons that he or they will be treated as having declared in response to the notice that the relevant circumstances were as specified unless, by that date, he states or they state any respects in which they were not.

(3) "Relevant circumstances" means circumstances (other than income) affecting—

(a) the entitlement of the person, or joint entitlement of the persons, to the tax credit, or

(b) the amount of the tax credit to which he was entitled, or they were jointly entitled, for the tax year.

(4) The notice must either—

(a) require that the person or persons must, by the date specified for the purposes of this subsection, declare that the amount of the current year income or estimated current year income (depending on which is specified) was the amount, or fell within the range, specified or comply with subsection (5), or

(b) inform the person or persons that he or they will be treated as having declared in response to the notice that the amount of the current year income or estimated current year income (depending on which is specified) was the amount, or fell within the range, specified unless, by that date, he complies or they comply with subsection (5).

(5) To comply with this subsection the person or persons must either—
(a) state the current year income or his or their estimate of the current year income (making clear which); or
(b) declare that, throughout the period to which the award related, subsection (1) of section 7 did not apply to him or them by virtue of subsection (2) of that section.
(6) The notice may—
(a) require that the person or persons must, by the date specified for the purposes of subsection (4), declare that the amount of the previous year income was the amount, or fell within the range, specified or comply with subsection (7), or
(b) inform the person or persons that he or they will be treated as having declared in response to the notice that the amount of the previous year income was the amount, or fell within the range, specified unless, by that date, he complies or they comply with subsection (7).
(7) To comply with this subsection the person or persons must either—
(a) state the previous year income, or
(b) make the declaration specified in subsection (5)(b).
(8) The notice must inform the person or persons that if he or they—
(a) makes or make a declaration under paragraph (a) of subsection (4), or is or are treated as making a declaration under paragraph (b) of that subsection, in relation to estimated current year income (or the range within which estimated current year income fell); or
(b) states or state under subsection (5)(a) his or their estimate of the current year income;

he or they will be treated as having declared in response to the notice that the amount of the (actual) current year income was as estimated unless, by the date specified for the purposes of this subsection, he states or they state the current year income.

(9) "Specified", in relation to a notice, means specified in the notice.
(10) Regulations may—
(a) provide that, in prescribed circumstances, one person may act for another in response to a notice under this section, and
(b) provide that, in prescribed circumstances, anything done by one member of a married couple or an unmarried couple in response to a notice given under this section is to be treated as also done by the other member of the married couple or unmarried couple.

AMENDMENTS

Subsection (10) is modified as it applies to polygamous units by Tax Credits (Polygamous Marriages) Regulations 2003 (SI 2003/742), reg.14.

DEFINITIONS

"the Board"—see s.67.
"current year income"—see s.7(4).
"joint claims"—see s.3(8).
"married couple"—see s.3(5).
"prescribed"—see s.67.
"previous year income"—see s.7(5).

"relevant circumstances"—see subs.(3).
"specified"—see subs.(9).
"tax credit"—see s 1(2).
"tax year"—see s.47.
"unmarried couple"—see s.3(6).

GENERAL NOTE

What are now ss.17 and 18 were originally drafted as one clause. It was divided by amendments in the House of Lords into the notice provisions (s.17) and the decision provisions (s.18), to avoid it being overlong. Together the two sections provide the regime for checking the s.14 initial decision on an award before turning it into an entitlement, and then for making the entitlement decision. The underlying pattern is that the award decision must be made in response to a claim. Payment is then made under the award decision for a tax year. At the end of the tax year, the Inland Revenue uses the s.17 powers to check whether the claimant is, or remains, entitled to the tax credit awarded, or to some higher or lower rate of tax credit. After checking, a "final decision" is made on entitlement. **1.379**

The effect of subs.(1) is that all awards of tax credit must be checked. In every case a notice must be sent to a claimant (or joint claimants). Notices must take one of two forms. One is a demand for a declaration that there has been no change of relevant circumstances (subs.(2)(a)). It can also demand details (or an estimate) of the current year's income (subs.(4)(a)). The other is a notice telling people that it will be assumed that there is no change of circumstances unless any changes are reported by a given date (subs.(2)(b)). It can also tell people that it is assumed that their income is of an assumed level or range unless a declaration is made stating otherwise (subs.(4)(b)). The notice may also take either of those approaches about the previous year's income (subs.(6)). Further provisions are laid down in the Tax Credits (Claims and Notifications) Regulations 2002 (SI 2002/2014). The section also states the ways in which people must comply with these notices. Penalties may be imposed on failures to reply and wrong replies (ss.31 and 32).

Decisions after final notice

18.—(1) After giving a notice under section 17, the Board must decide— **1.380**

(a) whether the person was entitled, or the persons were jointly entitled, to the tax credit, and

(b) if so, the amount of the tax credit to which he was entitled, or they were jointly entitled, for the tax year.

(2) But, subject to subsection (3), that decision must not be made before a declaration or statement has been made in response to the relevant provisions of the notice.

(3) If a declaration or statement has not been made in response to the relevant provisions of the notice on or before the date specified for the purposes of section 17(4), that decision may be made after that date.

(4) In subsections (2) and (3) "the relevant provisions of the notice" means—

(a) the provision included in the notice by virtue of subsection (2) of section 17,

(b) the provision included in the notice by virtue of subsection (4) of that section, and

(c) any provision included in the notice by virtue of subsection (6) of that section.

(5) Where the Board make a decision under subsection (1) on or before the date referred to in subsection (3), they may revise it if a new declaration or statement is made on or before that date.

(6) If the person or persons to whom a notice under section 17 is given is or are within paragraph (a) or (b) of subsection (8) of that section, the Board must decide again—

(a) whether the person was entitled, or the persons were jointly entitled, to the tax credit, and

(b) if so, the amount of the tax credit to which he was entitled, or they were jointly entitled, for the tax year.

(7) But, subject to subsection (8), that decision must not be made before a statement has been made in response to the provision included in the notice by virtue of subsection (8) of section 17.

(8) If a statement has not been made in response to the provision included in the notice by virtue of that subsection on or before the date specified for the purposes of that subsection, that decision may be made after that date.

(9) Where the Board make a decision under subsection (6) on or before the date referred to in subsection (8), they may revise it if a new statement is made on or before that date.

(10) Before exercising a function imposed or conferred on them by subsection (1), (5), (6) or (9), the Board may by notice require the person, or either or both of the persons, to whom the notice under section 17 was given to provide any further information or evidence which the Board consider they may need for exercising the function by the date specified in the notice.

(11) Subject to sections 19 and 20 and regulations under section 21 (and to any revision under subsection (5) or (9) and any appeal)—

(a) in a case in which a decision is made under subsection (6) in relation to a person or persons and a tax credit for a tax year, that decision, and

(b) in any other case, the decision under subsection (1) in relation to a person or persons and a tax credit for a tax year,

is conclusive as to the entitlement of the person, or the joint entitlement of the persons, to the tax credit for the tax year and the amount of the tax credit to which he was entitled, or they were jointly entitled, for the tax year.

AMENDMENTS

Subsection (10) is modified as it applies to polygamous units by Tax Credits (Polygamous Marriages) Regulations 2003 (SI 2003/742), reg.15.

DEFINITIONS

"the Board"—see s.67.
"prescribed"—see s.67.
"relevant provisions of the notice"—see subs.(4).
"tax credit"—see s.1(2).
"tax year"—see s.47.

General Note

See the note to s.17 for the general scheme of which this is part. Subsection (1) of this section imposes the duty on the Inland Revenue to make a decision on entitlement in every case, but only after the s.17 notice procedure has been followed (subs.(2)) or the full time to comply has been allowed (subs.(3)). Subsection (4) links the procedures under this section with the relevant notice provisions in s.17. Subsection (5) allows an entitlement decision under subs.(1) to be revised if there is a reply or further reply from a claimant after a decision has been made. The use of "revise" was avoided in earlier sections in favour of "amend" (despite their headings: see ss.15 and 16), but is here applied to changes to a final decision. Such revisions can be of the whole or only part of the decision. The language avoids attaching formalities or threshold conditions to the process. Subsections (6)–(9) repeat the substance of subss.(1)–(5) for claimants who estimated their current year income in their claims or initial responses to the s.17 notice. In either case, the Inland Revenue may require further information (subs.(10)). The standard penalty regime applies to subs.(10). Subsection (11) makes a subs.(1) or subs.(6) decision conclusive unless it is revised under subss.(5) or (9), or it is appealed under s.38, or it is altered under any of the powers in ss.19–21. **1.381**

Power to enquire

19.—(1) The Board may enquire into— **1.382**

(a) the entitlement of a person, or the joint entitlement of persons, to a tax credit for a tax year, and

(b) the amount of the tax credit to which he was entitled, or they were jointly entitled, for the tax year,

if they give notice to the person, or each of the persons, during the period allowed for the initiation of an enquiry.

(2) As part of the enquiry the Board may by notice—

(a) require the person, or either or both of the persons, to provide any information or evidence which the Board consider they may need for the purposes of the enquiry, or

(b) require any person of a prescribed description to provide any information or evidence of a prescribed description which the Board consider they may need for those purposes, by the date specified in the notice.

(3) On an enquiry the Board must decide—

(a) whether the person was entitled, or the persons were jointly entitled, to the tax credit, and

(b) if so, the amount of the tax credit to which he was entitled, or they were jointly entitled,

for the tax year.

(4) The period allowed for the initiation of an enquiry is the period beginning immediately after the relevant section 18 decision and ending—

(a) if the person, or either of the persons, to whom the enquiry relates is required by section 8 of the Taxes Management Act 1970 (c.9) to make a return, with the day on which the return becomes final (or, if both of the persons are so required and their returns become final on different days, with the later of those days), or

(b) in any other case, one year after the beginning of the relevant section 17 date.

(5) "The relevant section 18 decision" means—

(a) in a case in which a decision must be made under subsection (6) of section 18 in relation to the person or persons and the tax year to which the enquiry relates, that decision; and

(b) in any other case, the decision under subsection (1) of that section in relation to the person or persons and that tax year.

(6) "The relevant section 17 date" means—

(a) in a case in which a statement may be made by the person or persons in response to provision included by virtue of subsection (8) of section 17 in the notice given to him or them under that section in relation to the tax year, the date specified in the notice for the purposes of that subsection, and

(b) in any other case, the date specified for the purposes of subsection (4) of that section in the notice given to him or them under that section in relation to the tax year.

(7) A return becomes final—

(a) if it is enquired into under section 9A of the Taxes Management Act 1970 (c.9), when the enquiries are completed (within the meaning of section 28A of that Act), or

(b) otherwise, at the end of the period specified in subsection (2) of that section in relation to the return.

(8) An enquiry is completed at the time when the Board give notice to the person or persons of their decision under subsection (3); but if the Board give notice to the persons at different times the enquiry is completed at the later of those times.

(9) The person, or either of the persons, to whom the enquiry relates may at any time before such notice is given apply for a direction that the Board must give such a notice.

(10) Such an application is to be heard and determined in the same way as an appeal against a decision under subsection (3), and the General Commissioners or Special Commissioners hearing the application must give the direction applied for unless satisfied that the Board have reasonable grounds for not making the decision or giving the notice.

(11) Where the entitlement of a person, or the joint entitlement of persons, to a tax credit for a tax year has been enquired into under this section, it is not to be the subject of a further notice under subsection (1).

(12) Subject to section 20 and regulations under section 21 (and to any appeal), a decision under subsection (3) in relation to a person or persons and a tax credit for a tax year is conclusive as to the entitlement of the person, or the joint entitlement of the persons, to the tax credit for the tax year and the amount of the tax credit to which he was entitled, or they were jointly entitled, for the tax year.

AMENDMENTS

Subsections. (2), (4) and (9) are modified for polygamous units by Tax Credits (Polygamous Marriages) Regulations 2003 (SI 2003/742), reg.16.

DEFINITIONS

"the Board"—see s.67.
"General Commissioners"—see s.47.
"prescribed"—see s.67.
"Special Commissioners"—see s.47 .
"the relevant section 17 date"—see subs.(6).
"the relevant section 18 decision"—see subs.(5).
"tax credit"—see s.1(2).

GENERAL NOTE

This provision gives the Inland Revenue a broad general power similar to that in s.9A of the TMA 1970 (power to enquire into self-assessment returns) to enquire into the correctness of a s.18 entitlement decision. An enquiry under this section can be opened at any time after the s.18 decision is made until a year after the final date for replying to a s.17 notice, unless the Revenue uses its power to issue a demand for a personal tax return under s.8 of the TMA 1970 on the claimant. A return for a year must be made by January 31 next after the tax year ends (each April) or, if demanded later, three months after it is required. Section 9A (which entitles the Inland Revenue to issue a notice of enquiry into a return under s.8) allows about a year (the period is defined precisely) for a Revenue enquiry to follow a personal return. 1.383

An individual who is the subject of an enquiry has the same power to apply to a tribunal to stop the enquiry as exists for the equivalent income tax provisions, save that the application goes to the appeal tribunal (see s.63), not a tax tribunal.

The power to look into a decision about entitlement to tax credits is referred to both in this section and in practice as an enquiry. This is to be distinguished from an investigation into a claim for, or award of, a tax credit, which is referred to by the Inland Revenue as an examination. The key difference is that an award is provisional, while an enquiry relates to an award that has been or is being finalised to give rise to entitlement. In practice, however, it is likely that any decision to enquire into the entitlement of a claimant for a past year will be accompanied by an examination of any current claim or award and that the enquiry and examination will be conducted and concluded together. An enquiry is to be conducted in accordance with the terms of Inland Revenue Code of Practice 27 *Child Tax Credit and Working Tax Credit, Local Office Enquiries.* This code is, as might be expected, essentially the same as Code of Practice 23 (Local Office Examinations) set out at the end of this volume, and Code of Practice 27 is therefore not set out fully in the volume. The key difference, detailed in Code of Practice 27, is that this section gives a claimant a power to apply to an appeal tribunal to stop an enquiry. No such power exists to stop an examination. However, from a practical point of view examinations are inevitably time-limited as they will be overtaken by the need to consider entitlement at the end of the year, while (based on income tax practice) enquiries could continue for a considerable period in some cases.

Decisions on discovery

20.—(1) Where in consequence of a person's income tax liability being revised the Board have reasonable grounds for believing that a conclusive decision relating to his entitlement to a tax credit for a tax year (whether or not jointly with another person) is not correct, the Board may decide to revise that decision. 1.384

(2) A person's income tax liability is revised—

(a) on the taking effect of an amendment of a return of his under section 9ZA(1) of the Taxes Management Act 1970,

(b) on the issue of a notice of correction under section 9ZB of that Act amending a return of his (provided that he does not give a notice of rejection before the end of the period of thirty days beginning with the date of issue of the notice of correction),

(c) on the amendment of an assessment of his by notice under section 9C of that Act,

(d) on the amendment of a return of his under section 12ABA(3)(a) of that Act,

(e) on the amendment of a return of his under subsection (6)(a) of section 12ABB of that Act after the correction of a partnership return under that section (provided that the amendment does not cease to have effect by reason of the rejection of the correction under subsection (4) of that section),

(f) on the issue of a closure notice under section 28A of that Act making amendments of a return of his;

(g) on the amendment of a return of his under section 28B(4)(a) of that Act,

(h) on the making of an assessment as regards him under section 29(1) of that Act,

(i) on the vacation of the whole or part of an assessment of his under section 32 of that Act,

(j) on giving him relief under section 33 of that Act, or

(k) on the determination (or settlement) of an appeal against the making, amendment or vacation of an assessment or return, or a decision on a claim for relief, under any of the provisions mentioned in paragraphs (c), (f) and (h) to (j).

(3) But no decision may be made under subsection (1)—

(a) unless it is too late to enquire into the person's entitlement under section 19, or

(b) after the period of one year beginning when the person's income tax liability is revised.

(4) Where the Board have reasonable grounds for believing that—

(a) a conclusive decision relating to the entitlement of a person, or the joint entitlement of persons, to a tax credit for a tax year is not correct, and

(b) that is attributable to fraud or neglect on the part of the person, or of either of the persons, or on the part of any person acting for him, or either of them,

the Board may decide to revise that decision.

(5) But no decision may be made under subsection (4)—

(a) unless it is too late to enquire into the entitlement, or joint entitlement, under section 19, or

(b) after the period of five years beginning with the end of the tax year to which the conclusive decision relates.

(6) "Conclusive decision", in relation to the entitlement of a person, or joint entitlement of persons, to a tax credit for a tax year, means—

(a) a decision in relation to it under section 18(1), (5), (6) or (9) or 19(3) or a previous decision under this section, or

(b) a decision under regulations under section 21 relating to a decision within paragraph (a),

including a decision made on an appeal against such a decision.

(7) Subject to any subsequent decision under this section and to regulations under section 21 (and to any appeal), a decision under subsection (1) or (4) in relation to a person or persons and a tax credit for a tax year is conclusive as to the entitlement of the person, or the joint entitlement of the persons, to the tax credit for the tax year and the amount of the tax credit to which he was entitled, or they were jointly entitled, for the tax year.

AMENDMENTS

Subsection (4) is modified as it applies to polygamous units by Tax Credits (Polygamous Marriages) Regulations 2003 (SI 2003/742), reg.17.

CROSS-REFERENCES

TMA 1970: 1.385

s.9ZA	Amendment of personal or trustee return by taxpayer
s.9ZB	Correction of personal return by taxpayer
s.9C	Amendment of self-assessment during enquiry to prevent loss of tax
s.12ABA	Amendment of partnership return by taxpayer
s.12ABB	Correction of partnership return by Revenue
s.28A	Completion of enquiry into personal or trustee return
s.28B	Completion of enquiry into partnership return
s.29	Assessment where loss of tax discovered
s.32	Double assessment
s.33	Error or mistake

DEFINITIONS

"conclusive decision"—see subs.(6).
"income tax"—see ICTA 1988, s.1.
"prescribed"—see: s.67.
"tax credit"—see s.1(2).

GENERAL NOTE

Discovery is the traditional term used for finding out or taking informed guesses about undisclosed income for income tax purposes. The power to make assessments where loss of tax is discovered is in s.29 of the TMA 1970. This section is wider than that, although in part it flows from it. Section 29 allows an officer who discovers unassessed tax or excessive relief to make an assessment of the amount which, in the officer's opinion, ought to be charged to tax, and also imposes other conditions before the power can be used. This section, by contrast, allows action by the Inland Revenue in two sets of circumstances. 1.386

The first is if the Inland Revenue has reasonable grounds for believing an otherwise conclusive decision about tax credit (defined in subs.(6)) is not correct because of a revision of income tax liability (subs.(1)). The Inland Revenue may act if one of the TMA 1970 powers listed in subs.(2) has been used for a revision. These include s.29 and also the powers to revisit personal and partnership tax returns and decisions made by settlement or on appeal. Revisions under this power can be made only if it is too late to use s.19. And they cannot be made unless the revision is made within a year of the income tax revision (subs.(3)).

The second power (in subs.(4)) arises where the Inland Revenue has reasonable grounds to believe that an otherwise conclusive decision is wrong because of "fraud or neglect". That phrase is not defined in this Act but is the phrase used in similar TMA 1970 provisions (such as s.29). This power cannot be used if the s.19 power is available, and is subject to a time limit of five years from the end of the tax year to which the tax credit relates (subs.(5)). This is the usual time limit for similar actions in the TMA 1970.

A decision made under this section is itself conclusive, subject only to further decisions under this section or on appeal or because of official error (subs.(7)).

Decisions subject to official error

1.387 **21.**—Regulations may make provision for a decision under section 14(1), 15(1), 16(1), 18(1), (5), (6) or (9), 19(3) or 20(1) or (4) to be revised in favour of the person or persons to whom it relates if it is incorrect by reason of official error (as defined by the regulations).

General Note

1.388 "Official error" is defined by the Tax Credits (Official Error) Regulations 2003 (SI 2003/692). See the note on those regulations. The provision is significantly narrower than the equivalent provision for income tax in s.33 of the TMA 1970 (error or mistake), which applies to any error or mistake.

Information etc. requirements: supplementary

1.389 **22.**—(1) Regulations may make provision as to the manner and form in which—

(a) information or evidence is to be provided in compliance with a requirement imposed by a notice under section 14(2), 15(2), 16(3), 18(10) or 19(2), or

(b) a declaration or statement is to be made in response to a notice under section 17.

(2) Regulations may make provision as to the dates which may be specified in a notice under section 14(2), 15(2), 16(3), 17, 18(10) or 19(2).

General Note

1.390 These regulation-making powers are necessary because the standard regulations applying to social security decision-making (the Social Security and Child Support (Decisions and Appeals) Regulations 1999 (SI 1999/991)) do not apply and there are no equivalents in the TMA 1970. The regulations made under these powers are the Tax Credits (Claims and Notifications) Regulations 2002, (SI 2002/2014).

Notice of decisions

1.391 **23.**—(1) When a decision is made under section 14(1), 15(1), 16(1), 18(1), (5), (6) or (9), 19(3) or 20(1) or (4) or regulations under section 21, the Board must give notice of the decision to the person, or each of the persons, to whom it relates.

(2) Notice of a decision must state the date on which it is given and include details of any right to appeal against the decision under section 38.

(3) Notice need not be given of a decision made under section 14(1) or 18(1) or (6) on the basis of declarations made or treated as made by the person or persons in response to the notice given to him or them under section 17 if—

(a) that notice, or
(b) in the case of a decision under subsection (6) of section 18, that notice or the notice of the decision under subsection (1) of that section,

stated what the decision would be and the date on which it would be made.

DEFINITION

"the Board"—see s.67.

GENERAL NOTE

This section requires the Inland Revenue to adopt the same approach as for social security decisions of giving formal notice of every decision (save in limited cases where notice has already been given). The notice must set out any appeal rights. Section 45 makes provision for the form of a notice. Further details are laid down in the Tax Credits (Claims and Notifications) Regulations 2002 (SI 2002/2014). However, it may be viewed as significant that this provision is in primary legislation, while the equivalent for social security purposes (Social Security and Child Support (Decisions and Appeals) Regulations 1999 (SI 1999/991), reg.28) is made by regulation only. It is suggested therefore that the mandatory terms of subs.(1) (the Board *must* give notice) and subs.(2) (the notice *must* state) are not amenable to the somewhat relaxed approach to formalities applied to the social security equivalent (see the note to reg.28 of those Regulations). In particular, if no notice is given, it is arguable that no effective decision has been made, or alternatively that the decision is not final and the appeal period cannot start running. **1.392**

Payment

Payments

24.—(1) Where the Board have made an award of a tax credit, the amount of the tax credit awarded must be paid to the person to whom the award is made, subject to subsections (2) and (3). **1.393**

(2) Where an award of a tax credit is made to the members of a married couple or an unmarried couple, payments of the tax credit, or of any element of the tax credit, are to be made to whichever of them is prescribed.

(3) Where an award of a tax credit is made on a claim which was made by one person on behalf of another, payments of the tax credit, or of any element of the tax credit, are to be made to whichever of those persons is prescribed.

(4) Where an award of a tax credit has been made to a person or persons for the whole or part of a tax year, payments may, in prescribed circumstances, continue to be made for any period, after the tax year,

within which he is or they are entitled to make a claim for the tax credit for the next tax year.

(5) Payments made under subsection (4) are to be treated for the purposes of this section and the following provisions of this Part as if they were payments of the tax credit for the next tax year.

(6) Subject to section 25, payments of a tax credit must be made by the Board.

(7) Regulations may make provision about the time when and the manner in which a tax credit, or any element of a tax credit, is to be paid by the Board.

(8) If the regulations make provision for payments of a tax credit, or any element of a tax credit, to be made by the Board by way of a credit to a bank account or other account notifiedto the Board, the regulations may provide that entitlement to the tax credit or element is dependent on an account having been notifiedto the Board in accordance with the regulations.

AMENDMENTS

Subsection (2) is modified as it applies to polygamous units by Tax Credits (Polygamous Marriages) Regulations 2003 (SI 2003/742), reg.18.

DEFINITIONS

"claim"—see s.3(8).
"the Board"—see s.67.
"married couple"—see s.3(5).
"prescribed"—see s.67.
"tax credit"—see s.1(2).
"tax year"—see s.47.
"unmarried couple"—see s.3(6).

GENERAL NOTE

1.394 This section imposes a duty on the Inland Revenue to pay the amount of all tax credits, unless payment is made by an employer under s.25. The policy is that the employer will pay the WTC apart from the childcare element (if there is one). The Inland Revenue has stated that it will pay the CTC and the childcare element of WTC to the main carer direct. There is a potential for problems if employers fail to make these payments, and the duty to pay then reverts to the Inland Revenue. Details of how, when and to whom the payment is to be made are provided in the Tax Credits (Payments by the Board) Regulations 2002 (SI 2002/2173). Payment is to be either weekly or four-weekly, where possible to a bank account by credit transfer.

Payments of working tax credit by employers

1.395 **25.**—(1) Regulations may require employers, when making [payments of, or on account of, PAYE income] 1 and in any such other circumstances as may be prescribed, to pay working tax credit, or prescribed elements of working tax credit, to employees.

(2) The regulations may, in particular, include provision—

(a) requiring employers to make payments of working tax credit, or prescribed elements of working tax credit, in accordance with notices given to them by the Board,

(b) for the payment by the Board of working tax credit in cases where an employer does not make payments of working tax credit, or prescribed elements of working tax credit, in accordance with the regulations and with any notices given by the Board,
(c) prescribing circumstances in which employers are not required to make, or to continue making, payments of working tax credit, or prescribed elements of working tax credit,
(d) for the provision of information or evidence for the purpose of enabling the Board to be satisfied whether employers are complying with notices given by the Board and with the regulations,
(e) requiring employers to provide information to employees (in their itemised pay statements or otherwise),
(f) for the funding by the Board of working tax credit paid or to be paid by employers (whether by way of set off against income tax, national insurance contributions or student loan deductions for which they are accountable to the Board or otherwise),
(g) for the recovery by the Board from an employer of funding under para.(f) to the extent that it exceeds the amount of working tax credit paid by the employer,
(h) for the payment of interest at the prescribed rate on sums due from or to the Board, and for determining the date from which interest is to be calculated, and
(i) for appeals with respect to matters arising under the regulations which would otherwise not be the subject of an appeal.

(3) Section 20 of the Taxes Management Act 1970 (c.9) (power to call for documents etc.) applies (with section 20B and 20BB) in relation to an employer's compliance with regulations under this section as in relation to a person's tax liability (but subject to the modifications provided by subsection (4)).

(4) Those sections apply by virtue of subsection (3) as if—
(a) the references to the taxpayer, a taxpayer or a class of taxpayers were to the employer, an employer or a class of employers,
(b) the reference to any provision of the Taxes Acts were to regulations under this section,
(c) the references to the proper assessment or collection of tax were to the proper award or payment of working tax credit,
(d) the reference to an appeal relating to tax were to an appeal relating to compliance with regulations under this section, and
(e) the reference to believing that tax has been, or may have been, lost to the Crown were to believing that the Crown has, or may have, incurred a loss.

(5) In this Part—
"employee" means a person who receives any [payment of, or on account of, PAYE income][1]; and
"employer", in relation to an employee, means a person who makes any such payment to the employee.

(6) [. . .][1]

(7) "Student loan deductions" means deductions in accordance with regulations under section 22(5) of the Teaching and Higher Education Act 1998 (c.30), section 73B(3) of the Education (Scotland) Act 1980

(c.44) or Article 3(5) of the Education (Student Support) (Northern Ireland) Order 1998 (SI 1998/1760 (N.I. 14)).

AMENDMENTS

1. Subsection (6) repealed and words changedby ITEPA 2003, Sch.6, para.265 (April 6, 2003).

DEFINITIONS

"employee"—see subs.(5).
"employer"—*ibid.*
"PAYE income"—see ITEPA 2003, s.683.
"prescribed"—see s.67.
"student loan deduction"—see subs.(7).
"working tax credit"—see s.10.

GENERAL NOTE

The Chancellor of the Exchequer announced in the 2004 Budget that measures would be taken to transfer the duty to pay working tax credit from employers back to the Inland Revenue. No details had been announced at the date of writing.

1.396 Unusually, this section deals with WTC only. It continues the policy introduced by s.6 of the TCA 1999 to pay WTC where possible to employees in their pay packets. It does not apply to CTC, which must be paid by the Inland Revenue. The text is derived from that section. The section empowers regulations to impose the duty on employers, and gives the Inland Revenue the same powers as for income tax to ensure compliance by employers. Under the rewording following ITEPA 2003, the powers are contingent on an employer making PAYE payments. This is based on the provisions under ITEPA, Pt 12 (Pay As You Earn) and regulations made under that Part. Section 683 of ITEPA defines "PAYE income" as including not only PAYE employment income but also PAYE pension income and PAYE social security income. However, the duty in this section applies only to employers and therefore to PAYE employment income. This is any taxable earnings or taxable specific income from an employment (ITEPA, s.10). The powers are wide and include the necessary powers to allow employers to set off the amount of WTC paidout against income tax, NI contributions or student loan repayments collected in. See further the Working Tax Credit (Payment by Employers) Regulations 2002 (SI 2002/2172).

For the penalty regime supporting the operation of this section, see s.33.

Liability of officers for sums paid to employers

1.397 **26.**—(1) Regulations may provide that where—

(a) an employer which is a body corporate has failed to repay any funding to the Board in accordance with regulations made under s.25(2)(g); and
(b) the provision of the funding, or the failure by the employer to repay the funding, appears to the Board to be attributable to fraud or neglect on the part of one or more individuals who, at the time of the fraud or neglect, were officers of the body corporate ("culpable officers"), the culpable officers are required to pay to the Board the amount of funding recoverable by the Board from the employer.

(2) Regulations under this section must include provision—

(a) for any amount paid to the Board by a culpable officer in accordance with the regulations to be deducted from the amount of funding liable to be repaid by the employer,

(b) for the amount which a culpable officer is liable to pay under the regulations to be reduced where the amount of funding recoverable from the employer is reduced by payments made to the Board by the employer, and

(c) for the Board to repay to a culpable officer the amount (if any) by which the amount that he has paid to the Board pursuant to the regulations exceeds the reduced amount that he is liable to pay by virtue of paragraph (b).

(3) Regulations under this section may include provision—

(a) requiring payments by culpable officers to be made in accordance with notices given to them by the Board,

(b) for determining, in cases of an employer in relation to which there is more than one culpable officer, the proportion of the amount of funding recoverable from the employer that is payable by each culpable officer,

(c) for the payment of interest at the prescribed rate on sums due to or from the Board, and for determining the date from which interest is to be calculated, and

(d) for appeals with respect to matters arising under the regulations.

(4) "Officer", in relation to a body corporate, means—

(a) any director, manager, secretary or other similar officer of the body corporate, or any person purporting to act as such, and

(b) in a case where the affairs of the body corporate are managed by its members, any member of the body corporate exercising functions of management with respect to it or purporting to do so.

DEFINITIONS

"the Board"—see s.67.
"employee"—see s.25(5).
"employer"—*ibid.*
"officer"—see subs.(4).
"prescribed"—see s.67.

GENERAL NOTE

This regulation-making power follows the equivalent provision in s.11 of the TCA 1999. It provides for regulations to be made to impose a liability directly on any "culpable officer" of a "body corporate" for excess funding paid from the Inland Revenue because of fraud or neglect by that officer. However, unlike s.11 of the TCA 1999, this section does not rely on social security legislation, but provides for specific regulations to be introduced. No regulations have been made to date. **1.398**

Rights of employees

27.—Schedule 1 (rights of employees not to suffer unfair dismissal or other detriment) has effect. **1.399**

DEFINITIONS

"employee"—see s.25(5).

GENERAL NOTE

1.400 This section introduces Sch.1. Both this section and the Schedule are based on s.7 of, and Sch.3 to, the TCA 1999. The aim is to provide employees with direct rights to ensure that employers do not discriminate against them because of WTC. The underlying fear is that employers would rather get rid of employees than implement the WTC process. Schedule 1 makes the necessary amendments to the Employment Rights Act (GB) and Order (NI) to give employees a right not to suffer detriment and a right not to be unfairly dismissed because of tax credits. The text of Sch.1 is not included here as it is a matter of employment law.

Overpayments

1.401 **28.**—(1) Where the amount of a tax credit paid for a tax year to a person or persons exceeds the amount of the tax credit to which he is entitled, or they are jointly entitled, for the tax year (as determined in accordance with the provision made by and by virtue of sections 18 to 21), the Board may decide that the excess, or any part of it, is to be repaid to the Board.

(2) In this Part such an excess is referred to as an overpayment.

(3) For overpayments made under awards on single claims, the person to whom the tax credit was awarded is liable to repay the amount which the Board decide is to be repaid.

(4) For overpayments made under awards on joint claims, the persons to whom the tax credit was awarded are jointly and severally liable to repay the amount which the Board decide is to be repaid unless the Board decide that each is to repay a specified part of that amount.

(5) Where it appears to the Board that there is likely to be an overpayment of a tax credit for a tax year under an award made to a person or persons, the Board may, with a view to reducing or eliminating the overpayment, amend the award or any other award of any tax credit made to the person or persons; but this subsection does not apply once a decision is taken in relation to the person or persons for the tax year under section 18(1).

(6) Where the Board decide under section 16 to terminate an award of a tax credit made to a person or persons on the ground that at no time during the period to which the award related did the person or persons satisfy—

(a) section 8(1) (if the award related to child tax credit), or

(b) section 10(1) (if it related to working tax credit),

the Board may decide that the amount paid under the award, or any part of it, is to be treated for the purposes of this Part (apart from subsection (5)) as an overpayment.

DEFINITIONS

"the Board"—see s.67.
"joint claim"—see s.3(8).
"overpayment"—see subs.(2).

"single claim"—see s.3(8).
"tax credit"—see s.1(2).
"tax year"—see s.47.

General Note

An overpayment is an excess of a tax credit awarded and paid as against the amount of tax credit to which a claimant is entitled under a final decision about entitlement (subs.(2)). This will usually arise where the final decision on entitlement is for a lesser amount than the amount awarded. It may also arise under a later revision under s.19 or 20, or when an award was made that should not have been made (subs.(6)). Subsection (1) gives a power to (but does not impose a duty on) the Inland Revenue to collect overpayments. The decision of the Inland Revenue whether or not to collect an overpayment is not subject to appeal, and is not conditional on the fulfilment of any test by the claimant. This is a different approach from that taken for social security purposes, and by the previous tax credits regime, where it had to be shown in most cases that the claimant had caused the overpayment by a failure to disclose, or a misrepresentation of, a material fact. In addition, the decision on recoverability for social security purposes is subject to appeal. 1.402

The Inland Revenue published in November 2003 *New Tax Credits – Ensuring compliance*. This notes the high level of overpayments estimated to have been made under the working families' tax credit system. The estimate was that overpayments were an estimated 10–14 per cent of the total of £5.05 billion awarded for 2000–01. The paper sets out the Inland Revenue strategy for using the powers in TCA 2002 to combat fraudulent claims and for using the information powers in the Act.

Overpayments proved a generally controversial subject in the first year of operation of the TCA 2002. There was a very considerable level of overpayment in the initial start-up period. The *Financial Statement and Budget Report* for 2004–05, (H.M. Treasury), Table C8 records an increase in net public expenditure on tax credits between 2002–03 and 2003–04 of £1.4 billion from £3.4 billion to £4.8 billion, with net cost falling back in 2004–05 to £4.1 billion. This was significantly more than the estimate in the Report for 2003–04. The 2004–05 Report comments at para.C67 that this also involves some £0.5 billion "reprofiling of payment schedules" (overpayments recovered outside the original award periods) in these years. On this basis there were many very substantial overpayments made on initial awards.

Recovery of overpayments

29.—(1) Where an amount is liable to be repaid by a person or persons under section 28, the Board must give him, or each of them, a notice specifying the amount. 1.403

(2) The notice must state which of subsections (3) to (5) is to apply in relation to the amount or any specifiedpart of the amount; and a notice may at any time be replaced by another notice containing a different statement.

(3) Where a notice states that this subsection applies in relation to an amount (or part of an amount), it is to be treated for the purposes of Part 6 of the Taxes Management Act 1970 (c.9) (collection and recovery) as if it were tax charged in an assessment and due and payable by the person or persons to whom the notice was given at the end of the period of 30 days beginning with the day on which the notice is given.

(4) Where a notice states that this subsection applies in relation to an amount (or part of an amount), it may, subject to provision made by regulations, be recovered by deduction from payments of any tax credit under an award made for any period to the person, or either or both of the persons, to whom the notice was given.

(5) Where a notice states that this subsection applies in relation to an amount (or part of an amount), [PAYE regulations][1] apply to it as if it were an underpayment of tax for a previous year of assessment by the person or persons to whom the notice was given.

AMENDMENTS

1. Words amended by ITEPA 2003, Sch.6, para.266 (April 6, 2003). Subs.(4) is modified by the Tax Credits (Polygamous Marriages) Regulations 2003 (SI 2003/742), reg.12 as it applies to polygamous units.

DEFINITIONS

"the Board"—see s.67.
"overpayment"—see s.28(2).

GENERAL NOTE

1.404 There is no appeal against a decision about either recovery or recoverability under this Act. The decision that can be appealed is the entitlement decision under which the overpayment arises. That decision must be notified to the claimant under s.23, save where one of the exceptions in s.23(3) applies. It may be anticipated that, following equivalent experience in social security cases, some recipients will only object, and attempt to appeal, when they receive notice of an overpayment under this section rather than notice of the decision that gives rise to the overpayment. Whether this can amount to an effective and timely appeal against the entitlement decision will depend on part on how and when the required notices are given, and is for decision under s.39.

This section is the equivalent of s.30 of the TMA 1970. The Inland Revenue may give a formal notice to someone whom it has decided has been overpaid tax credit. The notice may activate all or any of three alternative methods of recovering the overpaid tax credit. The first, under subs.(3), is by using ss.60–70A of the TMA 1970. These empower the Inland Revenue's collection and recovery powers for unpaid income tax demands. These allow distraint and action in both civil courts and magistrates' courts. Subsection (4) entitles the Inland Revenue to collect the overpayment by deducting it from other payments of tax credit: see further Tax Credits (Payments by the Board) Regulations 2002 (SI 2002/2173), reg.12A, inserted by the Tax Credits (Miscellaneous Amendments) Regulations 2004 (SI 2004/762), reg.18. Subsection (5), likely to be used for WTC, empowers the collection by an alteration to the PAYE coding for the claimant (where the tax credit is paid through an employer) in the same way as underpaid past income tax. These powers also apply to interest charged under s.37. The Inland Revenue did not have power to use the PAYE system to recover overpayments in 2003–04, and therefore used the power to deduct overpayments from other awards of tax credit, or carried the overpayments forward to 2004–05.

The effect on an ongoing basis of changes in this way will be to increase the amount of income tax, or reduce the amount of tax credit, over the following year, so further severing the immediate practical link that social security benefits usually seek to achieve between the needs of the claimant and the amount received. For example, the award for tax credits in 2003–04 is initially based on the income of 2001–02. If the income for 2003–04 is more than £2,500 higher than that of 2001–02, then there will have been an overpayment of the tax credit for 2003–04, in addition to a probable reduction of tax credits in 2004–05 compared with the previous year. This will be compounded if the overpayment of the previous year is collected by a reduction of the tax credit actually paid in 2004–05.

The Inland Revenue issued a new Code of Practice 26, *What happens if we have paid you too much tax credit?* in December 2003. The full text is set out at the end of the volume. This sets out the Inland Revenue procedure in overpayments cases and its policy for dealing with recovery of overpayments in cases that cause hardship. Any dispute about recovery of an overpayment can take place, if at all, in the civil courts.

Underpayments

30.—(1) Where it has been determined in accordance with the provision made by and by virtue of sections 18 to 21 that a person was entitled, or persons were jointly entitled, to a tax credit for a tax year and either— **1.405**

(a) the amount of the tax credit paid to him or them for that tax year was less than the amount of the tax credit to which it was so determined that he is entitledor they are jointly entitled, or

(b) no payment of the tax credit was made to him or them for that tax year,

the amount of the difference, or of his entitlement or their joint entitlement, must be paid to him or to whichever of them is prescribed.

(2) Where the claim for the tax credit was made by one person on behalf of another, the payment is to be made to whichever of those persons is prescribed.

DEFINITIONS

"prescribed"—see s.67.
"tax credit"—see s.1(2).
"tax year"—see s.47.

GENERAL NOTE

This provision is the converse of s.28. However, the procedure that triggers it is not a mirror of the provisions giving rise to an overpayment. In particular, see the note to s.6 on notifications of changes of circumstances. If there is an underpayment, this section requires the Inland Revenue to make it good. But underpayments, unlike repayments of income tax, or overpayments of tax credit, do not carry interest. Nor does the section impose any time-limit on the payment. **1.406**

Penalties

Incorrect statements etc.

31.—(1) Where a person fraudulently or negligently— **1.407**

(a) makes an incorrect statement or declaration in or in connection with a claim for a tax credit or a notification of a change of circumstances given in accordance with regulations under section 6 or in response to a notice under section 17, or

(b) gives incorrect information or evidence in response to a requirement imposed on him by virtue of section 14(2), 15(2), 16(3), 18(10) or 19(2) or regulations under section 25,

a penalty not exceeding £3,000 may be imposed on him.

(2) Where a person liable to a penalty under subsection (1) is a person making, or who has made, a claim for a tax credit for a period jointly with another and the penalty is imposed—

(a) under paragraph (a) of that subsection in respect of the claim, a notification relating to the tax credit claimed or a notice relating to the tax credit awarded on the claim, or

(b) under paragraph (b) of that subsection in respect of a requirement imposed on him with respect to the tax credit for the period,

a penalty of an amount not exceeding £3,000 may be imposed on the other person unless subsection (3) applies.

(3) This subsection applies if the other person was not, and could not reasonably have been expected to have been, aware that the person liable to the penalty under subsection (1) had fraudulently or negligently made the incorrect statement or declaration or given the incorrect information or evidence.

(4) Where penalties are imposed under subsections (1) and (2) in respect of the same statement, declaration, information or evidence, their aggregate amount must not exceed £3,000.

(5) Where a person acts for another—

(a) in or in connection with a claim or notification referred to in subsection (1), or

(b) in response to a notice so referred to,

subsection (1) applies to him (as well as to any person to whom it applies apart from this subsection).

AMENDMENTS

Subsection (2) is modified as it applies to polygamous units by Tax Credits (Polygamous Marriages) Regulations 2003 (SI 2003/742), reg.20.

DEFINITIONS

"change of circumstances"—see s.(1).
"claim"—see s.3(8).
"joint claim"—*ibid.*
"tax credit"—see s.1(2).

GENERAL NOTE

1.408 The response in this Act to concern about the potential for fraud in the tax credits system by both claimants and employers is the two-stage decision-making process, backed at each stage by wide information powers and a penalty regime applicable to all those who either fail to provide information or who provide wrong information.

Sections 31–34 and Sch.2 set out a full penalty regime to support the operation of tax credits. It is an enhanced version of the provisions of s.9 of, and Sch.4 to, the TCA 1999, and it draws on the approach in Pt X (Penalties, ss.93–107) in the TMA 1970.

This section deals with the problem where anyone required to make a declaration, statement or notification or to give information or evidence does so "incorrectly" and where the person does so "fraudulently or negligently". It applies both to the person making the declaration, etc., and to anyone acting for that person (subs.(5)), and both could be subject to penalty proceedings in connection with the same matter. This wording echoes the terms of s.98(2) of the TMA 1970, the main penalty-imposing section in that Act. The maximum penalty of £3,000 is also the same as that in s.98 (a figure last adjusted in 1989). It is the same level as in s.9(5) of the TCA 1999. The section also makes provision for the penalty to be imposed on both of two joint claimants in appropriate cases, though subject to a joint maximum of £3,000.

The Inland Revenue have published two leaflets of guidance about the exercise of their penalty powers: WTC3, *Tax Credit Penalties, How tax credit examinations are settled*, and WTC4, *Tax Credit penalties, How tax credit enquiries are settled.* They apply to penalties under both this section and s.32. These reflect the differences between examinations (taking place about current claims or awards) and enquiries (taking place when an award is finalised or after entitlement has been established) but otherwise have very similar content. The full text of WTC3 is set out at the end of this volume. The leaflets set out the procedure for dealing with the imposition of penalties and the basis on which the Inland Revenue decide at what level a penalty will be set. The Inland Revenue's practice follows that applying for similar income tax examinations and enquiries. Discounts to the maximum penalty will be applied to reflect: the extent to which the error was disclosed voluntarily by the claimant; the extent to which the claimant has cooperated with the Inland Revenue in the examination or enquiry; the seriousness of the errors or omissions; and whether this is a first or subsequent occasion on which there has been an error or omission. Any decision about a penalty is open to appeal to an appeals tribunal and to a Social Security Commissioner and they are, of course, not bound by these policy statements. However, it is the Inland Revenue's practice to seek settlement of a penalty with the individual under s.54 of the Taxes Management Act 1970. It is rare for an income tax penalty appeal not to be settled at some stage.

Fraudulently or negligently

Those sections in the TMA 1970 have been subject to consideration in the courts on a number of occasions, and it is to be expected that the common phraseology of those sections and these (such as "fraudulently or negligently") will receive a similar interpretation. On this basis, the fraud or neglect of an agent will be regarded as the fraud or neglect of the claimant: *Clixby v Pountney* (1968) 44 T.C. 515. It is clearly established in income tax law that the onus of proving fraud or neglect is on the Inland Revenue. *Hillenbrand v IRC* (1966) 42 T.C. 617 established that there is no presumption of fraud or neglect because of an omission, although the omission might give a factual basis for a decision on this point. However, if the Inland Revenue establish the fraud or neglect, then the burden shifts to the taxpayer to show that any assessment made by the Inland Revenue as a result is incorrect. It is also established that the Inland Revenue does not have to show the precise nature of discovered income: *Hudson v Humbles* (1965) 42 T.C. 380. That is part of the process of making and appealing an assessment. It is suggested that the same approaches would be appropriate here, save that in addition the Inland Revenue and appeal tribunal will be able to take account of evidence gathered for income tax purposes in deciding the outcome of a s.20 review. 1.409

Additionally, since the Human Rights Act 1998 came into effect, it is arguable that this section imposes a "criminal" liability under Art.6(3) of the European Convention on Human Rights. (For the text, see Vol.III of this work). Courts have applied the criminal standard to equivalent provisions in income tax and

VAT legislation. If Art.6(3) applies then close consideration needs to be given to the burden of proof under this section, the evidence available for establishing or resisting the application of the section and the availability of legal aid.

A penalty under this section bears interest under s.37. It is treated as unpaid tax for the purposes of recovery and collection (Sch.2, para.7). Appeals against penalty decisions are dealt with in Sch.2 (see s.34).

Subsections (2) and (3) deal with a problem that is no longer relevant to income tax, namely the case where one of a couple making a joint claim has failed fully to co-operate with the other, so that the declaration is wrong but one of the joint claimants is not aware that this is so. In such cases responsibility remains joint and several unless one of the claimants can show that the defence in subs.(3) applies. This imposes a double test of both fact and reasonableness.

Failure to comply with requirements

1.410 **32.**—(1) Where a person fails—

(a) to provide any information or evidence which he is required to provide by virtue of section 14(2), 15(2), 16(3), 18(10) or 19(2) or regulations under section 25, or

(b) to comply with a requirement imposed on him by a notice under section 17 by virtue of subsection (2)(a), (4)(a) or (6)(a) of that section,

the penalties specified in subsection (2) may be imposed on him.

(2) The penalties are—

(a) a penalty not exceeding £300, and

(b) if the failure continues after a penalty is imposed under paragraph (a), a further penalty or penalties not exceeding £60 for each day on which the failure continues after the day on which the penalty under that paragraph was imposed (but excluding any day for which a penalty under this paragraph has already been imposed).

(3) Where a person fails to give a notification required by regulations under section 6(3), a penalty not exceeding £300 may be imposed on him.

(4) No penalty under subsection (2) may be imposed on a person in respect of a failure after the failure has been remedied.

(5) For the purposes of this section a person is to be taken not to have failed to provide information or evidence, comply with a requirement or give a notification which must be provided, complied with or given by a particular time—

(a) if he provided, complied with or gave it within such further time (if any) as the Board may have allowed,

(b) if he had a reasonable excuse for not providing, complying with or giving it by that time, or

(c) if, after having had such an excuse, he provided, complied with or gave it without unreasonable delay.

(6) Where the members of a married couple or an unmarried couple both fail as mentioned in subsection (1)(b), the aggregate amount of any penalties under subsection (2) imposed on them in relation to their failures must not exceed the amounts specified in that subsection; and where the members of a married couple or an unmarried couple both fail as

mentioned in subsection (3), the aggregate amount of any penalties imposed on them in relation to their failures must not exceed £300.

DEFINITIONS

"the Board"—see s.67.
"married couple"—see s.3(5).
"unmarried couple"—see s.3(6).

GENERAL NOTE

See the note to s.31 on the penalty regime as a whole. This section imposes penalties on those who fail to comply with any notices under s.17, who fail to provide information or evidence under any of the powers to require this, or who fail to give notification of a change of circumstances under s.6. It is a parallel to s.9(1) of the TMA 1970, and replaces s.9(3) of the TCA 1999. In common with those Acts, this section imposes a potential penalty on all failures, regardless of the reason for the failure. There is no test of fraud or negligence. The policy of all these measures is to impose a relatively low initial maximum penalty (£300 in all cases), but then to provide a cumulatively daily penalty as a strong deterrent to those who choose to ignore not only the notices and requirements but also the initial penalty. In each case, the maximum daily rate is £60. But the daily rate stops when the failure is remedied. 1.411

A penalty under this section bears interest under s.37. It is treated as unpaid tax for the purposes of recovery and collection (Sch.2, para.7). Appeals against penalty decisions are dealt with in Sch.2 (see s.34). By contrast with s.31, this section does not demand proof of fraud or negligence, and may therefore impose a civil penalty rather than a criminal penalty for the purposes of the European Convention on Human Rights.

For details of Inland Revenue's practice in setting and dealing with penalties, see the note to s.31 and Inland Revenue leaflets: WTC3, *Tax Credit Penalties, How tax credit examinations are settled*, and WTC4, *Tax Credit penalties, How tax credit enquiries are settled.* The full text of WTC3 is set out at the end of the volume. The Inland Revenue has announced that it will, on a concessionary basis, not seek penalties from those who fail to comply with the mandatory provisions in this section when the award made to the individual is a nil award.

Failure by employers to make correct payments

33.—(1) Where an employer refuses or repeatedly fails to make to an employee payments of tax credits which he is required to make to him by regulations under section 25 and, as a result, the Board make payments to the employee in accordance with regulations under subsection (2)(b) of that section, a penalty not exceeding £3,000 may be imposed on the employer. 1.412

(2) Where an employer has, by reason of his fraud or neglect, not paid to an employee for a tax year the correct amount of any tax credit which he is required by regulations under section 25 to pay to him for that tax year, a penalty not exceeding £3,000 may be imposed on the employer.

(3) But no penalty may be imposed on an employer under subsection (2) in respect of payments which are incorrect only because of a refusal or failure in respect of which a penalty is imposed on him under subsection (1).

DEFINITIONS

"the Board"—see s.66.
"employee"—see s.25(5).
"employer"—*ibid.*
"tax credits"—see s.1(2).

GENERAL NOTE

1.413 This section imposes a specific penalty to enforce the correct operation of the system of paying tax credits (in practice, at present, only WTC) in the pay packet (see s.25). A penalty applies to any employer refusing or repeatedly failing to make payments of tax credits to "an employee" with the result that the Inland Revenue has to make the payment. It would therefore seem to apply to each individual employee separately, so a general failure might incur a potentially large penalty.

There is a separate penalty for an employer who pays the wrong amount of tax credit to an employee during a tax year (otherwise than by failing to pay) if the wrong payment was because of fraud or neglect.

Appeals by employers go to the tax appeal tribunals, unlike all other appeals (s.63). They will in practice probably be linked with other Inland Revenue enquiries into the operation of the PAYE system, on which any appeals go to the tax appeal tribunals. Provision is made for the appeals to go to General or Special Commissioner of Income Tax in Tax Credits (Employer Penalty Appeals) Regulations 2003 (SI 2003/1382).

Supplementary

1.414 **34.**—Schedule 2 (penalties: supplementary) has effect.

GENERAL NOTE

1.415 This section incorporates Sch.2 into the Act. The Schedule sets out the procedure for determining, appealing and collecting penalties. Paragraph 1 provides for determination of penalties in terms similar to s.100 of the TMA 1970. The appeal procedures in paras 2 and 3 echo those in the TMA 1970. However, they are replaced by the modifications operating for the time being under s.63 of the Act. This routes appeals to appeal tribunals and the Social Security Commissioners rather than to the General Commissioners, Special Commissioners and courts. There were similar provisions in Sch.4 to the TCA 1999.

Paragraph 5 of the Schedule gives the Inland Revenue the same power to mitigate penalties as in s.102 of the TMA 1970. This is in practice how the Inland Revenue prefers to deal with penalties. It first indicates what penalty it considers appropriate by reference to its published practice. It then seeks to deal with both the outstanding tax and interest, together with the penalty, by what is known as a contract settlement. In exchange for the taxpayer paying an agreed sum of money, the Inland Revenue agrees to waive its rights to any tax, interest and penalties. The outcome is a contract separate from any specific tax provision. This approach was long ago endorsed by the courts: see *AG v Johnstone* (1926) 10 T.C. 758. Conduct of these "back duty" cases, as they are known, on behalf of taxpayers is regarded as a specific specialist skill by tax experts. The approach of agreeing a monetary settlement may be the practical answer to the issues arising under Art.6(3) of the European Convention on Human Rights as noted under s.31.

Paragraph 6 imposes similar time limits to those in s.103 of that Act.

Fraud

Offence of fraud

35.—(1) A person commits an offence if he is knowingly concerned in any fraudulent activity undertaken with a view to obtaining payments of a tax credit by him or any other person. 1.416

(2) A person who commits an offence under subsection (1) is liable—

(a) on summary conviction, to imprisonment for a term not exceeding six months, or a fine not exceeding the statutory maximum, or both, or

(b) on conviction on indictment, to imprisonment for a term not exceeding seven years, or a fine, or both.

DEFINITION

"tax credit"—see s.1(2).

GENERAL NOTE

Like the penalties provisions, this section reflects the fear of fraud by claimants and others abusing the tax credits system. There is no equivalent of this section in the TCA 1999. The new offence is briefly stated and is clearly intended to have a wide reach. It is not confined to claimants or employers and could be applied, for example, to a childcare provider. 1.417

Powers in relation to documents

36.—(1) Section 20BA of the Taxes Management Act 1970 (c.9) (orders for delivery of documents) applies (with Schedule 1AA and section 20BB) in relation to offences involving fraud in connection with, or in relation to, tax credits as in relation to offences involving serious fraud in connection with, or in relation to, tax. 1.418

(2) Section 20C (entry with warrant to obtain documents) of that Act applies (with section 20CC) in relation to offences involving serious fraud in connection with, or in relation to, tax credits as in relation to offences involving serious fraud in connection with, or in relation to, tax (but subject to the modification provided by subsection (3)).

(3) Subsection (1A) of section 20C applies by virtue of subsection (2) as if the references to the proper assessment or collection of tax were to the proper award or payment of a tax credit.

(4) Any regulations under Schedule 1AA to the Taxes Management Act 1970 which are in force immediately before the commencement of subsection (1) apply, subject to any necessary modifications, for the purposes of that Schedule as they apply by virtue of that subsection (until amended or revoked).

DEFINITION

"tax credit"—see s.1(2).

GENERAL NOTE

This applies specific powers available to the Inland Revenue for dealing with tax fraud to tax credit fraud. Sections 20BA and 20BB of the TMA 1970 deal 1.419

with orders for delivery of documents and offences of fraud respectively. Section 20C is a power to enter premises on a warrant, but is available only in cases of serious fraud and can only be obtained from a judicial authority. The statutory instrument currently made under Sch.1AA is the Orders for the Delivery of Documents (Procedure) Regulations 2000 (SI 2000/2875).

Interest

Interest

1.420 **37.**—(1) If an overpayment of a tax credit for a period is attributable to fraud or neglect on the part of the person, or either or both of the persons, to whom the award of the tax credit was made (or a person acting for him, or for either or both of them, in making the claim for the tax credit), the Board may decide that the whole or any part of the overpayment is to carry interest.

(2) Where the Board so decide the overpayment (or part of the overpayment) carries interest at a prescribed rate from the date 30 days after the appropriate date.

(3) "The appropriate date" is—

(a) in the case of an amount treated as an overpayment by virtue of section 28(6), the date of the decision under section 16 to terminate the award; and

(b) in any other case, the date specified for the purposes of subsection (4) of section 17 in the notice given to the person or persons under that section in relation to the tax credit.

(4) The Board must give notice of a decision under subsection (1) to the person, or each of the persons, to whom it relates; and the notice must state the date on which it is given and include details of the right to appeal against the decision under section 38.

(5) A penalty under any of sections 31 to 33 carries interest at the prescribed rate from the date on which it becomes due and payable; but the Board may in their discretion mitigate any interest or entirely remit any interest which wouldotherwise be carried by a penalty.

(6) Any interest carried under this section by an overpayment or penalty is to be regarded for the purposes of section 29(3) to (5) or paragraph 7 of Schedule 2 as if it were part of the overpayment or penalty.

Amendments

Subsection (1) is modified as it applies to polygamous units by Tax Credits (Polygamous Marriages) Regulations 2003 (SI 2003/742), reg.21.

Definitions

"the Board"—see s.67.
"prescribed"—*ibid.*
"overpayment"—see s.28.
"tax credit"—see s.1(2).

GENERAL NOTE

Interest has long been imposed on taxpayers who do not make timely payments of income tax. This includes an underpayment (or repayment) of tax reliefs and deductions (see TMA 1970, s.86). By contrast, interest is not imposed on those required to repay an overpayment of social security benefits. Interest was not imposed on overpayments under the TCA 1999, although penalties under s.9 of that Act carried interest (Sch.4, para.8 to that Act). **1.421**

This section adopts a compromise in imposing interest payments on overpayments caused by fraud or neglect, but not generally. It also imposes again an interest charge on payments of penalties. Interest does not run unless a decision is made to impose it, and that cannot start until either the date on which the award of tax credit was terminated under s.16 or the closing date of a notice issued under s.17.

The "prescribed rate" is set out in the Tax Credits (Interest Rate) Regulations 2003 (SI 2003/123).

Appeals

Appeals

38.—(1) An appeal may be brought against— **1.422**

(a) a decision under section 14(1), 15(1), 16(1), 19(3) or 20(1) or (4) or regulations under section 21,

(b) the relevant section 18 decision in relation to a person or persons and a tax credit for a tax year and any revision of that decision under that section,

(c) a determination of a penalty under paragraph 1 of Schedule 2, and

(d) a decision under section 37(1).

(2) "The relevant section 18 decision" means—

(a) in a case in which a decision must be made under subsection (6) of section 18 in relation to the person or persons and the tax credit for the tax year, that decision, and

(b) in any other case, the decision under subsection (1) of that section in relation to the person or persons and the tax credit for the tax year.

DEFINITIONS

"tax credit"—see s.1(2).
"tax year"—see s.47.

GENERAL NOTE

This section creates a series of specific rights of appeal. The following decisions or actions of the Inland Revenue are subject to the appeal process: **1.423**

(a) an initial decision to award or refuse tax credits under s.14(1);

(b) a decision whether (and if so, how) to amend a s.14 decision under s.15(1);

(c) a decision amending or terminating a s.14 decision under s.16(1);

(d) a decision on entitlement made under s.18(1) or (6);

(e) a decision after an enquiry under s.19(3);

(f) a decision revising a previous decision on entitlement under s.20(1);

(g) a decision revising a previous decision on entitlement on the grounds of fraud or neglect under s.20(4);

(h) a decision to revise a decision on entitlement because of official error under s.21;

(i) a determination of a penalty under Sch.2 para.1;

(j) a decision to impose interest under s.37(1).

There have been very few appeals heard by appeal tribunals during the first year of operation of tax credits under the TCA 2002, and none by the Social Security Commissioners. In part this reflects the Inland Revenue approach of conducting local office examinations of doubtful or unclear claims and of issuing awards on a provisional basis and then reconsidering them during the year (see ss.14 and 16). In part it also reflects the Inland Revenue's power to reach a settlement (see s.54 of the Taxes Management Act 1970) rather than let the matter go forward for a tribunal determination. There appear also to be delays in the system and some holding-over of appeals so that they are heard as issues of entitlement rather than as provisional awards. Whether these are appropriate explanations for the absence of appeal hearings may depend on the precise reason for an appeal. But the Act clearly gives separate appeal rights from award decisions under s.14(1) as well as from entitlement decisions under s.18, as this section makes clear. And as there is a clear right of appeal, the Inland Revenue is under a duty not to obstruct a properly conducted exercise of that right by reason of the application to it of Art.6(1) of the European Convention on Human Rights and s.3 of the Human Rights Act 1998. See Vol.III of this work.

Separately from these, the appellate authorities can be invoked in two other situations. The Inland Revenue cannot itself make a determination of daily penalties under s.32(2) and must instead start proceedings for such penalties before the appellate authorities. This is not technically an appeal (see Sch.2, para.3). An individual subject to an enquiry under s.19 can, under s.19(8), apply to the appellate authorities to direct the enquiry to end. Such an application is to be treated as if it was an appeal (s.19(10)).

Exercise of right of appeal

1.424 **39.**—(1) Notice of an appeal under section 38 against a decision must be given to the Board in the prescribed manner within the period of 30 days after the date on which notice of the decision was given (or, in the case of a decision to which section 23(3) applies, the date of the decision).

(2) Notice of such an appeal must specify the grounds of appeal.

(3) An appeal under section 38 is to the General Commissioners but the appellant may elect (in accordance with section 46(1) of the Taxes Management Act 1970 (c.9)) to bring the appeal before the Special Commissioners instead.

(4) Subsections (2) to (7) of section 31D of the Taxes Management Act 1970 (which relate to an election to bring proceedings before the Special Commissioners) have effect in relation to an election under subsection (3) (as in relation to an election under subsection (1) of that section).

(5) On the hearing of an appeal under section 38 the General Commissioners or Special Commissioners may allow the appellant to put

forward grounds not specified in the notice, and take them into consideration if satisfied that the omission was not wilful or unreasonable.

(6) Part V of the Taxes Management Act 1970 (appeals to Commissioners) applies in relation to appeals under section 38 (as in relation to appeals under the Taxes Acts, within the meaning of that Act), but subject to such modifications as are prescribed.

(7) Any regulations under section 56B of the Taxes Management Act 1970 (c.9) which are in force immediately before the commencement of subsection (6) apply, subject to any necessary modifications, for the purposes of appeals under section 38 (until amended or revoked).

DEFINITIONS

"the Board"—see s.67.
"General Commissioners"—see s.47.
"modifications"—see s.67.
"prescribed"—*ibid.*
"Special Commissioners"—see s.47.

GENERAL NOTE

This section *must* be read subject to s.63. The Government's original plan was that appeals would all go to the General Commissioners and Special Commissioners of Income Tax. It became clear after the Bill had been published that this would not be possible because of ongoing reforms of the tax tribunals. The decision was therefore taken to leave most forms of appeal with the appeal tribunals constituted under the SSA 1998, as happened under the TCA 1999, at least for the time being. The mechanism adopted was to leave this section in place, but to provide in s.63 an alternative set of provisions that take effect automatically and stop only when the Treasury so orders. Under s.63, until the Treasury order is made, all appeals apart from appeals about employer penalties go to the appeal tribunals. Section 39 therefore applies as it stands only to appeals by employers against penalties under ss.31–33. In all other cases, s.39 is to be read subject to the modifications in s.63. These replace all references to the General Commissioners and Special Commissioners with references to the appeal tribunals constituted under the SSA 1998. Further appeals go to the Social Security Commissioners instead of the courts. Subsections (3) and (4) do not apply (s.63(5)), and nor do subss.(6) or (7) (s. 63(9)). For convenience, the resulting modified form of s.39 is set out below: **1.425**

"39 Exercise of right of appeal

(1) Notice of an appeal under section 38 against a decision must be given to the Board in the prescribed manner within the period of thirty days after the date on which notice of the decision was given (or, in the case of a decision to which section 23(3) applies, the date of the decision).

(2) Notice of such an appeal must specify the grounds of appeal.

(5) On the hearing of an appeal under section 38 the appeal tribunal may allow the appellant to put forward grounds not specified in the notice, and take them into consideration if satisfied that the omission was not wilful or unreasonable."

Subs. (1)

This gives a 30-day time-limit on appeals (the usual Inland Revenue time-limit), compared with a normal time-limit of one month from social security decisions to those tribunals. For the prescribed manner of notice of appeal see Tax **1.426**

Credits (Notice of Appeal) Regulations 2002 (SI 2002/3119), reg.2, and for late appeals see reg.5 of those Regulations.

Subs. (2)

1.427 This requires the grounds of appeal to be specified. The equivalent social security requirement is that particulars of the grounds be stated.

Subs. (5)

1.428 This raises a more significant difference in procedures as compared with the previous social security procedures. It gives a limited discretion to the appeal tribunal to consider other grounds. In social security cases, tribunals and Commissioners operate on an investigative basis so should consider all relevant issues, though s.12(8)(a) of the SSA 1998 provides a power not to consider points not in issue.

Supplementary

Annual reports

1.429 **40.**—(1) The Board must make to the Treasury an annual report about—

(a) the matters required by section 2(5) to be set forth in the accounts mentioned in section 13 of the Inland Revenue Regulation Act 1890 (c.21),
(b) the number of awards of child tax credit and of working tax credit,
(c) the number of enquiries conducted under section 19,
(d) the number of penalties imposed under this Part, and
(e) the number of prosecutions and convictions for offences connected with tax credits.

(2) The Treasury must publish each annual report made to it under subsection (1) and lay a copy before each House of Parliament.

DEFINITIONS

"the Board"—see s.67.
"child tax credit"—see s.8.
"tax credits"—see s 1(2).
"working tax credit"—see s.10.

GENERAL NOTE

1.430 This section derives from a clause adopted by the House of Lords against the wishes of government, and represents the one major amendment in the Act not moved by the Government itself. The aim is to ensure a specific report that would be put before Parliament each year about both the scale of the tax credits system and the extent of fraud within it. The wording of the section comes from a government amendment moved to replace the Lords clause in the House of Commons. It was recognised that to some extent it duplicates figures already published by the Inland Revenue in its more general reports.

Annual review

1.431 **41.**—(1) The Treasury must, in each tax year, review the amounts specified in subsection (2) in order to determine whether they have retained their value in relation to the general level of prices in the United Kingdom as estimated by the Treasury in such manner as it considers appropriate.

(2) The amounts are monetary amounts prescribed—

(a) under subsection (1)(a) of section 7;
(b) for the purposes of any of paragraphs (a) to (d) of subsection (3) of that section;
(c) under section 9;
(d) under section 11, otherwise than by virtue of section 12, or
(e) under subsection (2) of section 13, otherwise than by virtue of subsection (3) of that section.

(3) The Treasury must prepare a report of each review.

(4) The report must include a statement of what each amount would be if it had fully retained its value.

(5) The Treasury must publish the report and lay a copy of it before each House of Parliament.

DEFINITIONS

"prescribed"—see s.67

GENERAL NOTE

This provides for the annual uprating review of the monetary amounts used in awarding tax credits. 1.432

Persons subject to immigration control

42.—(1) Regulations may make provision in relation to persons subject to immigration control or in relation to prescribed descriptions of such persons— 1.433

(a) for excluding entitlement to, or to a prescribed element of, child tax credit or working tax credit (or both), or
(b) for this Part to apply subject to other prescribed modifications.

(2) "Person subject to immigration control" has the same meaning as in section 115 of the Immigration and Asylum Act 1999 (c.33).

DEFINITIONS

"child tax credit"—see s.8.
"modifications"—see s.67.
"persons subject to immigration control"—see Immigration and Asylum Act 1999, s.115.
"prescribed"—see s.67.
"working tax credit"—see s.10.

GENERAL NOTE

Although listed in the "supplementary" part of Pt I of the Act, this makes provision for excluding anyone from entitlement to tax credits if he or she is "subject to immigration control", a phrase derived from the Immigration and Asylum Act 1999. The definition covers those who are not nationals of an EEA state and who require leave to enter the United Kingdom or have certain forms of conditional leave. This carries forward the exclusion from WFTC of all such people (s.115(1)(f) of that Act). For the detailed application of this section, see the Tax Credits (Immigration) Regulations 2003 (SI 2003/653). 1.434

Polygamous marriages

1.435 **43.**—(1) Regulations may make provision for this Part to apply in relation to persons who are parties to polygamous marriages subject to prescribed modifications.

(2) A person is a party to a polygamous marriage if—

(a) he is a party to a marriage entered into under a law which permits polygamy, and

(b) either party to the marriage has a spouse additional to the other party.

Definition

"modifications"—see s.67.

General Note

1.436 This is another of the necessary compromises between the general approach to income tax and the general approach to social security. Social security benefits have long contained special provisions dealing with polygamous marriages, if only to prevent more than two of the marriage partners benefiting for a particular benefit as a married couple. In contrast, the point is not so significant in the context of income tax as there is now individual assessment. The standard treatment of monogamous marriages is set out in s.3.

Effect is given to this section by the Tax Credits (Polygamous Marriages) Regulations 2003 (SI 2003/742). Where those regulations provide for a modification of the sections of this Act, that is noted in this volume as an amendment to the section.

Crown employment

1.437 **44.** This Part applies in relation to persons employed by or under the Crown (as in relation to other employees).

Definitions

"Crown"—see Interpretation Act 1978, Sch.1.
"employed"—see s.25(5).

General Note

1.438 This section avoids any unintended exclusion of civil and other public servants by reason of the Crown Proceedings Act 1947 or otherwise. The Tax Credits (Residence) Regulations 2003 (SI 2003/642) extend this further by applying the Act to Crown Servants working overseas and their partners. The main concern of both this section and those regulations is that Crown servants receive full entitlement to CTC.

Inalienability

1.439 **45.**—(1) Every assignment of or charge on a tax credit, and every agreement to assign or charge a tax credit, is void; and, on the bankruptcy of a person entitled to a tax credit, the entitlement to the tax credit does not pass to any trustee or other person acting on behalf of his creditors.

(2) In the application of subsection (1) to Scotland—

(a) the reference to assignment is to assignation ("assign" being construed accordingly), and

(b) the reference to the bankruptcy of a person is to the sequestration of his estate or the appointment on his estate of a judicial factor under section 41 of the Solicitors (Scotland) Act 1980 (c.46).

DEFINITION

"tax credit"—see s.1(2).

GENERAL NOTE

This mirrors (and repeats much of the wording of) SSAA 1992, s.187. While informal pledges of both benefit and benefit books occur, that section renders any such arrangement unenforceable in the courts or as against government departments. This section ensures that this also applies to tax credits. **1.440**

Giving of notices by Board

46. The Board may give any notice which they are required or permitted to give under this Part in any manner and form which the Board consider appropriate in the circumstances. **1.441**

DEFINITION

"the Board"—see s.67.

GENERAL NOTE

No provision is made in this section for regulations or for deemed notice. There is no equivalent of TMA 1970, s.114 (want of form not to invalidate assessments) or 115 (delivery and service of documents) provided for in the Act. However, it is suggested that this does not discharge the Inland Revenue from the duty of complying with specific provisions as to content in this Act, in the Tax Credits (Claims and Notifications) Regulations 2002 (SI 2002/2014), or elsewhere. **1.442**

Consequential amendments

47. Schedule 3 (consequential amendments) has effect. **1.443**

GENERAL NOTE

This section gives effect to Sch.3 (not included in this volume). Section 68(1) ensures that those provisions are co-extensive with the provisions they affect. Most of the provisions are concerned to replace WFTC with WTC and to substitute a reference to CTC in place of references to the various previous child benefits and credits. Paragraph 25 amends s.30C of the SSCBA 1992, and para.30 amends s.42 of that Act. Both deal with transfers between benefit and tax credit. **1.444**

Interpretation

48. In this Part— **1.445**
"child" has the meaning given by section 8(3),
"the current year income" has the meaning given by section 7(4),
"employee" and "employer" have the meaning given by section 25(5),
"the General Commissioners" means the Commissioners for the general purposes of the income tax appointed under section 2 of the Taxes Management Act 1970 (c.9),

"the income threshold" has the meaning given by section 7(1)(a),
"joint claim" has the meaning given by section 3(8),
"married couple" has the meaning given by section 3(5),
"overpayment" has the meaning given by section 28(2) and (6),
"the previous year income" has the meaning given by section 7(5),
"qualifying remunerative work", and being engaged in it, have the meaning given by regulations under section 10(2),
"qualifying young person" has the meaning given by section 8(4),
"the relevant income" has the meaning given by section 7(3),
"responsible", in relation to a child or qualifying young person, has the meaning given by regulations under section 8(2) (for the purposes of child tax credit) or by regulations under section 10(4) (for the purposes of working tax credit),
"single claim" has the meaning given by section 3(8),
"the Special Commissioners" means the Commissioners for the special purposes of the Income Tax Acts appointed under section 4 of the Taxes Management Act 1970 (c.9),
"tax year" means a period beginning with 6th April in one year and ending with 5th April in the next, and
"unmarried couple" has the meaning given by section 3(6).

General Note

1.446 See also s.67 for further definitions.

Part 2

Child Benefit and Guardian's Allowance

Transfer of functions etc.

Functions transferred to Treasury

1.447 **49.**—(1) The functions of the Secretary of State under—
(a) section 77 of the Social Security Contributions and Benefits Act 1992 (c.4) (guardian's allowance: Great Britain),
(b) Part IX of that Act (child benefit: Great Britain), except section 142(1)(c) and (2) and paragraphs 5 and 6(1) of Schedule 10,
(c) section 80 of the Social Security Administration Act 1992 (c.5) (overlap with benefits under legislation of other member States: Great Britain), and
(d) section 72 of the Social Security Act 1998 (c.14) (power to reduce child benefit for lone parents: Great Britain),

are transferred to the Treasury.

(2) The functions of the Northern Ireland Department under—
(a) section 77 of the Social Security Contributions and Benefits (Northern Ireland) Act 1992 (c.7) (guardian's allowance: Northern Ireland),

(b) Part IX of that Act (child benefit: Northern Ireland), except section 138(1)(c) and (2) and paragraphs 5 and 6(1) of Schedule 10,
(c) section 76 of the Social Security Administration (Northern Ireland) Act 1992 (c.8) (overlap with benefits under legislation of other member States: Northern Ireland), and
(d) Article 68 of the Social Security (Northern Ireland) Order 1998 (SI 1998/1506 (N.I. 10)) (power to reduce child benefit for lone parents: Northern Ireland),

are transferred to the Treasury.

(3) The functions of the Secretary of State under Part X of the Social Security Administration Act 1992 (c.5) (review and alteration of benefits: Great Britain) so far as relating to child benefit and guardian's allowance are transferred to the Treasury.

(4) The functions of the Northern Ireland Department under sections 132 to 134 of the Social Security Administration (Northern Ireland) Act 1992 (c.8) (review and alteration of benefits: Northern Ireland) so far as relating to child benefit and guardian's allowance are transferred to the Treasury.

DEFINITION

"the Northern Ireland Department"—see s.67.

GENERAL NOTE

This section transfers responsibility for policy matters relating to child benefit and guardian's allowance from the DWP to the Treasury. Such matters include both the rules governing entitlement to these two benefits (subs.(1)) and the setting of actual benefit rates (subs.(3)). The parallel powers exercised by the Department for Social Development in Northern Ireland are also transferred to the Treasury (subss.(2) and (4)). This section does not affect the validity of any action taken by the Secretary of State or the Northern Ireland Department before it is brought into force (s.54(3)). This transfer follows the precedent of the transfer of responsibility for WFTC (formerly family credit) from the then DSS to the Treasury under the TCA 1999. The justification for this further transfer is that as the Treasury has responsibility for CTC, it makes sense for this role to encompass other benefits for children to ensure a streamlined system of support for families with children. 1.448

Functions transferred to the Board

50.—(1) The functions of the Secretary of State and the Northern Ireland Department under the provisions specified in subsection (2), so far as relating to child benefit and guardian's allowance, are transferred to the Board. 1.449

(2) The provisions referred to in subsection (1) are—
(a) the Social Security Contributions and Benefits Act 1992 (c.4);
(b) the Social Security Administration Act 1992, except Part XIII (advisory bodies and consultation: Great Britain),
(c) the Social Security Contributions and Benefits (Northern Ireland) Act 1992 (c.7),
(d) the Social Security Administration (Northern Ireland) Act 1992, except Part XII (advisory bodies and consultation: Northern Ireland),

(e) Chapter 2 of Part I of the Social Security Act 1998 (c.14) (social security decisions and appeals: Great Britain);
(f) Chapter 2 of Part II of the Social Security (Northern Ireland) Order 1998 (SI 1998/1506 (N.I. 10)) (social security decisions and appeals: Northern Ireland), and
(g) any subordinate legislation made under any of the provisions specified in section 49 or any of the preceding provisions of this subsection.

(3) This section has effect subject to section 49.

DEFINITIONS

"the Board"—see s.67.
"the Northern Ireland Department"—*ibid.*

GENERAL NOTE

1.450 Whereas the previous section transfers policy responsibility for child benefit and guardian's allowance from the DWP to the Treasury, this section transfers the operational responsibilities for both benefits from the DWP and its Northern Ireland equivalent to the Revenue. This section does not affect the validity of any action taken by the Secretary of State or the Northern Ireland Department before it is brought into force (s.54(3)).

Consequential amendments

1.451 **51.**—Schedule 4 (amendments consequential on transfer of functions made by sections 49 and 50) has effect.

GENERAL NOTE

1.452 This section introduces Sch.4, which makes a series of amendments consequential to the transfer of functions relating to child benefit and guardian's allowance under ss.49 and 50 above.

52. *Omitted*

General functions of the Board

1.453 **53.**—(1) Child benefit and guardian's allowance are to be under the care and management of the Board.

(2) For the purposes of the Inland Revenue Regulation Act 1890 (c.21) the definition of "inland revenue" in section 39 of that Act is to be taken to include child benefit and guardian's allowance.

(3) The reference in section 4(1) of that Act (appointment of collectors, officers and other persons) to collecting, receiving, managing and accounting for Inland Revenue is to be taken to include a reference to paying and managing child benefit and guardian's allowance.

(4) The duties of the Board under section 13 of that Act (Board to keep accounts) are to include a duty to set forth in the accounts mentioned in that section—

(a) the amounts of the several payments made by them of or in respect of child benefit and guardian's allowance;
(b) the amounts of the expenses of paying and managing child benefit and guardian's allowance, and

(c) the amounts received by them in respect of child benefit and guardian's allowance,

distinguishing in each case between amounts relating to child benefit and amounts relating to guardian's allowance.

(5) In any declaration for the purposes of section 6 of the Taxes Management Act 1970 (c.9) (declarations on taking office), whether made before or after the commencement of this section, the reference to an offence relating to Inland Revenue is to be taken to include a reference to an offence relating to child benefit or guardian's allowance.

DEFINITION

"the Board"—see s.67.

GENERAL NOTE

This section brings child benefit and guardian's allowance under the statutory "care and management" of the Inland Revenue. See further s.2 above, which makes similar provision for the new tax credits. The section makes it clear that child benefit and guardian's allowance remain social security benefits, notwithstanding the transfer of responsibilities effected by ss.49 and 50 above. Both benefits remain social security benefits for European Union law purposes under EC Council Regulation 1408/71 in any event. **1.454**

Transitional provisions

54.—(1) Any function covered by section 49 which is a function of making subordinate legislation may be exercised by the Treasury at any time after the passing of this Act if the subordinate legislation made in the exercise of the function comes into force after the commencement of that section. **1.455**

(2) Any function covered by section 50 which is a function of making subordinate legislation may be exercised by the Board at any time after the passing of this Act if the subordinate legislation made in the exercise of the function comes into force after the commencement of that section.

(3) Nothing in section 49 or 50 affects the validity of anything done by or in relation to the Secretary of State or the Northern Ireland Department before its commencement.

(4) Anything (including legal proceedings) relating to any functions transferred by section 49, or any property, rights or liabilities transferred by section 52(1), which is in the course of being done or carried on by or in relation to the Secretary of State or the Northern Ireland Department immediately before the transfer may be continued by or in relation to the Treasury.

(5) Anything (including legal proceedings) relating to any functions transferred by section 50, or any property, rights or liabilities transferred by section 52(2), which is in the course of being done or carried on by or in relation to the Secretary of State or the Northern Ireland Department immediately before the transfer may be continued by or in relation to the Board.

(6) Anything done by the Secretary of State or the Northern Ireland Department for the purposes of or in connection with any functions transferred by section 49, or any property, rights or liabilities transferred

by section 52(1), which is in effect immediately before the transfer has effect afterwards as if done by the Treasury.

(7) Anything done by the Secretary of State or the Northern Ireland Department for the purposes of or in connection with any functions transferred by section 50, or any property, rights or liabilities transferred by section 52(2), which is in effect immediately before the transfer has effect afterwards as if done by the Board.

(8) The Treasury is substituted for the Secretary of State or the Northern Ireland Department in any subordinate legislation, any contracts or other documents and any legal proceedings relating to any functions transferred by section 49, or any property, rights or liabilities transferred by section 52(1), made or commenced before the transfer.

(9) The Board are substituted for the Secretary of State or the Northern Ireland Department in any subordinate legislation, any contracts or other documents and any legal proceedings relating to any functions transferred by section 50, or any property, rights or liabilities transferred by section 52(2), made or commenced before the transfer.

(10) Any order made under section 8 of the Electronic Communications Act 2000 (c.7) which—

(a) modifies provisions relating to child benefit or guardian's allowance, and

(b) is in force immediately before the commencement of this subsection,

is to continue to have effect for the purposes of child benefit and guardian's allowance, despite subsection (7) of that section, until regulations made by the Board under section 132 of the Finance Act 1999 (c.16) which are expressed to supersede that order come into force.

DEFINITIONS

"the Board"—see s.67.
"the Northern Ireland Department"—*ibid.*

GENERAL NOTE

1.456 This section makes the necessary transitional provisions to cover the process of transfer from the social security departments to the Treasury and the Inland Revenue. The Treasury and the Board are given the power to make regulations after Royal Assent but before the transfer takes place in order to prepare for these changes (subss.(1) and (2)). Any action taken by the Secretary of State or the Northern Ireland Department prior to the transfer of functions remains valid (subs.(3)). In addition, any actions so taken before transfer will continue to have effect after the date of transfer as if they were the actions of the Treasury or the Board (subss.(4)–(9)). Finally, the Social Security (Electronic Communications) (Child Benefit) Order 2002 (SI 2002/1789) remains in force (subs.(10)).

Minor amendments

Continuing entitlement after death of child

1.457 **55.**—(1) Insert the section set out in subsection (2)—

(a) in the Social Security Contributions and Benefits Act 1992 (c.4) after section 145 (as section 145A), and

(b) in the Social Security Contributions and Benefits (Northern Ireland) Act 1992 (c.7) after section 141 (as section 141A).

(2) The section is—

"Entitlement after death of child

(1) If a child dies and a person is entitled to child benefit in respect of him for the week in which his death occurs, that person shall be entitled to child benefit in respect of the child for a prescribed period following that week.

(2) If the person entitled to child benefit under subsection (1) dies before the end of that prescribed period and, at the time of his death, was—

(a) a member of a married couple and living with the person to whom he was married, or
(b) a member of an unmarried couple,

that other member of the married couple or unmarried couple shall be entitled to child benefit for the period for which the dead person would have been entitled to child benefit under subsection (1) above but for his death.

(3) If a child dies before the end of the week in which he is born, subsections (1) and (2) apply in his case as if references to the person entitled to child benefit in respect of a child for the week in which his death occurs were to the person who would have been so entitled if the child had been alive at the beginning of that week (and if any conditions which were satisfied, and any facts which existed, at the time of his death were satisfied or existed then).

(4) Where a person is entitled to child benefit in respect of a child under this section, section 77 applies with the omission of subsections (4) to (6).

(5) In this section—
"married couple" means a man and a woman who are married to each other and are neither—

(a) separated under a court order, nor
(b) separated in circumstances in which the separation is likely to be permanent, and

"unmarried couple" means a man and a woman who are not a married couple but are living together as husband and wife."

DEFINITIONS

"married couple"—see SSCBA 1992, s.145A(5).
"unmarried couple"—*ibid.*
"week"—see SSCBA 1992, s.147(1).

GENERAL NOTE

This section, which inserts a new s.145A into the SSCBA 1992 (and a new s.141A into the parallel Northern Ireland legislation), extends entitlement to child benefit after the death of the child who is the subject of the claim. Under present rules, entitlement ceases immediately on the child's death. The period of extended entitlement is to be laid down in regulations (see subs.(1)) and is intended to be eight weeks, as with CTC. If the child benefit claimant dies as well as the child, the claimant's surviving partner will be eligible for child benefit during this extension period (subs.(2)). In addition, child benefit entitlement always **1.458** starts on a Monday (see the definition of "week" in SSCBA 1992, s.147(1)), which has had the effect of excluding from entitlement those parents whose newborn children do not survive until the Monday following their birth. Such parents will now also be entitled to child benefit for this extension period (subs.(3)). The same concessions apply equally to guardian's allowance (subs.(4)). See also s.8(5) above, which allows a similar provision to be made for CTC.

Presence in United Kingdom

1.459 **56.**—(1) For section 146 of the Social Security Contributions and Benefits Act 1992 (c.4) (persons outside Great Britain) substitute—

"146 Presence in Great Britain

(1) No child benefit shall be payable in respect of a child for a week unless he is in Great Britain in that week.

(2) No person shall be entitled to child benefit for a week unless he is in Great Britain in that week.

(3) Circumstances may be prescribed in which a child or other person is to be treated for the purposes of this section as being, or as not being, in Great Britain."

(2) For section 142 of the Social Security Contributions and Benefits (Northern Ireland) Act 1992 (c.7) (persons outside Northern Ireland) substitute—

"142 Presence in Northern Ireland

(1) No child benefit shall be payable in respect of a child for a week unless he is in Northern Ireland in that week.

(2) No person shall be entitled to child benefit for a week unless he is in Northern Ireland in that week.

(3) Circumstances may be prescribed in which a child or other person is to be treated for the purposes of this section as being, or as not being, in Northern Ireland."

DEFINITIONS

"prescribed"—see SSCBA 1992, s.147(1).
"week"—*ibid.*

GENERAL NOTE

1.460 This section makes a further change to the rules governing entitlement to child benefit which is favourable to claimants in certain circumstances. It does so by substituting a new SSCBA 1992, s.146, which abolishes the requirement that both the claimant and the child must have been present in Great Britain for 182 days before entitlement can begin. However, it remains the case that both the claimant and the child must actually be in Great Britain (or Northern Ireland, as appropriate), though this is subject to modification under European Union law. In addition, the existing provision enabling regulations to provide for entitlement to continue during periods of temporary absence is retained. This regulation-making power will allow the presence test to be common for both the CTC and child benefit. CTC is, however, a United Kingdom tax credit, so the presence tests applied to it cover the whole United Kingdom.

Abolition of exclusion of tax exempt persons

57.—In Schedule 9 to— 1.461

(a) the Social Security Contributions and Benefits Act 1992, and
(b) the Social Security Contributions and Benefits (Northern Ireland) Act 1992,

omit paragraph 4 (person not entitled to child benefit if he or other prescribed person is exempt from tax under prescribed provisions).

DEFINITION

"prescribed"—see SSCBA 1992, s.147(1).

GENERAL NOTE

Schedule 9 to the SSCBA 1992 (and its companion Northern Ireland legislation) sets out a number of situations in which a claimant is excluded from entitlement to child benefit. These disqualifications include persons with any income which is exempt from United Kingdom income tax (even if they pay income tax on the rest of their income). This rule dates from the origins of child benefit as being derived in part from a former income tax relief. This section removes the exclusion, as no such exclusion applies to CTC. 1.462

PART 3

SUPPLEMENTARY

Information etc.

Administrative arrangements

58.—(1) This section applies where regulations under— 1.463

(a) section 4 or 6 of this Act,
(b) section 5 of the Social Security Administration Act 1992 (c.5), or
(c) section 5 of the Social Security Administration (Northern Ireland) Act 1992 (c.8),

permit or require a claim or notification relating to a tax credit, child benefit or guardian's allowance to be made or given to a relevant authority.

(2) Where this section applies, regulations may make provision—

(a) for information or evidence relating to tax credits, child benefit or guardian's allowance to be provided to the relevant authority (whether by persons by whom such claims and notifications are or have been made or given, by the Board or by other persons),
(b) for the giving of information or advice by a relevant authority to persons by whom such claims or notifications are or have been made or given, and
(c) for the recording, verification and holding, and the forwarding to the Board or a person providing services to the Board, of claims and notifications received by virtue of the regulations referred to in subsection (1) and information or evidence received by virtue of paragraph (a).

(3) "Relevant authority" means—

(a) the Secretary of State,
(b) the Northern Ireland Department, or

(c) a person providing services to the Secretary of State or the Northern Ireland Department.

DEFINITION

"child benefit"—see SSCBA 1992, s.141.
"claim"—see s.3(8).
"guardian's allowance"—see SSCBA 1992, s.77.
"relevant authority"—see subs.(3).
"tax credit"—see s.1(2).

GENERAL NOTE

1.464 Section 5 of the SSAA 1992 and its Northern Ireland equivalent provide the authority for the Social Security (Claims and Payments) Regulations 1987 (SI 1987/1968) under which regulations for all aspects of claiming benefits are detailed. This section enables claims and notifications for tax credits and child benefit being validly given to both the Inland Revenue and the social security authorities, and to anyone acting under contract to the social security authorities. It will, for example, allow claims for child benefit and CTC to be made together to one authority. See also the Tax Credits (Administrative Arrangements) Regulations 2002 (SI 2002/3036).

Use and disclosure of information

1.465 **59.**—Schedule 5 (use and disclosure of information) has effect.

GENERAL NOTE

1.466 This section incorporates Sch.5 into the Act. The Schedule adds further provisions to the statutory authority already available so that tax authorities, social security authorities, other government departments, and local authorities can exchange information. The widest power is the power to give information to anyone for the purposes of the Learning and Skills Act 2000 (para.10). This wide power is linked to a new criminal offence if it is misused (para.10(4)). Paragraph 11 includes disclosures about tax credits in the general offence of disclosing information held by a person in connection with tax, tax credit and social security functions unless the information is disclosed with lawful authority or certain other conditions are met. This replaces the inclusion of tax credits within that section under s.12 of the TCA 1999. Paragraph 9 of the Schedule has given effect by the Tax Credits (Provision of Information) (Functions Relating to Health) Regulations 2003 and No.2 Regulations (SI 2003/731) and the Tax Credits (Provision of Information) (Functions Relating to Health) (No.2) Regulations 2003 (SI 2003/1650).

Other supplementary provisions

Repeals

1.467 **60.**—Schedule 6 (repeals) has effect.

GENERAL NOTE

1.468 This section incorporates the standard repeals Schedule into the Act. It provides the authority for the abolitions flagged up in s.1(3). It confirms that this Act replaces the whole of the TCA 1999.

Commencement

61.—Apart from section 54(1) and (2), the preceding provisions of this Act come into force in accordance with orders made by the Treasury. **1.469**

General Note

See end of the introductory General Note to the Act as a whole. **1.470**

Transitional provisions and savings

62.—(1) The Secretary of State may by order make as respects England and Wales and Scotland, and the Northern Ireland Department may by order make as respects Northern Ireland, any transitional provisions or savings which appear appropriate in connection with the commencement of the abolition of the increases referred to in section 1(3)(e). **1.471**

(2) Subject to any provision made by virtue of subsection (1), the Treasury may by order make any transitional provisions or savings which appear appropriate in connection with the commencement of any provision of this Act.

General Note

See the note to the previous section. **1.472**

Tax credits appeals etc.: temporary modifications

63.—(1) Until such day as the Treasury may by order appoint, Part I of this Act has effect subject to the modifications specified in this section; and an order under this subsection may include any transitional provisions or savings which appear appropriate. **1.473**

(2) Except in the case of an appeal against an employer penalty, an appeal under section 38 is to an appeal tribunal (rather than to the General Commissioners or Special Commissioners).

(3) The function of giving a direction under section 19(10) is a function of an appeal tribunal (rather than of the General Commissioners or Special Commissioners).

(4) Except in the case of an employer information penalty, proceedings under paragraph 3 of Schedule 2 are by way of information made to an appeal tribunal (rather than to the General Commissioners or Special Commissioners).

(5) So far as is appropriate in consequence of subsections (2) to (4)—

(a) the references to the General Commissioners or Special Commissioners in sections 19(10) and 39(5) and paragraphs 2 and 3(2) of Schedule 2 are to the appeal tribunal, and

(b) subsections (3) and (4) of section 39 do not apply.

(6) An appeal under paragraph 2(2) or 4(1) of Schedule 2 from a decision of, or against the determination of a penalty by, an appeal tribunal lies to a Social Security Commissioner (rather than to the High Court or Court of Session).

(7) So far as is appropriate in consequence of subsection (6), the references in paragraphs 2(2) and 4 of Schedule 2 to the High Court and the Court of Session are to the Social Security Commissioner.

(8) Regulations may apply any provision contained in—

(a) Chapter 2 of Part I of the Social Security Act 1998 (c.14) (social security appeals: Great Britain),

(b) Chapter 2 of Part II of the Social Security (Northern Ireland) Order 1998 (SI 1998/1506 (N.I. 10)) (social security appeals: Northern Ireland), or

(c) section 54 of the Taxes Management Act 1970 (c.9) (settling of appeals by agreement),

in relation to appeals which, by virtue of this section, are to an appeal tribunal or lie to a Social Security Commissioner, but subject to such modifications as are prescribed.

(9) Except in the case of appeals against employer penalties, subsections (6) and (7) of section 39 do not apply.

(10) "Appeal tribunal" means an appeal tribunal constituted—

(a) in Great Britain, under Chapter 1 of Part I of the Social Security Act 1998, or

(b) in Northern Ireland, under Chapter 1 of Part II of the Social Security (Northern Ireland) Order 1998.

(11) "Employer penalty" means—

(a) a penalty under section 31 or 32 relating to a requirement imposed by virtue of regulations under section 25, or

(b) a penalty under section 33.

(12) "Employer information penalty" means a penalty under section 32(2)(a) relating to a requirement imposed by virtue of regulations under section 25.

(13) "Social Security Commissioner" means—

(a) in Great Britain, the Chief Social Security Commissioner or any other Social Security Commissioner appointed under the Social Security Act 1998 (c.14) or a tribunal of three or more Commissioners constituted under section 16(7) of that Act, and

(b) in Northern Ireland, the Chief Social Security Commissioner or any other Social Security Commissioner appointed under the Social Security Administration (Northern Ireland) Act 1992 (c.8) or a tribunal of two or more Commissioners constituted under Article 16(7) of the Social Security (Northern Ireland) Order 1998 (SI 1998/1506 (N.I. 10)).

DEFINITIONS

"appeal tribunal"—see subs.(10).
"employer information penalty"—see subs.(12).
"employer penalty"—see subs.(11).
"General Commissioners"—see s.47.
"modifications"—see s.67.
"Social Security Commissioner"—see subs.(13).
"Special Commissioners"—see s.47.

GENERAL NOTE

1.474 See the general note to s.38 for this important transitional provision.

Northern Ireland

64.—(1) The Northern Ireland Act 1998 (c.47) has effect subject to the amendments in subsections (2) and (3). **1.475**

(2) In Schedule 2 (excepted matters), after paragraph 10 insert—

"10A. Tax credits under Part 1 of the Tax Credits Act 2002.

10B. Childbenefit and guardian's allowance."

(3) In section 87 (consultation and co-ordination on social security matters), after subsection (6) insert—

"(6A) But this section does not apply to the legislation referred to in subssection (6) to the extent that it relates to child benefit or guardian's allowance."

(4) For the purposes of that Act, a provision of—

(a) an Act of the Northern Ireland Assembly; or

(b) a Bill for such an Act,

which amends or repeals any of the provisions of the Employment Rights (Northern Ireland) Order 1996 (SI 1996/1919 (N.I. 16)) dealt with in Schedule 1 shall not be treated as dealing with tax credits if the Act or Bill deals with employment rights conferred otherwise than by that Schedule in the same way.

DEFINITION

"tax credits"—see s.1(2).

GENERAL NOTE

The provisions on Northern Ireland are necessary because of the transfer of the administration of child benefit and guardian's allowance from the Northern Ireland authorities to the Home Civil Service. The amendments also confirm the effect of s.16 of the Tax Credits Act 1999 in reserving tax credits as excepted matters. **1.476**

65–66. *Omitted.*

Interpretation

67.—In this Act— **1.477**

"the Board" means the Commissioners of Inland Revenue,

"modifications" includes alterations, additions and omissions, and "modifies" is to be construed accordingly,

"the Northern Ireland Department" means the Department for Social Development in Northern Ireland,

"prescribed" means prescribed by regulations, and

"tax credit" and "tax credits" have the meanings given by section 1(2).

68–70. *Omitted.*

Sch.1. *Omitted.*

SCHEDULE 2

PENALTIES: SUPPLEMENTARY

Determination of penalties by Board

1.478 **1.**—(1) The Board may make a determination—

(a) imposing a penalty under section 31, 32(2)(b) or (3) or 33; and

(b) setting it at such amount as, in their opinion, is appropriate.

(2) The Board must give notice of a determination of a penalty under this paragraph to the person on whom the penalty is imposed.

(3) The notice must state the date on which it is given and give details of the right to appeal against the determination under section 38.

(4) After the notice of a determination under this paragraph has been given the determination must not be altered except on appeal.

(5) A penalty determined under this paragraph becomes payable at the end of the period of 30 days beginning with the date on which the notice of determination is given.

2.—(1) On an appeal to them under section 38 against the determination of a penalty under para.1, the General Commissioners or Special Commissioners may—

(a) if it appears that no penalty has been incurred, set the determination aside,

(b) if the amount determined appears to be appropriate, confirm the determination,

(c) if the amount determined appears to be excessive, reduce it to such other amount (including nil) as they consider appropriate, or

(d) if the amount determined appears to be insufficient, increase it to such amount not exceeding the permitted maximum as they consider appropriate.

(2) An appeal from a decision of the Commissioners under sub-paragraph (1) lies, at the instance of the person on whom the penalty was imposed, to—

(a) the High Court, or

(b) in Scotland, the Court of Session as the Court of Exchequer in Scotland,

and on such an appeal the court has a similar jurisdiction to that conferred on the Commissioners by sub-paragraph (1).

Penalty proceedings before Commissioners

1.479 **3.**—(1) The Board may commence proceedings for a penalty under section 32(2)(a).

(2) Proceedings under this paragraph are by way of information in writing, made to the General Commissioners or Special Commissioners, and upon summons issued by them to the defendant (or defender) to appear before them at a time and place stated in the summons; and they must hear and decide each case in a summary way.

4.—(1) An appeal against the determination of a penalty in proceedings under paragraph 3 lies to the High Court or, in Scotland, the Court of Session as the Court of Exchequer in Scotland—

(a) by any party on a question of law, and

(b) by the defendant (or, in Scotland, the defender) against the amount of the penalty.

(2) On any such appeal the court may—

(a) if it appears that no penalty has been incurred, set the determination aside,

(b) if the amount determined appears to be appropriate, confirm the determination,

(c) if the amount determined appears to be excessive, reduce it to such other amount (including nil) as the court considers appropriate, or

(d) if the amount determined appears to be insufficient, increase it to such amount not exceeding the permitted maximum as the court considers appropriate.

Mitigation of penalties

1.480 **5.**—The Board may in their discretion mitigate any penalty under this Part or stay or compound any proceedings for any such penalty and may also, after judgment, further mitigate or entirely remit any such penalty.

Time limits for penalties

1.481 **6.**—(1) In the case of a penalty under s.31 relating to a tax credit for a person or persons for the whole or part of a tax year (other than a penalty to which sub-paragraph (3) applies), the Board may determine the penalty at any time before the latest of—

(a) the end of the period of one year beginning with the expiry of the period for initiating an enquiry under section 19 into the entitlement of the person, or the joint entitlement of the persons, for the tax year,
(b) if such an enquiry is made, the end of the period of one year beginning with the day on which the enquiry is completed, and
(c) if a decision relating to the entitlement of the person, or the joint entitlement of the persons, for the tax year is made under section 20(1) or (4), the end of the period of one year beginning with the day on which the decision is made.

(2) In the case of a penalty under section 32 relating to a tax credit for a person or persons for the whole or part of a tax year (other than a penalty to which sub-paragraph (3) applies), the Board may determine the penalty, or commence proceedings for it, at any time before—
(a) if an enquiry into the entitlement of the person, or the joint entitlement of the persons, for the tax year is made under section 19, the end of the period of one year beginning with the day on which the enquiry is completed, and
(b) otherwise, the end of the period of one year beginning with the expiry of the period for initiating such an enquiry.

(3) In the case of—
(a) a penalty under section 31 or 32 relating to a requirement imposed by virtue of regulations under section 25; or
(b) a penalty under section 33,
the Board may determine the penalty, or commence proceedings for it, at any time before the end of the period of six years after the date on which the penalty was incurred or began to be incurred.

Recovery of penalties

7.—(1) A penalty payable under this Part is to be treated for the purposes of Part VI of the Taxes Management Act 1970 (c.9) (collection and recovery) as if it were tax charged in an assessment and due and payable. **1.482**

(2) Regulations under section 203(2)(a) of the Income and Corporation Taxes Act 1988 (c.1) (PAYE) apply to a penalty payable under this Part as if it were an underpayment of tax for a previous year of assessment.

Sch.3–Sch.6. *Omitted.*

Employment Act 2002

(2002 c.22)

ARRANGEMENT OF SECTIONS

PART I

STATUTORY LEAVE AND PAY

CHAPTER 1

PATERNITY AND ADOPTION

Rights to leave and pay

3. Adoption leave [*omitted*]
4. Statutory adoption pay [*omitted*]*

Administration and enforcement: pay

1.484 5. General functions of the Board
6. Financial arrangements
7. Funding of employers' liabilities
8. Regulations about payment
9. Decisions and appeals
10. Powers to require information
11. Penalties: failures to comply
12. Penalties: fraud, etc.
13. Supply of information held by the Board
14. Supply of information held by the Secretary of State
15. Use of information by the Board
16. Interpretation

CHAPTER 2

MATERNITY

1.485 17. Rights during and after maternity leave [*omitted*]
18. Maternity pay period[*omitted*]*
19. Rate of statutory maternity pay [*omitted*]*
20. Entitlement to statutory maternity pay [*omitted*]*
21. Funding of employers' liabilities: statutory maternity pay [*omitted*]*

PART II

TRIBUNAL REFORM

22–28. [*omitted*]

PART III

DISPUTE RESOLUTION, ETC.

1.486 29–40. [*omitted*]

PART IV

MISCELLANEOUS AND GENERAL

1.487 41–55. [*omitted*]

Schedule 1—Penalties: procedure and appeals
Schedules 2–8 [*omitted*]

*These sections make amendments to SSCBA 1992 which are incorporated in the text of that legislation elsewhere in this volume.

General Note

On the background to the Employment Act 2002, see the General Note to SSCBA 2002, Part 12ZA. **1.488**

Schedule 1—Penalties: procedure and appeals

Part I

Statutory Leave and Pay

Chapter 1

Paternity and Adoption

Administration and enforcement: pay

General functions of the Board

5.—(1) For the purposes of the Inland Revenue Regulation Act 1890 (c.21), except sections 21, 22 and 35, everything that relates to statutory paternity pay or statutory adoption pay shall be taken to relate to inland revenue; and the expressions "in relation to Inland Revenue", "Collector of Inland Revenue" and "Officer of Inland Revenue" are to be read accordingly. **1.489**

(2) The reference in section 4(1) of that Act (appointment of collectors, officers and other persons) to collecting, receiving, managing and accounting for Inland Revenue shall be taken to include a reference to paying and managing statutory paternity pay and statutory adoption pay.

(3) In any declaration for the purposes of section 6 of the Taxes Management Act 1970 (c.9) (declarations on taking office), whether made before or after the commencement of this section, the reference to an offence relating to Inland Revenue shall be taken to include a reference to an offence relating to statutory paternity pay or statutory adoption pay.

General Note

This section ensures that the overall legal framework which governs the operation of the Inland Revenue applies also to SPP and SAP. **1.490**

Financial arrangements

6.—[*omitted*]

General Note

1.491 This section amends SSAA 1992 and SSCBA 1992 to ensure that SPP and SAP are treated in the same was as SPP and SMP in terms of their administration.

Funding of employers' liabilities

1.492 **7.**—(1) The Secretary of State shall by regulations make provision for the payment by employers of statutory paternity pay and statutory adoption pay to be funded by the Board to such extent as the regulations may specify.

(2) Regulations under subsection (1) shall—

(a) make provision for a person who has made a payment of statutory paternity pay or statutory adoption pay to be entitled, except in such circumstances as the regulations may provide, to recover an amount equal to the sum of—

(i) the aggregate of such of those payments as qualify for small employers' relief; and

(ii) an amount equal to 92 per cent of the aggregate of such of those payments as do not so qualify; and

(b) include provision for a person who has made a payment of statutory paternity pay or statutory adoption pay qualifying for small employers' relief to be entitled, except in such circumstances as the regulations may provide, to recover an additional amount equal to the amount to which the person would have been entitled under section 167(2)(b) of the Social Security Contributions and Benefits Act 1992 (corresponding provision for statutory maternity pay) had the payment been a payment of statutory maternity pay.

(3) For the purposes of subsection (2), a payment of statutory paternity pay or statutory adoption pay qualifies for small employers' relief if it wouldhave so qualified were it a payment of statutory maternity pay, treating the period for which the payment is made, in the case of statutory paternity pay, or the payee's adoption pay period, in the case of statutory adoption pay, as the maternity pay period.

(4) Regulations under subsection (1) may, in particular—

(a) make provision for funding in advance as well as in arrear;

(b) make provision for funding, or the recovery of amounts due under provision made by virtue of subsection (2)(b), by means of deductions from such amounts for which employers are accountable to the Board as the regulations may provide, or otherwise;

(c) make provision for the recovery by the Board of any sums overpaid to employers under the regulations.

(5) Where in accordance with any provision of regulations under subsection (1) an amount has been deducted from an employer's contributions payments, the amount so deducted shall (except in such cases as the Secretary of State may by regulations provide) be treated for the purposes

of any provision made by or under any enactment in relation to primary or secondary Class 1 contributions—

(a) as having been paid (on such date as may be determined in accordance with the regulations), and

(b) as having been received by the Board, towards discharging the employer's liability in respect of such contributions.

(6) Regulations under this section must be made with the concurrence of the Board.

(7) In this section, "contributions payments", in relation to an employer, means any payments which the employer is required, by or under any enactment, to make in discharge of any liability in respect of primary or secondary Class 1 contributions.

DEFINITIONS

"the Board"—see s.16.
"contributions payments"—see subs.(7).
"employer"—see *ibid.*

GENERAL NOTE

See further the SPP and SAP (Administration) Regs 2002, especially regs 3–8. **1.493**

Regulations about payment

8.—(1) The Secretary of State may make regulations with respect to the payment by employers of statutory paternity pay and statutory adoption pay. **1.494**

(2) Regulations under subsection (1) may, in particular, include provision—

(a) about the records to be kept by employers in relation to payments of statutory paternity pay and statutory adoption pay, including the length of time for which they are to be retained;

(b) for the production of wages sheets and other documents and records to officers of the Board for the purpose of enabling them to satisfy themselves that statutory paternity pay and statutory adoption pay have been paid and are being paid, in accordance with the regulations, to employees who are entitled to them;

(c) for requiring employers to provide information to employees (in their itemised pay statements or otherwise);

(d) for requiring employers to make returns to the Board containing such particulars with respect to payments of statutory paternity pay and statutory adoption pay as the regulations may provide.

(3) Regulations under subsection (1) must be made with the concurrence of the Board.

DEFINITIONS

"the Board"—see s.16.
"employer"—see *ibid.*

GENERAL NOTE

See further the SPP and SAP (Administration) Regs 2002, regs 9 and 10. **1.495**

Decisions and appeals

9.—[*omitted*]

GENERAL NOTE

1.496 This section amends ss.8, 11 and 14 of the Social Security Contributions (Transfer of Functions, etc.) Act 1999; the relevant amendments are incorporated elsewhere in this volume.

Powers to require information

1.497 **10.**—(1) The Secretary of State may by regulations make provision enabling an officer of the Board authorised by the Board for the purposes of this section to require persons of a description specified in the regulations to provide, or produce for inspection, within such period as the regulations may require, such information or documents as the officer may reasonably require for the purpose of ascertaining whether statutory paternity pay or statutory adoption pay is or was payable to or in respect of any person.

(2) The descriptions of person which may be specified by regulations under subsection (1) include, in particular—

(a) any person claiming to be entitled to statutory paternity pay or statutory adoption pay,
(b) any person who is, or has been, the spouse or partner of such a person as is mentioned in paragraph (a),
(c) any person who is, or has been, an employer of such a person as is mentioned in paragraph (a),
(d) any person carrying on an agency or other business for the introduction or supply to persons requiring them of persons available to do work or to perform services, and
(e) any person who is a servant or agent of any such person as is specified in paragraphs (a) to (d).

(3) Regulations under subsection (1) must be made with the concurrence of the Board.

DEFINITIONS

"the Board"—see s.16.
"employer"—see *ibid.*

GENERAL NOTE

1.498 See further the SPP and SAP (Administration) Regs 2002, especially regs 11–14.

Penalties: failures to comply

1.499 **11.**—(1) Where a person—

(a) fails to produce any document or record, provide any information or make any return, in accordance with regulations under section 8, or
(b) fails to provide any information or document in accordance with regulations under section 10,

he shall be liable to the penalties mentioned in subsection (2) below (subject to subsection (4)).

(2) The penalties are—

(a) a penalty not exceeding £300, and

(b) if the failure continues after a penalty is imposed under paragraph (a), a further penalty or penalties not exceeding £60 for each day on which the failure continues after the day on which the penalty under that paragraph was imposed (but excluding any day for which a penalty under this paragraph has already been imposed).

(3) Where a person fails to keep records in accordance with regulations under section 8, he shall be liable to a penalty not exceeding £3,000.

(4) Subject to subsection (5), no penalty shall be imposed under subsection (2) or (3) at any time after the failure concerned has been remedied.

(5) Subsection (4) does not apply to the imposition of a penalty under subsection (2)(a) in respect of a failure within subsection (1)(a).

(6) Where, in the case of any employee, an employer refuses or repeatedly fails to make payments of statutory paternity pay or statutory adoption pay in accordance with any regulations under section 8, the employer shall be liable to a penalty not exceeding £3,000.

(7) Section 118(2) of the Taxes Management Act 1970 (c.9) (extra time for compliance, etc.) shall apply for the purposes of subsections (1), (3) and (6) as it applies for the purposes of that Act.

(8) Schedule 1 to this Act (penalties: procedure and appeals) has effect in relation to penalties under this section.

DEFINITIONS

"the Board"—see s.16.
"employer"—see *ibid.*

GENERAL NOTE

This provision, imposing penalties on employers who fail to comply with the requirements of the SPP and SAP schemes, is modelled on the equivalent provision for tax credits: TCA 2002, s.32. **1.500**

Penalties: fraud etc.

12.—(1) Where a person fraudulently or negligently— **1.501**

(a) makes any incorrect statement or declaration in connection with establishing entitlement to statutory paternity pay, or

(b) provides any incorrect information or document of a kind mentioned in regulations under section 10(1) so far as relating to statutory paternity pay,

he shall be liable to a penalty not exceeding £300.

(2) Where a person fraudulently or negligently—

(a) makes any incorrect statement or declaration in connection with establishing entitlement to statutory adoption pay, or

(b) provides any incorrect information or document of a kind mentioned in regulations under section 10(1) so far as relating to statutory adoption pay,

he shall be liable to a penalty not exceeding £3,000.

(3) Where an employer fraudulently or negligently makes incorrect payments of statutory paternity pay, he shall be liable to a penalty not exceeding £300.

(4) Where an employer fraudulently or negligently makes incorrect payments of statutory adoption pay, he shall be liable to a penalty not exceeding £3,000.

(5) Where an employer fraudulently or negligently—

(a) produces any incorrect document or record, provides any incorrect information or makes any incorrect return, of a kind mentioned in regulations under section 8; or

(b) receives incorrect payments in pursuance of regulations under section 7;

he shall be liable to a penalty not exceeding £3,000 or, if the offence relates only to statutory paternity pay, £300.

(6) Schedule 1 (penalties: procedure and appeals) has effect in relation to penalties under this section.

DEFINITIONS

"the Board"—see s.16.
"employer"—see *ibid.*

GENERAL NOTE

1.502 This provision, imposing penalties on employers who act fraudulently in connection with the SPP and SAP schemes, is modelled on the equivalent provision for tax credits: TCA 2002, s.31.

Supply of information held by the Board

1.503 **13.**—(1) This section applies to information which is held for the purposes of functions relating to statutory paternity pay or statutory adoption pay—

(a) by the Board, or

(b) by a person providing services to the Board, in connection with the provision of those services.

(2) Information to which this section applies may be supplied—

(a) to the Secretary of State or the Department; or

(b) to a person providing services to the Secretary of State or the Department;

for use for the purposes of functions relating to social security, child support or war pensions.

DEFINITIONS

"the Board"—see s.16.
"the Department"—see *ibid.*

Supply of information held by the Secretary of State

1.504 **14.**—(1) This section applies to information which is held for the purposes of functions relating to statutory paternity pay or statutory adoption pay—

(a) by the Secretary of State or the Department, or

(b) by a person providing services to the Secretary of State or the Department, in connection with the provision of those services.

(2) Information to which this section applies may be supplied—

(a) to the Board, or

(b) to a person providing services to the Board,

for use for the purposes of functions relating to statutory paternity pay or statutory adoption pay.

DEFINITIONS

"the Board"—see s.16.

"the Department"—see *ibid.*

Use of information by the Board

15.—(1) Information which is held— **1.505**

(a) by the Board, or

(b) by a person providing services to the Board, in connection with the provision of those services,

for the purposes of any functions specifiedin any paragraph of subsection (2) below may be used for the purposes of, or for any purposes connected with, the exercise of any functions specified in any other paragraph of that subsection, and may be supplied to any person providing services to the Board for those purposes.

(2) The functions referred to in subsection (1) above are—

(a) the functions of the Board in relation to statutory paternity pay;

(b) their functions in relation to statutory adoption pay, and

(c) their functions in relation to tax, contributions, statutory sick pay, statutory maternity pay or tax credits, or functions under Part III of the Pension Schemes Act 1993 (c.48) (certification of pension scheme, etc.) or Part III of the Pension Schemes (Northern Ireland) Act 1993 (c.49) (corresponding provisions for Northern Ireland).

(3) In subsection (2)(c) above, "contributions" means contributions under Part I of the Social Security Contributions and Benefits Act 1992 (c.4) or Part I of the Social Security Contributions and Benefits (Northern Ireland) Act 1992 (c.7).

DEFINITIONS

"the Board"—see s.16.

Interpretation

16.—In sections 5 to 15— **1.506**

"the Board" means the Commissioners of Inland Revenue;

"the Department" means the Department for Social Development or the Department for Employment and Learning;

"employer" and "employee" have the same meanings as in Parts 12ZA and 12ZB of the Social Security Contributions and Benefits Act 1992.

Chapter 2

Maternity

17.–21. [*omitted*]

General Note

1.507 Section 17 amends the provisions governing the right to maternity leave under the Employment Rights Act 1996. Sections 18–20 amend ss.164 and 165 of the SSCBA 1992, and substitutes a new s.166 of that Act, while s.21 substitutes a new s.167 of the same Act. These amendments are incorporated elsewhere in this volume.

SCHEDULE 1

Penalties: Procedure and Appeals

Determination of penalties by officer of Board

1.508 **1.**—(1) Subject to sub-paragraph (2) and except where proceedings have been instituted under paragraph 5, an officer of the Board authorised by the Board for the purposes of this paragraph may make a determination—

(a) imposing a penalty under section 11 or 12, and
(b) setting it at such amount as, in his opinion, is correct or appropriate.

(2) Sub-paragraph (1) does not apply to the imposition of such a penalty as is mentioned in section 11(2)(a).

(3) Notice of a determination of a penalty under this paragraph shall be served on the person liable to the penalty and shall state the date on which it is issued and the time within which an appeal against the determination may be made.

(4) After the notice of a determination under this paragraph has been served the determination shall not be altered except in accordance with this paragraph or on appeal.

(5) If it is discovered by an officer of the Board authorised by the Board for the purposes of this paragraph that the amount of a penalty determined under this paragraph is or has become insufficient, the officer may make a determination in a further amount so that the penalty is set at the amount which, in his opinion, is correct or appropriate.

Provisions supplementary to paragraph 1

1.509 **2.**—(1) A penalty determined under paragraph 1 above shall be due and payable at the end of the period of thirty days beginning with the date of the issue of the notice of determination.

(2) Part 6 of the Taxes Management Act 1970 (c.9) shall apply in relation to a penalty determined under para.1 as if it were tax charged in an assessment and due and payable.

Appeals against penalty determinations

1.510 **3.**—(1) An appeal may be brought against the determination of a penalty under paragraph 1.

(2) The provisions of the Taxes Management Act 1970 relating to appeals, except section 50(6) to (8), shall have effect in relation to an appeal against such a determination as they have effect in relation to an appeal against an assessment to tax.

(3) On an appeal by virtue of sub-paragraph (2) against the determination of a penalty under paragraph 1, the General or Special Commissioners may—

(a) if it appears to them that no penalty has been incurred, set the determination aside,
(b) if the amount determined appears to them to be appropriate, confirm the determination,
(c) if the amount determined appears to them to be excessive, reduce it to such other amount (including nil) as they consider appropriate,

(d) if the amount determined appears to them to be insufficient, increase it to such amount not exceeding the permitted maximum as they consider appropriate.

(4) An appeal from a decision of the Commissioners against the amount of a penalty which has been determined under paragraph 1 or this paragraph shall lie, at the instance of the person liable to the penalty—

(a) to the High Court, or

(b) in Scotland, to the Court of Session as the Court of Exchequer in Scotland, and on that appeal the court shall have the like jurisdiction as is conferred on the Commissioners by virtue of this paragraph.

Penalty proceedings before Commissioners

4.—(1) An officer of the Board authorised by the Board for the purposes of this paragraph may commence proceedings for any penalty to which sub-paragraph (1) of paragraph 1 does not apply by virtue of sub-paragraph (2) of that paragraph. **1.511**

(2) Proceedings under this paragraph shall be by way of information in writing, made to the General or Special Commissioners, and upon summons issued by them to the defendant (or, in Scotland, the defender) to appear before them at a time and place stated in the summons; and they shall hear and decide each case in a summary way.

(3) Part 6 of the Taxes Management Act 1970 (c.9) shall apply in relation to a penalty determined in proceedings under this paragraph as if it were tax charged in an assessment and due and payable.

(4) An appeal against the determination of a penalty in proceedings under this paragraph shall lie to the High Court or, in Scotland, to the Court of Session as the Court of Exchequer in Scotland—

(a) by any party on a question of law; and

(b) by the defendant (or, in Scotland, the defender) against the amount of the penalty.

(5) On any such appeal the court may—

(a) if it appears that no penalty has been incurred, set the determination aside;

(b) if the amount determined appears to be appropriate, confirm the determination;

(c) if the amount determined appears to be excessive, reduce it to such other amount (including nil) as the court considers appropriate;

(d) if the amount determined appears to be insufficient, increase it to such amount not exceeding the permitted maximum as the court considers appropriate.

Penalty proceedings before court

5.—(1) Where in the opinion of the Board the liability of any person for a penalty under section 11 or 12 arises by reason of the fraud of that or any other person, proceedings for the penalty may be instituted before the High Court or, in Scotland, the Court of Session as the Court of Exchequer in Scotland. **1.512**

(2) Subject to sub-paragraph (3), proceedings under this paragraph shall be instituted—

(a) in England and Wales, in the name of the Attorney General; and

(b) in Scotland, in the name of the Advocate General for Scotland.

(3) Sub-paragraph (2) shall not prevent proceedings under this paragraph being instituted in England and Wales under the Crown Proceedings Act 1947 (c.44) by and in the name of the Board as an authorised department for the purposes of that Act.

(4) Any proceedings under this paragraph instituted in England and Wales shall be deemed to be civil proceedings by the Crown within the meaning of Part II of the Crown Proceedings Act 1947.

(5) If in proceedings under this paragraph the court does not find that fraud is proved but considers that the person concerned is nevertheless liable to a penalty, the court may determine a penalty notwithstanding that, but for the opinion of the Board as to fraud, the penalty would not have been a matter for the court.

Mitigation of penalties

6.—The Board may in their discretion mitigate any penalty under section 11 or 12, or stay or compound any proceedings for a penalty, and may also, after judgment, further mitigate or entirely remit the penalty. **1.512.1**

Time-limits for penalties

1.513 **7.**—A penalty under section 11 or 12 may be determined by an officer of the Board, or proceedings for the penalty may be commenced before the Commissioners or the court, at any time within six years after the date on which the penalty was incurred or began to be incurred.

Interest on penalties

1.514 **8.**—(1) After paragraph (p) of section 178(2) of the Finance Act 1989 (c.26) (setting rates of interest) there shall be inserted—

"(q) paragraph 8 of Schedule 1 to the Employment Act 2002."

(2) A penalty under section 11 or 12 shall carry interest at the rate applicable under section 178 of the Finance Act 1989 from the date on which it becomes due and payable until payment.

Interpretation

1.515 **9.** In this Schedule—

"the Board" means the Commissioners of Inland Revenue;

"General Commissioners" and "Special Commissioners" have the same meanings as in the Taxesdd Management Act 1970 (c.9).

Income Tax (Earnings and Pensions) Act 2003

(2003 c.1)

ARRANGEMENT OF SELECTED SECTIONS

PART I

OVERVIEW

PART 2

EMPLOYMENT INCOME: CHARGE TO TAX

CHAPTER 1

INTRODUCTION

CHAPTER 2

TAX ON EMPLOYMENT INCOME

6. Nature of charge to tax on employment income **1.517**
7. Meaning of "employment income", "general earnings" and "specific employment income"
8. Meaning of "exempt income"

CHAPTER 3

OPERATION OF TAX CHARGE

9. Amount of employment income charged to tax **1.518**
10. Meaning of "taxable earnings" and "taxable specific income"
11. Calculation of "net taxable earnings"
12. Calculation of "net taxable specific income"
13. Person liable for tax

CHAPTER 7

APPLICATION OF PROVISIONS TO AGENCY WORKERS

Agency workers

44. Treatment of workers supplied by agencies **1.519**

PART 3

EMPLOYMENT INCOME: EARNINGS AND BENEFITS, ETC. TREATED AS EARNINGS

CHAPTER 1

EARNINGS

62. Earnings **1.523**

CHAPTER 2

TAXABLE BENEFITS: THE BENEFITS CODE

The benefits code

63. The benefits code **1.524**
64. Relationship between earnings and benefits code

65. Dispensations relating to benefits within provisions not applicable to lower-paid employment

General definitions for benefits code

1.525 66. Meaning of "employment" and related expressions

CHAPTER 3

TAXABLE BENEFITS: EXPENSES PAYMENTS

1.526 70. Sums in respect of expenses
71. Meaning of paid or put at disposal by reason of the employment
72. Sums in respect of expenses treated as earnings

CHAPTER 4

TAXABLE BENEFITS: VOUCHERS AND CREDIT-TOKENS

Cash vouchers: introduction

1.527 73. Cash vouchers to which this chapter applies
74. Provision for, or receipt by, member of employee's family

Meaning of "cash voucher"

1.528 75. Meaning of "cash voucher"
76. Sickness benefits-related voucher

Benefit of cash voucher treated as earnings

1.529 81. Benefit of cash voucher treated as earnings

Non-cash vouchers: introduction

1.530 82. Non-cash vouchers to which this chapter applies

Meaning of "non-cash voucher"

1.531 84. Meaning of "non-cash voucher"

Benefit of non-cash voucher treated as earnings

1.532 87. Benefit of non-cash voucher treated as earnings

Credit-tokens: introduction

90. Credit-tokens to which this chapter applies **1.533**

Meaning of "credit-token"

92. Meaning of "credit-token" **1.534**

Benefit of credit-token treated as earnings

94. Benefit of credit-token treated as earnings **1.535**

General supplementary provisions

95. Disregard for money, goods or services obtained **1.536**

CHAPTER 6

TAXABLE BENEFITS: CARS, VANS AND RELATED BENEFITS

General

114. Cars, vans and related benefits **1.537**
115. Meaning of "car" and "van"
116. Meaning of when car or van is available to employee
117. Meaning of car or van made available by reason of employment
118. Availability for private use

Cars: benefit treated as earnings

120. Benefit of car treated as earnings **1.538**
121. Method of calculating the cash equivalent of the benefit of a car

Car fuel: benefit treated as earnings

149. Benefit of car fuel treated as earnings **1.539**
150. Car fuel: calculating the cash equivalent
151. Car fuel: nil cash equivalent

CHAPTER 10

TAXABLE BENEFITS: RESIDUAL LIABILITY TO CHARGE

Introduction

201. Employment-related benefits **1.540**
202. Excluded benefits

Cash equivalent of benefit treated as earnings

1.541 203. Cash equivalent of benefit treated as earnings

Determination of the cost of the benefit

1.542 204. Cost of the benefit: basic rule
210. Exemption of minor benefits

CHAPTER 11

TAXABLE BENEFITS: EXCLUSION OF LOWER-PAID EMPLOYMENTS FROM PARTS OF BENEFIT CODE

Introduction

1.543 216. Provisions not applicable to lower-paidemployments

What is lower-paid employment?

1.544 217. Meaning of "lower-paid employment"
218. Calculation of earnings rate for a tax year
219. Extra amounts to be added in connection with a car

PART 5

EMPLOYMENT INCOME: DEDUCTIONS ALLOWED FROM EARNINGS

CHAPTER 1

DEDUCTIONS ALLOWED FROM EARNINGS: GENERAL RULES

Introduction

1.545 327. Deductions from earnings: general

General rules

1.546 328. The income from which deductions may be made
329. Deductions from earnings not to exceed earnings
330. Prevention of double deductions
331. Order for making deductions
332. Meaning of "the deductibility provisions"

CHAPTER 2

DEDUCTIONS FOR EMPLOYEE'S EXPENSES

Introduction

333. Scope of this chapter: expenses paid by the employee **1.547**
334. Effect of reimbursement, etc.

General rule for deduction of employee's expenses

336. Deductions for expenses: the general rule **1.548**

Travel expenses

337. Travel in performance of duties **1.549**
338. Travel for necessary attendance
339. Meaning of "workplace" and "permanent workplace"

Fees and subscriptions

343. Deduction for professional membership fees **1.550**
344. Deduction for annual subscriptions

PART 9

PENSION INCOME

CHAPTER 1

INTRODUCTION

565. Structure of Part 9 **1.551**

CHAPTER 2

TAX ON PENSION INCOME

566. Nature of charge to tax on pension income and relevant definitions **1.552**
567. Amount charged to tax
568. Person liable for tax

CHAPTER 3

UNITED KINGDOAM SOCIAL SECURITY PENSIONS

1.553 569. United Kingdom pensions
570. "Pension": interpretation
571. Taxable pension income
572. Person liable for tax

CHAPTER 5

UNITED KINGDOM SOCIAL SECURITY PENSIONS

1.554 577. United Kingdom social security pensions
578. Taxable pension income
579. Person liable for tax

CHAPTER 6

APPROVED RETIREMENT BENEFITS SCHEMES

Pensions and annuities

1.555 580. Pensions and annuities
581. Taxable pension income
582. Person liable for tax

Interpretation etc.

1.556 586. Meaning of "retirement benefits scheme", etc.
588. Meaning of "employee" and "ex-spouse"

CHAPTER 15

VOLUNTARY ANNUAL PAYMENTS

1.557 633. Voluntary annual payments
634. Taxable pension income: UK voluntary annual payments
635. Taxable pension income: foreign voluntary annual payments
636. Person liable for tax

CHAPTER 16

EXEMPTION FOR CERTAIN LUMP SUMS

PART 10

SOCIAL SECURITY INCOME

CHAPTER 1

INTRODUCTION

CHAPTER 2

TAX ON SOCIAL SECURITY INCOME

CHAPTER 3

TAXABLE UK SOCIAL SECURITY BENEFITS

CHAPTER 4

TAXABLE UK SOCIAL SECURITY BENEFITS: EXEMPTIONS

Incapacity benefit

Income support

1.563 665. Exempt unless payable to member of couple involved in trade dispute
666. Child maintenance bonus
667. Amounts in excess of taxable maximum
668. Taxable maximum
669. Interpretation

Jobseeker's allowance

1.564 670. Child maintenance bonus
671. Amounts in excess of taxable maximum
672. Taxable maximum: general
673. Taxable maximum: income-based jobseeker's allowance
674. Taxable maximum: contribution-based jobseeker's allowance
675. Interpretation

Increases in respect of children

1.565 676. Increases in respect of children

CHAPTER 5

UK SOCIAL SECURITY BENEFITS WHOLLY EXEMPT FROM INCOME TAX

1.566 677. UK social security benefits wholly exempt from tax: Table B

CHAPTER 6

TAXABLE FOREIGN BENEFITS

1.567 678. Taxable benefits: foreign benefits
679. Taxable social security income
680. Person liable for tax

PART 13

SUPPLEMENTARY PROVISIONS

Interpretation

1.568 720. Meaning of "the Inland Revenue", etc.
721. Other definitions

Schedule 1—Abbreviations and defined expressions
Part 1—Abbreviations of Acts and instruments
Part 2—Index of expressions defined in this Act or ICTA

INTRODUCTION AND GENERAL NOTE

This Act (destined to be known as ITEPA or ITEPA 2003) is the second of the major income tax Acts produced by the Tax Law Rewrite Project, and the first that repeals and replaces a major part of the Income and Corporation Taxes Act 1988 (ICTA). (The first was the Capital Allowances Act 2001.) It took effect from and including the start of the 2003–04 income tax year, April 6, 2003, the same day that the TCA 2002 came fully into effect. It is of considerable importance to tax credits because it entirely rewrites the income tax rules dealing with earnings from employments and offices, pension income, and social security income. The time-hallowed "Schedule E" and its charge to tax on "offices and employments on emoluments therefrom" has at last been relegated to history and a codified set of provisions taxing employment income, pension income and social security income put in its place. The approach of TCA 2002 is to rely on income tax rules for the calculation of income for tax credits purposes. The provisions of ITEPA are therefore the rules that will apply to the great majority of claimants for tax credits. **1.569**

ITEPA is of considerable length and detail, running to 725 sections and 8 Schedules on enactment. (And that is despite a decision in principle to minimise the use of schedules in Rewrite Bills.) Besides consolidating the existing statute law from the ICTA 1988 and its many amendments, and incorporating provisions previously in schedules and regulations into the main part of the Act, ITEPA also includes in codified form relevant decisions of the courts. It also turns into legislative form some of the extra statutory concessions and Revenue practices by which the previous legislation was operated. It also removes redundant legislation, corrects inconsistencies, and makes other minor changes to the previous law. Some policy changes were also made in other legislation before ITEPA was enacted, and these were then incorporated into ITEPA. It is therefore more than simply a consolidation of the law, and is better viewed as a code. It has been drafted in the form of a code, and therefore includes signposting provisions and a far stronger internal structure than the previous legislation.

ITEPA also uses, where possible, plain English. Its language is therefore updated from the "old" language of "Sch.E" and "emoluments".

The Tax Credits (Definition and Calculation of Income) Regulations 2002, as amended to take into account ITEPA, refer to a considerable number of provisions of ITEPA. This selection of sections from ITEPA includes the more important of those sections, together with the sections that set out the internal signposting of ITEPA and its definitions. It is not a complete reproduction of all ITEPA sections, as some of the anti-avoidance provisions that are applied to tax credits are highly technical and, in practice, sometimes quite controversial in application, while others will, it is anticipated, rarely be directly relevant to tax credits claims. In particular, the following parts are entirely omitted:

Part 4: Employment income: Exemptions
Part 6: Employment Income: Income which is not earnings or share-related
Part 7: Employment income: Share-related income and exemptions
Part 8: Former employees: Deductions for liabilities
Part 9: Pay As You Earn
Schs 2–8

Part 2, Chapter 8 of ITEPA (ss.48–61) deal with the so-called IR35 provisions, namely the provisions under which income of a "pocket book" company could be treated as the employment income of the individual who owned the company so that income was not diverted so as to be excluded from income tax. It was understood that these sections would apply to tax credits and they were therefore included in the 2003–04 edition of this volume. However, amendments to the Working Tax Credit (Entitlement and Maximum Rate) Regulations 2002 were made by the Tax Credits (Miscellaneous Amendments No.2) Regulations 2003 (SI 2003/2815) to clarify the intended policy that these provisions do not apply to tax credits. They are therefore no longer of relevance to this volume.

Part 7 of ITEPA was repealed completely and replaced by new provisions by the Finance Act 2003, s.140 and Sch.22 with effect from April 15, 2003. The original Pt 7 was outside the scope of tax credits income calculations. The new Pt 7 is not, by reason of amendment of the Tax Credits (Definition and Calculation of Income) Regulations 2002 (SI 2002/2006), reg.4. See the note to that regulation. The text of the new Pt 7 is not reproduced in this volume.

But particular attention has been paid to sections making special provision for those who are sick or disabled, and to the taxation of state pensions and social security benefits.

Interpreting and applying ITEPA

1.570 While from a technical viewpoint ITEPA is a consolidation measure, it varies in several ways from the consolidation performed by the ICTA 1988, part of which it repeals and replaces. There are a series of both policy and technical changes in ITEPA, compared with the sections of ICTA 1988 that it replaces. But ITEPA, as noted above, is also used to incorporate both practices and case law. The ITEPA Bill was accompanied by the usual tables of origins and destinations. But it also provides two other aids to those interpreting and applying it. Schedule 1 includes a full index of defined terms used in ITEPA, including terms it derives from ICTA 1988 and other income tax legislation. Reference should be made to Sch.1 Pt 2 for any phrase that needs interpretation. The ITEPA Bill was publishedfully in draft before submission to Parliament. The draft Bill was accompanied by a commentary. The draft Bill was then amended before publication as a Parliamentary Bill, accompanied by three volumes of explanatory notes. Volumes I and II contain extensive notes on clauses. Much of Vol.II comprises Annex 1. This is a detailed explanation of 183 changes made by the Bill to the previous law. Volume III consists of Annex 2. These are 72 separate notes on technical points in clauses. Finally, Annex 3 lists former extra statutory concessions now enacted for the first time.

There is another significant change to the way the ITEPA Bill was handled compared with not only ICTA 1988 but most Public Acts. It was not debated in substance in Parliament. Instead, it was considered by a Joint Committee of the Houses. The Joint Committee recommended the Bill to both Houses with a few further (minimal, and technical) changes. With those changes only, the Bill received royal assent. In effect, the debating process of Parliament was bypassed in favour of the much wider consultation conducted as part of the Tax Law Rewrite Project. But that also means that the interpretative techniques described as ascertaining the "intention of Parliament" cannot be applied in the form of *Pepper v Hart* arguments. Rather, in so far as there is any change with the previous law, the intention is in the notes presented with the Bill. And, in addition, the reports of the Tax Law Rewrite Project give a definitive, if technically non-authoritative, account of what the previous legislation is understood to mean.

The result should be an Act in which there is far less room for genuine doubt or dispute about what the words mean, if full regard is had to the pedigree of the Act. Bearing that pedigree in mind, no attempt is made in this volume to do more than indicate these sources.

PART 1

OVERVIEW

Overview of contents of this Act

1.—(1) This Act imposes charges to income tax on— **1.571**

(a) employment income (see Parts 2 to 7),

(b) pension income (see Part 9), and

(c) social security income (see Part 10).

(2) Those charges to tax have effect for the purposes of section 1(1) of ICTA (the general charge to income tax).

(3) This Act also—

(a) confers certain reliefs in respect of liabilities of former employees (see Part 8);

(b) provides for the assessment, collection and recovery of income tax in respect of employment, pension or social security income that is PAYE income (see Part 2); and

(c) allows deductions to be made from such income in respect of payroll giving (see Part 12).

Abbreviations and general index in Schedule 1

2.—(1) Schedule 1 (abbreviations and defined expressions) applies for the purposes of this Act. **1.572**

(2) In Schedule 1—

(a) Part 1 gives the meaning of the abbreviated references to Acts and instruments used in this Act; and

(b) Part 2 lists the places where expressions used in this Act are defined or otherwise explained.

(3) *Omitted*

PART 2

EMPLOYMENT INCOME: CHARGE TO TAX

CHAPTER 1

INTRODUCTION

Structure of employment income Parts

3.—(1) The structure of the employment income Parts is as follows— **1.573**

This Part imposes the charge to tax on employment income, and sets out—

(a) how the amount charged to tax for a tax year is to be calculated; and

(b) who is liable for the tax charged;

Part 3 sets out what are earnings and provides for amounts to be treated as earnings;

Part 4 deals with exemptions from the charge to tax under this Part (and, in some cases, from other charges to tax);

Part 5 deals with deductions from taxable earnings;

Part 6 deals with employment income other than earnings or share-related income; and

Part 7 deals with share-related income and exemptions.

(2) In this Act "the employment income Parts" means this Part and Parts 3 to 7.

GENERAL NOTE

1.574 Part 4 (Employment income: Exemptions)—ss.227–326—is entirely omitted from this work. It comprises a codified list of all exemptions from the charge to income tax otherwise imposed by ITEPA on various earnings and benefits, under the following chapter heads: mileage allowances and passenger payments; transport travel and subsistence; education and training; recreational benefits; non-cash vouchers and credit-tokens; removal benefits and expenses; special kinds of employee; pension provision; termination of employment; and miscellaneous. The general rule of income tax law is that it is for a claimant to claim for, and show that he or she is entitled to, the benefit of an exemption.

Part 6 is also entirely omitted. It comprises ss.386–416, and deals with payments to, and benefits from, non-approved pension schemes, and payments on termination of employment.

Part 7 is also entirely omitted. It is a lengthy part—ss.417–564 and Schs 2–5. They deal with the detail of the various kinds of tax charge on, and exemption of, share-related income including all forms of benefits obtained by shares or interests in shares.

"Employment" for the purposes of the employment income Parts

1.575 **4.**—(1) In the employment income Parts "employment" includes in particular—

(a) any employment under a contract of service,

(b) any employment under a contract of apprenticeship, and

(c) any employment in the service of the Crown.

(2) In those Parts, "employed", "employee" and "employer" have corresponding meanings.

GENERAL NOTE

1.576 There are no general income tax (or, more generally, tax) rules defining whether an individual is an employee or self-employed, or whether a relationship is an employment relationship. That is a matter to be decided by general law. There is considerable case law on the subject, some of it deriving from income tax and some from social security cases. Under the Social Security (Transfer of Functions) Act 1999, s.8, decisions about the same question for the purposes of the Social Security Contributions and Benefits Act 1992 were transferred to the Inland Revenue and, on appeal, to the tax appeal tribunals. There is, however, no equivalent provision in the TCA 2002. It would seem, therefore, that appeals about Revenue decisions about employment for tax credit purposes go to appeal tribunals, not tax appeal tribunals.

Application to offices and office-holders

5.—(1) The provisions of the employment income Parts that are expressed to apply to employments apply equally to offices, unless otherwise indicated. 1.577

(2) In those provisions as they apply to an office—

(a) references to being employed are to being the holder of the office;

(b) "employee" means the office-holder;

(c) "employer" means the person under whom the office-holder holds office.

(3) In the employment income Parts "office" includes in particular any position which has an existence independent of the person who holds it and may be filled by successive holders.

Chapter 2

Tax on Employment Income

Nature of charge to tax on employment income

6.—(1) The charge to tax on employment income under this Part is a charge to tax on— 1.578

(a) general earnings; and

(b) specific employment income.

The meaning of "employment income", "general earnings" and "specific employment income" is given in section 7.

(2) The amount of general earnings or specific employment income which is chargedto tax in a particular tax year is set out in section 9.

(3) The rules in Chapters 4 and 5 of this Part, which are concerned with—

(a) the residence and domicile of an employee in a tax year; and

(b) the tax year in which amounts are receivedor remitted to the United Kingdom;

apply for the purposes of the charge to tax on general earnings but not that on specific employment income.

(4) The person who is liable for any tax chargedon employment income is set out in section 13.

(5) Employment income is not chargedto tax under this Part if it is within the charge to tax under Case I of Schedule D by virtue of section 314(1) of ICTA (divers and diving supervisors).

Meaning of "employment income", "general earnings" and "specific employment income"

7.—(1) This section gives the meaning for the purposes of the Tax Acts of "employment income", "general earnings" and "specific employment income". 1.579

(2) "Employment income" means—

(a) earnings within Chapter 1 of Part 3;

(b) any amount treated as earnings (see subsection (5)); or
(c) any amount which counts as employment income (see subsection (6)).

(3) "General earnings" means—
(a) earnings within Chapter 1 of Part 3; or
(b) any amount treated as earnings (see subsection (5));
excluding in each case any exempt income.

(4) "Specific employment income" means any amount which counts as employment income (see subsection (6)), excluding any exempt income.

(5) Subsection (2)(b) or (3)(b) refers to any amount treated as earnings under—
(a) Chapters 7 and 8 of this Part (application of provisions to agency workers and workers under arrangements made by intermediaries),
(b) Chapters 2 to 11 of Part 3 (the benefits code),
(c) Chapters 12 of Part 3 (payments treated as earnings), or
(d) section 262 of CAA 2001 (balancing charges to be given effect by treating them as earnings).

(6) Subsection (2)(c) or (4) refers to any amount which counts as employment income by virtue of—
(a) Part 6 (income which is not earnings or share-related),
(b) Part 7 (share-related income and exemptions), or
(c) any other enactment.

Meaning of "exempt income"

1.580 **8.**—For the purposes of the employment income Parts, an amount of employment income within paragraph (a), (b) or (c) of section 7(2) is "exempt income" if, as a result of any exemption in Part 4 or elsewhere, no liability to income tax arises in respect of it as such an amount.

CHAPTER 3

OPERATION OF TAX CHARGE

Amount of employment income charged to tax

1.581 **9.**—(1) The amount of employment income which is charged to tax under this Part for a particular tax year is as follows.

(2) In the case of general earnings, the amount charged is the net taxable earnings from an employment in the year.

(3) That amount is calculated under section 11 by reference to any taxable earnings from the employment in the year (see section 10(2)).

(4) In the case of specific employment income, the amount charged is the net taxable specific income from an employment for the year.

(5) That amount is calculated under section 12 by reference to any taxable specific income from the employment for the year (see section 10(3)).

(6) Accordingly, no amount of employment income is charged to tax under this Part for a particular tax year unless—

(a) in the case of general earnings, they are taxable earnings from an employment in that year; or
(b) in the case of specific employment income, it is taxable specific income from an employment for that year.

Meaning of "taxable earnings" and "taxable specific income"

10.—(1) This section explains what is meant by "taxable earnings" and "taxable specific income" in the employment income Parts. 1.582

(2) "Taxable earnings" from an employment in a tax year are to be determined in accordance with—
(a) Chapter 4 of this Part (rules applying to employees resident, ordinarily resident and domiciled in the UK); or
(b) Chapter 5 of this Part (rules applying to employees resident, ordinarily resident or domiciled outside the UK).

(3) "Taxable specific income" from an employment for a tax year means the full amount of any specific employment income which, by virtue of Part 6 or 7 or any other enactment, counts as employment income for that year in respect of the employment.

Calculation of "net taxable earnings"

11.—(1) For the purposes of this Part, the "net taxable earnings" from an employment in a tax year are given by the formula— 1.583

TE – DE,

where—

TE means the total amount of any taxable earnings from the employment in the tax year; and

DE means the total amount of any deductions allowed from those earnings under provisions listed in sections 327(3) to (5) (deductions from earnings: general).

(2) If the amount calculated under subsection (1) is negative, the net taxable earnings from the employment in the year are to be taken to be nil instead.

(3) Relief may be available under section 380(1) of ICTA (set-off against general income)—
(a) where TE is negative; or
(b) in certain exceptional cases where the amount calculated under subsection (1) is negative.

(4) If a person has more than one employment in a tax year, the calculation under subsection (1) must be carried out in relation to each of the employments.

Calculation of "net taxable specific income"

12.—(1) For the purposes of this Part the "net taxable specific income" from an employment for a tax year is given by the formula— 1.584

TSI – DSI,

where—

TSI means the amount of any taxable specific income from the employment for the tax year; and

DSI means the total amount of any deductions allowed from that income under provisions of the Tax Acts not included in the lists in section 327(3) and (4) (deductions from earnings: general).

(2) If the amount calculated under subsection (1) is negative, the net taxable specific income from the employment for the year is to be taken to be nil instead.

(3) If a person has more than one kind of specific employment income from an employment for a tax year, the calculation under subsection (1) must be carried out in relation to each of those kinds of specific employment income; and in such a case the "net taxable specific income" from the employment for that year is the total of all the amounts so calculated.

Person liable for tax

1.585 **13.**—(1) The person liable for any tax on employment income under this Part is the taxable person mentioned in subsection (2) or (3). This is subject to subsection (4).

(2) If the tax is on general earnings, "the taxable person" is the person to whose employment the earnings relate.

(3) If the tax is on specific employment income, "the taxable person" is the person in relation to whom the income is, by virtue of Part 6 or 7 or any other enactment, to count as employment income.

(4) If the tax is on general earnings received, or remitted to the United Kingdom, after the death of the person to whose employment the earnings relate, the person's personal representatives are liable for the tax.

(5) In that event the tax is accordingly to be assessed on the personal representatives and is a debt due from and payable out of the estate.

CHAPTER 7

APPLICATION OF PROVISIONS TO AGENCY WORKERS

Agency workers

Treatment of workers supplied by agencies

1.586 **44.**—(1) This section applies if—

(a) an individual ("the worker") personally provides, or is under an obligation personally to provide, services (which are not excluded services) to another person ("the client");
(b) the services are supplied by or through a third person ("the agency") under the terms of an agency contract;
(c) the worker is subject to (or to the right of) supervision, direction or control as to the manner in which the services are provided; and
(d) remuneration receivable under or in consequence of the agency contract does not constitute employment income of the worker apart from this chapter.

(2) If this section applies—
(a) the services which the worker provides, or is obliged to provide, to the client under the agency contract are to be treated for income tax purposes as duties of an employment held by the worker with the agency; and
(b) all remuneration receivable under or in consequence of the agency contract (including remuneration which the client pays or provides in relation to the services) is to be treated for income tax purposes as earnings from that employment.

Part 3

Employment Income: Earnings and Benefits, etc. Treated as Earnings

Chapter 1

Earnings

Earnings

62.—(1) This section explains what is meant by "earnings" in the employment income Parts. **1.596**

(2) In those Parts, "earnings", in relation to an employment, means—
(a) any salary, wages or fee;
(b) any gratuity or other profit or incidental benefit of any kind obtained by the employee if it is money or money's worth; or
(c) anything else that constitutes an emolument of the employment.

(3) For the purposes of subsection (2), "money's worth" means something that is—
(a) of direct monetary value to the employee; or
(b) capable of being converted into money or something of direct monetary value to the employee.

(4) Subsection (1) does not affect the operation of statutory provisions that provide for amounts to be treated as earnings (and see section 721(7)).

Chapter 2

Taxable Benefits: The Benefits Code

The benefits code

The benefits code

63.—(1) In the employment income Parts "the benefits code" means— **1.597**
this chapter,
Chapter 3 (expenses payments),

Chapter 4 (vouchers and credit-tokens),
Chapter 5 (living accommodation),
Chapter 6 (cars, vans and related benefits),
Chapter 7 (loans),
[. . .][1]
Chapter 10 (residual liability to charge), and
Chapter 11 (exclusion of lower-paid employments from parts of benefits code).

(2) If an employment is an excluded employment, the general effect of section 216(1) (provisions not applicable to lower-paidemployments) is that only the following chapters apply to the employment—
this chapter,
Chapter 4 (vouchers and credit-tokens),
Chapter 5 (living accommodation), and
Chapter 11 (exclusion of lower-paidemployments from parts of benefits code).

(3) Section 216(5) and (6) explain and restrict the effect of section 216(1).

(4) In the benefits code, "excluded employment" means an employment to which the exclusion in section 216(1) applies.

AMENDMENT

1. Words repealed by FA 2003. Sch.43.

Relationship between earnings and benefits code

1.598 **64.**—(1) This section applies if, apart from this section, the same benefit would give rise to two amounts ("A" and "B")—

(a) A being an amount of earnings as defined in Chapter 1 of this Part; and
(b) B being an amount to be treated as earnings under the benefits code.

(2) In such a case—

(a) A constitutes earnings as defined in Chapter 1 of this Part; and
(b) the amount (if any) by which B exceeds A is to be treated as earnings under the benefits code.

(3) This section does not apply in connection with living accommodation to which Chapter 5 of this Part applies.

(4) In that case section 109 applies to determine the relationship between that chapter and Chapter 1 of this Part.

(5) [. . .][1].

(6) [. . .][1].

AMENDMENT

1. Subss.(5) and (6) repealed by FA 2003, Sch.43.

Dispensations relating to benefits within provisions not applicable to lower-paid employment

1.599 **65.**—(1) This section applies for the purposes of the listed provisions where a person ("P") supplies the Inland Revenue with a statement of the cases and circumstances in which—

(a) payments of a particular character are made to or for any employees; or
(b) benefits or facilities of a particular kind are provided for any employees,

whether they are employees of P or some other person.

(2) The "listed provisions" are the provisions listed in section 216(4) (provisions of the benefits code which do not apply to lower-paid employments).

(3) If the Inland Revenue are satisfied that no additional tax is payable by virtue of the listed provisions by reference to the payments, benefits or facilities mentioned in the statement, they must give P a dispensation under this section.

(4) A "dispensation" is a notice stating that the Inland Revenue agree that no additional tax is payable by virtue of the listed provisions by reference to the payments, benefits or facilities mentioned in the statement supplied by P.

(5) If a dispensation is given under this section, nothing in the listed provisions applies to the payments, or the provision of the benefits or facilities, covered by the dispensation or otherwise has the effect of imposing any additional liability to tax in respect of them.

(6) If in their opinion there is reason to do so, the Inland Revenue may revoke a dispensation by giving a further notice to P.

(7) That notice may revoke the dispensation from—
(a) the date when the dispensation was given; or
(b) a later date specified in the notice.

(8) If the notice revokes the dispensation from the date when the dispensation was given—
(a) any liability to tax that would have arisen if the dispensation had never been given is to be treated as having arisen; and
(b) P and the employees in question must make all the returns which they would have had to make if the dispensation had never been given.

(9) If the notice revokes the dispensation from a later date—
(a) any liability to tax that would have arisen if the dispensation had ceased to have effect on that date is to be treated as having arisen; and
(b) P and the employees in question must make all the returns which they would have had to make if the dispensation had ceased to have effect on that date.

General definitions for benefits code

Meaning of "employment" and related expressions

66.—(1) In the benefits code— 1.600
(a) "employment" means a taxable employment under Part 2; and
(b) "employed", "employee" and "employer" have corresponding meanings.

(2) Where a chapter of the benefits code applies in relation to an employee—

(a) references in that chapter to "the employment" are to the employment of that employee; and

(b) references in that chapter to "the employer" are to the employer in respect of that employment.

(3) For the purposes of the benefits code an employment is a "taxable employment under Part 2" in a tax year if the earnings from the employment for that year are (or would be if there were any) general earnings to which the charging provisions of Chapter 4 or 5 of Part 2 apply.

(4) In subsection (3)—

(a) the reference to an employment includes employment as a director of a company; and

(b) "earnings" means earnings as defined in Chapter of this Part.

CHAPTER 3

TAXABLE BENEFITS: EXPENSES PAYMENTS

Sums in respect of expenses

1.601 **70.**—(1) This chapter applies to a sum paid to an employee in a tax year if the sum—

(a) is paid to the employee in respect of expenses; and

(b) is so paid by reason of the employment.

(2) This chapter applies to a sum paid away by an employee in a tax year if the sum—

(a) was put at the employee's disposal in respect of expenses;

(b) was so put by reason of the employment; and

(c) is paid away by the employee in respect of expenses.

(3) For the purposes of this chapter it does not matter whether the employment is held at the time when the sum is paid or paidaway so long as it is held at some point in the tax year in which the sum is paid or paidaway.

(4) References in this chapter to an employee accordingly include a prospective or former employee.

(5) This chapter does not apply to the extent that the sum constitutes earnings from the employment by virtue of any other provision.

Meaning of paid or put at disposal by reason of the employment

1.602 **71.**—(1) If an employer pays a sum in respect of expenses to an employee it is to be treated as paid by reason of the employment unless—

(a) the employer is an individual, and

(b) the payment is made in the normal course of the employer's domestic, family or personal relationships.

(2) If an employer puts a sum at an employee's disposal in respect of expenses it is to be treated as put at the employee's disposal by reason of the employment unless—

(a) the employer is an individual, and
(b) the sum is put at the employee's disposal in the normal course of the employer's domestic, family or personal relationships.

Sums in respect of expenses treated as earnings

72.—(1) If this chapter applies to a sum, the sum is to be treated as earnings from the employment for the tax year in which it is paid or paid-away. **1.603**

(2) Subsection (1) does not prevent the making of a deduction allowed under any of the provisions listed in subsection (3).

(3) The provisions are—

section 336 (deductions for expenses: the general rule);
section 337 (travel in performance of duties);
section 338 (travel for necessary attendance);
section 340 (travel between group employments);
section 341 (travel at start or finish of overseas employment);
section 342 (travel between employments where duties performed abroad);
section 343 (deduction for professional membership fees);
section 344 (deduction for annual subscriptions);
section 346 (deduction for employee liabilities);
section 353 (deductions from earnings charged on remittance).

Chapter 4

Taxable Benefits: Vouchers and Credit-tokens

Cash vouchers: introduction

Cash vouchers to which this chapter applies

73.—(1) This chapter applies to a cash voucher provided for an employee by reason of the employment which is received by the employee. **1.604**

(2) A cash voucher provided for an employee by the employer is to be regarded as provided by reason of the employment unless—

(a) the employer is an individual; and
(b) the provision is made in the normal course of the employer's domestic, family or personal relationships.

(3) A cash voucher provided for an employee and appropriated to the employee—

(a) by attaching it to a card held for the employee; or
(b) in any other way;

is to be treated for the purposes of this chapter as having been received by the employee at the time when it is appropriated.

Provision for, or receipt by, member of employee's family

1.605 **74.**—For the purposes of this chapter any reference to a cash voucher being provided for or received by an employee includes a reference to it being provided for or received by a member of the employee's family.

Meaning of "cash voucher"

Meaning of "cash voucher"

1.606 **75.**—(1) In this chapter "cash voucher" means a voucher, stamp or similar document capable of being exchanged for a sum of money which is—

(a) greater than;
(b) equal to; or
(c) not substantially less than,

the expense incurred by the person at whose cost the voucher, stamp or similar document is provided.

(2) For the purposes of subsection (1) it does not matter whether the document—

(a) is also capable of being exchanged for goods or services;
(b) is capable of being exchanged singly or together with other vouchers, stamps, or documents;
(c) is capable of being exchanged immediately or only after a time.

(3) Subsection (1) is subject to section 76 (sickness benefits-related voucher).

Sickness benefits-related voucher

1.607 **76.**—(1) This section applies where—

(a) the expense incurred by the person at whose cost a voucher, stamp or similar document is provided ("the provision expense") includes costs to that person of providing sickness benefits ("sickness benefits costs"),
(b) the voucher, stamp or document would be a cash voucher (apart from this section) but for the fact that the sum of money for which it is capable of being exchanged ("the exchange sum") is substantially less than the provision expense, and
(c) the whole or part of the difference between the exchange sum and the provision expense represents the sickness benefits costs.

(2) The voucher, stamp or document is a cash voucher within the meaning of this chapter if—

$$E = \frac{PE}{D}$$

or

E is not substantially less than $\frac{PE}{D}$,

where—
E is the exchange sum;
PE is the provision expense; and
D is the amount of the difference between E and PE which represents the sickness benefits costs.

(3) In this section "sickness benefits" mean benefits in connection with sickness, personal injury or death.

Benefit of cash voucher treated as earnings

Benefit of cash voucher treated as earnings

81.—(1) The cash equivalent of the benefit of a cash voucher to which this chapter applies is to be treated as earnings from the employment for the tax year in which the voucher is received by the employee. **1.608**

(2) The cash equivalent is the sum of money for which the voucher is capable of being exchanged.

Non-cash vouchers: introduction

Non-cash vouchers to which this chapter applies

82.—(1) This chapter applies to a non-cash voucher provided for an employee by reason of the employment which is received by the employee. **1.609**

(2) A non-cash voucher provided for an employee by the employer is to be regarded as provided by reason of the employment unless—
(a) the employer is an individual; and
(b) the provision is made in the normal course of the employer's domestic, family or personal relationships.

(3) A non-cash voucher provided for an employee and appropriated to the employee—
(a) by attaching it to a card held for the employee; or
(b) in any other way,
is to be treated for the purposes of this chapter as having been received by the employee at the time when it is appropriated.

Meaning of "non-cash voucher"

Meaning of "non-cash voucher"

84.—(1) In this chapter "non-cash voucher" means— **1.610**
(a) a voucher, stamp or similar document or token which is capable of being exchanged for money, goods or services;
(b) a transport voucher, or

(c) a cheque voucher,

but does not include a cash voucher.

(2) For the purposes of subsection (1)(a) it does not matter whether the document or token is capable of being exchanged—

(a) singly or together with other vouchers, stamps, documents or tokens;

(b) immediately or only after a time.

(3) In this chapter "transport voucher" means a ticket, pass or other document or token intended to enable a person to obtain passenger transport services (whether or not in exchange for it).

(4) In this chapter "cheque voucher" means a cheque—

(a) provided for an employee; and

(b) intended for use by the employee wholly or mainly for payment for—

(i) particular goods or services; or

(ii) goods or services of one or more particular classes;

and, in relation to a cheque voucher, references to a voucher being exchanged for goods or services are to be read accordingly.

Benefit of non-cash voucher treated as earnings

Benefit of non-cash voucher treated as earnings

1.611 **87.**—(1) The cash equivalent of the benefit of a non-cash voucher to which this chapter applies is to be treated as earnings from the employment for the tax year in which the voucher is received by the employee.

(2) The cash equivalent is the difference between—

(a) the cost of provision; and

(b) any part of that cost made good by the employee to the person incurring it.

(3) In this chapter the "cost of provision" means, in relation to a non-cash voucher, the expense incurred in or in connection with the provision of—

(a) the voucher, and

(b) the money, goods or services for which it is capable of being exchanged,

by the person at whose cost they are provided.

(4) In the case of a transport voucher, the reference in subsection (3)(b) to the services for which the voucher is capable of being exchanged is to the passenger transport services which may be obtained by using it.

(5) If a person incurs expense in or in connection with the provision of non-cash vouchers for two or more employees as members of a group or class, the expense incurred in respect of one of them is to be such part of that expense as is just and reasonable.

(6) This section is subject to section 89 (reduction for meal vouchers).

Credit-tokens: introduction

Credit-tokens to which this chapter applies

90.—(1) This chapter applies to a credit-token provided for an employee by reason of the employment which is used by the employee to obtain money, goods or services. 1.612

(2) A credit-token provided for an employee by the employer is to be regarded as provided by reason of the employment unless—

(a) the employer is an individual; and
(b) the provision is made in the normal course of the employer's domestic, family or personal relationships.

Meaning of "credit-token"

Meaning of "credit-token"

92.—(1) In this chapter "credit-token" means a credit card, debit card or other card, a token, a document or other object given to a person by another person ("X") who undertakes— 1.613

(a) on the production of it, to supply money, goods or services on credit; or
(b) if a third party ("Y") supplies money, goods or services on its production, to pay Y for what is supplied.

(2) A card, token, document or other object can be a credit-token even if—

(a) some other action is required in addition to its production in order for the money, goods or services to be supplied;
(b) X in paying Y may take a discount or commission.

(3) For the purposes of this section—

(a) the use of an object given by X to operate a machine provided by X is to be treated as its production to X, and
(b) the use of an object given by X to operate a machine provided by Y is to be treated as its production to Y.

(4) A "credit-token" does not include a cash voucher or a non-cash voucher.

Benefit of credit-token treated as earnings

Benefit of credit-token treated as earnings

94.—(1) On each occasion on which a credit-token to which this chapter applies is used by the employee in a tax year to obtain money, goods or services, the cash equivalent of the benefit of the token is to be treated as earnings from the employment for that year. 1.614

(2) The cash equivalent is the difference between—

(a) the cost of provision; and

(b) any part of that cost made good by the employee to the person incurring it.

(3) In this section the "cost of provision" means the expense incurred—

(a) in or in connection with the provision of the money, goods or services obtained on the occasion in question; and

(b) by the person at whose cost they are provided.

(4) If a person incurs expense in or in connection with the provision of credit-tokens for two or more employees as members of a group or class, the expense incurred in respect of one of them is to be such part of that expense as is just and reasonable.

General supplementary provisions

Disregard for money, goods or services obtained

1.615 **95.**—(1) This section applies if the cash equivalent of the benefit of a cash voucher, a non-cash voucher or a credit-token—

(a) is to be treated as earnings from an employee's employment under this chapter; or

(b) would be so treated but for a dispensation given under section 96.

(2) Money, goods or services obtained—

(a) by the employee or another person in exchange for the cash voucher or non-cash voucher; or

(b) by the employee or a member of the employee's family by use of the credit-token,

are to be disregarded for the purposes of the Income Tax Acts.

(3) But the goods or services are not to be disregarded for the purposes of applying sections 362 and 363 (deductions where non-cash voucher or credit-token provided).

(4) In the case of a transport voucher, the reference in subsection (2)(a) to the services obtained in exchange for the voucher is to the passenger transport services obtained by using it.

Chapter 6

Taxable Benefits: Cars, Vans and Related Benefits

General

Cars, vans and related benefits

1.616 **114.**—(1) This chapter applies to a car or a van in relation to a particular tax year if in that year the car or van—

(a) is made available (without any transfer of the property in it) to an employee or a member of the employee's family or household;
(b) is so made available by reason of the employment (see section 117); and
(c) is available for the employee's or member's private use (see section 118).

(2) Where this chapter applies to a car or van—
(a) sections 120 to 148 provide for the cash equivalent of the benefit of the car to be treated as earnings;
(b) sections 149 to 153 provide for the cash equivalent of the benefit of any fuel provided for the car to be treated as earnings; and
(c) sections 154 to 166 provide for the cash equivalent of the benefit of the van to be treated as earnings.

(3) This chapter does not apply if an amount constitutes earnings from the employment in respect of the benefit of the car or van by virtue of any other provision (see section 119).

(4) The following provisions of this chapter provide for further exceptions—
section 167 (pooled cars);
section 168 (pooled vans);
section 169 (car available to more than one member of family or household employed by same employer).

Meaning of "car" and "van"

115.—(1) In this chapter— 1.617
"car" means a mechanically propelled road vehicle which is not—
(a) a goods vehicle;
(b) a motor cycle;
(c) an invalid carriage; or
(d) a vehicle of a type not commonly used as a private vehicle and unsuitable to be so used;
"van" means a mechanically propelled road vehicle which—
(a) is a goods vehicle; and
(b) has a design weight not exceeding 3,500 kilograms, and
which is not a motor cycle.

(2) For the purposes of subsection (1)—
"design weight" means the weight which a vehicle is designed or adapted not to exceed when in normal use and travelling on a road laden;
"goods vehicle" means a vehicle of a construction primarily suited for the conveyance of goods or burden of any description;
"invalid carriage" has the meaning given by section 185(1) of the Road Traffic Act 1988 (Chapter 52);
"motor cycle" has the meaning given by section 185(1) of the Road Traffic Act 1988.

Meaning of when car or van is available to employee

116.—(1) For the purposes of this chapter a car or van is available to an employee at a particular time if it is then made available, by reason of 1.618

the employment and without any transfer of the property in it, to the employee or a member of the employee's family or household.

(2) References in this chapter to—

(a) the time when a car is first made available to an employee are to the earliest time when the car is made available as mentioned in subsection (1); and

(b) the last day in a year on which a car is available to an employee are to the last day in the year on which the car is made available as mentioned in subsection (1).

(3) This section does not apply to section 138 (automatic car for a disabled employee).

Meaning of car or van made available by reason of employment

1.619 **117.**—For the purposes of this chapter a car or van made available by an employer to an employee or a member of the employee's family or household is to be regarded as made available by reason of the employment unless—

(a) the employer is an individual; and

(b) it is so made available in the normal course of the employer's domestic, family or personal relationships.

Availability for private use

1.620 **118.**—(1) For the purposes of this chapter a car or van made available in a tax year to an employee or a member of the employee's family or household is to be treated as available for the employee's or member's private use unless in that year—

(a) the terms on which it is made available prohibit such use; and

(b) it is not so used.

(2) In this chapter "private use", in relation to a car or van made available to an employee or a member of the employee's family or household, means any use other than for the employee's business travel (see section 171(1)).

Cars: benefit treated as earnings

Benefit of car treated as earnings

1.621 **120.**—(1) If this chapter applies to a car in relation to a particular tax year, the cash equivalent of the benefit of the car is to be treated as earnings from the employment for that year.

(2) In such a case the employee is referred to in this chapter as being chargeable to tax in respect of the car in that year.

Method of calculating the cash equivalent of the benefit of a car

1.622 **121.**—(1) The cash equivalent of the benefit of a car for a tax year is calculated as follows—

Step 1

Find the price of the car in accordance with sections 122 to 124.

Step 2

Add the price of any accessories which fall to be taken into account in accordance with sections 125 to 131.

Step 3

Make any deduction under section 132 for capital contributions made by the employee to the cost of the car or accessories.

Step 4

If the amount carried forward from step 3 exceeds £80,000, the interim sum is £80,000.

In any other case, the interim sum is the amount carried forward from step 3.

Step 5

Find the appropriate percentage for the car for the year in accordance with sections 133 to 142.

Step 6

Multiply the interim sum by the appropriate percentage for the car for the year.

Step 7

Make any deduction under section 143 for any periods when the car was unavailable.

The resulting amount is the provisional sum.

Step 8

Make any deduction from the provisional sum under section 144 in respect of payments by the employee for the private use of the car.

The result is the cash equivalent of the benefit of the car for the year.

(2) The method of calculation set out in subs.(1) is modified in the special cases dealt with in—

section 146 (cars that run on roadfuel gas); and

section 147 (classic cars: 15 years of age or more).

(3) The cash equivalent may be reduced under s.148 where the car is shared.

(4) This section is subject to any regulations made by the Treasury under section 170(4) (power to reduce the appropriate percentage).

Benefit of car fuel treated as earnings

1.623 **149.**—(1) If in a tax year—

(a) fuel is provided for a car by reason of an employee's employment; and

(b) that person is chargeable to tax in respect of the car by virtue of section 120;

the cash equivalent of the benefit of the fuel is to be treated as earnings from the employment for that year.

(2) The cash equivalent of the benefit of the fuel is calculated in accordance with sections 150 to 153.

(3) Fuel is to be treated as provided for a car, in addition to any other way in which it may be provided, if—

(a) any liability in respect of the provision of fuel for the car is discharged;

(b) a non-cash voucher or a credit-token is used to obtain fuel for the car;

(c) a non-cash voucher or a credit-token is used to obtain money which is spent on fuel for the car; or

(d) any sum is paid in respect of expenses incurred in providing fuel for the car.

(4) References in this section to fuel do not include any facility or means for supplying electrical energy for an electrically propelled vehicle.

Car fuel: calculating the cash equivalent

1.624 **150.**—(1) The cash equivalent of the benefit of the fuel is the appropriate percentage of £14,400.

(2) The "appropriate percentage" means the appropriate percentage determined in accordance with sections 133 to 142 for the purpose of calculating the cash equivalent of the benefit of the car for which the fuel is provided.

(3) But the cash equivalent may be—

(a) nil where either of the conditions in section 151 is met;

(b) proportionately reduced under section 152;

(c) reduced under section 153.

Car fuel: nil cash equivalent

1.625 **151.**—(1) The cash equivalent of the benefit of the fuel is nil if condition A or B is met.

(2) Condition A is met if in the tax year in question—

(a) the employee is required to make good to the person providing the fuel the whole of the expense incurred by that person in connection with the provision of the fuel for the employee's private use; and

(b) the employee does make good that expense.

(3) Condition B is met if in the tax year in question the fuel is made available only for business travel (see section 171(1)).

Chapter 10

Taxable Benefits: Residual Liability to Charge

Introduction

Employment-related benefits

201.—(1) This chapter applies to employment-related benefits. 1.626

(2) In this chapter—

"benefit" means a benefit or facility of any kind;

"employment-related benefit" means a benefit, other than an excluded benefit, which is provided in a tax year—

(a) for an employee; or

(b) for a member of an employee's family or household;

by reason of the employment.

For the definition of "excluded benefit" see section 202.

(3) A benefit provided by an employer is to be regarded as provided by reason of the employment unless—

(a) the employer is an individual; and

(b) the provision is made in the normal course of the employer's domestic, family or personal relationships.

(4) For the purposes of this chapter it does not matter whether the employment is held at the time when the benefit is provided so long as it is held at some point in the tax year in which the benefit is provided.

(5) References in this chapter to an employee accordingly include a prospective or former employee.

Excluded benefits

202.—(1) A benefit is an "excluded benefit" for the purposes of this chapter if— 1.627

(a) any of Chapters 3 to 9 of the benefits code applies to the benefit;

(b) any of those chapters would apply to the benefit but for an exception; or

(c) the benefit consists in the right to receive, or the prospect of receiving, sums treated as earnings under section 221 (payments where employee absent because of sickness or disability).

(2) In this section, "exception", in relation to the application of a chapter of the benefits code to a benefit, means any enactment in the chapter which provides that the chapter does not apply to the benefit. But for this purpose section 86 (transport vouchers under pre-26th March 1982 arrangements) is not an exception.

Cash equivalent of benefit treated as earnings

1.628 **203.**—(1) The cash equivalent of an employment-related benefit is to be treated as earnings from the employment for the tax year in which it is provided.

(2) The cash equivalent of an employment-related benefit is the cost of the benefit less any part of that cost made good by the employee to the persons providing the benefit.

(3) The cost of an employment-related benefit is determined in accordance with section 204 unless—

(a) section 205 provides that the cost is to be determined in accordance with that section; or

(b) section 206 provides that the cost is to be determined in accordance with that section.

Determination of the cost of the benefit

Cost of the benefit: basic rule

1.629 **204.**—The cost of an employment-related benefit is the expense incurred in or in connection with provision of the benefit (including a proper proportion of any expense relating partly to provision of the benefit and partly to other matters).

Exemption of minor benefits

1.630 **210.**—(1) The Treasury may make provision by regulations for exempting from the application of this Chapter such minor benefits as may be specified by regulation.

(2) An exemption conferred by such regulations is conditional on the benefit being made available to the employer's employees generally on similar terms.

General Note

1.631 For regulations made under this section see the Income Tax (Exemption of Minor Benefits) Regulations 2002 (SI 2002/205) as amended by the income Tax (Exemption of Minor Benefits)(Amendment) Regulations 2003 (SI 2003/1434). These regulations are not included in this volume. They remove taxation from minor benefits, such as free meals, provided by employers that would otherwise be liable to taxation.

CHAPTER 11

TAXABLE BENEFITS: EXCLUSION OF LOWER-PAID EMPLOYMENT FROM PARTS OF BENEFITS CODE

Introduction

Provisions not applicable to lower-paid employments

216.—(1) The chapters of the benefits code listed in subsection (4) do not apply to an employment in relation to a tax year if— 1.632
(a) it is lower-paid employment in relation to that year (see section 217); and
(b) condition A or B is met.

(2) Condition A is that the employee is not employed as a director of a company.

(3) Condition B is that the employee is employed as a director of a company but has no material interest in the company and either—
(a) the employment is as a full-time working director; or
(b) the company is non-profit-making or is established for charitable purposes only.

"Non-profit-making" means that the company does not carry on a trade and its functions do not consist wholly or mainly in the holding of investments or other property.

(4) The chapters referred to in subsection (1) are—
Chapter 3 (taxable benefits: expenses payments);
Chapter 6 (taxable benefits: cars, vans and related benefits);
Chapter 7 (taxable benefits: loans);
[. . .][1]
Chapter 10 (taxable benefits: residual liability to charge).

(5) Subsection (1)—
(a) means that in any of those chapters a reference to an employee does not include an employee whose employment is within the exclusion in that subsection, if the context is such that the reference is to an employee in relation to whom the chapter applies; but
(b) does not restrict the meaning of references to employees in other contexts.

(6) Subsection (1) has effect subject to—
section 188(2) (discharge of loan: where employment becomes lower-paid);
[. . .][1], and
section 220 (employment in two or more related employments).

AMENDMENT

1. Words repealed by FA 2003, Sch. 43.

What is lower-paid employment?

Meaning of "lower-paid employment"

1.633 **217.**—(1) For the purposes of this chapter an employment is "lower-paid employment" in relation to a tax year if the earnings rate for the employment for the year (calculated under section 218) is less than £8,500.

(2) Subsection (1) is subject to section 220 (employment in two or more related employments).

Calculation of earnings rate for a tax year

1.634 **218.**—(1) For any tax year the earnings rate for an employment is to be calculated as follows—

Step 1

Find the total of the following amounts—

(a) the total amount of the earnings from the employment for the year within Chapter 1 of this Part;

(b) the total of any amounts that are treated as earnings from the employment for the year under the benefits code (see subsections (2) and (3));

(c) the total of any amounts that are treated as earnings from the employment for the year under Chapter 12 of this Part (payments treated as earnings); and

(d) in the case of an employment within section 56(2) (deemed employment of worker by intermediary), the amount of the deemed employment payment for the year (see section 54), excluding any exempt income.

Step 2

Add to that total any extra amount required to be added for the year by section 219 (extra amounts to be added in connection with a car).

Step 3

Subtract the total amount of any authorised deductions (see subsection (4)) from the result of step 2.

Step 4

The earnings rate for the employment for the year is given by the formula—

$$\frac{Y}{R \times E}$$

where—

R is the result of step 3;

Y is the number of days in the year; and

E is the number of days in the year when the employment is held.

(2) Section 216(1) (provisions not applicable to lower-paid employment) is to be disregarded for the purpose of determining any amount under step 1.

(3) If the benefit of living accommodation is to be taken into account under step 1, the cash equivalent is to be calculated in accordance with section 105 (even if the cost of providing the accommodation exceeds £75,000).

(4) For the purposes of step 3, "authorised deduction" means any deduction that would (assuming it was an amount of taxable earnings) be allowed from any amount within step 1 under—

section 346 (employee liabilities);
section 352 (agency fees paid by entertainers);
section 355 (corresponding payments by non-domiciled employees with foreign employers);
section 368 (fixed sum deductions from earnings payable out of public revenue);
section 370 (travel costs and expenses where duties performed abroad: employee's travel);
section 371 (travel costs and expenses where duties performed abroad: visiting spouse's or child's travel);
section 373 (non-domiciled employee's travel costs and expenses where duties performed in United Kingdom);
section 374 (non-domiciled employee's spouse's or child's travel costs and expenses where duties performed in United Kingdom);
section 376 (foreign accommodation and subsistence costs and expenses (overseas employments));
section 377 (costs and expenses in respect of personal security assets and services);
section 713 (payroll giving to charities); section 592(7) of ICTA (contributions to exempt approved schemes); section 594 of ICTA (contributions to exempt statutory schemes); or section 262 of CAA 2001 (capital allowances to be given effect by treating them as deductions).

Extra amounts to be added in connection with a car

219.—(1) The provisions of this section apply for the purposes of section 218(1) in the case of a tax year in which a car is made available as mentioned in section 114(1) (cars, vans and related benefits) by reason of the employment. 1.635

(2) Subsection (3) applies if in the tax year—

(a) an alternative to the benefit of the car is offered; and
(b) the amount that would be earnings within Chapter 1 of this Part if the benefit of the car were to be determined by reference to the alternative offered exceeds the benefit code earnings (see subsection (4)).

(3) The amount of the excess is an extra amount to be added under step 2 in section 218(1).

(4) For the purposes of subsection (2) "the benefit code earnings" is the total for the year of—

(a) the cash equivalent of the benefit of the car (calculated in accordance with Chapter 6 of this Part); and
(b) the cash equivalent (calculated in accordance with that chapter) of the benefit of any fuel provided for the car by reason of the employment.

(5) Subsection (6) applies if in the tax year there would be an amount of general earnings consisting of—
(a) earnings within Chapter 1 of this Part; or
(b) an amount treated as earnings from the employment under c.3 (expenses payments) or Chapter 4 (vouchers and credit-tokens) of this Part, if section 239 or 269 (exemptions in respect of payments or benefits connected with taxable cars, etc.) did not apply to the discharge of a liability, or to a payment or benefit, in connection with the car.

(6) The amount of general earnings mentioned in subsection (5) is an extra amount to be added under step 2 in section 218(1).

(7) Section 216(1) (provisions not applicable to lower-paid employment) is to be disregarded for the purpose of determining any amount under this section.

PART 5

EMPLOYMENT INCOME: DEDUCTIONS ALLOWED FROM EARNINGS

CHAPTER 1

DEDUCTIONS ALLOWED FROM EARNINGS: GENERAL RULES

Introduction

Deductions from earnings: general

1.636 **327.**—(1) This Part provides for deductions that are allowed from the taxable earnings from an employment in a tax year in calculating the net taxable earnings from the employment in the tax year for the purposes of Part II (see section 11(1)).

(2) In this Part, unless otherwise indicated by the context—
(a) references to the earnings from which deductions are allowed are references to the taxable earnings mentioned in subsection (1); and
(b) references to the tax year are references to the tax year mentioned there.

(3) The deductions for which this Part provides are those allowed under—

Chapter 2 (deductions for employee's expenses);

Chapter 3 (deductions from benefits code earnings);
Chapter 4 (fixed allowances for employee's expenses);
Chapter 5 (deductions for earnings representing benefits or reimbursed expenses); and
Chapter 6 (deductions from seafarers' earnings).

(4) Further provision about deductions from earnings is made in—
section 232 (giving effect to mileage allowance relief);
section 619 of ICTA (contributions under retirement annuity contracts); and
section 262 of CAA 2001 (capital allowances to be given effect by treating them as deductions from earnings).

(5) Further provision about deductions from income including earnings is made in—
Part 12 (payroll giving);
section 592(7) of ICTA (contributions to exempt approved schemes); and
section 594(1) of ICTA (contributions to exempt statutory schemes).

General rules

The income from which deductions may be made

328.—(1) The general rule is that deductions under this Part are allowed— 1.637
(a) from any earnings from the employment in question; and
(b) not from earnings from any other employment. This is subject to subsections (2) to (4).

(2) Deductions under section 351 (expenses of ministers of religion) are allowed from earnings from any employment as a minister of a religious denomination.

(3) Deductions under section 368 (fixed sum deductions from earnings payable out of public revenue) are allowed only from earnings payable out of the public revenue.

(4) Deductions limited to specified earnings (see subsection (5)) are allowed—
(a) only from earnings from the employment that are taxable earnings under certain of the charging provisions of Chapters 4 and 5 of Part 2; and
(b) not from other earnings from it.

(5) "Deductions limited to specified earnings" are deductions under—
sections 336 to 342 (deductions from earnings charged on receipt: see sections 335(2) and 354);
section 353 (deductions from earnings charged on remittance);
sections 370 to 374 (travel deductions from earnings charged on receipt), and Chapter 6 of this Part (deductions from seafarers' earnings: see section 378(1)(a)).

Deductions from earnings not to exceed earnings

1.638 **329.**—(1) The amount of a deduction allowed under this Part may not exceed the earnings from which it is deductible.

If two or more deductions allowed under this Part are deductible from the same earnings, the amounts deductible may not in aggregate exceed those earnings.

(3) If deductions allowed otherwise than under this Part fall to be allowed from the same earnings as amounts deductible under this Part, the amounts deductible under this Part may not exceed the earnings remaining after the other deductions.

(4) Subsections (1) and (2) do not apply to a deduction under section 351 (expenses of ministers of religion), and subsection (3) applies as if such a deduction were allowed otherwise than under this Part.

(5) This section is to be disregarded for the purposes of the deductibility provisions (see section 332).

(6) See also section 380 of ICTA (which provides that where a loss in an employment is sustained, relief may be given against other income).

Prevention of double deductions

1.639 **330.**—(1) A deduction from earnings under this Part is not allowed more than once in respect of the same costs or expenses.

(2) If apart from this subsection—

(a) a deduction would be allowed under Chapter 4 of this Part (fixed allowances for employee's expenses) for a sum fixed by reference to any kind of expenses; and

(b) the employee would be entitled under another provision to a deduction for an amount paid in respect of the same kind of expenses;

only one of those deductions is allowed.

Order for making deductions

1.640 **331.**—(1) This Part needs to be read with section 835(3) and (4) of ICTA (general rule that deductions are to be allowed in the order resulting in the greatest reduction of liability to income tax).

In the case of deductions under this Part, the general rule in that section is subject to—

(a) section 23(3) (which requires certain deductions to be made in order to establish "chargeable overseas earnings"); and

(b) section 381 (which requires deductions under other provisions to be taken into account before deductions under Chapter 6 of this Part (seafarers)).

Meaning of "the deductibility provisions"

1.641 **332.**—For the purposes of this Part, "the deductibility provisions" means the following provisions (which refer to amounts or expenses that would be deductible if they were incurred and paid by an employee)—

the definition of "business travel" in section 171(1) (definitions for Chapter 6 of Part 3),
section 179(6) (exception for certain advances for necessary expenses), the definition of "business travel" in section 236(1) (definitions for Chapter 2 of Part 4),
section 240(1)(c) and (5) (exemption of incidental overnight expenses and benefits),
section 252(3) (exception from exemption of work-related training provision for non-deductible travel expenses),
section 257(3) (exception from exemption for individual learning account training provision for non-deductible travel expenses),
section 305(5) (offshore oil and gas workers: mainland transfers),
section 310(6)(b) (counselling and other outplacement services),
section 311(5)(b) (retraining courses),
section 361(b) (scope of Chapter 3 of this Part: cost of benefits deductible as if paid by employee),
section 362(1)(c) and (2)(b) (deductions where non-cash voucher provided),
section 363(1)(b) and (2)(b) (deductions where credit-token provided),
section 364(1)(b) and (2) (deductions where living accommodation provided),
section 365(1)(b) and (2) (deductions where employment-related benefit provided).

Chapter 2

Deductions for Employee's Expenses

Introduction

Scope of this chapter: expenses paid by the employee

333.—(1) A deduction from a person's earnings for an amount is allowed under the following provisions of this chapter only if the amount— 1.642
(a) is paid by the person; or
(b) is paid on the person's behalf by someone else and is included in the earnings.

(2) In the following provisions of this chapter, in relation to a deduction from a person's earnings, references to the person paying an amount include references to the amount being paid on the person's behalf by someone else if or to the extent that the amount is included in the earnings.

(3) Subsection (1)(b) does not apply to the deductions under—
(a) section 351(2) and (3) (expenses of ministers of religion); and

(b) section 355 (deductions for corresponding payments by non-domiciled employees with foreign employers),

and subsection (2) does not apply in the case of those deductions.

(4) Chapter 3 of this Part provides for deductions where—

(a) a person's earnings include an amount treated as earnings under Chapter 4, 5 or 10 of Part 3 (taxable benefits: vouchers, etc., living accommodation and residual liability to charge); and

(b) an amount in respect of the benefit in question would be deductible under this chapter if the person had incurred and paid it.

Effect of reimbursement, etc.

1.643 **334.**—(1) For the purposes of this chapter, a person may be regarded as paying an amount despite—

(a) its reimbursement; or

(b) any other payment from another person in respect of the amount.

(2) But where a reimbursement or such other payment is made in respect of an amount, a deduction for the amount is allowed under the following provisions of this chapter only if or to the extent that—

(a) the reimbursement; or

(b) so much of the other payment as relates to the amount; is included in the person's earnings.

(3) *Omitted*

General rule for deduction of employee's expenses

Deductions for expenses: the general rule

1.644 **336.**—(1) The general rule is that a deduction from earnings is allowedfor an amount if—

(a) the employee is obliged to incur and pay it as holder of the employment; and

(b) the amount is incurred wholly, exclusively and necessarily in the performance of the duties of the employment.

(2) The following provisions of this chapter contain additional rules allowing deductions for particular kinds of expenses and rules preventing particular kinds of deductions.

(3) No deduction is allowed under this section for an amount that is deductible under sections 337 to 342 (travel expenses).

Travel expenses

Travel in performance of duties

1.645 **337.**—(1) A deduction from earnings is allowed for travel expenses if—

(a) the employee is obliged to incur and pay them as holder of the employment; and

(b) the expenses are necessarily incurred on travelling in the performance of the duties of the employment.

(2) This section needs to be read with section 359 (disallowance of travel expenses: mileage allowances and reliefs).

Travel for necessary attendance

338.—(1) A deduction from earnings is allowed for travel expenses if— **1.646**

(a) the employee is obliged to incur and pay them as holder of the employment; and

(b) the expenses are attributable to the employee's necessary attendance at any place in the performance of the duties of the employment.

(2) Subsection (1) does not apply to the expenses of ordinary commuting or travel between any two places that is for practical purposes substantially ordinary commuting.

(3) In this section, "ordinary commuting" means travel between—

(a) the employee's home and a permanent workplace; or

(b) a place that is not a workplace and a permanent workplace.

(4) Subsection (1) does not apply to the expenses of private travel or travel between any two places that is for practical purposes substantially private travel.

(5) In subsection (4), "private travel" means travel between—

(a) the employee's home and a place that is not a workplace; or

(b) two places neither of which is a workplace.

(6) This section needs to be read with section 359 (disallowance of travel expenses: mileage allowances and reliefs).

Meaning of "workplace" and "permanent workplace"

339.—(1) In this Part, "workplace", in relation to an employment, means a place at which the employee's attendance is necessary in the performance of the duties of the employment. **1.647**

(2) In this Part "permanent workplace", in relation to an employment, means a place which—

(a) the employee regularly attends in the performance of the duties of the employment; and

(b) is not a temporary workplace.

This is subject to subsections (4) and (8).

(3) In subsection (2), "temporary workplace", in relation to an employment, means a place which the employee attends in the performance of the duties of the employment—

(a) for the purpose of performing a task of limited duration; or

(b) for some other temporary purpose.

This is subject to subsections (4) and (5).

(4) A place which the employee regularly attends in the performance of the duties of the employment is treated as a permanent workplace and not a temporary workplace if—

(a) it forms the base from which those duties are performed; or

(b) the tasks to be carried out in the performance of those duties are allocated there.

(5) A place is not regarded as a temporary workplace if the employee's attendance is—

(a) in the course of a period of continuous work at that place—

(i) lasting more than 24 months, or

(ii) comprising all or almost all of the period for which the employee is likely to hold the employment; or

(b) at a time when it is reasonable to assume that it will be in the course of such a period.

(6) For the purposes of subsection (5), a period is a period of continuous work at a place if over the period the duties of the employment are performed to a significant extent at the place.

(7) An actual or contemplated modification of the place at which duties are performed is to be disregarded for the purposes of subsections (5) and (6) if it does not, or would not, have any substantial effect on the employee's journey, or expenses of travelling, to and from the place where they are performed.

(8) An employee is treated as having a permanent workplace consisting of an area if—

(a) the duties of the employment are defined by reference to an area (whether or not they also require attendance at places outside it);

(b) in the performance of those duties the employee attends different places within the area;

(c) none of the places the employee attends in the performance of those duties is a permanent workplace; and

(d) the area would be a permanent workplace if subsections (2), (3), (5), (6) and (7) referred to the area where they refer to a place.

Fees and subscriptions

Deduction for professional membership fees

1.648 **343.**—(1) A deduction from earnings from an employment is allowed for an amount paid in respect of a professional fee if—

(a) the duties of the employment involve the practice of the profession to which the fee relates; and

(b) the registration, certification, licensing or other matter in respect of which the fee is payable is a condition, or one of alternative conditions, which must be met if that profession is to be practised in the performance of those duties.

(2) In this section, "professional fee" means a fee mentioned in the following Table.

TABLE 1.649

Health professionals

1. Fee payable for entry or retention of a name in any of the following—
 (a) the Register of Chartered Psychologists;
 (b) the register maintained by the Registrar of Chiropractors;
 (c) a roll or record kept for a class of dental auxiliaries;
 (d) the dentists register;
 (e) the register of dispensing opticians;
 (f) the register maintained by the Health Professions Council;
 (g) the register maintained by the registrar appointed by the Hearing Aid Council;
 (h) the register of medical practitioners;
 (i) the register maintained by the Nursing and Midwifery Council;
 (j) either of the registers of ophthalmic opticians;
 (k) the register maintained by the Registrar of Osteopaths;
 (l) the Register of Pharmaceutical Chemists.

2. Fee payable by a chartered psychologist on the issue of a practising certificate.

Animal health professionals

3. Fee payable for entry or retention of a name in any of the following—
 (a) the register maintained by the registrar appointed by the Farriers Registration Council;
 (b) the supplementary veterinary register;
 (c) the register of veterinary surgeons.

Legal professionals

4. Fee payable to the Council for Licensed Conveyancers on the issue of a licence to practise as a licensed conveyancer.

5. Fee and contribution to the compensation fundor Guarantee Fund payable on the issue of a solicitor's practising certificate.

Architects

6. Fee payable for entry or retention of a name in the Register of Architects.

Teachers

7. Fee payable for entry or retention of a name in any of the following—
 (a) the register maintained by the General Teaching Council for England;

(b) the register maintained by the General Teaching Council for Scotland;
(c) the register maintained by the General Teaching Council for Wales.

Patent agents and trade mark agents

8. Registration fee payable by—
(a) a registered patent agent;
(b) a registered trade mark agent.
9. Practising fee payable by—
(a) a registered patent agent;
(b) a registered trade mark agent.

Occupations in the transport sector

10. Fee payable by a driving instructor for entry or retention of a name in the register of approved instructors or on the issue or renewal of a licence authorising its holder to give paid instruction in the driving of a motor car.

11. Fee (including any related medical or technical examination fee) payable, on the issue or renewal of a licence by the Civil Aviation Authority, by—
(a) an aircraft maintenance engineer;
(b) an air traffic controller or student air traffic controller;
(c) a member of the flight crew of an aircraft registered in the United Kingdom;
(d) a flight information service officer.

12. Fee (including any related medical examination fee) payable—
(a) on the issue or renewal of a licence authorising its holder to drive a large goods vehicle or a passenger-carrying vehicle;
(b) by an officer or other seaman on the issue, renewal or endorsement of a certificate, licence or other document which is required as evidence of his qualification or competence to serve in a ship.

13. Fee payable by a seafarer employed in a sea-going United Kingdom ship on the issue or renewal of a medical fitness certificate.

(3) The Board of Inland Revenue may make an order adding such fee as is specified in the order to the table of fees mentioned in subsection (2).

(4) The Board may make an order if they consider that such fee is payable in respect of any registration, certification, licensing or other matter if it is required as a condition, or one of alternative conditions, of the practice of a profession.

Deduction for annual subscriptions

1.650 **344.**—(1) A deduction from earnings from an employment is allowed for an amount paid in respect of an annual subscription if—
(a) it is paid to a body of persons approved under this section; and

(b) the activities of the body which are directed to one or more of the objects within subsection (2) are of direct benefit to, or concern the profession practised in, the performance of the duties of the employment.

(2) The objects are—

(a) the advancement or dissemination of knowledge (whether generally or among persons belonging to the same or similar professions or occupying the same or similar positions),

(b) the maintenance or improvement of standards of conduct and competence among the members of a profession,

(c) the provision of indemnity or protection to members of a profession against claims in respect of liabilities incurred by them in the exercise of their profession.

(3) The Inland Revenue may approve a body of persons under this section if, on an application by the body, they are satisfied that—

(a) the body is not of a mainly local character,

(b) its activities are carried on otherwise than for profit, and

(c) its activities are wholly or mainly directed to objects within subsection (2).

(4) The Inland Revenue must give notice to the body of their decision on the application.

(5) If the activities of the body are to a significant extent directed to objects other than objects within subsection (2), the Inland Revenue may—

(a) determine the proportion of the activities directed to objects within subsection (2); and

(b) determine that only such corresponding part of the subscription as is specifiedby the Inland Revenue is allowable under this section.

(6) In determining that part, the Inland Revenue must have regard to the proportion of expenditure of the body attributable to objects other than objects within subsection (2) and all other relevant circumstances.

(7) If a body applies for approval under this section and is approved, a subscription paid to it—

(a) before it has applied but in the same tax year as the application; or

(b) after it has applied but before it is approved, is treated for the purposes of this section as having been paid to an approved body.

PART 9

PENSION INCOME

CHAPTER 1

INTRODUCTION

Structure of Part 9

1.651 **565.**—The structure of this Part is as follows—

Chapter 2—

(a) imposes the charge to tax on pension income; and

(b) provides for deductions to be made from the amount of income chargeable;

Chapters 3 to 15 set out the types of income which are charged to tax under this Part and, for each type of income, identify—

(a) the amount of income chargeable to tax for a tax year; and

(b) the person liable to pay any tax charged;

Chapters 16 to 18 deal with exemptions from the charge to tax (whether under this Part or any other provision).

GENERAL NOTE

1.652 In the ICTA, most forms of pension income were taxed in the same way as emoluments under Schedule E. One of the main changes undertaken as part of the Tax Law Rewrite Project was to extract all the various provisions relating to the taxation of pensions of employees and office holders (both in the United Kingdom and overseas) and put them together in a single code. That code now forms Part 9 of ITEPA 2003. It contains all the primary legislation from the ICTA 1988 and successive Finance Acts on the taxation of state pensions (including social security pensions), occupational pensions payable to officeholders and employees, and personal pensions. It recognises the division between earnings and pensions, but prevails over the separate provisions in Part 10, dealing with social security income. It includes provisions in separate chapters dealing with foreign pension income.

The Tax Credits (Definition and Calculation of Income) Regulations 2002 rely on that code for defining pension income for the purposes of the tax credits income test. This selection of sections sets out the key provisions from that code. Foreign pensions, are not, however, included as pension income for tax credits purposes, so no reference is made to those chapters of Part 9 of ITEPA. Foreign pensions should therefore be considered as foreign income, not pension income, for tax credits purposes. Those chapters and chapters on closed schemes are not included in this selection. The selection reflects the main rules on United Kingdom pensions (ch.3), United Kingdom social security pensions (ch.5), and the rules on approved retirement benefit schemes (the main occupations schemes) (ch.6). There are similar rules, not repeated, to those in ch.7 (former approved superannuation schemes) and also ch.8 (approved personal pension schemes), ch.9 (retirement annuity contracts), and ch.10 (other employment-related annuities).

Chapters 11, 12 and 14 deal with specialist funds. Chapter 17, listing exemptions, and ch.18, listing exemptions for non-United Kingdom residents are, where thought appropriate, reflected in s.19 of the Tax Credits (Definition and Calculation of Income) Regulations 2002 without reference to these provisions, which are therefore not selected.

CHAPTER 2

TAX ON PENSION INCOME

Nature of charge to tax on pension income and relevant definitions

566.—(1) The charge to tax on pension income under this Part is a charge to tax on that income excluding any exempt income. **1.653**

(2) "Pension income" means the pensions, annuities and income of other types to which the provisions listed in subsection (4) apply.

This definition applies for the purposes of the Tax Acts.

(3) "Exempt income" means pension income on which no liability to income tax arises as a result of any provision of Chapters 16 to 18 of this Part.

This definition applies for the purposes of this Part.

(4) These are the provisions referred to in subsection (2)—

Provision	*Income*	*Chapter (of this Part)*
Section 569	United Kingdom pensions	Chapter 3
Section 573	Foreign pensions	Chapter 4
Section 577	United Kingdom social security pensions	Chapter 5
Section 580	Pensions or annuities from approved retirement benefits schemes	Chapter 6
Section 583	Unauthorised payments from— (a) approved retirement benefits schemes; or (b) former approved superannuation funds (see section 593)	Chapter 6
Section 590	Annuities paid under former approved superannuation funds	Chapter 7
Section 595	Annuities from approved personal pension schemes	Chapter 8
Section 598	Income withdrawals under approved personal pension Arrangements	Chapter 8

Provision	*Income*	*Chapter (of this Part)*
Section 601	Unauthorised personal pension payments	Chapter 8
Section 605	Annuities under retirement annuity contracts	Chapter 9
Section 609	Annuities for the benefit of dependants	Chapter 10
Section 610	Annuities under sponsored superannuation schemes	Chapter 10
Section 611	Annuities in recognition of another's services	Chapter 10
Section 615	Certain overseas government pensions paid in the United Kingdom	Chapter 11
Section 619	The House of Commons Members' Fund	Chapter 12
Section 623	Return of surplus employee additional voluntary contributions	Chapter 13
Section 629	Pre-1973 pensions paid under OPA 1973	Chapter 14
Section 633	Voluntary annual payments	Chapter 15

Amount charged to tax

1.654 **567.**—(1) The amount of pension income which is charged to tax under this Part for a particular tax year is as follows.

(2) In relation to each pension, annuity or other item of pension income, the amount charged to tax is the "net taxable pension income" for the tax year.

(3) The net taxable pension income for a pension, annuity or other item of pension income for a tax year is given by the formula—

$$\frac{\text{TPI}}{\text{DPI}}$$

where—

TPI means the amount of taxable pension income for that pension, annuity or item of pension income for that year (see subsection (4)); and

DPI means the total amount of any deductions allowed from the pension, annuity or item of pension income (see subsection (5)).

(4) For the purposes of this Act—

(a) the amount of taxable pension income for a pension, annuity or other item of pension income for a tax year is determined in accordance with Chapters 13 to 15 of this Part (which contain provisions relating to this amount for each type of pension income); and

(b) in determining the amount of taxable pension income for a pension, annuity or other item of pension income, any exempt income is to be excluded.

(5) The deductions allowed from a pension, annuity or other item of pension income are those under—
section 617 (10% deduction from an overseas government pension to which section 615 applies);
Part 22 (payroll giving).

Person liable for tax

568.—For the provision identifying which person is liable for any tax charged under this Part on a pension, annuity or other item of pension income, see Chapters 3 to 15. 1.655

CHAPTER 3

UNITED KINGDOM PENSIONS: GENERAL RULES

United Kingdom pensions

569.—(1) This section applies to any pension paid by or on behalf of a person who is in the United Kingdom. 1.656
(2) But this section does not apply to a pension if any provision of Chapters 5 to 14 of this Part applies to it.
(3) For pensions paid by or on behalf of a person who is outside the United Kingdom, see Chapter 4 of this Part.

"Pension": interpretation

570.—In this chapter, "pension" includes a pension which is paid voluntarily or is capable of being discontinued. 1.657

Taxable pension income

571.—If section 569 applies, the taxable pension income for a tax year is the full amount of the pension accruing in that year, irrespective of when any amount is actually paid. 1.658

Person liable for tax

572.—If section 569 applies, the person liable for any tax charged under this Part is the person receiving or entitled to the pension. 1.659

CHAPTER 5

UNITED KINGDOM SOCIAL SECURITY PENSIONS

United Kingdom social security pensions

1.660 **577.**—(1) This section applies to—
the state pension;
graduated retirement benefit;
industrial death benefit;
widowed mother's allowance;
widowed parent's allowance; and
widow's pension.

(2) In this section—

"state pension" means any pension payable under—

(a) section 44, 48A, 48B, 48BB, 51 or 78 of SSCBA 1992; or

(b) section 44, 48, 48B, 48BB, 51 or 78 of SSCB(NI)A 1992;

"graduated retirement benefit" means any benefit payable under—

(a) section 36 or 37 of the National Insurance Act 1965 (Chapter 51); or

(b) section 35 or 36 of the National Insurance Act (Northern Ireland) 1966 (Chapter 6 (NI));

"industrial death benefit" means any benefit payable under—

(a) section 94 of, and Part 6 of Schedule 7 to SSCBA 1992; or

(b) section 94 of, and Part 6 of Schedule 7 to SSCB(NI)A 1992;

"widowed mother's allowance" means any allowance payable under—

(a) section 37 of SSCBA 1992; or

(b) section 37 of SSCB(NI)A 1992;

"widowed parent's allowance" means any allowance payable under—

(a) section 39A of SSCBA 1992; or

(b) section 39A of SSCB(NI)A 1992;

"widow's pension" means any pension payable under—

(a) section 38 of SSCBA 1992; or

(b) section 38 of SSCB(NI)A 1992.

(3) In subsection (2), in paragraph (b) of the definition of state pension, the reference to section 48 of SSCB(NI)A 1992 is a reference to the section 48 inserted by paragraph 3(1) of Schedule 2 to the Pensions (Northern Ireland) Order 1995 (SI 1995/3213 (NI 22)).

(4) Chapter 17 of this Part provides a partial exemption for a pension to which this section applies in respect of any part of the pension which is attributable to an increase in respect of a child (see section 645).

Taxable pension income

1.661 **578.**—If section 577 applies, the taxable pension income for a tax year is the full amount of the pension, benefit or allowance accruing in that year, irrespective of when any amount is actually paid.

Person liable for tax

579.—If section 577 applies, the person liable for any tax charged under this Part is the person receiving or entitled to the pension, benefit or allowance. 1.662

Chapter 6

Approved Retirement Benefits Schemes

Pensions and annuities

Pensions and annuities

580.—This section applies to— 1.663

(a) any pension or annuity paid under a retirement benefits scheme which is either approved or being considered for approval; and

(b) any annuity acquired using funds held for the purposes of a retirement benefits scheme which is either approved or being considered for approval.

Taxable pension income

581.—If section 580 applies, the taxable pension income for a tax year is the full amount of the pension or annuity accruing in that year, irrespective of when any amount is actually paid. 1.664

Person liable for tax

582.—If section 580 applies, the person liable for any tax charged under this Part is the person receiving or entitled to the pension or annuity. 1.665

Meaning of "retirement benefits scheme", etc.

586.—(1) In this chapter— 1.666

"retirement benefits scheme" has the meaning given in section 611 of ICTA;

"approved", in relation to such a scheme, means that the scheme is approved by the Board of Inland Revenue for the purposes of—

(a) Chapter 2 of Part 2 of FA 1970; or

(b) Chapter 1 of Part 14 of ICTA.

(2) Any reference in this chapter to a pension or annuity paid under a retirement benefits scheme includes a reference to a pension or annuity paid under a contract which—

(a) is made for purposes of the scheme; and

(b) is made between—

(i) the administrator of the scheme;

(ii) the employer; or

(iii) the employee or an ex-spouse of the employee;
and a third party.

(3) In subsection (2) the reference to the employer is a reference to the person who is the employer in relation to the scheme.

(4) In subsection (2)(b)(i), "administrator of the scheme" is to be construed in accordance with section 611AA of ICTA.

(5) References in this chapter to approved retirement benefits schemes are extended by section 587 (marine pilots' benefit fund).

Meaning of "employee" and "ex-spouse"

1.667 **588.**—(1) In this chapter—

"employee"—

(a) includes a person who is to be, or has been, an employee; and
(b) in relation to a company, includes any officer or director of the company and any other person taking part in the management of the affairs of the company;

"ex-spouse" means a party to a marriage which has been dissolved or annulled and, in relation to any person, means the other party to a marriage with that person which has been dissolved or annulled.

(2) For the purposes of the definition of "employee" in subsection (1), "director", in relation to a company, includes—

(a) in the case of a company the affairs of which are managed by a board of directors or similar body, a member of that board or body;
(b) in the case of a company the affairs of which are managed by a single director or similar person, that person;
(c) in the case of a company the affairs of which are managed by the members themselves, a member of that company,

and includes a person who is to be or has been a director.

CHAPTER 15

VOLUNTARY ANNUAL PAYMENTS

Voluntary annual payments

1.668 **633.**—(1) This section applies to an annual payment which—

(a) is paid voluntarily; or
(b) is capable of being discontinued, if conditions A and B are met.

(2) Condition A is that the payment is paid to—

(a) a former employee or a former officeholder;
(b) the widow or widower of a former employee or former officeholder; or
(c) any child, relative or dependant of a former employee or a former officeholder.

(3) Condition B is that the payment is paid by or on behalf of—
(a) the person—
(i) who employed the former employee; or
(ii) under whom the former officeholder held the office; or
(b) the successors of that person.

(4) But this section applies to a payment which is paid by or on a behalf of a person who is outside the United Kingdom only if it is paid to a person resident in the United Kingdom.

(5) In this section "office" includes in particular any position which has an existence independent of the person who holds it and may be filled by successive holders.

Taxable pension income: United Kingdom voluntary annual payments

634.—(1) The taxable pension income for payments to which section 633 applies is determined in accordance with this section if the payments are made by or on behalf of a person who is in the United Kingdom. **1.669**

(2) The taxable pension income for a tax year is the full amount of the payments accruing in that year irrespective of when any amount is actually paid.

Taxable pension income: foreign voluntary annual payments

635.—(1) The taxable pension income for payments to which section 633 applies is determined in accordance with this section if the payments are made by or on behalf of a person who is outside the United Kingdom. **1.670**

(2) The taxable pension income for a tax year is the amount on which tax would be chargeable if the pension were charged to tax under Case V of Schedule D for that year (see in particular the provisions of ICTA listed in subsection (3)).

(3) Those provisions of ICTA are—
(a) sections 65 and 68 (calculation of the amount of the income on which tax is to be charged in the tax year);
(b) section 584 (relief for unremittable overseas income);
(c) section 585 (relief on delayed remittances).

Person liable for tax

636.—If section 633 applies, the person liable for any tax charged under this Part is the person receiving or entitled to the payment. **1.671**

CHAPTER 16

EXEMPTION FOR CERTAIN LUMP SUMS

Exemption for lump sums provided under certain pension schemes, etc.

1.672 **637.**—(1) No liability to income tax arises on a lump sum provided under—

(a) approved personal pension arrangements;
(b) a tax-exempt pension scheme; or
(c) a retirement annuity contract.

(2) But subsection (1)(b) applies to a lump sum paid in compensation for loss of office or employment, or for loss or diminution of earnings, only if—

(a) the payment is properly regarded as earned by past services; or
(b) the loss of office or employment, or the loss or diminution of earnings, is due to ill health.

(3) Subsection (1)(b) does not apply to a lump sum to which section 583 (approved retirement benefits schemes: unauthorised payments) or section 623 (return of surplus AVCs) applies.

This includes cases where section 583 applies by virtue of section 593.

(4) Subsection (1)(c) applies to a lump sum only if it is provided in consequence of a right which meets the conditions in paras (a) and (b) of section 620(3) of ICTA.

(5) In this section—

"approved personal pension arrangements" has the same meaning as in Chapter 4 of Part 14 of ICTA (see section 630(1) of ICTA);

"earnings" means earnings or amounts treated as earnings which constitute employment income (see section 7(2)(a) or (b));

"office" includes in particular any position which has an existence independent of the person who holds it and may be filled by successive holders;

"retirement annuity contract" has the same meaning as in Chapter 9 of this Part (see section 606).

(6) In this section, "tax-exempt pension scheme" means—

(a) a retirement benefits scheme which is—
   (i) an approved scheme;
   (ii) a relevant statutory scheme; or
   (iii) a scheme set up by a government outside the United Kingdom for the benefit, or primarily for the benefit, of its employees; or
(b) any such scheme or fund as was described in section 221(1) and (2) of ICTA (schemes to which payments could be made without charge to tax under section 220 of that Act).

(7) For the purposes of subsection (6)—

"relevant statutory scheme" has the meaning given in section 611A(1) of ICTA;

"retirement benefits scheme" has the meaning given in section 611 of ICTA;

"approved", in relation to a retirement benefits scheme, means that the scheme is approved by the Board of Inland Revenue for the purposes of—

(a) Chapter 2 of Part 2 of FA 1970; or

(b) Chapter 1 of Part 14 of ICTA.

PART 10

SOCIAL SECURITY INCOME

CHAPTER 1

INTRODUCTION

Structure of Part 10

655.—(1) The structure of this Part is as follows— **1.673**

Chapter 2—

(a) imposes the charge to tax on social security income; and

(b) provides for deductions to be made from the amount of income chargeable;

Chapter 3 sets out the United Kingdom social security benefits which are charged to tax under this Part and identifies—

(a) the amount of income chargeable to tax for a tax year; and

(b) the person liable to pay any tax charged;

Chapters 4 and 5 deal with exemptions from the charge to tax on United Kingdom social security benefits (whether under this Part or any other provision);

Chapters 6 and 7 make provisions about foreign benefits.

(2) For other provisions about the taxation of social security benefits see—

section 151 of FA 1996 (power for the Treasury to make orders about the taxation of benefits payable under Government pilot schemes);

section 84 of FA 2000 (exemption of payments under New Deal 50plus);

section 85 of FA 2000 (exemption of payments under Employment Zones programme).

(3) For the charge to tax on social security pensions see Part 9.

GENERAL NOTE

"Social security income" is another head of charge created from the Tax Law Rewrite Project. Previously, all forms of social security income were fitted, sometimes somewhat uncomfortably, in Schedule E. Part 10 of ITEPA is now used to codify the charge to income tax on all forms of social security benefit and **1.674** allowance other than pensions. As this section records, Part 9 deals with pensions. The opportunity has also been taken to set out the various provisions in a systematic way, and dealing with both United Kingdom and other benefits.

Because of the general importance of these provisions for social security purposes, the Part has been included more extensively than other Parts of ITEPA for social security purposes, and not restricted to those relevant only for tax credits purposes.

Subsection (1) is a signposting provision.

Subsection (2) lists the three sections (not included in this volume) under which limited exemptions from income tax may be made for social security benefits. The power under s.151 of FA 1996 is used to exempt payments made to claimants under pilot schemes. For current exemptions under this provision, see: the Taxation of Benefits under Government Pilot Schemes (Return to Work Credit and Employment Retention and Advancements Schemes) Order 2003 (SI 2003/2339) (not reproduced in this volume), in effect from October 1, 2003; and the Taxation of Benefits under government Pilot Schemes (Working Neighbourhoods Pilot and In Work Credit) Order 2004 (SI 2004/575), in effect from April 6, 2004. Both orders fully exempt payments under those schemes form income tax. The reference to s.84 of FA 2000 is superseded from the start of working tax credit as New Deal payments have now been incorporated into the credit.

Subsection (3) is a signpost to s.577 (United Kingdom social security pensions).

CHAPTER 2

TAX ON SOCIAL SECURITY INCOME

Nature of charge to tax on social security income

1.675 **656.**—(1) The charge to tax on social security income is a charge to tax on that income excluding any exempt income.

(2) "Exempt income" is social security income on which no liability to income tax arises as a result of any provision of Chapters 4, 5 or 7 of this Part.

This definition applies for the purposes of this Part.

DEFINITIONS

1.676 "social security income"—see s.657(2).

"tax" – see ICTA, s.832(3).

GENERAL NOTE

1.677 This section is extremely important because it emphasises that the exemption provisions in the Part override the charges to tax. In practice, very few forms of UK social security income are chargeable to tax under this Part. Remember that pensions are chargeable under Part 9. In most cases statutory sick pay and the other statutory payments are chargeable to tax under Part 2. Any such payments that are not caught by Part 2 are caught by a "safety net" provision in this Part.

Provisions in this part exempt child benefit, guardian's allowance and child tax credit and so exclude all child-related benefit. Other provisions exempt all disablement related benefits payable to the disabled or incapacitated individual.

Tax credits under the TCA 2002 are themselves exempted from tax under this Part. So are the local government benefits of housing benefit and council tax benefit. Benefits received from the national health service, in kind or in cash, are not income for any income tax purpose, and are not affected by this Part. Welfare benefits in kind, such as welfare foods and publicly provided accommodation, are not within the definition of "social security income" in s.657 and so are excluded from the charge to tax under this Part. They do not fall to be charged under any other part of ITEPA 2003.

This leaves income tax payable only on some parts of some payments of income support, jobseeker's allowance and incapacity benefit, and also on bereavement allowance (in practice linked with pension entitlements but not a form of pension income) and carer's allowance (formerly known as invalid care allowance).

The equivalent approach is adopted for foreign social security payments.

Meaning of "social security income", "taxable benefits", etc.

657.—(1) This section defines— 1.678

"social security income" for the purposes of the Tax Acts; and

"taxable benefits", "Table A" and "Table B" for the purposes of this Part.

(2) "Social security income" means—

(a) the United Kingdom social security benefits listed in Table A;

(b) the United Kingdom social security benefits listed in Table B;

(c) the foreign benefits to which section 678 applies; and

(d) the foreign benefits to which section 681(2) applies.

(3) "Taxable benefits" means—

(a) the United Kingdom social security benefits listed in Table A; and

(b) the foreign benefits to which section 678 applies.

(4) Subsections (2) and (3) are subject to section 660(2).

(5) "Table A" means Table A in section 660.

(6) "Table B" means Table B in section 677.

General Note

This section defines the term "social security income" used in s.656, which is the charging section. Unless a form of income is within the scope of the definition in subs.(2), it is not liable to income tax under this Part. Nor will it be liable to income tax under any other general provision in the Taxes Act. However, the interpretation of the scope of this section must take into account the very wide provisions dealing with benefits provided by employers in Part 2, which in practice covers some forms of payments that are in principle social security payments (such as statutory maternity pay). Further, anything that is a "pension" is taxable under Part 9 and is removed from this Part by s.655(3). 1.679

Amount charged to tax

658.—(1) The amount of social security income which is charged to tax under this Part for a particular tax year is as follows. 1.680

(2) In relation to a taxable benefit, the amount charged to tax is the net taxable social security income for the tax year.

(3) The net taxable social security income for a taxable benefit for a tax year is given by the formula—

$$TSSI - PGD$$

where—

TSSI means the amount of taxable social security income for that benefit for that year (see subsections (4) to (7)); and

PGD means the amount of the deduction (if any) allowed from the benefit under Part 12 (payroll giving).

(4) In relation to bereavement allowance, carer's allowance, incapacity benefit and income support (which are listed in Table A), the amount of taxable social security income is determined in accordance with section 661.

(5) In relation to any other benefit listed in Table A, the amount of taxable social security income is the amount of the benefit that falls to be charged to tax.

(6) In relation to foreign benefits to which section 678 applies, the amount of taxable social security income is determined in accordance with section 679.

(7) In determining for the purposes of this Act the amount of taxable social security income, any exempt income is to be excluded.

DEFINITIONS

"exempt income"—see s.656(2)
"social security income"—see s.657(2)
"tax year"—see s.721(1)
"taxable benefit"—see s.657(3)

Person liable for tax

1.681 **659.**—The person liable for any tax charged under this Part is identified in—

(a) section 662 (United Kingdom benefits); or
(b) section 680 (foreign benefits).

CHAPTER 3

TAXABLE UNITED KINGDOM SOCIAL SECURITY BENEFITS

Taxable benefits: United Kingdom benefits—Table A

1.682 **660.**—(1) This is Table A:

1.683 TABLE A

TAXABLE UK BENEFITS

Social security benefit	*Payable under*	
Bereavement allowance	SSCBA 1992	Section 39B
	SSCB(NI)A 1992	Section 39B
Carer's allowance	SSCBA 1992	Section 70
	SSCB(NI)A 1992	Section 70

Social security benefit	*Payable under*	
Incapacity benefit	SSCBA 1992	Section 30A(1) or (5), 40 or 41
	SSCB(NI)A 1992	Section 30A(1) or (5), 40 or 41
Income support	SSCBA 1992	Section 123
	SSCB(NI)A 1992	Section 124
Jobseeker's allowance	JSA 1995	Section 1
	JS(NI)O 1995	Article 3
Statutory adoption pay	SSCBA 1992	Section 171ZL
	Any provision made for Northern Ireland which corresponds to section 171ZL of SSCBA 1992	
Statutory maternity pay	SSCBA 1992	Section 164
	SSCB(NI)A 1992	Section 160
Statutory paternity pay	SSCBA 1992	Section 171ZA or 171ZB
	Any provision made for Northern Ireland which corresponds to section 171ZA or section 171ZB of SSCBA 1992	
Statutory sick pay	SSCBA 1992	Section 151
	SSCB(NI)A 1992	Section 147.

(2) A benefit listed below is not "social security income" or a "taxable benefit" if it is charged to tax under another Part of this Act—

statutory adoption pay;
statutory maternity pay;
statutory paternity pay;
statutory sick pay.

DEFINITIONS

"social security income"—see s.657(2)
"taxable benefit"—see s.657(3)

GENERAL NOTE

For the full forms of the abbreviations in Table A see Sch.1, part 1 to the Act. Subsection (2) provides that a charge to tax under Part 2 of the Act takes priority over this Part, but the section ensures that all statutory payments are taxable. 1.684

Taxable social security income

661.—(1) This section applies in relation to each of the following taxable benefits listed in Table A— 1.685

bereavement allowance;
carer's allowance;
incapacity benefit; and
income support.

(2) The amount of taxable social security income for a taxable benefit for a tax year is the full amount of the benefit accruing in the tax year irrespective of when any amount is actually paid.

Definitions

"tax year"—see s.721(1)
"taxable benefit"—see s.675(3)

General Note

1.686 This is a new rule under ITEPA introduced to replace both inconsistent previous legislation and a lack of legislation, the rules apparently varying from one benefit to another for no good reason. "Accrued" is standard income tax language not normally used for social security purposes. In social security terms, as the section makes clear, it means payable not paid.

Person liable for tax

1.687 **662.**—The person liable for any tax charged under this Part on a taxable benefit listed in Table A is the person receiving or entitled to the benefit.

General note

1.688 "Received or entitled" is familiar income tax language applied to social security income by ITEPA in place of a lack of any clear previous rule. As the wording indicates it covers both the person for whom the benefit is payable and the person who actually receives it. The wording will make joint claimants for jobseeker's allowance both liable for any income tax on the allowance. It is, however, not clear how this is applied to appointees appointed to receive income support for a claimant.

Chapter 4

Taxable UK Social Security Benefits: Exemptions

Incapacity benefit

Long-term incapacity benefit: previous entitlement to invalidity benefit

1.689 **663.**—(1) No liability to income tax arises on long-term incapacity benefit if—

(a) a person is entitled to the benefit for a day of incapacity for work which falls in a period of incapacity for work which is treated for the purposes of that benefit as having begun before April 13, 1995; and
(b) the part of that period which is treated as having fallen before that date includes a day for which that person was entitled to invalidity benefit.

(2) In this section—
"invalidity benefit" means invalidity benefit under—
(a) Part 2 of SSCBA 1992; or
(b) Part 2 of SSCB(NI)A 1992;
"long-term incapacity benefit" means incapacity benefit payable under—
(a) section 30A(5), 40 or 41 of SSCBA 1992; or
(b) section 30A(5), 40 or 41 of SSCB(NI)A 1992.

Short-term incapacity benefit not payable at the higher rate

664.—(1) No liability to income tax arises on short-term incapacity benefit unless it is payable at the higher rate. **1.690**

(2) In this section—
(a) "short-term incapacity benefit" means incapacity benefit payable under—
(i) section 30A(1) of SSCBA 1992; or
(ii) section 30A(1) of SSCB(NI)A 1992;
(b) the reference to short-term incapacity benefit payable at the higher rate is to be construed in accordance with—
(i) section 30B of SSCBA 1992; or
(ii) section 30B of SSCB(NI)A 1992.

Income support

Exempt unless payable to member of couple involved in trade dispute

665.—(1) No liability to income tax arises on income support unless— **1.691**
(a) the income support is payable to one member of a married or unmarried couple ("the claimant"); and
(b) section 126 of SSCBA 1992 or section 125 of SSCB(NI)A 1992 (trade disputes) applies to the claimant but not to the other member of the couple.

(2) In this section, "married couple" and "unmarried couple" have the same meaning as in section 137(1) of SSCBA 1992 or section 133(1) of SSCB(NI)A 1992.

Child maintenance bonus

666.—No liability to income tax arises on a part of income support which is attributable to a child maintenance bonus (within the meaning of section 10 of CSA 1995 or Article 4 of CS(NI)O 1995). **1.692**

Amounts in excess of taxable maximum

667.—(1) If the amount of income support paid to a person ("the claimant") for a week or a part of a week exceeds the claimant's taxable maximum for that period, no liability to income tax arises on the excess. **1.693**

(2) The claimant's taxable maximum for a period is determined under section 668.

Taxable maximum

1.694 **668.**—(1) A claimant's taxable maximum for a week is determined under this subsection if the applicable amount for the purpose of calculating the income support consists only of an amount in respect of the relevant couple.

The taxable maximum is equal to one half of the applicable amount.

(2) A claimant's taxable maximum for a week is determined under this subsection if the applicable amount includes amounts that are not in respect of the relevant couple.

The taxable maximum is equal to one half of the amount which is included in the applicable amount in respect of the relevant couple.

(3) A claimant's taxable maximum for a part of a week is determined as follows—

Step 1

Assume that the income support is paid to the claimant for the whole of, rather than part of, the week.

Step 2

Determine under subsection (1) or (2) what the claimant's taxable maximum for that week would be on that assumption.

Step 3

Determine the claimant's taxable maximum for the part of the week using this formula—

$$\frac{N}{7} \times TMW$$

where—

N is the number of days in the part of the week for which the claimant is actually paid the income support; and

TMW is the taxable maximum for the whole week determined under step 2.

Interpretation

1.695 **669.**—(1) In section 668, except in relation to Northern Ireland—

"applicable amount" means the amount prescribed in relation to income support in regulations made under section 135 of SSCBA 1992;

"married couple" and "unmarried couple" have the same meaning as in section 137(1) of SSCBA 1992.

(2) In section 668, in relation to Northern Ireland—

"applicable amount" means the amount prescribed in relation to income support in regulations made under section 131 of SSCB(NI)A 1992;

"married couple" and "unmarried couple" have the same meaning as in section 133(1) of SSCB(NI)A 1992.

(3) In section 668, "relevant couple", in relation to a claimant, means the married or unmarried couple of which the claimant is a member.

General Note

This applies the social security definitions of "married couple" and "unmarried couple" to ITEPA for the purposes of taxing social security income. The general approach to treating husband and wife as a married couple for income tax purposes is in s.282 of ICTA. The fact that a taxpayer is a member of an unmarried couple, or of a same-sex couple, is irrelevant for income tax purposes save for this part of ITEPA. **1.696**

Jobseeker's allowance

Child maintenance bonus

670.—No liability to income tax arises on a part of a jobseeker's allowance which is attributable to a child maintenance bonus (within the meaning of section 10 of CSA 1995 or Article 4 of CS(NI)O 1995). **1.697**

Amounts in excess of taxable maximum

671.—(1) If the amount of jobseeker's allowance paid to a person ("the claimant") for a week or a part of a week exceeds the claimant's taxable maximum for that period, no liability to income tax arises on the excess. **1.698**

(2) The claimant's taxable maximum for a period is determined under sections 672 to 674.

Taxable maximum: general

672.—(1) A claimant's taxable maximum for a week is determined— **1.699**

(a) under section 673, if the claimant is paid an income-based jobseeker's allowance for that week; or

(b) under section 674, if the claimant is paid a contribution-based jobseeker's allowance for that week.

(2) A claimant's taxable maximum for a part of a week is determined as follows—

Step 1

Assume that the jobseeker's allowance is paid to the claimant for the whole of, rather than part of, the week.

Step 2

Determine under section 673 or 674 what the claimant's taxable maximum for that week would be on that assumption.

Step 3

Determine the claimant's taxable maximum for the part of the week using this formula—

$$\frac{N}{7} \times TMW$$

where—

N is the number of days in the part of the week for which the claimant is actually paidthe jobseeker's allowance; and

TMW is the taxable maximum for the whole week determined under step 2.

Taxable maximum: income-based jobseeker's allowance

1.700 **673.**—(1) A claimant's taxable maximum for a week is determined under this section if—

(a) the claimant is paid an income-based jobseeker's allowance for that week, or

(b) the claimant is assumed under section 672(2) to be paid an income-based jobseeker's allowance for that week.

(2) If the claimant is not a member of a married or unmarried couple, the claimant's taxable maximum for the week is equal to the age-related amount which would be applicable to the claimant if a contribution based jobseeker's allowance were payable to the claimant for that week.

(3) If the claimant is a member of a married or unmarried couple, the claimant's taxable maximum for the week is equal to the portion of the applicable amount which is included in the jobseeker's allowance in respect of the couple for that week.

(4) But if—

(a) the claimant is a member of a married or unmarried couple; and

(b) the other member of that couple is prevented by section 14 of JSA 1995 or Article 16 of JS(NI)O 1995 (trade disputes) from being entitled to a jobseeker's allowance;

the claimant's taxable maximum for that week is equal to half the portion of the applicable amount which is included in the jobseeker's allowance in respect of the couple for that week.

Taxable maximum: contribution-based jobseeker's allowance

1.701 **674.**—(1) A claimant's taxable maximum for a week is determined under this section if—

(a) the claimant is paid a contribution-based jobseeker's allowance for that week; or

(b) the claimant is assumed under section 672(2) to be paid a contribution-based jobseeker's allowance for that week.

(2) If the claimant is not a member of a married or unmarried couple, the claimant's taxable maximum for the week is equal to the age-related amount which is applicable to the claimant for that week.

(3) If the claimant is a member of a married or unmarried couple, the claimant's taxable maximum for the week is equal to the portion of the

applicable amount which would be included in the jobseeker's allowance in respect of the couple if an income-based jobseeker's allowance were payable to the claimant for that week.

Interpretation

675.—(1) In sections 671 to 674, except in relation to Northern Ireland— 1.702

"age-related amount" and "applicable amount" mean the amounts determined as such in accordance with regulations made under section 4 of JSA 1995;

"contribution-based jobseeker's allowance" and "income-based jobseeker's allowance" have the same meaning as in section 1(4) of JSA 1995;

"married couple" and "unmarried couple" have the same meaning as in section 35(1) of JSA 1995.

(2) In sections 671 to 674, in relation to Northern Ireland—

"age-related amount" and "applicable amount" mean the amounts determined as such in accordance with regulations made under Article 6 of JS(NI)O 1995;

"contribution-based jobseeker's allowance" and "income-based jobseeker's allowance" have the same meaning as in Article 3(4) of JS(NI)O 1995;

"married couple" and "unmarried couple" have the same meaning as in Article 2(2) of JS(NI)O 1995.

Increases in respect of children

Increases in respect of children

676.—No liability to income tax arises on a part of a taxable benefit listed in Table A which is attributable to an increase in respect of a child. 1.703

General Note

This is superseded from 2003–04 for incapacity benefit and carer's allowance, and from 2004–05 for income support and jobseeker's allowance, by the introduction of child tax credit, which is exempt from tax. 1.704

Chapter 5

UK Social Security Benefits Wholly Exempt from Income Tax

UK social security benefits wholly exempt from tax: Table B

677.—(1) No liability to income tax arises on the United Kingdom social security benefits listed in Table B. 1.705

TABLE B—PART 1

1.706 BENEFITS PAYABLE UNDER PRIMARY LEGISLATION

Social security benefit	*Payable under*
Attendance allowance	SSCBA 1992, s.64 SSCB(NI)A 1992, s.64
Back to work bonus	JSA 1995, s.26 JS(NI)O 1995, Article 28
Bereavement payment	SSCBA 1992, s.36 SSCB(NI)A 1992, s.36
Child benefit	SSCBA 1992, s.141 SSCB(NI)A 1992, s.137
Child's special allowance	SSCBA 1992, s.56 SSCB(NI)A 1992, s.56
Child tax credit	TCA 2002, Part 1
Council tax benefit	SSCBA 1992, s.131
Disability living allowance	SSCBA 1992, s.71 SSCB(NI)A 1992, s.71
Guardian's allowance	SSCBA 1992, s.77 SSCB(NI)A 1992, s.77
Housing benefit	SSCBA 1992, s.130 SCB(NI)A 1992, s.129
Industrial injuries benefit (apart from industrial death benefit)	SSCBA 1992, s.94 SSCB(NI)A 1992, s.94
Pensioner's Christmas bonus	SSCBA 1992, s.148 SSCB(NI)A 1992, s.144
Payments out of the social fund	SSCBA 1992, s.138 SSCB(NI)A 1992, s.134
Severe disablement allowance	SSCBA 1992, s.68 SSCB(NI)A 1992, s.68
State maternity allowance	SSCBA 1992, s.35 SSCB(NI)A 1992, s.35
State pension credit	SPCA 2002, s.1 SPCA(NI) 2002, s.1
Working tax credit	TCA 2002, Part 1

TABLE B—PART 2

1.707 BENEFITS PAYABLE UNDER REGULATIONS

Social security benefit	*Payable under regulations made under*
Compensation payments where child support reduced because of a change in legislation	CSA 1995, s.24 CS(NI)O 1995, Article 17

Social security benefit	*Payable under regulations made under*
Payments to reduce under-occupation by housing benefit claimants	WRPA 1999, s.79 WRP(NI)O 1999, Article 70

(2) Industrial death benefit is charged to tax under Part 9 (see section 577).

(3) In this section "industrial death benefit" means any benefit payable under—

(a) section 94 of, and Part 6 of Schedule 7 to, SSCBA 1992; or
(b) section 94 of, and Part 6 of Schedule 7 to, SSCB(NI)A 1992.

Chapter 6

Taxable Foreign Benefits

Taxable benefits: foreign benefits

678.—(1) This section applies to any benefit which is payable under the law of a country or territory outside the United Kingdom if— 1.708

(a) it is substantially similar in character to a benefit listed in Table A, and
(b) it is payable to a person resident in the United Kingdom.

(2) But this section does not apply to a benefit which is charged to tax under Part 9 (pension income).

General Note

This is a new statutory provision in ITEPA. Until its enactment, the Inland Revenue refrained from taxing foreign social security benefits on the basis of an extra-statutory concession. The only real problem area is the divide between social security income, exempt under this provision, and pension income, taxed under Part 9. 1.709

Taxable social security income

679.—(1) If section 678 applies, the taxable social security income for a taxable benefit for a tax year is the amount on which tax would be chargeable if the benefit were chargeable to tax under Case V of Schedule D (see in particular the provisions of ICTA listed in subsection (2)). 1.710

(2) Those provisions of ICTA are—

(a) sections 65 and 68 (calculation of the amount of the income on which tax is to be charged in the tax year);
(b) section 584 (relief for unremittable overseas income);
(c) section 585 (relief on delayed remittances).

Person liable for tax

1.711 **680.**—The person liable for any tax charged under this Part on a benefit to which section 678 applies is the person receiving or entitled to the benefit.

PART 13

SUPPLEMENTARY PROVISIONS

Interpretation

Meaning of "the Inland Revenue" etc.

1.712 **720.**—(1) In this Act "the Inland Revenue" means any officer of the Board of Inland Revenue.

(2) In this Act "the Board of Inland Revenue" means the Commissioners of Inland Revenue (as to which, see in particular the Inland Revenue Regulation Act 1890 (c.21)).

(3) Functions conferred on the Board of Inland Revenue by this Act are within section 4A of that Act (functions of Board exercisable by officer acting with their authority).

Other definitions

1.713 **721.**—(1) In this Act—

"cash voucher" has the same meaning as in Chapter 4 of Part 3 (see section 75);

"credit-token" has the same meaning as in Chapter 4 of Part 3 (see section 92);

"foreign employer" means—

- (a) in the case of an employee resident in the United Kingdom, an individual, partnership or body of persons resident outside the United Kingdom and not resident in the United Kingdom or the Republic of Ireland, and
- (b) in the case of an employee not resident in the United Kingdom, an individual, partnership or body of persons resident outside and not resident in the United Kingdom;

"non-cash voucher" has the same meaning as in Chapter 4 of Part 3 (see section 84);

"the normal self-assessment filing date", in relation to a tax year, means the 31st January following the tax year;

"personal representatives", in relation to a person who has died, means—

- (a) in the United Kingdom, persons responsible for administering the estate of the deceased; and
- (b) in a country or territory outside the United Kingdom, those persons having functions under its law equivalent to those of administering the estate of the deceased;

"tax year" means, in relation to income tax, a year for which any Act provides for income tax to be charged; and

"the tax year 2003–04" means the tax year beginning on 6th April, 2003 (and any corresponding expression in which two years are similarly mentioned is to be read in the same way).

(2) In the application of this Act to Scotland, "assignment" means an assignation.

(3) Any reference in this Act to being domiciledin the United Kingdom is to be read as a reference to being domiciled in any part of the United Kingdom.

(4) For the purposes of this Act the following are members of a person's family—

(a) the person's spouse,
(b) the person's children and their spouses,
(c) the person's parents, and
(d) the person's dependants.

(5) For the purposes of this Act the following are members of a person's family or household—

(a) members of the person's family,
(b) the person's domestic staff, and
(c) the person's guests.

(6) The following provisions (which relate to the legal equality of illegitimate children) are to be disregarded in interpreting references in this Act to a child or children—

(a) section 1 of the Family Law Reform Act 1987 (Chapter 42),
(b) the paragraph inserted in Schedule 1 to the Interpretation Act 1978 (Chapter 30) by paragraph 73 of Schedule 2 to the 1987 Act,
(c) section 1(2) of the Law Reform (Parent and Child) (Scotland) Act 1986 (Chapter 9),
(d) Article 155 of the Children (Northern Ireland) Order 1995 (SI 1995 No. 755 (NI 2)).

(7) In the employment income Parts any reference to earnings which is not limited by the context—

(a) to earnings within Chapter 1 of Part 3, or
(b) to any other particular description of earnings; includes a reference to any amount treated as earnings by any of the provisions mentioned in section 7(5) (meaning of "employment income" etc.).

SCHEDULE 1

Abbreviations and Defined Expressions

Part 1

Abbreviation of Acts and Instruments

TMA 1970	The Taxes Management Act 1970 (c.9)	**1.714**
ICTA 1970	The Income and Corporation Taxes Act 1970 (c.10)	
FA 1970	The Finance Act 1970 (c.24)	
FA 1971	The Finance Act 1971 (c.68)	
OPA 1973	The Overseas Pensions Act 1973 (c.21)	
FA 1973	The Finance Act 1973 (c.51)	

FA 1974	The Finance Act 1974 (c.30)
FA 1976	The Finance Act 1976 (c.40)
FA 1977	The Finance Act 1977 (c.36)
ICTA	The Income and Corporation Taxes Act 1988 (c.1)
FA 1988	The Finance Act 1988 (c.39)
FA 1989	The Finance Act 1989 (c.26)
SSCBA 1992	The Social Security Contributions and Benefits Act 1992 (c.4)
SSCB(NI)A 1992	The Social Security Contributions and Benefits (Northern Ireland) Act 1992 (c.7)
TCGA 1992	The Taxation of Chargeable Gains Act 1992 (c.12)
VERA 1994	The Vehicle Excise and Registration Act 1994 (c.22)
FA 1995	The Finance Act 1995 (c.4)
JSA 1995	The Jobseekers Act 1995 (c.18)
CSA 1995	The Child Support Act 1995 (c.34)
CS(NI)O 1995	The Child Support (Northern Ireland) Order 1995 (SI 1995/2702 (NI 13))
JS(NI)O 1995	The Jobseekers (Northern Ireland) Order 1995 (SI 1995/2705 (NI 15))
FA 1996	The Finance Act 1996 (c.8)
ERA 1996	The Employment Rights Act 1996 (c.18)
ER(NI)O 1996	The Employment Rights (Northern Ireland) Order 1996 (SI 1996/1919 (NI 16))
FA 1999	The Finance Act 1999 (c.16)
WRPA 1999	The Welfare Reform and Pensions Act 1999 (c.30)
WRP(NI)O 1999	The Welfare Reform and Pensions (Northern Ireland) Order 1999 (SI 1999/3147 (NI 11))
FA 2000	The Finance Act 2000 (c.17)
CAA 2001	The Capital Allowances Act 2001 (c.2)
FA 2001	The Finance Act 2001 (c.9)
SPCA 2002	The State Pension Credit Act 2002 (c.16)
TCA 2002	The Tax Credits Act 2002 (c.21)
SPCA(NI) 2002	The State Pension Credit Act (Northern Ireland) 2002 (c.14 (NI))

Part 2

Index of Expressions Defined in this Act or ICTA

1.715 *Note:* this index does not apply to expressions used in any of Chapters 6 to 9 of Part 7 (share incentive plans and other arrangements for acquiring shares): separate indexes appear at the end of Schedules 2 to 5.

accessory (in c.6 of Pt 3)	section 125(2)
acquisition (in c.8 of Pt 3)	section 197(2)
the acquisition (in c.8 of Pt 3)	section 192(4)
acquisition (in c.9 of Pt 3)	section 200(2)
age of a car or van (in c.6 of Pt 3)	section 171(3)
agency contract (in c.7 of Pt 2)	section 47(1)
annual rental value (in c.10 of Pt 3)	section 207
annual value (in c.5 of Pt 3)	section 110
approved (in c.8 of Pt 9)	section 604
approved (in relation to retirement benefits scheme) (in c.6 of Pt 9)	sections 586(1)
approved retirement benefits scheme (in c.6 of Pt 9)	section 587(1)
as a director or employee, in relation to the acquisition of an interest in shares (in c.2 of Pt 7)	section 423
asset (in c.4 of Pt 11)	section 701
assignment (in the application of the Act to Scotland)	section 721(2)
associate (in c.8 of Pt 2)	section 60
associated company (in c.8 of Pt 2)	section 61(1)
available for private use (in c.6 of Pt 3)	section 118(1)

basic rate	section 832(1) of ICTA
benefit (in c.10 of Pt 3)	section 201(2)
benefit (in c.3 of Pt 6)	section 402
the benefits code (in the employment income Parts)	section 63(1)
the Board of Inland Revenue	section 720(2)
body of persons	section 832(1) of ICTA
business (in c.8 of Pt 2)	section 61(1)
business travel (in c.6 of Pt 3)	section 171(1)
business travel (in c.2 of Pt 4)	section 236(1)
capital allowance	section 832(1) of ICTA
car (in c.6 of Pt 3)	section 115(1)
car (in c.2 of Pt 4)	section 235(2)
car (in c.3 of Pt 4)	section 249
var is available to an employee (in c.6 of Pt 3)	section 116(1)
car first made available to an employee (in c.6 of Pt 3)	section 116(2)(a)
car made available by reason of employment (in c.6 of Pt 3)	section 117
car with a CO_2 emissions figure (in c.6 of Pt 3)	section 134(1)
car without a CO_2 emissions figure (in c.6 of Pt 3)	section134(2)
cash voucher	s.721(1)
charging provisions of c.4 of Pt 2 (in the employment income Parts)	section 14(3)
charging provisions of c.5 of Pt 2 (in the employment income Parts)	section 20(3)
cheque voucher (in c.4 of Pt 3)	section 84(4)
child, children	section 832(5) of ICTA, and see section 721(6)
close company	section 832(1) of ICTA
company	section 832(1) of ICTA
company (in c.8 of Pt 2)	section 61(1)
connected (in the context of "connected person" or one person being connected" with another)	section 839 of ICTA (see section 718)
control section 840 of ICTA (see	section 719)
control (in the benefits code)	section 69
cost of provision in relation to non-cash voucher (in c.4 of Pt 3)	section 87(3)
credit-token	section 721(1)
date of first registration (in relation to a car or van) (in c.6 of Pt 3)	section 171(2)
the deductibility provisions (in Pt 5)	section 332
diesel (in c.6 of Pt 3)	section 171(1)
director (in the benefits code)	section 67(1)
director, full-time working (in the benefits code)	section 67(3)
disabled person's badge (in c.6 of Pt 3)	section 171(4)
distribution	section 832(1) of ICTA
domiciled in the United Kingdom	section 721(3)
donations (in Pt 12)	section 714(1)
earnings (in the employment income Parts)	section 62 and see section 721(7)
earnings (from which deductions are allowed) (in Pt 5)	section 327(2)(a)
earnings charged on receipt (in Pt 5)	section 335(4)
earnings charged on remittance (in Pt 5)	section 335(4)
earnings "for" a tax year (in c.4 of Pt 2)	section 16
earnings "for" a tax year (in c.5 of Pt 2)	section 29

earnings-only exemption	section 227(2)
EC certificate of conformity (in c.6 of Pt 3)	section 171(1)
EC type-approval certificate (in c.6 of Pt 3)	section 171(1)
eligible period (in c.6 of Pt 5)	section 378(2)
employed (in the employment income Parts)	sections 4 and 5(2)(a)
employed (in the benefits code)	section 66(1)(b)
employee (in the employment income Parts)	sections 4 and 5(2)(b)
employee (in the benefits code)	section 66(1)(b) (see also section 216(5))
employee (in c.3 of Pt 3)	section 70(4)
employee (in c.8 of Pt 3)	section 197(1)
employee (in c.9 of Pt 3)	section 200(1)
employee (in c.10 of Pt 3)	section 201(5)
employee (in c.1 of Pt 6)	section 386(5)
employee (in c.2 of Pt 6)	section 400(1)
employee (in c.6 of Pt 9)	section 588(1)
employee (in c.13 of Pt 9)	section 628(1)
employee (in Pt 11)	section 712(1)
employer (in the employment income Parts)	sections 4 and 5(2)(c)
employer (in the benefits code)	section 66(1)(b)
the employer (in the benefits code)	section 66(2)(b)
employer (in Pt 11)	section 712(1)
employer's national insurance contributions (in c.8 of Pt 2)	section 61(1)
employment (in the employment income Parts)	sections 4 and 5(1)
employment (in the benefits code)	section 66(1)(a)
the employment (in the benefits code)	section 66(2)(a)
employment (in c.5 of Pt 11)	section 707
employment as a seafarer (in c.6 of Pt 5)	section 384(1)
the employment change (in c.7 of Pt 4)	section 275
employment income	section 7(2)
the employment income Parts	section 3(2)
employment income exemption	section 227(3)
employment-related benefit (in c.10 of Pt 3)	section 201(2)
employment-related loan (in c.7 of Pt 3)	section 174
employment-related shares (in c.9 of Pt 3)	section 198(2)
the employment-related shares (in c.8 of Pt 3)	section 192(4)
engagement to which c.8 of Pt 2 applies (in c.8 of Pt 2)	section 49(5)
excluded benefits (in c.10 of Pt 3)	section 202
excluded employment (in the benefits code)	section 63(4)
excluded services (in c.7 of Pt 2)	section 47(2)
exempt approved scheme (in c.13 of Pt 9)	section 628(1)
exempt income (for the purposes of the employment income Parts)	section 8
exempt income (for the purposes of Pt 9)	section 566(3)
exempt income (for the purposes of Pt 10)	section 656(2)
ex-spouse (in c.2 of Pt 6)	section 400(1)
ex-spouse (in c.6 of Pt 9)	section 588(1)
foreign employer	section 721(1)
former approved superannuation fund (in c.7 of Pt 9)	section 594(1)
General Commissioners	section 2 of TMA 1970
general earnings	section 7(3)
House of Commons Members' Fund (in c.12 of Pt 9)	section 620
the included amount (in c.5 of Pt 5)	section 369(2)
income withdrawal (in c.8 of Pt 9)	section 604
initial extra accessory (in c.6 of Pt 3)	section 126(2)
the Inland Revenue	section 720(1)

interest	section 832(1) of ICTA
interest in shares (in c.8 of Pt 3)	section 197(1)
interest in shares (in c.9 of Pt 3)	section 200(1)
last day on which car available (in c.6 of Pt 3)	section 116(2)(b)
later accessory (in c.6 of Pt 3)	section 126(3)
list price (of a car) (in c.6 of Pt 3)	section 123(1)
list price (of accessories) (in c.6 of Pt 3)	section 127
loan (in c.7 of Pt 3)	section 173(2)(a)
local authority	section 842A of ICTA
lower-paid employment (in c.11 of Pt 3)	section 217
making a loan (in c.7 of Pt 3)	section 173(2)(b)
market value (in c.8 of Pt 3)	section 197(1)
market value (in c.9 of Pt 3)	section 200(1)
market value (of asset) (in c.10 of Pt 3)	section 208
material interest (in company) (in the benefits code)	section 68
members of a person's family	section 721(4)
member of a person's family or household	section 721(5)
mileage allowance payments (in c.2 of Pt 4)	section 229(2)
national insurance contributions (in c.8 of Pt 2)	section 61(1)
net taxable earnings (for the purposes of Pt 2)	section 11
net taxable specific income (for the purposes of Pt 2)	section 12
non-cash voucher	section 721(1)
non-standard accessory (in c.6 of Pt 3)	section 125(4)
the normal self-assessment filing date	section 721(1)
notice	section 832(1) of ICTA
notional price (of a car) (in c.6 of Pt 3)	section 124(1)
notional price (of accessories) (in c.6 of Pt 3)	section 130(1)
office (in the employment income Parts)	section 5(3)
official rate of interest (in c.7 of Pt 3)	section 181
ordinary commuting (in c.3 of Pt 4)	section 249
ordinary share capital	section 832(1) of ICTA
original pensioner (in c.14 of Pt 9)	section 630(1)
passenger payments (in c.2 of Pt 4)	section 233(3)
PAYE income	section 683
PAYE provisions (in c.8 of Pt 2)	section 61(1)
PAYE regulations	section 684(8)
payment for the employment-related shares (in c.8 of Pt 3)	section 7(3)
pension (in c.3 of Pt 9)	section 570
pension (in c.4 of Pt 9)	section 574
pension (in c.11 of Pt 9)	section 615(7)
pension (in c.18 of Pt 9)	section 647(4)
pension income	section 566(2)
permanent workplace (in Pt 5)	section 339(2)
person involved in providing the accommodation (in c.5 of Pt 3)	section 112
person paying an amount (in c.2 of Pt 5)	section 333(2)
personal pension arrangements (in c.8 of Pt 9)	section 604
personal pension scheme (in c.8 of Pt 9)	section 604
personal representatives	section 721(1)
persons providing a benefit (in c.10 of Pt 3)	section 209
post-employment earnings (in relation to former employee) (in Pt 8)	section 563
premium (in relation to qualifying insurance contract) (in c.2 of Pt 5)	section 346(3)(a)
pre-1973 pension (in c.14 of Pt 9)	section 630(2)
prescribed (in c.5 of Pt 11)	section 707
price of a car (in c.6 of Pt 3)	section 122

private use (in c.6 of Pt 3)	section 118(2)
the property, in relation to living accommodation (in c.5 of Pt 3)	section 113
provision of cash voucher for employee (in c.4 of Pt 3)	section 74
provision of credit-token for employee (in c.4 of Pt 3)	section 91(a)
provision of non-cash voucher for employee (in c.4 of Pt 3)	section 83
published price of the manufacturer, importer or distributor of the accessory (in c.6 of Pt 3)	section 129(1)
published price of the manufacturer, importer or distributor of the car (in relation to accessory) (in c.6 of Pt 3)	section 128(1)
qualifying accessory (in c.6 of Pt 3)	section 125(1)
readily convertible asset (in c.4 of Pt 11)	section 702
receipt of cash voucher by employee (in c.4 of Pt 3)	section 74
receipt of money earnings (in c.4 of Pt 2)	section 18
receipt of money earnings (in c.5 of Pt 2)	section 31
receipt of non-cash voucher by employee (in c.4 of Pt 3)	section 83
receipt of non-money earnings (in c.4 of Pt 2)	section 19
receipt of non-money earnings (in c.5 of Pt 2)	section 32
relevant engagements (in c.8 of Pt 2)	section 50(4)
relevant statutory scheme (in c.13 of Pt 9)	section 628(1)
relevant taxes (in c.6 of Pt 3)	section 171(1)
remittance of earnings (in c.5 of Pt 2)	section 33
remuneration (in c.7 of Pt 2)	section 47(3)
residence, former residence and new residence (in c.7 of Pt 4)	section 276(1), (2)
retirement annuity contract (in c.9 of Pt 9)	section 606
retirement benefits scheme (in c.1 of Pt 6)	section 387(1)
retirement benefits scheme (in c.6 of Pt 9)	section 586(1)
road fuel gas (in c.6 of Pt 3)	section 171(1)
Schedule A business	section 832(1) of ICTA
shares (in c.8 of Pt 3)	section 197(1)
shares (in c.9 of Pt 3)	section 200(1)
ship (in c.6 of Pt 5)	section 385
social security income	section 657(2)
Special Commissioners	section 4 of TMA 1970
specific employment income	section 7(4)
standard accessory (in c.6 of Pt 3) section 125(4)	
51% subsidiary	section 838(1) of ICTA
Table A (in Pt 10)	section 657(5)
Table B (in Pt 10)	section 657(6)
tax	section 832(3) of ICTA
tax credit	section 832(1) of ICTA
taxable benefit (in c.5 of Pt 11)	section 707
taxable benefits (in Pt 10)	section 657(3)
taxable cheap loan (in c.7 of Pt 3)	section 175(2)
taxable earnings (in the employment income Parts)	section 10(2)
taxable employment under Pt 2 (in the benefits code)	section 66(3)
taxable pension income (in Pt 9)	section 567(3), (4)
the taxable period (in c.5 of Pt 3)	section 102(2)
taxable person (in c.3 of Pt 6)	section 403(6)
taxable social security income (in Pt 10)	section 658(4)–(7)
taxable specific income (in the employment income Parts)	section 10(3)
tax year	section 721(1)
the tax year (in Pt 5)	section 327(2)(b)
the tax year 2003–04 etc.	section 721(1)

total income	section 835 of ICTA
trade	section 832(1) of ICTA
transport voucher (in c.4 of Pt 3)	section 84(3)
United Kingdom	section 830 of ICTA
UK approval certificate (in c.6 of Pt 3)	section 171(1)
use of credit-token by employee (in c.4 of Pt 3)	section 91(b)
van (in c.6 of Pt 3)	section 115(1)
van is available to an employee (in c.6 of Pt 3)	section 116(1)
van made available by reason of employment (in c.6 of Pt 3)	section 117
workplace (in Pt 5)	section 339(1)

GENERAL NOTE

The note at the head of this Schedule is in the Act. The list of definitions set out here is not the complete list in the Schedule, as definitions of relevance only to Parts of the Act not included in this selection have been excluded. **1.716**

PART II

TAX CREDITS

Tax Credits Act 2002 (Commencement No.1) Order 2002

(SI 2002 No. 1727 (c.52))

The Treasury, in exercise of the powers conferred upon them by sections 61 and 62(2) of the Tax Credits Act 2002 and after the signifying of Royal Assent to that Act, hereby make the following Order:

ARRANGEMENT OF ARTICLES

Citation and interpretation

1.—(1) This Order may be cited as the Tax Credits Act 2002 (Commencement No.1) Order 2002. 2.02

(2) In this Order—

"the Act" means the Tax Credits Act 2002;

"award" means an award of a tax credit for a period commencing on or after 6th April 2003.

Commencement of certain provisions of the Act

2. The following provisions of the Act come into force on the dates and for the purposes mentioned in relation to each provision: 2.03

Provision	*Date*	*Purposes*
Section 1(1) and (2) (introductory)	9th July 2002	All purposes of Part I of the Act and, as respects tax credits, Part III of the Act
Section 2 (functions of Board)	9th July 2002	All purposes of Part I of the Act and, as respects tax credits, Part III of the Act
Section 3(1) and (3) (claims)	9th July 2002	Making regulations about claims
Section 3(1) and (3)	1st August 2002	Making claims
Section 3(1) and (3)	1st January 2003	Making decisions on claims

Provision	*Date*	*Purposes*
Section 3(1) and (3)	6th April 2003	All other purposes of Part I of the Act and, as respects tax credits, Part III of the Act
Section 3(2)(a)	1st January 2003	All purposes of Part I of the Act and, as respects tax credits, Part III of the Act
Section 3(2)(b)	1st January 2003	All purposes of Part I of the Act and, as respects tax credits, Part III of the Act
Section 3(4)	1st August 2002	Entitlement to make a claim
Section 3(5) to (8)	9th July 2002	All purposes of Part I of the Act and, as respects tax credits, Part III of the Act
Section 4(1) (claims: supplementary)	9th July 2002	Making regulations
Section 4(2)	1st August 2002	All purposes mentioned in section 4(2) of the Act
Section 5(1) and (3) (period of awards)	1st January 2003	Making decisions on claims made before beginning of tax year
Section 5(2) and (3)	6th April 2003	Making decisions on other claims
Section 6 (notifications of changes of circumstances)	9th July 2002	Making regulations
Section 7(1) to (5) (income test)	9th July 2002	Making regulations
Section 7(1) to (5)	1st August 2002	Making claims
Section 7(1) to (5)	1st January 2003	Making decisions on claims
Section 7(1) to (5)	6th April 2003	Entitlement to payment of award
Section 7(6) to (9)	9th July 2002	Making regulations

Provision	*Date*	*Purposes*
Section 7(10)	1st August 2002	Estimating income for the purposes of making, amending or terminating awards
Section 8 (entitlement to child tax credit)	9th July 2002	Making regulations
Section 8	1st August 2002	Making claims
Section 8	1st January 2003	Making decisions on claims
Section 8	6th April 2003	Entitlement to payment of award
Section 9 (maximum-rate child tax credit)	9th July 2002	Making regulations
Section 9	1st August 2002	Making claims
Section 9	1st January 2003	Making decisions on claims
Section 9	6th April 2003	Entitlement to payment of award
Section 10 (entitlement to working tax credit)	9th July 2002	Making regulations
Section 10	1st August 2002	Making claims
Section 10	1st January 2003	Making decisions on claims
Section 10	6th April 2003	Entitlement to payment of award
Section 11 (maximum-rate working tax credit)	9th July 2002	Making regulations
Section 11	1st August 2002	Making claims
Section 11	1st January 2003	Making decisions on claims

Provision	*Date*	*Purposes*
Section 11	6th April 2003	Entitlement to payment of award
Section 12(1) to (5) (childcare element working tax credit)	9th July 2002	Making regulations
Section 12(1) to (5)	1st August 2002	Making claims
Section 12(1) to (5)	1st January 2003	Making decisions on claims
Section 12(1) to (5)	6th April 2003	Entitlement to payment of award
Section 12(5) to (8)	9th July 2002	Making schemes
Section 13 (rate of tax credit)	9th July 2002	Making regulations
Section 13	1st August 2002	Making claims
Section 13	1st January 2003	Making decisions on claims
Section 13	6th April 2003	Entitlement to payment of award
Section 14(1) and (3) (initial decisions on claims)	1st January 2003	Making decisions on claims
Section 14(2)	9th July 2002	Making regulations
Section 14(2)	1st August 2002	Dealing with claims
Section 15(1) (revised decisions after notifications)	1st January 2003	Making decisions on whether to amend awards
Section 15(2)	9th July 2002	Making regulations
Section 15(2)	1st August 2002	Dealing with notifications of change of circumstances

Provision	*Date*	*Purposes*
Section 16(1) (other revised decisions)	1st January 2003	Making decisions on whether to amend or terminate awards
Section 16(2) and (3)	1st January 2003	Giving of notice under section 16(2) and (3) of the Act
Section 16(3)	9th July 2002	Making regulations
Section 17(1) to (9) (final notice)	6th April 2003	Giving final notice on award
Section 17(10)	9th July 2002	Making regulations
Section 18 (decisions after final notice)	6th April 2003	Making decisions after final notice
Section 19 (power to enquire into awards)	6th April 2003	Enquiring into awards
Section 19(2)	9th July 2002	Making regulations
Section 20 (decisions on discovery)	6th April 2003	Making decisions under section 20(1) and (4) of the Act
Section 21 (decisions subject to official error)	9th July 2002	Making regulations for the purposes of revising decisions under sections 14(1), 15(1), 16(1), 18(1), (5), (6) and (9), 19(3) and 20(1) and (4) of the Act.
Section 22 (information, etc. requirements: supplementary)	9th July 2002	Making regulations
Section 23 (notice of decisions)	1st January 2003	Giving notices of decisions under sections 14(1), 15(1) and 16(1) of the Act, and of revised decisions under those sections by virtue of regulations under section 21 of the Act

Provision	*Date*	*Purposes*
Section 23	6th April 2003	Giving notices of decisions under sections 18(1), (5), (6) and (9), 19(3) and 20(1) and (4) of the Act, and of revised decisions under those sections by virtue of regulations under section 21 of the Act
Section 24 (payments of a tax credit)	9th July 2002	Making regulations
Section 24	1st August 2002	Making claims
Section 24	1st January 2003	Making decisions on claims
Section 24	6th April 2003	Entitlement to payment of award
Section 25(1), (2) and (5) to (7) (payments of working tax credit by employers)	9th July 2002	Making regulations
Section 25(3), (4) and (5)	6th April 2003	Power to call for documents etc. in relation to employer's compliance with regulations under section 25
Section 26 (liability of officers for sums paid to employers)	1st January 2003	Making regulations
Section 27 and Schedule 1 (rights of employees)	1st September 2002	Rights conferred on employees by virtue of regulations under section 25 of the Act
Sections 28 to 30 (overpayments, recovery of overpayments and underpayments of a tax credit)	6th April 2003	Liability to repay overpayments or to be paid full entitlement where underpayment
Section 30 (underpayments)	1st January 2003	Making regulations under section 30 of the Act
Section 31 (incorrect statements, etc.)	1st August 2002	Imposition of penalties for incorrect statement or

Provision	*Date*	*Purposes*
		declaration in or in connection with a claim for a tax credit or a notification given in accordance with regulations under s.6 of the Act, or for incorrect information or evidence in response to a requirement imposed by virtue of regulations under section 25 of the Act
Section 31	1st January 2003	Imposition of penalties for incorrect information or evidence in response to a requirement imposed by virtue of section 14(2), 15(2) or 16(3) of the Act
Section 31	6th April 2003	Imposition of penalties for incorrect information or evidence in response to a requirement imposed by virtue of section 18(10) or 19(2) of the Act, or for incorrect statement or declaration in response to a notice under section 17 of the Act
Section 32 (failure to comply with requirements)	1st August 2002	Imposition of penalty for failure to provide information or evidence required by regulations under section 25 of the Act, or for failure to give notification required by regulations under section 6(3) of the Act
Section 32	1st January 2003	Imposition of penalty for failure to provide information or evidence under section 14(2), 15(2) or 16(3) of the Act
Section 32	6th April 2003	Imposition of penalty for failure to provide information or evidence

Provision	*Date*	*Purposes*
		under section 18(10) or 19(2) of the Act, or to comply with requirement imposed by notice under section 17 of the Act by virtue of subsection (2)(a), (4)(a) or (6)(a) of that section
Section 33 (failure by employers to make correct payments)	6th April 2003	Imposition of penalty for failure by employer to make correct payment to employee
Section 34 and Schedule 2 (penalties: supplementary)	1st August 2002	Imposition of penalties under section 31 of the Act for incorrect statement or declaration in or in connection with a claim for a tax credit or a notification given in accordance with regulations under s.6 of the Act, or for incorrect information or evidence in response to a requirement imposed by regulations under section 25 of the Act; mitigation of such penalties, appeals against such penalties and recovery of such penalties
Section 34 and Schedule 2	1st January 2003	Imposition of penalties under section 31 of the Act for incorrect information or evidence in response to a requirement imposed by virtue of section 14(2), 15(2) or 16(3) of the Act; mitigation of such penalties, appeals against such penalties and recovery of such penalties
Section 34 and Schedule 2	6th April 2003	Imposition of penalties under section 31 of the Act for incorrect information or evidence in response to a requirement imposed by

Provision	Date	Purposes
		virtue of section 18(10) or 19(2) of the Act, or for incorrect statement or declaration in response to a notice under section 17 of the Act; mitigation of such penalties, appeals against such penalties and recovery of such penalties
Section 34 and Schedule 2	1st August 2002	Imposition of penalties under section 32(2)(b) or (3) of the Act for failure to provide information or evidence required by regulations under section 25 of the Act, or for failure to give notification required by regulations under section 6(3) of the Act; bringing of proceedings for penalties under section 32(2)(a) before Commissioners for failure to provide information or evidence required by regulations under section 25 of the Act; mitigation of such penalties, appeals against such penalties and recovery of such penalties
Section 34 and Schedule 2	1st January 2003	Imposition of penalties under section 32(2)(b) of the Act for failure to provide information or evidence under section 14(2), 15(2) or 16(3) of the Act; bringing of proceedings for such penalties under section 32(2)(a) before Commissioners; mitigation of such penalties, appeals against such penalties and recovery of such penalties
Section 34 and Schedule 2	6th April 2003	Imposition of penalties under section 32(2)(b) of the Act for failure to provide

Provision	*Date*	*Purposes*
		information or evidence under section 18(10) or 19(2) of the Act, or for failure to comply with requirement imposed by notice under section 17 of the Act by virtue of subsections (2)(a), (4)(a) or (6)(a) of that section; bringing of proceedings for such penalties under section 32(2)(a) before Commissioners; mitigation of such penalties, appeals against such penalties and recovery of such penalties
Section 34 and Schedule 2	6th April 2003	Imposition of penalties under section 33 of the Act for failure by employer to make correct payment to employee; mitigation of such penalties, appeals against such penalties and recovery of such penalties
Section 35 (offence of fraud)	1st August 2002	Instituting criminal proceedings for fraud in connection with obtaining payments of a tax credit
Section 36 (powers in relation to documents)	1st August 2002	Obtaining of documents in relation to offences involving fraud or serious fraud in connection with, or in relation to, tax credits
Section 37(1) to (4) and (6) (interest)	6th April 2003	Interest on overpayment of a tax credit
Section 37(2) and (5)	9th July 2002	Making regulations to prescribe rates of interest
Section 37(5) and (6)	1st August 2002	Interest on penalties under section 31 of the Act for incorrect statement or declaration in or in connection with a claim for a tax credit or a notification

Provision	*Date*	*Purposes*
		given in accordance with regulations under section 6 of the Act, or for incorrect information or evidence in response to a requirement imposed by virtue of regulations under section 25 of the Act
Section 37(5) and (6)	1st January 2003	Interest on penalties under section 31 of the Act for incorrect information or evidence in response to a requirement imposed by virtue of section 14(2), 15(2) or 16(3) of the Act
Section 37(5) and (6)	6th April 2003	Interest on penalties under section 31 of the Act for incorrect information or evidence in response to a requirement imposed by virtue of section 18(10) or 19(2) of the Act, or for incorrect statement or declaration in response to a notice under section 17 of the Act
Section 37(5) and (6)	1st August 2002	Interest on penalties under section 32 of the Act for failure to provide information or evidence required by regulations under section 25 of the Act, or for failure to give notification required by regulations under section 6(3) of the Act
Section 37(5) and (6)	1st January 2003	Interest on penalties under section 32 of the Act for failure to provide information or evidence under section 14(2), 15(2) or 16(3) of the Act
Section 37(5) and (6)	6th April 2003	Interest on penalties under section 32 of the Act for

Provision	*Date*	*Purposes*
		failure to provide information or evidence under section 18(10) or 19(2) of the Act, or to comply with requirement imposed by notice under section 17 of the Act by virtue of subsection (2)(a), (4)(a) or (6)(a) of that section
Section 37(5) and (6)	6th April 2003	Interest on penalties under section 33 of the Act for failure by employer to make correct payment to employee
Sections 38 and 39 (appeals and exercise of right of appeal)	1st September 2002	Appeal against determination of penalty under paragraph 1 of Schedule 2 to the Act where the penalty is imposed under section 31 of the Act for incorrect statement or declaration in or in connection with a claim for a tax credit or a notification given in accordance with regulations under section 6 of the Act, or for incorrect information or evidence in response to a requirement imposed by virtue of regulations under section 25 of the Act
Sections 38 and 39	1st January 2003	Appeal against determination of penalty under paragraph 1 of Schedule 2 to the Act where the penalty is imposed under section 31 of the Act for incorrect information or evidence in response to a requirement imposed by virtue of section 14(2), 15(2) or 16(3) of the Act

Provision	*Date*	*Purposes*
Sections 38 and 39	6th April 2003	Appeal against determination of penalty under paragraph 1 of Schedule 2 to the Act where the penalty is imposed under section 31 of the Act for incorrect information or evidence in response to a requirement imposed by virtue of section 18(10) or 19(2) of the Act, or for incorrect statement or declaration in response to a notice under section 17 of the Act
Sections 38 and 39	1st September 2002	Appeal against determination of penalty under paragraph 1 of Schedule 2 to the Act where the penalty is imposed under section 32(2)(b) or (3) of the Act for failure to provide information or evidence required by regulations under section 25 of the Act, or for failure to give notification required by regulations under section 6(3) of the Act
Sections 38 and 39	1st January 2003	Appeal against determination of penalty under paragraph 1 of Schedule 2 to the Act where the penalty is imposed under section 32(2)(b) of the Act for failure to provide information or evidence under section 14(2), 15(2) or 16(3) of the Act
Sections 38 and 39	6th April 2003	Appeal against determination of penalty under paragraph 1 of Schedule 2 to the Act where the penalty is imposed

Provision	*Date*	*Purposes*
		under section 32(2)(b) of the Act for failure to provide information or evidence under section 18(10) or 19(2) of the Act, or to comply with requirement imposed by notice under section 17 of the Act by virtue of subsections (2)(a), (4)(a) or (6)(a) of that section
Sections 38 and 39	6th April 2003	Appeal against a determination of a penalty under paragraph 1 of Schedule 2 to the Act where the penalty is imposed under section 33 of the Act for failure by employer to make correct payment to employee
Section 38 and 39	1st January 2003	Appeal against a decision under section 14(1), 15(1) or 16(1) of the Act, or under regulations under section 21 of the Act
Sections 38 and 39	6th April 2003	Appeal against a decision under section 18 (falling within section 38(1)(b)), 19(3), 20(1) to (4) or 37(1) of the Act
Section 40 (annual reports)	6th April 2004	Making of annual report by the Board to the Treasury
Section 41 (annual review)	6th April 2003	Review of prescribed monetary amounts
Sections 42 and 43 (persons subject to immigration control and polygamous marriages)	9th July 2002	Making regulations
Section 44 (Crown employment)	9th July 2002	Application of Part I of the Act to persons employed by or under the Crown

Provision	Date	Purposes
Section 45 (inalienability)	1st January 2003	All purposes of Part I of the Act and, as respects tax credits, Part III of the Act
Section 46 (giving of notices by Board)	August 1, 2002	All purposes of Part I of the Act and, as respects tax credits, Part III of the Act
Section 48 (interpretation)	9th July 2002	All purposes of Part I of the Act
Section 58 (administrative arrangements)	9th July 2002	For the purposes of making regulations in relation to tax credits only
Section 59 and Schedule 5 (use and disclosure of information)	1st August 2002	All purposes of Part I of the Act and, as respects tax credits, Part III of the Act
Section 60 and Schedule 6 (repeals) so far as concerns section 6 of the Tax Credits Act 1999 (c.10) (payment of tax credit by employers, etc.) and regulations made under that section	27th August 2002	For the purposes of awards of Working Families' Tax Credit and Disabled Person's Tax Credit commencing on or after 27th August 2002
Section 60 and Schedule 6 so far as concerns section 6 of the Tax Credits Act 1999 and regulations made under that section	The day immediately following the expiry of the period of 26 weeks from the date of commencement of the award	For the purposes of awards of Working Families' Tax Credit and Disabled Person's Tax Credit that commence on or after 4th June 2002 but before 27th August 2002 and are existing on August 27, 2002

[[1]Claims for a tax credit relating to the tax year 2003–04—transitional provision

3.—(1) For the purposes of the definition of "the previous year income" in section 7(5) of the Act— 2.04

(a) any claim under the Act for a tax credit relating to the tax year 2003–04 shall be treated as if it were a claim for the tax year 2002–03, and

(b) accordingly the previous year income in relation to such a claim shall be income for the tax year 2001–02.

(2) In paragraph (1)—

"the tax year 2001–02" means the tax year beginning on 6th April 2001 and ending on 5th April 2002,

"the tax year 2002–03" means the tax year beginning on 6th April 2002 and ending on 5th April 2003, and

"the tax year 2003–04" means the tax year beginning on 6th April 2003 and ending on 5th April 2004.]

AMENDMENT

1. Tax Credits (Claims) (Transitional Provision) (Amendment) Order 2002 (SI 2002/2158) (Order made August 20, 2002).

GENERAL NOTE

2.05 The normal rule for assessing entitlement to child tax credit and working tax credit is to have regard to the claimant's "relevant income" by reference to the previous tax year (TCA 2002, s.7). This transitional provision means that, for the purposes of claims relating to the tax year 2003–04 (*i.e.* the first year of the operation of the new scheme), the relevant previous year is 2001–02, and not 2003–03. The reason for this is that in the great majority of cases 2001–02 should be a "closed year" and thus provide a sound database for claims to the new tax credits.

Tax Credits Act 2002 (Commencement No.2) Order 2003

(SI 2003 No. 392 (c.25))

The Treasury, in exercise of the powers conferred upon them by sections 61 and 62(2) of the Tax Credits Act 2002, hereby make the following Order:

ARRANGEMENT OF ARTICLES

Citation and interpretation

2.07 **1.**—(1) This Order may be cited as the Tax Credits Act 2002 (Commencement No.2) Order 2003.

(2) In this Order, "the Act" means the Tax Credits Act 2002.

Commencement of certain provisions of the Act

2.08 **2.** Subject to article 3 (savings), the following provisions of the Act come into force on the dates and for the purposes mentioned in relation to each provision:

Provision	*Date*	*Purposes*
Part II of the Act (child benefit and guardian's allowance) including Schedule 4 but excluding sections 49, 50 and 54(1) and (2)	26th February 2003	Making subordinate legislation relating to child benefit and guardian's allowance
Part II of the Act including Schedule 4 but excluding section 54(1) and (2)	1st April 2003	Transfer of functions, etc. relating to child benefit and guardian's allowance, other than functions of making subordinate legislation, and minor amendments
Part II of the Act including Schedule 4 but excluding sections 54(1) and (2)	7th April 2003	Entitlement to payment of child benefit and guardian's allowance
Section 58 (administrative arrangements)	26th February 2003	Making subordinate legislation relating to child benefit and guardian's allowance
Section 59 and Schedule 5 (use and disclosure of information)	26th February 2003	Making subordinate legislation relating to the use and disclosure of information in connection with child benefit and guardian's allowance
Section 59 and Schedule 5	1st April 2003	Use and disclosure of information relating to child benefit and guardian's allowance
Section 60 and Schedule 6 so far as concerns section 145(5) of the Social Security Contributions and Benefits Act 1992 and section141(5) of the Social Security Contributions and Benefits (Northern Ireland) Act 1992 (rate of child benefit)	1st April 2003	Repeal of power of Secretary of State and Department for Social Development in Northern Ireland to make regulations prescribing rate of child benefit

Provision	*Date*	*Purposes*
Section 60 and Schedule 6 so far as concerns the words "of Part I or VI of this Act" in paragraph (a) of section 175(1A) of the Social Security Contributions and Benefits Act 1992 and paragraph (b) of section 175(1A) of that Act and the word "and" before it (regulations, orders and schemes) and, in section 172 of the Social Security Contributions and Benefits (Northern Ireland) Act 1992 (Assembly, etc. control of regulations and orders), the words "or 141" in subsection (2)(a) and the words "(other than section 141)" in subsection (3)(c)	1st April 2003	Repeals consequential on repeal of power of Secretary of State and Department for Social Development in Northern Ireland to make regulations prescribing the rate of child benefit
Section 60 and Schedule 6 so far as concerns paragraph 4 of Schedule 9 to the Social Security Contributions and Benefits Act 1992 and paragraph 4 of Schedule 9 to the Social Security Contributions and Benefits (Northern Ireland) Act 1992 (exclusions from entitlement to child benefit—persons exempt from tax)	7th April 2003	Repeal of exclusion from entitlement to child benefit by reason of exemption from tax
Section 60 and Schedule 6 so far as concerns section	1st April 2003	Repeal of regulatory power to reduce amount of guardian's allowance

Provision	*Date*	*Purposes*
154(2)(b) and (c) of the Social Security Administration Act 1992 (c.5) and section 134 (2)(b) and (c) of the Social Security Administration Northern Ireland) Act 1992 (c.8) (social security benefit in respect of children)		or increase for child dependants where there is an increase in the rate of child benefit
Section 60 and Schedule 6 so far as concerns the word "other" in section 189(1) of the Social Security Administration Act 1992	26th February 2003	Making subordinate legislation relating to child benefit and guardian's allowance

Savings

3.—(1) Notwithstanding the commencement of section 56 of the Act (presence in the United Kingdom) by virtue of article 2 on 26th February 2003 for the purposes of making subordinate legislation relating to child benefit, the Child Benefit (Residence and Persons Abroad) Regulations 1976 and the Child Benefit (Residence and Persons Abroad) Regulations (Northern Ireland) 1976 shall continue to have effect as follows. **2.09**

(2) Except as provided in paragraphs (3) and (4), both those Regulations shall continue to have effect up to and including 6th April 2003.

(3) Regulation 7 of both those Regulations shall continue to apply to persons referred to in sub-paragraph (c) of regulation (1) of both those Regulations and, to the extent applicable to that sub-paragraph, persons referred to in sub-paragraphs (d) and (e) of that regulation, whose absence begins before 7th April 2003 and continues on and after that date until—

(a) the absence ceases; or

(b) 2nd April 2006;

whichever first occurs.

(4) Regulation 9 of, and the Schedule to, both those Regulations (modification of the Child Benefit Act 1975 and the Child Benefit (Northern Ireland) Order 1975 to take account of reciprocal agreements relating to family allowances) shall continue to have effect indefinitely.

Tax Credits Act 2002 (Commencement No.3 and Transitional Provisions and Savings) Order 2003

(SI 2003 No. 938)

The Treasury, in relation to articles 1 and 2, in exercise of the powers conferred upon them by section 61 of the Tax Credits Act 2002 and the Secretary of State for Work and Pensions, in relation to articles 1 and 3 to 5 in exercise of the powers conferred on him by s.62(1) of that Act and of all other powers enabling each of them in that behalf, hereby make the following Order:

ARRANGEMENT OF ARTICLES

Citation and interpretation

2.11 **1.**—(1) This Order may be cited as the Tax Credits Act 2002 (Commencement No.3 and Transitional Provisions and Savings) Order 2003.

(2) In this Order—

"the 2002 Act" means the Tax Credits Act 2002; the Administration Act" means the Social Security Administration Act 1992;

"the Contributions and Benefits Act" means the Social Security Contributions and Benefits Act 1992.

Appointed day

2.12 **2.** The day appointed for the coming into force of—

(a) section 1(3)(e) of the 2002 Act (abolition of increases in benefits in respect of children under sections 80 and 90 of the Contributions and Benefits Act);

(b) section 60 of, and Schedule 6, to, the 2002 Act, in so far as they repeal the provisions specified in the Schedule to this Order, is 6th April 2003.

Saving provision

2.13 **3.**—(1) Notwithstanding the coming into force of the specified provisions, the Contributions and Benefits Act and the Administration Act shall, in cases to which paragraph (2) applies, subject to paragraph (3), continue to have effect from the commencement date as if those provisions had not come into force.

(2) This paragraph applies where a person—

(a) is entitled to a relevant increase on the day before the commencement date; or

(b) claims a relevant increase on or after the commencement date and it is subsequently determined that he is entitled to a relevant increase in respect of a period which includes the day before the commencement date.

(3) The provisions saved by paragraph (1) shall continue to have effect until—

(a) subject to sub-paragraph (c), where a relevant increase ceases to be payable to a person to whom paragraph (2) applies for a period greater than 58 days beginning with the day on which it was last payable, on the day 59 days after the day on which it was last payable; or

(b) in any other case, subject to sub-paragraph (c), on the date on which entitlement to a relevant increase ceases;

(c) where regulation 6(19) or (23) of the Social Security (Claims and Payments) Regulations 1987 applies to a further claim for a relevant increase, on the date on which entitlement to that relevant increase ceases.

(4) In this article—

"the commencement date" means 6th April 2003;

"a relevant increase" means an increase under section 80 or 90 of the Contributions and Benefits Act;

"the specified provisions" means the provisions of the 2002 Act which are brought into force by article 2.

Transitional application of sections 37 and 39A of the Contributions and Benefits Act

4. For the purposes of the continuing application of sections 37 (widowed mother's allowance) and 39A (widowed parent's allowance) of the Contributions and Benefits Act in cases to which article 3(2) applies, those sections shall apply as if the amendments specified in paragraphs 26 and 28 of Schedule 3 to the 2002 Act had not come into force. **2.14**

Transitional application of section 154 of the Administration Act

5. For the purposes of the continuing application of section 154(2)(c) of the Administration Act in cases to which article 3(2) applies, that section shall apply as if it had not been repealed in Schedule 6 to the 2002 Act and the reference to child benefit in that section shall be treated as including a reference to child tax credit under section 8 of the 2002 Act. **2.15**

Article 2 SCHEDULE

REPEALS SPECIFIED IN SCHEDULE 6 TO THE 2002 ACT WHICH ARE COMMENCED BY THIS ORDER

2.16

Act	*Provision*
Contributions and Benefits Act	In section 20(1), the words "(with increase for child dependants)" (in each place) and in paragraph (f)(i), the words "and child". In section 30B(3), the word "80,". In section 56(1), the words "(and in particular to those of section 81 below)". Section 60(6). In sections 61(1) and (2), the words "on account of a child or an adult". In section 63(c) and (f)(i), the words "and child". In section 77(1), the words following paragraph (b). In section 78(4)(d), the word "80". Sections 80 and 81. In section 89(1), the words "section 80 and" and in the heading the words "child or". In section 90, the words "child or". In section 91(1)(b), the words "for an adult dependant". In Schedule 4, in Part IV, in column (1), the entries relating to widowed mother's allowance, widowed parent's allowance and child's special allowance and col.(2). In Schedule 5, in paragraph 2(5)(b) the word "80".
Administration Act	In section 3(3), the words "(together with any increase under section 80(5) of the Contributions and Benefits Act)". Section 150(1)(f).

Tax Credits Act 2002 (Commencement No.4, Transitional Provisions and Savings) Order 2003

(SI 2003 No. 962 (c.51))

The Treasury, in exercise of the powers conferred upon them by sections 61 and 62(2) of the Tax Credits Act 2002, hereby make the following Order:

ARRANGEMENT OF ARTICLES

2.17

Citation and interpretation

1.—(1) This Order may be cited as the Tax Credits Act 2002 (Commencement No.4, Transitional Provisions and Savings) Order 2003. **2.18**

(2) In this Order—

"the Act" means the Tax Credits Act 2002;

"the 1999 Act" means the Tax Credits Act 1999; and

"the superseded tax credits" means working families' tax credit and disabled person's tax credit.

Commencement of provisions of the Act

2.—(1) Subject to the provisions of articles 3 and 4 (savings and transitional provisions), the provisions of the Act specified in this article shall come into force in accordance with the following paragraphs of this article. **2.19**

(2) Section 47 (consequential amendments), so far as it relates to paragraphs 4 to 7 of Schedule 3, shall come into force on 1st April 2003.

(3) The following provisions of the Act shall come into force on 6th April 2003—

(a) section 1(3)(a) and (f) (abolition of Children's Tax Credit under section 257AA of the Income and Corporation Taxes Act 1988 and employment credit);
(b) section 47, so far as it relates to the provisions of Schedule 3 specified in sub-paragraph (d);
(c) section 60 (repeals), so far as it relates to the provisions of Schedule 6 specified in sub-paragraph (e);
(d) in Schedule 3 (consequential amendments)—
  (i) paragraphs 1–3;
  (ii) para.8 and 9, and
  (iii) paragraphs 13–59, and
(e) in Schedule 6, the entries relating to the enactments specified in column 1 of Schedule 1 to this Order to the extent shown in column 2 of that Schedule.

(4) The following provisions of the Act shall come into force on 8th April 2003—

(a) section 1(3)(b) and (c) (abolition of working families' tax credit and disabled person's tax credit);
(b) section 47 so far as concerns the provisions of Schedule 3 mentioned in this paragraph;
(c) section 60 so far as concerns the entries in Schedule 6 referred to in sub-paragraph (e);

(d) paragraph 10 to 12 of Schedule 3 to the Act; and

(e) in Schedule 6 to the Act, the entries relating to the enactments specified in column 1 of Schedule .2 to this Order to the extent shown in column 2 of that Schedule.

(5) Section 1(3)(d) of the Act (child premia in respect of income support and income-based jobseeker's allowance) shall come into force on 6th April 2005.

Savings

2.20 **3.**—(1) This article applies to any claim for either of the superseded tax credits made—

(a) on or before 6th July, 2003; and

(b) in respect of a period ending on or before 8th April 2003.

Such a claim is referred to in the following provisions of this article as "a relevant claim".

(2) Notwithstanding the commencement of the repeals specified in paragraph (6)—

(a) a relevant claim may be made, inquired into by an officer of the Board, or decided by an officer of the Board; and

(b) a decision of an officer of the Board on a relevant claim may be—

(i) revised,

(ii) superseded, or

(iii) the subject of an appeal,

in accordance with the provisions specified in paragraph (3) as if the repeals specified in paragraph (6) had not taken place.

(3) The provisions specified are—

(a) Chapter 2 of Part I of the Social Security Act 1998;

(b) in Northern Ireland, ch.II of Part II of the Social Security (Northern Ireland) Order 1998; and

(c) regulations under the provisions mentioned in sub-paragraphs (a) and (b), as applied for the purposes of the superseded tax credits by section 21 or 23 of the 1999 Act (as the case may be).

(4) Notwithstanding the commencement of the repeals specified in paragraph (6), payment of a superseded tax credit may be made on or after 8th April 2003 in pursuance of a decision of an officer of the Board on a relevant claim (including such a decision as revised, superseded or varied on appeal).

(5) Notwithstanding the commencement of the repeals specified in paragraph (6)—

(a) an officer of the Board may make any decision in respect of an overpayment of a superseded tax credit, the recovery of such an overpayment, or the imposition of any penalty in respect of a superseded tax credit which he might have made but for the repeal in question, and

(b) the like consequences shall flow from the decision mentioned in sub-paragraph (a), including any right of appeal, as would have flowed but for the repeal in question.

(6) The repeals specified in this paragraph are those contained in Schedule 6 to the Act relating to—

(a) the 1999 Act, other than section 6;
(b) sections 122(1), 123(1), 128, 129 and 135(5) of the Social Security Contributions and Benefits Act 1992;
(c) sections 5(2), 11, 71(11), 121DA(1), 124(2), 154(2), 163(2), 179(5), and 191 of the Social Security Administration Act;
(d) sections 121(1), 122(1), 127, 128 and 131(5) of the Social Security Contributions and Benefits (Northern Ireland) Act 1992; and
(e) sections 5(2), 9, 69(11), 115CA(1), 134(2), 155(5) and 167(1) of the Social Security Administration (Northern Ireland) Act 1992.

Savings

4. Notwithstanding the repeal in Schedule 6 of words in section 84 of the Finance Act 2000, section 84 of that Act shall apply to a payment of an employment credit made on or after 6th April 2003 as if the repeal had not occurred. 2.21

Transitional provisions

5.—(1) If a claim has been made for a tax credit under the Act by two (or more) persons, at least one of whom was in receipt of either or both of the superseded tax credits immediately before the repeal of the 1999 Act, the Board may make any payment of a tax credit, due to them under the Act on or before 5th October 2003, to either or any of them, notwithstanding any provision of the Tax Credits (Payment by Employers) Regulations 2002 or the Working Tax Credit (Payment by the Board) Regulations 2002. 2.22

(2) In respect of a person who claims the higher rate of short-term incapacity benefit, or long-term incapacity benefit on or before 6th April 2005 section 30C of the Social Security Contributions and Benefits Act 1992 and section 30C of the Social Security Contributions and Benefits (Northern Ireland) Act 1992 shall have effect as if, after subsection (5A), there were inserted—

"(5B) A person also satisfies the relevant tax credit conditions on any day before 7th April 2003 if that day falls within a week for which he is entitled to a disabled person's tax credit."

(3) In respect of a person who claims incapacity benefit on or before 6th April 2005 under section 40 or 41 of either the Social Security Contributions and Benefits Act 1992 or the Social Security Contributions and Benefits (Northern Ireland) Act 1992, section 42 of the respective Act shall have effect as if, after subsection (1A), there were inserted—

"(1B) A person also satisfies the relevant tax credit conditions on any day before 7th April 2003 if that day falls within a week for which he is entitled to a disabled person's tax credit.".

(4) Notwithstanding regulation 7 of the Tax Credits (Claims and Notifications) Regulations 2002, a person shall not be entitled to a tax credit in respect of any day prior to the day on which he makes a claim for it ("the earlier day") if—

(a) the earlier day falls—

(i) before 23rd October 2003 in a case where the claimant, or in the case of a joint claim, either of the claimants is not less than 60, or

(ii) before 6th April 2004 in any other case; and

(b) on the earlier day the claimant is entitled, or in the case of a joint claim, either of the claimants is entitled, to an income-based job-seeker's allowance or income support other than by virtue of regulation 6(2) of the Income Support (General) Regulations 1987 or regulation 6(2) of the Income Support (General) Regulations (Northern Ireland) 1987.

Article 2(3)(e) SCHEDULE 1

PROVISIONS OF SCHEDULE 6 TO THE ACT COMING INTO FORCE ON 6TH APRIL 2003

2.23

Enactment	*Extent of repeal or revocation commenced*
Taxes Management Act 1970	The whole entry in Schedule 6
Income and Corporation Taxes Act 1988	The whole entry in Schedule 6
Children Act 1989	The whole entry in Schedule 6
Education Reform (Northern Ireland) Order 1989	The whole entry in Schedule 6
Disability Living Allowance and Disability Working Allowance Act 1991	The whole entry in Schedule 6
Child Support Act 1991	The whole entry in Schedule 6
Disability Living Allowance and Disability Working Allowance (Northern Ireland) Order 1991	The whole entry in Schedule 6
Child Support (Northern Ireland) Order 1991	The whole entry in Schedule 6
Social Security Contributions and Benefits Act 1992	So much of the entry in Schedule 6 as concerns sections 21(5A)(b) and 45A
Social Security Administration Act 1992	So much of the entry in Schedule 6 as concerns sections 3(3) and 189(1)
Social Security Contributions and Benefits (Northern Ireland) Act 1992	So much of the entry in Schedule 6 as concerns sections 20(1), 21(5A)(b), 30B(3), 45A, 56(1), 60(6), 61(1) and (2), 63(c) and (f)(i), 77(1), 78(4)(d), 80, 81, 89(1), 90, 91(1)(b) and Schedules 4 and 5
Social Security Administration (Northern Ireland) Act 1992	So much of the entry in Schedule 6 as concerns section 3(3)
Local Government Finance Act 1992	The whole entry in Schedule 6
Finance Act 1994	The whole entry in Schedule 6
Social Security (Incapacity for Work) Act 1994	The whole entry in Schedule 6
Social Security (Incapacity for Work) (Northern Ireland) Order 1994	The whole entry in Schedule 6

Enactment	*Extent of repeal or revocation commenced*
Pensions Act 1995	The whole entry in Schedule 6
Pensions (Northern Ireland) Order 1995	The whole entry in Schedule 6
Employment Tribunals Act 1996	The whole entry in Schedule 6
Employment Rights (Northern Ireland) Order 1996	The whole entry in Schedule 6
Finance Act 1999	The whole entry in Schedule 6
Access to Justice Act 1999	The whole entry in Schedule 6
Welfare Reform and Pensions Act 1999	The whole entry in Schedule 6
Welfare Reform and Pensions (Northern Ireland) Order 1999	The whole entry in Schedule 6
Finance Act 2000	The whole entry in Schedule 6
Finance Act 2001	The whole entry in Schedule 6.

Article 2(4)(e) SCHEDULE 2

PROVISIONS OF SCHEDULE 6 TO THE ACT COMING INTO FORCE ON 8TH APRIL 2003 **2.24**

Enactment	*Extent of repeal or revocation commenced*
Social Security Contributions and Benefits Act 1992	So much of the entry in Schedule 6 as relates to sections 122(1), 123(1), 128, 129 and 135(5)
Social Security Administration Act 1992	So much of the entry in Schedule 6 as relates to sections 5(2), 11, 71(11), 121DA(1), 124(2), 163(2), 179(5) and 191
Social Security Contributions and Benefits (Northern Ireland) Act 1992	So much of the entry in Schedule 6 as relates to sections 121(1), 122(1), 127, 128 and 131(5)
Social Security Administration (Northern Ireland) Act 1992	So much of the entry in Schedule 6 as relates to sections 5(2), 9, 69(11), 115CA(1), 134(2), 155(5) and 167(1)
Jobseekers Act 1995	The whole entry in Schedule 6
Jobseekers (Northern Ireland) Order 1995	The whole entry in Schedule 6
Finance Act 1997	The whole entry in Schedule 6
Social Security Act 1998	The whole entry in Schedule 6
Tax Credits (Initial Expenditure) Act 1998	The whole entry in Schedule 6
Social Security (Northern Ireland) Order 1998	The whole entry in Schedule 6
Tax Credits Act 1999	The whole entry in Schedule 6, in so far as it has not already been commenced
Employment Relations Act 1999	The whole entry in Schedule 6
Immigration and Asylum Act 1999	The whole entry in Schedule 6

Enactment	*Extent of repeal or revocation commenced*
Employment Relations (Northern Ireland) Order 1999	The whole entry in Schedule 6
Government Resources and Accounts Act 2000	The whole entry in Schedule 6
Social Security Fraud Act 2001	The whole entry in Schedule 6
Social Security Fraud Act (Northern Ireland) 200	The whole entry in Schedule 6
Employment Act 2002	The whole entry in Schedule 6
Criminal Injuries Compensation (Northern Ireland) Order 2002	The whole entry in Schedule 6.

Working Tax Credit (Entitlement and Maximum Rate) Regulations 2002

(SI 2002 No. 2005)

Whereas a draft of this instrument, which prescribes the amount in excess of which, by virtue of subsection (2) of section 12 of the Tax Credits Act 2002, charges are not to be taken into account for the purposes of that subsection, and which also contains the first regulations made under sections 11 and 12 of that Act, has been laid before, and approved by resolution of, each House of Parliament:

Now, therefore, the Treasury, in exercise of the powers conferred upon them by sections 10, 11, 12, 65(1) and (7) and 67 of the Tax Credits Act 2002, hereby make the following Regulations:

Regulations

Part 1

General

Part II

Conditions of Entitlement

Basic element

4. Entitlement to basic element of working tax credit: qualifying remunerative work. 2.26
5. Time off in connection with maternity, paternity and adoption.
5A. Time off in connection with childbirth and placement for adoption: further provisions.
6. Periods of illness or incapacity for work.
7. Term-time and other seasonal workers.
7A. Strike periods.
7B. Persons suspended from work.
7C. Pay in lieu of notice.
8. Gaps between jobs.

Disability element

9. Disability element and workers who are to be treated as at a disadvantage in getting a job. 2.27
9A. Initial claims.
9B. Training for work, etc.

30-hour element

10. 30-hour element. 2.28

Second-adult element

11. Second-adult element. 2.29

Lone-parent element

12. Lone-parent element. 2.30

Childcare element

Severe disability element

50 Plus element

Death of a child or qualifying young person for whom the claimant is responsible

PART III

MAXIMUM RATE

PART I

GENERAL

Citation, commencement and effect

2.36 **1.** These Regulations may be cited as the Working Tax Credit (Entitlement and Maximum Rate) Regulations 2002 and shall come into force—

(a) for the purpose of enabling claims to be made, on 1st August 2002;
(b) for the purpose of enabling decisions on claims to be made, on 1st January 2003; and
(c) for all other purposes, on April 6, 2003;

and shall have effect for the tax year beginning on 6th April 2003 and subsequent tax years.

DEFINITIONS

"claim"—see TCA 2002, s.3(8).
"tax year"—see TCA 2002, s.47.

GENERAL NOTE

These regulations give substance to ss.10 (entitlement) and 11 (maximum rate) of the TCA 2002. These are the only sections in the Act that apply specifically to the award and entitlement to working tax credit. Most of the provisions in those sections are enabling only. These are the regulations giving substance to working tax credit. **2.37**

Interpretation

2.—(1) In these Regulations, except where the context otherwise requires— **2.38**

"the Act" means the Tax Credits Act 2002, and a reference without more to a numbered section is a reference to the section of the Act bearing that number;

"the Board" means the Commissioners of Inland Revenue;

"the Contributions and Benefits Act" means the Social Security Contributions and Benefits Act 1992;

"child" has the same meaning as it has in the Child Tax Credit Regulations 2002;

"claim" means a claim for working tax credit and "joint claim" and "single claim" have the meanings respectively assigned in [[1]section 3(8)];

"claimant" means the person making a claim and, in the case of a joint claim, means either of the claimants;

"couple" means a married couple or an unmarried couple;

"the determination of the maximum rate" means the determination of the maximum rate of working tax credit;

[[1]"employed", except in the expression "self-employed" means employed under a contract of service or apprenticeship where the earnings under the contract are chargeable to income tax as employment income under Parts II–VII of the Income Tax (Earnings and Pensions) Act 2003 [[2] otherwise than by reason of Chapter 8 of Part 2 of that Act (deemed employment in respect of arrangements made by intermediaries)];]

"employment zone" means an area within Great Britain designated by the Employment Zones Regulations 2000 for the purposes of section 60 of the Welfare Reform and Pensions Act 1999;

"employment zone programme" means a programme which is—

(a) established for one or more employment zones; and

(b) designed to assist claimants for a jobseeker's allowance to obtain sustainable employment;

[1"initial claim" shall be construed in accordance with regulation 9A;]

"local authority" means—

(a) in relation to England, the council of a county or district, a metropolitan district, a London Borough, the Common Council of the City of London or the Council of the Isles of Scilly;

(b) in relation to Wales, the council of a county or county borough; or;

(c) in relation to Scotland, a council constituted under section 2 of the Local Government, etc. (Scotland) Act 1994;

[1"partner" means a member of a married or unmarried couple making a joint claim;]

"patient" means a person (other than a person who is serving a sentence, imposed by a court, in a prison or youth custody institution or, in Scotland, a young offenders' institution) who is regarded as receiving free in-patient treatment within the meaning of the Social Security (Hospital In-Patients) Regulations 1975;

"period of award" shall be construed in accordance with [1section 5];

"qualifying young person" means a person who satisfies regulation 5 of the Child Tax Credit Regulations 2002;

"relevant childcare charges" has the meaning given by regulation 14;

[1. . .]

"self-employed" means engaged in the carrying on of a trade profession or vocation;

"sports award" means an award made by one of the Sports Councils named in section 23(2) of the National Lottery etc. Act 1993 out of sums allocated to it for distribution under that section;

"surrogate child" means a child in respect of whom an order has been made under section 30 of the Human Fertilisation and Embryology Act 1990;

[1. . .]

"training allowance" means an allowance (whether by way of periodical grants or otherwise) payable—

(a) out of public funds by a Government department or by or on behalf of the Secretary of State, Scottish Enterprise or Highlands and Islands Enterprise or the Department for Employment and Learning ("the relevant paying authority");

(b) to a person in respect of his maintenance or in respect of a member of his family; and

(c) for the period, or part of the period, during which he is following a course of training or instruction—

(i) provided by, or in pursuance of arrangements made with, the relevant paying authority; or

(ii) approved by the relevant paying authority in relation to him, but does not include an allowance, paid by a Government department, Northern Ireland department or the Scottish Executive to or in respect of a person by reason of the fact that he is training as a teacher, or is following a course of full-time education, other than under arrangements made under section 2 of the Employment and Training Act 1973, section 2 or 3 of the Disabled Persons (Employment) Act (Northern Ireland) 1945, or section 1(1) of the Employment and Training Act (Northern Ireland) 1950;

[[1]"training for work" shall be construed in accordance with regulation 9B;]

"week" means a period of seven days beginning with midnight between Saturday and Sunday.

(2) For the purposes of these Regulations a person is responsible for a child or qualifying young person if he is treated as being responsible for that child or qualifying young person in accordance with the rules contained in regulation 3 of the Child Tax Credit Regulations 2002.

(3) A reference in these Regulations to an enactment applying to Great Britain but not to Northern Ireland shall, unless the context otherwise requires, include a reference to the corresponding enactment applying in Northern Ireland.

[[1](4) In these Regulations as they apply to an office a reference to being employed includes a reference to being the holder of an office.]

AMENDMENTS

1. Working Tax Credit (Entitlement and Maximum Rate) (Amendment) Regulations 2003 (SI 2003/701), reg.3 (April 6, 2003).

2. Tax Credits (Miscellaneous Amendments No.2) Regulations 2003 (SI 2003/2815), reg.13 (November 26, 2003).

DEFINITIONS

See also the definitions in TCA 2002, s.47 and, for the purposes of income tax, the full list of terms defined in both ICTA 1988 and ITEPA 2003 set out in Sch.1 to ITEPA 2003.

Other elements ofworking tax credit

3.—(1) For the purposes of determining the maximum rate of working tax credit, in addition to the basic element and the disability element, the following elements are prescribed— 2.39

(a) a 30 hour element;
(b) a second adult element;
(c) a lone parent element;
(d) a childcare element;
(e) a severe disability element; and
(f) a 50 Plus element.

(2) It is a condition of entitlement to the other elements of working tax credit that the person making the claim for working tax credit is entitled to the basic element.

(3) If the claim for working tax credit is a joint claim, and both members of the couple satisfy the conditions of entitlement for—

(a) the disability element;
(b) the severe disability element; or
(c) the 50 Plus element,

the award must include two such elements.

DEFINITIONS

"basic element"—see TCA 2002, s.11(4).
"claim"—see reg.2.
"joint claim"—see reg.2.

GENERAL NOTE

2.40 Section 11(2) of the TCA 2002 requires that all awards of working tax credit must contain a common element (known as the basic element—see s.11(4)). Section 11(3) requires that there be an element related to those with disabilities putting them at a disadvantage in getting a job. The list of other elements in s.11(6) is, however, permissive only. This regulation sets out the other elements to which claimants may for the time being be entitled as part of their working tax credit award, save one: the childcare element is not included because it is dealt with separately under s.12 of the TCA 2002.

The structure adopted is to require all claimants to show that they are entitled to the basic element in accordance with reg.4. Unless a claimant establishes that entitlement, he or she does not qualify for working tax credit at all. Once entitlement to the basic element is shown, a claimant may claim any or all of the other elements—subject, of course, to showing additional separate entitlement to each of them.

PART II

CONDITIONS OF ENTITLEMENT

Basic element

Entitlement to basic element of working tax credit: qualifying remunerative work

2.41 **4.**—(1) Subject to the qualification in paragraph (2), a person shall be treated as engaged in qualifying remunerative work if, and only if, he satisfies all of the following conditions.

First condition

2.42 The person—
- (a) is working at the date of the claim; or
- (b) has an offer of work which he has accepted at the date of the claim and the work is expected to commence within 7 days of the making of the claim.

In relation to a case falling within sub-paragraph (b) of this condition, references in the second third and fourth conditions below to work which the person undertakes are to be construed as references to the work which the person will undertake when it commences.

In such a case the person is only to be treated as being in qualifying remunerative work when he begins the work referred to in that subparagraph.

Second condition

The person— 2.43

[1(a) is aged at least 16 and—

(i) undertakes work for not less than 16 hours per week,

(ii) either he or his partner is responsible for a child or qualifying young person, or he has a physical or mental disability which puts him at a disadvantage in getting a job and satisfies regulation 9(1)(c),]

(b) satisfies the conditions in regulation 18, or

(c) is aged at least 25 and undertakes not less than 30 hours work per week in any other case.

Third condition

The work which the person undertakes is expected to continue for at least 4 weeks after the making of the claim or, in a case falling within sub-paragraph (b) of the first condition, after the work starts. 2.44

Fourth condition

The work is done for payment or in expectation of payment. Paragraphs (3) and (4) provide the method of determining the number of hours of qualifying remunerative work that a person undertakes. 2.45

Regulations 5 to 8 apply in relation to periods of absence from work connected with childbirth or adoption, sickness, seasonal absence from work in relation to which there is a recognised yearly cycle of employment and those who have a gap between periods of work.

Regulation 9 prescribes the conditions which must be satisfied by, or exist in relation to, a person so that he is to be treated as having a physical or mental disability which puts him at a disadvantage in getting a job.

(2) A person who would otherwise satisfy the conditions in paragraph (1) shall not be regarded as engaged in qualifying remunerative work to the extent that he is—

(a) engaged by a charitable or voluntary organisation, or is a volunteer, if the only payment received by him or due to be paid to him is a payment by way of expenses which falls to be disregarded under item 1 in Table 7 in regulation 19 of the Tax Credits (Definition and Calculation of Income) Regulations 2002;

(b) engaged in caring for a person who is not a member of his household but is temporarily residing with him if the only payment made to him for providing that care is disregarded income by virtue of item 3 or 4 in Table 8 in regulation 19 of the Tax Credits (Definition and Calculation of Income) Regulations 2002;

(c) engaged on a scheme for which a training allowance is being paid;

(d) participating in the Intensive Activity Period specified in regulation 75(1)(a)(iv) of the Jobseeker's Allowance Regulations 1996 or the Preparation for Employment Programme specified in regulation 75(1)(a)(v) of the Jobseeker's Allowance Regulations (Northern Ireland) 1996;

(e) engaged in an activity in respect of which—

(i) a sports award has been made, or is to be made, to him, and
(ii) no other payment is made, or is expected to be made, to him; or

(f) participating in an employment zone programme, that is to say a programme established for one or more areas designated pursuant to section 60 of the Welfare Reform and Pensions Act 1999, and subject to the Employment Zones Regulations 2000 if he receives no payments under that programme other than—
(i) discretionary payments disregarded in the calculation of a claimant's income under item 6(b) in [1 Table 6] in regulation 19 of the Tax Credits (Definition and Calculation of Income) Regulations 2002; or
(ii) training premiums.

[2 This is subject to the following qualification.

(2A) Neither sub-paragraph (c) nor sub-paragraph (d) of paragraph (2) applies if—

(a) in a case falling within sub-paragraph (c), the training allowance, or
(b) in a case falling within sub-paragraph (d), any payment made by the Secretary of State, or, in Northern Ireland, by the Department for Social Development, in connection with the Intensive Activity Period,

is chargeable to income tax as the profits of a trade, profession or vocation.]

(3) The number of hours for which a person undertakes qualifying remunerative work is—

(a) in the case of an apprentice, employee or officeholder, the number of hours of such work which he normally performs—
(i) under the contract of service or of apprenticeship under which he is employed, or
(ii) in the office in which he is employed;
(b) in the case of an agency worker, the number of hours in respect of which remuneration is normally paid to him by an employment agency with whom he has a contract of employment; or
(c) in the case of a person who is self-employed, the number of hours he normally performs for payment or in expectation of payment.

This is subject to the following qualification.

(4) In reckoning the number of hours of qualifying remunerative work which a person normally undertakes—

(a) any period of customary or paid holiday; and
(b) any time allowed for meals or refreshment, unless the person is, or expects to be paid earnings in respect of that time, shall be disregarded.

[1(5) In reckoning the number of hours of qualifying remunerative work which a person normally undertakes, any time allowed for visits to a hospital, clinic or other establishment for the purpose only of treating or monitoring the person's disability shall be included; but only if the person is, or expects to be, paid in respect of that time.]

AMENDMENTS

1. Working Tax Credit (Entitlement and Maximum Rate) (Amendment) Regulations 2003 (SI 2003/701), reg.4 (April 6, 2003).

2. Tax Credits (Miscellaneous Amendments) Regulations 2004 (SI 2004/762), reg.5 (April 6, 2004).

DEFINITIONS

"agency worker"—see ITEPA 2003, s.44.
"child"—see reg.2.
"claim"—see reg.2.
"employed"—see reg.2.
"Employment Zone programme"—see reg.2.
"office-holder"—see ITEPA 2003, s.5.
"partner"—see reg.2.
"qualifying young person"—see reg.2.
"responsible for a child"—see TCA 2002, s.48.
"self-employed"—see reg.2.
"sports award"—see reg.2.
"training allowance"—see reg.2.
"week"—see reg.2.

GENERAL NOTE

The structure of this key regulation is somewhat misleading. It suggests that there are four conditions for qualifying for entitlement to the basic element of working tax credit. This somewhat disguises the fact that there are four different and alternative bases for claiming working tax credit, all of which are wrapped up together in the "second condition", while the other three conditions are common to all groups of claimant. 2.46

First condition

Section 10(1) requires that all claimants for working tax credit must be in "qualifying remunerative work". This condition defines the scope of being "in" work. A claimant cannot receive working tax credit until he or she has started work (or, in the case of joint claimants or members of a polygamous unit, one of them has started work), or the work is to start within seven days. 2.47

Second condition

As noted above, this creates four alternative conditions, or routes to entitlement: 2.48

Route 1 is for a claimant working 16 or more hours a week and who, or whose partner, is responsible for a child or qualifying young person. This replaces the adult element of WFTC. The requirement of responsibility for a child or qualifying young person is the same test as for child tax credit purposes, and the regulations adopt the relevant definitions from the Child Tax Credit Regulations. In practical terms, they are the same tests as those for claiming child benefit for a child. The 16-hour test and the reference to remunerative work reflect the similar test in reg.5 of the Income Support (General) Regulations 1987 (SI 1987/1967).

Route 2 is for a disabled claimant suffering prejudice in the job market. It replaces the former disabled person's tax credit. Few qualified for that credit, and it is not likely to have a much wider practical scope under the new route. The full conditions for this route are in reg.9. It again uses the 16-hour test.

Route 3 is for those over 50 who would, before these tax credits were introduced, have been entitled to a grant from the "New Deal 50 Plus" scheme of the former Department for Education and Employment. The conditions are set out in reg.18.

Route 4 is the safety net basis of claim for anyone over 25 who is working full time (defined as 30 hours a week) but receiving only minimal earnings. The assumption behind working tax credit is that all employees are receiving the national minimum wage (and it is the task of the Inland Revenue to enforce the national minimum wage legislation). But this will not take a claimant who is working substantially less than the national maximum working week of 48 hours above the income threshold for working tax credit. And there will be many self-employed (for example, subsistence farmers) who will meet the 30-hour work test but also have an income below the working tax credit threshold. This route, like Route 3 to the working tax credit, is not a social security benefit of any kind. It is a subsidy to the low paid without reference to any social circumstances, and its effect is, as noted, to link with the national minimum wage to provide a national minimum take-home pay for all workers, whether employed or self-employed, over 25.

Third condition

2.49 This imposes a minimum level of continuity before working tax credit can be claimed. For WFTC the equivalent test was that the work was likely to continue for five weeks. It is separate from, but presumably to be read with, the 16 and 30-hour requirements of the second condition. In other words, it would seem that it has in cases of doubt to be shown that the work will be at a level of 16 or 30 hours a week for those four weeks. That will be a question of fact in all cases. The self-employed may have to show that they are, in that sense, "ordinarily self employed", which is the test for payment of Class 2 NI contributions. In the modern context of flexible employment and allegedly zero-hours contracts, close attention may have to be paid not only to the terms of agreement between the two parties to the work relationship but also to whether there is "an irreducible minimum of obligation on each side to create a contract of service": Stephenson L.J. in *Nethermere (St Neots) Ltd v Gardiner* [1984] I.C.R. 612, CA. If there is, the question is then whether on the facts it is shown that it will (or, at the end of the year, did) last for four weeks at the required level. But there is a possible practical problem of timing for a claimant in this sort of work because of the interaction of this requirement with the terms of the first condition—requiring that the work start within seven days of the offer of work— and the backdating rule that prevents a claim being made more than three months after entitlement starts.

Fourth condition

2.50 This echoes the well known test from the previous family credit reg.4 of the former Family Credit (General) Regulations 1987 (SI 1987/1973) and from income support (reg.5 of the Income Support (General) Regulations 1987 (SI 1987/1967)). The test is that the work is done either for payment or in the expectation of it. There is considerable case law from the Courts and Commissioners on whether work is, in this sense, remunerative. It is to be expected that the same test will apply to tax credits also. For the question whether work is remunerative, see in particular *R(IS) 22/95* and the decision of the Court of Appeal in *Chief Adjudication Officer v Ellis* (reported as the appendix to that decision). In *R(FIS) 1/86* it was established that the remuneration did not come from the work. That may cause other problems for tax credits, as it may not be clear whether money received in this way from work is "employment income". However, the courts have found, for example, that tips paid to a taxi driver are earnings from the driver's employment even though paid by third parties: see *Shilton v Wilmshurst* [1991] S.T.C. 88, HL. But, as with WFTC, the question whether the work is remunerative, and the question of the level of earnings from the work, are for separate determination.

Paragraph (2)

This paragraph lists six specific activities that are excepted from "work" for working tax credit purposes. It echoes the six exceptions from remunerative work for WFTC purposes listed in reg.4(3) of the former Family Credit (General) Regulations 1987 (SI 1987/1973), as amended. They are now redefined to fit them in with the income tax legislation. **2.51**

The number of hours worked

Paragraphs (3)–(5), together with regs 5–8, help define the number of hours worked by a claimant or partner. Subject to the specific provisions, it is essentially a question of fact to be determined over the claim period which will (unlike for the previous benefits replaced by working tax credit) normally be a full year. The practical approach of *R(FC) 1/92* was to look at the hours actually worked, rather than the contractual requirements. The wording of this form of the rule would suggest that this is the proper approach to be taken. **2.52**

Paragraph (3) provides the starting point for deciding the number of hours, but each category of work is tested against what is "normal". The main previous test was by reference to the hours worked in the week of claim, or either of the two previous weeks, or the following week, or the week next following any current holiday. Anyone meeting those tests was then assumed to be "normally" employed at the relevant level. This makes it clearer that the issue is one of fact, and is for most claimants a significant simplification of the rules. Paragraph (4) repeats the previous disregard of paid holidays and unpaid breaks, and para.(5) extends this to allow the inclusion of paid medical visits.

Regulation 4 of the Family Credit (General) Regulations 1987 (SI 1987/1973) contained a very dense set of rules within a single regulation all dealing with the question of hours worked or deemed to be worked. The new "decompressed" drafting that transfers part of those rules to regs 5–8 of these regulations is to be welcomed.

[1Time off in connection with [2childbirth] and adoption

5.—(1) This regulation applies for any period during which a person— **2.53**

(a) is paid maternity allowance,

(b) is paid statutory maternity pay,

(c) is absent from work during an ordinary maternity leave period under section 71 of the Employment Rights Act 1996 or Article 103 of the Employment Rights (Northern Ireland) Order 1996;

(d) is paid statutory paternity pay,

(e) is absent from work during a paternity leave period under s.80A of the Employment Rights Act 1996 or Article 112A of the Employment Rights (Northern Ireland) Order 1996,

(f) is paid statutory adoption pay, or

(g) is absent from work during an ordinary adoption leave period under section 75A of the Employment Rights Act 1996 or Article 107A of the Employment Rights (Northern Ireland) Order 1996.

(2) For the purposes of the conditions in regulation 4(1), the person is treated as being engaged in qualifying remunerative work during the period.

This is subject to paragraph (3).

(3) The person must have been engaged in qualifying remunerative work immediately before the beginning of the period.

(4) A person who is self-employed is treated as engaged in qualifying remunerative work for the requisite number of hours during any period for which paragraph (1) would have applied in his case but for the fact that the work he performed in the week immediately before the period began, although done for payment or in the expectation of payment, was not performed under a contract of service or apprenticeship.]

AMENDMENTS

1. Working Tax Credit (Entitlement and Maximum Rate) (Amendment) Regulations 2003 (SI 2003/701), reg.5 (April 6, 2003).
2. Tax Credits (Miscellaneous Amendments) Regulations 2004 (SI 2004/762), reg.6 (April 6, 2004).

DEFINITIIONS

"qualifying remunerative employment"—see reg.4.
"self-employed"—see reg.2.
"week"—see reg.2

GENERAL NOTE

2.54 This regulation was rewritten to take account of the extended rights of mothers and fathers, including adoptive parents, to parental leave as from 2003. It is designed to stop an award of working tax credit being terminated by such leave. See also reg.5A.

2.55 **[1 Time off in connection with childbirth and placement for adoption: further provisions**

5A.—(1) This regulation applies to a person for any period –
(a) which falls within a period to which regulation 5 applies; and
(b) which follows the birth or the placement for adoption of the child in connection with whose birth or placement entitlement to the allowance, pay or leave mentioned in regulation 5(1) arises.

(2) A person who was undertaking qualifying remunerative work for at least 16 hours per week, immediately before the beginning of a period to which regulation 5 applies, shall be treated as satisfying the requirements of regulation 4(1) during the period mentioned in paragraph (1) above.

(3) Paragraph (4) of regulation 5 applies for the purpose of this regulation as it applies for the purpose of that regulation.]

AMENDMENT

1. Tax Credits (Miscellaneous Amendments) Regulations 2004 (SI 2004/762), reg.7 (April 6, 2004).

GENERAL NOTE

2.56 This regulation reduces the number of hours, for which a person must have been engaged in qualifying remunerative work immediately before beginning a period of statutory leave in connection with the birth or placement for adoption of a child, in order to qualify for tax credit for so much of that period as follows the birth or placement for adoption of the relevant child.

[[1]Periods of illness or incapacity for work

6.—(1) This regulation applies for any period during which a person— 2.57

(a) is paid statutory sick pay;

(b) is paid short-term incapacity benefit at the lower rate under sections 30A–30E of the Contributions and Benefits Act;

(c) is paid income support on the grounds of incapacity for work under paragraphs 7 and 14 of Schedule 1B to the Income Support (General) Regulations 1987, or

(d) receives national insurance credits on the grounds of incapacity for work under reg.8B of the Social Security (Credits) Regulations 1975.

(2) For the purposes of the conditions in regulation 4(1), the person is treated as being engaged in qualifying remunerative work during the period.

This is subject to paragraphs (3) and (4).

(3) The person must have been engaged in qualifying remunerative work immediately before the beginning of the period.

(4) If the person is paid income support as specified in paragraph (1)(c) or receives national insurance credits as specified in paragraph (1)(d) he is treated as being engaged in qualifying remunerative work for a period of 28 weeks only, beginning with the day on which he is first paid income support or receives national insurance credits (as the case may be).

(5) A person who is self-employed is treated as engaged in qualifying remunerative work for the requisite number of hours during any period for which paragraph (1) would have applied in his case but for the fact that the work he performed in the week immediately before the period began, although done for payment or in the expectation of payment, was not performed under a contract of service or apprenticeship.]

AMENDMENT

1. Working Tax Credit (Entitlement and Maximum Rate) (Amendment) Regulations 2003 (SI 2003/701), reg.6 (April 6, 2003).

DEFINITIONS

"incapacity for work"—see Social Security Contributions and Benefits Act 1992, s.171A.

"qualifying remunerative employment"—see reg.4.

"self-employed"—see reg.2.

"week"—see reg.2.

GENERAL NOTE

2.58 This paragraph allows continuity of a claim for working tax credit into a period of sickness or disability, provided that one of the four alternative forms of benefit is received for the period. Paragraph 7 of Sch.1B to the Income Support (General) Regulations 1987 (SI 1987/1967) deal with those treated as incapable of work under the SSCBA 1992 and those entitled to statutory sick pay. Paragraph 14 deals with pregnant women who are incapable of work by reason of the pregnancy or are within 11 weeks before the expected date of confinement or seven weeks after the pregnancy ends. There is a 28-week limit on the overlap between working tax credit and either income support or contribution credits.

Term time and other seasonal workers

2.59 **7.**—(1) For the purposes of the conditions in regulation 4(1), paragraph (2) applies if a person—

(a) works at a school, other educational establishment or other place of employment;

(b) there is a recognisable cycle to his employment there; and

(c) the length of that recognisable cycle is one year and includes periods of school holidays or similar vacations during which he does not work.

(2) If this paragraph applies, the periods mentioned in paragraph (1)(c) are disregarded in determining whether the conditions in regulation 4(1) are satisfied.

GENERAL NOTE

2.60 This carries forward to working tax credit the provisions of reg.4(4) of the Family Credit (General) Regulations 1987 (SI 1997/1973) dealing with cyclical and "term-time only" employments. But it puts the effect of those employments on a claimant's entitlement in an entirely new context. This is because the question of hours worked and sums earned are now entirely divorced from each other. To claim working tax credit the claimant must establish normal work of 16 hours a week. But that no longer carries with it an assumption of normal earnings during that assumed work. The income test is by reference to actual earnings over the entire year. As a consequence, this rule will operate to the advantage of those such as supply teachers, school learning support assistants and seasonal staff. They will continue to get their working tax credit throughout the year if the conditions of this regulation are met, while their earnings will be established without reference to assumed earnings during assumed hours of work. For example, someone working 20 hours a week for 40 weeks a year at, say, £100 a week, will meet the hours test for every week of the year if the conditions of this regulation are met, but will earn from that source only £4,000 so will be below the minimum figure of earnings for claiming working tax credit in full. This means also a continuing entitlement to claim childcare charges when appropriate. In addition, because child tax credit is now separated from working tax credit and will be separated from all other benefits, there will be no adverse effect on any child tax credit entitlement from fluctuating work patterns.

[1Strike periods

2.61 **7A.**—(1) This regulation applies for any period during which a person is on strike.

(2) For the purposes of the conditions in regulation 4(1), the person is treated as being engaged in qualifying remunerative work during the period.

This is subject to paragraph (3).

(3) The person—

(a) must have been engaged in qualifying remunerative work immediately before the beginning of the period, and

(b) must not be on strike for longer than a period of 10 consecutive days on which he should have been working.]

AMENDMENT

1. Working Tax Credit (Entitlement and Maximum Rate) (Amendment) Regulations 2003 (SI 2003/701), reg.7 (April 6, 2003).

DEFINITION

"qualifying remunerative employment"—see reg.4.

GENERAL NOTE

This rule is a relaxation from the strict set of rules preventing workers benefiting during a strike. It reflects, perhaps, the provision under reg.6(11) of the Working Tax Credit (Payment by Employers) Regulations 2002 (SI 2002/2172) by which an employer is not required to make a payment of working tax credit if no payment of PAYE income is being made for a payment period, and an underlying doubt whether a claimant who is on strike is still qualified for tax credits. The effect of this regulation is to stop a break in entitlement occurring for a strike of 10 consecutive days or less. That being so, the entitlement for working tax credit will continue and the duty to pay will revive with the next payment of PAYE income. 2.62

[[1]Persons suspended from work

7B.—(1) This regulation applies for any period during which a person is suspended from work while complaints or allegations against him are investigated. 2.63

(2) For the purposes of the conditions in regulation 4(1), the person is treated as being engaged in qualifying remunerative work during the period.

This is subject to paragraph (3).

(3) The person must have been engaged in qualifying remunerative work immediately before the beginning of the period.]

AMENDMENT

1. Working Tax Credit (Entitlement and Maximum Rate) (Amendment) Regulations 2003 (SI 2003/701), reg.7 (April 6, 2003).

DEFINITIONS

"qualifying remunerative employment"—see reg.4.

GENERAL NOTE

This deals with a practical problem similar in part to that behind reg.7A. However, in the case of someone is suspended from work, for example while a complaint is investigated, the period of suspension will often not be known. The individual will still be "working" in the contractual sense of being obliged to remain with that employer, but in some cases the employer will be under no obligation to make a PAYE income payment. That being so, the duty of the employer to pay tax credits under the Working Tax Credit (Payment by Employers) Regulations 2002 (SI 2002/2172) lapses. It is not clear if the duty of the Inland 2.64

Revenue to pay under reg.6(14) of those Regulations comes into effect in such cases or, if it does, when. See the note to reg.6 of those Regulations.

[1Pay in lieu of notice

2.65 **7C.**—(1) This regulation applies if a person stops work and receives pay in lieu of notice.

(2) For the purposes of the conditions in regulation 4(1), the person shall not be treated as being engaged in qualifying remunerative work during the period for which he receives the pay.]

AMENDMENT

1. Working Tax Credit (Entitlement and Maximum Rate) (Amendment) Regulations 2003 (SI 2003/701), reg.7 (April 6, 2003).

DEFINITION

"qualifying remunerative employment"—see reg.4.

GENERAL NOTE

2.66 This deals in a pragmatic way with the problem caused when someone stops work before a period of notice has ended, but who receives pay in lieu of notice (often abbreviated to PILON). As the employer will not be making any further payments of earnings to the employee, there will be no PAYE income with which to pay any working tax credit entitlement (see Working Tax Credit (Payment by Employers) Regulations 2002 (SI 2002/2172)). This regulation resolves any potential obligation on the employer by excluding the claimant from entitlement to working tax credit. But a problem may arise if the employee does not find other work during that period (and he or she may be prevented from doing so). The provisions about calculating earnings from employment for jobseeker's allowance purposes allow sums to be spread over the period for which they are paid, unless they are excluded from earnings for that purpose, and so may exclude entitlement to JSA. See regs 94 and 98 of the Jobseeker's Allowance Regulations 1996 (SI 1996/207) and the notes to them in Vol.II of this work. So the individual may be excluded from both working tax credit and jobseeker's allowance.

Gaps between jobs

2.67 **8.** For the purposes of the conditions in regulation 4(1), a person shall be treated as being engaged in qualifying remunerative work for the requisite number of hours if he has been so engaged within the past seven days.

DEFINITION

"qualifying remunerative employment"—see reg.4.

GENERAL NOTE

2.68 Regulation 4 allows someone to make a claim for working tax credit if he or she has an offer of a job starting within seven days of the claim (see the first condition in reg.4). However, if there is a gap of not more than that period between jobs, this regulation allows the gap to be bridged so as to avoid the need to make a new claim. This is also consistent with the provisions of the Tax Credits (Claims and Notifications) Regulations 2002 (SI 2002/2014), reg.10, allowing claims for working tax credit seven days in advance.

Disability element

[1Disability element and workers who are to be treated as at a disadvantage in getting a job

9.—(1) The determination of the maximum rate must include the disability element if the claimant, or, in the case of a joint claim, one of the claimants— 2.69

(a) undertakes qualifying remunerative work for at least 16 hours per week;

(b) has any of the disabilities listed in Part I of Schedule 1, or in the case of an initial claim, satisfies the conditions in Part II of Schedule 1; and

(c) is a person who satisfies any of Cases A to G on a day for which the maximum rate is determined in accordance with these Regulations.

(2) Case A is where the person has been in receipt of the higher rate of short-term incapacity benefit, long-term incapacity benefit or severe disablement allowance for at least one day in the preceding 182 days.

(3) Case B is where, for at least one day in the preceding 182 days, the person has been a person [2 for whom at least one of the following benefits has been payable and for whom the applicable amount] included a higher pensioner or disability premium [2in respect of him] determined—

(a) in the case of income support, in accordance with [2 paragraphs 10(1)(b) or (2)(b) or 11, and where applicable 12,] of Part III of Schedule 2 to the Income Support (General) Regulations 1987;

(b) in the case of income-based jobseeker's allowance, in accordance with [2 paragraphs 12(1)(a), or (b)(ii), or (c), or 13, and where applicable 14 of Part 3 of] Schedule 1 to the Jobseeker's Allowance Regulations 1996;

(c) in the case of housing benefit, in accordance with [2 paragraphs 10(1)(b) or (2)(b) or 11, and where applicable, 12], of Part III of Schedule 2 to the Housing Benefit (General) Regulations 1987;

(d) in the case of Council Tax Benefit, in accordance with [2 paragraphs 11(1)(b) or (2)(b) or 12, and where applicable, 13] of Part III of Schedule 1 to the Council Tax Benefit (General) Regulations 1992.

For the purposes of this Case "the applicable amount" has the meaning given by section 135 of the Contributions and Benefits Act.

(4) Case C is where the person is a person to whom at least one of the following is payable—

(a) a disability living allowance;

(b) an attendance allowance;

(c) a mobility supplement or a constant attendance allowance which is paid, in either case, in conjunction with a war pension or industrial injuries disablement benefit.

(5) Case D is where the person has an invalid carriage or other vehicle provided under—

(a) section 5(2)(a) of, and Schedule 2 to, the National Health Service Act 1977,

(b) section 46 of the National Health Service (Scotland) Act 1978; or

(c) Article 30(1) of the Health and Personal Social Services (Northern Ireland) Order 1972.

(6) Case E is where the person—

(a) has received, on account of his incapacity for work, statutory sick pay, occupational sick pay, short-term incapacity benefit payable at the lower rate or income support, for a period of 140 qualifying days, or has been credited with Class 1 or Class 2 contributions under the Contributions and Benefits Act for a period of 20 weeks on account of incapacity for work, and where the last of those days or weeks (as the case may be) fell within the preceding 56 days;

(b) has a disability which is likely to last for at least six months, or for the rest of his life if his death is expected within that time; and

(c) has gross earnings which are less than they were before the disability began by at least the greater of 20 per cent and £15 per week.

For the purpose of this Case "qualifying days" are days which form part of a single period of incapacity for work within the meaning of Part XI of the Contributions and Benefits Act.

(7) Case F is where the person—

(a) has undertaken training for work for at least one day in the preceding 56 days; and

(b) has received the higher rate of short-term incapacity benefit, long-term incapacity benefit or severe disablement allowance within 56 days before the first day of that period of training for work.

Regulation 9B explains the meaning of "training for work" and of a period of training for work.

(8) Case G is where the person was entitled, [2 for at least one day in the preceding 56 days], to the disability element of working tax credit or to disabled person's tax credit by virtue of his having satisfied the requirements of Case A, B, E or F at some earlier time.

For the purposes of this Case a person is treated as having an entitlement to the disability element of working tax credit if that element is taken into account in determining the rate at which the person is entitled to a tax credit.

(9) For the purposes of the Act, a person who satisfies paragraph (1)(b) is to be treated as having a physical or mental disability which puts him at a disadvantage in getting a job.]

AMENDMENTS

1. Working Tax Credit (Entitlement and Maximum Rate) (Amendment) Regulations 2003 (SI 2003/701), reg.8 (April 6, 2003).

2. Tax Credits (Miscellaneous Amendments No.2) Regulations 2003 (SI 2003/2815), reg.14 (November 26, 2003).

DEFINITIONS

"claim"—see reg.2.
"initial claim"—see reg.9A.
"joint claim"—see reg.2.
"qualifying remunerative employment"—see reg.4.
"training for work"—see reg.9B.
"week"—see reg.2.

GENERAL NOTE

This complex regulation in effect replaces the whole of the Disability Work Allowance (General) Regulations 1991 (SI 1991/2887), so its complexity has to be viewed as a considerable simplification! It provides the conditions for a claim to working tax credit by Route 2, and replaces DPTC. It imposes three separate sets of conditions, all of which must be met to meet the second condition in reg.4 of these Regulations. The first of the three conditions is the requirement that the claimant work 16 or more hours a week in qualifying remunerative work. This restates one of the requirements of the second condition, but with the specific addition of the reference to "qualifying remunerative" work. The other two conditions may be termed the "disability conditions". 2.70

First disability condition

To come within this condition, the claimant must have one or more of the disabilities listed in Pt 1 of Sch.1 to these Regulations (see below). These have been brought forward from the conditions of entitlement to DPTC and disability working allowance. Paragraph (5) emphasises that a person meeting this condition is to be treated as being put at a disadvantage by reason of the disability. 2.71

Second disability condition

To come within this condition, the claimant must meet the conditions of one or more of seven separate "cases" labelled Case A to Case G. Briefly these link with other benefits or activities as follows: 2.72

Case A: entitlement to long-term incapacity benefit or the higher rate of short-term incapacity benefit, or severe disablement allowance;

Case B: entitlement to a higher pensioner or disability premium of income support, income-based jobseeker's allowance, housing benefit and/or council tax benefit;

Case C: entitlement to disability living allowance, attendance allowance, mobility supplement or constant attendance allowance;

Case D: membership of the Motability scheme;

Case E: entitlement to occupational or statutory sick pay, short-term incapacity benefit, income support or "disability credits"; a continuing disability; and earnings that have reduced since the disability started by 20 per cent or £15 a week;

Case F: training for work linked with payment of the benefits in Case A;

Case G: immediate previous entitlement to the disability element of WTC or DPTC under Cases A, B, E or F.

There are special rules that apply to initial claims, noted under reg.9A below.

[1Initial claims

2.73 **9A.**—(1) In regulation 9(1)(b) an "initial claim" means a claim which—

(a) is made for the disability element of working tax credit, and

(b) relates to a person who has not had an entitlement to that element or to disabled person's tax credit during the two years immediately preceding the making of the claim.

(2) In paragraph (1) any reference to the making of a claim includes the giving of notification, in accordance with regulation 20 of the Tax Credits (Claims and Notifications) Regulations 2002, of a change of circumstances falling within that regulation.

(3) For the purposes of paragraph (1)(b), a person is treated as having an entitlement to the disability element of working tax credit if, by virtue of the person being a person who satisfies regulation 9, that element is taken into account in determining the rate at which the person is entitled to a tax credit.]

AMENDMENT

1. Working Tax Credit (Entitlement and Maximum Rate) (Amendment) Regulations 2003 (SI 2003/701), reg.8 (April 6, 2003).

DEFINITIONS

"claim"—see reg.2.
"claimant"—see reg.2.
"disability element"—see reg.9.

GENERAL NOTE

2.74 This regulation makes clear that an "initial claim" for the purposes of regulation 9 is a first claim involving disability, or a notification that may involve the addition of a disability element to an award already made on other grounds. This clarifies the scope of reg.9(1), which extends the test of disability under the second disability condition for a first claim. An initial claim will have an extended relevance for working tax credit as compared with its predecessors as the claim will, in normal course of events, last for the balance of the tax year from the effective date of claim.

[1Training for work, etc.

2.75 **9B.**—(1) In [2regulation 9], "training for work" means training for work received—

(a) in pursuance of arrangements made under—

(i) section 2(1) of the Employment and Training Act 1973,

(ii) section 2(3) of the Enterprise and New Towns (Scotland) Act 1990, or

(iii) section 1(1) of the Employment and Training Act 1950, or

(b) on a course whose primary purpose is the teaching of occupational or vocational skills, and which the person attends for 16 hours or more a week.

(2) For the purposes of regulation 9(7), a period of training for work means a series of consecutive days of training for work, there being disregarded any day specified in paragraph (3).

(3) Those days are any day on which the claimant was—

(a) on holiday;

(b) attending court as a justice of the peace, a party to any proceedings, a witness or a juror;

(c) suffering from some disease or bodily or mental disablement as a result of which he was unable to attend training for work, or his attendance would have put at risk the health of other persons;

(d) unable to participate in training for work because—

(i) he was looking after a child because the person who usually looked after that child was unable to do so;

(ii) he was looking after a member of his family who was ill;

(iii) he was required to deal with some domestic emergency; or

(iv) he was arranging or attending the funeral of his partner or a relative; or

(e) authorised by the training provider to be absent from training for work.

(4) For the purposes of paragraph (3)(d)(iv) "relative" means close relative, grandparent, grandchild, uncle, aunt, nephew or niece; and in this paragraph "close relative" means parent, parent-in-law, son, son-in-law, daughter, daughter-in-law, step-parent, step-son, step-daughter, brother, sister, or the spouse of any of the preceding persons or, if that person is one of an unmarried couple, the other member of that couple.]

AMENDMENTS

1. Working Tax Credit (Entitlement and Maximum Rate) (Amendment) Regulations 2003 (SI 2003/701), reg.8 (April 6, 2003).

2. Tax Credits (Miscellaneous Amendments) Regulations 2004 (SI 2004/762), reg.8 (April 6, 2004).

DEFINITIONS

"claim"—see reg.2.
"claimant"—see reg.2.
"week"—see reg.2.

GENERAL NOTE

This definition is necessary to clarify the scope of Case F in reg.9(7). 2.76

30 hour element

30 hour element

10.—(1) The determination of the maximum rate must include a 30 hour element if the claimant, or in the case of a joint claim, at least one of the claimants, is engaged in qualifying remunerative work for at least 30 hours per week. 2.77

(2) The determination of the maximum rate must also include the 30-hour element if—

(a) the claim is a joint claim,

(b) at least one of the claimants is responsible for one or more children or qualifying young people,

(c) the aggregate number of hours for which the couple engage in qualifying remunerative work is at least 30 hours per week, and

(d) at least one member of the couple engages in qualifying remunerative work for at least 16 hours per week.

[[1](3) For the purposes of determining whether the condition in paragraph (2)(c) is met, the words "for not less than 16 hours per week" in paragraph (a) of the second condition in regulation 4(1) are omitted.]

AMENDMENT

1. Working Tax Credit (Entitlement and Maximum Rate) (Amendment) Regulations 2003 (SI 2003/701), reg.9 (April 6, 2003).

DEFINITION

"child"—see reg.2.
"claim"—see reg.2.
"claimant"—see reg.2.
"couple"—see reg.2.
"joint claim"—see TCA 2002, s.3.
"qualifying remunerative work"—see reg.4.
"qualifying young person"—see reg.2.
"responsible"—see TCA 2002, s.48.
"week"—see reg.2.

GENERAL NOTE

2.78 An additional element of £640 a year is payable if the claimant or couple work 30 hours a week. Paragraphs (1) and (2) together ensure that the total of 30 hours can be worked by either of the couple or by both together if one or both of them are responsible for a child or qualifying young person. Paragraph (3) deals with a drafting problem in applying the second condition in reg.4 for establishing that a claimant is engaged in qualifying remunerative work to both members of a couple jointly working 30 hours a week but where only one is working over 16 hours.

Second adult element

[[1]Second adult element

2.79 **11.**—(1) The determination of the maximum rate must include the second adult element if the claim is a joint claim.

This is subject to the following provisions of this regulation.

(2) The determination of the maximum rate shall not include the second adult element if—

(a) one of the claimants is aged 50 or over;

(b) the 50 plus element is payable, and

(c) neither of the claimants is engaged in qualifying remunerative work for at least 30 hours per week.

(3) But subsection (2) does not apply if at least one of the claimants—
(a) is responsible for a child or a qualifying young person, or
(b) satisfies regulation 9(1).

(4) The determination of the maximum rate shall also not include the second adult element if—
(a) neither claimant has responsibility for a child or qualifying young person; and
(b) one claimant is serving a custodial sentence of more than twelve months.]

AMENDMENT

1. Working Tax Credit (Entitlement and Maximum Rate) (Amendment) Regulations 2003 (SI 2003/701), reg.10 (April 6, 2003).

DEFINITIONS

"50 Plus element"—see reg.18.
"child"—see reg.2.
"claimant"—see reg.2.
"joint claim"—see reg.2.
"qualifying remunerative work"—see reg.4.
"qualifying young person"—see reg.2.
"responsible"—see TCA 2002, s.48.
"week"—see reg.2.

GENERAL NOTE

The value of the second adult element is a little less than the basic element (£1,545 as against £1,570 in 2004–05). The effect of para.2 is therefore to limit entitlement of claimants fall within it, as the 50 plus element is £1,075 for those working under 30 hours a week. The rule appears to be that if the claimant is over 50 and working over 30 hours and there is a second adult, then both this element and the increased 30-hour element (£1,610) can be claimed. The phraseology avoids calling the second adult an "adult dependant". The assumption is that neither member of a couple is to be regarded as dependent on the other. **2.80**

Lone parent element

Lone parent element

12. The determination of the maximum rate must include the lone parent element if— **2.81**
(a) the claim is a single claim; and
(b) the claimant is responsible for [[1]a child or qualifying young person].

AMENDMENT

1. Working Tax Credit (Entitlement and Maximum Rate) (Amendment) Regulations 2003 (SI 2003/701), reg.11 (April 6, 2003).

DEFINITION

"child"—see reg.2.
"claim"—see reg.2.

"qualifying young person"—see reg.2.
"responsible"—see TCA 2002, s.48.

General Note

2.82 The value of the lone parent element is the same as that of the second adult element.

Childcare element

Entitlement to childcare element of working tax credit

2.83 **13.**—(1) The determination of the maximum rate must include a childcare element where that person, or in the case of a joint claim at least one of those persons, is incurring relevant childcare charges and—

(a) is a person, not being a member of a married or unmarried couple, engaged in [1qualifying remunerative work];

[1(b) is a member or are members of a married or unmarried couple where both are engaged in qualifying remunerative work; or

(c) is a member or are members of a married or unmarried couple where one is engaged in qualifying remunerative work and the other—

(i) is incapacitated;

(ii) is an in-patient in hospital; or

(iii) is in prison (whether serving a custodial sentence or remanded in custody awaiting trial or sentence).]

(2) For the purposes of paragraph (1), a person is not treated as incurring relevant childcare charges where the average weekly charge calculated in accordance with regulation 15 is nil or where an agreement within regulation 15(4) has not yet commenced.

[1(3) [2. . .]

(4) For the purposes of para.(1)(c)(i), the other member of a couple is incapacitated in any of the circumstances specified in paragraphs (5) to (8).]

(5) The circumstances specified in this paragraph are where either council tax benefit or housing benefit is payable under Part VII of the Contributions and Benefits Act to the other member or his partner and the applicable amount of the person entitled to the benefit includes—

(a) a disability premium; or

(b) a higher pensioner premium by virtue of the satisfaction of—

(i) in the case of council tax benefit, paragraph 11(2)(b) of Schedule 1 to the Council Tax Benefit (General) Regulations 1992;

(ii) in the case of housing benefit, paragraph 10(2)(b) of Schedule 2 to the Housing Benefit (General) Regulations 1987,

on account of the other member's incapacity or either regulation 13A(1)(c) of Council Tax Benefit (General) Regulations 1992 (treatment of childcare charges) or, as the case may be, regulation 21A(1)(c) of the Housing Benefit (General) Regulations 1987 (treatment of childcare charges) applies in that person's case;

(6) The circumstances specified in this paragraph are where there is payable in respect of him one or more of the following pensions or allowances—

(a) short-term incapacity benefit [1payable at the higher rate] under section 30A of the Contributions and Benefits Act;
(b) long-term incapacity benefit under section 40 or 41 of the Contributions and Benefits Act;
(c) attendance allowance under section 64 of that Act;
(d) severe disablement allowance under section 68 of that Act;
(e) disability living allowance under section 71 of that Act;
(f) increase of disablement pension under section 104 of that Act;
(g) a pension increase under a war pension scheme or an industrial injuries scheme which is analogous to an allowance or increase of disablement pension under sub-paragraph (b), (d) or (e) above.

(7) The circumstances specified in this paragraph are where a pension or allowance to which sub-paragraph [1(c)], (d), (e) or (f) of paragraph (6) refers, was payable on account of his incapacity but has ceased to be payable only in consequence of his becoming a patient.

(8) The circumstances specified in this paragraph are where he has an invalid carriage or other vehicle provided to him under section 5(2)(a) of and Schedule 2 to the National Health Service Act 1977, section 46 of the National Health Service (Scotland) Act 1978; or Article 30(1) of the Health and Personal Social Services (Northern Ireland) Order 1972.

AMENDMENTS

1. Working Tax Credit (Entitlement and Maximum Rate) (Amendment) Regulations 2003 (SI 2003/701), reg.12 (April 6, 2003).

2. Tax Credits (Miscellaneous Amendments) Regulations 2004 (SI 2004/762), reg.9 (April 6, 2004).

DEFINITIONS

"child"—see reg.2.
"childcare"—see reg.14.
"claimant"—see reg.2.
"joint claim"—see reg.2.
"married or unmarried couple"—see TCA 2002, s.3.
"partner"—see reg.2.
"patient"—see reg.2.
"qualifying remunerative work"—see reg.4.
"relevant childcare charges"—see reg.14.

GENERAL NOTE

Specific provision is made for the childcare element in TCA 2002, s.12. The element may be claimed by those entitled to working tax credit and incurring relevant childcare charges for a child for whom a claimant is responsible in three circumstances: **2.84**

(a) a lone parent working 16 hours a week;
(b) a couple both of whom are working 16 hours a week; or
(c) a couple, one of whom is working 16 hours a week and the other of whom is incapacitated, in hospital or in prison.

Incapacitated

2.85 The test of incapacity is set out in paras (4)–(8). Each of these tests refers to entitlement to a form of benefit to which only the disabled or incapacitated are entitled. This follows the policy of the tax credits legislation in relying on the determination by others of disability or incapacity in most cases. Paragraph (5) is by reference to housing benefit and council tax benefit, paras (6) and (7) by reference to benefits awarded by the Department for Work and Pensions, and para.(8) by reference to the Motability scheme.

Entitlement to childcare element of working tax credit

2.86 **14.**—(1) [1Subject to paragraph (1A),] for the purposes of section 12 of the Act charges incurred for childcare are charges paid by the person, or in the case of a joint claim, by either or both of the persons, for childcare provided for any child for whom the person, or at least one of the persons, is responsible [3 within the meaning of regulation 3 of the Child Tax Credit Regulations 2002].

In these Regulations, such charges are called "relevant childcare charges".

[1(1A) Childcare charges do not include charges in respect of care provided by a relative of a child wholly or mainly in the child's home.

(1B) For the purposes of this regulation—

(a) "relative" means parent, grandparent, aunt, uncle, brother or sister whether by blood, half blood, marriage or affinity;

(b) "the child's home" means the home of the person, or in the case of a joint claim of either or both of the persons, responsible for the child.]

(2) "Child care" means care provided for a child—

(a) in England and Wales—

(i) by persons registered under Part XA of the Children Act 1989;

(ii) in schools or establishments which are exempted from registration under Part XA of the Children Act 1989 by virtue of paragraph 1 or 2 of Schedule 9A to that Act;

(iii) in respect of any period between his eighth birthday [2 and the last day he is treated as a child for the purposes of this regulation,] where the care is provided out of school hours, by a school on school premises or by a local authority; or

(iv) by a childcare provider approved by an accredited organisation within the meaning given by regulation 4 of the Tax Credit (New Category of Child Care Provider) Regulations 1999;

(b) in Scotland—

(i) by a person in circumstances where the care service provided by him consists of child minding or of day care of children within the meaning of section 2 of the Regulation of Care (Scotland) Act 2001 and is registered under Part I of that Act; or

(ii) by a local authority in circumstances where the care service provided by the local authority consists of child minding or of day care of children within the meaning of section 2 of the Regulation of Care (Scotland) Act 2001 and is registered under Part II of that Act;

(c) in Northern Ireland—
(i) by persons registered under Part XI of the Children (Northern Ireland) Order 1995; or
(ii) by institutions and establishments exempt from registration under that Part by virtue of Article 121 of that Order; or
(d) [1anywhere outside the United Kingdom]—
(i) by a childcare provider approved by an accredited organisation within the meaning given by regulation 4 of the Tax Credit (New Category of Child Care Provider) Regulations 2002; or
(ii) [1. . .]
[1(e) in England—
(i) wholly or mainly in the child's home by a childcare provider approved in accordance with the Tax Credits (Approval of Home Child Care Providers) Scheme 2003; or
(ii) by a domiciliary care worker under the Domiciliary Care Agencies Regulations 2002.]

(3) For the purposes of this regulation a person is a child until the last day of the week in which falls 1st September following that child's 15th birthday (or 16th birthday if the child is disabled).

(4) For the purposes of paragraph (3), a child is disabled where—
(a) a disability living allowance is payable in respect of that child, or has ceased to be payable solely because he is a patient;
(b) the child is registered as blind in a register compiled by a local authority under section 29 of the National Assistance Act 1948 (welfare services) or, in Scotland, has been certified as blind and in consequence is registered as blind in a register maintained by or on behalf of a local authority in Scotland, or, in Northern Ireland has been certified as blind and in consequence is registered as blind in a register maintained by or on behalf of a Health and Social Services Board; or
(c) the child ceased to be registered as blind in such a register within the 28 weeks immediately preceding the date of claim.

(5) Charges paid in respect of the child's compulsory education or charges paid by a person to a partner or by a partner to the person in respect of any child for whom either or any of them is responsible are not relevant childcare charges.

(6) Where regulation 15(4) (agreement for the provision of future childcare) applies—
(a) the words "charges paid" in paragraph (1) include charges which will be incurred; and
(b) the words "childcare provided" in paragraph (1) include care which will be provided.

(7) [3. . .]

(8) Relevant childcare charges are calculated on a weekly basis in accordance with regulation 15.

AMENDMENTS

1. Working Tax Credit (Entitlement and Maximum Rate) (Amendment) Regulations 2003 (SI 2003/701), reg.13 (April 6, 2003).

2. Tax Credits (Miscellaneous Amendments No.2) Regulations 2003 (SI 2003/2815), reg.15 (November 26, 2003).

3. Tax Credits (Miscellaneous Amendments) Regulations 2004 (SI 2004/762), reg.10 (April 6, 2004).

DEFINITIONS

"child"—see reg.2.
"claim"—see reg.2.
"partner"—see reg.2.
"patient"—see reg.2.

GENERAL NOTE

2.87 The main content of this regulation is the definition of the main phrases on which reg.13 relies. "Child" receives a slightly limited definition compared with the standard approach for child tax credit and working tax credit, as para.(3) puts an upper limit on the relevant age of a child. The provision does not apply at all to those over 16, who are known as "qualifying young persons" for working tax credit and child tax credit purposes. There is an upwards extension of the age limit for disabled children in paras (3) and (4). This is by reference to payment of any level of disability living allowance or by blindness. There is also a limit applying to the youngest children. Paragraph (7) links with reg.13(3) to exclude a claim by someone on maternity, paternity or adoption leave by reference only to the child in respect of whom the leave is granted.

"Child care" is given an extensive definition. This is necessary because responsibility for childcare legislation is part of the devolved responsibilities of the Scottish and Northern Irish parliaments and the Welsh assembly. In addition, the definition has been extended to childcare outside the United Kingdom. This links with the provisions in the Tax Credits (Residence) Regulations 2003 (SI 2003/642) under which Crown servants outside the United Kingdom, and their partners, are regarded as being in the United Kingdom for tax credits purposes. Accordingly, staff provided with approved childcare facilities by, for example, defence establishments, can qualify for the childcare element of working tax credit. Any dispute about whether someone is providing "childcare" is for the authorities responsible for that particular set of registration rules.

"Relevant childcare charges" is defined by reference to charges for "childcare", with the important exception in para.(1A) of childcare provided by a (registered) relative in the child's home. It can, however, be provided in the carer's home even though the carer is, say, a grandparent. The condition ensures that both the carer, and the carer's premises, are open to inspection. Paragraph (5) excludes charges for education as against care, and payments made by one of a married or unmarried couple to the other (although the one to whom the payments are made may not be responsible for the child).

Calculation of relevant childcare charges

2.88 **15.**—(1) Relevant childcare charges are calculated by aggregating the average weekly charge paid for childcare for each child in respect of whom charges are incurred [[1]and rounding up the total to the nearest whole pound]. This is subject to [[1]paragraphs (1A) and (2)].

[[1](1A) In any case in which the charges in respect of childcare are paid weekly, the average weekly charge for the purposes of paragraph (1) is established—

(a) where the charges are for a fixed weekly amount, by aggregating the average weekly charge paid for childcare for each child in respect of whom charges are incurred in the most recent four complete weeks; or

(b) where the charges are for variable weekly amounts, by aggregating the charges for the previous 52 weeks and dividing the total by 52.]

(2) In any case in which the charges in respect of childcare are paid monthly, the average weekly charge for the purposes of paragraph (1) is established—

(a) where the charges are for a fixed monthly amount, by multiplying that amount by 12 and dividing the product by 52; or

(b) where the charges are for variable monthly amounts, by aggregating the charges for the previous 12 months and dividing the total by 52.

(3) In a case where there is insufficient information for establishing the average weekly charge paid for childcare in accordance with paragraphs (1) and (2), an officer of the Board shall estimate the charge—

(a) in accordance with information provided by the person or persons incurring the charges; and

(b) by any method which in the officer's opinion is reasonable.

(4) If a person—

(a) has entered into an agreement for the provision of childcare; and

(b) will incur under that agreement relevant childcare charges in respect of childcare during the period of the award, the average weekly charge for childcare is based upon a written estimate of the future weekly charges provided by that person.

AMENDMENTS

1. Working Tax Credit (Entitlement and Maximum Rate) (Amendment) Regulations 2003 (SI 2003/701), reg.14 (April 6, 2003).

DEFINITIONS

"child"—see reg.14(3).
"childcare"—see reg.14(2).
"relevant childcare charges"—see reg.14(1).

GENERAL NOTE

This regulation sets out the methods to be used in calculating the amount of childcare charges on which the childcare element is to be based. The regulation was amended just before it came into effect because the previous form of the regulation was accepted as being seriously flawed. This is because it had attempted to use weekly payment rules from the previous approach used for WFTC for the new system of annual calculation and award. This created potential unfairness as between those who pay monthly for their childcare on an annualised basis and those who pay weekly on an actual basis. While the monthly payers usually have a steady pattern of payments, the weekly payers often pay more during school terms than during school holidays. **2.89**

The rules deal with monthly payments by either using the fixed monthly charge, or the average of the last 12 monthly charges, to determine the weekly figure. Varying weekly charges are calculated by reference to the last 52 weeks, while fixed weekly charges are calculated by reference to the last four weeks. Presumably, however, regard must be had to more than four past weeks in applying this rule to avoid the problem of assessing the charges for the wrong four weeks.

There are two important provisos to these rules. The first is that the Inland Revenue may rely on estimates based on "any method . . . which is reasonable". This should allow a solution to the problem of increases in the charges that should be reflected in increases in the childcare element. The second proviso, in para.(4), allows an estimate of the future charges to be taken into account provided that the claimant has entered into a written agreement for the provision of childcare.

Change of circumstances

2.90 **16.**—(1) There is a relevant change in circumstances if—

(a) [[1]. . .]

(b) [[1]during the period of an award, the weekly relevant childcare charges, rounded up to the nearest whole pound]—

(i) exceed the average weekly charge calculated in accordance with regulation 15 by £10 a week or more;

(ii) are less than the average weekly charge calculated in accordance with regulation 15 by £10 a week or more; or

(iii) are nil.

If there is a relevant change in circumstances, the amount of the childcare element of working tax credit shall be recalculated with effect from the specified date.

[[1](2) For the purposes of paragraph (1), the weekly relevant childcare charge—

(a) where the childcare charges are for a fixed weekly amount, is the aggregate of the weekly charge paid for childcare for each child in respect of whom charges are incurred in each of the four consecutive weeks in which the change occurred; or

(b) where the childcare charges are for variable weekly amounts, is established by aggregating the anticipated weekly charge paid for childcare for each child in respect of whom charges will be incurred for the following 52 weeks and dividing the total by 52.]

(3) If in any case the charges in respect of childcare are paid monthly, the weekly relevant childcare charge for the purposes of paragraph (1) is established—

(a) where the charges are for a fixed monthly amount, by multiplying that amount by 12 and dividing the product by 52; or

(b) where the charges are for variable monthly amounts, by aggregating the [[1]anticipated] charges for the [[1]next] 12 months and dividing the total by 52.

(4) In a case where there is insufficient information for establishing the weekly relevant childcare charge paid for childcare in accordance with paragraphs (2) and (3), an officer of the Board shall estimate the charge—

(a) in accordance with information provided by the person or persons incurring the charges; and

(b) by any method which in the officer's opinion is reasonable.

(5) For the purpose of paragraph (1) the specified date is—

(a) where the childcare charges are increased, the later of—

(i) the first day of the week in which the change occurred, and
(ii) the first day of the week in which falls the day which is three months prior to the date notification of the change is given,

(b) where the childcare charges are decreased, the first day of the week following

the four consecutive weeks in which the change occurred.

AMENDMENTS

1. Working Tax Credit (Entitlement and Maximum Rate) (Amendment) Regulations 2003 (SI 2003/701), reg.15 (April 6, 2003).

DEFINITIONS

"award"—see TCA 2002, s.14.
"change of circumstances"—see TCA 2002, s.6.

GENERAL NOTE

This regulation brings into play the mechanisms for amending or terminating an award of working tax credit. Section 6(3) of the TCA 2002 makes provision for regulations to impose a duty on a claimant to report a change of circumstances that may decrease the rate of entitlement to a tax credit. Regulation 21 of the Tax Credits (Claims and Notifications) Regulations 2002 (SI 2002/2014) imposes the requirement that notification of a change of circumstances as defined in this regulation must be given within three months of the change occurring. Regulations 22–24 of those Regulations set out how and by whom this is to be done. 2.91

Failure to notify may make the claimant liable to a penalty of £300 under s.32(3) of the TCA 2002.

Severe disability element

Severe disability element

17.—(1) The determination of the maximum rate must include the severe disability element if the claimant, or, in the case of a joint claim, one of the claimants satisfies paragraph (2). 2.92

(2) A person satisfies this paragraph if a disability living allowance, attributable to the care component payable at the highest rate prescribed under section 72(3) of the Contributions and Benefits Act or an attendance allowance at the higher rate prescribed under section 65(3) of that Act—

(a) is payable in respect of him; or
(b) would be so payable but for a suspension of benefit by virtue of regulations under section 113(2) of the Contributions and Benefits Act (suspension during hospitalisation), or an abatement as a consequence of hospitalisation.

DEFINITIONS

"claimant"—see reg.2.
"joint claim"—see reg.2.

General Note

2.93 This is in addition to the disability element provided for in reg.9. It adds a further £890 to the entitlement of the claimant or claimants. But it is restricted to the case where the disabled individual is receiving the highest rate of the care component of disability living allowance (or the attendance allowance equivalent), which means that both day and night attention or supervision are needed. The regulations referred to in para.(2)(b) are the Social Security (Hospital In-Patients) Regulations 1975 (SI 1975/555), set out in Vol.I of this work.

50 Plus element

50 Plus element

2.94 **18.**—(1) The determination of the maximum rate must include the 50 plus element if—

(a) in the case of a single claim, the claimant satisfies paragraph(3); or
(b) in the case of a joint claim, at least one of the claimants satisfies that paragraph.

This is subject to the qualification in paragraph (2).

(2) The 50 plus element shall not be payable in respect of a claimant—
(a) for a continuous period of longer than 12 months; or
(b) for periods amounting in aggregate to more than 12 months if the gap between any consecutive pair of those periods is not more than 26 weeks.

(3) A claimant satisfies this paragraph if—
[1 (a) he is aged at least 50; and
(b) he starts qualifying remunerative work; and]
(c) he undertakes qualifying remunerative work for at least 16 hours per week; and
(d) he satisfies the condition in para.(4), (6), (7), (8) or (9).

(4) The condition is that—
(a) for a period of at least six months immediately before his starting [1qualifying remunerative] work as mentioned in paragraph (3)(b); or
(b) for consecutive periods, amounting in the aggregate to at least six months, the last of which ends immediately before his starting [1qualifying remunerative] work as mentioned in paragraph (3)(b), paragraph (5) is satisfied.

[2 (4A) For the purposes of paragraph (4)(b) "consecutive periods" are periods, any pair of which is separated by a gap of not more than 12 weeks.]

(5) This paragraph is satisfied while the claimant is receiving—
(a) income support;
(b) a jobseeker's allowance;
(c) incapacity benefit;
(d) severe disablement allowance; [2. . .]
(e) both a state retirement pension and [2state pension credit within the meaning of the State Pension Credit Act 2002; or]

[2 (f) a training allowance paid by the Secretary of State under section 2(1) of the Employment and Training Act 1973 to a person in his capacity as a participant in either of the schemes provided by, or under arrangements made with, the Secretary of State and known as "Work-Based Learning for Adults" and "Training for Work".]

(6) The condition is that for at least six months immediately prior to his starting [1qualifying remunerative] work—

(a) another person was receiving—

(i) the payment mentioned in sub-paragraphs (a) to (d) of paragraph (5); or

(ii) both the payments mentioned in paragraph (5)(e); and

(b) an increase in respect of the claimant, as a dependant of the other person—

(i) in a case falling within sub-paragraph (a)(i) was payable with that payment; or

(ii) in a case falling within sub-paragraph (a)(ii) was payable with that pension.

(7) The condition is that for at least six months immediately prior to his starting [1qualifying remunerative] work as mentioned in paragraph (3)(b) he satisfied the conditions entitling him to be credited with contributions or earnings in accordance with the Social Security (Credits) Regulations 1975.

(8) The condition is that—

(a) the condition in paragraph (4)(a), (6) or (7) would have been satisfied if the reference to six months were omitted;

(b) immediately prior to the period during which that condition, as modified by sub-paragraph (a), is satisfied there is a period during which the condition in paragraph (9) is satisfied; and

(c) the total of the periods during which—

(i) the condition in paragraph (4)(a), (6) or (7), as modified by sub-para.(a), is satisfied; and

(ii) the condition in para.(9) is satisfied, equals or exceeds six months.

(9) The condition is that the claimant, or, in the case of a joint claim, one of the claimants, is receiving—

(a) [1carer's] allowance;

(b) bereavement allowance; or

(c) widowed parent's allowance.

DEFINITIONS

"claimant"—see reg.2.
"joint claim"—see reg.2.
"qualifying remunerative work"—see reg.4.

AMENDMENTS

1. Tax Credits (Miscellaneous Amendments No.2) Regulations 2003 (SI 2003/2815), reg. 16 (November 26, 2003).

2. Tax Credits (Miscellaneous Amendments) Regulations 2004 (SI 2004/762), reg. 11 (April 6, 2004).

GENERAL NOTE

2.95 Unlike all the other elements of working tax credit, this is limited in time. It is payable only for a maximum of 12 months in total (though not necessarily in one period): para.(2). This is one of the routes to working tax credit that does not involve a social security element. It is instead the replacement of the former "New Deal 50 Plus" payable by the former Department for Employment under employment legislation. Its aim is to give an encouragement for those over 50 and on benefit to get back to work. The regulation lays down two sets of requirements for the element to be paid: first, the claimant must now have qualifying remunerative work for 16 hours a week, and secondly, he or she must have been claiming benefits or incapacity credits before the work, or someone else was claiming benefits for him or her, for a period of at least six months. Part of the period of six months may be counted, under paras (8) and (9), by reference to the award of invalid care allowance (now covers allowance) or an award to a widow or widower.

Death of a child or qualifying young person for whom the claimant is responsible

Entitlement after death of a child or qualifying young person for whom the claimant is responsible

2.96 **19.**—(1) Paragraph (2) applies if—

(a) the death occurs of a child or qualifying young person;

(b) working tax credit is payable to a person who was, or to a couple at least one of whom was, immediately before the death responsible for that child or qualifying young person;

(c) the prescribed conditions for an element of working tax credit were satisfied because the claimant, or at least one of the claimants, was responsible for that child or qualifying person, but would not have been satisfied but for that responsibility; and

(d) the prescribed conditions would have continued to be satisfied but for the death.

(2) If this paragraph applies, working tax credit shall continue to be payable, as if the child or qualifying young person had not died, for the period for which child tax credit continues to be payable in accordance with regulation 6 of the Child Tax Credit Regulations 2002.

DEFINITIONS

"child"—see reg.2.
"qualifying young person"—see reg.2.

GENERAL NOTE

2.97 Section 55 of the TCA 2002 provides an extension of the payment of child benefit for a period of eight weeks after the death of a child for whom the benefit is paid. Section 5(5) makes similar provision for child tax credit, and effect is given to this by reg.6 of the Child Tax Credit Regulations 2002 (SI 2002/2007). This regulation matches those extensions for working tax credit also, s.10(3)(d) of the TCA 2002 providing authority for this.

PART III

MAXIMUM RATE

Maximum rates of elements of Working Tax Credit

20.—(1) The maximum annual rate of working tax credit (excluding the childcare element) payable to a single claimant or to a couple making a joint claim is the sum of whichever of the following elements are applicable— 2.98

(a) the basic element specified in col.(2) of the table in Schedule 2 at paragraph 1;

(b) in respect of a claimant who satisfies regulation 9(1), the disability element specified in column (2) of the table in Schedule 2 at paragraph 2;

(c) the 30-hour element specified in column (2) of the table in Schedule 2 at paragraph 3 in respect of—

(i) a single claimant who works for not less than 30 hours per week;

(ii) a couple either or both of whom work for not less than 30 hours per week; or

(iii) a couple, at least one of whom is responsible for a child or a qualifying young person and at least one of whom works for 16 hours per week if their hours of work when aggregated amount to at least 30 hours per week;

(d) the second-adult element specified in column (2) of the table in Schedule 2 at paragraph 4 where regulation 11 so provides;

(e) the lone-parent element specified in column (2) of the table in Schedule 2 at paragraph 5 where regulation 12 applies;

(f) the severe disability element specified in column (2) of the table in Schedule 2 at para.6—

(i) in respect of a single claimant who satisfies regulation 17; or

(ii) in respect of a member of a couple making a joint claim who satisfies regulation 17; and

(g) the 50 Plus element in respect of a person who satisfies regulation 18(2) at whichever of the rates specified in column 2 of the Table in Schedule 2 at paragraph 7 applies in his case.

(2) The maximum rate of the childcare element of a working tax credit is 70 per cent. of the maxima specified in paragraph (3).

(3) The maxima are—

(a) £135 per week, where the [[1]claimant or, in the case of a joint claim, at least one of the claimants, is responsible for] only one child in respect of whom relevant childcare charges are paid; and

(b) £200 per week where the [[1]claimant or, in the case of a joint claim, at least one of the claimants, is responsible for] more than one child in respect of whom relevant childcare charges are paid.

AMENDMENTS

1. Working Tax Credit (Entitlement and Maximum Rate) (Amendment) Regulations 2003 (SI 2003/701), reg.16 (April 6, 2003).

Definitions

"claimant"—see reg.2.
"joint claim"—see reg.2.

General Note

2.99 This regulation emphasises that the entitlement of a claimant or claimants to working tax credit is made up of each of the elements to which there is entitlement. It is "the sum of whichever of the . . . elements are applicable". However, as noted above, there must be entitlement under reg.4. to the basic element in all cases. Paragraph (1) provides the necessary drafting provision to tie each of the other elements (save for the childcare element), the conditions for which have been defined above, into the rate of award and entitlement to working tax credit to the claimant or claimants under s.11 of the TCA 2002.

Paragraphs (2) and (3) then provide the effective rate of the childcare element. They set the maximum weekly childcare element at £140 for care for two or more children, and £94.50 for care for a single child.

The current figures for the maximum rates of all elements other than the childcare element are in Sch.2.

The varying levels of working tax credit by reference to these differing elements and the different routes by which, under reg.4, claims can be made for working tax credit can be illustrated by some short examples. The examples show the maximum entitlement to working tax credit in each case. They do not take into account the income or benefit entitlements of the claimant(s).

Route 1: Lone-parent with three children, working 32 hours a week, and incurring childcare costs of £250 a week.

Her entitlement is:

Basic element	*£ 1,570*
30-hour element	*£ 640*
Lone parent element	*£ 1,545*
Childcare element	*£ 7,280 (limited to 70 per cent of £200 a week)*
Maximum entitlement	*£ 11,035*

In addition, the lone parent will be entitled to child benefit, and child tax credit for herself and the three children.

Route 2: Married couple, one working 35 hours a week, the other needing day and night care for which disability living allowance at the highest rate has been awarded.

Their entitlement is:

Basic element	*£1,570*
30-hour element	*£ 640*
Second adult element	*£1,545*
Disability element	*£2,100*
Severe disability element	*£ 890*
Maximum entitlement	*£6,745*

Route 3: Married couple, both over 70. One has just started working 20 hours a week, the couple having previously been in receipt of their retirement pension and the minimum income guarantee (income support) for some time. They have no disabilities.

(SI 2002 No. 2005, reg.20)

Their entitlement is:

Basic entitlement	*£1,570*
50 Plus element	*£1,075 (lower rate)*
Maximum entitlement	*£2,645*

There is no entitlement to the second adult element in this case: see reg.11(2).

Route 4: Unmarried couple. He is 26 and working 32 hours a week. She is 18, expecting their child soon, and is not and has not been working.

Their entitlement is:

Basic entitlement	*£1,570*
30-hour element	*£ 640*
Second adult element	*£1,545*
Maximum entitlement	*£3,755*

The couple will be entitled to child benefit, maternity benefits and child tax credit when the child is born.

SCHEDULE 1 — **Regulation 9 (1)**

Disability Which puts a Person at a Disadvantage in Getting a Job

Part I

1. When standing he cannot keep his balance unless he continually holds onto something. **2.100**

2. Using any crutches, walking frame, walking stick, prosthesis or similar walking aid which he habitually uses, he cannot walk a continuous distance of 100 metres along level ground without stopping or without suffering severe pain.

3. He can use neither of his hands behind his back as in the process of putting on a jacket or of tucking a shirt into trousers.

4. He can extend neither of his arms in front of him so as to shake hands with another person without difficulty.

5. He can put neither of his hands up to his head without difficulty so as to put on a hat.

6. Due to lack of manual dexterity he cannot, with one hand, pick up a coin which is not more than 2½ centimetres in diameter.

7. He is not able to use his hands or arms to pick up a full jug of 1 litre capacity and pour from it into a cup, without difficulty.

8. He can turn neither of his hands sideways through 180 degrees.

9. He—

(a) is registered as blind or registered as partially sighted in a register compiled by a local authority under section 24(9)(g) of the National Assistance Act 1948;

(b) has been certified as blind or as partially sighted and, in consequence, registered as blind or partially sighted in a register maintained by or on behalf of a council constituted under the Local Government (Scotland) Act 1994; or

(c) has been certified as blind and in consequence is registered as blind in a register maintained by or on behalf of a Health and Social Services Board in Northern Ireland.

10. He cannot see to read 16 point print at a distance greater than 20 centimetres, if appropriate, wearing the glasses he normally uses.

11. He cannot hear a telephone ring when he is in the same room as the telephone, if appropriate, using a hearing aid he normally uses.

12. In a quiet room he has difficulty in hearing what someone talking in a loud voice at a distance of 2 metres says, if appropriate, using a hearing aid he normally uses.

13. People who know him well have difficulty in understanding what he says.

14. When a person he knows well speaks to him, he has difficulty in understanding what that person says.

15. At least once a year during waking hours he is in a coma or has a fit in which he loses consciousness.

16. He has a mental illness for which he receives regular treatment under the supervision of a medically qualified person.

17. Due to mental disability he is often confused or forgetful.

18. He cannot do the simplest addition and subtraction.

19. Due to mental disability he strikes people or damages property or is unable to form normal social relationships.

20. He cannot normally sustain an 8-hour working day or a 5-day working week due to a medical condition or intermittent or continuous severe pain.

PART II

2.101 **21.** As a result of an illness or accident he is undergoing a period of habilitation or rehabilitation.

GENERAL NOTE

2.102 Under reg.9 of these Regulations, a person is treated as having a disability which puts him or her at a disadvantage in getting a job only if one of the paragraphs of this Schedule applies to him or her. If a paragraph does apply, reg.9 deems the claimant to be at a disadvantage in getting a job, whether or not the disability actually has that effect. See the notes to regs 9 and 9A for the application of these tests to initial and repeat claims.

The Schedule requires the exercise of a considerable amount of judgement. For instance, the words "without difficulty" frequently appear. The difficulty need not be severe and plainly a person may have difficulty with an action without necessarily suffering pain when performing it. Slowness may well be sufficient.

Attention is drawn to the final condition in para.20 before detailed comment is made on the specific disabilities. This is the overarching condition that a person cannot sustain a full working day or a full working week due either to a medical condition (of any nature, physical or mental) or intermittent or continuous severe pain. *R(S) 11/51* emphasised that this has to be determined by what a claimant can reasonably be expected to do with regard to his or her age, education, training and other personal factors. It is suggested that this should be the starting point for consideration of the application of this Schedule, with reference being made to the specific disabilities in that context.

Para. 2

2.103 Note that this test is not the same as the test prescribed in reg.12(1)(a)(ii) of the Social Security (Disability Living Allowance) Regulations 1991 (SI 1991/2890) in respect of the mobility component of disability living allowance. Not only is the distance of 100 metres prescribed, but the question is whether that distance can be walked "without stopping" or without "severe pain" (rather than "severe discomfort"). It should also be noted that only artificial aids which are habitually used are to be taken into account, so there is no need to consider whether an aid which is not used might be suitable. In *R(M) 2/89*, the Commissioner held that a person walks only when putting one foot in front of the other, so that a person who has to swing through crutches, rather than using them to help him or her move both legs separately, cannot walk.

Para. 6

2.104 Two-and-a-half centimetres (1 inch) is the diameter of a 50 pence coin. Since their reduction in size, other coins, apart from the £2 coin, are smaller. Note that the claimant satisfies the test (and so may qualify for benefit) if he or she can pick up a large coin in one hand but not the other. In *CDWA 3123/1997* the claimant had no thumb on his left hand and the terminal joint of his right thumb was missing. He maintained that he was only able to pick up a coin of 2.5 centimetres in diameter by pushing it across a surface and catching it in his hand. The Commissioner holds that the tests in Sch.1 were to be performed in the normal way and not by employing some unusual or awkward manoeuvre. The normal way of picking up coins with one hand was to use the pinch grip between the thumb and fingers. An ability to pick up with the fingers alone was irrelevant because that ability did not demonstrate the presence or absence of the pinch grip. The Commissioner also confirmed that para.6 would be satisfied if the claimant could not pick up a coin of the prescribed size with one hand even if he could with the other.

Para. 7

This is a test of both steadiness and strength, using both hands or arms at once if necessary. The Commissioner in *CDWA 3123/1997* confirmed that the position was different under para.7 (as compared with para.6) since, here, the question was whether the claimant could perform the pouring task using both hands and arms together. An inability to do so with either hand alone is immaterial if he or she can manage the task with both hands. But any realistic difficulty, however slight, in carrying out that task would satisfy the test in para.7. Arguably, an ability to pick up and pour with one hand alone, where the claimant has no use of the other arm at all, would mean that the claimant would not qualify under this paragraph, although that question did not arise in that case. **2.105**

Para. 8

Presumably, this is a test of wrist movements and is intended to be performed with the elbows kept still. **2.106**

Para. 10

16 point print is 4 mm high. It is this size. **2.106/1**

Paras 12–14

If hearing or understanding is possible, but only with difficulty (perhaps after repetition), the claimant still qualifies. The precise relationship between paras 12 and 14 is unclear. Difficulty in understanding may arise for reasons other than loss of hearing and, indeed, a person without hearing may be able to understand through lip-reading. Can a person who can hear a loud voice, but not an ordinary conversational voice, at a distance of 2 metres qualify under para.14 if he or she cannot lip-read? In principle, the answer would seem to be "yes". That would not mean that para.12 had no effect because the person would only be able to qualify under para.14 if he or she was further disadvantaged by an inability to make use of other methods of comprehending speech. **2.107**

Para. 16

Medication taken on prescription will be enough, provided that it is regular. Mental illness is not defined, but, if a person is receiving treatment there is likely to be a diagnosis of an illness and if it is an illness of the mind it will be mental illness. **2.108**

Para. 17

Mental disability is not defined and neither is the extent of confusion or forgetfulness required. On one view, any confusion or forgetfulness suggests some disability of the mind and the question is whether the degree of confusion or forgetfulness is sufficient to warrant the view that the legislator intended such a claimant to qualify (see the approach of the Court Appeal in *W v L* [1974] Q.B. **2.109**

711). On the other hand, in *R(A) 2/92*, a Commissioner considered that a specific diagnosis was required and that suggests that the first question is whether there is such a diagnosis. Only after that has been answered does one go on to consider whether there is any resulting confusion or forgetfulness.

Para. 19

2.110 See the note to para.17. The approach taken in *R(A) 2/92* would create real difficulties here given the view expressed there that "personality disorder" can be distinguished from "mental disability".

Para. 21

2.111 This applies only on an initial claim.

SCHEDULE **2 Regulation 20(1)**

MAXIMUM RATES OF THE ELEMENTS OF A WORKING TAX CREDIT

2.112

[1*Relevant element of Working Tax Credit*	*Maximum annual rate*
1. Basic element	£1,570
2. Disability element	£2,100
3. 30 hour element	£640
4. Second adult element	£1,545
5. Lone parent element	£1,545
6. Severe disability element	£890
7. 50 Plus element—	
(a) in the case of a person who normally undertakes qualifying remunerative work for at least 16 hours but less than 30 hours per week; and	£1,075
(b) in the case of a person who normally undertakes qualifying remunerative work for at least 30 hours per week	£1,610]

AMENDMENT

1. Tax Credits Up-rating Regulations 2004 (SI 2004/941), reg.3 and Sch.2 (April 6, 2004).

Tax Credits (Definition and Calculation of Income) Regulations 2002

(SI 2002/2006)

Whereas a draft of this instrument, which contains the first regulations made under section 7(8) and (9) of the Tax Credits Act 2002, has been laid before, and approved by resolution of, each House of Parliament:

Now, therefore, the Treasury, in exercise of the powers conferred upon them by sections 7(8) and (9), 65(1), (7) and (9) and 67 of the Tax Credits Act 2002, hereby make the following Regulations:

(SI 2002/2006)

PART I

General provisions

1. Citation, commencement and effect. 2.113
2. Interpretation.

PART II

INCOME FOR THE PURPOSES OF TAX CREDITS

General

3. Calculation of income of claimant. 2.114

CHAPTER 2

Employment income

4. Employment income. 2.115

CHAPTER 3

Pension income

5. Pension income 2.116

CHAPTER 4

Trading income

6. Trading income. 2.117

Chapter 5

Social security income

2.118 7. Social security income.

Chapter 6

Student income

2.119 8. Student income.

9. Payments of income in connection with students to be disregarded for the purposes of regulation 3.

Chapter 7

Investment income

2.120 10. Investment income.

Chapter 8

Property income

2.121 11. Property income.

Chapter 9

Foreign income

2.122 12. Foreign income.

Chapter 10

Notional income

2.123 13. Introduction.

14. Claimants treated for any purpose as having income by virtue of the Income Tax Acts.

15. Claimants depriving themselves of income in order to secure entitlement.

16. Claimants to whom income becomes available upon the making of a claim.

17. Claimants providing services to other persons for less than full earnings.

CHAPTER 11

Miscellaneous income

18. Miscellaneous income. 2.124

PART III

Sums disregarded in the calculation of income

General disregards in the calculation of income

19. General disregards in the calculation of income. 2.125

INTRODUCTION AND GENERAL NOTE

Section 7 of the Act ("income test") provides that entitlement to any tax credit is subject to an income test. These regulations set out the rules to be used for calculating the income of claimants for the purposes of that test. Until the introduction of these new rules, the means-tested or income-related benefits provided in the United Kingdom were subject to complex rules for assessing both income and capital that evolved over years from the original discretionary benefits for the poor. These evolved into the parallel and extremely complex sets of rules for determining both income and capital of claimants applying for income support, jobseeker's allowance, family credit (and WFTC), disability working allowance (and DPTC), housing benefit and council tax benefit. At the same time, entirely different sets of rules assessed income for income tax purposes and again for National Insurance (NI) contribution purposes. Such complexity had been subject to much criticism by employers as well as by advisers to those directly affected by the rules. 2.126

The Government announced some time ago that it accepted the arguments that income tax was too complex, and that the—in effect—competitive systems of means-testing were expensive and unproductive. A series of reforms have taken place to remove this unnecessary duplication of testing. One that is not evident on the face of these rules but lies behind them is the slow merger of the rules dealing with Class 1 and Class 2 NI contributions and income tax. Since the Social Security (Transfer of Functions, etc) Act 1999, NI contributions have been entirely handled by the Inland Revenue, and changes in both primary law and practice have removed a number of differences in the way those rules apply, in particular, to determining the income of employees.

Two other reforms are reflected in these rules. The first is a project to rewrite and, to the extent possible, to simplify, income tax law. The second is a rebasing of entitlement from the previous social security approach ("means-testing" of all forms of income and capital) to an approach based on the income tax approach. These rules therefore set out a series of tests based on income tax law. But it is not, as they say, "income tax as we know it"—the time hallowed and distinctly antique collection of obscure provisions in the ICTA. Instead, it is looking ahead to the rewriting of income tax law as part of the Tax Law Rewrite Project, and the structure of these Regulations reflects the pattern of that rewrite.

The Tax Law Rewrite Project

2.127 By a convenient coincidence, one of the major Acts of that project, the Income Tax (Earnings and Pensions) Act 2003 (ITEPA), took effect on the same day as tax credits first became payable—April 6, 2003. This abolished the former "Schedule" charge on emoluments, replacing it with separate charges on employment income, pension income and social security income. These regulations were amended following the Royal Assent to ITEPA to adopt the provisions from that Act, but the original Regulations had been drafted on the assumption that ITEPA would come into effect at the time it did. The Regulations are also assuming that the next two Bills on which the Tax Law Rewrite Project is still working will also come into effect.

The current task of the Tax Law Rewrite Project is to conduct a thorough review of existing income tax law and practice. As part of that review, it examines all existing legislation and the case law, practices and concessions that have arisen from the legislation. As part of the exercise, the team identifies any suggested changes of underlying approach to the law, but not requiring changes of the law itself; changes of both law and policy; and changes of law but not of policy. Any major changes required enactment separately in a Finance Act before being absorbed into the Rewrite Bill. There is then a full consultative process on published exposure drafts of the legislation, and then a final consultation on the full draft. At the same time, the Rewrite teams prepare a new codified draft of the relevant legislative provisions, entirely rewritten into a common form. This is supported by a full commentary and a list of derivations and origins. The whole is then recommended to Parliament, where it is considered by a joint committee. In effect, the consultative process is used to eliminate any change that can be regarded as a policy change (one that has a direct adverse effect on individual taxpayers being a key test), so that the resulting draft is put to Parliament as a whole. ITEPA was accepted and given Royal Assent in this way following minimal parliamentary discussion but extremely thorough discussion at the drafting stages. Is the result a consolidation? Technically it is, so it may be assumed that no substantive change is intended, but it is very different in character to previous consolidations, not least in that the draft is the subject of an extremely detailed analysis. The whole of the output of the Tax Law Rewrite Project is available on the Project's website, and the commentaries are published by the Inland Revenue (see further www.inlandrevenue.gov.uk).

A fundamental change in approach

2.128 It must be stressed that the income test used for working tax credit and child tax credit is fundamentally different from the approach laid out in the Family Credit (General) Regulations 1987 (SI 1987/1973) and still used in the Income Support (General) Regulations 1987 (SI 1996/207), Jobseeker's Allowance Regulations 1996 (SI 1987/1967) and Housing Benefit (General) Regulations 1987 (SI 1987/1971). The main differences may be summarised as follows:

(1) *There is no capital rule.* There has never been a wealth tax in the United Kingdom, save for that, in effect, imposed on those claiming means-tested benefits. The approach is to tax income from capital as (and if) it arises. This is the approach now adopted for tax credits.

(2) *Capital gains are irrelevant.* Income tax is supplemented for individuals by a separate capital gains tax, e.g. on the capital gain made on selling an asset. Capital gains are also ignored for tax credits purposes.

(3) *There are no rules deeming income from capital held.* The rules treating capital as income, and attributing tariff income to capital, have been abolished and not replaced.

(4) *There is no all-inclusive definition of income.* The previous approach was to base the calculation of non-earned income on "gross income and any capital treated as income" (Family Credit (General) Regulations 1987, reg.24). The income tax based approach is to calculate income from each named source and to then aggregate the totals to establish the relevant income. If income arises from a source that is not one of the named sources, it is excluded from the calculation.

(5) *Claimants may choose forms of income that avoid the calculation.* The assumption behind the rules in the Family Credit (General) Regulations 1987, and their application, is that all forms of capital and income should be taken into account in assessing entitlement to a means-tested benefit. Not only is capital now entirely ignored, but under the new rules claimants have the same freedom as they have as income tax payers to minimise their income for calculation purposes. For example, they may choose to receive capital gains from their savings instead of income (e.g. by investing in premium bonds), or they may chose to invest any savings in tax-exempt forms (such as individual savings accounts). However, there are some important anti-avoidance provisions that must be taken into account, as noted below.

Differences between tax credits income calculations and income tax assessments

The approach taken in the new rules is to abandon almost all of the previous rules and to use instead those that can be found in the current income tax legislation. This allows the Inland Revenue to base its tax credits calculations on its income tax assessments or, in most cases, on the self-assessments of those individuals to income tax or the assessment and collection of income tax from employees by employers and agencies through the PAYE (Pay As You Earn) system. There are, however, some important differences from income tax assessments and these should also be noted: **2.129**

(1) *Couples are assessed jointly, not separately.* The income tax system was transferred from a system in which married couples were assessed on their joint incomes in the name of the husband to a system of separate assessment of each partner in 1990. One reason for this was the growing concern about discrimination against couples who were married, and assessed jointly, as against those who were unmarried and separately assessed. The new rules require both married and unmarried couples to make joint applications for working tax credit and child tax credit. This is the first time that the Inland Revenue has been concerned to calculate the joint income of unmarried couples, and it will bring sharply into focus the need to look carefully at when two individuals are required to make a joint claim. The starting point in any calculation of income for tax credits purposes is therefore to establish who the claimant is or claimants are. If two people become a couple,

or a couple breaks up, then that fact must be reported to the Inland Revenue and a new claim made.

(2) *The income tax personal allowances do not apply to tax credits.* Instead, claimants are entitled to the appropriate "elements". One important effect of this, combined with the first point, is that the widespread practice of transferring income from the working partner of a couple to the non-working partner, so as to claim the maximum value from personal allowances and to minimise higher-rate tax, and so to reduce income tax, will not work to reduce income for tax credits purposes.

(3) *The taxable forms of income are not identical to those used for income tax.* They are similar, but include some additional items, including rules dealing with income foregone and income of which a person has deprived himself or herself (these rules being carried forward from the Family Credit (General) Regulations 1987).

(4) *Claimants are taxed on worldwide income.* This is linked to (3). Tax credits may only be claimed by those who are ordinarily resident in the United Kingdom, but they are subject to the obligation to declare their full incomes, regardless of any reliefs by way of double taxation or exemption that they might receive under the Income Tax Acts or double taxation agreements.

(5) *Claimants are assessed on the basis both of this year's income and last year's income.* The income tax rules operate a tax year at a time. For tax credits, however, it is necessary to calculate both the current year income and the previous year income, as either may be the relevant income for tax credits purposes.

(6) *The thresholds for income tax and each tax credit are different.* In practice, the threshold for income tax is the personal allowance to which that taxpayer is entitled that year. There used to be a separate starting point for National Insurance contributions, but this has now been aligned with the income tax starting point. For those under 65, no income tax is payable on the first £4,745 of taxable income in 2004–05. Income tax is then charged at 10 per cent on the next £2,020, before the basic rate of 22 per cent starts. The threshold for working tax credit is £5,060, and that for child tax credit is £13,480. The rate of reduction is, however, the same for both—37 per cent. There is also a higher threshold for the family element of child tax credit, which is £50,000.

(7) *Deductions and exclusions are not identical.* Nor are specific inclusions, so the assessment of income from employment for income tax purposes will not be identical, and nor will the total income.

(8) *Claimants receiving income support or jobseeker's allowance receive maximum child tax credit.* This is passported through, and no calculation of income is necessary. But a claimant for income support or jobseeker's allowance will, by definition, not be entitled to working tax credit save under any transitional or temporary rule.

The drafting techniques used in these Regulations are also those of the Rewrite Project, for example in the use of signposting provisions and the use of the "command" tense of verbs in taking the user step by step through a calculation. Following this approach, reg.3 lays down in clear terms how income is to be calculated. But it is, in practice, the fifth of five questions that need to be answered to establish the relevant income of a claimant or claimants.

The questions to be decided:

(1) Who is claiming? 2.130

(2) IS or JSA . . . or SPC?

(3) Which tax year?

(4) Are there any income changes during the tax year?

(5) What income?

The questions are as follows:

(1) Who is claiming?

Is the claim a single claim, a joint claim or a claim by a polygamous unit? The income of each claimant must be calculated. 2.131

(2) IS, JSA, SPC?

If the claimant is claiming income support or jobseeker's allowance or state pension credit, then there is an automatic entitlement to child tax credit after the transitional period of 2003–2005 for income support and jobseeker's allowance and after October 2003 for state pension credit. The conditions of entitlement to those benefits will in practice exclude the claimant from entitlement to working tax credit. 2.132

(3) Which tax year?

As noted above, the income test is calculated for both the current year's income and the previous year's income. The relevant rules are in s.7 of the Act together with these Regs and the Tax Credits (Income Thresholds and Determination of Rates) Regulations 2002. 2.133

(4) Are there any changes during the year?

The award of tax credit under ss.5 and 14 of the Act are by reference initially to the income of the previous year. But there may be relevant changes of circumstances that lead to a revision of the award if there is a notified change of circumstances under reg.6. The decision on entitlement is made only after the end of the tax year under s.19. 2.134

(5) What kinds of income?

This is determined by the current regulations. 2.135

CROSS-REFERENCES

The notes to each paragraph set out in full the Parts, Chapters and section titles to all Chapters and Sections of the Taxes Act, ITEPA and Finance Acts referred to in these regulations. The regulations include cross references to a considerable number of income tax provisions, only some of which will be of more than occasional importance to tax credits assessments. In addition, as explained below, major parts of both Acts are of no relevance to tax credits. The volume contains a selection of the more important provisions from both Acts, and the cross references supplement that by noting the full title of each Chapter and section referred to in these Regulations. 2.136

PART I

General provisions

Citation, commencement and effect

2.137 **1.** These Regulations may be cited as the Tax Credits (Definition and Calculation of Income) Regulations 2002 and shall come into force—

(a) for the purpose of enabling claims to be made, on 1st August 2002;
(b) for the purpose of enabling awards to be made, on 1st January 2003; and
(c) for all other purposes, on 6th April 2003;

and shall have effect for the tax year beginning on 6th April 2003 and subsequent tax years.

DEFINITIONS

"award"—see TCA 2002, s.5.
"claim"—see TCA 2002, s.3.
"tax year"—see reg.2.

Interpretation

2.138 **2.**—(1) In these Regulations, unless the context otherwise requires—

"the Act" means the Tax Credits Act 2002;

"the Contributions and Benefits Act" means the Social Security Contributions and Benefits Act 1992; [3. . .]

"the Employment Act" means the Employment and Training Act 1973 [3; and

"the Northern Ireland Contributions and Benefits Act" means the Social Security Contributions and Benefits (Northern Ireland) Act 1992.]

(2) In these Regulations except where the context otherwise requires—

"the 1992 Fund" means moneys made available from time to time by the Secretary of State for Social Security for the benefit of persons eligible for payment in accordance with the provisions of a scheme established by him on 24th April 1992 as respects England and Wales and Northern Ireland and on 10th April 1992 as respects Scotland;

"the Board" means the Commissioners of Inland Revenue;

"child" has the meaning given in the Child Tax Credit Regulations 2002;

"claim" means a claim for child tax credit or working tax credit and "joint claim" and "single claim" shall be construed in accordance with [2section 3(8)] of the Act and "claimant" shall be construed accordingly;

[1"earnings" shall be construed in accordance with section 62 of the ITEPA;]

"the Eileen Trust" means the charitable trust of that name established on 29th March 1993 out of funds provided by the Secretary of State for Social Security for the benefit of persons eligible in accordance with its provisions;

[1. . .];

"employment zone" means an area within Great Britain designated by the Employment Zones Regulations 2000 for the purposes of section 60 of the Welfare Reform and Pensions Act 1999;

"employment zone programme" means a programme which is—

(a) established for one or more employment zones; and

(b) designed to assist claimants for a Jobseeker's Allowance to obtain sustainable employment;

"family" means—

(a) in the case of a joint claim, the married or unmarried couple by whom the claim is made and any child or qualifying young person for whom at least one of them is responsible, in accordance with regulation 3 of the Child Tax Credit Regulations 2002; and

(b) in the case of a single claim, the claimant and any child or qualifying young person for whom he is responsible in accordance with regulation 3 of the Child Tax Credit Regulations 2002;

"the Independent Living Fund" means the charitable trust of that name established out of funds provided by the Secretary of State for Social Services for the purpose of providing financial assistance to those persons incapacitated by or otherwise suffering from very severe disablement who are in need of such assistance to enable them to live independently;

"the Independent Living Funds" means the Independent Living Fund, the Independent Living (Extension) Fund and the Independent Living (1993) Fund;

"the Independent Living (Extension) Fund" means the trust of that name established on 25th February 1993 by the Secretary of State for Social Security and Robin Glover Wendt and John Fletcher Shepherd;

"the Independent Living (1993) Fund" means the trust of that name established on 25th February 1993 by the Secretary of State for Social Security and Robin Glover Wendt and John Fletcher Shepherd;

[1"ITEPA" means the Income Tax (Earnings and Pensions) Act 2003;]

"the Macfarlane (Special Payments) Trust" means the trust of that name established on 29th January 1990 partly out of funds provided by the Secretary of State for Health for the benefit of certain persons suffering from haemophilia;

"the Macfarlane (Special Payments) (No.2) Trust" means the trust of that name established on 3th May 1991 partly out of funds provided by the Secretary of State for Health for the benefit of certain persons suffering from haemophilia and other beneficiaries;

"the Macfarlane Trust" means the charitable trust established partly out of funds provided by the Secretary of State for Health to the Haemophilia Society for the relief of poverty or distress among those suffering from haemophilia;

"the Macfarlane Trusts" means the Macfarlane Trust, the Macfarlane (Special Payments) Trust and the Macfarlane (Special Payments) (No.2) Trust;

"pensionable age" has the meaning given by the rules in paragraph 1 of Schedule 4 to the Pensions Act 1995;

"pension fund holder", in relation to a personal pension scheme or a retirement annuity contract, means the trustees, managers or scheme administrators of the scheme or contract;

"personal pension scheme"—

(a) has the meaning given by section 1 of the Pensions Schemes Act 1993 or section 1 of the Pension Schemes (Northern Ireland) Act 1993; and

(b) includes a scheme approved by the Board under Chapter 4 of Part XIV of the Income and Corporation Taxes Act 1988;

"qualifying young person" has the meaning given in the Child Tax Credit Regulations 2002;

"retirement annuity contract" means a contract or trust scheme approved by the Board under or by virtue of any provision of Chapter 3 of Part XIV of the Taxes Act;

"retirement benefits scheme" has the meaning given in s.611 of the Taxes Act;

"Schedule D" means the Schedule set out in section 18 of the Taxes Act;

[1. . .];

"the Service Pensions Order" means the Naval, Military and Air Forces, etc. (Disablement and Death) Service Pensions Order 1983;

"tax year" means a period beginning with the 6th April in one year and ending with 5th April in the next;

"the Taxes Act" means the Income and Corporation Taxes Act 1988;

"voluntary organisation" means a body, other than a public or local authority, the activities of which are carried on otherwise than for profit;

"war pension" has the meaning given in section 25(4) of the Social Security Act 1989.

(3) For the purposes of these Regulations, whether a person is responsible for a child or a qualifying young person is determined in accordance with regulaton 3 of the Child Tax Credit Regulations 2002.

(4) In these Regulations—

(a) a reference to a claimant's partner is a reference to a claimant's spouse or a person with whom the claimant lives as a spouse; and

(b) a reference to a claimant's former partner is a reference to a claimant's former spouse or a person with whom the claimant has lived as a spouse; and

(c) a reference in these Regulations to an Extra Statutory Concession is a reference to that Concession as published by the Inland Revenue on 1st July 2002.

AMENDMENTS

1. Tax Credits (Definition and Calculation of Income) (Amendment) Regulations 2003 (SI 2003 No., 732), reg.4 (April 6, 2003).

2. Tax Credits (Miscellaneous Amendments No.2) Regulations 2003 (SI 2003/2815), reg.3 (November 26, 2003).
3. Tax Credits (Miscellaneous Amendments) Regulations 2004 (SI 2004/762), reg.13 (April 6, 2004).

GENERAL NOTE

See also the definitions in TCA 2002, ss.48 and 67. 2.139

For a full list of definitions and phrases for income tax, see ITEPA, Sch.1. This includes not only the words and phrases used in ITEPA but also those used in the Taxes Act and Finance Acts.

PART II

INCOME FOR THE PURPOSES OF TAX CREDITS

CHAPTER 1

General

Calculation of income of claimant

3.—(1) The manner in which income of a claimant, or, in the case of a joint claim, the aggregate income of the claimants, is to be calculated for a tax year for the purposes of Part I of the Act is as follows. 2.140

Step 1

Calculate and then add together— 2.141
(a) the pension income (as defined in regulation 5(1));
(b) the investment income (as defined in regulation 10);
(c) the property income (as defined in regulation 11);
(d) the foreign income (as defined in regulation 12); and
(e) the notional income (as defined in regulation 13),
of the claimant, or, in the case of a joint claim, of the claimants.

If the result of this step is £300 or less, it is treated as nil.

If the result of this step is more than £300, only the excess is taken into account in the following steps.

Step 2

Calculate and then add together— 2.142
(a) the employment income (as defined in regulation 4);
(b) the social security income (as defined in regulation 7);
(c) the student income (as defined in regulation 8); and
(d) the miscellaneous income (as defined in regulation 18), of the claimant, or in the case of a joint claim, of the claimants.

Step 3

2.143 Add together the results of steps 1 and 2.

Step 4

2.144 Calculate the trading income (as defined in regulation 6) of the claimant, or in the case of a joint claim, of the claimants.

Add the result of this step to that produced by step 3 [1. . .] in the year.

If there has been a trading loss in the year, [1subtract] the amount of that loss from the result of step 3.

[2Any trading loss in the year not set off as a result of the calculations in Steps One to Four above due to an insufficiency of income may be carried forward and set off against trading income (if any) of the same trade, profession or vocation in subsequent years (taking earlier years first) for the purposes of calculation of income under this regulation.]

(2) Subject to the qualifications in the following paragraphs of this regulation, and the provisions of Part III, the result of step 4 in paragraph (1) is the income of the claimant, or, in the case of a joint claim, of the claimants, for the purposes of the Act.

(3) Income which—

(a) arises in a territory outside the United Kingdom; and

(b) is, for the time being, unremittable for the purposes of section 584 of the Taxes Act,

is disregarded in calculating the income of the claimant or, in the case of a joint claim, of the claimants.

(4) Paragraph (5) applies in the case of a claimant who is [1, for income tax purposes]

(a) resident [1and domiciled but not ordinarily resident] in the United Kingdom; [2. . .]

(b) resident and ordinarily resident but not domiciled in the United Kingdom [2or]

[2 (c) resident but neither ordinarily resident nor domiciled in the United Kingdom.]

(5) In the case of a person to whom this paragraph applies—

[1(a) any income arising outside the United Kingdom is to be taken into account, subject to any specific provision of these Regulations, regardless of the domicile or residence of the claimant; and;]

(b) references to a sum being [1taken into account] are to be construed as including a sum which would be taxable if he were resident, ordinarily resident and domiciled in the United Kingdom.

[1(5A) Any income is to be taken into account, subject to any specific provision of these Regulations, notwithstanding the provision of any Order in Council under section 788 of the Taxes Act (double taxation agreements).]

(6) In the case of a claimant who would be chargeable to income tax but for some special exemption or immunity from income tax, income shall be calculated on the basis of the amounts which would be so chargeable but for that exemption or immunity.

[1(6A) Income paid to a claimant in a currency other than sterling shall be converted into sterling at the average of the exchange rates applicable for the conversion of that currency into sterling in the period of 12 months ending on 28th March in the tax year in which the income arises.]

(7) In calculating income under this Part there shall be deducted [1. . .]—

(a) [1the amount of] any banking charge or commission payable in converting to sterling a payment of income which is made in a currency other than sterling;

(b) [1the grossed up amount of] any qualifying donation (within the meaning of section 25 of the Finance Act 1990 (donations to charity by individuals)), made by the claimant or, in the case of a joint claim, by either or both of the claimants; [2. . .]

(c) [1the amount of] any contribution made by the claimant, or in the case of a joint claim, by either or both of the claimants to—

(i) a retirement benefits scheme approved under Chapter 1 of Part XIV of the Taxes Act, including a pilots benefit fund approved under section 607 of that Act and a relevant statutory scheme within the meaning of section 611A of that Act;

(ii) a retirement annuity contract approved under Chapter 3 of Part XIV of that Act; or

(iii) a personal pension scheme, approved under [1Chapter 4 of Part XIV of that Act] [2and]

[2(d) any contribution made by the claimant, or in the case of a joint claim, by either or both of the claimants, if made in accordance with Inland Revenue Extra Statutory Concession A9.]

[1together with the amount of any tax relief due on those contributions.]

[2(8) If—

(a) a claimant has sustained a loss in relation to a Schedule A business or an overseas property business; and

(b) the relief to which he is entitled in accordance with section 379A(2) and (3) of the Taxes Act exceeds the amount of his property income or foreign income for tax credits purposes, for the year in question;

the amount of his total income for tax credit purposes, computed in accordance with the preceding provisions of this regulation, shall be reduced by the amount of the excess.

In this paragraph "Schedule A business" and "overseas property business" have the same meanings as they have in the Taxes Act.]

AMENDMENTS

1. Tax Credits (Definition and Calculation of Income) (Amendment) Regulations 2003 (SI 2003/732), reg.5 (April 6, 2003).

2. Tax Credits (Miscellaneous Amendments No.2) Regulations 2003 (SI 2003/2815), reg.4 (November 26, 2003).

CROSS-REFERENCES

FA 1990, s.25	Charities: donations to charities by individuals
Taxes Act, s.584	Relief for unremittable overseas income
Taxes Act, Pt XIV, ch. 1	Pension Schemes, etc.: retirement benefit schemes

ch.3	Retirement annuities
ch.4	Personal pension schemes
Taxes Act, s.607	Pilots' benefit fund
Taxes Act, s.611	Retirement benefit schemes: definition of relevant statutory scheme
Taxes Act, s.788	Double taxation relief: relief by agreement with other countries

General Note

2.145 Regulation 3(1) and (2) state that there are four steps to calculating the aggregate income of a claimant or joint claimants for a tax year, but it is suggested that this would be better presented as five steps. The four steps are:

(1) Add the totals of income from sources subject to the £300 discount and deduct that discount.
(2) Add the totals from all other sources, apart from trading income.
(3) Add the totals of (1) and (2).
(4) Add to, or subtract from, the total from (3) the net income (or net loss) from trading income.

The "fifth step" is then to deduct from that sum the various general deductions, exclusions, exemptions and disregards in these regulations. These are set out in reg.3(3) (unremittable income), reg.3(7) (other general deductions), reg.9 (exempt scholarship income) and the Tables 6, 7 and 8 in reg.19 (general disregards).

The balance of reg.3 is a motley of provisions. Paragraph (3) applies Taxes Act, s.584 to these Regulations. Paragraphs (4) and (5) are somewhat curious, and may have been formulated before the Tax Credits (Residence) Regulations 2003 (SI 2003/654) were written. Paragraph (4) states that para.(5) applies in the case of a claimant "who is", in case (a), resident but not ordinarily resident. However, reg.3 of the Tax Credits (Residence) Regulations 2003 prevents such a person claiming a tax credit, or being one of a couple making a joint claim. So reg.3(5) of these Regulations can strictly never apply to a claimant. Perhaps what is intended is that if a person is in the current year ordinarily resident, but was not in the previous year, then para.(5) applies to that previous year. This would be important because the purpose of paras (4) and (5) is to disapply the "remittance basis" of taxation under Case V of Sch.D (restricting the charge to income tax in the United Kingdom to tax on income remitted to the United Kingdom only). This, together with para.(5A), would bring into charge the full worldwide income of the claimant in the previous year even if none of it had been taxable in the United Kingdom in that year. Paragraph (5A) brings into charge any worldwide income that would be excluded from United Kingdom taxation by reason of a double taxation agreement concluded between the United Kingdom and any other state.

It is not clear what para.(6) covers. Perhaps it enforces the avoidance of exemption provisions in Taxes Act, s.829(4). It is difficult to see how it applies [compensating out] to remove the privileges granted to diplomats and consuls under the Diplomatic Privileges Act 1964 and the Consular Relations Act 1968. The income tax provisions in ITEPA dealing with (in the broad sense) diplomatic income are not applied to the calculation of tax credits income, suggesting that the assumption behind the rules is that this income is not within the scope of tax credits calculations.

Paragraph (7) is part of the "fifth step", along with para.(3). It provides for two important deductions commonly made against income for income tax purposes. The first is to allow the deduction from income for tax credits purposes of any sums given to charities within the terms of the FA 1990, s.25. That is the provision authorising the tax deduction for "gift aid" payments for all non-refundable gifts of money to charities made otherwise than by covenant, the charity being treated as receiving the sum under deduction of tax at the basic rate. The other allows deduction from total income of contributions to approved pension schemes, including personal pension schemes.

CHAPTER 2

Employment income

Employment income

4.—(1) In these Regulations, "employment income" means— 2.146

(a) any [1earnings] from an office or employment received in the tax year;

(b) so much of any payment made to a claimant in that year in respect of expenses as is chargeable to income tax [1by virtue of section 62 or section 72 of ITEPA];

(c) [1the cash equivalent of] any non-cash voucher received by the claimant in that year and chargeable to income tax under [1section 87 of ITEPA];

(d) [1the cash equivalent of] any credit-token received by the claimant in that year and chargeable to income tax under [1section 94 of ITEPA];

(e) [1the cash equivalent of] any cash voucher received by the claimant in that year and chargeable to income tax under [1section 81 of ITEPA];

[1(f) any amount chargeable to tax under Chapter 3 of Part VI of ITEPA;]

(g) so much of a payment of statutory sick pay, received by the claimant during the year, as is subject to income tax [1by virtue of section 660 of ITEPA;]

(h) the amount (if any) by which a payment of [1statutory maternity pay, statutory paternity pay or statutory adoption pay] exceeds £100 per week;

(i) any amount charged to income tax for that year [1under section 120 or section 149 of ITEPA;]

[1(j) any sum to which section 225 of ITEPA applies;]

(k) any amount paid in that year by way of strike pay to the claimant as a member of a trade union;

[2(l) any amount charged to income tax for that year under Part 7 of ITEPA.]

For the purposes of this paragraph, references to the receipt of a payment of any description are references to its receipt by or on behalf of the claimant, or in the case of a joint claim of either of the claimants, in any part of the world.

This paragraph is subject to the following qualifications.

(2) Employment income does not include pension income.

[3 (2A) Paragraph (2B) applies if a claimant is a member of the Brigade of Gurkhas, to whom the voluntary settlement of tax liabilities of certain members of those units between the Ministry of Defence and the Board ("the voluntary settlement") applies.

(2B) In the case of a claimant to whom this paragraph applies, the amount of his employment income from that employment for a particular tax year shall be the amount published by the Ministry of Defence as the UK equivalent rate in his case.]

[2 (3) This paragraph applies if (apart from section 64 of ITEPA) the same benefit would give rise to two amounts ("A" and "B")—

(a) "A" being an amount of earnings from a claimant's employment as defined in section 62 of ITEPA, and

(b) "B" being an amount to be treated as earnings under any provision of Chapter 10 of Part 3 of ITEPA.

In such a case, the amount to be taken into account in computing the claimant's employment income is the greater of A and B, and the lesser amount shall be disregarded.]

(4) In calculating employment income, the payments and benefits listed in Table 1 shall be disregarded.

Table 1. Payments [1and benefits] disregarded in the calculation of employment income

2.147 **1.** Any payment in respect of qualifying removal expenses, or the provision of any qualifying removal benefit, within the meaning of [1Chapter 7 of Part IV of ITEPA].

[1**2A.** The payment or reimbursement of expenses incurred in the provision of transport to a disabled employee (as defined in section 246(4) of ITEPA) by his employer, if no liability to income tax arises in respect of that payment or reimbursement (as the case may be) by virtue of section 246 of ITEPA.

2B. The provision to a disabled employee (as defined in section 246(4) of ITEPA) by his employer of a car, the provision of fuel for the car, or the reimbursement of expenses incurred in connection with the car, if no liability to income tax arises in respect of that provision or reimbursement (as the case may be) by virtue of section 247 of ITEPA.

2C. The payment or reimbursement of expenses incurred on transport, if no liability to income tax arises in respect of that payment or reimbursement (as the case may be) by virtue of section 248 of ITEPA.]

3. Travel facilities provided for the claimant as a member of the naval, military or air forces of the Crown for the purpose of going on, or returning from, leave.

4. Payment or reimbursement of expenses in connection with the provision for, or use by, the claimant as a person holding an office or employment of a car-parking space at or near his place of work.

5. Any benefit or non-cash voucher provided to the claimant, or to any member of his family or household, [1in respect of which no liability to income tax arises by virtue of Chapter 5 of Part IV of ITEPA.]

6. Any payment of incidental overnight expenses [[1]in respect of which no liability to income tax arises by virtue of section 240 of ITEPA.]

[[1]7. Food, drink and mess allowances for the armed forces and training allowances payable to members of the reserve forces in respect of which no liability to income tax arises by virtue of section 297 or 298 of ITEPA.]

8. The value of meal vouchers issued to the claimant as an employee [[1]if section 89 of ITEPA applies to the vouchers.]

9. Any cash payment received by the claimant as a miner in lieu of free coal, or the provision of the coal itself, [[1]in respect of which no liability to income tax arises by virtue of section 306 of ITEPA.]

10. An award made to the claimant as a director or employee by way of a testimonial to mark long service [[1]if, or to the extent that, no liability to income tax arises in respect of it by virtue of section 323 of ITEPA.]

11. Payment of a daily subsistence allowance [[1]in respect of which no liability to income tax arises by virtue of section 304 of ITEPA.].

[[1]**11A.** The payment or reimbursement of reasonable expenses incurred by an employee who has a permanent workplace at an offshore installation, on transfer transport, related accommodation and subsistence or local transport, if no liability to income tax arises in respect of that payment or reimbursement (as the case may be) by virtue of section 305 of ITEPA.

For the purposes of this item, expressions which are defined in section 305 of ITEPA have the same meaning here as they do there.

11B. Payment of an allowance to a person in employment under the Crown in respect of which no liability to income tax arises by virtue of section 299 of ITEPA.

11C. The payment or reimbursement to an employee of any sum in connection with work-related training, or individual learning account training (as respectively defined in sections 251 and 256 of ITEPA) if no liability to income tax arises in respect of that payment or reimbursement (as the case may be) by virtue of any provision of Chapter 4 of Part IV of ITEPA.

11D. The provision for an employee of a non-cash voucher or a credit-token, to the extent that liability to income tax does not arise in respect of that voucher or credit-token (as the case may be), under Chapter 4 of [[2] Part 3 of ITEPA, by virtue of any provision of Chapter 6 of Part 4 of ITEPA.]

11E. The provision for an employee of free or subsidised meal vouchers or tokens (within the meaning of section 317(5) of ITEPA), if no liability to income tax arises in respect of that provision by virtue of section 317 of ITEPA.]

12. An award made to the claimant under a Staff Suggestion Scheme, if the conditions specified in [[1]sections 321 and 322 of ITEPA [[3] are satisfied].]

13. Travelling and subsistence allowances paid to or on behalf of the claimant by his employer [[1]in respect of which no liability to income tax arises by virtue of section 245 of ITEPA.]

14. Any gift consisting of goods, or a voucher or token to obtain goods, [1in respect of which no liability to income tax arises by virtue of section 270 or 324 of ITEPA.]

[1 14A. Any payment or reimbursement of expenses incurred in connection with an employment-related asset transfer (as defined in section 326(2) of ITEPA), if no liability to income tax arises in respect of that payment or reimbursement (as the case may be) by virtue of section 326 of ITEPA.

14B. Any payment of expenses incurred by an employee in connection with a taxable car if no liability to income tax arises in respect of the payment by virtue of section 239(2) of ITEPA.]

[2 **14C.** The discharge of any liability of an employee in connection with a taxable car if no liability to income tax arises by virtue of section 239(1) of ITEPA.

14D. A benefit connected with a taxable car if no liability to income tax arises by virtue of section 239(4) of ITEPA.]

15. A cash voucher, non-cash voucher or credit-token to the extent that it is used by the recipient for the provision of childcare, the costs of which if borne by the recipient would be relevant childcare charges within the meaning of regulation 14 of the Working Tax Credit (Entitlement and Maximum Rate) Regulations 2002.

[3 **16.** A payment made by the Department for Work and Pensions under section 2 of the Employment Act—

(a) by way of In-Work Credit, Job Grant or Return to Work Credit, or
(b) under the Employment Retention and Advancement Scheme or the Working Neighbourhoods Pilot.]

[2 17. The payment or reimbursement of reasonable additional household expenses incurred by an employee who works from home, within the meaning of section 316A of ITEPA.

18. The payment or reimbursement of retraining course expenses within the meaning of the section 311 of ITEPA.]

(5) From the amount of employment income, calculated in accordance with the preceding provisions of this regulation, there shall be deducted the amount of any deduction permitted in calculating [1calculating earnings by virtue of any provision of sections [2231 to 232,] 336–344, or s.346, 347, 351, 352, 362, 363, 367, 368, 370, 371, 373, 374, 376, 377 or 713 of ITEPA].

Amendments

1. Tax Credits (Definition and Calculation of Income) (Amendment) Regulations 2003 (SI 2003/732), reg.6 (April 6, 2003).

2. Tax Credits (Miscellaneous Amendments No.2) Regulations 2003 (SI 2003/2815), reg.5 (November 26, 2003).

3. Tax Credits (Miscellaneous Amendments) Regulations 2004 (SI 2004/762), reg.14 (April 6, 2004).

Cross-references

The regulation adopts for tax credits purposes the following chapters and sections of ITEPA, all relating to employment income:

Pt 3: Employment income: Earnings and benefits etc treated as earnings
s.62 Earnings
Pt 3, ch.4 Taxable benefit: vouchers and credit-tokens
s.72 Sums in respect of expenses treated as earnings
s.81 Benefit of cash voucher treated as earnings
s.87 Benefit of non-cash voucher treated as earnings
s.89 Reduction for meal vouchers
s.94 Benefit of credit-token treated as earnings
Pt 3, ch.6 Taxable benefits: cars, vans and related vehicles
s.120 Benefit of car treated as earnings
s.149 Benefit of car fuel treated as earnings
Pt 3, ch.10 Taxable benefits: residual liability to charge
s.201 Employment-related benefits
s.211 Special rules for scholarships: introduction
Pt 3, ch.11 Taxable benefits: exclusion of lower-paid employments
Pt 3, ch.12 Payments treated as earnings
s.225 Payments for restrictive covenants
Pt 4: Employment income: exemptions
s.239 Payments and benefits connected with taxable cars and vans and exempt heavy goods vehicles
s.240 Incidental overnight expenses and benefits
s.245 Travelling and subsistence during public transport strikes
s.246 Transport between work and home for disabled employees
s.247 Provision of cars for disabled employees
s.248 Transport home: late-night working and failure of car-sharing arrangements
Pt 4, ch.4 Exemptions: education and training
s.251 Meaning of "work-related training"
s.256 Meaning of "individual learning account training"
Pt 4, ch.5 Exemptions; recreational benefits
Pt 4, ch.6 Exemptions: non-cash vouchers and credit-tokens
s.270 Exemptions of small gifts of vouchers and tokens from third parties
Pt 4, ch.7 Exemptions: removal benefits and expenses
s.297 Armed forces' food, drink and mess allowances
s.298 Reserve and auxiliary forces' training allowances
s.299 Crown employees' foreign service allowances
s.304 Experts seconded to the European Commission
s.305 Offshore oil and gas workers: mainland transfers
s.306 Miners, etc.: coal and allowances in lieu of coal
s.317 Subsidised meals
s.321 Suggestion awards
s.322 Suggestion awards: "the permitted maximum"
s.323 Long service awards
s.324 Small gifts from third parties
s.326 Expenses incidental to transfer of a kind not normally met by transferor
Pt 5: Employment income: deductions allowed from earnings
s.336 Deductions for expenses: the general rule
s.337 Travel in performance of duties
s.338 Travel for necessary attendance
s.339 Meaning of "workplace" and "permanent workplace"
s.340 Travel between group employments
s.341 Travel at start and finish of overseas employment
s.342 Travel between employments where duties performed abroad

s.343	Deduction for professional membership fees
s.344	Deduction for annual subscriptions
s.346	Deduction for employee liabilities
s.347	Payments made after leaving employment
s.351	Expenses of ministers of religion
s.352	Limited deduction for agency fees paid by entertainers
s.362	Deductions where non-cash voucher provided
s.363	Deductions where credit-token provided
s.367	Fixed sum deductions for repairing and maintaining work equipment
s.368	Fixed sum deductions from earnings payable out of public revenue
s.370	Travel costs and expenses where duties performed abroad: employee's travel
s.371	Travel costs and expenses where duties performed abroad: visiting spouse's or child's travel
s.373	non-domiciled employee's travel costs and expenses where duties performed in United Kingdom
s.374	Non-domiciled employee's spouse's or child's travel costs and expenses where duties performed in United Kingdom
s.376	Foreign accommodation and subsistence costs and expenses (overseas employments)
s.377	Costs and expenses in respect of personal security assets and services

Pt 6, ch.3 Payments and benefits on termination of employment

s.660	Taxable benefits; United Kingdom benefits: Table A

Pt 12: Payroll giving

s.713	Donations to charity: payroll deduction scheme

General Note

2.148 This regulation defines "employment income" for the purposes of reg.3. Although the result may be obvious in most cases, four questions have to be asked to set the context of a tax credits calculation of employment income when regard is had to a particular source of income:

What income is relevant?
What exemptions and deductions apply?
Whose income is it?
When is the income brought into calculation?

These are discussed in turn. The same pattern is followed in the notes on other regulations.

What income is relevant? The scope of ITEPA and regulation 4

2.149 The former charge to tax in this area (the Sch.E that was abolished from April 6, 2003) defined the scope of the charge in deceptively compact terms. It was on "offices or employments on emoluments therefrom". The decompacting has not removed the need to deal with both the question whether something is an "office or employment" and what earnings are derived from those activities.

Employment and self-employment

2.150 The common context of a dispute about whether an activity is or is not an employment is the contention by the individual concerned that he or she is self-employed. This issue is discussed in the general note to reg.6 below. "Office" used to be a separate provision in the old Sch.E, reflecting the antiquity of the phraseology used. ITEPA, s.5 now relegates the status of office-holders (rightly in terms of relative importance) to a secondary status in the legislation. It also codifies the common law definition of "office". For all tax credits purposes, as for all ITEPA purposes, "employee" is to be read as including office holders, and "being employed" includes holding an office. "Office" is now defined (in words adopted from the income tax case of *GWR v Bater* [1920] 3 K.B. 266) as including "any position which has an existence independent of the person who holds it and may be filled by successive holders". For a discussion of that in the context of the borderline between holding an office and being self-employed see *Edwards v Clinch* [1982] A.C. 543.

Employment income

ITEPA deals with the income taxation of employment income in Pts 1–8 of the Act. For the structure of those Parts, see s 3 of ITEPA, and for the main charge to tax, see s 6. As can be seen from the list of cross-references, the policy and drafting approaches taken for the purposes of calculating employment income for tax credits purposes are to select from the provisions of those parts (ss.1–564), rather than simply to adopt the whole code, or those parts of the code felt appropriate. TCTM04101 directs Board officers to "Note that, although based on income tax law, not all of the additional rules for income chargeable to tax under Schedule E have been included in the tax credit employment income rules", and "not all of the general exemptions and reliefs from inclusion as income chargeable under Schedule E have been included . . .". This will also apply to ITEPA. The only major part of the code omitted as a whole is Part 7 (Employment income: share-related income and exemptions—ss.417–554), although Pt 8 (relating to former employees) is also excluded. Elsewhere, close attention has to be paid to those charges and exemptions that are included (as listed in the cross-reference list derived from reg.3) and those that are excluded. 2.151

So, for example, while most sections in Pt 3 (Employment Income: earnings and benefits etc treated as earnings) are adopted, ch.5 (taxable benefits: living accommodation) is not, nor is ch.7 (taxable benefits: loans). Similarly, while most of the sections in Pt 4 (Employment income: exemptions) are allowed also as exemptions for tax credits purposes, again the approach has been to select those that are applied and those that are not. The same is true of Pt 5 (Employment income: deductions allowed from earnings). This reflects in part an assessment of the provisions that are not relevant (*e.g.* Pt 4, ch.10 (exemptions on termination of employment)) are excluded as not relevant either to working tax credit or to child tax credit, but that does not always appear to explain the omission. For example, the exemption for subsidised meals in s.317 is applied, but not the exemption for care for children in s.318.

The resulting picture is one of some complexity, because one cannot simply adopt the income tax assessment of all employees for tax credits without looking through at least some of them to see on which sections of ITEPA the charge to tax is based or the exemption or deduction is claimed. In any case, other than the most straightforward, it may therefore be necessary to look at the breakdown of any charge to tax not based simply on earnings and the usual expenses and deductions. That also means that the approach of adopting a figure from the P45 or P60 supplied to an employee at the end of an employment or the end of a tax year may not be enough in those cases. While this might sound an over-exact approach to the calculation of income, it has to be borne in mind that the effective value of any charge or exemption for tax credit purposes is, at the margin, 37 per cent of the amount charged or claimed. So, a failure to allow a deduction for a £150 expense (which, if deductible at the basic rate of income tax, will have in effect cost the employee not £150 but £117) will "cost" the employee £55 in lost tax credits, or nearly half the actual cost to the employee of the amount for which the deduction is claimed.

To follow that point with a relevant example, it would seem from the exclusion of s.317 that a claimant for WTC may claim for childcare charges if paid by the employee, but is liable to have the value of the advantage of employer-provided childcare taken into account as income for tax credits purposes although, of course, the employee will not be paying for, and therefore not able to claim for, that provision. However, this depends how the employer provides the advantage. If the employer provides childcare through the mechanism of providing the employee with a cash voucher, non-cash voucher or credit token, the exclusion from calculation of that value by Table 1, Item 15, is broader than the income tax exclusion. As the working tax credit childcare element is not itself taxable to income tax (Taxes Act, s.617A), the justification for this mismatch is not clear.

Differences between income tax assessments and tax credit calculations of employment income

2.152 The only full way of noting the differences between total net (i.e. after deductions) employment income for income tax purposes and for tax credits purposes is by precise reference to individual provisions in ITEPA. This must cover the ITEPA sections included in, and excluded from, reg.4 together with those provisions that are included in reg.4 but not by reference to specific provisions in ITEPA. Cross-references from reg.4 are not assisted by the reenactment of the employment income provisions since the regulation was drafted, as the previous drafting order of the regulation has been lost. As ITEPA is an immediately contemporary codification of employment income taxation, no reference for 2003–04 need be made to any other provision. In future years, it may be assumed that changes will, where appropriate, be made in parallel.

The full list of sections of ITEPA included by cross reference is set out above, and from that the obvious gaps can be identified. There are no differences with regard to cash earnings or equivalent (see ss.62 and 72 of ITEPA). But only some parts of the Pt 3 provisions on taxable benefits apply. Chapter 3 (expense payments), ch.4 (vouchers and credit-tokens), ch.6 (cars, vans and related benefits) and ch.10 (residual liability) apply, but no part of ch.5 (living accommodation), ch.7 (loans), ch.8 (notional loans in respect of acquisition of shares), or ch.9 (disposals of shares for more than market value) apply. And of the six specific payments treated as earnings by ch.12, only one (restrictive covenants under s.225) is expressly brought into the calculation.

Two kinds of income only are mentioned in reg.4 that are not related directly to specific provisions in ITEPA. Regulation 4(1)(h) requires inclusion of only the excess of statutory maternity pay over £100. For income tax purposes the sum is fully taxable. Regulation 4(1)(k) requires the inclusion of strike pay, whether or not that is otherwise taxable under this or any other head of income. These both reflect social security rules rather than income tax rules.

What exemptions and deductions apply?

2.153 The exclusions from para.(4) are far harder to summarise. Part 4 deals with exemptions. Chapter 1 deals with general exemptions rules. Of the specific rules, ch.2 (mileage allowances and passenger payments) is not within the scope of tax credits, and nor are many of the specific exemptions related to transport, travel and subsistence in ch.3. Of ss.237–248 in that Chapter, only ss.239, 240 and 245–8 are permitted exclusions for tax credits calculations. Chapter 4 (education and training) exemptions are allowed, as are ch.5 (recreational benefits) and ch.7 (removal expenses). But the exemptions in ch.8 (special kinds of employees) and ch.11 (miscellaneous exemptions) are included on a selected basis only. In part, this selection excludes exemptions related to foreign elements, and to living accommodation (the benefit of which is excluded from the calculation of income), and so reflects the broader policy of the definition of relevant income. But there is no substitute in this Part of the Act for a detailed comparison of individual provisions.

There are only three exemptions mentioned in reg.4 without express reference to ITEPA provisions. In the Table, Item 3 (forces' leave) is defined broadly rather than in terms of s.296 of ITEPA, which is to the same effect. Item 4 (parking) is also broader than the equivalent s.237. Likewise, item 15 (cash vouchers, etc.) is broader than ss.266–267.

By comparison, the deductions rules incorporated in para.(5) by section number follow closely the equivalent rules in Pt 5 of ITEPA, with only minor omissions. The differences are restricted largely to foreign issues or irrelevant categories of deduction, such as those related to (non-included) living accommodation.

TCTM confirms the Revenue view that most of the provisions in this regulation "mirror" or "are identical with" the equivalent ITEPA provisions. The guidance is to apply the same considerations for tax credits calculations in those cases as for income tax on employment income (and there are specific cross-references to the Inspectors Manual on Sch.E—to become employment income). It may in general be thought that the tax credits appeal authorities and tax appeal authorities would also strive to a common approach, as it may be predicted that that is the approach that superior courts would take if asked to consider the same rules in the different contexts.

Whose income is it?

This is rarely in issue in a tax credits context. One of the few practical problems arises where income is shared between husband and wife, but the joint claimant rules render that irrelevant here. The identity of the income tax payer, applying here also, is set out in ITEPA, s.13. The taxable person, and therefore the person whose income it is for tax credits purposes, is the person to whose employment the earnings relate. **2.154**

When is the income brought into calculation?

The employment income to be calculated for tax credits is the income "received by the claimant . . . in" or "paid to" the claimant in the tax year in question: para.(1). That tax year will either be the current year or the previous year, as determined under s.7(3) of the TCA 2002. The income for a tax year is therefore the income, in that sense, of the year. This is consistent with the general income tax rules for assessment on a current year basis. ITEPA, s.19 provides for taxation to be based on the "net taxable earnings from an employment in the year". It is calculated when received, not when earned. That is a question of fact. This may be important for bonuses and other non-regular payments. In practice, that is also how the PAYE system operates. **2.155**

One problem that the regulation does not expressly address is the calculation of the income for a previous year. ITEPA only applies directly to the tax years from 2003 to 2004. But the previous year for employment income purposes in 2003–04 is the tax year 2001–02 when, of course, ITEPA was not enacted. This is a point that the drafter appears to have overlooked when replacing references to the Taxes Act and subsequent Acts by ITEPA in the Amendment Regulations. While it is only a transitional provision, it is difficult to see how an ordinary reading of the language can conclude that something is taxed, or exempted, by virtue of a section or paragraph that was not enacted at the relevant time. On a very strict reading, that means that employment income would appear to be outside the scope of tax credit calculations for 2001–02. That is obviously not the intention, and the proper intention can be found in the original, unamended version of reg.4. In practice, there will in most cases be little difference between the two versions, but there may be some cases where there is a relevant difference.

CHAPTER 3

Pension income

Pension income

2.156 **5.**—[[1](1) In these Regulations, except where the context otherwise require, "pension income" means—

(a) any pension to which section 577 or 629 of ITEPA applies;
(b) any pension to which section 569 of ITEPA applies;
(c) any voluntary annual payment to which section 633 of ITEPA applies;
(d) any pension or annuity to which section 580 of ITEPA applies;
(e) any unauthorised personal pension payment to which section 601 of ITEPA applies;
(f) any periodical payment to which section 619 of ITEPA applies;
(g) any annuity paid from a fund to which section 590 of ITEPA applies;
(h) any unauthorised payment from a retirement benefits scheme to which section 583 ITEPA applies;
(i) any annuity to which section 595 of ITEPA applies;
(j) any income withdrawal to which section 598 of ITEPA applies;
(k) any annuity to which section 605 of ITEPA applies;
(l) any annuity to which section 609, 610 or 611 of ITEPA applies; and
(m) any payment to which section 623 of ITEPA applies.]

(2) In calculating the amount of a person's pension income there shall be disregarded any [[1]payment or benefit mentioned] in Column 1 of Table 2 to the extent specified in the corresponding entry in Column 2.

Table 2. [[1]Pensions, other payments and benefits] disregarded in the calculation of pension income

2.157

1. Payment	*2. Extent of disregard*
1. A wounds pension or disability pension to which [[1]section 641 of ITEPA] applies.	So much of the payment as is disregarded by virtue of [[1]section 641 of ITEPA].
2. An annuity or additional pension payable to a holder of the Victoria Cross, George Cross or any other decoration mentioned in [[1]section 638 of ITEPA].	The whole of the annuity or additional pension and, if both are payable, the whole of both such annuity and additional pension.

1. Payment	*2. Extent of disregard*
3. A pension or allowance to which [[1]section 639 of ITEPA] applies.	[[1]The amount of the pension or allowance.]
4. A pension or allowance by reason of payment of which a pension or allowance specified in [[1]section 639 of ITEPA] is withheld or abated.	[[1]The amount treated as falling within section 639 of ITEPA by virtue of section 640(2) of that Act.]
5. In the case of a claimant in receipt of a pension under the Service Pensions Order, any increase in the rate of that pension in respect of a dependant who is not a member of the claimant's family.	The amount of the increase.
6. A mobility supplement, or a payment in respect of attendance, paid in conjunction with a war pension.	The amount of the supplement or payment.
7. Any supplementary pension under Article 29(1A) of the Service Pensions Order.	The amount of the supplementary pension.
8. A pension awarded at the supplementary rate under article 27(3) of the Personal Injuries (Civilians) Scheme 1983.	The amount for the time being specified in paragraph 1(c) of Schedule 4 to the Scheme.
9. A pension awarded on retirement through disability caused by injury on duty or by a work-related illness.	[[1]The exempt amount of the pension calculated in accordance with section 644(3) of ITEPA.]
[[1]**10.** A lump sum on which no liability to income tax arises by virtue of section 637 of ITEPA.	The amount of the lump sum.
11. Coal or smokeless fuel provided as mentioned in section 646(1) of ITEPA, or an allowance in lieu of such provision.	The amount on which no liability to income tax arises by virtue of that section.]

[[1](3) From the amount of pension income, calculated in accordance with the preceding provisions of this regulation, there shall be deducted any amount deductible for income tax purposes in computing pension income (as defined in ITEPA) under section 713 of that Act.]

AMENDMENTS

1. Tax Credits (Definition and Calculation of Income) (Amendment) Regulations 2003 (SI 2003/732), reg.7 (April 6, 2003).

CROSS-REFERENCES

The regulation adopts for tax credits purposes the following chapters of, or sections in, Pt 9 of ITEPA (Pension income):

Chapter 3,	United Kingdom pensions: general rules
s.569	United Kingdom pensions
Chapter 5,	United Kingdom social security pensions
s.577	United Kingdom social security pensions
Chapter 6,	Approved retirement benefits schemes
s.580	Pensions and annuities
s.583	unauthorised payments
Chapter 7,	Former approves superannuation schemes
s.590	Annuities
Chapter 8,	Approved personal pension schemes
s.595	Annuities
s.598	Income withdrawals
s.601	Unauthorised personal pension payments
Chapter 9,	Retirement annuity contracts
s.605	Annuities
Chapter 10,	Other employment-related annuities
s.609	Annuities for the benefit of dependants
s.610	Annuities under sponsored superannuation schemes
s.611	Annuities in recognition of another's services
Chapter 12,	House of Commons Members' Fund
s.619	The House of Commons Members' Fund
Chapter 13,	Return of Surplus employee additional voluntary contributions
s.623	Return of surplus employee additional voluntary contributions
Chapter 14,	Pre-1973 pensions paid under the Overseas Pensions Act 1973
s.629	Pre-1973 pensions paid under the Overseas Pensions Act 1973
Chapter 15,	Voluntary annual payments
s.633	Voluntary annual payments
Chapter 16,	Exemption for certain lump sums
s.637	Exemption for lump sums provided under certain pension schemes
Chapter 17,	Exemptions: any taxpayer s.638 Awards for bravery
s.639	Pensions in respect of death due to military or war service
s.640	Exemption under
s.639	where income withheld
s.641	Wounds and disability pensions
s.644	Pensions payable where employment ceased due to disablement
s.646	Former miners etc: coal and allowances in lieu of coal

The following section in Pt 12 (Payroll giving) is also included:
s.713 (donations to charity: payroll deduction scheme)

GENERAL NOTE

2.158 This regulation defines "pension income" for the purposes of reg.3. "Pension income" is a new concept evolved by the Tax Law Rewrite Project and launched in ITEPA. Previously, taxation of pensions has mainly been as if pensions were emoluments, and therefore subject to Sch.E, with other rules bringing certain kinds of pension into various cases of Sch.D. The pension income provisions in ITEPA bring together most of the various charges to tax on different kinds of pensions, including some pensions payable to the former self-employed, and also pensions payable without reference to work of any kind. It also includes social security provisions by way of pension.

What income is relevant?

ITEPA, Pt 9 (pension income) is a comprehensive code on the taxation of most forms of United Kingdom and foreign pensions, whether public or private. Regulation 5 adopts that code in so far as it relates to both public and private pensions in the United Kingdom, but not the foreign pensions. The codification of pensions income taxation by ITEPA happened after the first draft of these regulations, with the unfortunate result that reg.5 does not follow the pattern or numerical order of the code. But it applies directly all the relevant provisions in Pt 9, without the selectivity found in reg.4. **2.159**

The pattern of ITEPA, Pt 9, as adopted in this regulation, is as follows. Chapter 1 (structure of part) and ch.2 (tax on pension income) set out the general income tax rules. The succeeding chapters deal with specific forms of pension provision. Of these, the following apply directly to the calculation of tax credits: Chapter 3 General rules (and definition of "pension")

Chapter 5	United Kingdom social security pensions
Chapter 6	Approved retirement benefit schemes
Chapter 7	Former approved retirement benefit schemes
Chapter 8	Approved personal pension schemes
Chapter 9	Retirement annuity contracts
Chapter 10	Other employment-related annuities
Chapter 12	House of Commons members fund
Chapter 13	Return of surplus additional voluntary contributions
Chapter 14	Pre-1973 pensions paid under the Overseas pensions Act 1973
Chapter 15	Voluntary annual payments

The following are not applied for tax credits:

Chapter 4	Foreign pensions: general rules
Chapter 11	Certain overseas government pensions paid in the United Kingdom.

TCTM04200 and following deal with pension income. It emphasises that, to the extent set out above, the intention is that the tax credits rules mirror the income tax provisions. It emphasises that pensions paid under the SSCBA 1992 are pension income and not social security income.

What exemptions and deductions apply?

Again, the pattern is to adopt all relevant provisions in ITEPA, Pt 9. Of the three chapters dealing with exemptions, ch.16 (exemption for certain lump sums) applies fully. Chapter 17 (exemptions: any taxpayer) applies in large part. The sections not applied relate for the most part to foreign pensions, and are dealt with under the foreign income provision in reg.12. This also applies to ch.18 (exemptions: non-United Kingdom resident taxpayers). The only other section not applied is ITEPA, s.645 (social security pensions: increases for children), which does not apply by reason of the repeal of those provisions and their replacement by child tax credit by TCA 2002 (save for the oversight of the rare payments under s.85 of the SSCBA 1992 not being repealed by the Act). **2.160**

Whose income is it?

ITEPA, s.572 provides that the person liable for any tax charged is the person receiving or entitled to the pension. This is therefore the operative rule for inclusion of pension income for the calculation of tax credits income. It is the alternative to deal with those who are not entitled to a pension being received (as with voluntary pensions), but will rarely present problems. There is no significance for tax credits purposes in most cases about pensions to couples. If it **2.161** is significant then, of course, entitlement is a question of law and receipt a question of fact.

When is the income brought into the calculation?

2.162 This also follows from s.572. As a result, pension income is to be included when entitlement arises. If there is no entitlement, as with voluntary pensions, then it is when the pension is received. That should follow the income tax treatment.

CHAPTER 4

Trading income

Trading income

2.163 **6.** The claimant's trading income is—

(a) the amount of his taxable profits for the tax year from—
  (i) any trade carried on in the United Kingdom or elsewhere;
  (ii) any profession or vocation the income from which does not fall under any other provisions of these Regulations; or

(b) if the claimant is a partner in the trade, profession or vocation, his taxable profit for the year arising from his share of the partnership's trading or professional income.

Here, "taxable profits" has the same meaning as it has for Cases I, II and V of Schedule D but disregarding sections 95A and 96 of the Taxes Act (averaging of fluctuating profits: rules for creative artists, farmers and market gardeners).

CROSS-REFERENCES

Taxes Act, s.95A	Creative artists: relief for fluctuating profits
s.96	Farming and market gardening: relief for fluctuating profits

GENERAL NOTE

2.164 This regulation defines "trading income" for the purposes of reg.3. "Trading income" is the Tax Law Rewrite Project's title for income chargeable to tax under both Cases I and II of Sch.D of the income tax (Taxes Act, s.18). Case I imposes tax on "trade", and Case II on "professions and vocations" not taxed elsewhere in the Taxes Act. Regulation 6 adopts these charging provisions without the formal title by repeating the key words from the definitions of the scope of Cases I and II in s.18 of the Taxes Act. In contrast to regs 4 and 5, the rest of reg.6 is very compact, but its effect is to apply most of the income tax rules and practices relevant to assessment of the self-employed.

Employment and self-employment

2.165 The critical distinction in the case of many of those with smaller incomes who claim to be traders or self-employed is whether that is a true description in both law and fact of the individual's status. This is directly relevant for the calculation of tax credits because it must be decided if reg.4 or 6 applies. Following from that decision are subsidiary questions about the exemptions and deductions that must be calculated in finding the net income; the question of which period of income is to be taken into account; and the provision in Step 4 of reg.3 allowing trading losses to be deducted from other income. The rules assume that there cannot be a net loss by way of employment income, and do not allow for it. But this is an important overall change in the tax credit rules because previously no income losses were allowed.

The status of employee or self-employed is important for several reasons besides the current context:

Income tax: employment income or trading income?
NI contributions: Class 1 or Class 2 contributions?
VAT: is the person carrying on registerable activities?
Benefits: is the individual entitled to benefits available only to employees?

In addition, there are other issues that arise from the employment status, such as the minimum wage, holiday entitlements, and employer liability, that are again to be decided separately.

Drawing a line between employment and self-employment has always been difficult. It is also wide open to abuse, for example to reduce NI contributions but to increase benefit entitlement. This has led to people claiming to be an employee for some purposes and self-employed for others, and to different government agencies in the past adopting different answers to an individual's status in different contexts.

One result has been a series of initiatives to concentrate the decision-making on this issue so as to avoid inconsistent official decisions. Another is a series of legislative initiatives to define more clearly where the borderline is and to deal with abusive situations.

As a result of various initiatives, the Inland Revenue are now the effective deciders, subject to appeal, of employment status. The Social Security (Transfer of Functions, etc.) Act 1999 transferred NI contribution administration to the Inland Revenue. In addition, s.8 of that Act transferred to the Inland Revenue the decision whether someone is employed or self-employed for most social security benefit purposes. Appeals from a Revenue decision under s.8, about contributions, and about income tax liability, all go to the tax appeal commissioners. In the case of the s.8 decisions, most of these were previously dealt with on appeal by social security appeal tribunals, so this was a transfer of appeal jurisdiction. The Inland Revenue has also inherited responsibility for the national minimum wage legislation.

Any need to decide between reg.4 and 6 now goes on appeal (back) to the appeal tribunals. This may arise in a more subtle way than directly in connection with identification of income. This is because of the methods of payment of working tax credit. If an individual is an employee, then it is for the employer in most cases to pay the WTC. See the Working Tax Credit Payment by Employer's 2002 (SI 2002/2172) Regulations. The self-employed are paid directly by the Board. There is also another issue behind this, also of concern to the Inland Revenue and to the practical application of working tax credit. Employees are entitled and required to be paid by their employers at the level of the national minimum wage. The safety-net earnings rules for working tax credit are designed to act as a backup to the national minimum wage for employees. But there is no national minimum earnings level for the self-employed. This is entirely for the individual and the market place. The finding that someone is self-employed therefore means that no employer has a duty to pay working tax credit, and also that the individual's earnings cannot be assumed to be at the national minimum wage level. Indeed, they may be negative. As noted, that is of a further concern to the Inland Revenue because it is the duty of the Inland Revenue to enforce the national minimum wage legislation.

There are several provisions that now provide that someone is, or is to be treated as, an employee rather than self-employed. Two of these deserve emphasis.

The first is the category of workers who in practical terms are somewhere between the two main groups—agency workers. ITEPA, Pt 1, ch.7 deals with agency workers. Section 44 provides that in most such cases the worker is regarded as the employee of the agency even if that is not the formal status adopted. The second concerns ch.8 of that Part, which codifies the controversial "IR35" rules for what are sometimes known as "pocket book companies". These rules provide that in stated situations an individual who is under an obligation to provide services to a third party via an intermediary in circumstances where the worker is not paid as an employee by the intermediary can be treated as being an employee of the intermediary with a deemed employment income from that intermediary. This is used, for example, where someone works for a genuine third party, but where the contractual relationship with the third party is, typically, through a company of which the individual is the only shareholder. The company then pays the individual in some indirect way—benefits, loans, dividends—which the individual claims (if asked) to be either not income at all or not employment income.

What income is relevant? What exemptions and deductions apply?

2.166 "Trade" is defined in the Taxes Act, s.832 as "every trade, manufacture, adventure or concern in the nature of trade". There is considerable case law on this meaning, of which reference might be made in the marginal case to the decisions of the House of Lords in *Ransom v Higgs* [1974] 1 W.L.R. 1594 and *Ensign Tankers v Stokes* [1992] 1 A.C. 655. In *Ransom*, the House of Lords made clear the wide factual scope of "trade", in the light of the extending definition. The fact, for example, that no particular name could be given to the activity did not stop it being a trading activity if it was an economic or commercial activity aimed at generating profit (even if it did not do so). The converse of this is that activities that appear to be commercial but are not aimed at making a profit may be regarded in some cases as tax avoidance manoeuvres and not as trading (*Ensign Tankers*). Reference in marginal cases is usually made to the so-called "badges of trade". The badges were first identified by the Royal Commission on the Taxation of Income in 1952 as:

(a) the subject-matter of the sale or realisation;
(b) the length of the period of ownership of assets realised;
(c) the frequency or number of similar transactions by that person;
(d) whether there was supplementary work on or in connection with the assets realised or the realisation;
(e) the reasons for the realisation of the assets;
(f) motive.

Two other points should be emphasised. First, there is a need to distinguish activities generating capital from those generating income. For the calculation of tax credits income, all activities generating capital should be ignored. (This introduces into the tax credits context a much fought-over income tax borderline removed in part for income tax purposes by the introduction of capital gains tax.) Secondly, and seemingly by contrast to the first, a "one off" activity generating profit may be a trading activity. The statutory definition indicates that a single activity may be caught as an "adventure" or a "concern in the nature of trade". From these follow a third point: a payment is either a trading payment or it is capital. There is no middle ground. If a receipt is not a trading receipt, it cannot be brought into charge to income tax (and it is therefore suggested to tax credits either) under other income charging provisions. See *Jones v Leeming* [1930] A.C. 415.

"Profession" is not defined by statute, and has been taken by the courts to cover activities consisting of, or involving significant levels of, intellectual skill. An example is the profession of author: *Wain v Cameron* [1995] S.T.C. 555. "Vocation" has been defined as "the way in which a man passes his life": *Partridge v Mallandine* (1886) 18 Q.B.D. 276. These are both seen as continuing activities. Single payments of the nature of a profession or vocation are to be regarded as income within reg.18.

As reg.6 reflects, the charge to income tax on the self-employed is based on the accounts of the business. Increasingly, both the legislative provision for, and the Inland Revenue practice relating to, the taxation of commercial activity is accounts-based. The concern in calculating income for tax credits is therefore with the claimant's business accounts for any trade. This is to be calculated in accordance with the rules for Cases I and II of Sch.D, set out in ss.74–99 of the Taxes Act.

In practice, in the simplest cases, the accounts will be "three-liners". The Inland Revenue will accept these for income tax purposes and presumably also for tax credits purposes. The three lines are:

(a) income;
(b) deductions (including capital allowances if any);
(c) net income.

It is assumed that the net income is the difference between the other two! Three-line accounts in this form are accepted where the gross income (turnover) of the trading activity is less than £15,000 a year. If turnover is over that limit, then full accounts itemising income and expenditure will need to be provided, or at least the individual will have to provide all the details required in the standard self-employment pages to the self-assessment form for income tax. In the more complex cases, there should be two sets of accounts: the ordinary working accounts produced for the business (be it company, partnership or individual) and the tax computations or adjustments necessary to change the accounts from the approach adopted for the business to the approach necessary for income tax purposes. For example, the standard item "depreciation" on capital assets held for the business must be removed and replaced by a claim for any specific capital allowances to which the taxpayer is entitled. A second and further set of such computations may be necessary for tax credits purposes—or at least points may need following up. It is common for a business run by a husband to make a payment to an otherwise-non-earning wife. That is a deduction for trading purposes, but must be added back in for the joint claim they should be making for tax credits purposes as earnings of the wife. The business may be paying rent for the accommodation to the owners of the premises used. If that is the jointly owned (or owned in common) home of the joint claimants, again the rental income needs to go back into the tax credits calculation as property income.

This is the primary territory of the financially qualified panel members of appeal tribunals. In less formal English, they are accountants. It is for the President of the Appeals Service, acting normally through regional judicial officers, to decide if a case involves an issue of complexity about accounts justifying the appointment of an accountant to the tribunal membership. Where the task of the tribunal is to pick its way through accounts provided by accountants—as it will be in the more complex issues about trading income—then the presence on the tribunal of an accountant will obviously give it directly relevant expertise. As questions of accounts, and accounts practice, are primarily questions of fact, not of law, an expert appeal tribunal will not only have the first say on these issues, but usually also the final say! This is the clear approach taken by the courts in considering equivalent appeals from the Special and General Commissioners of Income Tax. For that reason, further explanation of the taxation of the self-employed is regarded as beyond the scope of this work.

The other reason why business tax accounts are normally a matter of accounting expertise is that since 1998 it is required that:

> For the purposes of Case I or II of Schedule D the profits of a trade, profession or vocation must be computed in accordance with generally accepted

accounting practice, subject to any adjustment required or authorised by law in computing profits for those purposes: FA 1998, s42(1).

In addition, since 2000, all accounts for the purposes of taxing income from a profession must be on an earnings basis and not a cash basis. Most trades have accounts on a similar basis. This involves bringing in income as it is earned, rather than received, and accounting for stock in trade, work in progress, and the present value of future liabilities. Further, the general accounting practices adopted for these issues must be applied consistently from year to year or adjustments made in the year of change to reflect any change to the profit levels because of any change in the accounting method.

Whose income is it?

2.167 It is the income of the individual or partner running the business. The tax credits rules are silent as to partners' shares, so it will be the same share of the trading income as for income tax. That is based on the proposition that for English law purposes (but not Scottish law) a partnership is not a separate entity, so the trading income of the partnership is directly the trading income of the partners, divided as they decide or, by default, under the general rules of the Partnership Act 1890.

When is the income to be brought into the calculation?

2.168 The standard rule for determining the income tax on trading profits is that the tax payable in any one tax year is based on the "full amount of the profits of the year of assessment". But where there is a "basis period" for the trade, that basis period is used: Taxes Act, s.60. The "basis period" is, for an ongoing business, the accounts year of the business. It is defined as the period of 12 months immediately following the basis period for the previous tax year. That is designed to prevent gaps or overlaps occurring between tax years and the actual accounts of the business. There are detailed rules dealing with the opening period of a business, the closing period, and also any changes in accounting period, or "overlap periods". These are in the Taxes Act, ss.60–63A.

The other point to be watched is that this kind of income covers all trading income, while the claimant's business activities may consist of two or more separate trades. Whether someone is conducting one trade or two is a question of fact, save where special rules apply. The main special rule is the Taxes Act s.53, under which "all farming and market gardening in the United Kingdom shall be treated as the carrying on of a trade or, as the case may be, a part of a trade". However, the other special rule applying to the income taxation of farming— the provision allowing profits and losses to be averaged over several years in the Taxes Act, s.95—does not apply. Subject to that, the accounts of each business must be brought into the calculation separately to produce an overall trading income.

The trading income of an individual for any year, and for each business if more than one, is therefore the trading income of the accounting year ending in either the current year or the previous year (depending on the application of s.7(3) of the Act). For example, if a business produces annual accounts for the calendar year, then the accounts year relevant for income tax in 2003–04 is the accounts for the calendar year 2003. The income tax year 2003–04 runs from April 6, 2003 to April 5, 2004. So the accounts year ending in that year is the accounts year ending on December 31, 2003. For tax credit calculation purposes, the *current year income* is therefore the income for the year from January 1, 2003 to December 1, 2003. In 2003–04, the previous year income is (exceptionally) the income for 2001–02. The accounts year for that year is the calendar year 2001. It is for the business itself to choose its accounting year. So a small business may, to maximise delay between accounting period and taxation, adopt a year starting on May 1. The effect of the rule is to base the tax credits calculation for 2003–04 in this example on either the profits of the accounts year ending April 30, 2003 (current year) or April 30, 2001 (previous year).

There are special rules for the opening and closing years of a business: Taxes Act ss.61 and 63. These will apply for tax credits purposes also.

CHAPTER 5

Social security income

Social security income

7.—(1) The claimant's social security income is the total amount payable— 2.169

(a) under any provision of the Social Security Act 1988, the Contributions and Benefits Act or the Jobseekers Act 1995 or under section 69 of the Child Support, Pensions and Social Security Act 2000;

(b) [1. . .];

(c) by the Secretary of State in respect of the non-payment of a payment which ought to have been made under a provision mentioned in sub-paragraph (a); and

(d) by way of an ex-gratia payment made by the Secretary of State, or in Northern Ireland by the Department for Social Development, in connection with a benefit, pension or allowance under the Contributions and Benefits Act.

This is subject to the following provisions of this regulation.

(2) Pensions under the Contributions and Benefits Act which are pension income by virtue of regulation 5(1)(a) are not social security income.

(3) In calculating the claimant's social security income the payments in Table 3 shall be disregarded.

Table 3. Payments under, or in connection with, the Act, the Social Security Act 1988, the Contributions and Benefits Act or the Jobseekers Act 1995 disregarded in calculation of social security income

1. An attendance allowance under section 64 of the Contributions and Benefits Act.	2.170
2. A back to work bonus under section 26 of the Jobseekers Act 1995.	
3. A bereavement payment under section 36 of the Contributions and Benefits Act.	

4. Child benefit under Part II of the Act.
5. A Christmas bonus under section 148 of the Contributions and Benefits Act.
6. Council tax benefit under section 131 of the Contributions and Benefits Act.
7. A disability living allowance under section 71 of the Contributions and Benefits Act.
8. Disabled person's tax credit under section 129 of the Contributions and Benefits Act.
9. Any discretionary housing payment pursuant to regulation 2(1) of the Discretionary Financial Assistance Regulations 2001.
10. An ex-gratia payment by the Secretary of State or, in Northern Ireland, the Department for Social Development, to a person over pensionable age by way of supplement to incapacity benefit.
11. A guardian's allowance under section 77 of the Contributions and Benefits Act.
12. Housing benefit under section 130 of the Contributions and Benefits Act.
13. Income support under section 124 of the Contributions and Benefits Act, unless it is chargeable to tax under [[1]section 665 of ITEPA.].
14. Incapacity benefit which is— (a) short term incapacity benefit payable at the lower rate; or (b) payable to a person who had received invalidity benefit before 13th April 1995 if the period of incapacity for work is treated, by virtue of regulation 2 of the Social Security (Incapacity Benefit) (Transitional) Regulations 1995 (days to be treated as days of incapacity for work) as having begun before that date.
15. Industrial injuries benefit [[1](except industrial death benefit)] under section 94 of the Contributions and Benefits Act.
16. A contribution-based jobseeker's allowance under the Jobseekers Act 1995, to the extent that it exceeds the maximum contained in [[1]section 674 of ITEPA.].
17. An income-based jobseeker's allowance under the Jobseekers Act 1995.
18. A maternity allowance under section 35 of the Contributions and Benefits Act.

19. A severe disablement allowance under section 68 or 69 of the Contributions and Benefits Act
20. A social fund payment under Part VIII of the Contributions and Benefits Act.
[1**20A.** Statutory adoption pay under Part XIIZB of the Contributions and Benefits Act.
21A. Statutory paternity pay under Part XIIZA of the Contributions and Benefits Act.]
21. Statutory maternity pay under Part XII of the Contributions and Benefits Act.
22. Statutory sick pay under Part IX of the Contributions and Benefits Act.
23. Working families' tax credit under section 128 of the Contributions and Benefits Act.
24. A payment by way of compensation for the non-payment of, or in respect of loss of entitlement (whether wholly or partly) of, income support, jobseeker's allowance, [2 or housing benefit].
25. A payment in lieu of milk tokens or the supply of vitamins under the Welfare Foods Regulations 1996.

(4) If an increase in respect of a child dependant is payable with an allowance, benefit, pension or other payment ("the main payment") listed in Table 3, the increase shall also be wholly disregarded in calculating the income of the recipient of the main payment.

(5) [1. . .]

[1(5A) From the amount of social security income, calculated in accordance with the preceding provisions of this regulation, there shall be deducted any amount deductible for income tax purposes in computing social security income (as defined in ITEPA) under section 713 of ITEPA.]

(6) A reference in this regulation to an enactment applying only in Great Britain includes a reference to a corresponding enactment applying in Northern Ireland.

AMENDMENTS

1. Tax Credits (Definition and Calculation of Income) (Amendment) Regulations 2003 (SI 2003/732), reg.8 (April 6, 2003).
2. Tax Credits (Miscellaneous Amendments No.2) Regulations 2003 (SI 2003/2815), reg.6 (November 26, 2003).

CROSS-REFERENCE

ITEPA, s.713	Donations to charity: payroll giving scheme

General Note

2.171 This regulation defines "social security income" for the purposes of reg.3. "Social security income" is another creation of the Tax Law Rewrite Project. Like pension income, it has been taken out from under the general Sch.E charge, and now forms a separate code in Part X of ITEPA (ss.655–681). But, unlike the employment income and pensions income regulations, this regulation adopts the approach of parallel legislation to Pt X of ITEPA rather than adopting ITEPA provisions themselves. Nonetheless, the relevant ITEPA provisions are included in this volume both for cross-reference and for more general reference in handling social security benefits.

Part 10 of ITEPA is in the following pattern. Chapter 1 sets out the structure of the Part. Ch.2 deals with general points on tax on social security income, including a definition of the terms used. Ch.3 lists the taxable United Kingdom social security benefits. This is in the form of Table A to s.660. Chapter 4 lists exemptions from the ch.3 charge to specific benefits. Chapter 5 lists benefits wholly exempt from tax, in the form of Table B to s.677. Chapter 6 lists taxable foreign benefits, and ch.7 lists exemptions from the benefits brought in under ch.6. Of those chapters, chs 6 and 7 are irrelevant to the head of the tax credits income calculation as it is limited to United Kingdom benefits only.

What income is relevant?

2.172 As just noted, reg.7 is expressly limited to benefits to which a claimant is entitled under United Kingdom legislation only. Foreign social security benefits are to be included under foreign income. There are two other limitations on social security income. The first, deriving from a parallel with ITEPA, is that state retirement benefits are treated as pension income not as social security income. The second, not deriving from that source, is the treatment of the statutory payments (sick, maternity, adoption, paternal) as employment income. ITEPA treats these as social security income (although this is a default rule— if they are taxed as employment income then they are excluded here: ITEPA s.660(2)).

With those exclusions, the other benefits that are taxable under Table A in ITEPA, and also relevant for calculating tax credit income, are:

Widowed mother's/parent's allowance
Carer's allowance
Incapacity benefit (some)
Income support (some)
Jobseeker's allowance (some)

In each case there are provisions about how much of the income is taxed. In practice, much of that tax is collected under the PAYE scheme.

What exclusions and deductions apply?

2.173 The list in Table 3 parallels the list in Table B to s.677 of ITEPA (payments wholly exempt), along with the provisions, in particular, for jobseeker's allowance and incapacity benefit, save for the statutory payments (noted above) and the treatment of present and past tax credits. CTC and WTC are not taxable. The list is very extensive, and it leaves relevant to tax credits only the short list of benefits noted in the previous paragraph.

There is no specific provision in the regulations dealing with overpayments of benefit. In practice, this may not be a major problem because of the limited extent to which account is taken of benefits. But the position might arise where, say, a widowed parent's allowance was overpaid (perhaps because of the living together rule) so that income previously paid was required to be repaid. For income tax purposes, late account can be taken of this for up to five years after the event. For tax credits purposes, the reduction in income for the relevant period will be relevant only in so far as there can be a recalculation of the income for tax credits, and there is a timely claim made. As the main time-limit is three months, there will only be a limited extent to which such adjustments can be requested, even with the benefit of a rapid notification of the change of circumstances. The two benefits administered by the Revenue, child benefit and guardian's allowance, are exempt in any event.

Social security beneficiaries may also set charitable giving against their income.

Whose income is it?

The regulation is silent on this point, which therefore falls to be decided by reference to the social security rules. ITEPA, s.662 imposes the income tax on the person receiving or entitled to the benefit, so covering appointees as well as claimants. 2.174

When is the income brought into the calculation?

The calculation is based on the amount actually received in the year, regardless of the period for which it is received. 2.175

Chapter 6

Student income

[1 Student Income

8. "Student income" means, in relation to a student— 2.176

(a) in England and Wales, any grant—
  (i) under regulation 15 of the Education (Student Support) Regulations 2002 other than a grant under paragraph (1)(c) or (8) of that regulation or
  (ii) under regulation 15 of the Education (Student Support) (No.2) Regulations 2002 other than a grant for Parents Learning Allowance as defined in regulation 15(7) of those Regulations;

(b) in Scotland, any dependant's grant payable under regulation 4(1)(c) of the Students' Allowances (Scotland) Regulations 1999; and

(c) in Northern Ireland, any grant which corresponds to income treated as student income in England and Wales by virtue of paragraph (a).]

Amendment

1. Tax Credits (Miscellaneous Amendments No.2) Regulations 2003 (SI 2003/2815), reg.7 (November 26, 2003).

General Note

This regulation defines "student income" for the purposes of reg.3. "Student income" is not a head of taxation under the Taxes Act or under the scheme used 2.177

by the Tax Law Rewrite Project. Instead, this is taken from social security law. It must be read with the exemptions in regs 9 and 19, and the general principles of income tax.

The effect of the narrow point in reg.8 with the various exemptions is to exclude most forms of income that students receive (other than earnings). While part of an educational support grant is included (so going towards excluding the claimant from WTC), s.331 of the Taxes Act exempts all scholarship income if it meets the conditions in the section. Section 331A exempts any interest on the reimbursement of student loan repayments. (It may be remembered that the Inland Revenue also collects repayments of student loans under the national scheme.)

Two other sources of student "income", in the widest sense, are or may be exempt from inclusion under general principles: loans and gifts. The extent to which this is so illustrates the difference between the means-tested benefits approach to assessing a claimant's income, and the rules for calculating tax credits income.

The question of the status of loans was discussed by the Court of Appeal at some length in *Morrell v Secretary of State for Work and Pensions* [2003] E.W.C.A. Civ.526. A claimant for income support had been receiving regular monthly sums from her mother by way of loan. Some of the money was paid by the mother to the claimant's landlord. The question was whether the sums were income for the purposes of income support. The Court of Appeal followed the recent decision of that Court in *Leeves v Chief Adjudication Officer* [1999] 1 All E.R. 90. In that case the question was whether a student grant was to be treated as income for income support purposes. Potter L.J. adopted the submission for the claimant that "income" should be given its ordinary and natural meaning, and that money accruing in respect of which there was an obligation of immediate and equivalent repayment was not income. On the facts, the student grant for maintenance was income but immediately repayable debts were not. The grant was income until the demand for repayment was made, when it ceased to be income.

But a further question arises for tax credits purposes. The payments must not only have the quality of income, but must fall under one of the kinds of income being taken into account. The definition of "student income" in reg.8 does not cover these loans, nor gifts, even if they are recurring. The question is whether such loans or gifts are income within any of the other kinds of income in the regulations. We shall return to that at para.2.207.

Further sources of income linked to education and training are exempt under the specific provisions listed in Table 6 of reg.19—items 4, 5, 6 and 7 are all relevant.

Payments of income in connection with students to be disregarded for the purposes of regulation 3

2.178 **9.** Income which is exempt from income tax by virtue of section 331 or 331A of the Taxes Act (which deal respectively with scholarship income and interest on the repayment of sums recovered by way of deductions in respect of student loans) is disregarded in calculating a claimant's income under regulation 3.

CROSS-REFERENCES

Taxes Act, s.331	Scholarship income
s.331A	Student loans: certain interest to be disregarded

GENERAL NOTE

2.179 This regulation is an exempting regulation only. See note to reg.8.

CHAPTER 7

Investment income

Investment income

10.—(1) In these Regulations, "investment income" means the gross amount of— **2.180**

(a) any interest of money whether yearly or otherwise, or any annuity or other annual payment, whether such payment is payable within or out of the United Kingdom, either as a charge on any property of the person paying it by virtue of any deed or will or otherwise, or as a reservation out of it, or as a personal debt or obligation by virtue of any contract, or whether the payment is received and payable half-yearly or at any shorter or longer periods, but not including property income;

(b) any discounts on securities;

(c) any income from securities payable out of the public revenues of the United Kingdom or Northern Ireland;

(d) dividends and other distributions of a company resident in the United Kingdom and any tax credit associated with that payment; and

(e) any amount treated as forming part of the individual's income for the year for income tax purposes by virtue of section 547(1)(a) of the Taxes Act.

This is subject to the following qualification.

(2) In calculating investment income, there shall be disregarded—

(a) any amount listed in column 1 of Table 4 to the extent shown in the corresponding entry in column 2;

(b) any amount listed in column 1 of Table 5 during the period shown in the corresponding entry in column 2;

(c) any income arising from savings certificates, and interest on tax reserve certificates, exempted from tax by section 46 of the Taxes Act (savings certificates and tax reserve certificates);

(d) the first £70 in any tax year of interest on deposits with National Savings and Investments, exempted from income tax by section 325 of the Taxes Act (interest on deposits with National Savings and Investments);

(e) any payment to a claimant which does not form part of his income for the purposes of income tax by virtue of section 347A(1)(b) of the Taxes Act (general rule about annual payments otherwise subject to tax under Case III of Schedule D).

Table 4. Payments disregarded in the calculation of investment income

2.181

1. Description of income to be disregarded	*2. Extent of disregard*
1. Any interest, dividends, distributions, profits or gains in respect of investments under— (a) a Personal Equity Plan; or (b) an Individual Savings Account; in respect of which the claimant is entitled to relief from income tax under section 333 of the Taxes Act, or which is taxed only in accordance with regulation 23 of the Individual Savings Account Regulations 1998.	The whole amount, unless it is interest under a personal equity plan to which regulation 17A(2) of the Personal Equity Plan Regulations 1989 applies. Interest to which that paragraph applies is disregarded only to the extent that it does not exceed the annual limit of £180 mentioned in that regulation.
2. Any interest or bonus payable on an account which is a tax-exempt special savings account for the purposes of section 326A of the Taxes Act.	The whole amount.
3. Any terminal bonus, or interest or other sum, payable under a share option linked scheme which is a certified contractual savings scheme for the purposes of section 326 of the Taxes Act.	The whole amount.
4. Any winnings from betting, including pool betting, or lotteries or games with prizes.	The whole amount.
5. Any interest on a payment of £10,000 made by the Secretary of State to a person who was held prisoner by the Japanese during the Second World War or to the spouse of such a person, if the payment is held in a distinct account and no payment (other than	The whole amount of the interest.

1. Description of income to be disregarded	*2. Extent of disregard*
interest) has been added to the account.	
6. Any interest on a payment made to the claimant by, or on behalf, of a government of country outside the United Kingdom, either from its own resources or with contributions from any other organisation, by way of compensation for a victim of National Socialism if the payment is held in a distinct account and no payment (other than interest) has been added to the account. Here a reference to a victim of National Socialism is a reference to a person who was required to work as a slave or a forced labourer for National Socialists or their sympathisers during the Second World War, or suffered property loss, or suffered injury or is the parent of a child who died, at the hands of National Socialists or their sympathisers during the Second World War.	The whole amount of the interest.
7. Any monies paid to the claimant by a bank or building society as compensation in respect of an unclaimed account held by a Holocaust victim and which vested in the Custodian of Enemy Property under section 7 of the Trading with the Enemy Act 1939 and treated as exempt from income tax by Extra Statutory Concession A100.	The amount treated as exempt by the Extra Statutory Concession.
8. Any interest, or payment in respect of interest, which is disregarded for income tax purposes by virtue of—	The amount so disregarded.

1. Description of income to be disregarded	*2. Extent of disregard*
(a) section 329 of the Taxes Act (interest or damages for personal injuries); or (b) section 329AA of the Taxes Act (personal injury damages in the form of periodical payments).	
[[1]**9**]. Annuity payments under an award of compensation made under the Criminal Injuries Compensation Scheme (within the meaning of s.329AB(2) of the Taxes Act).	The amount of any payment which is treated as not being income of the claimant or his partner by virtue of section 329AA of the Taxes Act.
[[1]**10**]. A payment under a life annuity.	The amount of interest eligible for relief under section 353 of the Taxes Act by virtue of section 365 of that Act.
[[1]**11**]. Any interest, or payment in respect of interest, which is compensation to a person who is under the age of 18 years for the death of one or both of his parents.	The whole of the interest or payment.
12. A purchased life annuity to which section 656 of the Taxes Act applies.	The capital element of the annity as defined and calculated in section 656 of the Taxes Act.

Table 5. Payments in connection with very severe disablement, Creutzfeldt–Jakob disease and haemophilia

2.182

1. Description of income to be disregarded	*2. Applicable period*
1. A trust payment made to— (a) a diagnosed person; (b) the diagnosed person's partner; or (c) the person who was his partner at the date of his death.	The period beginning on the date on which the trust payment is made and ending with the death of the person to whom the payment is made.

1. Description of income to be disregarded	*2. Applicable period*
2. A trust payment made to a parent of a deceased diagnosed person, or a person acting in the place of his parent.	The period beginning on the date on which the trust payment is made and ending two years after that date.
3. The amount of any payment out of the estate of a person to whom a trust payment has been made, which is made to the person who was the diagnosed person's partner at the date of his death.	The period beginning on the date on which the payment is made and ending on the date on which that person dies.
4. The amount of any payment out of the estate of a person to whom a trust payment has been made, which is made to a parent of a deceased diagnosed person, or a person acting in the place of his parent.	The period beginning on the date on which the payment is made and ending two years after that date.

(3) The amounts disregarded under Items 3 and 4 in Table 5 shall not exceed the total amount of any trust payments made to the person to whom the trust payment had been made.

(4) In this regulation, "diagnosed person" means—

(a) a person who has been diagnosed as suffering from, or who after his death has been diagnosed has having suffered from, variant Creutzfeldt–Jakob disease;

(b) a person who is suffering or has suffered from haemophilia; or

(c) a person in respect of whom a payment has been made from the 1992 Fund, the Eileen Trust or the Independent Living Funds; and

a reference to a person being a member of the diagnosed person's household at the date of the diagnosed person's death includes a person who would have been a member of his household but for the diagnosed person being in residential accommodation, a residential care home or a nursing home on that date.

(5) In this regulation—

"relevant trust" means—

(a) a trust established out of funds provided by the Secretary of State in respect of persons who suffered, or who are suffering, from variant Creutzfeldt–Jakob disease for the benefit of persons eligible for payments in accordance with its provisions;

(b) the Macfarlane Trusts; or

(c) the 1992 Fund, the Eileen Trust or the Independent Living Funds.

"residential accommodation", "residential care home" and "nursing home" have the meanings given by regulation 2(1) of the Income Support (General) Regulations 1987; and

"trust payment" means a payment under a relevant trust.

AMENDMENTS

1. Tax Credits (Definition and Calculation of Income) (Amendment) Regulations 2003 (SI 2003 No., 732), reg.9 (April 6, 2003).

2. Tax Credits (Miscellaneous Amendments No.2) Regulations 2003 (SI 2003/2815), reg.8 (November 26, 2003).

CROSS-REFERENCES

Taxes Act,	
s.325	Interest on deposits with National Savings Bank
s.326	Interest, etc., under contractual savings schemes
s.326A	Tax-exempt special savings accounts
s.329	Interest on damages for personal injuries
s.329AA	Personal injuries damages in the form of periodical payments
s.329AB	Compensation for personal injury under statutory or other schemes
s.333	Personal equity plans
s.347A	Annual payments: general rule
s.353	Relief for payments of interest: general provision
s.365	Loan to buy life annuity
s.547	Life policies, life annuities and capital redemption polices: method of charging gain to tax.

GENERAL NOTE

2.183 This regulation defines "investment income" for the purposes of reg.3. It reflects more than any other the fundamental change of approach taken for "new" tax credits compared with WFTC and DPTC and their predecessors. For those purposes, as with income support, there were two kinds of income: earnings, and income other than earnings. That broad brush approach is abandoned under these regulations.

"Investment income" used to mean, for income tax purposes, income other than earned income, reflecting the same broad division as for income support. But here it has a much narrower meaning. It is designed so as to catch, in the same way as income tax, only income from capital, in the broad sense of income from some form of asset. But at the same time it includes the exemptions and deductions that many taxpayers use to reduce their non-earned income.

What income is relevant to the calculation?

2.184 The scope of the charge in reg.10(1) is not expressly based by reference on any particular main provision in the Taxes Act. Instead, it adopts the wording of a number of such provisions. The wording of para.(1)(a), (b) and (c) repeats the key wording from Sch.D, Case III to the Taxes Act, s.18. The wording in para.(1)(d) covers the charge on dividends and other distributions from United Kingdom companies under Sch.F in the Taxes Act, s.20. Only para.(1)(e) makes an explicit provision to the Taxes Act, s.547. This covers the separate charges to income tax under Pt XIII, ch.2 of the Taxes Act (life policies, life annuities and capital redemption policies). However, as we shall see, much of the income potentially caught by these wide words is then removed from the scope of the provision by the various exceptions and exemptions. The regulation is best approached by breaking it down into the forms of income it covers.

Dividends and other distributions

The regulation includes the gross amount (that is, with the value of the associated tax credit) of all dividends and other distributions paid by United Kingdom companies. The term "dividends and other distributions" is defined extensively in ss.20 and 209–211 of the Taxes Act. It covers not only ordinary dividends, but also capital dividends, and other forms of payment out by a company. But it is limited to United Kingdom companies. A dividend or other payment from a foreign company is excluded (as it is from the income tax charge under Sch.F). Instead, foreign source payments are "foreign income" for current purposes. **2.185**

However, if the United Kingdom shares are held through a Personal Equity Plan or Individual Savings Account, then the dividends and distributions are tax-exempt. It should also be noted that shares held in connection with employment, or income from those shares, is not treated as employment income for tax credits purposes, even where it is treated in that way for income tax purposes.

Interest

"Interest" is a payment for the use of money by reference to time: *Bennett v Ogston* (1930) 15 T.C. 374. It is a major source of income for those with smaller savings, but in practice smaller amounts of interest, or interest earned from specialist funds for the disabled, will be excluded from tax credit calculations—at least if the funds are invested in an appropriate way. This is emphasised by the number of exceptions and exemptions in reg.10. These are in addition to the fact that the first £300 of non-earned income is ignored in addition to the specific exemptions. There are major exemptions in para.(1)(c) and (1)(d) for National Savings, plus other exemptions in Table 4, Items 1, 2, 3, 5, 6, 8 and 11. Several of these are investments of choice, or tax shelters, such as TESSAs, ISAs, PEPs and SAYE schemes. **2.186**

Annuities

Although annuities are within the scope of Case III of the Schedule, this is in practice limited in its significance. Retirement annuities are taken into the calculation as pension income, and not as investment income. In addition, the exemptions at Items 9 and 10 of Table 4 are also important. These reflect income tax provisions, but exclude taxation of the income element, and not the element of return of capital, of purchased annuities. **2.187**

Annual payments

The law about the scope of "annual payments" is extremely complex, with significant case law. But in practice this does not now matter for income tax purposes because of the limitations put on the provision by s.347A of the Taxes Act. The same limit is expressly applied here. The effect is to exclude from any deduction for tax purposes, and accordingly from the charge to tax under Case III, all annual payments other than payments of interest; payments made for bona fide commercial reasons in connection with the individual's trade profession or vocation; or payments to which Taxes Act, s.125 applies. The provision dealing with commercial payments covers such things as annual payments made by current partners of a partnership to a former partner. Section 125 is an anti-avoidance provision dealing with annual payments for non-taxable consideration. It is designed to prevent tax avoidance schemes exploiting a gap between Cases I and II of Sch.D by providing an annual payment that is charged under Case III in exchange for a liability incurred in money or money's worth but in such a form that it is excluded from the trading accounts of the person making it. In effect, this backs up the exclusion of trading covenants. Save, therefore, for interest and for these limited exceptions, the reference to "annual payments" can be ignored. **2.188**

Gains on life policies and similar

2.189 The reference in reg.10 to s.547 brings into investment income any gains chargeable to income tax under a series of provisions in Pt XIII, ch.2 of the Taxes Act. These impose "in the manner and to the extent therein provided, charges to tax in respect of gains to be treated in accordance with this Chapter as arising in connection with policies of life assurance, contracts for life annuities and capital redemption policies": s.539(1). There are important limits on the scope of these charge, for example removing mortgage protection policies, approved life assurance policies and policies linked to personal pension schemes. (These may, instead, be pension income.) In other cases, a charge to income tax may arise, for example, on the death of an assured life. If a gain does arise, then it is treated as income for income tax purposes in the year in which the event triggering the charge occurred, and accordingly that will also apply to tax credits.

Whose income is it?

2.190 Income tax on the various items chargeable as investment income is normally collected, at least in part, from the payers or paying agents. So the Inland Revenue is normally only concerned with those liable to higher-rate payments. Here, the concern is with all recipients. The general Sch.D rule applies for defining chargeability: it is the person "receiving or entitled to" the income.

The most common problem with regard to "receiving" or "entitled to" is with the joint investments of husband and wife, or other partners (both personal and business). The general rule with regard to husbands and wives is in the Taxes Act, s.282A. Savings held jointly are assumed to generate income equally to the two spouses, unless they elect otherwise under s.282B. There is no such assumption for unmarried couples, although the requirement of a joint claim from such couples means that this is of no importance for tax credits calculations.

The general rule for other partners, including joint tenants, tenants in common or coparceners is that each is to be treated according to his or her share: Taxes Act, s.277.

When is the income brought into calculation?

2.191 The general rule for Case III assessments, and therefore for investment income calculations, is that the charge is on the "full amount of the income arising within the year": Taxes Act, s.64. No deductions are allowed from such income. Further, where—as is often the case—the income is received after deduction of tax, the income for tax credits purposes is the grossed-up amount.

CHAPTER 8

Property income

Property income

2.192 **11.**—(1) In these Regulations, "property income" means the annual taxable profits arising from a business carried on for the exploitation, as a source of rents or other receipts, of any estate, interest or rights in or over land in the United Kingdom.

Expressions which are used in this paragraph which are defined in section 15 of the Taxes Act for the purposes of that section bear the same meaning here as they bear in that section.

This paragraph is subject to the following [1qualifications].

(2) In calculating property income there shall be disregarded any profits or gains—

(a) treated as nil by paragraph 9 of Schedule 10 to the Finance (No.2) Act 1992; or

(b) excluded from profits or gains by paragraph 11 of that Schedule.

[1 (3) Where a Schedule A business (as defined within Schedule A set out in section 15 of the Taxes Act) makes a loss to which the relief provisions of section 379A of the Taxes Act apply, then such relief as may arise under subsection (1) of that section shall be applied in calculating property income for the purposes of this regulation.]

AMENDMENT

1. Tax Credits (Miscellaneous Amendments No.2) Regulations 2003 (SI 2003/2815), reg.9 (November 26, 2003).

CROSS-REFERENCE

F(2)A 1992, Sch.10	Furnished accommodation.

GENERAL NOTE

This regulation defines "property income" for the purposes of reg.3. "Property income" is another of the labels identified by the Tax Law Rewrite Project for restructuring income tax. But it is the label that has caused the most disagreement because of the inherent legal ambiguity in it. The charge to income tax is the same as that of Sch.A, set down in s.15 of the Taxes Act. It is a charge on income from a business deriving profit from the exploitation of land in the United Kingdom. It does not apply to land outside the United Kingdom, and it does not apply to other forms of property. The rules for Sch.A have been rewritten in their entirety in the last 40 years, with substantial changes in the last few years. The effect has been to codify the rules ahead of the Rewrite Project. Another result is that there is minimal case law on the Sch.A rules, save for some issues on the borderlines between Sch.A and Sch.D. On the latter point—and the difference between what a farmer calls land and what a lawyer calls land—see *Lowe v Ashmore* [1971] Ch. 545. For a statutory provision providing that income from mines and other forms of exploitation of the resources provided by land, see the Taxes Act, s.55. **2.193**

The Sch.A rules are in s.15 and then ss.21–43G of the Taxes Act. They catch all forms of rental income from land in the United Kingdom, and prescribe the allowable deductions from that income. The general approach since 1998 is to allow computation of profits from a Sch.A business to be "computed in the same way as the profits of a trade are computed for the purposes of Case I of Schedule D": Taxes Act, s 21A(1).

The exception provided for in F(2)A 1992, Sch.10, is the "rent-a-room" scheme. In brief, this provides, subject to set conditions, that an owner–occupier who lets out rooms in his or her home to others is not liable to account for income tax on rent or other payments received up to £4,250 a year. So if a claimant for tax credits has a lodger paying, say, £50 a week to live in one of the bedrooms in the claimant's house, then the entire income is excluded from calculation for tax credits purposes. If the total received is above £4,250, then the claimant can elect either to have the first £4,250 omitted or to be charged to tax on the profits.

The tax charge, and therefore the tax credits calculation, is made by reference to the person "receiving or entitled to" the income and by reference to the full amounts of the profits arising in the year": s.21.

CHAPTER 9

Foreign income

2.194 **12.**—(1) In these Regulations, "foreign income" means income arising, in the year in question, from possessions or from securities out of the United Kingdom which are not—

(a) employment income;
(b) trading income; or
(c) investment income falling within regulation 10(1)(e).

This is subject to the following provisions of this regulation.

(2) The reference in paragraph (1) to income arising from or possessions or from securities out of the United Kingdom shall be construed in accordance with section 18(3B) of the Taxes Act.

(3) In calculating the claimant's foreign income there shall be disregarded—

(a) any payment by way of an annuity or pension payable under any special provision for victims of National Socialist persecution which is made by the law of the Federal Republic of Germany, or any part of it, or of Austria;
(b) if the claimant's foreign income comprises or includes a pension to which section 65(2) or [1. . .] of the Taxes Act applies [1or to which sections 567(5) and 617 of ITEPA apply], the amount authorised to be deducted by [1the relevant provision]; and
(c) any amount which would be disregarded for the purposes of income tax by virtue of—
  (i) Extra Statutory Concession A10 (lumps sums paid by overseas pension schemes);
  (ii) [1s.681 of ITEPA];
  (iii) Extra Statutory Concession A30 (interest on damages for personal injuries awarded by a foreign court); or
  (iv) Extra Statutory Concession A44 (education allowances payable to public officials of overseas territories).

[2 (4) Where an overseas property business (within the meaning of the Taxes Act) makes a loss to which the relief provisions of section 379A of the Taxes Act apply, by virtue of section 379B of that Act, then such relief as may arise under section 379A(1) shall be applied in calculating foreign income for the purposes of this regulation.]

AMENDMENTS

1. Tax Credits (Definition and Calculation of Income) (Amendment) Regulations 2003 (SI 2003/732), reg.10 (April 6, 2003).

2. Tax Credits (Miscellaneous Amendments No.2) Regulations 2003 (SI 2003/2815), reg.10 (November 26, 2003).

CROSS-REFERENCES

Taxes Act,

s.18	Schedule D
s.65	Cases IV and V assessments: general

s.196	Foreign pensions
ITEPA,	
s.681	Foreign social security benefits
Extra Statutory Concessions,	
A10	Lump sums paid under overseas pension schemes
A30	Interest or damages for personal injuries (foreign court awards)
A44	Education allowances under overseas service aid scheme

General Note

This regulation defines "foreign income" for the purposes of reg.3. The reference to "possessions" "out of the United Kingdom" in the definition is a reference to Case V of Sch.D, and the reference to "securities" is to Case IV of Sch.D: Taxes Act, s.18. **2.195**

The definition makes clear that this head of calculation does not apply to employment income, to trading income, or to investment income. The question of interaction is, perhaps, a little less clear than the regulation implies.

There are two important issues to note about the scope of this regulation that are raised by reg.3. In practice, most kinds of foreign income are taxed by the income tax authorities of the source state—that is, the state from which the income comes. Also in practice, the United Kingdom will probably have agreed a double taxation agreement under the Taxes Act, s.788, and this will determine the extent to which, if at all, the foreign income can be taxed in the United Kingdom. It will also provide relief to stop double taxation by the foreign state and the United Kingdom on the same income. Regulation 3(5) provides that any such double taxation agreement is to be ignored for tax credits purposes. The second point is that some forms of foreign income are only taxable to a limited extent in the United Kingdom if the taxpayer is not ordinarily resident here or is not domiciled here. Regulation 3(4) and (5) provide that those limitations are also to be ignored for tax credits purposes. Both therefore widen the scope of the tax credits provision as compared with a United Kingdom income tax assessment.

Turning to specific kinds of income, interactions must be dealt with by reference to each kind of income. In the case of employment income under reg.4, the commentary on that kind of income makes clear that some kinds of foreign income that are charged to tax under ITEPA as employment income have not been applied for tax credits purposes. Similarly specific forms of employment expense that are related to foreign employments have not been included by reg.4. Is the intention to include here what has been excluded from the scope of reg.4, or is the intention to exclude from foreign income anything that is within the scope of employment income but has been omitted from the specific scope of reg.4? This problem arises because there is old authority that a foreign office or employment can be a foreign possession. But arguably that approach has not survived the codification and enactment of employment income law under ITEPA.

The definition of "pension income" in reg.5 does not extend to foreign pensions, as the relevant chapters of Pt 10 of ITEPA have not been incorporated for tax credits purposes into that definition. Again, therefore, the question arises whether they form part of foreign income. It would seem clear that foreign pensions are part of foreign income as the rights to the pension would constitute a foreign possession (see also s.58 of the Taxes Act, charging foreign pensions as foreign possessions if they are not caught under the employment income rules). That is confirmed by the need to exclude certain kinds of pension from the scope of this regulation by para.(3). Paragraph (3)(b) applies s.65(2) of the Taxes Act for tax credits purposes. That subsection charges income tax under Case IV or V of Sch.D on a foreign pension on 9/10ths of the pension, subject to s.330 of the Act. Section 330 excludes from income tax those pensions within the scope of para.(3)(a) of this regulation. The effect of para.(3)(b) is therefore to allow the same 10 per cent deduction as for income tax. The same is applied under ITEPA, ss.567 and 617 to some foreign pensions.

Foreign trading income appears to be within reg.6, and therefore properly excluded from this regulation. That is confirmed not only by the reference to trade "in the United Kingdom or elsewhere" but also by the reference in reg.6 to Case V of Sch.D. The distinction between Case I and Case V is between a trade within the United Kingdom and a trade with the United Kingdom, that is, a trade that takes place here and one that takes place elsewhere but with the results of the trade coming here. The location of a trade is usually defined in British practice by the place where the contracts for the trade are made. As double taxation agreements are irrelevant for tax credits purposes, and the rules for calculating Case V trading income are treated as being the same as for Case I trading income, the effect is to bring in worldwide trading income, regardless of the location of the source. Foreign social security income is not within reg.7. Nor is it any longer covered by the old "Sch.E" rules as those have gone with the enactment of ITEPA. Foreign social security benefits are also kept out of the scope of this regulation (if they were in it) by the exclusion adopted from ITEPA, s.681 of foreign social security benefits.

The definition of student income in reg.8 prevents this applying to foreign grants for students. There may be, of course, a question whether a foreign student is ordinarily resident in the United Kingdom in any event.

Regulation 10 concentrates on United Kingdom investment income. In particular, para.10(1)(c) repeats the underlying income tax rule by treating income from United Kingdom securities as investment income while leaving income from foreign securities (which otherwise fall under Case IV of Sch.D) to be treated as foreign income. Similarly, income from United Kingdom dividends and other distributions are within reg.10(1)(d) while foreign dividends and other disctributions fall within this regulation.The exclusions in para.(3)(c) of this regulation are necessary to bring in extra-statutory equivalents of explicit exemptions from United Kingdom investment income incorporated in reg.10. The reference in para.(1)(c) of this regulation to reg.10(1)(e) is to the anti-avoidance provisions on life policies and similar discussed in the note to reg.10. Regulation 11 is another provision expressly limited, as is Sch.A of the income tax, to land in the United Kingdom. Foreign land is a foreign possession and rent from such land is within this regulation. See the Taxes Act, s.65A, which applies the Sch.A rules (and therefore the Sch.D, Case I rules) to the charge under Case V of Sch.D on income from exploitation of foreign land. However, this will rarely turn up in United Kingdom income tax assessments in practice as the standard rule of international tax law (and of double taxation agreements) is to tax income from land where it is.

The regulations on notional income may apply to capture items that are broadly described as foreign income. Section 761 of the Taxes Act, for example, charges offshore gains. That is an anti-avoidance provision designed to convert receipts of offshore funds outside the jurisdiction of United Kingdom taxation into something within the scope of United Kingdom taxation. Those provisions in reg.14 that have this effect are designed to deal with cases where there is no security or possession of the taxpayer within the United Kingdom under the ordinary rules, so have the effect of supporting this regulation.

These may be an overlap in practice between this regulation and reg.16 on miscellaneous income. The reference in that regulation to Case VI confines it, as the note on that regulation indicates, to certain narrow forms of income only. But those might also be forms of income that can be regarded as coming from a foreign possession (e.g. proceeds from writing an article in the form of overseas royalty rights). It is assumed that if there is such an overlap, the standard income tax rule preventing double taxation (in this case double calculation) would be applied. But will the rule that allows the Revenue to choose which head of income is to be used where there is an overlap between heads of the same Schedule also apply?

The extra statutory concessions

The Regulations have followed the precedent of the Social Security (Contributions) Regulations 2001 (SI 2001/1004) in adopting by express reference the terms of Inland Revenue published extra statutory concessions into the text of secondary legislation. The purpose is to ensure alignment between the income tax rule and the tax credits rule so as to ensure fairness. The dubious legality of the practice from the standpoint of income tax (on which see *Vestey v IRC* [1980] A.C. 1148) would appear to have been ratified for current purposes. The three concessions each deal with narrow points where statute law makes an allowance for a payment in the United Kingdom but does not make equivalent allowance for the same treatment for a foreign-sourced payment. The effect is to provide equivalent treatment for those foreign payments. **2.196**

CHAPTER 10

Notional Income

Introduction

13. In these Regulations, "notional income" means income which, by virtue of regulations 14 to 17 a claimant is treated as having, but which he does not in fact have. **2.197**

GENERAL NOTE

This regulation emphasises that the provisions of regs 14–17 are not parallels to income tax in the ordinary sense, in that the income is not in fact income of the claimant (or any of the joint claimants). It may, as the notes to the following regulations show, be the income of someone else. **2.198**

This, and the regulations that follow, are a good example of the much clearer drafting style now adopted by the Inland Revenue as compared with the former concentrated style of regulations. In particular, regs 15–17 between them cover only part of what used to be reg.26 of the Family Credit (General) Regulations 1987 (SI 1987/1973). The pattern adopted is to include as income, in reg.14, sums treated as income by reference to selected anti-avoidance provisions. Regulations 15–17 then continue the treatment as income of other sums that were so treated under the Family Credit (General) Regulations 1987.

Claimants treated for any purpose as having income by virtue of the Income Tax Acts

14.—(1) If an amount is treated for any purpose as the claimant's income under any provision mentioned in paragraph (2), he is to be treated as having that amount of income. **2.199**

(2) The provisions mentioned in paragraph (1) are—

(a) the following provisions of the Taxes Act—

(i) section 34 (treatment of premiums, etc. as rent);

(ii) section 56 (transactions in deposits with and without certificates or in debts) or 56A (disposal or exercise of rights in pursuance of deposits);

(iii) section 249 (stock dividends treated as income);

(iv) section 421 (taxation of borrower when loan to participators in a close company released, etc.);

(v) section 660A (income arising under settlement where settlor retains an interest);

(vi) section 660B (payments to unmarried minor children of settlor);

(vii) section 677 (sums paid to settlor otherwise than as income) or 678 (capital sums paid by body connected with settlement);

(viii) section 695 (limited interests in residue of estate in administration) or 696 (absolute interests in residue of estate in administration);

(ix) section 714 (transfers of securities: treatment of deemed sums and reliefs) or 716 (transfer of unrealised interest);

(x) section 730 (transfer of income arising from securities);

(xi) section 730A (treatment of price differential on sale and repurchase of securities;

(xii) section 739 (prevention of avoidance of income tax);

(xiii) section 740 (liability of non-transferors);

(xiv) section 761 (charge to income tax of offshore income gain); and

(xv) section 776 (transactions in land: taxation of chargeable gains); and

(b) paragraph 1 of Schedule 13 to the Finance Act 1996 (discounted securities: charge to tax on realised profit comprised on a discount).

General Note

2.200 This regulation brings into calculation for tax credits purposes any sum that is treated as income by the Inland Revenue for income tax purposes under any of the named sections of the Taxes Act. Under the Taxes Act, the selected sections provide for sums to be treated as being income, or of being income of a stated person, and are subject to a charge to tax in a stated year of assessment. That charge is usually under either Case VI of Sch.D (see the note to reg.18) or Sch.F.

The wording of the regulation ensures that the operative decision is that for income tax purposes (carrying rights of appeal and settlement to the tax appeal tribunals and courts). Once the matter is settled for those purposes it will also apply for these purposes. The Revenue will be able to do that by using its powers to enquire and on discovery under ss.19 and 20 of the Act.

In summary, the sections of the Taxes Act selected by para.(2) are:

s.34 treats a stated proportion of a capital sum received for granting a lease for a period of under 50 years as income chargeable under Sch.D, Case VI.

ss.56 and 56A treat the rights to receive amounts, with or without interest, under certificates of deposit, or similar arrangements, or the proceeds of sale of such instruments or assets, or the advantages obtained by exercising rights under such arrangements, as income chargeable under Sch.D, Case VI.

s.249 is designed to stop avoidance of a charge under Sch.F by the issue of share capital as a cash or stock dividends or bonuses or similar arrangements.

s.421 is the charge to tax under Sch.F where a loan to a participator in a close company is released to that participator.

s.660A is a key provision, along with s.660B, in dealing with avoidance of income tax by the use of "settlements", a term that is defined widely. The effect of this section is to treat any income arising under a settlement as being the income of the settlor, and not the income of any other person, unless the income arises from property in which the settlor has no interest. Those terms are defined robustly.

s.660B supports s.660A by dealing in the same way as that section with payments made to children of the settlor if they are unmarried and under 18.

s.677 is another provision aimed at preventing avoidance through the use of trusts. It treats capital sums paid to the settlor as being income of the settlor unless certain strict conditions are met. Section 678 buttresses s.677 by bringing in also sums paid by bodies connection with a settlement.

ss.695 and 696 are the charging provisions to deal with estates of deceased persons in the course of administration. Section 695 deals with sums paid to someone with a limited interest in residue, while s.696 deals with someone with an absolute interest in residue.

ss.714, 716, 730 and 730A are some of the charging provisions for Pt XVII, ch.2 of the Taxes Act. This chapter charges tax arising on transfers of securities with or without interest. They impose charges to income tax under Sch.D, Case VI on individuals receiving sums under the arrangements caught by this chapter if they are not treated as trading income.

s.739 is a powerful section entitled "prevention of avoidance of income tax" under the chapter title "transfer of assets abroad". Section 740 supports the section by catching non-transferors. The sections apply where assets are transferred broad by those ordinarily resident in the United Kingdom and are extremely widely drawn.

s.761 is the charging section imposing a charge to tax on offshore income gains. It applies to gains from non-resident companies, unit trusts, or other arrangements which are "non-qualifying" as defined by ss.757–764 of the Taxes Act.

s.776 is another anti-avoidance provision, although one that is little used in practice (probably because it is effective in blocking avoidance). The section "is enacted to prevent the avoidance of tax by persons concerned with land or the development of land", and is again very widely drawn. If it applies, it treats capital gains so derived as income.

Sch.13 to the FA 1996 lays down income tax provisions for dealing with gains from discounted securities, imposing tax charges on the gains it identifies under either Case III or Case IV of Sch.D.

Claimants depriving themselves of income in order to secure entitlement

15. If a claimant has deprived himself of income for the purpose of securing entitlement to, or increasing the amount of, a tax credit, he is treated as having that income. 2.201

General Note

This provision is carried forward from the Family Credit (General) Regulations 1987 (SI 1987/1973). It is equivalent to Income Support (General) Regulations 2.202

1987 (SI 1987/1967), reg.42(1), and the note on that in Vol.II in this series should be consulted. Note, however, that this provision is defined by reference to deprivation for the purposes of securing or increasing entitlement to tax credits (and not, for example, income support). TCTM04920 gives the example of someone who transfers entitlement to an occupational pension to someone else by deed of gift. Without reference to authority, it emphasises that securing or increasing entitlement to tax credit may not be a claimant's main motive but it must be a significant one. That is a question of fact.

Claimants to whom income becomes available upon the making of a claim

2.203 **16.**—(1) If income would become available to a claimant upon the making of an application for that income, he is treated as having that income.

This is subject to the following qualification.

(2) Paragraph (1) does not apply in relation to income—

(a) under a trust derived from a payment made in consequence of a personal injury;

(b) under a personal pension scheme or retirement annuity contract;

(c) consisting in a sum to which Item 8 of Table 4 in regulation 10 refers (compensation for personal injuries which is administered by the Court); or

(d) consisting in a rehabilitation allowance made under section 2 of the Employment Act.

[1 (3) Paragraph (1) also does not apply to income by way of—

(a) a Category A or Category B retirement pension,

(b) a graduated retirement benefit, or

(c) a shared additional pension,

payment of which has been deferred.

Here –

"Category A retirement pension" means a pension to which a person is entitled by virtue of section 44 of the Contributions and Benefits Act or the Northern Ireland Contributions and Benefits Act;

"Category B retirement pension" means a pension to which a person is entitled by virtue of any of sections 48A to 48C of the Contributions and Benefits Act or sections 48A to 48C of the Northern Ireland Contributions and Benefits Act;

"graduated retirement benefit" means a pension payable under –

(a) sections 36 and 37 of the National Insurance Act 1965; or

(b) sections 35 and 36 of the National Insurance Act (Northern Ireland) 1966; and

"shared additional pension" means a pension to which a person is entitled by virtue of section 55A of the Contributions and Benefits Act or section 55A of the Northern Ireland Contributions and Benefits Act.]

AMENDMENT

1. Tax Credits (Miscellaneous Amendments) Regulations 2004 (SI 2004/762), reg.15 (April 6, 2004).

DEFINITIONS

"Category A retirement pension"—see para. (3).
"Category B retirement pension"—see *ibid.*
"graduated retirement benefit"—see *ibid.*
"shared additional pension"—see *ibid.*

GENERAL NOTE

This continues the provision previously in Family Credit (General) Regulations 1987 (SI 1987/1967), reg.26(2). See the note to the similar provision in Income Support (General) Regulations 1987 (SI 1987/1967), reg.42(2)–(4). The precise operative scope of this provision is not clear. For income support, sums not received may not count as earnings or other income. But most of the charges to income tax, as noted above, are on those "receiving or entitled to". So entitlement is enough to bring the sums in both for income tax purposes and tax credit purposes, even if they are not received. This regulation could, however, extend that to cover sums to which entitlement had not arisen, for example because no demand had been made for the sum under a contractual entitlement operative on such demand. 2.204

Claimants providing services to other persons for less than full earnings

17.—(1) If a claimant provides a service for another person and— 2.205

(a) the other person makes no payment of earnings or pays less than those paid for a comparable employment (including self-employment) in the area; and

(b) the Board are satisfied that the means of the other person are sufficient for him to pay for, or to pay more for, the service,

the claimant is to be treated as having such an amount of employment income, or in the case of a service provided in the course of a trade or business, such an amount of trading income as is reasonable for the employment of the claimant to provide the service.

This is subject to the following qualification.

(2) Paragraph (1) does not apply where—

(a) the claimant is a volunteer or is engaged to provide the service by a charitable or voluntary organisation and the Board are satisfied that it is reasonable for the claimant to provide the service free of charge; or

(b) the service is provided in connection with the claimant's participation in an employment or training programme—

(i) in Great Britain in accordance with regulation 19(1)(q) of the Jobseeker's Allowance Regulations 1996 other than where it is provided in connection with the claimant's participation in the Intensive Activity period specified in regulation 75(1)(a)(iv) of those Regulations; or

(ii) in Northern Ireland in accordance with regulation 19(1)(p) of the Jobseeker's Allowance Regulations (Northern Ireland) 1996 other than where it is provided in connection with the claimant's participation in the Preparation for Employment Programme specified in regulation 75(1)(a)(v) of those Regulations.

General Note

2.206 This continues the provision previously in the Family Credit (General) Regulations 1987 (SI 1987/1973), reg.26(4), save that it is drafted in a clearer and less dense form. See the note in Vol.II in this series to the similar (though differently drafted) provision in Income Support (General) Regulations 1987 (SI 1987/1967), reg.42(6).

Chapter 11

Miscellaneous income

Miscellaneous income

2.207 **18.** In these Regulations, "miscellaneous income" means income which does not fall within any other provision of these Regulations and which is subject to income tax under Case VI of Schedule D.

General Note

2.208 This defines "miscellaneous income" for the purposes of reg.3. It does so by reference to Case VI of Sch.D in the Taxes Act, s.18. As amended by ITEPA, Case VI reads: "tax in respect of any annual profits or gains not falling under any other Case or Schedule D and not charged by virtue or Schedule A or by virtue of ITEPA 2003 as employment income, pension income or social security income."

Case VI is the "sweeper" provision in the Taxes Act charge to income tax, but it is not of unlimited scope. The courts have held that the words must be construed in the context of the other charges to income tax. It does not, therefore, allow capital gains to be brought into tax, because they are not "annual profits or gains" in the income tax sense. Nor are gifts or other payments that are not "annual" in the sense that they are not income or do not create a "profit or gain". The wide definition of "trade" as noted in reg.6 prevents this head of charge being used to charge income tax on receipts arising from trade-type situations aside from Case I of Sch.D. However, Case VI does catch payments of an income nature that fall outside Case II of Sch.D because the recipient of the sum is not carrying on a profession or vocation (for example, one-off payments for newspaper articles).

Case VI is also used in the Taxes Act to impose a charge on a wide range of sums treated as income by anti-avoidance and other provisions. So far as relevant to tax credits, these sums are dealt with by reg.14 and do not come into the calculation under this head.

Part III

Sums disregarded in the calculation of income

General disregards in the calculation of income

2.209 **19.**—(1) For the purposes of regulation 3—

(a) the sums specified in Table 6 are disregarded in the calculation of income;

(b) the sums specified in column 1 of Table 7 are disregarded in the calculation of income if the condition in the corresponding entry in column 2 of that Table is satisfied; and
(c) the sums specified in column 1 of Table 8 are disregarded in the calculation of income to the extent specified in the corresponding entry in column 2 of that Table.

(2) In this regulation—

"the JSA Regulations" means the Jobseeker's Allowance Regulations 1996; and

"the JSA (NI) Regulations" means the Jobseeker's Allowance (Northern Ireland) Regulations 1996.

Table 6. Sums disregarded in the calculation of income

2.210

1. Any payment of an employment credit under a scheme under section 2(2) of the Employment Act known as "New Deal 50 Plus" or the corresponding scheme under section 1 of the Employment and Training Act (Northern Ireland) 1950.
2. Any payment made— (a) under section 15 of the Disabled Persons (Employment Act) 1944 or section 15 of the Disabled Persons (Employment) Act (Northern Ireland) 1945; or (b) in accordance with arrangements made under section 2 of the Employment Act or section 1 of the Employment and Training Act (Northern Ireland) 1950 to assist disabled persons to obtain or retain employment despite their disability.
3. Any mandatory top-up payment made pursuant to— (a) section 2 of the Employment Act [3 or section 1 of the Employment and Training Act (Northern Ireland) 1950] in respect of the claimant's participation in— (i) an employment programme specified in regulation 75(1)(a)(ii)(bb) of the JSA Regulations or regulation 75(1)(a)(ii) of the JSA (NI) Regulations (Voluntary Sector Option of the New Deal); (ii) an employment programme specified in regulation 75(1)(a)(ii)(cc) of the JSA Regulations (Environmental Task Force Option of the New Deal) or regulation 75(1)(a)(iii) of the JSA (NI) Regulations; or (iii) the Intensive Activity Period of the New Deal Pilots for 25 Plus specified in regulation 75(1)(a)(iv) of the JSA Regulations or, in Northern Ireland, the Preparation for Employment Programme specified in regulation 75(1)(a)(v) of the JSA (NI) Regulations; or (b) a written arrangement entered into between— (i) the Secretary of State and the person who has arranged for the claimant's participation in the Intensive Activity Period of the New Deal for 25 Plus and which is made in respect of his participation in that Period; or

(ii) the Department for Employment and Learning and the person who has arranged for the claimant's participation in the Preparation for Employment Programme and which is made in respect of the claimant's participation in the Programme. [3This item applies only to the extent that the payment is not taxable as a profit of a trade, profession or vocation.]
4. Any discretionary payment pursuant to section 2 of the Employment Act, or, in Northern Ireland, section 1(1) of the Employment and Training Act (Northern Ireland) 1950 to meet, or help to meet, special needs in respect of the claimant's participation in the Full-Time Education and Training Option of the New Deal as specified in regulation 75(1)(b)(ii) of the JSA Regulations or of the JSA (NI) Regulations.
5. Any— (a) education maintenance allowance in accordance with regulations made under section 518 of the Education Act 1996 (payment of school expenses; grant of scholarships, etc.); or (b) payment (not within sub-paragraph (a)) in respect of a course of study attended by a child or qualifying young person payable— (i) in accordance with regulations made under section 518 of the Education (Scotland) Act 1980 (power to assist persons to take advantage of educational facilities) or section 12(2)(c) of the Further and Higher Education (Scotland) Act 1992 (provision of financial assistance to students); or (ii) by virtue of regulations made in Article 50, 51 or 55(1) of the Education and Libraries (Northern Ireland) Order 1986 (provisions to assist persons to take advantage of educational facilities).
6. Any payment made by an employment zone contractor payable in respect of the claimant's participation in the employment zone programme by way of— (a) a training premium; (b) a discretionary payment, being a fee, grant, loan or otherwise; or (c) any arrears of subsistence allowance paid as a lump sum.
7. [3. . .]
8. An amount of income equal to any qualifying maintenance payment within section 347B of the Taxes Act.
[2 9. Any payment by way of foster care receipts to the extent that those receipts qualify for relief under Schedule 36 to the Finance Act 2003.]
10. Any payment of maintenance, whether under a court order or not, which is made or due to be made by— (a) the claimant's former partner, or the claimant's partner's former partner; or

(b) the parent of a child or qualifying young person where that child or qualifying young person is a member of the claimant's household except where that parent is the claimant or the claimant's partner.

11. Any payment in respect of a child or qualifying young person who is a member of the claimant's household made—

[2 (a) to adopters which is exempt from income tax by virtue of section 327A of the Taxes Act;]

(b) by a local authority in pursuance of paragraph 15(1) of Schedule 1 to the Children Act 1989 (local authority contribution to child's maintenance);

[3(bb) by a local authority by way of special guardianship support services pursuant to regulations under section 14F(1)(b) of the Children Act 1989; or]

(c) by an authority, as defined in Article 2 of the Children (Northern Ireland) Order 1995, in pursuance of Article1 5 of, and paragraph 17 of Schedule 1 to, that Order (contribution by an authority to child's maintenance).

12. Any payment in respect of travelling expenses—

(a) in relation to England and Wales, under regulation 3, 5 or 8 of the National Health Service (Travelling Expenses and Remission of Charges) Regulations 1988;

(b) in relation to Scotland, under regulation 3, 5 or 8 of the National Health Service (Travelling Expenses and Remission of Charges) (Scotland) Regulations 1988;

(c) in relation to Northern Ireland under regulation 3, 5 or 8 of the Travelling Expenses and Remission of Charges Regulations (Northern Ireland) 1989; or

(d) made by the Secretary of State for Health, the Scottish Ministers, the Secretary of State for Wales, or the Department of Health, Personal Social Services and Public Safety and which is analogous to a payment specified in paragraph (a), (b) or (c).

13. Any payment made by the Secretary of State or the Scottish Ministers under a scheme established to assist relatives and other persons to visit persons in custody.

[2 14. Any payment under the Community Care (Direct Payments) Act 1996, section 57 of the Health and Social Care Act 2001, section 12B of the Social Work (Scotland) Act 1968, Article 15A of the Health and Personal Social Services (Direct Payments) (Northern Ireland) Order 1996 or section 8 of the Carers and Direct Payments Act (Northern Ireland) 2002.]

[1 14A. Any payment made under the "Supporting People" programme—

(a) in England and Wales, under section 93 of the Local Government Act 2000;

(b) in Scotland, under section 91 of the Housing (Scotland) Act 2001; or (c) in Northern Ireland, under Article 4 of the Housing Support Services (Northern Ireland) Order 2002.]
15. [[1]Any payment or a voucher] provided under section 95 or 98 of the Immigration and Asylum Act 1999 for any former asylum-seeker or his dependants.
16. Any payment of a provident benefit by a trade union. Here— "provident benefit" has the meaning given in section 467(2) of the Taxes Act; and "trade union" has the meaning given in section 467(4) of the Taxes Act.

Table 7. Sums disregarded in calculating income if conditions are satisfied

2.211

1. Description of payment	*2. [[3]Conditions] that must be satisfied*
1. Any payment in respect of any expenses incurred by a claimant who is engaged by a charitable or voluntary organisation or is a volunteer.	The claimant does not receive remuneration or profit from the engagement and is not treated as possessing any employment income under regulation 17 in respect of that engagement.
2. A payment by way of— (a) travelling expenses reimbursed to the claimant; (b) a living away from home allowance under section 2(2)(d) of the Employment Act, section 2(4)(c) of the Enterprise and New Towns (Scotland) Act 1990 or section 1 of the Employment and Training Act (Northern Ireland) 1950; (c) training grant; or (d) childcare expenses reimbursed to the claimant in respect of	The claimant— (a) participates in arrangements for training made under— (i) section 2 of the Employment Act; (ii) section 2 of the Enterprise and New Towns (Scotland) Act 1990; or (iii) section 1 of the Employment and Training Act (Northern Ireland) 1950; or (b) attends a course at an employment rehabilitation centre

1. Description of payment	*2. [3Conditions] that must be satisfied*
his participation in— (i) a New Deal option; (ii) the Intensive Activity Period of the New Deal Pilots for 25 Plus; or (iii) the Preparation for Employment Programme.	established under section 2 of the Employment Act. [3The payment is not taxable as a profit of a trade, profession or vocation.]

Table 8. Sums partly disregarded in the calculation of income

2.212

Type of payment to be disregarded	*Limit on, or exception to, the extent of disregard*
1. Any discretionary payment made pursuant to section 2 of the Employment Act, or, in Northern Ireland, section 1(1) of the Employment and Training Act (Northern Ireland) 1950 to meet, or help meet, the claimant's special needs in undertaking a qualifying course within the meaning of regulation 17A(7) of the JSA Regulations or regulation 17A(7) of the JSA (NI) Regulations.	A payment is not within this item to the extent that it relates to travel expenses incurred as a result of the claimant's attendance on the course if an amount in respect of those expenses has already been disregarded pursuant to regulation 8.
2. Any payment made in respect of a career development loan paid pursuant to section 2 of the Employment Act.	A payment is not within this item to the extent that the loan has been applied for or paid in respect of living expenses for the period of education and training supported by the loan.
3. Any payment made to the claimant or his partner in respect of a person who is not normally a member of the claimant's household but is temporarily in his care, by— (a) a health authority; (b) a local authority;	A payment is only to be disregarded by virtue of this item if [1(a)] any profits or gains arising from the payment mentioned in col.1 are treated as nil by paragraph 9 of Schedule 10 to

Type of payment to be disregarded	*Limit on, or exception to, the extent of disregard*
(c) a voluntary organisation; (d) that person pursuant to section 26(3A) of the National Assistance Act 1948; (e) a primary care trust established under section 16A of the National Health Service Act 1977.	the Finance (No.2) Act 1992; or [1(b) excluded from profits or gains by paragraph 11 of that Schedule.]
4. Any payment made in Northern Ireland to the claimant or his partner in respect of a person who is not normally a member of the claimant's household but is temporarily in his care— (a) pursuant to Article 36(7) of the Health and Personal Social Services (Northern Ireland) Order 1972 by an authority; a voluntary organisation; or the person concerned; or (b) by a training school within the meaning of section 137 of the Children and Young Persons Act (Northern Ireland) 1968. In this item "an authority" has the meaning given by Article 2 of the Children (Northern Ireland) Order 1995.	A payment is only to be disregarded by virtue of this item if [1(a)] any profits or gains arising from the payment mentioned in column 1 are treated as nil by paragraph 9 of Schedule 10 to the Finance (No.2) Act 1992; or [1(b) excluded from profits or gains by paragraph 11 of that Schedule.]
5. Any payment under an insurance policy taken out to insure against the risk of being unable to maintain the repayments— (a) on a loan which is secured on the	A payment is only to be disregarded by virtue of this item to the extent that it is used to— (a) maintain the repayments referred to in col.(1); and

Type of payment to be disregarded	*Limit on, or exception to, the extent of disregard*
dwelling house which the claimant occupies as his home; or (b) under a regulated agreement or under a hire-purchase agreement or a conditional sale agreement. For the purposes of paragraph (b)— "regulated agreement" has the meaning given in the Consumer Credit Act 1974; and "hire-purchase agreement" and "conditional sale agreement" have the meanings given in Part 3 of the Hire-Purchase Act 1964.	(b) meet any amount due by way of premiums on— (i) that policy; or (ii) in a case to which paragraph (a) of this item applies, an insurance policy taken out to insure against loss or damage to any building or part of a building which is occupied by the claimant as his home and which is required as a condition of the loan referred to in column (1).
[1**6]**. Any payment in respect of the claimant's attendance at court as a juror or witness.	This item applies only to the extent that the payment is not compensation for loss of earnings or for the loss of payment of social security income.
[17]. Any payment of a sports award except to the extent that it has been made in respect of living expenses.	For the purposes of this item "living expenses" does not include— (a) the cost of vitamins, minerals or other special dietary supplements intended to enhance the performance of the claimant in the sport in respect of which the award was made; or (b) accommodation costs incurred as a consequence of living away from home whilst training for, or competing in, the

Type of payment to be disregarded	*Limit on, or exception to, the extent of disregard*
	sport in respect of which the award was made.

AMENDMENTS

1. Tax Credits (Definition and Calculation of Income) (Amendment) Regulations 2003 (SI 2003/732), reg.11 (April 6, 2003).
2. Tax Credits (Miscellaneous Amendments No.2) Regulations 2003 (SI 2003/2815), reg.11 (November 26, 2003).
3. Tax Credits (Miscellaneous Amendments) Regulations 2004 (SI 2004/762), reg.16 (April 6, 2004).

CROSS-REFERENCES

Taxes Act, s.347B	Qualifying maintenance payments
F(2)A 1992, Sch.10	Furnished Accommodation

GENERAL NOTE

2.213 This regulation adds to the exemptions and exceptions in regs 3 and 9 that apply generally to income. Exceptions, exemptions and deductions that are specific to one or more kinds of income, but not all kinds of income, are detailed under the specific regulations.

The broad thrust of this regulation is to remove from the calculation for tax credits those sums that were also excluded for the old tax credits by Sch.2 to the Family Credit (General) Regulations 1987 (SI 1987/1973) (sums to be disregarded in the calculation of income other than earnings). The disregards in Sch.1 to those Regulations (sums to be disregarded in the calculation of earnings) are dealt with in reg.4. Schedule 3 (capital to be disregarded) is now irrelevant because all capital is now disregarded. The approach taken by the regulation is again to unpack the dense wording of the predecessor rules. The former Sch.2 was a list of items (from 1 to 71 in its final form, with several inserts) set out in an undifferentiated way without any obvious pattern to it. The pattern of this regulation is much clearer, not least because of the sub-division of the items into three separate tables so that full exemptions are separated from partial exemptions, and unconditional exemptions from conditional exemptions. Together, the tables are in total shorter than the list in the former Sch.2 because some exclusions have been moved to the regulations dealing with individual sources of income and others are no longer relevant.

Table 6

2.214 This sets out the sums to be disregarded in total. For fuller notes, see the equivalent provisions to the similar items in Income Support (General) Regulations 1987 (SI 1987/1967), Sch.9 (in Vol. II in this series). Several of the provisions are wider than the equivalent provision in the Income Support (General) Regulations 1987 because these provisions also apply to Northern Ireland, while the Income Support (General) Regulations 1987 apply to Great Britain only.

Paragraph 1—see Sch.9, para.63.
Paragraph 2—see Sch.9, para.51.
Paragraph 3—see Sch.9, para.62.

Paragraph 4—see Sch.9, para.13.
Paragraph 5—see Sch.9, para.11.
Paragraph 6—see Sch.9, para.72.
Paragraph 7—this is redefined to cover post-training sums.
Para.8—this excludes all sums within the scope of Taxes Act, s.347B (certain periodic payments made by one party to a marriage or former marriage to the other party for the maintenance of the other party or their children under a court order or agreement).
Paragraph 9—see Sch.9, para.26.
Paragraph 10—this widens out the scope of para.8.
Paragraph 11—see Sch.9, para.25.
Paragraph 12—see Sch.9, para.48.
Paragraph 13—see Sch.9, para.50.
Paragraph 14—see Sch.9, para.58.
Paragraph 14A—this is a new provision.
Paragraph 15—this is specifically focussed on former asylum-seekers or dependants.
Paragraph 16—s. 467 of the Taxes Act provides exemption from tax to trade unions that provide provident benefits to their members not exceeding £4,000 as a capital sum or £825 a year as an annuity during sickness, incapacity or old age, or after an accident, theft or death. The excludes the annuities from counting as income of claimants.

Table 7

This table details two conditional exclusions, both also in the former Sch.2 to the Family Credit (General) Regulations 1987 (SI 1987/1973). For item 1 see also the Income Support (General) Regulations 1987 (SI 1987/1967), Sch.9 para.2. For Item 2, see Sch.9, para.13. **2.215**

Table 8

The final table lists those disregards that apply to part only of a payment. Item 1 is to the same effect as Income Support (General) Regulations 1987 (SI 1987/1967) , Sch.9, para.65. Item 2 is based on Sch.9, para.59. Item 3 is similar to Sch.9, para.27, but excepts from it any payments that are or would be protected from income tax under the rent-a-room provisions (see reg.11). Item 4 is the equivalent provision for Northern Ireland. Item 5 parallels Sch.9, paras 29 and 30ZA. Item 6 is the same as Sch.9, para.43. Item 7 is based on Sch.9, para.69. **2.216**

Child Tax Credit Regulations 2002

(SI 2002/2007)

Whereas a draft of this instrument, which contains the first regulations made under section 9 of the Tax Credits Act 2002 has been laid before, and approved by resolution of, each House of Parliament:

Now, therefore, the Treasury, in exercise of the powers conferred on them by sections 8, 9, 65 and 67 of the Tax Credits Act 2002, hereby make the following Regulations:

ARRANGEMENT OF REGULATIONS

Citation, commencement and eVect

2.218 **1.** These Regulations may be cited as the Child Tax Credit Regulations 2002 and shall come into force—

(a) for the purpose of enabling claims to be made, on 1st August 2002;
(b) for the purpose of enabling awards to be made, on 1st January 2003; and
(c) for all other purposes on 6th April 2003; and shall have effect for the tax year beginning on 6th April 2003 and subsequent tax years.

Interpretation

2.219 **2.**—(1) In these Regulations, unless the context otherwise requires—

"the Act" means the Tax Credits Act 2002;

"advanced education" means full-time education for the purposes of—

(a) a course in preparation for a degree, a diploma of higher education, a higher national diploma, a higher national diploma or higher national certificate of Edexcel or the Scottish Qualifications Authority, or a teaching qualification; or
(b) any other course which is of a standard above ordinary national diploma, a national diploma or national certificate of Edexcel [2. . .], a general certificate of education (advanced level), [2or Scottish national qualifications at higher or advanced higher level];

[1"the Board" means the Commissioners of Inland Revenue;]

"the Careers Service" means—

(a) in England and Wales, a person with whom the Secretary of State or the National Assembly of Wales has made arrangements under s.10(1) of the Employment Act, and a local education authority to whom the Secretary of State or the National Assembly of Wales has given a direction under section 10(2) of that Act;
(b) in Scotland, a person with whom the Scottish Ministers have made arrangements under section 10(1) of the Employment Act and any education authority to which a direction has been given by the Scottish Ministers under section 10(2) of that Act; and
(c) [1. . .];

"child" means a person who has not attained the age of sixteen or who falls within the terms of regulation 4;

"claimant" has the meaning in section 9(8) of the Act, except in regulation 7, where that expression and "joint claimants" have the meanings given in regulation 7(1);

"the Connexions Service" means a person of any description with whom the Secretary of State has made an arrangement under section 114(2)(a) of the Learning and Skills Act 2000 and section 10(1) of the Employment Act, and any person to whom he has given a direction under section 114(2)(b) of the former Act and section 10(2) of the latter Act;

"the Contributions and Benefits Act" means the Social Security Contributions and Benefits Act 1992;

"custodial sentence"—

(a) in England and Wales, has the meaning in section 76 of the Powers of Criminal Courts (Sentencing) Act 2000;

(b) in Scotland, means detention under a sentence imposed by a court under section 44, 205, 207 or 208 of the Criminal Procedure (Scotland) Act 1995; and

(c) in Northern Ireland, means a custodial sentence under the Criminal Justice (Children) (Northern Ireland) Order 1998;

"disability living allowance" means a disability living allowance under section 71 of the Contributions and Benefits Act;

"the Employment Act" means the Employment and Training Act 1973;

"the family element of child tax credit" and "the individual element of child tax credit" shall be construed in accordance with section 9(3) of the Act;

"joint claim" and "single claim" shall be construed in accordance with section 3(8) of the Act;

"looked after by a local authority" has the meaning in section 22 of the Children Act 1989, section 17(6) of the Children (Scotland) Act 1995 or (in Northern Ireland) Article 25 of the Children (Northern Ireland) Order 1995 (with the modification that for the reference to a local authority there is substituted a reference to an authority within the meaning in Article 2 of that Order);

the "main responsibility test" has the meaning given in rule 2.2. of regulation 3;

the "normally living with test" has the meaning given in rule 1.1. of regulation 3;

"Part I" means Part I of the Act;

"patient" means a person (other than a person who is serving a custodial sentence) who is regarded as receiving free in-patient treatment within the meaning of the Social Security (Hospital In-patients) Regulations 1975, or the Social Security (Hospital In-patients) Regulations (Northern Ireland) 1975;

"placing for adoption" means placing for adoption in accordance with the Adoption Agencies Regulations 1983, the Adoption Agencies (Scotland) Regulations 1984 or the Adoption Agencies Regulations (Northern Ireland) 1989;

"qualifying young person" means a person, other than a child, who—
(a) has not attained the age of 19; and
(b) satisfies the conditions in regulation 5(3) and (4);

"recognised educational establishment" means an establishment recognised by the Secretary of State, the Scottish Ministers or the Department for Employment and Learning, as the case may be, as being, or as comparable to, a university, college or school;

"relevant training programme" means—
(a) arrangements made under section 2 of the Employment Act, section 2 of the Enterprise and New Towns (Scotland) Act 1990 or section 1 of the Employment and Training Act (Northern Ireland) 1950;
[1(aa) provision secured by the Learning and Skills Council for England or the National Council for Education and Training for Wales under Parts I or II of the Learning and Skills Act 2000;]
(b) arrangements made by the Secretary of State for persons enlisted in Her Majesty's forces for any special term of service specified in regulations made under section 2 of the Armed Forces Act 1966; or
(c) for the purposes of the application of Council Regulation (EEC)/1408/71, any corresponding provisions operated in another Member State;

"remunerative work" means work which is—
(a) done for payment or in expectation of payment;
(b) undertaken for not less than 24 hours a week, calculated in accordance with regulation 4(3) of the Working Tax Credit (Entitlement and Maximum Rate) Regulations 2002; and
(c) not excluded from the meaning of engagement in remunerative work by regulation 4(2) of those Regulations;

and other expressions have the same meanings as defined in the Act.

(2) In the application of these Regulations to Northern Ireland, a reference to a provision of an enactment which applies only to Great Britain or England and Wales, shall be construed, so far as necessary, as including a reference to the corresponding enactment applying to Northern Ireland.

AMENDMENTS

2.220 1. Child Tax Credit (Amendment) Regulations 2003 (SI 2003/738), reg.3 (April 6, 2003).

2. Tax Credits (Miscellaneous Amendments No.2) Regulations 2003 (SI 2003/2815), reg.17 (November 26, 2003).

Circumstances in which a person is or is not responsible for a child or qualifying young person

2.221 **3.**—(1) For the purposes of child tax credit the circumstances in which a person is or is not responsible for a child or qualifying young person shall be determined in accordance with the following Rules.

Rule 1

1.1. A person shall be treated as responsible for a child or qualifying young person who is normally living with him (the "normally living with test"). 2.222

1.2. This Rule is subject to rules 2 to 4.

Rule 2 (Competing claims)

2.1. This Rule applies where— 2.223

(a) a child or qualifying young person normally lives with two or more persons in—
  (i) different households; or
  (ii) the same household, where those persons are not limited to the members of a married couple or unmarried couple; or
  (iii) a combination of (i) and (ii); and
(b) two or more of those persons make separate claims (that is, not a single joint claim made by a married couple or unmarried couple) for child tax credit in respect of the child or qualifying young person.

2.2. The child or qualifying young person shall be treated as the responsibility of—

(a) only one of those persons making such claims; and
(b) whichever of them has (comparing between them) the main responsibility for him (the "main responsibility test");

subject to rules 3 and 4.

Rule 3

3.1. The persons mentioned in rule 2.2. (other than the child or qualifying young person) may jointly elect as to which of them satisfies the main responsibility test for the child or qualifying young person, and in default of agreement the Board may determine that question on the information available to them at the time of their determination. 2.224

Rule 4

4.1. A child or qualifying young person shall be treated as not being the responsibility of any person during any period in which any of the following Cases applies. 2.225

Case A	The child or qualifying young person is provided with, or placed in, accommodation under Part III of the Children Act 1989, Part II of the Children (Scotland) Act 1995 or Part IV of the Children (Northern Ireland) Order 1995, and the cost of that child's or qualifying young person's accommodation or maintenance is borne wholly or partly— (i) out of local authority funds under section 23 of the Children Act 1989 or section 26 of the Children (Scotland) Act 1995; (ii) in Northern Ireland, by an authority, within the meaning in Article 2, and under Article 27, of that Order; or

	(iii) out of other public funds. This Case shall not apply in the circumstances prescribed in regulation 3 of the Child Benefit (General) Regulations 1976, or regulation 3 of the Child Benefit (General) Regulations (Northern Ireland) 1979.
Case B	The child or qualifying young person— (i) is being looked after by a local authority; and (ii) has been placed for adoption by that authority in the home of a person proposing to adopt him, and a local authority is making a payment in respect of the child's or qualifying young person's accommodation or maintenance, or both, under section 23 of the Children Act 1989, section 26 of the Children (Scotland) Act 1995 or Article 27 of the Children (Northern Ireland) Order 1995. This Case applies in Northern Ireland with the modification that for references to a local authority there are substituted references to an authority (within the meaning in Article 2 of that Order).
Case C	A custodial sentence— (a) for life; (b) without limit of time; (c) of detention during Her Majesty's pleasure; (d) in Northern Ireland, of detention during the pleasure of the Secretary of State; or (e) for a term or period of more than four months, has been passed on the child or qualifying young person.
Case D	The child (having attained the age of sixteen or qualifying young person claims and is awarded child tax credit in his or her own right, in respect of a child for whom he or she is responsible, for that period.
[[1] Case E	The child (having attained the age of sixteen) or the qualifying young person, claims incapacity benefit in his or her own right and that benefit is paid to or in respect of him or her for that period. This Case does not apply at any time ("the later time") during a period of incapacity for work which began before 6th April 2004 in the case of a person in respect of whom, at a time— (a) during that period of incapacity, and (b) before that date, both incapacity benefit and child tax credit were payable, if child tax credit has been payable in

	respect of him or her continuously since 5th April 2004 until that later time. For the purposes of this Case "period of incapacity" shall be construed in accordance with section 30C of the 1992 Act (incapacity benefit: days and periods of incapacity for work) but disregarding subsections (5) and (5A) of that section.]

(2) Where—

(a) a claimant is treated as responsible for a child or qualifying young person by virtue of the preceding Rules, and

(b) the child or qualifying young person has a child of his or her own, normally living with him or her,

the claimant shall also be treated as responsible for, and as having made a claim for child tax credit in respect of, the child of the child or qualifying young person (but without prejudice to the facts as to which of them is mainly responsible for that child).

AMENDMENT

1. Tax Credits (Miscellaneous Amendments) Regulations 2004 (SI 2004/762), reg.2 (April 6, 2004).

DEFINITIONS

"child"—see reg.2(1).
"claimant"—see *ibid.*
"custodial sentence"—see *ibid.*
"joint claim"—see *ibid.*
"looked after by a local authority"—see *ibid.*
"main responsibility test"—see *ibid.*
"normally living with test"—see *ibid.*
"placing for adoption"—see *ibid.*
"qualifying young person"—see *ibid.*

GENERAL NOTE

Section 8(1) of the TCA 2002 provides that entitlement to child tax credit is dependent upon the claimant (and/or his or her partner in the case of a joint claim) "being responsible for one or more children or qualifying young persons". The 2002 Act then provides that this expression may be defined further by regulations (s.8(2)).This regulation accordingly sets out a number of rules for determining whether a person is or is not responsible for a child or young person. The starting point is in r.1, namely that as a general rule, a person is responsible for a child or young person normally living with him or her. This presumption is then subject to r.2, which deals with competing claims, as well as r.3 (election by the parties or determination by the Board in default of such agreement) and r.4 (special cases, principally involving children or young persons being accommodated at public expense and so not to be the subject of a child tax credit award). **2.226**

Para. (1) **2.227**

2.228 *Rule 1:* The presumption is that a person is responsible for a child or qualifying young person "who is normally living with him" (r.1, para.1.1). This "normally living with test" has been inherited from WFTC (and, before that, family credit: see Family Credit (General) Regulations 1987 (SI 1987/1973, reg.7(1)). The "normally living with test" was new to family credit, although the phrase "living with" the claimant was (and still is) used in the child benefit legislation (SSCBA 1992, s.143 and see, in particular *R(F) 2/79* and *R(F) 2/81*).

In the context of family credit (and later WFTC), *CFC 1537/1995* decided that a child "normally lives with" a person for the purposes of reg.7(1) if he or she spent more time with that person than anyone else. This was the construction that made sense of reg.7(2) of the 1987 Regulations, which made provision for cases where a child either spent equal amounts of time in different households or there was doubt as to which household a child was living in. But reg.7(2) only applied in cases of real doubt; if there was simply a factual dispute this was not enough to bring it into play. Where reg.7(2) applied, there was then a series of tests. The first was receipt of child benefit, the rules for which include methods of establishing priorities between claimants. If no one was receiving child benefit then if only one person had claimed child benefit, that person had priority. If there had been no claims (or more than one claim), the final test was who had "primary responsibility".

2.229 *Rule 2:* Rule 2, which applies to competing claims for child tax credit, adopts a slightly different approach to the old reg.7(2). Accordingly, it does not necessarily follow that *CFC 1537/1995* applies in precisely the same way. Rule 2 applies where two or more people (not being a couple) make child tax credit claims and the relevant child or qualifying young person "normally lives with two or more persons" *either* in different households *or* in the same household (other than in the case of a couple with a child in the same household) *or* in an arrangement that is a combination of these two first possibilities (r.2, para.2.1). Thus, r.2 only comes into play when the child or young person may, as a matter of fact, already be regarded as "normally" (but separately) living with at least two persons. For example, a child might spend weekdays living with one parent and weekends with the other parent in a different household. Although the child will spend more time living with the weekday parent, it is perfectly proper to say that he or she *also* normally lives with the weekend parent, at least for part of the week. This being so, the definition of "normally living with" applied in *CFC 1537/1995* (*i.e.* spending more time with one person than anyone else) cannot apply for the purposes of the meaning of "normally lives" in r.2, para.2.1, as that is specifically designed to deal with the situation where a child or young person by definition "normally" lives in more than one place. However, where r.2 does so apply, the general rule is that, as between the competing claimants, the child or young person is treated as the responsibility of the person with "main responsibility" for him or her (r.2, para.2.2). Thus, although *CFC 1537/1995* should be applied with care in this context, ultimately it may be a distinction without a difference.

As we have seen, the former reg.7(2) of the 1987 Regulations resolved problematic cases by reference first to the person in receipt of child benefit and then, in the absence of a child benefit claim, to the person with "primary responsibility" for the child or young person. Rule 2 makes no reference to the child benefit position. Instead, cases of shared care—as these will inevitably be—are to be determined by reference to who has "main responsibility" for the child or young person. This is presumably likely to be determined on a time basis, and so the weekdays parent in the example above is likely to be regarded as the one with such responsibility. As with the former reg.7(2), "responsibility" has no special meaning in the legislation and so must be determined according to the ordinary everyday meaning of the word. It would not seem that there is any material difference between "primary responsibility" (reg.7) and "main responsibility" (r.2). It would also appear that under r.2, as under the former reg.7, responsibility or the normality of living may be judged on an overall basis over a period. This is different from the income support provision, where the test of responsibility still has to be applied week by week (*CIS 49/1991* and *Whelan v Chief Adjudication Officer, The Independent*, November 14, 1994).

It will be evident from the analysis above that there is, under these Rules, no provision for the division of child tax credit between competing parents. The Rules are premised on establishing which claimant (or which couple of joint claimants) is entitled to child tax credit for a given child or young person, not on apportioning child tax credit entitlement between separated individual claimants (*e.g.* 5/7 to the weekdays parent and 2/7 to the weekend parent). Although the practical and administrative difficulties with such an arrangement are obvious, it did appear from the primary legislation that this might be a possibility (see, *e.g.* TCA 2002, ss.8(2) and 9(7)). There remains, therefore, the prospect of human rights challenges in this area, as with social security benefits which have elements related to a child or children's presence in a particular household for part-weeks in cases of shared care: see the General Note to Income Support (General) Regulations 1987 (SI 1987/1967), reg.15, in Vol.II in this series).

The attribution of responsibility for a child or young person to a particular person under r.2 is itself subject to rules 3 and 4.

Rule 3: Where there are competing claims under r.2, the parties may by agreement notify the Board as to which of them satisfies the main responsibility test for the child or young person in question. If the adults in question fail to agree, the Board may determine that question on the information then available. 2.230

Rule 4: Rule 4 sets out a number of specific circumstances (or Cases) in which a child or young person is not to be treated as the responsibility of a tax credit claimant, even though any of rs 1–3 above might otherwise apply. Cases A–C all deal with situations in which a child or young person is being accommodated at public expense in one way or another and so payment of child tax credit is inappropriate. These are similar to the exclusions under the child benefit scheme. Case D covers the special case of a child (aged at least 16) or young person who has herself been awarded child tax credit in respect of her own child (see also para.(2) where child tax credit has not been awarded in such circumstances to the young parent). 2.231

Case A: This exclusion covers children or young persons who are provided with or placed in accommodation under Pt III of the Children Act 1989 or associated legislation. The exception in reg.3 of the Child Benefit (General) Regulations 1976 (now Child Benefit (General) Regulations 2003 (SI 2003/493), reg.2) deals with children or young persons who are provided with residential accommodation on account of their disability. 2.232

Case B: This exclusion applies where (i) a child or young person is being looked after by a local authority (in the sense that term is used under the Children Act 1989); (ii) he or she has been placed for adoption, and (iii) a fostering allowance is in payment. 2.233

Case C: CTC will continue to be paid unless the child or young person has been sentenced to detention for a period of four months or longer. This is more generous than the equivalent rules for income support and income-based jobseeker's allowance, under which benefit for the child or young person ceases immediately he or she is taken into custody (Income Support (General) Regulations 1987 (SI 2.234

1987/1967), reg.16(5)(f) and (6); see also reg.15(3) regarding home leave). It is also more generous than the former WFTC and DPTC rules, under which there was no entitlement to the elements of those tax credits relating to children where a custodial sentence had been passed (Family Credit (General) Regulations 1987 (SI 1987/1973), reg.8(2)(e)). The justifications for the change given by ministers are the extra costs associated with contact and the need to enable families to maintain contact with the child or young person for whom they are responsible, and to assist with that person's re-integration in the community. It is difficult to see how these arguments do not apply equally forcefully in the context of income support and income-based jobseeker's allowance.

2.235 *Case D:* See also para.(2) below.

2.236 *Case E:* The effect of this provision is that a person is not to be treated as responsible for a child or a qualifying young person in respect of whom incapacity benefit is payable. There is transitional protection during a period of incapacity which began before April 6, 2004 for cases where both incapacity benefit and child tax credit were in payment in respect of the child or qualifying young person before that date.

2.237 *Paragraph (2):* This deals with the special case where a person (the claimant) is found to be responsible for a child or young person under rs 1–4 above (and so the exception in Case D of r.4 does not apply) and that child or young person herself has a child. In such circumstances, the claimant is treated as responsible for child tax credit purposes for both his or her child (or young person) and that child's own child.

Period for which a person who attains the age of 16 remains a child

2.238 **4.** A person who attains the age of sixteen remains a child for the purposes of Part I from the date on which he attained that age until immediately before 1st September which next follows that date.

DEFINITIONS

"child"—see reg.2(1).
"Pt I"—see *ibid.*

GENERAL NOTE

2.239 Section 8(3) of the TCA 2002 defines a child as a person who "has not attained the age of sixteen", but the same provision enables regulations to be made allowing a person to remain a "child" for tax credit purposes "for a prescribed period or until a prescribed date". This regulation provides that a child remains a child for both child tax credit and working tax credit purposes until the September 1 following his or her 16th birthday.

Maximum age and prescribed conditions for a qualifying young person

2.240 **5.**—(1) For the purposes of Part I, a person ceases to be a qualifying young person (unless disqualified earlier under the following paragraphs) on the date on which he attains the age of nineteen.

(2) A person who is not a child, but has not attained the age of nineteen years, is a qualifying young person for any period during which the following conditions are satisfied with regard to him [1(and once a person

falls within the terms of paragraph (3)(b), he shall be treated as having satisfied the first condition from the date of leaving education mentioned in that paragraph)].

(3) The first condition is that he is either—

(a) receiving full-time education, not being—
 (i) advanced education, or
 (ii) education received by that person by virtue of his employment or of any office held by him; or

(b) under the age of eighteen years and—
 [2(i) he has ceased to receive full-time education (the date of that event being referred to as "the date of leaving education"),
 (ii) within three months of the date of leaving education, he has notified the Board (in the manner prescribed by regulation 22 of the Tax Credits (Claims and Notifications) Regulations 2002) that he is registered for work or training with the Careers Service, the Connexions Service or the Department for Employment and Learning; and
 (iii) not more than 20 weeks has elapsed since the date of leaving education.]

(4) The second condition is that the period in question is not (and does not include)—

(a) a week in which he (having ceased to receive full-time education) becomes engaged in remunerative work;

(b) a period—
 (i) in which training for that person is being provided under a relevant training programme; and
 (ii) in respect of which an allowance may be paid under that programme to that person; or

(c) a period in respect of which that person receives income support or income-based jobseeker's allowance within the meaning of section 1(4) of the Jobseekers Act 1995.

(5) For the purposes of paragraphs (3) and (4) full-time education is education received by a person attending a course of education—

(a) at a recognised educational establishment, or

(b) if the education is recognised by the Secretary of State, the Scottish Ministers [3, the Board] or the Department for Employment and Learning, elsewhere;

where in pursuit of that course, the time spent receiving instruction or tuition, undertaking supervised study, examination or practical work or taking part in any exercise, experiment or project for which provision is made in the curriculum of the course, exceeds or exceeds on average 12 hours a week in normal term-time, and shall include normal gaps between the ending of one course and the commencement of another, where the person is enrolled on and commences the latter course.

(6) In calculating the time spent in pursuit of the course, no account shall be taken of time occupied by meal breaks or spent on unsupervised study.

AMENDMENTS

1. Child Tax Credit (Amendment) Regulations 2003 (SI 2003/738), reg.4 (April 6, 2003).

2. Child Tax Credit (Amendment) Regulations 2003 (SI 2003/738), reg.5 (April 6, 2003).

3. Child Tax Credit (Amendment) Regulations 2003 (SI 2003/738), reg.6 (April 6, 2003).

DEFINITIONS

"advanced education"—see reg.2(1).
"Careers Service"—see *ibid.*
"Connexions Service"—see *ibid.*
"child"—see *ibid.*
"full-time education"—see para.(5).
"Pt I"—see reg.2(1).
"qualifying young person"—see *ibid.*
"recognised educational establishment"—see *ibid.*
"relevant training programme"—see *ibid.*
"remunerative work"—see *ibid.*

GENERAL NOTE

2.241 Section 8(4) of the TCA 2002 enables regulations to be made prescribing conditions to be met by a person in order to count as a "qualifying young person" (CTC being payable in respect of children and qualifying young persons (TCA 2002, s.8(1)). This regulation provides that the maximum age for a "qualifying young person" is the date on which he or she reaches the age of 19 (para.(1)). It also spells out the conditions which must be met by a person who is no longer a child (on which note the extended meaning of "child" in reg.4) in order to rank as a "qualifying young person" (paras (2)–(6)). Two conditions must be satisfied in this regard (they are cumulative and not alternative). First, the young person must *either* be receiving full-time education, as defined by para.(3)(a) (and see also paras (5) and (6)) *or* be aged under 18, have ceased to receive full-time education, be registered for work or training with one of the relevant official agencies, and have met the latter two criteria for no more than 20 consecutive weeks (para.(3)(b)). Secondly, the period in question must not be or include a week in which the young person becomes engaged in remunerative work (having ceased full-time education), or a period in which he or she received a training allowance under a training programme or received income support or income-based jobseeker's allowance (para.(4)).

These conditions are modelled on those that apply to child benefit, on which see SSCBA 1992, s.142 (and the commentary in Vol.I of this series). The definition of full-time education likewise is in identical terms to the relevant provision for child benefit purposes (Child Benefit (General) Regulations 2003 (SI 2003/493), reg.5.

Entitlement to child tax credit after death of child or qualifying young person

6. If—

2.242 (a) a child or qualifying young person dies; and

(b) a person is (or would, if a claim had been made, have been) entitled to child tax credit in respect of the child or qualifying young person immediately before the death,

that person shall be entitled to child tax credit in respect of the child or qualifying young person for the period of eight weeks immediately following the death or, in the case of a qualifying young person, until the date on which he or she would have attained the age of nineteen, if earlier.

DEFINITIONS

"child"—see reg.2(1).
"qualifying young person"—see *ibid.*

GENERAL NOTE

Section 8(5) of the TCA 2002 enables regulations to be made allowing entitlement to child tax credit to continue for a prescribed period notwithstanding the death of the relevant child or qualifying young person. This regulation makes provision for the continued payment of child tax credit for a further eight weeks in such a situation. The same concession has been made in relation to child benefit (SSCBA 1992, s.145A, inserted by TCA 2002, s.55). 2.243

Determination of the maximum rate at which a person or persons may be entitled to child tax credit

7.—(1) In the following paragraphs— 2.244

(a) in the case of a single claim (but not a joint claim), the person making the claim is referred to as the "claimant"; and
(b) in the case of a joint claim, the members of the married couple or unmarried couple making the claim are referred to as the "joint claimants".

(2) The maximum rate at which a claimant or joint claimants may be entitled to child tax credit shall be the aggregate of—

(a) the family element of child tax credit; and
(b) an individual element of child tax credit, in respect of each child or qualifying young person for whom—
  (i) the claimant; or
  (ii) either or both of the joint claimants;
  as the case may be, is or are responsible.

(3) The family element of child tax credit—

(a) in a case where any of the children referred to in paragraph (2)(b) above is under the age of one year, is £1,090; and
(b) in any other case, is £545.

(4) The individual element of child tax credit for any child or qualifying young person referred to in paragraph (2)(b) above—

(a) where the child is disabled, is [1 £3,840];
(b) where the child is severely disabled, is [1 £4,730];
(c) in the case of any other child, is [1 £1,625];
(d) where the qualifying young person is disabled, is [1 £3,840];
(e) where the qualifying young person is severely disabled, is [1 £4,730]; and
(f) in the case of any other qualifying young person, is [1 £1,625].

AMENDMENT

1. Tax Credits Up-rating Regulations 2004 (SI 2004/941), reg.2 (April 6, 2004).

DEFINITIONS

"child"—see reg.2(1).
"claimant"—see *ibid.* and para.(1)(a).

"the family element of child tax credit"—see reg.2(1).
"the individual element of child tax credit"—see *ibid.*
"joint claim"—see *ibid.*
"qualifying young person"—see *ibid.*
"single claim"—see *ibid.*

General Note

2.245 Section 9 of the TCA 2002 makes provision for the maximum rate of child tax credit. This regulation provides the detail on how this rate is to be arrived at (para.(2)). It also sets out the actual annual rates for the component elements (paras (3) and (4)). Claimants who are entitled to income support or income-based jobseeker's allowance are automatically entitled to the maximum child tax credit applicable in their circumstances (TCA 2002, s.7(2) and Tax Credits (Income Thresholds and Determination of Rates) Regulations 2002 (SI 2002/2008), reg.4). The entitlement of other claimants is dependent upon the operation of the thresholds and withdrawal rates specified in the Income Thresholds and Determination of Rates Regulations.

Prescribed conditions for a disabled or severely disabled child or qualifying young person

2.246 **8.**—(1) For the purposes of section 9 of the Act a child or qualifying young person—

(a) is disabled if he satisfies the requirements of paragraph (2); and
(b) is severely disabled if he satisfies the requirements of paragraph (3).

(2) A person satisfies the requirements of this paragraph if—

(a) disability living allowance is payable in respect of him, or has ceased to be so payable solely because he is a patient; or
(b) he is—
    (i) registered as blind in a register compiled by a local authority under section 29 of the National Assistance Act 1948 (welfare services);
    (ii) in Scotland, has been certified as blind in a register maintained by or on behalf of a local government area (as defined in the Local Government etc. (Scotland) Act 1994), or
    (iii) in Northern Ireland, has been certified as blind and in consequence is registered as blind in a register maintained by or on behalf of a Health and Social Services Board; or
(c) he ceased to be so registered or certified as blind within the 28 weeks immediately preceding the date of claim.

(3) A person satisfies the requirements of this paragraph if the care component of disability living allowance—

(a) is payable in respect of him; or
(b) would be so payable but for either a suspension of benefit in accordance with regulations under section 113(2) of the Contributions and Benefits Act or an abatement as a consequence of hospitalisation,

at the highest rate prescribed under section 72(3) of that Act.

Definitions

"the Act"—see reg.2(1).
"child"—see *ibid.*

"the Contributions and Benefits Act"—see *ibid.*
"disability living allowance"—see *ibid.*
"patient"—see *ibid.*
"qualifying young person"—see *ibid.*

General Note

Section 9(5)(d) and (6) of the TCA 2002 make provision for a disabled child element and a severely disabled child element to be component parts of child tax credit. This regulation defines those terms. Thus, a child or qualifying young person is disabled if disability living allowance (DLA) is payable for them (or has ceased to be payable but only because he or she is now a patient) or if he or she is a registered blind person (or has ceased to be so registered in the immediately preceding 28 weeks) (para.(2)). A child or qualifying young person is severely disabled if they are entitled to the highest rate of the DLA care component (*i.e.* they satisfy both the "day" and "night" conditions in terms of their need for personal care or supervision): para.(3). The rates for these elements are set out in reg.8(4)(a) and (b). **2.247**

Tax Credits (Income Thresholds and Determination of Rates) Regulations 2002

(SI 2002/2008)

Whereas a draft of this instrument, which contains the first regulations made under section 13(2) of the Tax Credits Act 2002, has been laid before, and approved by resolution of, each House of Parliament:

Now, therefore, the Treasury, in exercise of the powers conferred upon them by sections 8(1) to (3), 13(2) and (3), 65(1) and (7) and 67 of the Tax Credits Act 2002, hereby make the following Regulations:

Made by the Treasury under ss.8(1)–(3), 13(2) and (3), 65(1) and (7) and 67 of the Tax Credits Act 2002.

Citation, commencement and effect

1.—(1) These Regulations may be cited as the Tax Credits (Income Thresholds and Determination of Rates) Regulations 2002 and shall come into force— **2.249**

(a) for the purpose of enabling claims to be made, on August 1, 2002;
(b) for the purpose of enabling decisions on claims to be made, on 1st January 2003; and
(c) for all other purposes, on 6th April 2003.

(2) These Regulations shall have effect for the tax year beginning with 6th April 2003 and subsequent tax years.

DEFINITIONS

"claim"—see TCA 2002, s.3.
"decision on claim"—see TCA 2002, s.14.
"tax year"—see reg.2.

Interpretation

2.250 **2.** In these Regulations—
"the Act" means the Tax Credits Act 2002;
"the income threshold" has the meaning given by section 7(1)(a) of the Act;
"period of award" shall be construed in accordance with section 5 of the Act;
"the relevant income" has the meaning given by section 7(3) of the Act;
"tax year" means a period beginning with 6th April in one year and ending with 5th April in the next.

Manner in which amounts to be determined for the purposes of section 7(1)(a) of the Act

2.251 **3.**—(1) This regulation prescribes the manner in which amounts are to be determined for the purposes of section 7(1)(a) of the Act.

(2) In the case of a person or persons entitled to working tax credit, the amount in relation to that tax credit is £5,060.

(3) In the case of a person or persons entitled to child tax credit, the amount in relation to that tax credit is [1£13,480].

AMENDMENT

1. Tax Credits Up-rating Regulations 2004 (SI 2004/941), reg.4 (April 6, 2004).

DEFINITION

"the Act"—see reg.2.

GENERAL NOTE

2.252 This regulation makes the necessary provision to give full operative effect to s.7(1) of the Act (income test).

Subsection (1)

2.253 Section. 7(1) of TCA 2002 imposes an income test on all claimants for tax credits, the test being whether the relevant income of the claimant (or claimants) for the tax year exceeds "the amount" for that tax credit. If the relevant income does exceed the amount, then it must be calculated by how much it does so. This applies to all claimants apart from those within s.7(2) and reg.4 below. In other words, "the amount" is the income threshold for claiming that tax credit. Only those with no incomes or incomes below the threshold can claim the full tax credit for the year. The section allows, and this regulation provides, different thresholds for different tax credits.

The thresholds for 2003–04, the initial year, were:

Child tax credit	£13,230
Working tax credit	£ 5,060

For 2004–05, the WTC threshold has remained the same but the CTC threshold has been increased to £13,480.

The existence of separate thresholds means that in many cases separate calculations have to be made under s.7(1) about entitlement to each tax credit. The current thresholds have the effect that many more people are entitled to the child tax credit than to the working tax credit. Regulations 7 and 8 of these Regulations make provision for dealing with this.

Social security benefits prescribed for the purposes of section 7(2) of the Act

4. The following are social security benefits prescribed for the purposes of section 7(2) of the Act in relation to child tax credit and working tax credit— 2.254

(a) income support under Part VII of the Social Security Contributions and Benefit Act 1992 other than income support to which a person is entitled only by virtue of regulation 6(2) and (3) of the Income Support (General) Regulations 1987;

(b) income support under Part VII of the Social Security Contributions and Benefit (Northern Ireland) Act 1992 other than income support to which a person is entitled only by virtue of regulation 6(2) and (3) of the Income Support (General) Regulations (Northern Ireland) 1987;

(c) an income-based jobseeker's allowance within the meaning of the Jobseekers Act 1995 or the Jobseekers (Northern Ireland) Order 1995.

[[1] (d) state pension credit within the meaning of the State Pension Credit Act 2002 or the State Pension Credit Act (Northern Ireland) 2002.]

DEFINITION

"the Act"—see reg.2.

AMENDMENT

1. Tax Credits (Miscellaneous Amendments No.2) Regulations 2003 (SI 2003/2815), reg.18 (November 26, 2003).

GENERAL NOTE

Section 7(2) of the TCA 2002 provides that those entitled to any of the social security benefits prescribed for the purposes of that subsection are not to be subject to the income test in s.7(1). This does not apply to exclude the claimant from any other requirements for an award. 2.255

Three benefits only have been prescribed by this regulation. They are:

(a) income support payable to any claimant. The exception applies to anyone who is a lone parent treated by reg.6(2) or (3) of the Income Support

(General) Regulations 1987 (and its Northern Ireland equivalent) as being entitled to income support for the first 14 days of a period of remunerative work because he or she was a lone parent who was, for at least 26 weeks before the work started, receiving income support or income-based jobseeker's allowance;

(b) income-based jobseeker's allowance;

(c) State pension credit.

Although the regulation does not state this, the effect of these prescriptions is sharply different between the two tax credits. Child tax credit can, under these rules, be claimed *in full* by any recipient of income support (subject to the exception) or income-based jobseeker's allowance without an income calculation. But, given the threshold for child tax credit set by reg.3, it is unlikely in practice that a parent within reg.6(2) and (3) will have enough income to exclude her or him from entitlement to that credit. Likewise, most claimants for the contribution-based jobseeker's allowance will also have income below the child tax credit income threshold. The fact that the claimant does not have a job is irrelevant to a claim for that tax credit. But a claimant for working tax credit is, presumably, unable to claim either form of jobseeker's allowance as she or he is required to be in remunerative work. And she or he is unable to claim income support because that work is required to be for at least 16 hours a week.

Amounts prescribed for the purposes of section 7(3)(a) and (b) of the Act

2.256 **5.** The amount prescribed for the purposes of section 7(3)(a) and (b) of the Act is £2,500.

DEFINITIONS

"the Act"—see reg.2.

GENERAL NOTE

2.257 Section 7(3) of TCA 2002 defines "relevant income". The approach adopted in the Act is to require a calculation of the income of any claimant (including any joint claimant) both for the current tax year (defined as the "current year income") or the previous tax year (defined as the "previous year income"). (For 2003–04 only, the "previous tax year" is treated by transitional provisions as being 2001–02: see S.I. 2002/1727, Art. 3). Section 7(3) sets out five rules for choosing whether the "relevant income" for that claimant for that year is the current year income or the previous year income.

The first four of the rules are set out in paras (a), (b), (c) and (d) of the subsection, with para.(e) supplying the default rule. Each of the paras (a)–(d) starts with the words "if an amount is prescribed for the purposes of this paragraph", and then sets out the rule. So these regulations should supply the prescribed sums for each of the four paras. They do not. They provide the sums only for paras (a) and (b). It is not clear whether this is a deliberate restriction of the operation of s.7(3), or an oversight, but the effect is that paras (c) and (d) have not been put into effect. Paragraphs. (a) and (b) provide the cases where the current year income exceeds the previous year income, while paras (c) and (d) provide for the cases where the previous year income exceeds the current year income. Para. (e) provides that in all other cases the current year income is to be taken. The amount prescribed for both paras (a) and (b) is £2,500. The effect of s.7(3) read with reg.5 is therefore to set three rules (not five) for choosing between the current year and previous year.

These are as follows:

(a) if the current year income exceeds the previous year income by not more than £2,500, then the relevant income is the previous year income;

(b) if the current year income exceeds the previous year income by more than £2,500, then the relevant income is the current year income reduced by £2,500;

(c) in any other case (such as the case where s.7(1) did not apply in the previous year and presumably including all cases where the previous year income is greater than the current year income), the current year income.

The stated intention of these provisions, and the partial effect of them, is to create a "buffer" between the previous year income and current year income. This is a rough-and-ready way of dealing with "small" changes in income level between one year and the next. It is rough-and-ready because the policy is to ignore income variations of up to £2,500. Given that the operative rate of tax credits is 37 per cent, the cash "value" of a £2,400 variation is £888, or just over £17 a week—doubtless a significant sum to someone earning, say, £6,000 a year.

As presently implemented, the rules operate as follows. An initial award under s.14 of the Act is made by the Revenue on the basis of the previous year income, under its powers to estimate income under s.7(10) of the Act. At the end of the year, the Revenue make a final decision under s.18. If the difference between the previous year income and current year income is an increase of less than the £2,500 buffer, then there is no required change to the previous year income, and no change need be made between the estimated award and the final entitlement. If the change is an increase of more than the £2,500 buffer, then the entitlement decision will be different from the award decision, but still buffered. For example, if the current income is £250 higher than the previous year income, then that increase will be ignored. This is to the advantage of the claimant who might otherwise lose some, or all, entitlement. This will apply if the current year income is less than £2,500 more than the previous year income, but not in any other case. The buffer does not operate if the current year income is less than the previous year income. If the current year income, for example, is £250 less than the previous year income, then the entitlement will be higher than the award. The result will be an underpayment of tax credit.

Manner of determining the rate at which a person is, or persons are, entitled to a tax credit

6. Regulations 7, 8 and 9 make provision as to the manner of determining the rate (if any) at which a person is, or persons are, entitled to a tax credit in any case where— 2.258

(a) the relevant income exceeds the income threshold; and

(b) his or their entitlement does not arise by virtue of section 7(2) of the Act.

DEFINITIONS

"entitlement"—see TCA 2002, ss.8 and 10.
"income threshold"—see reg.2.
"relevant income"—see reg.2.
"the Act"—see reg.2.

General Note

2.259 This is, on its face, purely a signposting regulation. It serves to remind the reader of the exception from the income test in s.7 of the TCA 2002, and also to tie in the £26 rule in reg.9 with the two main regulations: reg.7 dealing with working tax credit, and reg.8 dealing with child tax credit. As will be seen from those regulations, that order is intentional as entitlement to working tax credit, if any, must be calculated before entitlement to child tax credit.

There is, however, a drafting mismatch between the wording of this regulation and the approach of regs 7 and 8, which appears to deflect its intention. Reg. 6 states that the other regulations make provision for determining the rate of *entitlement* to tax credits. By contrast, regs 7 and 8 talk about periods of *award.* "Period of award" is defined in reg.2 of these Regulations by reference to s.5 of the TCA 2002 (entitled "periods of award"). And regs 7 and 8 of these Regulations refer to the elements of the credits to which a claimant "may be entitled" (regs 7(2)(a) and 8(2)).

The purpose of s.5 of TCA 2002 is to determine the period for which an award of tax credit is made. Awards are made under s.14 of the Act, and are made in advance of, or at the start of, the year of claim, using s.7(10) of the Act to estimate the income. At that point, the "period of award" can in most cases only be the whole tax year, or the balance of that year from the effective starting date of the award. Awards must ignore uncertain future changes as they are not then known. Regulations 7 and 8 set out in considerable detail how to deal with part-years. But, save for the case of claims made only part-way through a year, the "relevant period" for an award will always be the whole year, and the complexities of regs 7 and 8 are not needed.

The full calculations under regs 7 and 8 of these Regulations cannot be made until the end of the tax year, when the task of the Revenue is to make entitlement decisions under s.18 of the Act. So why refer to periods of award rather than periods of entitlement? It would appear that this mismatch between *award* and *entitlement* is a leftover of the changes made to the Tax Credits Bill during its passage through Parliament (as discussed in the notes to those sections). It is suggested that, to make practical sense of this regulation, the definition of "period of award" as applied to both regs 7 and 8 has to take in periods of entitlement as well.

Determination of rate of working tax credit

2.260 **7.**—(1) In relation to a person or persons entitled to working tax credit, the rate shall be determined by finding the rate for each relevant period and, where necessary, adding together those rates.

(2) "Relevant period" means any part of the period of award throughout which—

(a) the elements of working tax credit (other than the childcare element) to which the person or persons may be entitled, remain the same; and

(b) there is no relevant change of circumstances for the purposes of the childcare element of working tax credit, within the meaning of reg.16(1) of the Working Tax Credit (Entitlement and Maximum Rate) Regulations 2002 (change of circumstances for the purposes of childcare element).

(3) The rate for each relevant period shall be found in accordance with the following steps—

Step 1—Finding the daily maximum rate for each element other than the childcare element

For each element of the tax credit (other than the childcare element) to be included in the case of the person or persons entitled to the tax credit, find the daily maximum rate using the following formula: 2.261

$$\frac{MR}{N1}$$

where:
"MR" is the maximum rate in relation to that element for the tax year to which the claim for the tax credit relates;
"N1" is the number of days in that tax year.

Step 2—Finding the maximum rate for the relevant period for each element other than the childcare element

For each element of the tax credit to be so included, find the amount produced by multiplying the daily maximum rate (found under Step 1 and rounded up to the nearest penny) by the number of days in the relevant period. 2.262

Step 3—finding the income for the relevant period

Find the income for the relevant period by using the following formula: 2.263

$$\frac{I}{NI} \times N2$$

where:
"I" is the relevant income for the tax year to which the claim for the tax credit relates;
"N1" is the number of days in that tax year;
"N2" is the number of days in the relevant period.

Step 4—Finding the threshold for the relevant period

Find the threshold for the relevant period using the following formula: 2.264

$$\frac{£5,060}{NI} \times N2$$

where:
"N1" is the number of days in that tax year;
"N2" is the number of days in the relevant period.

Step 5—Finding the amount of the reduction

Find the amount which is 37 per cent of the amount by which the income for the relevant period (found under Step 3 and rounded down to the nearest penny) exceeds the threshold for the relevant period (found under Step 4 and rounded up to the nearest penny). 2.265

Step 6—Reducing the elements of the tax credit (other than any childcare element)

2.266 If the amount found under Step 5 (rounded down to the nearest penny) is less than or equal to the total of the amounts found under Step 2 for the elements of the tax credit, deduct the amount found under Step 5 (rounded down to the nearest penny) from the total of those amounts found under Step 2.

Step 7—Finding the actual weekly childcare costs for the relevant period

2.267 Find the relevant childcare charges for the relevant period in accordance with reg.15 of the Working Tax Credit (Entitlement and Maximum Rate) Regulations 2002.

Step 8—Finding the actual childcare costs for the relevant period

2.268 Multiply the result of Step 7 by $\frac{52}{N1} \times N2$

Here, N1 and N2 have the same meanings as in Step 3.

The result of this step is the amount of actual childcare costs for the relevant period.

Step 9—Finding the prescribed maximum childcare costs for the relevant period

2.269 Divide whichever of the maxima in reg.20(3) of the Working Tax Credit (Entitlement and Maximum Rate) Regulations 2002 is applicable by seven, round the result up to the nearest penny and multiply the resulting figure by the number of days in the relevant period.

The result of this is the prescribed maximum childcare costs for the relevant period.

Step 10—Finding the childcare element for the period

2.270 Take the lesser of the results of Steps 8 and 9.

Multiply that figure by 70 per cent and round the result up to the nearest penny.

The result of this step is the maximum rate of the childcare element for the relevant period.

Step 11—Reducing the elements of the tax credit (including any childcare element)

2.271 If the amount found under Step 5 (rounded down to the nearest penny) exceeds the total of the amounts found under Step 2 for the elements of the tax credit—

(a) deduct the excess from the amount found under Step 10 for any childcare element; and
(b) reduce the total of the amounts found under Step 2 for the other elements of the tax credit to nil.

Step 12—Finding the rate for the relevant period

2.272 Add together—

(a) the total of the amounts found under Step 2 for the elements of the tax credit (other than any childcare element) after reduction in accordance with Step 6 or Step 11; and

(b) the amount found under Step 10 for any childcare element after any reduction in accordance with Step 11.

This is the rate for the relevant period.

(4) "Child care element" has the meaning given by section 12(2) of the Act.

DEFINITIONS

"childcare element"—see TCA 2002, s.12.
"period of award"—see reg.2.
"rate"—see TCA 2002, s.13.

GENERAL NOTE

See the general note to reg.6 above. The effect of this regulation and reg.8—both together and separately—is to limit the amount of tax credit that a claimant can have to the relevant daily (or in the case of childcare element of working tax credit only, weekly) amount of the credit, if circumstances of a claimant change during a tax year. This approach is, as a result, less generous than the personal allowances for income tax, including children's tax credit. For example, the main personal allowance of an individual is the same amount for that individual throughout the year as is, for example, a bereaved person's allowance or a blind person's allowance. By contrast, the basis of calculation imposed by this regulation and reg.8 is that the elements of both working tax credit and child tax credit are payable only for the precise periods of the year for which the claimant can meet the requirement for that credit and element. For example, the family element of child tax credit increases from £545 to £1,090 for a family with a child under one in it. But under reg.8 that only increases the total child tax credit from the day when the child is born. Parents will only receive the full £1,090 in the relevant year if the child is actually born on April 6. Equally, however, the additional child tax credit continues to be payable up to the day before the child's first birthday in the following year (subject to the income test and save for marginal cases). **2.273**

Paras (1) and (2)

As noted above, "period of award" must be read as including also "period of entitlement" to make sense of this regulation. Likewise, the reference to "may be entitled" in para.(2) should include "is entitled". **2.274**

Para. (3)

This paragraph is written in the "step-by-step" style, using the command tense of relevant verbs, that has been adopted as part of the Tax Law Rewrite approach to tax regulations. It is also written so that the rules in the paragraph can be operated in full by a computer. **2.275**

Relevant periods of a full year

In most cases, as noted above, the complexities of this rule can be sidestepped because the question of an award of, or entitlement to, a tax credit can be judged by the full tax year. If the decision relates to a full year, then the steps can be telescoped as follows: **2.276**

Step 1 with Step 2: Identify the annual amount of each element of working tax credit to which the claimant is entitled, apart from the childcare element, for that tax year. **2.277**

2.278 *Step 3:* Identify the relevant income for the tax year (current year income or previous year income).

2.279 *Step 4 with Step 5 and Step 6:* If the income from Step 3 exceeds the annual amount from Steps 1 and 2, reduce the amount from Steps 1 and 2 by 37 per cent of that excess. The result is the excess income for the tax year.

2.280 *Step 7 with Step 8:* Find the relevant childcare charges for the tax year.

2.281 *Step 9 with Step 10:* The childcare element is 70 per cent of either £10,400 (for two or more children) or £7,020 (for one child) or, if less, 70 per cent of the total childcare charges for the tax year.

2.282 *Steps 11 and 12:* If there is excess income for the tax year from Steps 4–6, reduce the annual amount from Steps 1 and 2 by the amount of that excess, if necessary to nil. If the excess is greater than that amount, next reduce the amount from Steps 9 and 10 by the amount by which that excess income exceeds the annual amount from Steps 1 and 2. If the excess income is greater than both amounts, then the amount of working tax credit for the tax year is nil.

Note from this that the childcare element of working tax credit is to be calculated on a weekly, not daily, basis in the event of any problem, and also is to be left in payment after the other elements have stopped being payable under these rules.

Relevant periods of less than a year

2.283 "Short" periods arise only in a limited number of situations according to this regulation. A "period of award" comes to an end if the award of (and entitlement to) any element of working tax credit other than the childcare element changes. This looks simple, but might in practice produce complicated cases. A "period of award" will end in every case if a single claimant becomes one of a married or unmarried couple, or if joint claimants stop being a couple: TCA 2002, s.3(4). All claimants are required to report these changes: TCA 2002, s.6 and Tax Credits (Claims and Notifications) Regulations 2002 (SI 2002/2014), reg.21. But it also ends if the claimant (or either of the joint claimants) stops working for 16 hours a week, and if the 30-hour element has been claimed and the claimant (or either of them, or both of them together) stop working for 30 hours a week. There is no duty to report a change of hours above or below 30 hours. Careful note of the relevant periods needs to be made if the claimant comes, or stops being, within the scope of the disability element.

The rules for ending and restarting a period of award by reference to the childcare element are separate, and are based expressly on the duty to notify. That arises only if there is a change of circumstances about the childcare costs as detailed in reg.16 of the Working Tax Credits (Entitlement and Maximum Rate) Regulations 2002 (SI 2002/2005). Regulation 16(1) provides that there is a change of circumstances if charges stop being paid. There is also a change of circumstances if the average weekly childcare charges go up or down by £10 a week or more. As a result of last-minute changes to reg.16, the changes must be against a forward estimate, so only reflect a long-term change. In each of these cases, the steps set out in this regulation are to be applied in full separately to the periods before and after the change (or, if more than one change occurs, before and after each change).

Determination of rate of child tax credit

2.284 **8.**—(1) In relation to a person or persons entitled to child tax credit, the rate shall be determined by finding the rate for each relevant period and, where necessary, adding together those rates.

(2) "Relevant period" means—

(a) in the case of a person or persons entitled to child tax credit only, any part of the period of award throughout which the maximum rate at which he or they may be entitled to the tax credit remains the same;

(b) in the case of a person or persons entitled to both child tax credit and working tax credit, any part of the period of award throughout which the maximum rate of child tax credit to which he or they may be entitled remains the same and both sub-paras (a) and (b) of reg.7(2) are met.

(3) The rate for each relevant period shall be found in accordance with the following steps—

Step 1—Finding the daily maximum rate for each element

For each element of the tax credit to be included in the case of the person or persons entitled to the tax credit, find the daily maximum rate using the following formula: 2.285

$$\frac{MR}{NI}$$

where:

"MR" is the maximum rate in relation to that element for the tax year to which the claim for the tax credit relates;

"NI" is the number of days in that tax year.

Step 2—Finding the maximum rate for the relevant period for each element

For each element of the tax credit to be so included, find the amount produced by multiplying the maximum rate (found under Step 1 and rounded up to the nearest penny) by the number of days in the relevant period. 2.286

Step 3—Finding income for the relevant period

Find the income for the relevant period by using the following formula: 2.287

$$\frac{I}{NI} \times N2$$

where:

"I" is the relevant income for the tax year to which the claim for the tax credit relates;

"NI" is the number of days in that tax year;

"N2" is the number of days in the relevant period.

Step 4—Finding the threshold for the relevant period

Find the amount produced by the following formula: 2.288

$$\frac{\pounds 13{,}230}{NI} \times N2$$

where:

"NI" is the number of days in that tax year;

"N2" is the number of days in the relevant period.

The threshold for the relevant period is—

(a) in the case of a person or persons entitled to child tax credit only, that amount;

(b) in the case of a person or persons entitled to both child tax credit and working tax credit—

(i) that amount; or

(ii) if greater, the lowest amount of income for the relevant period (found under Step 3) which, disregarding reg.9, would result in a determination in accordance with reg.7 providing for no rate of working tax credit in his or their case for that period.

Step 5—Finding the amount of the reduction of the elements of the tax credit (other than the family element)

2.289 Find the amount (if any) which is 37 per cent of the amount by which the income for the relevant period (found under Step 3 and rounded down to the nearest penny) exceeds the threshold for the relevant period (found under Step 4 and rounded up to the nearest penny).

Step 6—Reducing the elements of the tax credit (other than the family element)

2.290 If the amount found under Step 5 (rounded down to the nearest penny) is less than the total of the amounts found under Step 2 for the elements of the tax credit (other than the family element), deduct the amount found under Step 5 (rounded down to the nearest penny) from the total of those amounts.

Step 7—Reducing the elements of the tax credit (other than the family element) to nil

2.291 If the amount found under Step 5 (rounded down to the nearest penny) is equal to or exceeds the total of the amounts found under Step 2 for the elements of the tax credit (other than the family element), reduce the total of those amounts to nil.

Step 8—Finding the amount of the reduction of the family element

2.292 Find the amount (if any) which is 6.67 per cent of the amount by which the income for the relevant period (found under Step 3 and rounded down to the nearest penny) exceeds—

(a) in any case where the total of the amounts found under Step 2 for the elements of the tax credit (other than the family element) would be reduced in accordance with Step 7 to nil if the relevant income were £50,000 or less, "X";

(b) in any other case, "Y";

where:

"X" is the amount found in accordance with Step 9 and rounded up to the nearest penny;

"Y" is the lowest amount of income for the relevant period (found under Step 3 and rounded up to the nearest penny) which would result in the total of the amounts of the elements of the tax credit (other than the family element) being reduced to nil in accordance with Step 7.

Step 9—Finding "X" for the purposes of Step 8

Find "X" using the following formula: 2.293

$$\frac{\pounds 50{,}000}{N1} \times N2$$

where:
"N1" is the number of days in that tax year;
"N2" is the number of days in the relevant period.

Step 10—Reducing the family element

Deduct any amount found under Step 8 (rounded down to the nearest penny) from the amount found under Step 2 for the family element. 2.294

Step 11—Finding the rate for the relevant period

Add together— 2.295

(a) the total of the amounts found under Step 2 for the elements of the tax credit (other than the family element) after any reduction in accordance with Step 6 or Step 7; and
(b) the amount found under Step 2 for the family element after any reduction in accordance with Step 10.

This is the rate for the relevant period.

(4) "The family element" means the family element of child tax credit within the meaning given by section 9(3) of the Act.

DEFINITIONS

"period of award"—see reg.2.
"the Act"—see reg.2.

GENERAL NOTE

See the general note to reg.6 above and the opening note to reg.7. 2.296

Paras (1) and (2)

The same comments apply as those to paras (1) and (2) of reg.7. 2.297

Para. (3)

This appears to be the equivalent for child tax credit of reg.7, but it has two additional elements. First, the effect of the steps is to remove an award of or entitlement to working tax credit before that of child tax credit. This may be important where one of a couple is receiving one of the credits while the other is receiving the other tax credit. The effect is to take the credit from the earner (and the duty to pay from the employer) before it is taken from the carer. 2.298

Secondly, the family element of child tax credit is removed only when a second, higher income threshold of £50,000 is exceeded. Further, the family element (currently £545 a year, increased to £1,090 if any of the children are less than a year old: Child Tax Credit Regulations 2002 (SI 2002/2007), reg.7(3)) is reduced only by 6.67 per cent of the excess of relevant income over £50,000. As the cut-off point for payment of child tax credit is £26 (reg.9 below), this makes the top relevant income to receive any tax credit just under £66,000 in 2003–04, but only where there is a child aged under one.

Relevant periods of a full year

2.299 In parallel with reg.7, reg.8 is straightforward as applied to a period of award of a full year. Steps 1–6 require that the annual amount of all elements (including the family element) be found, that the income for the year also be found, and that the excess of the income over the £13,480 threshold, if any, be calculated. The maximum amount of child tax credit is found by reducing the annual amount of all elements *excluding* the family element by 37 per cent of the excess of the income over the threshold.

Relevant periods of less than a year

2.300 If a claimant or claimants are entitled to both working tax credit and child tax credit, then anything that changes the entitlement to working tax credit also stops the period of award of child tax credit. However, the level of award of child tax credit may not in fact change as a result of this. In addition, the period of award of child tax credit, whether paid on its own or with working tax credit, changes under para.(2) if the "maximum rate" of child tax credit changes. "Maximum rate" is defined in Step 1, and is determined by reference to reg.7 of the Child Tax Credits Regulations 2002 (SI 2002/2007). The maximum rate will change if: the claimants become, or cease to be, responsible for any child; if an individual who was a child or qualifying young person ceases to be either a child or a qualifying young person; if a child becomes or ceases to be disabled or severely disabled; and if a new child is born to, or a child under one otherwise becomes the responsibility of, the claimant or claimants. In each of these cases, the steps in this regulation have to be applied separately to the periods before and after the change. Where the change occurs because of the death of a child or young person, the change does not take effect until eight weeks after the death: Child Tax Credits Regulations, 2002 reg.6.

Cases in which there is no rate of tax credit

2.301 **9.**—(1) In the case of a person or persons entitled to working tax credit only or child tax credit only, where the rate at which the person or persons would be entitled to the tax credit (as determined in accordance with reg.7 or 8) would be less than £26, there is no rate in his or their case.

(2) In the case of a person or persons entitled to both working tax credit and child tax credit, where the total of the rates at which the person or persons would be entitled to the tax credits (as determined in accordance with regulations 7 and 8) would be less than £26, there are no rates in his or their case.

General Note

2.302 This cut-off provision is authorised by s.13(3)(b) of the Act.

Tax Credits (Claims and Notifications) Regulations 2002

(SI 2002/2014)

The Commissioners of Inland Revenue, in exercise of the powers conferred upon them by ss.4(1), 6, 14(2), 15(2), 16(3), 17(10), 19(2), 22(1)(b) and (2), 65(1), (2) and (7) and 67 of the Tax Credits Act 2002, hereby make the following Regulations:

ARRANGEMENT OF REGULATIONS

PART I

GENERAL

PART II

CLAIMS

Part III

Notifications of Changes of Circumstances

2.305 19. Interpretation of this Part.
20. Increases of maximum rate of entitlement to a tax credit as a result of changes of circumstances to be dependent on notification.
21. Requirement to notify changes of circumstances which may decrease the rate at which a person or persons is or are entitled to tax credit or mean that entitlement ceases.
22. Manner in which notifications to be given.
23. Person by whom notification may be, or is to be, given.
24. Amended notifications.
25. Date of notification—cases where change of circumstances which may increase the maximum rate.
26. Date of notification—disability element and severe disability element for working tax credit.
26A. Date of notification—disability element and severe disability element for child tax credit.
27. Advance notification.
28. Circumstances where one person may act for another in giving a notification—receivers, etc.
29. Circumstances where one person may act for another in giving a notification—other appointed persons.

Part IV

Notices to Provide Information or Evidence

2.306 30. Employers.
31. Persons by whom childcare is provided.
32. Dates to be specified in notices under section 14(2), 15(2), 16(3), 18(10) or 19(2) of the Act.

Part V

Final Decisions

2.307 33. Dates to be specified in notices under section 17 of the Act.
34. Manner in which declaration or statement in response to a notice under section 17 of the Act to be made.
35. Circumstances where one person may act for another in response to a notice under section 17 of the Act—receivers, etc.
36. Circumstances where one person may act for another in response to a notice under section 17 of the Act.

PART I

GENERAL

Citation, commencement and effect

1.—(1) These Regulations may be cited as the Tax Credits (Claims and Notifications) Regulations 2002 and shall come into force on 12th August 2002. **2.308**

(2) These Regulations have effect in relation to claims for a tax credit for periods of award beginning on or after 6th April 2003.

Interpretation

2. In these Regulations— **2.309**

"the Act" means the Tax Credits Act 2002;

"appropriate office" means an office of—

(a) the Board,

(b) the Department for Work and Pensions, or

(c) the Department for Social Development in Northern Ireland;

"the Board" means the Commissioners of Inland Revenue;

"disability element" shall be construed in accordance with section 11(4) of the Act;

"joint claim" has the meaning given by section 3(8) of the Act;

"married couple" has the meaning given by section 3(5) of the Act;

[[1]"relevant authority" means—

(a) the Board;

(b) the Secretary of State or the Department for Social Development in Northern Ireland; or

(c) a person providing services to the Board, the Secretary of State or that Department in connection with tax credits;]

"severe disability element" has the meaning in regulation 17 of the Working Tax Credit Regulations;

"single claim" has the meaning given by section 3(8) of the Act;

"tax year" means a period beginning on 6th April in one year and ending with 5th April in the next;

"unmarried couple" has the meaning given by section 3(6) of the Act;

"the Working Tax Credit Regulations" means the Working Tax Credit (Entitlement and Maximum Rate) Regulations 2002.

AMENDMENT

1. Tax Credits (Claims and Notifications and Payments by the Board) (Amendment) Regulations 2003 (SI 2003/723), reg.3(1) (April 6, 2003).

Use of electronic communications to make claims or to give notices or notifications

2.310 **3.**—(1) In these Regulations "writing" includes writing produced by electronic communications that are approved by directions issued by or on behalf of the Board.

(2) If a claim which is required by these Regulations to be made to [[1]a relevant authority at an appropriate office] is made in writing produced by electronic communications, it shall be treated for the purposes of these Regulations as having been made to, and received by, [[1]a relevant authority at an appropriate office] on the date on which it is recorded on an official computer system.

(3) If a notice or notification which is required by these Regulations to be given to [[1]a relevant authority at an appropriate office] is given in writing produced by electronic communications, it shall be treated for the purposes of these Regulations as having been given to, and received by, [[1]a relevant authority at an appropriate office] on the date on which it is recorded on an official computer system.

(4) In this regulation—

(a) "electronic communications" has the meaning given by section 132(10) of the Finance Act 1999;

(b) "official computer system" means a computer system maintained by or on behalf of the Board to—

(i) send or receive information, or

(ii) process or store information.

AMENDMENTS

1. Tax Credits (Claims and Notifications and Payments by the Board) (Amendment) Regulations 2003 (SI 2003/723), reg.3(2) (April 6, 2003).

DEFINITIONS

"appropriate office"—see reg.2.
"the Board"—see *ibid.*
"electronic communications"—see para.(4)(a).
"official computer system"—see para.(4)(b).
"relevant authority"—see reg.2.
"writing"—see para.(1).

PART II

CLAIMS

Interpretation of this Part

2.311 **4.** In this Part (and Part III) "the relevant date", in relation to a claim for a tax credit, means—

(a) in cases where regulation 6 applies, the date on which the claim would be treated as being made by that regulation disregarding regulations 7 and 8;
(b) in cases where sub-paragraph (b) of regulation 11(3) applies, the date on which the claim would be treated as being made by that sub-paragraph disregarding regulations 7 and 8;
(c) in any other case, the date on which the claim is received by [1a relevant authority at an appropriate office].

AMENDMENT

1. Tax Credits (Claims and Notifications and Payments by the Board) (Amendment) Regulations 2003 (SI 2003/723), reg.3(2) (April 6, 2003).

DEFINITIONS

"appropriate office"—see reg.2.
"relevant authority"—see *ibid.*
"the relevant date"—see reg.4.

GENERAL NOTE

The general rule is that the "relevant date" (or date of claim in social security terms) is the date on which the claim for tax credits is received by "a relevant authority at an appropriate office" (para.(c)). On the basis of the definition of these latter terms in reg.2, this will normally, but not always, be an Inland Revenue office. For the date of receipt of electronic communications, *e.g.* online claims for tax credits, see reg.3. There are two modifications to the general rule in para.(c). First, amended claims are treated as made on the date on which the amended claim is received (see para.(a) and reg.6(3)). Secondly, where a claimant responds to a final notice under TCA 2002, s.17 within the specified time, the date of claim is the previous April 6 (reg.11(3)(a)). If the claimant's declaration is submitted beyond that time limit, then the date of claim is the latest date on which such declaration is received (see para.(b) and reg.11(3)(b)). Note that there are special rules governing the effective date of claim by refugees who have made a successful application for asylum and who subsequently make a retrospective claim for tax credits (see Tax Credits (Immigration) Regulations 2003 (SI 2003/653), regs 3 and 4). 2.312

Manner in which claims to be made

5.—(1) This regulation prescribes the manner in which a claim for a tax credit is to be made. 2.313

(2) A claim must be made to [1a relevant authority at an appropriate office]—
(a) in writing on a form approved or authorised by the Board for the purpose of the claim; or
(b) in such other manner as the Board may accept as sufficient in the circumstances of any particular case.

(3) A claim must contain the information requested on the form (or such of that information as the Board may accept as sufficient in the circumstances of the particular case).

(4) In particular, a claim must include in respect of every person by whom the claim is made—

(a) a statement of the person's national insurance number and information or evidence establishing that that number has been allocated to the person; or

(b) information or evidence enabling the national insurance number that has been allocated to the person to be ascertained; or

(c) an application for a national insurance number to be allocated to the person which is accompanied by information or evidence enabling such a number to be so allocated.

This paragraph is subject to paragraph (6).

(5) "National insurance number" means the national insurance number allocated within the meaning of regulation 9 of the Social Security (Crediting and Treatment of Contributions, and National Insurance Numbers) Regulations 2001.

(6) Paragraph (4) does not apply if the Board are satisfied that the person or persons by whom the claim was made had a reasonable excuse for making a claim which did not comply with the requirements of that paragraph.

(7) At any time after a claim has been made but before the Board have given notice of their decision under section 14(1) of the Act in relation to the claim, the person or persons by whom the claim was made may amend the claim by giving notice orally or in writing to [[1]a relevant authority at an appropriate office].

AMENDMENTS

1. Tax Credits (Claims and Notifications and Payments by the Board) (Amendment) Regulations 2003 (SI 2003 No.723), reg.3(2) (April 6, 2003).

DEFINITIONS

"the Act"—see reg.2.
"appropriate office"—see *ibid.*
"the Board"—see *ibid.*
"National insurance number"—see para.(5).
"relevant authority"—see reg.2.
"writing"—see reg.3(1).

GENERAL NOTE

Para. (2)

2.314 This rule is similar to, but not identical to, the standard social security provision in reg.4(1) of the Social Security (Claims and Payments) Regulations 1987 (SI 1987/1968). The fundamental difference is that it is not possible to make an oral claim for a social security benefit under reg.4(1) of the 1987 Regulations. This appears to be possible in the case of tax credits as the requirement that the claim be in writing appears only in para.(a), which will cover the great majority of cases, and not in the residual category envisaged by para.(b).

Paras (4)–(6)

2.315 The requirement to provide a national insurance number (or the information or evidence specified) mirrors the requirement for social security benefits set out in SSAA 1992, s.1(1B). Note however the Board's discretion not to apply this requirement if satisfied that the claimant had a reasonable excuse for making a claim which failed to comply with it (para.(6)). There is no equivalent discretion to disapply the requirement in the social security scheme.

Para. (7)

This provision is similar to the social security rule in reg.5(1) of the Social Security (Claims and Payments) Regulations 1987 (SI 1987/1968). However, a tax credits claim can be amended by giving oral notice, whereas the social security rule requires written notice. See further reg.6 on the determination of the date of claim for amended claims for tax credits. **2.316**

Amended claims

6.—(1) In the circumstances prescribed by paragraph (2) a claim for a tax credit which has been amended shall be treated as having been made as amended and, subject to regulations 7 and 8, as having been made on the date prescribed by paragraph (3). **2.317**

(2) The circumstances prescribed by this paragraph are where a person has amended or persons have amended the claim in accordance with reg.5(7).

(3) The date prescribed by this paragraph is the date on which the claim being amended was received by [[1]a relevant authority at an appropriate office].

AMENDMENT

1. Tax Credits (Claims and Notifications and Payments by the Board) (Amendment) Regulations 2003 (SI 2003/723), reg.3(2) (April 6, 2003).

DEFINITIONS

"appropriate office"—see reg.2.
"relevant authority"—see *ibid.*

Time-limit for claims (if otherwise entitled to tax credit up to three months earlier)

7.—(1) In the circumstances prescribed by paragraph (2), a claim for a tax credit received by [[1]a relevant authority at an appropriate office] shall be treated as having been made on the date prescribed by paragraph (3). **2.318**

(2) The circumstances prescribed by this paragraph are those where the person or persons by whom the claim is made would (if a claim had been made) have been entitled to the tax credit either—

(a) on the date falling three months before the relevant date (or on 6th April 2003, if later); or
(b) at any later time in the period beginning on the date in sub-paragraph (a) and ending on the relevant date.

(3) The date prescribed by this paragraph is the earliest date falling within the terms of paragraph (2)(a) or (b) when the person or the persons by whom the claim is made would (if a claim had been made) have become entitled to the tax credit.

AMENDMENT

1. Tax Credits (Claims and Notifications and Payments by the Board) (Amendment) Regulations 2003 (SI 2003/723), reg.3(2) (April 6, 2003).

DEFINITIONS

"appropriate office"—see reg.2.
"relevant authority"—see *ibid.*

GENERAL NOTE

2.319 This provides for a standard rule for a tax credits claim to be "backdated" by up to three months (assuming that the person or persons by whom the claim is made would then have been entitled to tax credit if an earlier claim had been made).

However, this regulation is subject to a transitional provision set out in Art.5(4) of the Tax Credits Act 2002 (Commencement No.4, Transitional Provisions and Savings) Order 2003 (SI 2003/962). Article 5(4) provides that a person shall not be entitled to a tax credit in respect of any day prior to the day on which he makes a claim for it where two conditions are met. The first is that that earlier date falls before April 6, 2004 (or before October 23, 2003 in the case of a claimant aged 60 or over) (or, in the case of a joint claim, where at least one member is aged 60). The second is that as at that earlier date the claimant (or either claimant) was entitled to income support or income-based jobseeker's allowance (other than under the "lone parent run-on" provisions). This provision is in consequence of the decision to transfer pensioner claimants of income support (in future state pension credit) to the new regime with effect from October 2003 and those of working age on the main means-tested benefits as from April 2004.

Date of claims—disability element of working tax credit

2.320 **8.**—(1) In the circumstances prescribed by paragraph (2) the claim referred to in sub-paragraph (f) of that paragraph shall be treated as having been made on the date prescribed by paragraph (3).

(2) The circumstances prescribed by this paragraph are where—

(a) a claim for working tax credit including the disability element ("the original claim") was made by a person or persons;
(b) on the original claim, the decision of the Board under section 14(1) of the Act was not to make an award of the tax credit;
(c) the reason for that decision was that the person or any of the persons did not satisfy [1paragraph (1)(c) of regulation 9] of the Working Tax Credit Regulations;
(d) at the relevant date in relation to the original claim, the person or any of the persons had made a claim for any of the benefits referred to in that paragraph that had not been determined;
(e) after that date, the claim for the benefit was determined in favour of the person by whom it was made; and
(f) a further claim for working tax credit including the disability element is made by the person or persons, within 3 months of the date that the claim for the benefit was determined.

(3) The date prescribed by this paragraph is—
(a) the first date in respect of which the benefit claimed was payable; or
(b) if later, the date on which the original claim was made (or treated as made under regulation 7).

AMENDMENT

1. Tax Credits (Claims and Notifications) (Amendment) Regulations 2003 (SI 2003/3240), reg.3 (January 1, 2004).

DEFINITIONS

"the Act"—see reg.2.
"the Board"—see *ibid.*
"disability element"—see *ibid.*
"the original claim"—see para.(2)(a).
"the relevant date"—see reg.4.
"the Working Tax Credit Regulations"—see reg.2.

GENERAL NOTE

This makes special provision for the date of a claim for working tax credit including the disability element of that tax credit. It covers the situation where a claim for working tax credit on this basis is disallowed because the claimant is not entitled to a qualifying benefit, although a claim for that benefit is pending and is subsequently allowed, and a further claim for working tax credit is made within three months of the determination of the claim for the qualifying benefit (para.(2)). In such a case, the date of claim is either the first date in respect of which the qualifying benefit was payable or, if later, the date on which the original working tax credit claim was made (para.(3)). **2.321**

Advance claims before the year begins

9.—(1) In the circumstances prescribed by paragraph (2) a claim for a tax credit may be made for a period after the relevant date. **2.322**
(2) The circumstances prescribed by this paragraph are where a tax credit is claimed for a tax year by making a claim before the tax year begins.
(3) This regulation shall cease to have effect in relation to the tax year beginning on 6th April 2004 and subsequent tax years

DEFINITIONS

"the relevant date"—see reg.4.
"tax year"—see reg.2.

GENERAL NOTE

This regulation provides, at least at the outset of the tax credits scheme, for claims for such credits to be made before the beginning of the tax year to which they relate (see also reg.14). There is further provision in reg.10 for advance claims for working tax credit where a person is about to start work. **2.323**

Advance claims—working tax credit

2.324 **10.**—(1) In the circumstances prescribed by paragraph (2) a claim for a tax credit may be made for a period after the relevant date.

(2) The circumstances prescribed by this paragraph are where—

(a) the tax credit in question is working tax credit; and

(b) the case falls within sub-paragraph (b) of the First Condition in regulation 4(1) of the Working Tax Credit Regulations (person who has accepted an offer of work which is expected to commence within seven days).

(3) In the circumstances prescribed by paragraph (2)—

(a) an award on a claim for tax credit may be made subject to the condition that the requirements for entitlement are satisfied no later than the date prescribed by paragraph (4); and

(b) if those requirements are satisfied no later than that date, the claim shall be treated as being made on the date on which they are satisfied.

(4) The date prescribed by this paragraph is the date falling 7 days after the relevant date.

DEFINITIONS

"the relevant date"—see reg.4.
"the Working Tax Credit Regulations"—see reg.2.

GENERAL NOTE

2.325 Claims for WFTC or DPTC could be made up to three days in advance (Social Security (Claims and Payments) Regulations 1987 (SI 1987/1968), reg.13(6)). This rule allows for working tax credit claims to be made up to seven days in advance where a person has accepted an offer of employment and is expected to commence within that week.

Circumstances in which claims to be treated as made—notices containing provision under section 17(2)(a), (4)(a) or (6)(a) of the Act

2.326 **11.**—(1) In the circumstances prescribed by paragraph (2), a claim for a tax credit is to be treated as made.

(2) The circumstances prescribed by this paragraph are where (in the case where there has been a previous single claim) a person has or (in the case where there has been a previous joint claim) both persons have made a declaration in response to provision included in a notice under section 17 of the Act by virtue of—

(a) subsection (2)(a) of that section;

(b) subsection (4)(a) of that section;

(c) subsection (6)(a) of that section; or

(d) any combination of those subsections.

The declaration made shall (subject to regulation 5(3)) be treated as a claim for tax credit by that person or persons for the tax year following that to which the notice relates.

(3) The claim shall be treated as made—

[2 (a) in a case where the declaration is made by 30th September next following the end of the tax year to which the claim relates, on 6th April preceding that date;

(aa) in a case where the declaration, not having been made by the date mentioned in sub-paragraph (a), is made before 31st January next following the end of the tax year to which the claim relates, and, in the opinion of the Board, the claimant had good cause for not making the declaration as mentioned in that sub-paragraph, on 6th April preceding the date on which the declaration is made;]

(b) in any other case, on the latest date on which the declaration is received by [[1]a relevant authority at an appropriate office] (subject to the application of regulation 7).

[[2] (4) Paragraph (3) does not apply—

(a) in the case where there has been a previous single claim (to which the notice referred to in paragraph (2) relates) if the person by whom it was made could no longer make a single claim; or

(b) in the case where there has been a previous joint claim (to which the notice referred to in paragraph (2) relates) if the persons by whom it was made could no longer make a joint claim.]

AMENDMENTS

1. Tax Credits (Claims and Notifications and Payments by the Board) (Amendment) Regulations 2003 (SI 2003/723), reg.3(2) (April 6, 2003).

2. Tax Credits (Miscellaneous Amendments) Regulations 2004 (SI 2004/762), reg. 3(2) (April 6, 2004).

DEFINITIONS

"the Act"—see reg.2.
"appropriate office"—see *ibid.*
"the Board"—see *ibid.*
"joint claim"—see *ibid.*
"relevant authority"—see *ibid.*
"single claim"—see *ibid.*
"tax year"—see *ibid.*

GENERAL NOTE

This allows the claimant's (or claimants') declaration in response to a Revenue final notice under various provisions of the TCA 2002, s.17, to be treated as a claim for tax credits. This effectively eases the process of making renewal claims for subsequent tax years. This assumes that the claimant(s) provide the necessary information as requested on the official form (para.(2) and reg.5(3)). The date of claim is the preceding April 6, *i.e.* the start of the tax year, assuming the declaration is returned within the designated time (para.(3)). 2.327

There are further deeming rules under reg.12 in relation to s.17 final notices.

Circumstances in which claims to be treated as made—notices containing provision under section 17(2)(b), (4)(b) and (6)(b) of the Act

12.—(1) In either of the circumstances prescribed by paragraphs (2) and (4) a claim for a tax credit is to be treated as made. 2.328

(2) The circumstances prescribed by this paragraph are where a person is or persons are treated as having made a declaration in response to provision included in a notice under section 17 of the Act by virtue of—

(a) subsection (2)(b) of that section; and

(b) subsection (4)(b) of that section,
or a combination of those subsections and subsection (6)(b) of that secon.

(3) The declaration referred to in paragraph (2) shall (subject to regulation 5(3)) be treated as a claim by that person or persons for tax credit for the tax year following that to which the notice relates.

(4) The circumstances prescribed by this paragraph are where a person or any of the persons has—

(a) made a statement under paragraph (b) of subsection (2) of section 17 of the Act in response to such a notice by the date specified for the purposes of that subsection; or

(b) made a statement under paragraph (b) of subsection (4) of that section in response to such a notice by the date specified for the purposes of that subsection,

or a combination of any of those subsections and subsection (6)(b) of that section.

(5) The notice referred to in paragraph (4), together with (and as corrected by) the statement or statements there referred to, shall (subject to regulation 5(3)) be treated as a claim for tax credit by that person or persons for the tax year following that to which the notice relates.

(6) The claim shall be treated as made on 6th April preceding the dates specified in the notice for the purposes of subsection (2) or (4) of section 17 of the Act.

(7) Paragraph (5) shall not apply—

(a) in the case where there has been a previous single claim (to which the notice relates), the person by whom it was made could no longer make a single claim; or

(b) in the case where there has been a previous joint claim (to which the notice relates), the persons by whom it was made could no longer jointly make a joint claim.

DEFINITIONS

"the Act"—see reg.2.
"joint claim"—see *ibid.*
"single claim"—see *ibid.*
"tax year"—see *ibid.*

GENERAL NOTE

2.329 Regulation 11 makes provision for the claimant's declaration in response to an Inland Revenue final notice to be treated as a claim for tax credits for the following tax year. This regulation makes similar provision for those cases in which the claimant is sent a final notice informing them that they will be treated as having declared that their circumstances as are specified in the notice. On the position of couples, see further reg.13.

Circumstances in which claims made by one member of a couple to be treated as also made by the other member of the couple

13.—(1) In the circumstances prescribed by paragraph (2) a claim for a tax credit made by one member of a married couple or an unmarried couple is to be treated as also made by the other member of the married couple or unmarried couple. 2.330

(2) The circumstances prescribed by this paragraph are those where one member of a married couple or an unmarried couple is treated by regulation 12 as having made a claim for a tax credit in response to a notice under section 17 of the Act given to both members of the couple.

DEFINITIONS

"the Act"—see reg.2.
"married couple"—see *ibid.*
"unmarried couple"—see *ibid.*

GENERAL NOTE

This reflects the general rule in TCA 2002, s.3(3) that couples must make a claim for tax credits jointly. 2.331

Circumstances in which awards to be conditional and claims treated as made—decisions under section 14(1) of the Act made before 6th April 2003

14.—(1) In the circumstances prescribed by paragraph (2) an award on a claim for a tax credit may be made subject to the condition that the requirements for entitlement are satisfied on 6th April 2003. 2.332

(2) The circumstances prescribed by this paragraph are those where—

(a) an advance claim (under regulation 9) for a tax credit has been made for the tax year beginning on 6th April 2003; and

(b) the Board give notice of their decision under section 14(1) of the Act before that date.

(3) Where, in a case falling within the terms of paragraph (2)—

(a) notification is given before 6th April 2003 of a change of circumstances (other than one increasing the maximum rate at which a person or persons may be entitled to a tax credit) which is expected to continue at that date; or

(b) the Board have reasonable grounds before that date for believing that the requirements for entitlement are otherwise expected to differ on that date from those in the claim,

the person or persons making the claim shall be treated as making a new claim (on the basis of the altered requirements for entitlement, together with so much of those requirements stated in the original claim as remain unchanged) in the place of the original claim.

DEFINITIONS

"the Act"—see reg.2.
"the Board"—see *ibid.*
"tax year"—see *ibid.*

GENERAL NOTE

2.333 This provides for circumstances in which claims for tax credits made before April 6, 2003 (under reg.9) can be made subject to the condition that the requirements for entitlement are satisfied on that date.

Persons who die after making a claim

2.334 **15.**—(1) This regulation applies where any person who has made a claim for a tax credit dies—

(a) before the Board have made a decision in relation to that claim under section 14(1) of the Act;

(b) having given a notification of a change of circumstances increasing the maximum rate at which a person or persons may be entitled to the tax credit, before the Board have made a decision whether (and, if so, how) to amend the award of tax credit made to him or them; or

(c) where the tax credit has been awarded for the whole or part of a tax year, after the end of that tax year but before the Board have made a decision in relation to the award under section 18(1), (5), (6) or (9) of the Act.

(2) In the case of a single claim, the personal representatives of the person who has died may proceed with the claim in the name of that person.

(3) In the case of a joint claim where only one of the persons by whom the claim was made has died, the other person with whom the claim was made may proceed with the claim in the name of the person who has died as well as in his own name.

(4) In the case of a joint claim where both the persons by whom the claim was made have died, the personal representatives of the last of them to die may proceed with the claim in the name of both persons who have died.

(5) For the purposes of paragraph (4), where persons have died in circumstances rendering it uncertain which of them survived the other—

(a) their deaths shall be presumed to have occurred in order of seniority; and

(b) the younger shall be treated as having survived the elder.

DEFINITIONS

"the Act"—see reg.2.
"the Board"—see *ibid.*
"joint claim"—see *ibid.*
"single claim"—see *ibid.*
"tax year"—see *ibid.*

GENERAL NOTE

2.335 This regulation makes provision as to how a claim is to proceed after the person or persons die after making it. In short, the personal representatives of the deceased person(s) may proceed with the claim (paras (2) and (4)), although in the case of a couple where only one partner has died the survivor may proceed with the claim in both their names (para.(3); see further reg.16). Paragraph (5) reflects the property law rule on contemporaneous deaths to be found in Law of Property Act 1925, s.184.

Persons who die before making joint claims

16.—(1) This regulation applies where one member of a married couple or an unmarried couple dies and the other member of the married couple or the unmarried couple wishes to make a joint claim for a tax credit. **2.336**

(2) The member who wishes to make the claim may make and proceed with the claim in the name of the member who has died as well as in his own name.

(3) Any claim made in accordance with this regulation shall be for a tax credit for a period ending with—

(a) the date of the death of the member of the married couple or unmarried couple who has died; or

(b) if earlier, 5th April in the tax year to which the claim relates.

DEFINITIONS

"joint claim"—see reg.2.
"married couple"—see *ibid.*
"unmarried couple"—see *ibid.*

GENERAL NOTE

See note to reg.15. **2.337**

Circumstances where one person may act for another in making a claim—receivers, etc.

17.—(1) In the circumstances prescribed by paragraph (2), any receiver or other person mentioned in sub-paragraph (b) of that paragraph may act for the person mentioned in sub-paragraph (a) of that paragraph in making a claim for a tax credit. **2.338**

(2) The circumstances prescribed by this paragraph are where—

(a) a person is, or is alleged to be, entitled to a tax credit but is unable for the time being to make a claim for a tax credit; and

(b) there are any of the following—

(i) a receiver appointed by the Court of Protection with power to make a claim for a tax credit on behalf of the person;

(ii) in Scotland, a tutor, curator or other guardian acting or appointed in terms of law who is administering the estate of the person; and

(iii) in Northern Ireland, a controller appointed by the High Court, with power to make a claim for a tax credit on behalf of the person.

Circumstances where one person may act for another in making a claim—other appointed persons

18.—(1) In the circumstances prescribed by paragraph (2), any person mentioned in sub-paragraph (b) of that paragraph may act for the person **2.339**

mentioned in sub-paragraph (a) of that paragraph in making a claim for a tax credit.

(2) The circumstances prescribed by this paragraph are where—

(a) a person is, or is alleged to be, entitled to a tax credit but is unable for the time being to make a claim for a tax credit; and

(b) in relation to that person, there is a person appointed under—

(i) regulation 33(1) of the Social Security (Claims and Payments) Regulations 1987;

(ii) regulation 33(1) of the Social Security (Claims and Payments) Regulations (Northern Ireland) 1987; or

(iii) paragraph (3).

(3) Where there is no person mentioned in regulation 17(2)(b) in relation to the person who is unable to act, the Board may appoint under this paragraph a person who—

(a) has applied in writing to the Board to be appointed to act on behalf of the person who is unable to act; and

(b) if a natural person, is aged 18 years or more.

(4) An appointment under paragraph (3) shall end if—

(a) the Board terminate it;

(b) the person appointed has resigned from the appointment having given one month's notice in writing to the Board of his resignation; or

(c) the Board are notified that a receiver or other person mentioned in regulation 17(2)(b) has been appointed in relation to the person who is unable to make a claim.

DEFINITIONS

"the Board"—see reg.2.
"writing"—see reg.3(1).

PART III

NOTIFICATIONS OF CHANGES OF CIRCUMSTANCES

Interpretation ofthis Part

2.340 **19.** In this Part "the notification date", in relation to a notification, means—

(a) the date on which the notification is given to [1a relevant authority at an appropriate office]; or

(b) in cases where regulation 24 applies, the date on which the notification would be treated by that regulation as being given disregarding regulations 25 and 26.

AMENDMENT

1. Tax Credits (Claims and Notifications and Payments by the Board) (Amendment) Regulations 2003 (SI 2003 No.723), reg.3(2) (April 6, 2003).

DEFINITIONS

"appropriate office"—see reg.2.
"relevant authority"—see *ibid.*

Increases of maximum rate of entitlement to a tax credit as a result of changes of circumstances to be dependent on notification

20.—(1) Any change of circumstances of a description prescribed by para.(2) which may increase the maximum rate at which a person or persons may be entitled to tax credit is to do so only if notification of it has been given in accordance with this Part. 2.341

(2) The description of changes of circumstances prescribed by this paragraph are changes of circumstances other than those in consequence of which the Board have given notice of a decision under section 16(1) of the Act in accordance with section 23 of the Act.

DEFINITIONS

"the Act"—see reg.2.
"the Board"—see *ibid.*

GENERAL NOTE

The effect of this provision is that increases in the maximum rate of entitlement to a tax credit, as a result of some relevant change of circumstances, are dependent upon notification. The normal rule is that changes which have the effect of increasing entitlement are backdated for a maximum of three months from the date of notification (reg.25). 2.342

Requirement to notify changes of circumstances which may decrease the rate at which a person or persons is or are entitled to tax credit or mean that entitlement ceases

21.—(1) [[1]Subject to paragraph (1A),] where a person has or persons have claimed a tax credit, notification is to be given within the time prescribed by paragraph (3) if there is a change of circumstances of the description prescribed by paragraph (2) which may decrease the rate at which he is or they are entitled to the tax credit or mean that he ceases or they cease to be entitled to the tax credit. 2.343

[[1](1A) Paragraph (1) does not apply where advance notification has been given under regulation 27(1).]

(2) The description of changes of circumstances prescribed by this paragraph are changes of circumstances as a result of which—

(a) entitlement to the tax credit ceases by virtue of section 3(4) of the Act; or
(b) there is a change in the relevant childcare charges which falls within regulation 16(1)(b) (omitting paragraph (i)) of the Working Tax Credit Regulations.

(3) The time prescribed by this paragraph is the period of three months beginning on the date on which the change of circumstances occurs or, if later, the period of three months beginning on 6th April 2003.

AMENDMENTS

1. Tax Credits (Claims and Notifications and Payments by the Board) (Amendment) Regulations 2003 (SI 2003 No.723), reg.4 (April 6, 2003).

DEFINITIONS

"the Act"—see reg.2.
"Working Tax Credit Regulations"—see *ibid.*

GENERAL NOTE

2.344 This regulation requires the claimant to notify changes of circumstances which may decrease the rate at which a person is (or, in the case of a joint claim, persons are) entitled to a tax credit or mean that entitlement ceases altogether (para.(1)). However, it is not all such changes of circumstances which need to be so notified, but only those specified in para.(2). There are, at present, only two such notifiable changes of circumstances. The first is where entitlement to tax credits ceases by virtue of TCA 2002, s.3(4), which explicitly deals with changes in relationship status. Thus it covers the situation where either a couple separate (and so can no longer make a joint claim) or a single claimant becomes a member of a couple (and so can no longer make a claim as a single person). The second is where the change relates to the relevant childcare charges. The changes covered by reg.16(1)(b)(ii) and (iii) of the Working Tax Credits (Entitlement and Maximum Rate) Regulations 2002 (SI 2002/2005) are where such charges either cease or go down by more £10 a week on average.

The changes described above are the only ones currently listed in the Inland Revenue's guidance notes (TC 6000 Notes, p.42) as "Changes you *must* tell us about". It appears, however, that this list is not complete. This is because TCA 2002, s.3(4) refers to entitlement ceasing where a claimant is (or joint claimants are) no longer able to make a single or joint claim (as appropriate). This therefore refers back to the conditions for making a single or joint claim in TCA 2002, s.3(3). However, that section is not solely concerned with relationship status—it also requires that claimants "are in the United Kingdom". Moreover, being in the United Kingdom is defined in terms of being "ordinarily resident" in the country (Tax Credits (Residence) Regulations 2003 (SI 2003/654), reg.3(1)). Those Regulations also allow persons who are ordinarily resident in the United Kingdom to be treated as still in the country, even though temporarily absent, providing the period of absence is no more than eight weeks (or 12 weeks if abroad in connection with a family member's illness, disability or death; see Tax Credits (Residence) Regulations 2003, reg.4). That being so, long-term absence should also presumably be a notifiable change in circumstances for the purposes of this regulation.

It should be emphasised that these rules mean that there is an important change from the normal social security practice in terms of notifying changes in circumstances. There is no obligation under this regulation to report a change in overall *income*—such changes can be picked up in the end-of-year reconciliation process, although this runs the risk of an overpayment of tax credits accruing in the meantime.

The manner of notification of changes of circumstances is governed by reg.22; see also reg.23 on who may give a notification (but also regs 28 and 29 on the special cases of receivers and appointees) and reg.24 on amended notifications. Regulations 25 and 26 deal with the date of notification and reg.27 covers advance notification.

Manner in which notifications to be given

22.—(1) This regulation prescribes the manner in which a notification is to be given. 2.345

(2) A notification must be given to [[1]a relevant authority at an appropriate office].

(3) A notification may be given orally or in writing.

(4) At any time after a notification has been given but before the Board have made a decision under section 15(1) or 16(1) of the Act in consequence of the notification, the person or persons by whom the notification was given may amend the notification by giving notice orally or in writing to [[1]a relevant authority at an appropriate office].

AMENDMENTS

1. Tax Credits (Claims and Notifications and Payments by the Board) (Amendment) Regulations 2003 (SI 2003 No.723), reg.3(2) (April 6, 2003).

DEFINITIONS

"the Act"—see reg.2.
"appropriate office"—see *ibid.*
"the Board"—see *ibid.*
"relevant authority"—see *ibid.*
"writing"—reg. 3(1).

Person by whom notification may be, or is to be, given

23.—(1) In the case of a single claim, notification is to be given by the person by whom the claim for a tax credit was made. 2.346

(2) In the case of a joint claim, notification may be given by either member of the married couple or unmarried couple by whom the claim for a tax credit was made.

DEFINITIONS

"joint claim"—see reg.2.
"married couple"—see *ibid.*
"single claim"—see *ibid.*
"unmarried couple"—see *ibid.*

Amended notifications

24.—(1) In the circumstances prescribed by paragraph (2) a notification which has been amended shall be treated as having been given as amended and, subject to regulations [[2]25, 26 and 26A], as having been given on the date prescribed by paragraph(3). 2.347

(2) The circumstances prescribed by this paragraph are where the person or persons by whom the notification is given amends or amend the notification in accordance with regulation 22(4).

(3) The date prescribed by this paragraph is the date on which the notification being amended was given to [[1]a relevant authority at an appropriate office].

AMENDMENTS

1. Tax Credits (Claims and Notifications and Payments by the Board) (Amendment) Regulations 2003 (SI 2003 No.723), reg.3(2) (April 6, 2003).

2. Tax Credits (Miscellaneous Amendments) Regulations 2004 (SI 2004/762), reg.3(3) (April 6, 2004).

DEFINITIONS

"appropriate office"—see reg.2.
"relevant authority"—see *ibid.*

Date of notification—cases where change of circumstances which may increase the maximum rate

2.348 **25.**—(1) Where a notification of a change of circumstances which may increase the maximum rate at which a person or persons may be entitled to tax credit is given in the circumstances prescribed by para.(2), that notification is to be treated as having been given on the date specified by paragraph (3).

(2) The circumstances prescribed by this paragraph are where notification is given to [[1]a relevant authority at an appropriate office] of a change of circumstances which has occurred other than in the circumstances prescribed by regulation 26(2).

(3) The date specified by this paragraph is—

(a) the date falling three months before the notification date; or

(b) if later, the date of the change of circumstances.

AMENDMENT

1. Tax Credits (Claims and Notifications and Payments by the Board) (Amendment) Regulations 2003 (SI 2003 No.723), reg.3(2) (April 6, 2003).

DEFINITIONS

"appropriate office"—see reg.2.
"the notification date"—see reg.19.
"relevant authority"—see reg.2.

GENERAL NOTE

2.349 Where a change in circumstances leads to an increase in the claimant's entitlement to tax credits, the change can be backdated for up to three months before the date of notification. The requirement for notification itself in such circumstances is contained in reg.20.

Date of notification—disability element and severe disability element for working tax credit

2.350 **26.**—(1) In the circumstances prescribed by either paragraph (2) or (3), the notification of a change of circumstances referred to in subparagraph (f) of either of those paragraphs is to be treated as having been given on the date specified by paragraph (4).

(2) The circumstances prescribed by this paragraph are where—

(a) a claim for working tax credit including the disability element, the severe disability element, or both those elements ("the original claim") was made by a person or persons;

(b) on the original claim, the decision of the Board under section 14(1) of the Act was not to award the [1credit], or to award it without one or both of those elements;

(c) the reason for that decision was that the person or any of the persons was not entitled to the element because he did not satisfy [1regulation 9(1)(c)], or regulation 17(2), as the case may be, of the Working Tax Credit Regulations;

(d) at the relevant date in relation to the original claim, the person or any of the persons had made a claim for any of the benefits referred to in those regulations that had not been determined;

(e) after that date, the claim for the benefit was determined in favour of the person by whom it was made; and

(f) notification is given of the change of circumstances which results in the person or any of the persons becoming entitled to that element or those elements, as the case may be, within three months of the date that the claim for the benefit was determined.

(3) The circumstances prescribed by this paragraph are where—

(a) a notification was given of a change of circumstances which might result in the person or any of the persons by whom the claim was made becoming entitled to the disability element or the severe disability element of working tax credit ("the original notification");

(b) on the notification, the decision of the Board under section 15(1) of the Act was not to amend the award of the tax credit made to him or them;

(c) the reason for that decision was that the person or any of the persons was not entitled to the element because he did not satisfy [1regulation 9(1)(c)], or regulation 17(2), as the case may be, of the Working Tax Credit Regulations;

(d) at the notification date in relation to the original notification, the person or either of the persons had made a claim that had not been determined for any of the benefits referred to in those Regulations;

(e) after that date, the claim for the benefit was determined in favour of the person by whom it was made; and

(f) a further notification of the change of circumstances is given by the person or any of the persons, within three months of the date that the claim for benefit was determined.

(4) The date prescribed by this paragraph is—

(a) the first date in respect of which the benefit claimed is payable; or

(b) if later, the date on which—

(i) in the circumstances prescribed by paragraph (2), the original claim was made (or treated as made under regulation 7); or

(ii) in the circumstances prescribed by paragraph (3), the original notification was given (or treated as given under regulation 25).

AMENDMENT

1. Tax Credits (Claims and Notifications) (Amendment) Regulations 2003 (SI 2003/3240), reg.4 (January 1, 2004).

DEFINITIONS

"the Act"—see reg.2.
"the Board"—see *ibid.*
"disability element"—see *ibid.*
"the notification date"—see reg.19.
"the original claim"—see para.(2)(a).
"the original notification"—see para.(3)(a).
"relevant date"—see reg.4.
"severe disability element"—see reg.2.
"Working Tax Credit Regulations"—see *ibid.*

GENERAL NOTE

2.351 The effect of this regulation is that a claim for the disability or severe disability element of working tax credit, based on a claim made for a disability or incapacity benefit, may be backdated to the first date in respect which that benefit is payable, if the award of that benefit is notified to the Board within three months of its having been made.

[1 Date of notification—disability element and severe disability element for child tax credit

2.352 **26A.**—(1) In the circumstances prescribed by either paragraph (2) or (3), the notification of a change of circumstances referred to in sub-paragraph (f) of either of those paragraphs is to be treated as having been given on the date specified by paragraph (4).

(2) The circumstances prescribed by this paragraph are where—

(a) a claim for child tax credit including the disability element, the severe disability element or both those elements ("the original claim") was made by a person or persons in respect of a child;

(b) on the original claim the decision of the Board under section 14(1) of the Act was not to award the credit, or to award it without one or both of those elements;

(c) the reason for that decision was that the person or the persons were not entitled to the element because the child did not satisfy regulation 8(2) or (3), as the case may be, of the Child Tax Credit Regulations 2002;

(d) at the relevant date in relation to the original claim, the person or any of the persons had made a claim for a disability living allowance in respect of that child ("the other claim") and the other claim had not been determined;

(e) after that date, the other claim was determined in favour of the person by whom it was made; and

(f) notice is given of the change of circumstances which results in the person or any of the persons becoming entitled to that element or those elements, as the case may be, within three months of the date that the other claim was determined.

(3) The circumstances prescribed by this paragraph are where—

(a) a notification was given of a change of circumstances which might result in the person or any of the persons by whom the claim was made becoming entitled to the disability element or the severe disability element of child tax credit ("the original notification");

(b) on the notification, the decision of the Board under section 15(1) of the Act was not to amend the award of the tax credit made to him or them;

(c) the reason for that decision was that the person or any of the persons was not entitled to the element because regulation 8(2) or (3), as the case may be, of the Child Tax Credit Regulations 2002 was not satisfied in respect of the child in relation to whom the claim was made;

(d) at the notification date in relation to the original notification, the person or either of the persons had made, in respect of the child, a claim that had not been determined for a disability living allowance ("the other claim");

(e) after that date, the other claim was determined in favour of the person by whom it was made; and

(f) a further notification of the change of circumstances is given by the person or any of the persons, within three months of the date that the other claim was determined.

(4) The date prescribed by this paragraph is—

(a) the first date in respect of which the disability living allowance is payable; or

(b) if later, the date on which—

(i) in the circumstances prescribed by paragraph (2), the original claim was made (or treated as made under regulation 7); or

(ii) in the circumstances prescribed by paragraph (3), the original notification was given (or treated as given under regulation 25).]

AMENDMENT

1. Tax Credits (Miscellaneous Amendments) Regulations 2004 (SI 2004/762), reg.3(4) (April 6, 2004).

DEFINITIONS

"the Act"—see reg. 2.
"the Board"—see *ibid.*
"the disability element"—see *ibid.*
"the notification date"—see reg. 19.
"the original claim"—see para. (2)(a).
"the original notification"—see para. (3)(a).
"the other claim"—see paras. (2)(d) and 3(d).
"the severe disability element"—see reg. 2.

GENERAL NOTE

The effect of this regulation is that a claim for the disability or severe disability element of child tax credit, based on a claim made in respect of the child for 2.353

disability living allowance, may be backdated to the first date in respect which that allowance is payable, providing the award is notified to the Board within three months of its having been made.

Advance notification

2.354 **27.**—(1) In [[1]any] of the circumstances prescribed by paragraphs (2) [[1], 2A] and (3) a notification of a change of circumstances may be given for a period after the date on which it is given.

(2) The circumstances prescribed by this paragraph are those prescribed by regulation 10(2) (working tax credit: person who has accepted an offer of work expected to commence within seven days), the reference to "the claim" being read as a reference to the notification.

[[1](2A) The circumstances prescribed by this paragraph are where either regulation 15(4) (agreement for the provision of future childcare) or regulation 16(1) (relevant change in circumstances) of the Working Tax Credit Regulations applies.]

(3) The circumstances prescribed by this paragraph are where a tax credit has been claimed for the tax year beginning on 6th April 2003 by making a claim before that tax year begins, and the notification relates to that tax year and is given before that date.

(4) In the circumstances prescribed by paragraph (2), an amendment of an award of a tax credit in consequence of a notification of a change of circumstances may be made subject to the condition that the requirements for entitlement to the amended amount of the tax credit are satisfied at the time prescribed by paragraph (5).

(5) The time prescribed by this paragraph is the latest date which—

(a) is not more than seven days after the date on which the notification is given; and

(b) falls within the period of award in which the notification is given.

[[1] (5A) In the circumstances prescribed by paragraph (2A), an amendment of an award of tax credit in consequence of a notification of a change of circumstances may be made subject to the condition that the requirements for entitlement to the amended amount of the tax credit are satisfied at the time prescribed by paragraph (5B).

(5B) The time prescribed by this paragraph is the first day of the week—

(a) in which the agreement within regulation 15(4) of the Working Tax Credit Regulations commences or the relevant change of circumstances occurs; and

(b) which is not more than seven days after the date on which notification is given and falls within the period of award in which the notification is given.

(5C) For the purposes of paragraph (5B), "week" means a period of 7 days beginning with midnight between Saturday and Sunday.]

(6) "Period of award" shall be construed in accordance with section 5 of the Act.

AMENDMENTS

1. Tax Credits (Claims and Notifications and Payments by the Board) (Amendment) Regulations 2003 (SI 2003 No.723), reg.5 (April 6, 2003).

Definitions

"the Act"—see reg.2.
"the claim"—see para.(2).
"period of award"—see para.(6).
"tax year"—see reg.2.
"week"—see para.(5C).

Circumstances where one person may act for another in giving a notification—receivers etc.

28.—(1) In the circumstances prescribed by paragraph (2) any receiver or other person mentioned in sub-paragraph (b) of that paragraph may act for the person mentioned in sub-paragraph (a) of that paragraph in giving a notification. 2.355

(2) The circumstances prescribed by this paragraph are where—

(a) a person is unable for the time being to give a notification; and

(b) there are any of the following—

(i) a receiver appointed by the Court of Protection with power to proceed with a claim for a tax credit on behalf of the person;

(ii) in Scotland, a tutor, curator or other guardian acting or appointed in terms of law who is administering the estate of the person; and

(iii) in Northern Ireland, a controller appointed by the High Court, with power to proceed with a claim for a tax credit on behalf of the person.

General Note

See also reg.35 in respect of receivers, etc. acting in response to final notices under TCA 2002, s.17. 2.356

Circumstances where one person may act for another in giving a notification—other appointed persons

29.—(1) In the circumstances prescribed by paragraph (2) any person mentioned in sub-paragraph (b) of that paragraph may act for the person mentioned in sub-paragraph (a) of that paragraph in giving a notification. 2.357

(2) The circumstances prescribed by this paragraph are where—

(a) a person is unable for the time being to give a notification; and

(b) in relation to that person, there is a person appointed under—

(i) regulation 33(1) of the Social Security (Claims and Payments) Regulations 1987;

(ii) regulation 33(1) of the Social Security (Claims and Payments) Regulations (Northern Ireland) 1987; or

(iii) regulation 18(3);

and the provisions of regulation 18(3) shall apply to notifications and (under regulation 36) responses to notices under section 17 of the Act, as they apply to claims.

Definition

"the Act"—see reg.2.

GENERAL NOTE

2.358 See also reg.36 in respect of appointees acting in response to final notices under TCA 2002, s.17.

PART IV

NOTICES TO PROVIDE INFORMATION OR EVIDENCE

Employers

2.359 **30.**—(1) For the purposes of sections 14(2)(b), 15(2)(b), 16(3)(b) and 19(2)(b) of the Act the persons specified in paragraph (2) are prescribed, and, in relation to those persons, the information or evidence specified in paragraph (4) is prescribed.

(2) The persons specified in this paragraph are—

(a) any person named by a person or either of the persons by whom a claim for a tax credit is made as his employer or the employer of either of them; and

(b) any person whom the Board have reasonable grounds for believing to be an employer of a person or either of the persons by whom such a claim is made.

(3) "Employer" has the meaning given by section 25(5) of the Act.

(4) The information or evidence specified in this paragraph is information or evidence, including any documents or certificates, which relates to—

(a) the claim for the tax credit in question;

(b) the award of the tax credit in question; or

(c) any question arising out of, or under, that claim or award.

DEFINITIONS

"the Act"—see reg.2.
"the Board"—see *ibid.*
"employer"—see para.(3).

Persons by whom childcare is provided

2.360 **31.**—(1) For the purposes of sections 14(2)(b), 15(2)(b), 16(3)(b) and 19(2)(b) of the Act the persons specified in paragraph (2) are prescribed, and, in relation to those persons, the information or evidence specified in paragraph (3) is prescribed.

(2) The persons specified in this paragraph are—

(a) any person named by a person or persons by whom a claim for the childcare element of working tax credit is made as being, in relation to him or either of them, a person by whom childcare is provided; and

(b) any person whom the Board have reasonable grounds for believing to be, in relation to a person or persons by whom such a claim is made, a person by whom childcare is provided.

(3) The information or evidence specified in this paragraph is information or evidence, including any documents or certificates, which relates to—

(a) the claim for the tax credit in question;
(b) the award of the tax credit in question; or
(c) any question arising out of, or under, that claim or award.

(4) "Child care" has the meaning given by regulation 14(2) of the Working Tax Credit Regulations.

DEFINITIONS

"the Act"—see reg.2.
"the Board"—see *ibid.*
"childcare"—see para.(4).

Dates to be specified in notices under section 14(2), 15(2), 16(3), 18(10) or 19(2) of the Act

32. In a notice under section 14(2), 15(2), 16(3), 18(10) or 19(2) of the Act, the date which may be specified shall not be less than 30 days after the date of the notice. **2.361**

DEFINITION

"the Act"—see reg.2.

PART V

FINAL DECISION

[[1] Dates to be specified in notices under section 17 of the Act

33. In a notice under section 17 of the Act— **2.362**

(a) the date which may be specified for the purposes of subsection (2) or subsection (4) shall be not later than 30th September following the end of the tax year to which the notice relates, or 30 days after the date on which the notice is given, if later; and
(b) the date which may be specified for the purposes of subsection (8) shall be not later than 31st January following the end of the tax year to which the notice relates, or 30 days after the date on which the notice is given, if later.]

AMENDMENT

1. Tax Credits (Miscellaneous Amendments) Regulations 2004 (SI 2004/762), reg.3(5) (April 6, 2004).

DEFINITIONS

"the Act"—see reg.2.
"tax year"—see *ibid.*

[1 Manner in which declaration or statement in response to a notice under section 17 of the Act to be made

2.363 **34.**—(1) This regulation prescribes the manner in which a declaration or statement in response to a notice under section 17 of the Act must be made.

(2) A declaration or statement must be made—

(a) in writing in a form approved by the Board for that purpose;

(b) orally to an officer of the Board; or

(c) in such other manner as the Board may accept as sufficient in the circumstances of any particular case.

(3) In a case falling within paragraph (2)(b) one of two joint claimants may act for both of them in response to a notice under section 17 if, at the time the declaration or statement is made, a joint claim could be made by both of them.]

AMENDMENT

1. Tax Credits (Miscellaneous Amendments) Regulations 2004 (SI 2004/762), reg.3(5) (April 6, 2004).

DEFINITIONS

"the Act"—see reg.2.
"the Board"—see *ibid.*
"joint claim"—see *ibid.*

Circumstances where one person may act for another in response to a notice under section 17 of the Act—receivers, etc.

2.364 **35.**—(1) In the circumstances prescribed by paragraph (2) any receiver or other person mentioned in sub-paragraph (b) of that paragraph may act for the person mentioned in sub-paragraph (a) of that paragraph in response to a notice under section 17 of the Act.

(2) The circumstances prescribed by this paragraph are where—

(a) a person is unable for the time being to act in response to a notice under section 17 of the Act; and

(b) there are any of the following—

(i) a receiver appointed by the Court of Protection with power to proceed with a claim for a tax credit on behalf of the person;

(ii) in Scotland, a tutor, curator or other guardian acting or appointed in terms of law who is administering the estate of the person; and

(iii) in Northern Ireland, a controller appointed by the High Court, with power to proceed with a claim for a tax credit and proceed with the claim on behalf of the person.

DEFINITION

"the Act"—see reg.2.

Circumstances where one person may act for another in response to a notice under section 17 of the Act

36.—(1) In the circumstances prescribed by paragraph (2) any person mentioned in sub-paragraph (b) of that paragraph may act for the person mentioned in sub-paragraph (a) of that paragraph in response to a notice under section 17 of the Act. 2.365

(2) The circumstances prescribed by this paragraph are where—

(a) a person is unable for the time being to act in response to a notice under section 17 of the Act; and

(b) in relation to that person, there is a person appointed under—

(i) regulation 33(1) of the Social Security (Claims and Payments) Regulations 1987;

(ii) regulation 33(1) of the Social Security (Claims and Payments) Regulations (Northern Ireland) 1987; or

(iii) regulation 18(3).

Definition

"the Act"—see reg.2.

Working Tax Credit (Payment by Employers) Regulations 2002

(SI 2002/2172) (as amended)

The Commissioners of Inland Revenue, in exercise of the powers conferred upon them by sections 25(1) and (2), 65 and 67 of the Tax Credits Act 2002, and with the consent of the Scottish Ministers, hereby make the following Regulations: 2.366

GENERAL NOTE

2.367 The statutory presumption is that payments of working tax credit are to be paid by employers (see TCA 2002, ss.24(6) and 25). These Regulations accordingly set out the detailed provisions defining the nature and extent of employers' duties in this regard. Payments of child tax credit, however, are to be made by the Board, as are payments of working tax credit that are not covered by s.25 of the Act or by these Regulations, *e.g.* by virtue of reg.6(14) below (see further Tax Credits (Payments by the Board) Regulations 2002 (SI 2002/2173), in this volume at para.2.402). There is also an important transitional provision to note. Where a child tax credit or working tax credit claim has been made by a person who was previously entitled to either WFTC or DPTC under the TCA 1999, any payments due to such a person on or before October 5, 2003 may be made by the Board directly—irrespective of the duties laid down by either these Regulations or the Tax Credits (Payments by the Board) Regulations 2002 (see Tax Credits Act 2002 (Commencement No.4, Transitional Provisions and Savings) Order 2003 (SI 2003/962), art.5(1)).

The Chancellor of the Exchequer announced in the 2004 Budget that measures would be taken to transfer the duty to pay working tax credit from employers back to the Inland Revenue. No details had been announced at the date of writing.

Citation, commencement and effect

2.368 **1.**—(1) These Regulations may be cited as the Working Tax Credit (Payment by Employers) Regulations 2002 and shall come into force on 1st March 2003.

(2) These Regulations have effect in relation to payments of working tax credit for periods beginning on or after 6th April 2003.

Interpretation

2.369 **2.**—(1) In these Regulations—

"amendment notice" shall be construed in accordance with regulation 5(1);

"the Board" means the Commissioners of Inland Revenue;

"the Contributions Regulations" means the Social Security (Contributions) Regulations 2001;

[[1]. . .];

"employer" and "employee" shall be construed in accordance with section 25(5) of the Tax Credits Act 2002;

"employer's place of business" means—

(a) the place where the trade, profession, vocation or business of the employer is carried on, or

(b) if the trade, profession, vocation or business of the employer is carried on at more than one place, the head office or the place where it is mainly carried on,

[[2]. . .]

"income tax month" means the period beginning on the sixth day of any calendar month and ending on the fifth day of the following calendar month;

"income tax quarter" means the period beginning on the 6th April and ending on the 5th July in any income tax year, or beginning on the 6th July and ending on the 5th October in that year, or beginning on the 6th October and ending on the 5th January in that year, or beginning on the 6th January and ending on the 5th April in that year;

"income tax year" means a year beginning on 6th April in any year and ending on 5th April in the following year;

"the Management Act" means the Taxes Management Act 1970;

"pay period" means the period by reference to which an employee's [1PAYE income is] paid, whether weekly, monthly or otherwise;

[1"PAYE income" has the meaning given by section 683 of the Income Tax (Earnings and Pensions) Act 2003;]

[2"the PAYE Regulations" means the Income Tax (Pay as You Earn) Regulations 2003;]

"relevant employer" has the meaning given by regulation 3;

"start notice" shall be construed in accordance with regulation 4(1);

"stop notice" shall be construed in accordance with regulation 12(1);

"the Taxes Act" means the Income and Corporation Taxes Act 1988.

(2) Any notice given under these Regulations to or by the Board must be in writing.

(3) In paragraph (2), "writing" includes writing produced by electronic communications that are approved by the Board.

AMENDMENTS

1. Working Tax Credit (Payment by Employers) (Amendment) Regulations 2003 (SI 2003/715), reg.4 (April 6, 2003).

2. Tax Credits (Miscellaneous Amendments) Regulations 2004 (SI 2004/762), reg.17(2) (April 6, 2004).

Definition of "relevant employer"

3.—(1) In these Regulations "relevant employer" means— **2.370**

(a) an employer who is required, on making any payment of or on account of any [1PAYE income] to any person, to deduct tax in accordance with the Employments Regulations or to deduct contributions in accordance with the Contributions Regulations; or

(b) where a person is the employee of more than one such employer, the employer who normally employs the employee for the higher (or highest) number of hours each week.

This is subject to paragraph (2).

(2) "Relevant employer" does not include an employer who is authorised to make deductions in accordance with [2regulation 34 of the PAYE Regulations] (employee on fixed pay).

AMENDMENTS

1. Working Tax Credit (Payment by Employers) (Amendment) Regulations 2003 (SI 2003/715), reg.5 (April 6, 2003). Definitions

2. Tax Credits (Miscellaneous Amendments) Regulations 2004 (SI 2004/762), reg.17(3) (April 6, 2004).

DEFINITIONS

"the Contributions Regulations"—see reg.2.
"employee"—see *ibid.*
"PAYE income"—see *ibid.*
"PAYE Regulations"—see *ibid.*
"relevant employer"—see para.(1).

GENERAL NOTE

Para. (1)

2.371 This definition of "relevant employer" is based upon, but is not identical to, the definition used in reg.3 of the Tax Credits (Payments by Employers) Regulations 1999 (SI 1999/3219) for the purposes of WFTC. The basic definition in reg.3(1)(a) is fundamentally the same: the relevant employer—who is under a duty to pay working tax credit through the payroll by virtue of these Regulations—is an employer who is required to make deductions in respect of income tax or national insurance contributions from an employee's wages. There has been a slight change in terminology in the reference to "PAYE income" which reflects the change in nomenclature for Sch.E tax liabilities under ITEPA 2003. The main difference relates to employees who have more than one employer. Under the 1999 Regulations, the employer who paid the larger (or largest) net earnings to the employee was the "relevant employer". Under these Regulations, the test is one of hours, not net wages (reg.3(1)(b)).

Para. (2)

2.372 The definition of "relevant employer" excludes employers who are authorised to make deductions under reg.34 of the Income Tax (Pay as You Earn) Regulations 2003 (SI 2003/2682): see reg.3(2) and (4). Regulation 34 of the 2003 Regulations permits Inland Revenue inspectors to authorise employers to use the simplified tax tables for employees who are "in receipt of a fixed salary or wage". Accordingly these employees are not subject to the usual cumulative PAYE procedure. Regulation 34 was originally designed to deal with those employees such as domestic servants, who were paid without variation (*e.g.* through sickness) and who received no bonuses or overtime. This is known as the "Q" Scheme within the Revenue, and subject to an internal annual wages limit equivalent to the single person's allowance plus £700. It is not in common usage.

Notification to relevant employer of employee's entitlement to working tax credit (start notice)

2.373 **4.**—(1) Where an employee of a relevant employer becomes entitled to an amount of working tax credit equal to or exceeding 75 pence per day, the Board shall give notice to the relevant employer of the employee's entitlement in accordance with paragraphs (2) and (3) ("start notice").

(2) A start notice shall contain the following particulars—

(a) the date of issue of the start notice;
(b) the name of the employee;
(c) the employee's national insurance number and (if known) his payroll number;
(d) the date from which the employer is to be responsible for payment of working tax credit to the employee ("the commencement date");

(e) the daily rate of working tax credit applicable to each calendar day starting with the commencement date, and a table showing the multiples from 1 to 31 of that daily rate;

(f) instructions to the employer to pay working tax credit to the employee at the same time that the employer makes a payment of [[1]PAYE income] to the employee.

(3) The commencement date contained in the start notice shall not be earlier than the date which is 42 days after the date of issue of the start notice.

Amendment

1. Working Tax Credit (Payment by Employers) (Amendment) Regulations 2003 (SI 2003/715), reg.6 (April 6, 2003).

Definitions

"the Board"—see reg.2.
"the commencement date"—see para.(2)(d).
"employee"—see reg.2.
"employer"—see *ibid.*
"PAYE income"—see *ibid.*
"relevant employer"—see reg.3(1).
"start notice"—see para.(1).

General Note

This regulation sets out the Inland Revenue's obligations in terms of the information that must be supplied to employers in connection with employees who are entitled to payments of working tax credit. The detailed information to be contained in the start notice follows closely the model adopted under TCA 1999 for WFTC (Tax Credits (Payments by Employers) Regulations 1999 (SI 1999/3219), reg.4). However, for working tax credit purposes employers are entitled to 42 days' notice of the date for commencing payments of working tax credit in all cases (the WFTC rules provided for 14 days' notice for the weekly paid and 42 days' notice for employees paid at longer intervals). 2.374

Notification to relevant employer of amendment of amount of employee's entitlement to working tax credit (amendment notice)

5.—(1) Where— 2.375

(a) the amount of working tax credit to which an employee is entitled is amended; and

(b) the amended amount differs from the previous amount by an amount equal to or exceeding 30 pence per day,

the Board shall give notice to the relevant employer of the amended amount ("amendment notice").

(2) An amendment notice shall contain the following particulars—

(a) the date of issue of the amendment notice;

(b) the name of the employee;

(c) the employee's national insurance number and (if known) his payroll number;

(d) the date from which the employer is to be responsible for payment of the amended amount of working tax credit to the employee ("the commencement date");

(e) the daily rate of the amended amount of working tax credit applicable to each calendar day starting with the commencement date, and a table showing the multiples from 1 to 31 of that daily rate;

(f) instructions to the employer to pay the amended amount of working tax credit to the employee at the same time that the employer makes a payment of [1PAYE income] to the employee, commencing with the pay period in which the commencement date falls.

(3) The commencement date contained in the amendment notice shall not be earlier than the date which is 42 days after the date of issue of the amendment notice.

AMENDMENT

1. Working Tax Credit (Payment by Employers) (Amendment) Regulations 2003 (SI 2003/715), reg.6 (April 6, 2003).

DEFINITIONS

2.376 "amendment notice"—see para.(1).
"the Board"—see reg.2.
"the commencement date"—see para.(2)(d).
"employee"—see reg.2.
"employer"—see *ibid.*
"pay period"—see *ibid.*
"PAYE income"—see *ibid.*
"relevant employer"—see reg.3(1).

GENERAL NOTE

This regulation makes provision similar to that under reg.4, but in this case for the Inland Revenue to notify employers when there is an amendment to the working tax credit award currently in payment. This requirement does not apply where the difference is less than 30 pence a day in the working tax credit award (para.(1)(b)). This regulation had no parallel under the Tax Credits (Payments by Employers) Regulations 1999 (SI 1999/3219) for the simple reason that WFTC was paid at a fixed rate for a fixed six-month period. Although WFTC claims might in certain narrowly defined circumstances be terminated, they could not be amended as such.

Relevant employer's obligation to pay working tax credit

2.377 **6.**—(1) On receipt of a start notice in respect of an employee the relevant employer must, if he reasonably expects the employee to remain in his employment for three or more consecutive pay periods commencing with the pay period in which the commencement date contained in the start notice falls, take the following steps.

Step 1

2.378 Calculate the amount of working tax credit which the employee is entitled to be paid for each pay period in respect of which the employer will be responsible for paying working tax credit to the employee in accordance with the start notice.

Step 2

On making any payment of [1PAYE income] to the employee in respect of any date falling on or after the commencement date contained in the start notice, pay to the employee the amount of working tax credit to which he is entitled for the pay period in respect of which that payment of [1PAYE income] is made. **2.379**

(2) If the relevant employer receives a start notice in respect of an employee but—

(a) does not reasonably expect that employee to remain in his employment for three or more consecutive pay periods as mentioned in paragraph (1); or

(b) becomes aware before the first date on which a payment of [1PAYE income] is due in respect of any date falling on or after the commencement date contained in the start notice that the employee has left his employment, or will leave his employment before the end of the third consecutive pay period,

he must return the start notice to the Board, indicating on the notice his reasons for doing so.

(3) On receipt of an amendment notice in respect of an employee the relevant employer must, except where paragraph (4) applies, take the following steps.

Step 1

Calculate the amount of working tax credit which the employee is entitled to be paid for each pay period in respect of which the employer will be responsible for paying working tax credit to the employee in accordance with the amendment notice. **2.380**

Step 2

On making any payment of [1PAYE income] to the employee in respect of any date falling on or after the commencement date contained in the amendment notice, pay to the employee the amount of working tax credit to which he is entitled for the pay period in respect of which that payment of [1PAYE income] is made. **2.381**

(4) If the relevant employer receives an amendment notice in respect of an employee but becomes aware that the employee will leave his employment before the first date on which he is due to make a payment of [1PAYE income] to the employee following the commencement date contained in the amendment notice, he must return the amendment notice to the Board, indicating on the notice his reasons for doing so.

(5) The relevant employer must record on the employee's payslip for any pay period, as a credit described as "tax credit", the amount of working tax credit paid with the payment of [1PAYE income] to which the payslip relates.

(6) On making any payment of working tax credit to an employee the relevant employer must record on the deductions working sheet (P11) for that employee referred to in [3regulation 66 of the PAYE Regulations] the amount of the payment (whether or not the employer is required to complete the deductions working sheet for the purposes of that regulation or of the Contributions Regulations).

(7) The relevant employer must record on the certificate (P60) referred to in [3regulation 67 of the PAYE Regulations] the total amount of working tax credit paid to each employee for the income tax year to which the certificate relates (whether or not the employer is required to complete the certificate for the purposes of that regulation or of the Contributions Regulations).

(8) The relevant employer must record on the return (P35) referred to in [3regulation 73 of the PAYE Regulations] the total amount of working tax credit paid by him for the income tax year to which the return relates [2and the total amount of funding received from the Board for that year in accordance with regulation 8].

(9) The relevant employer must record on the particulars (P14) referred to in [3paragraph (4) of regulation 73 of the PAYE Regulations] the total amount of working tax credit paid to each employee for the income tax year to which the particulars relate.

(10) Where the relevant employer makes a payment of working tax credit to an employee which exceeds the amount which the employee is entitled to be paid in accordance with the particulars contained in the start notice or the amendment notice, the employer may recover from the employee an amount not exceeding the excess.

(11) Where no payment of [1PAYE income] is due from the relevant employer to an employee for a complete pay period the employer may choose either—

(a) not to make any payment of working tax credit to the employee for that period; or

(b) to continue to pay working tax credit to the employee for that period as if he had made a payment of [1PAYE income] in that period.

(12) Where the relevant employer chooses not to make any payment of working tax credit to an employee for a pay period in the circumstances mentioned in paragraph (11), he must, not later than seven days following the end of that pay period, inform the Board that he has made no payment of working tax credit for that pay period.

(13) No payment of working tax credit shall be capable of attachment under any enactment, or may be used by way of set-off or otherwise reduced, extinguished or terminated except in accordance with these Regulations.

(14) Where the relevant employer fails to make payments of working tax credit to an employee in accordance with paragraph (1) or (3), the Board shall make payments of working tax credit to that employee.

AMENDMENTS

1. Working Tax Credit (Payment by Employers) (Amendment) Regulations 2003 (SI 2003/715), reg.6 (April 6, 2003).

2. Working Tax Credit (Payment by Employers) (Amendment) Regulations 2003 (SI 2003/715), reg.7 (April 6, 2003).

3. Tax Credits (Miscellaneous Amendments) Regulations 2004 (SI 2004/762), reg.17(4) (April 6, 2004).

DEFINITIONS

"amendment notice"—see reg.5(1).
"the Board"—see reg.2.
"the commencement date"—see reg.4(2)(d).
"the Contributions Regulations"—see reg.2.
"employee"—see *ibid.*
"employer"—see *ibid.*
"Employments Regulations"—see *ibid.*
"income tax year"—see *ibid.*
"pay period"—see *ibid.*
"PAYE income"—see *ibid.*
"relevant employer"—see reg.3(1).
"start notice"—see reg.4(1).

GENERAL NOTE

Paras (1)–(4)

This regulation represents the heart of this set of Regulations. It sets out the obligations on a "relevant employer" (as defined by reg.3) to make payments of working tax credit. The basic duties to calculate the amount of working tax credit due on receipt of a start notice under reg.4 and to make such payments of working tax credit together with payments of PAYE income are specified as Steps 1 and 2 under para.(1). There is a parallel requirement imposed on employers on receipt of an amendment notice under reg.5 (para.(3)). **2.382**

The obligation only arises if the employer "reasonably expects the employee to remain in his employment for three or more consecutive pay periods" (para.(1)). Presumably the test of reasonableness is meant to be objective in this context. In the event that this expectation is not held by the employer, or the employer becomes aware that the employee has left or is leaving that employment, then the employer is entitled to return the start notice to the Revenue (para.(2)). The Regulations do not then prescribe what information should be supplied to the employee in these circumstances.

Subject to this, the employer's obligation to make payments of working tax credit then continues until one of the circumstances set out in reg.12 applies (*i.e.* the employee dies, otherwise ceases to work for the employer or the Board issue a "stop notice").

Para. (5)

Payments of tax credits must be identified as such on the employee's payslip (para.(5); thus such payments cannot be "hidden" as an offset against deductions from salary. Subject to that overriding requirement of transparency, employers are free to show the tax credit in the way that best suits the design of their payslips. The purpose of this provision is to ensure that the message that "work pays" is not lost on employees. Similarly, working tax credit must be paid in full; it cannot be subject to attachment, used by way of set-off or otherwise reduced (*e.g.* for court orders, attachment of earnings orders or child support orders) (see para.(13)). The only exception to this principle appears to be the power granted to employers to recover overpayments of working tax credit under para.(10). **2.383**

Paras (6)–(9)

2.384 These record-keeping requirements imposed on employers follow those that applied to the former WFTC scheme (Tax Credits (Payments by Employers) Regulations 1999 (SI 1999/3219), reg.6(5)–(7)).

Para. (10)

2.385 This provides that where an employer mistakenly pays the employee more by way of a tax credit than the latter is entitled to, then the employer "may recover from the employee an amount not exceeding the excess". There are no qualifications to this power on the face of the regulation. Let us assume, therefore, that an employee is paid net wages of £200 a week and is entitled to a tax credit of £40 a week, but is paid a tax credit of £60 a week for five weeks in error. This regulation would appear, on the face of it, to permit the employer to recover the £100 overpayment of tax credit out of one week's wages. Presumably one must hope that employers would adopt a more reasonable approach.

Paras (11)–(12)

2.386 The provision contained in para.(11) had no parallel under the previous arrangements relating to WFTC. Thus an employer who suspends an employee without pay or whose workforce are on strike (or indeed locked out) can choose, and presumably will choose, not to continue paying working tax credit. The only obligation in such circumstances is to inform the Board under para.(12). See also para.(14) below.

Para. (14)

2.387 Where an employer defaults on their obligation as contained in para.(1) or (3), by failing to implement a start notice or amendment notice, the responsibility for paying working tax credit reverts to the Revenue. There is no indication in the regulation as to at what point in time this obligation falls to be discharged by the Revenue. Nor is it clear that the obligation reverts to the Revenue if the employer declines to continue paying working tax credit for a period when PAYE income is not due, as where an employee is suspended without pay or is on strike (see paras (11)–(12)).

Funding of payment of working tax credit

2.388 7.—(1) In this regulation—

"amount A" is the total amount of tax which the relevant employer is required to pay to the collector of taxes in respect of deductions from the [1PAYE income] of his employees in accordance with the Employments Regulations for an income tax month or income tax quarter ("the relevant period");

"amount B" is the total amount of deductions made by the relevant employer from the [1PAYE income] of his employees for the relevant period in accordance with regulations made under section 22(5) of the Teaching and Higher Education Act 1998, section 73B(3) of the Education (Scotland) Act 1980, or Art.3(5) of the Education (Student Support) (Northern Ireland) Order 1998 (student loan repayments);

"amount C" is the total amount of earnings-related contributions which the relevant employer is required to pay to the collector of taxes in respect of the [1PAYE income] of his employees for the relevant period (whether by means of deduction or otherwise) in accordance with the Contributions Regulations;

"amount D" is the total amount of deductions which as a contractor the relevant employer is required to make from payments to which section 559 of the Taxes Act applies in accordance with the Income Tax (Sub-contractors in the Construction Industry) Regulations 1993 for the relevant period.

(2) The relevant employer shall fund payment of working tax credit for the relevant period in accordance with the following rules.

Rule 1

The relevant employer shall fund any payment of working tax credit for the relevant period from amount A for that period. Amount A shall accordingly be reduced by the amount of working tax credit which the employer has paid in respect of that period. **2.389**

Rule 2

If the total amount of working tax credit which the relevant employer is required to pay for the relevant period exceeds amount A for that period, the employer shall fund payment of working tax credit for that period (or so much of the payment as remains outstanding) from the aggregate of amount A and amount B for that period. That aggregate shall accordingly be reduced by the amount used to fund payment of working tax credit for that period. **2.390**

Rule 3

If the total amount of working tax credit which the relevant employer is required to pay for the relevant period exceeds the aggregate of amount A and amount B for that period, the employer shall fund payment of working tax credit for that period (or so much of the payment as remains outstanding) from the aggregate of amount A, amount B and amount C for that period. That aggregate shall accordingly be reduced by the amount used to fund payment of working tax credit for that period. **2.391**

Rule 4

If the total amount of working tax credit which the relevant employer is required to pay for the relevant period exceeds the aggregate of amount A, amount B and amount C for that period, the employer shall fund payment of working tax credit for that period (or so much of the payment as remains outstanding) from the aggregate of amount A, amount B, amount C and amount D for that period. That aggregate shall accordingly be reduced by the amount used to fund payment of working tax credit for that period. **2.392**

Rule 5

If the total amount of working tax credit which the relevant employer is required to pay for the relevant period exceeds the aggregate of amount A, amount B, amount C and amount D for that period, the employer may apply to the Board in accordance with reg.8 to fund payment of working tax credit for that period (or so much of the payment as remains outstanding). **2.393**

(3) References in para.(1) to the total amount in the case of each of amount A, amount B, amount C and amount D are references to that total amount unreduced by any other amount which the relevant employer is entitled by virtue of any enactment to set off against that total amount.

AMENDMENTS

1. Working Tax Credit (Payment by Employers) (Amendment) Regulations 2003 (SI 2003/715), reg.6 (April 6, 2003).

DEFINITIONS

2.394 "amount A"—see para.(1).
"amount B"—see *ibid.*
"amount C"—see *ibid.*
"amount D"—see *ibid.*
"the Board"—see reg.2.
"the Contributions Regulations"—see *ibid.*
"employee"—see *ibid.*
"employer"—see *ibid.*
"Employments Regulations"—see *ibid.*
"income tax month"—see *ibid.*
"income tax quarter"—see *ibid.*
"PAYE income"—see *ibid.*
"relevant employer"—see reg.3(1).
"the relevant period"—see para.(1).

GENERAL NOTE

2.395 This regulation sets out how employers are to fund payments of working tax credit and, in particular, the priority order of payments otherwise due to the Revenue from which such payments may be deducted. The starting assumption is that payments of working tax credit should be deducted from PAYE income tax withheld under the Income Tax (Employments) Regulations 1993 (SI 1993/744), described as "Amount A". If the total amount of tax deducted is insufficient to fund the working tax credit payable, the balance can be deducted from student loan repayments ("Amount B"). If those funds are still insufficient, deductions may be made against National Insurance contributions ("Amount D"). If that is still not enough, then payments can be offset against deductions due in respect of the special rules governing sub-contractors in the construction industry ("Amount D"). Failing that, the employer may apply to the Board for funding to meet the expense of working tax credit payments (reg.8). Further provision is made for determinations and recovery from employers of overpayments of such advances under reg.14, with the powers of the Board's inspectors set out in reg.15.

Application for funding

2.396 **8.**—(1) Where—

(a) rule 5 stated in regulation 7(2) applies; or
(b) the relevant employer considers that that rule will apply on the date of any subsequent payment of [1PAYE income] to one or more employees who are entitled to working tax credit,

the employer, or an agent authorised by him for that purpose, may apply to the Board for funding on a form provided, or in a form in writing that is approved, by the Board.

(2) For the purposes of paragraph (1), "writing" includes writing produced by electronic communications that are approved by the Board.

(3) If the relevant employer's application is accepted the Board shall pay to the employer such amount as the Board may determine in the circumstances to be reasonable having regard to all relevant matters including—

(a) the past obligations and the likely future obligations of the employer under the enactments referred to in regulation 7(1) (definitions of "amount A", "amount B", "amount C" and "amount D"); and

(b) the obligations of the employer under any start notice or amendment notice issued to him to make payments of working tax credit, and his fulfilment of those obligations.

(4) The Board may vary the amount payable in accordance with para.(3), or may make a determination superseding that amount, if it has become inappropriate for any reason or they have reason to believe that it was incorrect at the time it was determined as payable in accordance with that paragraph.

(5) The Board shall notify the employer of—

(a) their decision on an application under paragraph (1);

(b) the amount determined under paragraph (3); and

(c) any variation or supersession of that amount under paragraph (4).

(6) An employer may appeal to the General Commissioners against—

(a) the Board's refusal of an application under paragraph (1);

(b) the amount determined under paragraph (3); or

(c) any variation or supersession of that amount under paragraph (4).

(7) An appeal under paragraph (6) shall be made by giving notice to the Board within 30 days of the issue of the Board's notification under paragraph (5).

(8) An appeal under para.(6) shall be heard by the General Commissioners for the division in which the employer's place of business is situated.

(9) The provisions of Part V of the Management Act and of the General Commissioners (Jurisdiction and Procedure) Regulations 1994 shall apply with any necessary modifications to an appeal under paragraph (6) as they apply to appeals against assessments.

(10) On appeal the General Commissioners, having regard to the matters referred to in paragraph(3), may—

(a) confirm the Board's refusal of an application under paragraph (1), or allow the appeal against that refusal;

(b) confirm, increase or reduce the amount determined under paragraph (3); or

(c) confirm, increase or reduce any variation or supersession of that amount under paragraph (4).

(11) Subject to paragraph (9), the determination of the General Commissioners shall be final.

(12) Where—

(a) an employer appeals to the General Commissioners under paragraph (6); and

(b) the General Commissioners determine the appropriate amount of funding in a sum which exceeds the amount determined as payable under paragraph (3), or that amount as varied or superseded under paragraph (4).

the Board shall pay to the employer the amount of the excess.

(13) An amount which is paid to an employer by the Board under paragraph (12) shall carry interest at the rate applicable under section 178 of the Finance Act 1989 for the purposes of section 824 [2. . .] of the Taxes Act from the date on which the condition in rule 5 of regulation 7(2) satisfied until payment.

(14) Funds provided to an employer by the Board in accordance with this regulation shall be for the purpose only of payment by that employer of working tax credit under Step 2 of regulation 6(1) or (3) to one or more employees.

AMENDMENT

1. Working Tax Credit (Payment by Employers) (Amendment) Regulations 2003 (SI 2003/715), reg.6 (April 6, 2003). Definitions

2. Tax Credits (Miscellaneous Amendments) Regulations 2004 (SI 2004/762), reg.17(5) (April 6, 2004).

DEFINITIONS

"amendment notice"—see reg.5(1).
"the Board"—see reg.2.
"employee"—see *ibid.*
"employer"—see *ibid.*
"the Management Act"—see *ibid.*
"PAYE income"—see *ibid.*
"relevant employer"—see reg.3(1).
"start notice"—see reg.4(1).
"the Taxes Act"—see reg.2.
"writing"—see para.(2).

GENERAL NOTE

2.397 This regulation sets out the Board's powers to make what is effectively an advance payment of working tax credit to an employer who makes an appropriate application in circumstances where that employer is unable to fund some or all working tax credit liabilities by deduction from other payments due to the Inland Revenue (see further reg.7). It also details the appeal procedure for appeals (which lie to the General Commissioners: paras (6)–(12)).

Such funding can be renewed in subsequent years (reg.9). Employers are also under a duty to inform the Board if there is a relevant change of circumstances (reg.10). The situations in which the Board may terminate such funding are set out in reg.11(2). The Board may also determine the amount of funding to be repaid by an employer where such funds have not been used (in whole or in part) to make payments of working tax credit (reg.14).

Renewal of funding

2.398 **9.**—(1) Where—

(a) the Board have provided a relevant employer with funds in accordance with regulation 8 in an income tax year; and
(b) the employer's entitlement to receive funding from the Board has not terminated in accordance with regulation 11,

the Board shall, following the end of that year, send to the relevant employer a form for renewal of funding ("renewal form") containing details relating to the funding of payments of working tax credit made by him.

(2) Not later than 30 days following the date of issue of the renewal form, the relevant employer must return the form to the Board signed by him and either confirming that the details recorded on the form are correct as at the date of issue or amending the details if they are not so correct.

DEFINITIONS

"the Board"—see reg.2.
"employer"—see *ibid.*
"income tax year"—see *ibid.*
"relevant employer"—see reg.3(1).
"renewal form"—see para.(1).

Notification of change of circumstances by relevant employer in receipt of funding

10. If, in the course of an income tax year, as a result of a change of circumstances, whether in relation to the amount of funding requested or otherwise, any of the details recorded on an application for funding under regulation 8, or on a renewal form under regulation 9, cease to be correct, the relevant employer may give notice to the Board, on a form provided by the Board for that purpose, amending those details. **2.399**

DEFINITIONS

"the Board"—see reg.2.
"income tax year"—see *ibid.*
"relevant employer"—see reg.3(1).

Termination of funding

11.—(1) The Board shall continue to provide a relevant employer with funds in accordance with regulation 8 until the occurrence of any of the events specified in paragraph (2). **2.400**

(2) The events are—

(a) a request by the relevant employer that the Board should discontinue providing him with funds;
(b) the failure by the relevant employer to return to the Board within the time stated in regulation 9 (2) a renewal form duly signed and completed;
(c) the failure by the relevant employer to respond to attempts by the Board on more than one occasion to contact him in relation to the provision of funds to him.

DEFINITIONS

"the Board"—see reg.2.
"relevant employer"—see reg.3(1).
"renewal form"—see reg.9(1).

Termination of relevant employer's obligation to pay working tax credit (stop notice)

2.401 **12.**—(1) The relevant employer must continue to make payments of working tax credit to an employee in accordance with a start notice or an amendment notice issued to him until—

(a) the death of the employee;
(b) the employee ceases to be employed by the employer otherwise than by reason of the employee's death; or
(c) a stop notice is issued by the Board to the employer notifying the employer to cease payment of working tax credit to the employee.

(2) A stop notice under paragraph (1)(c) shall contain the following particulars—

(a) the date of issue of the stop notice;
(b) the name of the employee concerned;
(c) the employee's national insurance number and (if known) his payroll number;
(d) the latest date for which working tax credit is payable to the employee ("the latest payable date").

[[1](e) the commencement date referred to in regulation 4(2)(d).]

(3) Except where an earlier date has been agreed between the Board and the relevant employer, the latest payable date for the purposes of paragraph (2)(d) shall not be earlier than 42 days after the date of issue of the stop notice.

(4) The relevant employer shall not pay working tax credit to the employee after the latest payable date.

This is subject to paragraph (5).

(5) The relevant employer may, after the latest payable date, make a payment of working tax credit that is outstanding at that date in respect of the pay period in which the latest payable date falls.

(6) A stop notice shall be effective in respect of an employee unless and until a new start notice is issued by the Board to the relevant employer in respect of that employee.

(7) Where the relevant employer—

(a) makes a payment of working tax credit in respect of any day after the date of death of the employee; and
(b) subsequently becomes aware that the employee has died,

he must inform the Board, not later than seven days after becoming aware of the employee's death, of the latest day for which he has paid working tax credit in respect of the employee.

(8) Where the relevant employer—

(a) makes a payment of working tax credit in respect of any day after the employee ceases to be employed by the employer otherwise than by reason of the employee's death; and
(b) subsequently becomes aware that the employee has left his employment,

he must inform the Board, not later than seven days after becoming aware that the employee has left his employment, of the latest day for which he has paid working tax credit in respect of the employee.

(9) Where the employee dies and the relevant employer has not made payments of working tax credit up to the date of death in accordance with paragraph (1), the Board shall pay to the employee's personal representatives the amount of working tax credit outstanding at the date of death.

AMENDMENT

1. Working Tax Credit (Payment by Employers) (Amendment) Regulations 2003 (SI 2003/715), reg.8 (April 6, 2003).

DEFINITIONS

"amendment notice"—see reg.5(1).
"the Board"—see reg.2.
"employee"—see *ibid.*
"employer"—see *ibid.*
"the latest payable date"—see para.(2)(d).
"relevant employer"—see reg.3(1).
"start notice"—see reg.4(1).
"stop notice"—see reg.2.

GENERAL NOTE

The start notice issued by the Revenue to the relevant employer under reg.4 (and any subsequent amendment notice under reg.5) includes a commencement date from which time working tax credit is payable, but does not include any termination date. (Contrast this with the "start notification" of fixed term awards of WFTC under Tax Credits (Payments by Employers) Regulations 1999 (SI 1999/3219), reg.4(2)(d), which also included a termination date.) Under the working tax credit regime, the obligation of the relevant employer to continue making payments of working tax credit under reg.6 is thus potentially open-ended. This obligation ceases only where the employee dies, or otherwise ceases to work for the employer, or the Board issue a stop notice under this regulation. But note that the employer may elect *not* to pay working tax credit if the employee's normal PAYE income is not paid for a particular period (*e.g.* because of suspension without pay or strike action: see reg.6(11)). 2.402

There arrears to be no provision in this regulation for the Board to issue a stop notice where an appeal is pending, either in the case in question or in a similar case. In contrast the anti-test case rule permits the Board to postpone payment in such cases where it is responsible for making payments of tax credits (Tax Credits (Payments by the Board) Regulations 2002 (SI 2002/2173), reg.11).

Temporary break in relevant employer's payment of working tax credit (emergency stop notice and restart notice)

13.—(1) Where the relevant employer— 2.403
(a) having commenced to make payments of working tax credit in accordance with regulation 6(1) or (3), subsequently fails to pay an amount of working tax credit to an employee in accordance with that regulation; or
(b) chooses in the circumstances referred to in regulation 6(11) not to make a payment of working tax credit to an employee; and

(c) in either case reaches agreement with the Board as to the date from which he is to resume making payments of working tax credit to the employee,

the Board shall take the action specified in paragrpahs (2) to (4).

(2) The Board shall give notice to the relevant employer confirming that the employer has ceased to make payments of working tax credit to the employee concerned ("emergency stop notice").

(3) The Board shall in addition give notice to the relevant employer confirming the date from which the employer is to resume making payments of working tax credit to that employee ("restart notice").

(4) The Board shall pay to the employee the amount of working tax credit to which he is entitled until the relevant employer resumes making payments of working tax credit to the employee.

(5) An emergency stop notice under paragraph (2) shall contain the following particulars—

(a) the date of issue of the notice;
(b) the name of the employee;
(c) the employee's national insurance number and (if known) his payroll number;
(d) the commencement date referred to in regulation 4(2)(d) [[1]. . .];
(e) the latest date for which working tax credit is payable to the employee.

(6) A restart notice under paragraph (3) shall contain the following particulars—

(a) the date of issue of the notice;
(b) the name of the employee;
(c) the employee's national insurance number and (if known) his payroll number;
(d) the date from which the employer is to resume making payments of working tax credit to the employee ("restart date");
(e) the daily rate of working tax credit applicable to each calendar day starting with the restart date, and a table showing the multiples from 1 to 31 of that daily rate.

(7) Regulation 6(1) and (5) to (10) applies in relation to the receipt by the relevant employer of a restart notice under this regulation as it applies to the receipt by him of a start notice.

(8) Where the relevant employer fails to resume making payments of working tax credit to the employee in accordance with paragraph (3), the Board shall continue to make payments of working tax credit to the employee.

AMENDMENT

1. Working Tax Credit (Payment by Employers) (Amendment) Regulations 2003 (SI 2003/715), reg.9 (April 6, 2003).

DEFINITIONS

"the Board"—see reg.2.
"commencement date"—see regs 4(2)(d) and 5(2)(d)
"emergency stop notice"—see para.(2).
"employee"—see *ibid.*

"employer"—see *ibid.*
"relevant employer"—see reg.3(1).
"restart date"—see para.(6)(d).
"restart notice"—see para.(3).

GENERAL NOTE

This regulation makes provision for the Board to issue an emergency stop notice (followed by a restart notice) when there is a temporary break in the payment of working tax credit by an employer to an employee. During the "gap" period, the Board assumes responsibility to make payments of working tax credit to the employee concerned (para.(4)). **2.404**

Determination of working tax credit funding to be repaid

14.—(1) This regulation applies where funds have been provided to the employer under regulation 8 in respect of one or more employees and it appears to an officer of the Board that the employer has not used the whole or part of those funds to pay working tax credit. **2.405**

(2) The officer of the Board shall determine to the best of his judgment the amount of funds provided under regulation 8 and not used to pay working tax credit and shall serve notice of his determination on the employer.

(3) A determination under this regulation may cover funds provided under regulation 8—

(a) for any one pay period, or more than one pay period, in an income tax year; and

(b) in respect of a class or classes of employees specified in the notice of determination (without naming the individual employees), or in respect of one or more employees named in the notice of determination.

(4) Subject to the following provisions of this regulation, the following enactments shall apply with any necessary modifications to a determination under this regulation as if it were an assessment and as if the amount of funds determined were income tax charged on the employer—

Part IV of the Management Act (assessment and claims);
Part V of the Management Act (appeals and other proceedings), except s.55;
Part VI of the Management Act (collection and recovery);
the General Commissioners (Jurisdiction and Procedure) Regulations 1994;
the Special Commissioners (Jurisdiction and Procedure) Regulations 1994.

(5) An appeal against a determination under this regulation that is to be brought before the General Commissioners pursuant to paragraph

(4) shall be brought before the General Commissioners for the division in which the employer's place of business is situated.

(6) Where an amount of funds determined under this regulation relates to more than one employee, proceedings may be brought for the recovery of that amount without distinguishing the amounts making up that sum which the employer is liable to repay in respect of each employee and without specifying the employees in question, and the amount

determined under this regulation shall be one cause of action or one matter of complaint for the purposes of proceedings under section 65, 66 or 67 of the Management Act.

(7) Nothing in para.(6) prevents the bringing of separate proceedings for the recovery of any amount which the employer is liable to repay in respect of each employee.

DEFINITIONS

"the Board"—see reg.2.
"employee"—see *ibid.*
"employer"—see *ibid.*
"income tax year"—see *ibid.*
"the Management Act"—see *ibid.*
"pay period"—see *ibid.*

GENERAL NOTE

2.406 This regulation provides for the determination of an amount of funding to be repaid to the Board where it transpires that the amount has not been used by the employer to fund payment of working tax credit.

Inspection of employer's records

2.407 **15.**—(1) For the purpose of enabling the Board to be satisfied whether a relevant employer is complying with the provisions of these Regulations, he must, whenever called upon to do so by an authorised officer of the Board, produce the records specified in paragraph (2) to that officer for inspection, at such time as that officer may reasonably require and at the prescribed place.

(2) The records are—

(a) all wages sheets, deductions working sheets and other documents and records of any kind or description relating to the calculation or payment of the tax credits of his employees in respect of the tax years or income tax months specified by the authorised officer; or

(b) such of those wages sheets, deductions working sheets or other documents and records as may be specified by the authorised officer.

(3) The prescribed place for the purposes of paragraph (1) means—

(a) such place in the United Kingdom as the employer and the authorised officer may agree upon; or

(b) in default of such agreement, the place in the United Kingdom at which the documents and records referred to in paragraph (2)(a) are normally kept; or

(c) in default of such agreement and if there is no such place as is referred to in sub-paragraph (b), the employer's principal place of business in the United Kingdom.

(4) The authorised officer may—

(a) take copies of, or make extracts from, any document produced to him for inspection in accordance with paragraphs (1) and (2); and

(b) remove any document so produced if it appears to him to be necessary to do so, at a reasonable time and for a reasonable period.

(5) Where any document is removed in accordance with paragraph (4)(b), the authorised officer shall provide a receipt for that document.

(6) Where any document is removed in accordance with paragraph (4)(b) that is reasonably required for the proper conduct of a business, the authorised officer shall, not later than seven days following the date on which the document was removed, provide a copy of the document, free of charge, to the person by whom it was produced or caused to be produced.

(7) Where a lien is claimed on a document produced in accordance with paragraphs (1) and (2), the removal of the document in accordance with paragraph (4)(b) shall not be regarded as breaking the lien.

(8) Where records are maintained by computer, the person required to produce them for inspection must provide the authorised officer with all facilities necessary for obtaining information from them.

(9) For the purposes of paragraphs (1) and (2), the employer must retain the wages sheets, deductions working sheets and other documents and records referred to in those paragraphs for not less than three years after the end of the income tax year to which they relate.

DEFINITIONS

"the Board"—see reg.2.
"employer"—see *ibid.*
"employer's place of business"—see *ibid.*
"income tax month"—see *ibid.*
"the Management Act"—see *ibid.*
"relevant employer"—see reg.3.

Tax Credits (Payments by the Board) Regulations 2002

(SI 2002/2173, AS AMENDED)

The Commissioners of Inland Revenue, in exercise of the powers conferred upon them by sections 24(2), (3), (4), (7) and (8), 65(1), (2) and (7) and 67 of the Tax Credits Act 2002, hereby make the following Regulations: **2.408**

1. Citation, commencement and effect.
2. Interpretation.
3. Child tax credit and childcare element—member of a couple prescribed for the purposes of s.24(2) of the Act.
4. Working tax credit (excluding any childcare element)—member of a couple prescribed for the purposes of s.24(2) of the Act.
5. Member of a couple prescribed for the purposes of s.24(2) of the Act where one of the members of the couple has died.
6. Person prescribed for the purposes of s.24(3) of the Act where an award of a tax credit is made on a claim which is made by one person on behalf of another.
7. Prescribed circumstances for the purposes of s.24(4) of the Act.
8. Time of payment by way of a credit to a bank account or other account.

GENERAL NOTE

2.409 The statutory presumption is that payments of working tax credit are to be paid by employers (see TCA 2002, ss.24(6) and 25). The relevant provisions are laid down in the Working Tax Credit (Payment by Employers) Regulations 2002 (SI 2002/2172) (see para.2.361). Payments of child tax credit, however, are to be made by the Board, as are payments of working tax credit that are not covered by s.25 of the Act and the Payment by Employers Regulations (see especially reg.6(14) of those Regulations). These Regulations thus make provision for such payments by the Board. There is also an important transitional provision to note. Where a child tax credit or working tax credit claim has been made by a person who was previously entitled to either WFTC or DPTC under the TCA 1999, any payments due to such a person on or before October 5, 2003 may be made by the Board directly—irrespective of the duties laid down by either these Regulations or the Working Tax Credit (Payments by Employers) Regulations 2002 (see Tax Credits Act 2002 (Commencement No.4, Transitional Provisions and Savings) Order 2003 (SI 2003/962), art.5(1)).

Citation, commencement and effect

2.410 **1.**—(1) These Regulations may be cited as the Tax Credits (Payments by the Board) Regulations 2002 and shall come into force on 6th April 2003.

(2) These Regulations have effect in relation to payments of a tax credit, or any element of a tax credit, which must be made [[1] . . .] in relation to the tax year beginning with 6th April 2003 and subsequent tax years.

[[1](3) Regulations 8 to 14 have effect only in relation to such payments as must be made by the Board.]

AMENDMENTS

1. Tax Credits (Claims and Notifications and Payments by the Board) (Amendment) Regulations 2003 (SI 2003/723), reg.7 (April 6, 2003).

Interpretation

2.411 **2.** In these Regulations—

"the Act" means the Tax Credits Act 2002;

"the Board" means the Commissioners of Inland Revenue;

"employee" and "employer" have the meaning given by section 25(5) of the Act;

"married couple" has the meaning given by section 3(5) of the Act;

"period of award" shall be construed in accordance with section 5 of the Act;

"the relevant tax year" means the whole or part of the tax year for which an award of a tax credit has been made to a person or persons (referred to in section 24(4) of the Act);

"tax year" means a period beginning with 6th April in one year and ending with 5th April in the next;

"unmarried couple" has the meaning given by section 3(6) of the Act.

Child tax credit and childcare element—member of a couple prescribed for the purposes of section 24(2) of the Act

3.—(1) This regulation has effect in relation to payments of— 2.412

(a) child tax credit; and

(b) any childcare element of working tax credit.

(2) Subject to regulation 5, the member of a married couple or an unmarried couple prescribed by paragraph (3) is prescribed for the purposes of section 24(2) of the Act.

(3) The member of a married couple or an unmarried couple prescribed by this paragraph is—

(a) the member who is identified by both members of the married couple or unmarried couple as the main carer for the children and qualifying young persons for whom either or both of the members is or are responsible;

(b) in default of such a member, the member who appears to the Board to be the main carer for those children and qualifying young persons.

(4) "Children" means persons who have not attained the age of 16 or who fall within the terms of regulation 4 of the Child Tax Credit Regulations 2002.

(5) "Qualifying young persons" means persons, other than children, who—

(a) have not attained the age of nineteen; and

(b) satisfy the conditions in regulation 5(3) and (4) of the Child Tax Credit Regulations 2002.

(6) Where payments are being made to the member of a married couple or an unmarried couple prescribed by virtue of paragraph (3) and the members of the married couple or unmarried couple jointly give notice to the Board that, as a result of a change of circumstances, the payments should be made to the other member as the main carer, the other member shall be treated as prescribed by virtue of paragraph (3).

[[1](7) For the purposes of this regulation, a person is responsible for a child or qualifying young person if he is treated as being responsible for that child or qualifying young person in accordance with the rules contained in regulation 3 of the Child Tax Credit Regulations 2002.]

AMENDMENT

1. Tax Credits (Claims and Notifications and Payments by the Board) (Amendment) Regulations 2003 (SI 2003/723), reg.8 (April 6, 2003).

DEFINITIONS

"the Act"—see reg.2.
"the Board"—see *ibid.*
"children"—see para.(4).
"married couple"—see reg.2.
"qualifying young persons"—see para.(5).
"unmarried couple"—see reg.2.

GENERAL NOTE

2.413 Section 24(2) of the TCA 2002 permits payments of tax credits, or elements within tax credits, in the case of a joint claim to whichever member of a married or unmarried couple is prescribed. This regulation deals with the payment of child tax credit and any childcare element of working tax credit by the Board. It provides that such tax credits are payable by the Board to the partner identified by the couple as the main carer of the children concerned or, in default, the partner identified as such by the Board (para.(3)). The couple can ask the Board to change the method of payment to the other partner as the main carer (para.(6)).

Working tax credit (excluding any childcare element)—member of a couple prescribed for the purposes ofsection 24(2) of the Act

2.414 **4.**—(1) This regulation has effect in relation to payments of working tax credit other than payments of any childcare element.

(2) Subject to regulation 5, the member of a married couple or anunmarried couple prescribed by para.(3) is prescribed for the purposes of section 24(2) of the Act.

(3) The member of a married couple or an unmarried couple prescribed by this paragraph is—

(a) if only one member of the married couple or unmarried couple is engaged in remunerative work, that member;

(b) if both members of the married couple or unmarried couple are engaged in remunerative work—

(i) the member elected jointly by them; or

(ii) in default of any election, such of them as appears to the Board to be appropriate.

(4) Where payments are being made to the member of a married couple or an unmarried couple prescribed by virtue of paragraph (3)(b) and the members of the married couple or unmarried couple jointly give notice to the Board that, as a result of a change of circumstances, they wish payments to be made to the other member, the other member shall be treated as prescribed by virtue of paragraph (3)(b).

(5) For the purposes of paragraph (3), a member of a married couple or an unmarried couple is engaged in remunerative work if—

(a) he is engaged in qualifying remunerative work; or

(b) he works not less than 16 hours per week and the other member of the married or unmarried couple is engaged in qualifying remunerative work.

(6) "Qualifying remunerative work", and being engaged in it, have the meaning given by regulation 4 of the Working Tax Credit (Entitlement and Maximum Rate) Regulations 2002.

DEFINITIONS

"the Act"—see reg.2.
"the Board"—see *ibid.*
"married couple"—see *ibid.*
"qualifying remunerative work"—see para.(6).
"unmarried couple"—see reg.2.

GENERAL NOTE

This deals with payment of working tax credit (excluding any childcare element, on which see reg.3) by the Board. In the case of a couple, such working tax credit should be paid by the Board to the member of the couple who is in remunerative work for working tax credit purposes (see paras (5) and (6)) or, if they both are, to the partner nominated jointly by the couple or, in default, as the Board sees appropriate (para.(3)). As with reg.3, the couple have the option of changing their election (para.(4)). 2.415

Member of a couple prescribed for the purposes of section 24(2) of the Act where one of the members of the couple has died

5.—(1) This regulation applies where one of the members of a married couple or an unmarried couple has died. 2.416

(2) The member of the married or unmarried couple prescribed by paragraph (3) is prescribed for the purposes of section 24(2) of the Act.

(3) The member of the married or unmarried couple prescribed by this paragraph is the member who survives.

(4) For the purposes of this regulation, where persons have died in circumstances rendering it uncertain which of them survived the other—

(a) their deaths shall be presumed to have occurred in order of seniority; and
(b) the younger shall be treated as having survived the elder.

DEFINITIONS

"the Act"—see reg.2.
"married couple"—see *ibid.*
"unmarried couple"—see reg.2.

GENERAL NOTE

This regulation is self-explanatory. Paragraph (4) follows the general property law rule on survivorship laid down by s.184 of the Law of Property Act 1925. 2.417

Person prescribed for the purposes of section 24(3) of the Act where an award of a tax credit is made on a claim which is made by one person on behalf of another

6. For the purposes of section 24(3) of the Act, the person prescribed is— 2.418

(a) the person by whom the claim on behalf of another was made; or
(b) if at any time the Board do not consider it appropriate for payments of the tax credit to be made to that person, the person on behalf of whom the claim was made.

DEFINITIONS

"the Act"—see reg.2.
"the Board"—see *ibid.*

GENERAL NOTE

2.419 See also regs 17, 18, 28 and 29 of the Tax Credits (Claims and Notifications) Regulations 2002 (SI 2002/2014).

Prescribed circumstances for the purposes of section 24(4) of the Act

2.420 **7.**—(1) Either of the circumstances prescribed by paragraphs (2) and (3) are prescribed circumstances for the purposes of section 24(4) of the Act.

(2) The circumstances prescribed by this paragraph are where—

(a) a claim for a tax credit for the next tax year has been made or treated as made by the person or persons by the date specified for the purposes of subsection (4) of section 17 of the Act in the notice given to him or them under that section in relation to the relevant tax year; and

(b) the Board have not made a decision under section 14(1) of the Act in relation to that claim.

(3) The circumstances prescribed by this paragraph are where—

(a) a claim for a tax credit for the next tax year has not been made or treated as made by the person or persons; and

(b) the Board have not made a decision under section 18(1) of the Act in relation to the person and persons for the relevant tax year.

DEFINITIONS

"the Act"—see reg.2.
"the Board"—see *ibid.*
"the relevant tax year"—see *ibid.*
"tax year"—see *ibid.*

GENERAL NOTE

2.421 Section 24(4) of the TCA 2002 enables payments of tax credits to continue to be paid in a following tax year in the absence of a claim and award in certain circumstances. This regulation thus allows payments to continue to be made, without interruption, at the start of each tax year while claims are being renewed in two types of circumstances. The first is where a renewal claim has been made or treated as made but has yet to be determined by the Board (para.(2)). The second is a step further back, where no such renewal claim has been made but the Board similarly has yet to make its final decision on the previous year (para.(3)).

Time of payment by way of a credit to a bank account or other account

2.422 **8.**—(1) Subject to paragraph (3), this regulation applies where the tax credit or element is to be paid by way of a credit to a bank account or other account notified to the Board.

(2) [[1]Subject to paragraph (2A),] the tax credit or element shall be paid—

(a) each week; or
(b) every four weeks,

in accordance with any election given by the person to whom payment is to be made.

[1(2A) If a person makes elections under paragraph (2) for child tax credit and any childcare element of working tax credit to be paid at differing intervals, the elections shall have no effect and the Board may pay the child tax credit and any childcare element together either each week or every four weeks as appears to them to be appropriate.]

(3) In the case of an employee entitled to working tax credit, this regulation does not apply where the making of payments of the tax credit by the Board is in consequence of the employer—

(a) not being required to make payments of the tax credit in accordance with the Working Tax Credit (Payment by Employers) Regulations 2002 and with any notices given by the Board; or
(b) failing to make such payments in accordance with those Regulations and with any such notices.

(4) This regulation is subject to regulations 10 and 11.

AMENDMENTS

1. Tax Credits (Claims and Notifications and Payments by the Board) (Amendment) Regulations 2003 (SI 2003/723), reg.9 (April 6, 2003).

DEFINITIONS

"the Board"—see reg.2.
"employee"—see *ibid.*
"employer"—see *ibid.*

GENERAL NOTE

Employees paid tax credits by the Board direct to their bank accounts have the option of having such payments paid weekly or four-weekly (para.(2)). However, it is not possible to have child tax credit and the childcare element of working tax credit paid at different intervals (para.(2A)). The intervals for payment via methods other than direct to a bank account are left to the discretion of the Board (see reg.9). However, payment via bank accounts is clearly intended to be the standard method for the Board to pay tax credits (see regs 13 and 14). **2.423**

Time of payment other than by way of a credit to a bank account or other account, etc.

9.—(1) This regulation applies where— **2.424**

(a) the tax credit or element is to be paid other than by way of a credit to a bank account or other account notified to the Board; or
(b) in the case of an employee entitled to working tax credit, the making of payments of the tax credit by the Board is in consequence of the employer—
    (i) not being required to make payments of the tax credit in accordance with the Working Tax Credit (Payment by Employers) Regulations 2002 and with any notices given by the Board; or
    (ii) failing to make such payments of the tax credit in accordance with those Regulations and with any such notices.

(2) The tax credit or element shall be paid at such times as appear to the Board to be appropriate.

DEFINITIONS

"the Board"—see reg.2.
"employee"—see *ibid.*
"employer"—see *ibid.*

[[1]Single payment of small sums of tax credit

2.425 **10.** The tax credit or element may be paid by way of a single payment, and at such time, and in such manner, as appear to the Board to be appropriate, in any of the following cases—

(a) where the Board are paying only child tax credit to a person and the weekly rate at which it is payable is less than £2;
(b) where the Board are paying both any childcare element (but no other element) of working tax credit and child tax credit to a person and the total weekly rate at which they are payable is less than £2;
(c) where the Board are paying only working tax credit (apart from any childcare element) to a person and the weekly rate at which it is payable (excluding any such childcare element) is less than £2;
(d) where the Board are paying both working tax credit (including elements other than, or in addition to, any childcare element) and child tax credit to a person who has elected under regulation 8(2) to have them paid at the same intervals and the total weekly rate at which they are payable is less than £2;
(e) where the Board are paying both working tax credit (apart from any childcare element) and child tax credit to a person who has elected under regulation 8(2) to have them paid at differing intervals and—
    (i) the total weekly rate at which any such childcare element and the child tax credit are payable is less than £2; or
    (ii) the weekly rate at which the working tax credit is payable (excluding any such childcare element) is less than £2.]

AMENDMENT

1. Tax Credits (Claims and Notifications and Payments by the Board) (Amendment) Regulations 2003 (SI 2003/723), reg.10 (April 6, 2003).

DEFINITION

"the Board"—see reg.2.

GENERAL NOTE

2.426 The original version of this regulation, which was substituted by the version above before it came into force, was just one sentence long: so much for simplicity. The basic principle, however, remains the same: if tax credits are payable at an aggregate level of less than £2 a week, then the Board will pay them in such manner as it deems appropriate (typically by way of a lump sum).

Postponement of payment

2.427 **11.**—(1) The Board may postpone payment of the tax credit or element in any of the circumstances specified in paragraphs (2) and (3).

(2) The circumstances specified in this paragraph are where there is a pending determination of an appeal against a decision of an appeal tribunal, a Social Security Commissioner or a court relating to—

(a) the case in question; or

(b) another case where it appears to the Board that, if the appeal were to be determined in a particular way, an issue would arise as to whether the award in the case in question should be amended or terminated under section 16(1) of the Act.

(3) The circumstances specified in this paragraph are where confirmation is pending of—

(a) the details of a bank account or other account by way of a credit to which payment is to be made; or

(b) the address of the person to whom payment is to be made, where it appears to the Board that such details or address as were previously notified to them are incorrect.

(4) For the purposes of paragraph (2), the circumstances where a determination of an appeal is pending include circumstances where a decision of an appeal tribunal, a Social Security Commissioner or a court has been made and the Board—

(a) are awaiting receipt of the decision;

(b) in the case of a decision by an appeal tribunal, are considering whether to apply for a statement of reasons or have applied for, and are awaiting receipt of, a statement of reasons; or

(c) have received the decision or statement of reasons and are considering—

(i) whether to apply for permission to appeal; or

(ii) where permission is not needed or has been given, whether to appeal.

(5) "Appeal tribunal" has the meaning given by section 63(10) of the Act.

(6) "Social Security Commissioner" has the meaning given by section 63(13) of the Act.

DEFINITIONS

"the Act"—see reg.2.
"Appeal tribunal"—see para.(5).
"the Board"—see reg.2.
"Social Security Commissioner"—see para.(6).

GENERAL NOTE

This regulation sets out the two types of circumstances in which a payment of tax credits by the Board may be postponed. The first is the straightforward situation where the Board believes that either the bank details or recipient's address previously notified to them is incorrect (para.(3)). The second is where there is an appeal pending in relation either to the particular case or to another case in which the outcome might lead to the amendment or termination of the award in the instant case (para.(2)). This is, therefore, the tax credits equivalent of the anti-test case rule. (But note, however, that it is limited to the postponement of payment, and does not make provision for limiting the effect of test cases in terms of backdating entitlement to tax credits.) The "pending determination" **2.428** must be one against a decision of an appeal tribunal, Social Security Commissioner or court (para.(2)). The notion of "pending" is defined by para.(4). There are no explicit time limits stated within this regulation on the Board's consideration of whether or not to lodge an appeal, but there are, of course, fairly tight time constraints on the exercise of such a right in the first place. This power, it should be noted, only applies to cases where tax credits are in payment by the Board: there is no equivalent power in the Tax Credits (Payment by Employers) Regulations 2002 (SI 2002/2172). For example, the test case rule is not a situation listed as one of those entitling the Board to issue a stop notice under reg.12 of those Regulations. This raises the possibility of a lack of parity of treatment between different categories of claimant based solely upon the mechanism of payment.

Amounts of payments

2.429 **12.**—(1) The tax credit or element shall be paid in accordance with the most recent decision by the Board under section 14(1), 15(1) or 16(1) of the Act.

(2) Where the tax credit or element is to be paid other than by way of a single payment, it shall be paid so far as possible in such amounts as will result in the person to whom payment is to be made receiving regular payments of similar amounts over the entire period of award.

(3) Where an award of tax credit is amended, the total amount paid prior to the award being amended shall be taken into account by the Board in determining the amount of any further payments for the remainder of the period of award.

(4) Where payments under section 24(4) of the Act are to be made, the rate at which the person or persons were entitled to the tax credit for the relevant tax year shall be taken into account by the Board in determining the amounts of those payments.

DEFINITIONS

"the Act"—see reg.2.
"the Board"—see *ibid.*

GENERAL NOTE

2.430 This regulation provides for the amount of tax credits payable to be determined by the Board's most recent relevant decision (para.(1)). Such payments should, so far as possible, be apportioned equally over regular payment intervals (para.(2)). Where the amount is amended, prior payments are to be taken into account to arrive at the appropriate amount now due in payment (para.(3)). Amounts of tax credits for subsequent years can be based on a preceding year's tax credit entitlement (para.(4); see further reg.7).

[1 Recovery of overpayments of tax credit from other payments of tax credit

2.431 **12A.**—(1) This regulation applies where notice is given to a person or persons under subsection (4) of section 29 of the Act (deduction of overpayments from payments of tax credit).

(2) The maximum rate at which an overpayment may be recovered from payments of tax credit is—

(a) where the only amount of tax credit to which the person is, or, in the case of a joint claim, the persons are, entitled, is the family element of child tax credit, 100% of that tax credit;
(b) where the total amount of tax credit to which the person is, or, in the case of a joint claim, the persons are, entitled is not subject to reduction—
  (i) by virtue of section 7(2) of the Act; or
  (ii) because their income for the relevant year does not exceed the relevant income threshold prescribed in his or their case in regulation 3 of the Tax Credits (Income Thresholds and Determination of Rates) Regulations 2002;

 10% of that tax credit; and
(c) in any other case, 25% of the tax credit to which the person is, or in the case of a joint claim, the persons are, entitled.

(3) In paragraph (2) a reference to the amount to which a person is, or persons are, entitled is a reference to the amount to which they would be entitled but for the operation of that paragraph.]

AMENDMENT

1. Tax Credits (Miscellaneous Amendments) Regulations 2004 (SI 2004/762), reg.18 (April 6, 2004).

DEFINITION

"the Act"—see reg. 2.

Manner of payment

13.—(1) Subject to paragraph (2), the tax credit or element shall be paid by way of a credit to a bank account or other account notified to the Board by the person to whom payment is to be made. 2.432

(2) Where [[1]it does not appear to the Board to be appropriate] for the tax credit or element to be paid by way of a credit to a bank account or other account notified to the Board by the person to whom payment is to be made, the tax credit or element may be paid in such manner as appears to the Board to be appropriate.

(3) Subject to regulation 14, if no bank account or other account has been notified to the Board, the tax credit or element shall be paid in such manner as appears to the Board to be appropriate.

AMENDMENT

1. Tax Credits (Claims and Notifications and Payments by the Board) (Amendment) Regulations 2003 (SI 2003/723), reg.11 (April 6, 2003).

DEFINITION

"the Board"—see reg.2.

GENERAL NOTE

This regulation establishes the presumption in favour of payment by the Board of tax credits to be direct to recipients' bank accounts. 2.433

Entitlement to tax credit or element dependent on a bank account or other account having been notified to the Board

2.434 **14.**—(1) Subject to paragraphs (2) and (3), if by the end of the relevant period no bank account or other account has been notified to the Board by the person to whom payment of a tax credit or element is to be made, that person shall cease to be entitled to the tax credit or element for the remainder of the period of the award until a bank account or other account is notified to the Board.

(2) Where a person who has ceased to be entitled to a tax credit or an element by virtue of paragraph (1) subsequently notifies to the Board a bank account or other account, paragraph (1)—

(a) shall not have effect for the period of three months prior to the date on which the Board receive the notification; and

(b) shall cease to have effect for the remainder of the period of award.

(3) Where there are exceptional circumstances which are expected to result in a person not being able to obtain a bank account or other account throughout the period of award, paragraph (1) shall not have effect in relation to that person's entitlement to a tax credit or element for the period of award.

(4) "The relevant period" means whichever of the following periods ends latest—

(a) the period of eight weeks beginning on the date on which the Board [1give] notice in writing for the purposes of this regulation to the person to whom payment is to be made of the requirement that a bank account or other account be notified to them;

(b) in cases where, within the period mentioned in sub-paragraph (a), the person to whom payment is to be made—

(i) requests from the Board authority to open an account for which such authority is required; and

(ii) provides sufficient information from which the Board can give that authority,

the period of three weeks beginning on the date on which the Board [1give] that authority;

(c) in cases where the person to whom payment is to be made has a reasonable excuse—

(i) for not being able to take all necessary steps to obtain a bank account or other account within whichever of the periods set out in sub-paragraph (a) or (b) ends latest; or

(ii) for not being able to notify to the Board the bank account or other account within that period,

the period ending with the date by which the account can reasonably be expected to be notified to the Board.

(5) "Writing" includes writing produced by electronic communications that are approved by the Board.

AMENDMENTS

1. Tax Credits (Claims and Notifications and Payments by the Board) (Amendment) Regulations 2003 (SI 2003/723), reg.12 (April 6, 2003).

DEFINITIONS

"the Board"—see reg.2.
"the relevant period"—see para.(4).
"writing"—see para.(5).

GENERAL NOTE

This regulation further demonstrates that entitlement to a tax credit is to be dependent on a bank account or other account having been notified to the Board. 2.435

Tax Credits (Administrative Arrangements) Regulations 2002

(SI 2003/3036)

The Commissioners of Inland Revenue, in exercise of the powers conferred upon them by ss.58 and 65(1), (2), (7) and (9) of the Tax Credits Act 2002, hereby make the following Regulations:

ARRANGEMENT OF ARTICLES

GENERAL NOTE

Section 58 of the TCA 2002 provides for regulations to make provision as to the administrative arrangements to apply between a relevant authority (*i.e.* the Secretary of State, the equivalent Northern Ireland Department or a person providing services to either of these authorities: TCA 2002, s.58(3)) and the Commissioners of Inland Revenue, who have the care and management of tax credits (see TCA 2002, s.2). Section 58 applies where regulations under TCA 2002, s.4 or 6 permit or require a claim or notification relating to a tax credit to be made or given to such a relevant authority. These Regulations have therefore been made under s.58 in order to provide for administrative arrangements in relation to claims and notifications made or given to a relevant authority in accordance with the Tax Credits (Claims and Notifications) Regulations 2002 (SI 2002/2014). Regulation 5 of those Regulations requires claims to be made to "an appropriate office", which means an office of the Board, the DWP or its Northern Ireland equivalent (reg.2). 2.437

Citation and commencement

1. These Regulations may be cited as the Tax Credits (Administrative Arrangements) Regulations 2002 and shall come into force on 1st January 2003. 2.438

Interpretation

2.439 **2.** In these Regulations—

"the Board" means the Commissioners of Inland Revenue;

"the principal Regulations" means the Tax Credits (Claims and Notifications) Regulations 2002;

"relevant authority" means—

(a) the Secretary of State;

(b) the Department for Social Development in Northern Ireland; or

(c) a person providing services to the Secretary of State or that Department.

Provision of information or evidence to relevant authorities

2.440 **3.**—(1) Information or evidence relating to tax credits which is held—

(a) by the Board; or

(b) by a person providing services to the Board, in connection with the provision of those services,

may be provided to a relevant authority for the purposes of, or for any purposes connected with, the exercise of that relevant authority's functions under the principal Regulations.

(2) Information or evidence relating to tax credits may be provided to a relevant authority by persons other than the Board (whether or not persons by whom claims or notifications relating to tax credits are or have been made or given).

DEFINITIONS

"the Board" —see reg.2.
"the principal Regulations"—see *ibid.*
"relevant authority"—see *ibid.*

Giving of information or advice by relevant authorities

2.441 **4.** A relevant authority to which a claim or notification is or has been made or given by a person in accordance with the principal Regulations may give information or advice relating to tax credits to that person.

DEFINITIONS

"the principal Regulations"—see reg.2.
"relevant authority"—see *ibid.*

Recording, verification and holding, and forwarding, of claims etc. received by relevant authorities

2.442 **5.**—(1) A relevant authority may record and hold claims and notifications received by virtue of the principal Regulations and information or evidence received by virtue of regulation 3(2).

(2) Subject to paragraphs (3) and (4), a relevant authority must forward to the Board or a person providing services to the Board such a

claim or notification, or such information or evidence, as soon as reasonably practicable after being satisfied that it is complete.

(3) Before forwarding a claim in accordance with paragraph (2), a relevant authority must verify—

(a) that any national insurance number provided in respect of the person by whom the claim is made exists and has been allocated to that person;

(b) that the matters verified in accordance with sub-paragraph (a) accord with—

(i) its own records; or

(ii) in the case of a person providing services to the Secretary of State or the Department for Social Development in Northern Ireland, records held by the Secretary of State or that Department; and

(c) whether the details of any relevant claim for benefit that have been provided are consistent with those held by it.

(4) If a relevant authority cannot locate any national insurance number in respect of a person by whom such a claim is made, it must forward to the Board or a person providing services to the Board the claim (notwithstanding that it is not complete).

(5) "National insurance number" means the national insurance number allocated within the meaning of—

(a) regulation 9 of the Social Security (Crediting and Treatment of Contributions, and National Insurance Numbers) Regulations 2001; or

(b) regulation 9 of the Social Security (Crediting and Treatment of Contributions, and National Insurance Numbers) Regulations (Northern Ireland) 2001.

(6) "Claim for benefit" means a claim for—

(a) a benefit in relation to which—

(i) the Secretary of State has functions under the Social Security Contributions and Benefits Act 1992; or

(ii) the Department for Social Development in Northern Ireland has functions under the Social Security Contributions and Benefits (Northern Ireland) Act 1992; or

(b) a jobseeker's allowance under—

(i) the Jobseekers Act 1995; or

(ii) the Jobseekers (Northern Ireland) Order 1995.

DEFINITIONS

"the Board"—see reg.2.
"the principal Regulations"—see *ibid.*
"relevant authority"—see *ibid.*

Tax Credits (Notice of Appeal) Regulations 2002

(SI 2002/3119)

The Commissioners of Inland Revenue, in exercise of the powers conferred upon them by ss.39(1), 65(2) and 67 of the Tax Credits Act 2002, hereby make the following Regulations:

ARRANGEMENT OF ARTICLES

GENERAL NOTE

2.444 These Regulations prescribe the manner of giving notice of appeal under the TCA 2002 against decisions relating to child tax credit or working tax credit. For further provisions relating to tax credits appeals, see Vol.III in this series.

Citation and commencement

2.445 **1.** These Regulations may be cited as the Tax Credits (Notice of Appeal) Regulations 2002 and shall come into force on 7th January 2003.

Prescribed manner of notice of appeal

2.446 **2.**—(1) The prescribed manner of giving notice of appeal to the Board under section 39(1) of the Tax Credits Act 2002 is as follows.

(2) The notice must—

(a) be given in writing;

(b) contain sufficient information to identify the appellant and the decision against which the appeal is being made; and

(c) be signed by or on behalf of the appellant.

(3) In paragraph (2)(a), "writing" includes writing produced by electronic communications if those electronic communications are approved by the Board.

(4) In para.(2)(c), "signed", where the notice is in writing produced by electronic communications, means authenticated in such manner as may be approved by the Board.

(5) In this regulation, "the Board" means the Commissioners of Inland Revenue.

Tax Credits (Interest Rate) Regulations 2003

(SI 2003/123)

The Treasury, in exercise of the powers conferred upon them by ss.37(2) and (5), 65(1) and (8) and 67 of the Tax Credits Act 2002, hereby make the following Regulations:

ARRANGEMENT OF ARTICLES

Citation and commencement

1. These Regulations may be cited as the Tax Credits (Interest Rate) Regulations 2003 and shall come into force on 18th February 2003. **2.448**

GENERAL NOTE

The tax credits regime does not adopt quite the same approach to interest on overpayments as the Inland Revenue does for late payments of income tax. Whereas interest on late payments of income tax has long been a feature of revenue law, s.37 of the TCA 2002 adopts a compromise approach to tax credits. Thus, interest is charged on overpayments caused by fraud or neglect, but not otherwise. These regulations specify the rate of interest to be applied on such overpayments, and also on any penalty under ss.31–33 (penalties for incorrect statements, failure to comply with requirements, etc.). **2.449**

Interpretation

2.—(1) In these Regulations— **2.450**

"the Board" means the Commissioners of Inland Revenue;

"established rate" means—

(a) on the coming into force of these Regulations, 6.5 per cent per annum;

(b) in relation to any date after the first reference date after the coming into force of these Regulations, the reference rate found on the immediately preceding reference date;

"operative date" means the sixth day of each month;

"reference date" means the day of each month which is the 12 working day before the sixth day of the following month;

"tax credit" means child tax credit or, as the case may be, working tax credit, provision for which is made by the Tax Credits Act 2002;

"working day" means any day other than a non-business day within the meaning of section 92 of the Bills of Exchange Act 1882.

(2) For the purposes of regulation 4(2) the reference rate found on a reference date is the percentage per annum found by averaging the base lending rates at close of business on that date of—

(a) Bank of Scotland;
(b) Barclays Bank plc;
(c) Lloyds Bank plc;
(d) HSBC Bank plc;
(e) National Westminster Bank plc;
(f) The Royal Bank of Scotland plc,

and, if the result is not a whole number, rounding the result to the nearest such number, with any result midway between two whole numbers rounded down.

DEFINITION

"reference rate"—see reg.4(2).

Interest on overpayments of tax credit and penalties

2.451 **3.**—(1) Where the Board decide in accordance with section 37(1) of the Tax Credits Act 2002 that the whole or part of an overpayment of a tax credit which is attributable to fraud or neglect is to carry interest, the rate of interest for the purposes of section 37(2) of that Act is that prescribed by regulation 4.

(2) The rate of interest for the purposes of section 37(5) of the Tax Credits Act 2002 (interest on a penalty under any of sections 31–33 of that Act) is that prescribed by regulation 4.

DEFINITION

"the Board"—see reg.2(1).

Prescribed rate of interest

2.452 **4.**—(1) The rate of interest which is prescribed is, subject to paragraph (2), 6.5 per cent per annum.

(2) Where, on a reference date after the coming into force of these Regulations, the reference rate found on that date ("RR") differs from the established rate, the rate of interest which is prescribed shall, on and after the next operative date, be the percentage per annum found by applying the formula:

$$RR + 2.5.$$

DEFINITION

"established rate"—see reg.2(1).

Tax Credits (Approval of Home Child Care Providers) Scheme 2003

(SI 2003 No. 463)

Made by the Secretary of State for Education and Skills, being the appropriate national authority under section 12(6) of the Tax Credits Act 2002 and in exercise of the powers conferred on the Secretary of State by sections 12(5), (7) and (8) and 65(9) of that Act, and after consultation with the Council of Tribunals in accordance with section 8(1) of the Tribunals and Inquiries Act 1992.

Arrangement of Articles

Citation, commfencement and application

1.—(1) This Scheme shall be known as the Tax Credits (Approval of Home Child Care Providers) Scheme 2003. 2.454

(2) Articles 1 to 16, 21 and 22 shall come into force on 25th March 2003; articles 17 to 20 shall come into force on 1st April 2003.

(3) This Scheme applies in relation to England.

General Note

This Scheme establishes a system for approving childcare providers for the purposes of the Tax Credits Act 2002. The childcare element of working tax credit 2.455

provides assistance with childcare charges (see TCA 2002, s.12(1) and for further details the Working Tax Credit (Entitlement and Maximum Rate) Regulations 2002 (SI 2002/2005), regs 13–16). The definition of "childcare" includes the requirement that such care be "by a person of a prescribed description" (TCA 2002, s.12(5)(b)). This Scheme relates only to England (art.1(3)); this is because the "appropriate national authority" for establishing such a scheme is the Secretary of State in England. The relevant authorities for other parts of the United Kingdom are respectively the Scottish Ministers, the National Assembly for Wales and (in Northern Ireland) the Department of Health, Social Services and Public Safety (TCA 2002, s.12(6)).

So far as the Scheme for England is concerned, Her Majesty's Chief Inspector of Schools in England is the specified person for the purposes of giving approvals (art.3). The Chief Inspector determines applications for approval in accordance with criteria set out in a Code of Practice issued by the Secretary of State. The matters which are to be addressed by the approval criteria are set out in the Schedule to the Scheme. The Scheme provides that an approval may only be given to an applicant who is a registered child minder at the time of the application (art.5). The Chief Inspector is required to operate a system for the determination of applications for approval and for assessment of continued compliance with the approval criteria (art.6). The Chief Inspector may charge any person seeking approval a reasonable fee (art.22). The Chief Inspector is also required to give notice of his or her intention to take specified steps relating to the refusal, withdrawal or variation of an approval (art.11). There is a right of appeal against decisions of the Chief Inspector (arts 14–16). These appeals are heard by the Care Standards Tribunal, constituted under the Care Standards Act 2000. This tribunal has, since April 2002, subsumed the functions of the tribunal established under the Protection of Children Act 1999 (as well as those of the former Registered Homes Tribunal).

Definitions

2.456 **2.** In this Scheme—

"the 1989 Act" means the Children Act 1989;

"approval criteria" has the meaning given to it in art.8;

"the Chief Inspector" means Her Majesty's Chief Inspector of Schools in England;

"child" has the meaning attributed to it by the Child Tax Credit Regulations 2002;

"parent" includes a person who—

(a) has parental responsibility for a child;
(b) is a local authority foster parent in relation to a child;
(c) is a foster parent with whom a child has been placed by a voluntary organisation; and
(d) fosters a child privately;

"parental responsibility" and "fosters a child privately" have the meanings attributed to those respective expressions by ss.3 and 66 of the 1989 Act;

"qualifying childcare" means care provided—

(a) for reward; and
(b) in respect of a child other than a child to whom the provider is a parent or relative;

"relative" in relation to a child means a grand parent, brother, sister, uncle or aunt (whether of the full blood or half blood or by affinity) or step-parent;

"the Tribunal" means the Tribunal established by s.9 of the Protection of Children Act 1999;
"the Tribunal Regulations" means the Protection of Children and Vulnerable Adults and Care Standards Tribunal Regulations 2002;
"the Suspension Regulations" means the Child Minding and Day Care (Suspension of Registration) (England) Regulations 2003.

Specified person

3. The person specified for the purpose of giving approvals under this Scheme is the Chief Inspector. 2.457

DEFINITION

"the Chief Inspector"—see art.2.

Requirements of the Scheme

4. For the purposes of regulation 14(2) of the Working Tax Credit (Entitlement and Maximum Rate) Regulations 2002, a person shall only be a childcare provider approved in accordance with this Scheme— 2.458
(a) if he is for the time being approved by the Chief Inspector; and
(b) in respect of the provision by him of qualifying childcare.

DEFINITIONS

"the Chief Inspector"—see art.2.
"qualifying childcare"—see *ibid.*

Approved person

5.—(1) The Chief Inspector may give an approval under this Scheme only in respect of a person who at the time of making the application is registered for child minding pursuant to section 79F(1) of the 1989 Act. 2.459

(2) Subject to the requirement of paragraph (1), a person shall be given approval as a childcarer under this Scheme if the Chief Inspector is satisfied that the approval criteria are met in relation to that person.

(3) A person who has been given approval under paragraph (2) shall cease to be so approved if that approval is withdrawn by the Chief Inspector or by virtue of an order under article 21.

(4) The Chief Inspector may withdraw an approval if he is satisfied that the approval criteria, or any of the conditions attached by virtue of article 10 to which the giving of the approval is subject, are no longer met in relation to that person.

DEFINITIONS

"the 1989 Act"—see art.2.
"approval criteria"—see *ibid.* and art.8.
"the Chief Inspector"—see art.2.

Approval system

6. The Chief Inspector shall operate a system for— 2.460
(a) the determination of applications for approval made to him under this Scheme; and

(b) the assessment of the extent to which the approval criteria continue to be met by a person so approved,

and shall make adequate arrangements to publicise the details of that system.

DEFINITIONS

"approval criteria"—see arts 2 and 8.
"the Chief Inspector"—see art.2.

Approval system

2.461 **7.** Without prejudice to the generality of aricle 6, the approval system referred to in that article shall in particular—

(a) provide for a procedure by which applicants may apply for approval;
(b) set out requirements relating to the provision by an applicant of documentary or other evidence necessary to demonstrate that the approval criteria are met;
(c) provide for a procedure whereby approvals may be withdrawn;
(d) arrange for childcare provided by a person approved under this Scheme to be inspected or otherwise assessed at suitable intervals;

and may—

(e) provide that reports of inspections or assessments be published in such form and manner as the Chief Inspector may determine;
(f) provide for such inspections or assessments to be carried out by persons on behalf of the Chief Inspector.

DEFINITIONS

"approval criteria"—see arts 2 and 8.
"the Chief Inspector"—see art.2.

Approval criteria

2.462 **8.**—(1) The approval criteria shall be established by a Code of Practice issued by the Secretary of State for the purposes of this Scheme, which criteria shall address the matters referred to in the Schedule.

DEFINITION

"approval criteria"—see arts 2 and 8.

Approval criteria

2.463 **9.** In determining whether in respect of any person approved for the purposes of this Scheme it is appropriate for any step referred to in article 11, 17 or 21 to be taken, the Chief Inspector shall take into account the compliance by that person with the provisions of the Code of Practice.

DEFINITION

"the Chief Inspector"—see art.2.

Conditions

10. The giving of an approval under this Scheme may be made subject to any condition that the Chief Inspector considers appropriate and necessary having regard to the approval criteria, and the Chief Inspector may vary or remove any such condition, or may impose any such new condition. **2.464**

DEFINITIONS

"approval criteria"—see arts 2 and 8.
"the Chief Inspector"—see art.2.

Notice of intention to take steps

11. Where the Chief Inspector proposes— **2.465**
(a) to refuse an application for an approval;
(b) to withdraw an approval previously granted;
(c) to vary any condition to which an approval is subject or to impose any new condition; or
(d) to refuse to grant an application for the removal or variation of any condition to which an approval is subject,

the provisions of section 79L of the 1989 Act (notice of intention to take steps) shall apply to the taking of such step as they apply to the taking of a step referred to in the said section 79L and as if those provisions were set out in this Scheme, but with the modifications referred to in article 12.

DEFINITIONS

"the 1989 Act"—see art.2.
"the Chief Inspector"—see *ibid.*

Notice of intention to take steps

12. Section 79L of the 1989 Act shall apply as if any reference in that section to— **2.466**
(a) the registration of any person were a reference to an approval of any person given under this Scheme;
(b) the registration authority were a reference to the Chief Inspector;
(c) an applicant were a reference to an applicant for approval under this Scheme;
(d) a registered person were a reference to a person approved or seeking approval under this Scheme; and
(e) an appeal under section 79M (Appeals) of the 1989 Act were a reference to an appeal under article 14 of this Scheme.

DEFINITIONS

"the 1989 Act"—see art.2.
"the Chief Inspector"—see *ibid.*

List of home childcare providers

13. The Chief Inspector shall keep a list of childcare providers for the time being approved under this Scheme. **2.467**

DEFINITIONS

"the Chief Inspector"—see art.2.

Appeals

2.468 **14.** An appeal against the taking of any step referred to in article 11 or against an order under article 21 shall lie to the Tribunal.

DEFINITIONS

"the Tribunal"—see art.2.

Appeals

2.469 **15.**—(1) The provisions of the Tribunal Regulations shall apply to an appeal under article 14 as they apply to an appeal under section 79M of the 1989 Act and as if those provisions were set out in this Scheme, but with the modifications referred to in paragraph (2).

(2) Schedule 2 of the Tribunal Regulations shall apply as if any reference to—

(a) section 79L or 79M of the 1989 Act were a reference to article 11 or 14 respectively of this Scheme;

(b) an order under section 79K (protection of children in an emergency) of the 1989 Act were a reference to an order under article 21 of this Scheme;

(c) any registration were a reference to an approval given under this Scheme;

(d) the registration body and the respondent were a reference to the Chief Inspector.

DEFINITIONS

"the 1989 Act"—see art.2.
"the Chief Inspector"—see *ibid.*
"the Tribunal Regulations"—see *ibid.*

Appeals

2.470 **16.** On an appeal, the Tribunal may—

(a) confirm the taking of the step or the making of the order or direct that it shall not have, or shall cease to have, effect; and

(b) impose, vary or cancel any condition to which the approval was subject.

DEFINITION

"the Tribunal"—see art.2.

Suspension of approval

2.471 **17.**—(1) The Chief Inspector may suspend the approval of any person acting as a childcare provider under this Scheme if the Chief Inspector has reasonable cause to believe that the continued provision of that care by that person exposes or may expose one or more of the children to whom it is or may be provided to the risk of harm and the purpose of the suspension is for one or more of the purposes set out in paragraph (2).

(2) The purposes of suspension are—

(a) to allow time for the circumstances giving rise to the Chief Inspector's belief to be investigated;

(b) to allow time for steps to be taken to reduce or eliminate the risk of harm.

DEFINITIONS

"the Chief Inspector"—see article 2.
"child"—see *ibid.*

Suspension of approval

18. An appeal against the suspension of approval pursuant to article 17 shall lie to the Tribunal. 2.472

DEFINITION

"the Tribunal"—see art.2.

Suspension of approval

19.—(1) The provisions of regulations 4 to 8 of the Suspension Regulations shall apply to a suspension under article 17 as they apply to a suspension under regulation 3 of the Suspension Regulations and as if those provisions were set out in this Scheme, but with the modifications referred to in paragraph (2). 2.473

(2) The Suspension Regulations shall apply as if any reference to—

(a) the registration of any person were to the approval of any person under this Scheme;

(b) a registered person were to a person approved under this Scheme; and

(c) a suspension made under the Regulations were to a suspension under article 17,

and associated expressions shall be read accordingly.

DEFINITION

"the Suspension Regulations"—see art 2.

Suspension of approval

20.—(1) The provisions of the Tribunal Regulations shall apply to an appeal under article 18 as they apply to an appeal under regulation 8(1) of the Suspension Regulations and as if those provisions were set out in this Scheme, but with the modifications referred to in paragraph (2). 2.474

(2) The Suspension Regulations shall apply as if any reference to—

(a) an appeal under regulations 8(1)(a) and (b) of those Regulations were to an appeal under article 18 of this Scheme;

(b) the registration of a person were to the approval of a person under this Scheme;

(c) a suspension under those Regulations were to a suspension under article 17 of this Scheme; and

(d) the respondent were to the Chief Inspector,

and any associated expressions shall be read accordingly.

DEFINITIONS

"the Chief Inspector"—see art.2.
"the Suspension Regulations"—see *ibid.*
"the Tribunal Regulations"—see *ibid.*

Emergency steps

2.475 **21.**—(1) If, in the case of any person approved as a childcare provider under this Scheme—

(a) the Chief Inspector applies to a justice of the peace for an order—
  (i) withdrawing the approval;
  (ii) varying or removing any condition to which the approval is subject; or
  (iii) imposing a new condition; and
(b) it appears to the justice that a child who is being, or may be, looked after by that person is suffering, or is likely to suffer, significant harm,

the justice may make the order.

(2) The withdrawal, variation, removal or imposition shall have effect from the time when the order is made.

(3) An application under paragraph (1) may be made without notice.

(4) An order made under paragraph (1) shall be made in writing.

(5) Where an order is made under this article, the Chief Inspector shall serve on the childcare provider to whom the order relates, as soon as reasonably practicable after the making of the order—

(a) a copy of the order;
(b) a copy of any written statement of the Chief Inspector's reasons for making the application for the order which supported that application; and
(c) notice of any right of appeal conferred by article 14.

(6) Where an order has been so made, the Chief Inspector shall, as soon as is reasonably practicable after the making of the order, notify the fact that such order has been made to—

(a) any local authority known to the Chief Inspector in whose area the person concerned provides or provided childcare;
(b) any parent known to the Chief Inspector for whose child the person concerned provides or provided childcare.

DEFINITIONS

"the Chief Inspector"—see art.2.
"child"—see *ibid.*
"parent"—see *ibid.*

Fees

2.476 **22.** The Chief Inspector may charge any person seeking his approval under this Scheme such reasonable fee as he shall, subject to the approval of the Secretary of State, determine.

DEFINITION

"the Chief Inspector"—see art.2.

Article 8 SCHEDULE 1

MATTERS TO BE ADDRESSED BY APPROVAL CRITERIA

1. The suitability of the childcare provider to look after children. 2.477
2. Working in partnership with parents.
3. Acting with integrity and maintaining confidentiality.
4. Organisational skills.
5. Awareness of care, learning and play.
6. Health, safety and welfare of children.
7. Equal opportunities.
8. Special needs.
9. Managing behaviour.
10. Child protection.
11. Keeping of records.

Tax Credits (Immigration) Regulations 2003

(SI 2003/653)

The Treasury, in exercise of the powers conferred upon them by sections 42 and 65(1), (3), (7) and (9) of the Tax Credits Act 2002, hereby make the following Regulations:

ARRANGEMENT OF ARTICLES

Citation and commencement

1. These Regulations may be cited as the Tax Credits (Immigration) Regulations 2003 and shall come into force on 6th April 2003. 2.479

Interpretation

2. In these Regulations— 2.480
"the Act" means the Tax Credits Act 2002;
"the Child Tax Credit Regulations" means the Child Tax Credit Regulations 2002;

"immigration rules" has the meaning given by section 33 of the Immigration Act 1971;
"joint claim" has the meaning given by section 3(8) of the Act;
"limited leave" has the meaning given by section 33 of the Immigration Act 1971;
"married couple" and "unmarried couple" have the meanings given by section 3(5) and (6) of the Act respectively;
"person subject to immigration control" has the meaning in section 115(9) of thc Immigration and Asylum Act 1999;
"refugee" means a person who has been recorded by the Secretary of State as a refugee within the definition in Article 1 of the Convention relating to the Status of Refugees done at Geneva on 28th July 1951 as extended by Article 1(2) of the Protocol relating to the Status of Refugees done at New York on 31st January 1967;
"tax credit" refers to either child tax credit or working tax credit and references to tax credits are to both of them;
"the Working Tax Credit Regulations" means the Working Tax Credit (Entitlement and Maximum Rate) Regulations 2002.

Exclusion of persons subject to immigration control from entitlement to tax credits

2.481 **3.**—(1) No person is entitled to child tax credit or working tax credit while he is a person subject to immigration control, except in the following Cases, and subject to paragraphs (2) to (9).

Case 1

2.482 He is a person who—
(a) has been given leave to enter, or remain in, the United Kingdom by the Secretary of State upon the undertaking of another person or persons, pursuant to the immigration rules, to be responsible for his maintenance and accommodation; and
(b) has been resident in the United Kingdom for a period of at least five years commencing on or after the date of his entry into the United Kingdom, or the date on which the undertaking was given in respect of him, whichever is the later.

Case 2

2.483 He is a person who—
(a) falls within the terms of paragraph (a) of Case 1; and
(b) has been resident in the United Kingdom for less than the five years mentioned in para.(b) of Case 1,

but the person giving the undertaking has died or, where the undertaking was given by more than one person, they have all died.

Case 3

2.484 He is a person who satisfies the following conditions—
(a) he has limited leave to enter or remain in the United Kingdom;

(b) that leave was subject to a condition that he does not have recourse to public funds, during that period of limited leave;
(c) he has, during so much as has elapsed of that period of limited leave (including that period as extended), supported himself without recourse to public funds, other than any such recourse by reason of the previous satisfaction of these conditions;
(d) he is temporarily without funds during that period of leave because remittances to him from abroad have been disrupted;
(e) there is a reasonable expectation that his supply of funds will be resumed; and
(f) the period (or aggregate of periods) for which this Case applies does not exceed 42 days during any single period of limited leave (including any extension to that period).

Case 4

Where the claim is for working tax credit, he is— 2.485
(a) a national of a state which has ratified the European Convention on Social and Medical Assistance (done in Paris on 11th December 1953) or of a state which has ratified the Council of Europe Social Charter (signed in Turin on 18th October 1961); and
(b) lawfully present in the United Kingdom.
The Case so described also applies where—
(a) the claim is for child tax credit;
(b) the award of child tax credit would be made on or after 6th April 2004; and
(c) immediately before the award is made (and as part of the transition of claimants entitled to elements of income support and income-based Jobseeker's Allowance, to child tax credit) the person is, or will on the making of a claim be, entitled to any of the amounts in relation to income support or income-based Jobseeker's Allowance which are described in section 1(3)(d) of the Act.

Case 5

Where the claim is for child tax credit, he is— 2.486
(a) a person who is lawfully working in the United Kingdom; and
(b) a national of a State with which the Community has concluded an Agreement under Article 310 of the Treaty of Amsterdam amending the Treaty on European Union, the Treaties establishing the European Communities and certain related Acts providing, in the field of social security, for the equal treatment of workers who are nationals of the signatory State and their families.

(2) Where one member of a married couple or unmarried couple is a person subject to immigration control, and the other member is not or is within any of Cases 1 to 5 or regulation 5—
(a) the calculation of the amount of tax credit under the Act, the Child Tax Credit Regulations and the Working Tax Credit Regulations (including any second adult element or other element in respect of, or determined by reference to, that person);

(b) the method of making (or proceeding with) a joint claim by the couple; and

(c) the method of payment of the tax credit,

shall, subject to paragraph (3), be determined in the same way as if that person were not subject to such control.

(3) Where the other member is within Case 4 or 5 or regulation 5, para.(2) shall only apply to the tax credit to which he (in accordance with those provisions) is entitled.

(4) Where a person has submitted a claim for asylum as a refugee and in consequence is a person subject to immigration control, in the first instance he is not entitled to tax credits, subject to paragraphs (5) to (9).

(5) If that person—

(a) is notified that he has been recorded by the Secretary of State as a refugee; and

(b) claims tax credit within three months of receiving that notification,

paragraphs (6) to (9) and regulation 4 shall apply to him.

(6) He shall be treated as having claimed tax credits—

(a) on the date when he submitted his claim for asylum; and

(b) on every 6th April (if any) intervening between the date in subparagraph (a) and the date of the claim referred to in paragraph (5)(b),

rather than on the date on which he makes the claim referred to in paragraph (5)(b).

(7) Regulations 7 and 8 of the Tax Credits (Claims and Notifications) Regulations 2002 shall not apply to claims treated as made by virtue of paragraph (6).

(8) He shall have his claims for tax credits determined as if he had been recorded as a refugee on the date when he submitted his claim for asylum.

(9) The amount of support provided under—

(a) section 95 or 98 of the Immigration and Asylum Act 1999;

(b) regulations made under Schedule 9 to that Act, by the Secretary of State in respect of essential living needs of the claimant and his dependants (if any); or

(c) regulations made under paragraph 3 of Schedule 8 to that Act,

(after allowing for any deduction for that amount under regulation 21ZB(3) of the Income Support (General) Regulations 1987) shall be deducted from any award of tax credits due to the claimant by virtue of paragraphs (6) and (8).

DEFINITIONS

"the Act"—see reg.2.
"the Child Tax Credit Regulations"—see *ibid.*
"immigration rules"—see *ibid.*
"joint claim"—see *ibid.*
"limited leave"—see *ibid.*
"married couple"—see *ibid.*
"person subject to immigration control"—see *ibid.*
"refugee"—see *ibid.*
"tax credit"—see *ibid.*
"unmarried couple"—see *ibid.*
"the Working Tax Credit Regulations"—see *ibid.*

GENERAL NOTE

These regulations are made under s.42(1) of the Tax Credits Act 2002, which enables regulations to make provision for the exclusion of "persons subject to immigration control" from entitlement to child tax credit or working tax credit (or both). For these purposes, a "person subject to immigration control" has the same meaning as in s.115 of the Immigration and Asylum Act 1999. Section 115(9) of the 1999 Act is the starting point for this definition, and defines a "person subject to immigration control" as a person who *either* requires leave to enter or remain in the United Kingdom but does not have it *or* has such leave but this is (i) subject to a condition that he does not have recourse to public funds, or (ii) as a result of a maintenance undertaking, or (iii) through the continuation of leave pending certain appeals. For detailed commentary on this definition, see the annotations to reg.21(3) of the Income Support (General) Regulations 1987 (SI 1987/1967) in Vol.II in this series. It should be noted that a person who is a national of an EEA state (*i.e.* a national of an EU Member State or of Iceland, Liechtenstein or Norway) can *never* be a person subject to immigration control for the purposes of social security or tax credits. 2.487

The structure of reg.3 itself falls into three parts. Paragraph (1) sets out the general rule, along with certain exceptions. The position of couples, where one partner is a person subject to immigration control but the other is not, is dealt with in paras (2) and (3). Paragraphs (4)–(9) are concerned with the particular status of asylum seekers.

Para. (1)

The general rule is that a person subject to immigration control is not entitled to either child tax credit or working tax credit (para.(1)). This general rule is then subject to the five exceptions listed in Cases 1–5. These Cases have been adapted from the exceptions to the general rule precluding persons subject to immigration control from being entitled to the various means-tested benefits, as set out in the Schedule to the Social Security (Immigration and Asylum) Consequential Amendments Regulations 2000 (SI 2000/636: see Vol.II in this series). Thus, Case 1 in para.(1) mirrors para.3 in Pt I of the Schedule to the 2000 Regulations; Case 2 follows para.2 of Pt I of the Schedule and Case 3 is similar to para.1 in Pt I of the Schedule (but includes a 42-day limit in sub-para.(f)). These first three Cases operate as exceptions to the preclusionary rule for both child tax credit and working tax credit. The exception in Case 4 is in the same terms as para.4 in Pt I of the Schedule to the 2000 Regulations and applies to all working tax credit claims. It also applies to child tax credit claims in respect of awards made on or after April 6, 2004 where, immediately before the award the claimant was (or would have been) entitled to a child allowance or family or disabled child premium as part of an award of income support or income-based jobseeker's allowance. The exception in Case 5 is adapted from para.2 of Pt II of the Schedule to the 2000 Regulations, which deals with exceptions from the preclusionary rule in respect of certain noncontributory benefits. 2.488

There is also a special rule, applying to child tax credit only, which provides transitional relief for claimants moving from income support or income-based jobseeker's allowance to child tax credit (see reg.5).

Paras (2) and (3)

Paragraph (2) provides that where only one member of a married or unmarried couple is a person subject to immigration control, and the other is not, entitlement to tax credits is determined in the same way as if neither of them were so subject. The same applies where the other member is either within one of the excepted cases in para.(1) or covered by the transitional provisions in reg.5 below. Note also the qualification in para.(3). 2.489

Paras (4)–(9)

2.490 These provisions enable backdated claims to tax credits to be made where an asylum claim has been accepted. A claimant who has submitted a claim for asylum is a person subject to immigration control and so in the first instance is not entitled to tax credits (para.(4)). However, if such an application is accepted, the claimant may claim tax credits retrospectively (para.(5)). Any such retrospective claim must be made within three months of the notification from the IND (para.(5)(a)). This contrasts favourably with the 28 days allowed for retrospective claims for income support in similar situations (Income Support (General) Regulations 1987 (SI 1987/1967), reg.21ZB). In the event of a successful application for asylum, the claim for tax credits is treated as having been made on the date of the submission of the claim for asylum, not the post-acceptance date of the actual claim for tax credits (para.(6)(a)). The claim is also regarded as having been renewed on every intervening April 6, demonstrating an awareness of the delays which are well known in the system for determining asylum applications (para.(6)(b)). Accordingly, the normal time-limits in regs 7 and 8 of the Tax Credits (Claims and Notifications) Regulations 2002 (SI 2002/2014) for claiming tax credits are disapplied (para.(7)) and the claim treated as if the applicant had been recorded as a refugee on the date when the asylum application was actually made (para.(8)). Any arrears of tax credits which are due, following the application of these provisions, are then subject to an offset in recognition of any sums provided by way of asylum support under various statutory provisions (para.(9)).

Note that, by virtue of reg.4, the provisions of Pt I of the TCA 2002 apply to the determination of claims for tax credits made by refugees whose asylum claims have been accepted, subject to the omission of ss.14–17 and various modifications to ss.18 and 19 of the 2002 Act.

Modifications of Part I of the Act for refugees whose asylum claims have been accepted

2.491 **4.**—(1) For the purposes of claims falling within paragraph (2), Part I of the Act shall apply subject to the modifications set out in paras (3)–(5).

(2) A claim falls within this paragraph if it is a claim for tax credits which a person is treated as having made by virtue of regulation 3(6), other than a claim which he is treated as having made in the tax year in which he made his claim under regulation 3(5).

(3) Omit sections 14 to 17 (initial decisions, revised decisions and final notices).

(4) In section 18 (decisions after final notices)—

(a) in subsection (1) for "After giving a notice under section 17" substitute "In relation to each claim for a tax credit made by a person or persons for the whole or part of a tax year";

(b) omit subsections (2) to (9);

(c) for subsection (10) substitute—

"(10) Before making their decision the Board may by notice—

(a) require the person, or either or both of the persons, by whom the claim is made to provide any information or evidence which the Board consider they may need for making their decision; or

(b) require any person of a prescribed description to provide any information or evidence of a prescribed description which the Board consider they may need for that purpose,

by the date specified in the notice.";

(d) in subsection (11) omit—
(i) "any revision under subsection (5) or (9) and";
(ii) paragraph (a);
(iii) in paragraph (b), "in any other case,".

(5) In section 19 (enquiries)—
(a) in subsection (4), for paragraphs (a) and (b) substitute
"one year after that decision or, if—
(a) the person, or either of the persons, to whom the enquiry relates is required by section 8 of the Taxes Management Act 1970 to make a return; and
(b) the return becomes final on a day more than one year after that decision,
with that day (or, if both of the persons are so required and their returns become final on different days, with the later of those days).;"
(b) in subsection (5) omit paragraph (a) and, in paragraph (b) "in any other case,";
(c) omit subsection (6).

DEFINITIONS

"the Act"—see reg.2.
"tax credit"—see *ibid.*

GENERAL NOTE

See note to reg.3. **2.492**

Transitional relief—claimants moving from income support and income-based jobseeker's allowance to child tax credit

5. In relation to child tax credit, a person is not treated for the purposes of these Regulations as subject to immigration control where— **2.493**
(a) the award of child tax credit would be made on or after 6th April 2004;
(b) immediately before the award of child tax credit is made, he is, or will on the making of a claim be, entitled to any of the amounts in relation to income support or income-based jobseeker's allowance which are described in section 1(3)(d) of the Act; and
(c) he is a person who, immediately before the award of child tax credit is made—
(i) was receiving or entitled to income support by virtue of regulation 12(1) of the Social Security (Persons From Abroad) Miscellaneous Amendments Regulations 1996, and his claim for asylum has not been recorded by the Secretary of State as having been decided (other than on appeal) or abandoned; or
(ii) was receiving or entitled to income support or income-based jobseeker's allowance by virtue of regulation 12(3) of the Social Security (Immigration and Asylum) Consequential Amendments Regulations 2000, and his claim for asylum has not been so recorded as having been decided (other than on appeal) or abandoned.

Definitions

"the Act"—see reg.2.
"person subject to immigration control"—see *ibid.*

General Note

2.494 This provides for transitional relief (on or after 6th April 2004) for claimants moving over from the specified elements of income support or income-based jobseeker's allowance to child tax credit.

Tax Credits (Residence) Regulations 2003

(SI 2003/654)

The Treasury, in exercise of the powers conferred upon them by sections 3(7) and 65(1), (7) and (9) of the Tax Credits Act 2002, hereby make the following Regulations:

Regulations

Citation and commencement

2.496 **1.**—These Regulations may be cited as the Tax Credits (Residence) Regulations 2003 and shall come into force on 6th April 2003.

Interpretation

2.497 **2.**—(1) In these Regulations—

"the Act" means the Tax Credits Act 2002;

"child" has the same meaning as it has in the Child Tax Credit Regulations 2002;

"Crown servant posted overseas" has the meaning given in regulation 5(2);

"partner" means where a person is a member of a married or unmarried couple, the other member of that couple;

"qualifying young person" has the meaning given in regulation 2, read with reg.5, of the Child Tax Credit Regulations 2002;

"relative" means brother, sister, ancestor or lineal descendant.

(2) In these Regulations, a person is responsible for a child or qualifying young person if he is treated as being responsible for that child or

qualifying young person in accordance with the rules contained in regulation 3 of the Child Tax Credit Regulations 2002.

General Note

This regulation follows the pattern of all tax credit provisions in adopting the definitions of "child" and "qualifying young person" from the Child Tax Credit Regulations 2002 (SI 2002/2007). 2.498

Circumstances in which a person is treated as not being in the United Kingdom

3.—(1) A person shall be treated as not being in the United Kingdom for the purposes of Part I of the Act if he is not ordinarily resident in the United Kingdom. 2.499

(2) Paragraph (1) does not apply to a Crown servant posted overseas or his partner.

(3) A person who is in the United Kingdom as a result of his deportation, expulsion or other removal by compulsion of law from another country to the United Kingdom shall be treated as being ordinarily resident in the United Kingdom.

(4) For the purposes of working tax credit, a person shall be treated as being ordinarily resident if he is exercising in the United Kingdom his rights as a worker pursuant to Council Regulation (EEC) 1612/68 or Commission Regulation (EEC) 1251/70 or he is a person with a right to reside in the United Kingdom pursuant to Council Directive 8/360/ EEC or 73/148/EEC.

Definitions

"Crown servant posted overseas"—see reg.2.
"partner"—see reg.2.

General Note

Section 3(3) of the TCA 2002 makes it a requirement for entitlement to tax credits that the claimant is "in the United Kingdom". This regulation, authorised by s.3(7), imposes the income test of "ordinary residence" as an additional requirement for entitlement. Read together with the section, the regulations require that a claimant must show: 2.500

(a) ordinary residence in the United Kingdom, and
(b) presence in the United Kingdom or, if he or she is not present in the United Kingdom, that the absence is temporary.

The approach taken here is consistent with the general jurisdictional approach to income tax in the United Kingdom. In common with some other parts of the common law world, income tax is residence-based, rather than nationality-based (as in the United States) or source-based (as in other parts of Europe). Income tax uses two main tests: residence and ordinary residence. The Tax Credits (Definition and Calculation of Income) Regulations 2002 (SI 2002/2006), reg.3 removes the significance of both those tests for the purposes of defining the relevant income of a claimant. These Regulations impose the test at another level. Those Regulations also disapply the definitions of "residence" in the various United Kingdom double tax agreements (which, for income tax purposes, override the national legislation).

Ordinary residence

2.501 "Ordinary residence" was used as the test for WFTC (Family Credit (General) Regulations 1987 (SI 1987/1973), reg.3) where the test was worded as a requirement that the claimant be both present and ordinarily resident. In *R(M) 1/85*, the Commissioner followed *Shah* (below) for those purposes as defining the term. The new form of words appears to avoid the problem with the previous wording commented on in Vol.II of the 2002 edition of this work. One change, however, is that the test is now applied to the whole of the United Kingdom, as Northern Ireland no longer has a separate system for these purposes.

"Ordinary residence" is a question of fact, not law. For the only relevant provisions in income tax law, see the Taxes Act, ss.334–336. It is separate from the other test used for income tax, "residence". "Residence" is determined for income tax purposes by reference to each tax year. "Ordinary residence" is based on a longer view, though perhaps not so long a view as "habitual residence". It is clear from both case law and practice that a claimant can have two ordinary residences at the same time for income tax purposes, and that the status of ordinary residence can be acquired on arrival in the United Kingdom if the claimant arrives with the intention of staying. That may be compared with the approach often taken for social security purposes to "habitual residence". For the leading authorities on the approach to be taken to the test see *Levene v IRC* [1928] A.C. 217; *IRC v Lysaght* [1928] A.C. 234; and *Shah v Barnet LBC* [1983] 2 A.C. 309, HL.

The Inland Revenue has a code of practice, published as booklet IR20, which defines how the Revenue treat disputed issues of ordinary residence. The Revenue treat the question as partly one of intention and partly one of actual presence. The working practice is to treat someone as resident in the United Kingdom if he or she is present for more than 183 days in total in any one year (whenever that year starts), and to treat someone as ordinarily resident if present for more than an average of 91 days in each of four consecutive years. A new arrival who has a joblasting more than three years here and/or who buys a house here is likely to be treated as ordinarily resident on arrival, and the reverse will be true of those leaving. IR20 should be treated with some caution as it applies to tax credits. Commentators have taken the view on a number of occasions that the Revenue view is one that supports the Revenue's own approach to the definitions, rather than necessarily takes a neutral view on the issues. Secondly, and linked with this, the Revenue code in IR20 is designed to include people who would probably prefer to be excluded from the charge to United Kingdom income tax. Will the same approach be applied where the Revenue might wish to exclude the claimant, while the claimant's interest will be to be included? In other words, will the Revenue apply its allegedly expansive view of its jurisdiction under IR20 in the same way when paying out tax credits as when collecting in tax?

In practice, problems will usually arise in the following situations:

2.502 *(1) When someone who has been ordinarily resident in the United Kingdom goes overseas:* the usual issue here will be that the claimant is no longer as a matter of fact "in" the United Kingdom to claim child tax credit for any children. Subject to the temporary absence rule in reg.4, and the rules for Crown servants in regs 5 and 6, the claimant will cease to qualify for tax credits. However, if the person (or one of two joint claimants leaving together) returns often enough to remain "present", then it will be a question of fact whether the claimant is ordinarily resident despite the overseas link. Where one of two joint claimants goes overseas and the other does not, the claim should become a single claim.

2.503 *(2) When someone arrives in the United Kingdom:* the first practical requirement for working tax credit purposes is that the claimant has a job. If he or she has come to the United Kingdom to work and that work is likely to last at least 3 years, then current Revenue practice is to treat the person as ordinarily resident here on arrival. The position of the worker whose work here may not last that period but who has rights under EU law as a worker is protected by reg.3(4). It is suggested that if the person is accepted as ordinarily resident under either rule for working tax credit purposes then he or she should also be accepted as able to claim child tax credit as well. There will also be a practical argument in other cases that if the claimant is treated as liable to United Kingdom income tax, then he or she will expect United Kingdom tax credits. However, the liability to income tax may arise on residence alone before the individual becomes ordinarily resident in the United Kingdom.

(3) When someone has strong links with the United Kingdom and another state: **2.504** there may be ordinary residence in both states. This will be a question of fact. Unlike regs 5 and 6 below, this regulation does not deal expressly with partners making joint claims. The position is clear from s.3 of the Act. A couple must make a joint claim if both are "in" the United Kingdom. If one of the couple is not present or ordinarily resident here, then only the other partner can make the claim. But this will have the effect of excluding the non-resident partner's income from the income calculation. It may therefore be in the interests of some claimants for child tax credit to claim, say, that the mother is present and ordinarily resident, but that the father is not. This is not now a concern for income tax purposes as all married couples are assessed to income tax separately.

The Treasury published a consultative document with the 2003 Budget about the tests of residence, ordinary residence and domicile, entitled: *Reviewing the residence and domicile rules as they affect the taxation of individuals: a background paper.* It is available on the HM Treasury website. It contains a valuable summary of current practice and the problems it generates.

Para. (2)

Paragraph (2) relates to regs (5) and (6) below. Paragraph (3) deals with the problem that some of these individuals might not otherwise be regarded as ordinarily resident and so would be deprived of claims to either working tax credit or child tax credit. But see also the Tax Credits (Immigration) Regulations 2003 (SI 2003/653). Paragraph (4), which relates to working tax credit only, makes the necessary exception to protect the rights of movement of workers and others under EU law. See Vol.III of this work. It is not entirely clear why this is limited to working tax credit, as child tax credit would appear to be a social security family benefit for EU law purposes and therefore something to which someone with EU rights might also lay claim. Perhaps the aim is to ensure that in order to claim child tax credit in these situations the individual must first claim, or be entitled to claim, working tax credit. But that may exclude higher earners who are outside the income rules for working tax credit but not for child tax credit. **2.505**

Persons temporarily absent from the United Kingdom

4.—(1) A person who is ordinarily resident in the United Kingdom and is temporarily absent from the United Kingdom shall be treated as being in the United Kingdom during the first— **2.506**

(a) 8 weeks of any period of absence; or
(b) 12 weeks of any period of absence where that period of absence, or any extension to that period of absence, is in connection with—
  (i) the treatment of his illness or physical or mental disability;
  (ii) the treatment of his partner's illness or physical or mental disability;

(iii) the death of a person who, immediately prior to the date of death, was his partner;
(iv) the death, or the treatment of the illness or physical or mental disability, of a child or qualifying young person for whom either he or his partner is, or both of them are, responsible; or
(v) the death, or the treatment of the illness or physical or mental disability, of his or his partner's relative.

(2) A person is temporarily absent from the United Kingdom if at the beginning of the period of absence his absence is unlikely to exceed 52 weeks.

DEFINITIONS

"ordinarily resident"—see reg.3.
"partner"—see reg.2.

GENERAL NOTE

2.507 This regulation deals with the practical application of the requirement that a claimant be "in" the United Kingdom as well as ordinarily resident here. It adopts the approach long used in social security law of ignoring temporary absence. See, for comparison, Income Support (General) Regulations 1987 (SI 1987/1967), reg.4. The current rule appears reasonably generous as it ignores the first eight weeks of "any" period of absence. Presumably, a claimant could make a visit back to the United Kingdom before the end of eight (or 12) weeks to re-establish presence before starting a second period of absence, and so on. On the facts, this would also avoid the 52-week rule in para.(2). On the wording, it would seem that the 52-week rule reapplies at the beginning of each period of absence.

See reg.6 below for a modification of this regulation as it applies to the partners of Crown servants employed overseas.

Crown servants posted overseas

2.508 **5.**—(1) A Crown servant posted overseas shall be treated as being in the United Kingdom.

(2) A Crown servant posted overseas is a person performing overseas the duties of any office or employment under the Crown in right of the United Kingdom—
(a) who is, or was, immediately prior to his posting or his first of consecutive postings, ordinarily resident in the United Kingdom; or
(b) who, immediately prior to his posting or his first of consecutive postings, was in the United Kingdom in connection with that posting.

GENERAL NOTE

2.509 This regulation and reg.6 protect the position of British public servants and their partners (and therefore also their children) when working outside the United Kingdom. Section 44 of the TCA 2002 removes any doubt about the application of the tax credits scheme to Crown employees.

Partners of Crown servants posted overseas

2.510 **6.**—(1) The partner of a Crown servant posted overseas who is accompanying the Crown servant posted overseas shall be treated as being in the United Kingdom when he is either—

(a) in the country where the Crown servant is posted; or
(b) absent from that country in accordance with regulation 4 as modified by paragraphs (3) and (4).

(2) Regulation 4 applies to the partner of a Crown servant posted overseas with the modifications set out in paragraphs (3) and (4).

(3) Omit the words "ordinarily resident in the United Kingdom and is".

(4) In relation to a partner who is accompanying the Crown servant posted overseas the references to "United Kingdom" in the phrase "temporarily absent from the United Kingdom", in both places where it occurs, shall be construed as references to the country where the Crown servant is posted.

DEFINITIONS

"Crown servant posted overseas"—see reg.5.
"partner"—see reg.2.

Transitional provision—income support and income-based jobseeker's allowance

7.—A person is exempt from the requirement to be ordinarily resident in the United Kingdom (which is set out in regulation 3(1)) in respect of child tax credit on and for three years after the date on which the award of child tax credit is made where— 2.511

(a) the award of child tax credit would be made on or after 6th April 2004;
(b) immediately before the award of child tax credit is made, he is, or will be on the making of a claim, entitled to any of the amounts in relation to income support and income-based jobseeker's allowance which are described in section 1(3)(d) of the Act; and
(c) he is a person to which one or more of the following provisions applies—
    (i) paragraph (b) or (c) in the definition of "person from abroad" in regulation 21(3) of the Income Support (General) Regulations 1987;
    (ii) paragraph (b) or (c) in the definition of "person from abroad" in regulation 85(4) of the Jobseeker's Allowance Regulations 1996;
    (iii) paragraph (b) or (c) in the definition of "person from abroad" in regulation 21(3) of the Income Support (General) (Northern Ireland) Regulations 1987;
    (iv) paragraph (b) or (c) in the definition of "person from abroad" in regulation 85(4) of the Jobseeker's Allowance Regulations (Northern Ireland)1996.

GENERAL NOTE

This is a narrow three-year transitional provision for child tax credit only. It takes effect from or after April 6, 2004—the date when CTC replaces the child additions to income support and jobseeker's allowance. It is limited to: 2.512

(a) claimants receiving either income support or income-based jobseeker's allowance including child additions immediately before the rule comes into effect; but only if

(b) they are claiming those benefits as refugees or following a grant of exceptional leave to enter or remain in the United Kingdom under the Immigration Acts.

It should be read with the Tax Credits (Immigration) Regulations 2003 (SI 2003/653).

Tax Credits (Official Error) Regulations 2003

(SI 2003/692)

The Commissioners of Inland Revenue, in exercise of the powers conferred upon them by sections 21 and 65(2), (3), (7) and (9) of the Tax Credits Act 2002 hereby make the following Regulations:

ARRANGEMENT OF REGULATIONS

Citation and commencement

2.514 **1.** These Regulations may be cited as the Tax Credits (Official Error) Regulations 2003 and shall come into force on 6th April 2003.

Interpretation

2.515 **2.**—(1) In these Regulations—

"the Board" means the Commissioners of Inland Revenue;

"official error" means an error relating to a tax credit made by—

(a) an officer of the Board;
(b) an officer of the Department for Work and Pensions;
(c) an officer of the Department for Social Development in Northern Ireland; or
(d) a person providing services to the Board or to an authority mentioned in paragraph (b) or (c) of this definition, in connection with a tax credit or credits,

to which the claimant, or any of the claimants, or any person acting for him, or any of them, did not materially contribute, excluding any error of law which is shown to have been an error by virtue of a subsequent decision by a Social Security Commissioner or by a court;"

"Social Security Commissioner" has the meaning given by section 63(13);

"tax year" means a period beginning with 6th April in one year and ending with April 5 in the next.

(2) In these Regulations, references to a section are to that section of the Tax Credits Act 2002.

General Note

The double inverted commas at the end of the very last line of the definition of "official error" are a typographical error in the HMSO version of these regulations. The lack of a heading to reg.3 is also unfortunate. 2.516

3.—(1) A decision under section 14(1), 15(1), 16(1), 18(1), (5), (6) or (9), 19(3) or 20(1) or (4) may be revised in favour of the person or persons to whom it relates if it is incorrect by reason of official error, subject to the following paragraphs. 2.517

(2) In revising a decision, the officer or person in question need not consider any issue that is not raised by the application for revision by the claimant or claimants or, as the case may be, did not cause him to act on his own initiative.

(3) A decision mentioned in paragraph (1) may be revised at any time not later than five years after the end of the tax year to which the decision relates.

Definitions

"official error"—see reg.2(1).
"tax year"—see *ibid.*

General Note

These regulations, made under s.21 of the TCA 2002, provide for decisions under the various specified sections of the Act (see reg.3(1)) to be revised in favour of the claimant(s) if they are incorrect because of "official error". The definition of "official error" in reg.2(1) is identical in all material respects to that which applies in the social security scheme under the Social Security and Child Support (Decisions and Appeals) Regulations 1999 (SI 1999/991) (see reg.1(3) and the commentary in Vol. III of this series). However, whereas a social security decision may be revised on the basis of official error and arrears of benefit paid back to the date of the original claim (SSA 1998, s.9(3) and reg.3(5)(a) of the 1999 Regulations), a claim for tax credits is subject to a time limit of five years after the end of the tax year to which the decision relates (reg.3(3)). 2.518

Tax Credits (Provision of Information) (Functions Relating to Health) Regulations 2003

(SI 2003/731)

The Commissioners of Inland Revenue, in exercise of the powers conferred upon them by sections 65(2) and 67 of, and paragraph 9(2) of Schedule 5 to, the Tax Credits Act 2002, hereby make the following Regulations:

Arrangement of Regulations

Citation and commencement

2.520 **1.** These Regulations may be cited as the Tax Credits (Provision of Information) (Functions Relating to Health) Regulations 2003 and shall come into force on 6th April 2003.

GENERAL NOTE

2.521 Section 59 of and Sch.5 to the TCA 2002 make provision for the use and disclosure of information relating to claims by and between the Inland Revenue and government departments. These regulations prescribe functions for the purposes of para.9 of Sch.5 to the 2002 Act, which enables information relating to tax credits, child benefit or guardian's allowance to be provided by the Board of Inland Revenue to the Department of Health, the National Assembly for Wales, the Scottish Ministers, or the Department of Health, Social Services and Public Safety in Northern Ireland for the purposes of such functions relating to health as may be prescribed. These functions are set out in reg.3. Information may also be provided to persons providing services to, or exercising functions on behalf of, those Departments or persons.

These regulations are supplemented by the Tax Credits (Provision of Information) (Functions Relating to Health) (No. 2) Regulations 2003 (SI 2003/1650).

Interpretation

2.522 **2.** In these Regulations—

"child tax credit" shall be construed in accordance with section 8 of the Tax Credits Act 2002;

"disability element" means the disability element of working tax credit as specified in section 11(3) of the Tax Credits Act 2002;

"family" means—

(a) in the case of a joint claim for a tax credit under the Tax Credits Act 2002, the married or unmarried couple by whom the claim is made and any child or qualifying young person for whom at least one of them is responsible, in accordance with regulation 3 of the Child Tax Credit Regulations 2002;

(b) in the case of a single claim for a tax credit under the Tax Credits Act 2002, the claimant and any child or qualifying young person for whom he is responsible in accordance with regulation 3 of the Child Tax Credit Regulations 2002;

"qualifying family" means a family—

(a) that has a relevant income of £14,200 or less; and

(b) one member of which is receiving—

(i) working tax credit and child tax credit; or

(ii) working tax credit which includes a disability element; or

(iii) child tax credit, not being eligible for working tax credit;

"qualifying young person" has the meaning given by regulation 2(1), read with regulation 5(3) and (4), of the Child Tax Credit Regulations 2002;

"relevant income" has the same meaning as in section 7(3) of the Tax Credits Act 2002;

"working tax credit" shall be construed in accordance with section 10 of the Tax Credits Act 2002.

Prescribed functions relating to health

3. The following functions are prescribed for the purposes of paragraph 9 of Schedule 5 to the Tax Credits Act 2002 (provision of information by the Board of Inland Revenue for health purposes)— 2.523

(a) the issue by or on behalf of the Secretary of State, the National Assembly for Wales, the Scottish Ministers or the Department of Health, Social Services, and Public Safety in Northern Ireland of a certificate confirming that the family is a qualifying family;

(b) verification by or on behalf of the Secretary of State, the National Assembly for Wales, the Scottish Ministers or that Department at any time that a family is a qualifying family at that time;

(c) the issue on behalf of the Secretary of State or that Department of milk tokens and free vitamins to persons entitled to receive free of charge milk (including dried milk) or vitamins in accordance with the Welfare Food Regulations 1996 or the Welfare Food Regulations (Northern Ireland) 1988;

(d) the making on behalf of the Secretary of State or that Department of payments to such persons in accordance with those Regulations;

(e) the giving on behalf of the Secretary of State or that Department of information relating to milk tokens and related health matters to such persons in accordance with those Regulations.

DEFINITIONS

"family"—see reg.2.
"qualifying family"—see *ibid.*

The Tax Credits (Polygamous Marriages) Regulations 2003

(SI 2003/742)

The Treasury, in exercise of the powers conferred upon them by sections 3(7), 7(8) and (9), 8, 10 to 12, 42, 43 and 65(1), (3), (7) and (9) of the Tax Credits Act 2002, and the Commissioners of Inland Revenue, in exercise of the powers conferred on them by sections 4(1), 6, 24 and 65(2), (3), (7) and (9) of that Act, and of all other powers enabling them in that behalf, hereby make the following Regulations:

ARRANGEMENT OF REGULATIONS 2.524

INTRODUCTION AND GENERAL NOTE

2.525 These regulations provide alternative language to that of single claims and joint claims, and the associated definitions for single and joint claims, in cases where the claimant is a party to a polygamous marriage. Part I of the TCA 2002 and all relevant regulations are altered to give consistent effect to the policy that all the members of a polygamous marriage, or "unit" as it is called, must jointly claim for and be responsible for any tax credits payable to any of them. This is a different approach from that usually taken for social security benefits purposes, under which polygamous marriages are usually ignored for benefit purposes unless they are in fact monogamous. See the Social Security and Family Allowances (Polygamous Marriages) Regulations 1975 (SI 10975/561) in Vol.I of this work.

Section 43(1) of the TCA 2002 empowers regulations to apply Pt I of that Act to persons who are parties to a polygamous marriage. "Party to a polygamous marriage" is defined by s.43(2) to include any marriage entered into under a law which permits polygamy and under which any party to the marriage has more than one spouse, that is, more than one husband or wife. The drafters have chosen to adopt different language in these Regulations and the amendments made by these Regulations to the TCA 2002 and other regulations. Instead of "polygamous marriage", the term used throughout is "polygamous unit". The significance of this is discussed in reg.2 below.

The remaining regulations give effect to those modifications as necessary within the other regulations implementing the TCA 2002. Any necessary commentary is added to the relevant amended regulation.

Citation, commencement and effect

2.526 **1.**—(1) These Regulations may be cited as the Tax Credits (Polygamous Marriages) Regulations 2003 and shall come into force on 6th April 2003, immediately after the coming into force of the Child Tax Credit (Amendment) Regulations 2003.

(2) Regulations 22 to 56 only have effect in relation to members of polygamous units (and in the case of regulations 35 to 38, former members of such units).

Interpretation

2.527 **2.**—In these Regulations—

"the Act" means the Tax Credits Act 2002;

"polygamous couple" means a man and a woman who are married under a law which permits polygamy where—

(a) they are not separated under a court order or in circumstances in which the separation is likely to be permanent; and
(b) either of them has an additional spouse;

"polygamous unit" means—
(a) a polygamous couple; and
(b) any person who is married to either member of the polygamous couple and who is not separated from that member under a court order or in circumstances in which the separation is likely to be permanent.

GENERAL NOTE

Section 43(2) of the TCA 2002 provides that a person is a party to a polygamous marriage if: 2.528
(a) he or she is a party to a marriage entered into under a law which permits polygamy; and
(b) he or she has a spouse additional to any other party to the marriage.

The effect of this definition is to limit the scope of the operation of the modifications made under these Regulations to take account also of the definition of "married couple" in s.3(5) of the TCA 2002.

Modifications to Part I of the Act for members of polygamous units

3.—Regulations 4 to 21 prescribe modifications to Part I of the Act so far as it applies to members of polygamous units. 2.529

4. In section 3—
(a) in subsection (3)(a) after "United Kingdom", insert "(and neither of whom are members of a polygamous unit)";
(b) after subsection (3)(a) insert—
"(aa) jointly by the members of a polygamous unit all of whom are aged at least 16 and are in the United Kingdom, or";
(c) in subsection (3)(b) after "paragraphs (a)", insert "or (aa)";
(d) after subsection (4)(a), insert—
"(aa) in the case of a joint claim under subsection (3)(a), if a member of the married or unmarried couple becomes a member of a polygamous unit; and
(ab) in the case of a joint claim under subsection (3)(aa), if there is any change in the persons who comprise the polygamous unit, and";
(e) after subsection (6), insert—
"(6A) In this Part "polygamous unit" has the meaning given by regulation 2 of the Tax Credits (Polygamous Marriages) Regulations 2003.";
(f) in subsection (8), in the definition of "joint claim", after "para.(a)" insert "or para.(aa)".

5. In section 4(1)(g)—
(a) for "member of a married couple or an unmarried couple", substitute "or more members of a polygamous unit";
(b) for "of the married couple or unmarried couple", substitute "or members".

6. In section 7(2), for "either" substitute "any";

7. In section 8(1), for "either or both" substitute "any or all".

8. In section 9(2)(b), for "either or both" substitute "any or all".

9. In section 10—

(a) in subsection (1), for "either or both" substitute "any or all";

(b) in subsection (3), for "either" wherever it appears substitute "any".

10. In section 11—

(a) in subsection (3), for "either or both" substitute "any or all";

(b) in subsection (6)(a), for "either of the persons or the two" substitute "any of the persons or all";

(c) in subsection (6)(b), for "married couple or unmarried couple" substitute "polygamous unit";

(d) omit subsection (6)(c);

(e) in both subsection (6)(d) and (e), for "either or both" substitute "any or all".

11. In both section 12(3) and (4)(a), for "either or both" substitute "any or all".

12. In section 14(2)(a), for "either or both" substitute "any or all".

13. In section 16(3)(a), for "either or both" substitute "any or all".

14. In section 17(10)(b)—

(a) for "member of a married couple or an unmarried couple", substitute "or more members of a polygamous unit";

(b) for "married couple or unmarried couple", substitute "or members".

15. In section 18(10), for "either or both" substitute "any or all".

16. In section 19—

(a) in subsection (2)(a), for "either or both" substitute "any or all";

(b) in subsection (4)(a), for "either" substitute "any" and for "both" substitute "more than one";

(c) in subsection (9), for "either" substitute "any".

17. In section 20(4)(b), for "either" (wherever it appears) substitute "any".

18. In section 24(2)—

(a) for "married couple or an unmarried couple", substitute "polygamous unit";

(b) for "whichever of them" substitute "one or more of those persons as".

19. In section 29(4), for "either or both" substitute "any or all".

20. In section 31(2)—

(a) after "another" insert "or others";

(b) for "unless subsection (3) applies" substitute "or each of them unless subsection (3) applies to the person in question".

21. In section 37(1), for "either or both" (in each place they appear) substitute "any or all".

Amendments to the Child Tax Credit Regulations 2002

2.530 **22.**—Amend the Child Tax Credit Regulations 2002 (for members of polygamous units only) as follows.

23. In regulation 2(1)—

(a) for the definition of "joint claim", substitute the following definition—
" "joint claim" means a claim under section 3(3)(aa) of the Act, as inserted by regulation 4(b) of the Tax Credits (Polygamous Marriages) Regulations 2003;";
(b) insert at the appropriate place the following definition—" "polygamous unit" has the meaning in the Tax Credits (Polygamous Marriages) Regulations 2003;".

24. In regulation 3(1), in rule 2.1., for "married couple or unmarried couple" in each place it appears substitute "polygamous unit".

25. In regulation 7—
(a) in paragraph (1)(b), for "married couple or unmarried couple" substitute "polygamous unit";
(b) in paragraph (2)(b)(ii), for "either or both" substitute "any or all".

Amendments to the Working Tax Credit (Entitlement and Maximum Rate) Regulations 2002

26. Amend the Working Tax Credit (Entitlement and Maximum Rate) Regulations 2002 (for members of polygamous units only) as follows. 2.531

27. In regulation 2(1)—
(a) for the definition of "joint claim", substitute the following definition—" "joint claim" means a claim under section 3(3)(aa) of the Act (as inserted by regulation 4(b) of the Tax Credits (Polygamous Marriages) Regulations 2003);";
(b) insert at the appropriate place the following definition—" "polygamous unit" has the meaning in the Tax Credits (Polygamous Marriages) Regulations 2003;".

28. In regulation 3(3)—
(a) for "both members of the couple satisfy", substitute "more than one member of the polygamous unit satisfies"; and
(b) for "two such elements", substitute "one such element for each of them that satisfies those conditions".

29. In regulation 4(1), in paragraph (a)(ii) of the Second Condition, for "his partner" substitute "any other member of the polygamous unit".

30. In regulation 10(2)—
(a) in sub-paragraph (c), for "couple" substitute "members of the polygamous unit";
(b) in sub-paragraph (d), for "couple" substitute "unit".

31. In regulation 11—
(a) in paragraph (1), after "element" insert "(and an additional such element for each member of the polygamous unit exceeding two in number)";
(b) in paragraph (2)(c), for "neither of the claimants" substitute "no claimant";
(c) in paragraph (4), in the words preceding sub-paragraph (a), after "adult element" insert "for any claimant";
(d) in paragraph (4)(a), for "neither claimant" substitute "none of the claimants"; and

(e) in paragraph (4)(b), for "one claimant" substitute "the claimant in question".

32. In regulation 13—

(a) omit paragraph (1)(a);

(b) in paragraph (1)(b), for "married or unmarried couple where both" substitute "polygamous unit where at least two of them";

(c) in paragraph (1)(c), for the words preceding paragraph (i) substitute "is a member or are members of a polygamous unit where at least one member is engaged in qualifying remunerative work and at least one other".

(d) in paragraph (4), for "the other member of a couple" substitute "another member of the polygamous unit";

(e) in paragraph (5), for "the other member or his partner" substitute "him or another member of the polygamous unit".

33. In regulation 14—

(a) in paragraph (1), for "either or both" substitute "any or all";

(b) in paragraph (1B), for "either or both" substitute "any or all";

(c) in paragraph (5), for "a partner or by a partner" substitute "another member of the same polygamous unit or".

34. In regulation 20—

(a) in paragraph (1), for "single claimant or to a couple" substitute "polygamous unit";

(b) omit paragraph (1)(c)(i);

(c) in paragraph (1)(c)(ii), for "a couple either or both" substitute "the members of a polygamous unit, any or all of whom";

(d) in paragraph (1)(c)(iii), for "a couple" substitute "the members of a polygamous unit";

(e) omit paragraph (1)(e);

(f) omit paragraph (1)(f)(i);

(g) in paragraph (1)(f)(ii), for "couple" substitute "polygamous unit".

Amendments to the Tax Credits (Definition and Calculation of Income) Regulations 2002

2.532 **35.** Amend the Tax Credits (Definition and Calculation of Income) Regulations 2002 (for members or former members of polygamous units only) as follows.

36. In regulation 2 (interpretation)—

(a) in paragraph (2), in the definition of "family" for "married or unmarried couple" substitute "members of the polygamous unit";

(b) in paragraph (2), insert at the appropriate places the following definitions—

" "joint claim" means a claim under section 3(3)(aa) of the Act, as inserted by regulation 4(b) of the Tax Credits (Polygamous Marriages) Regulations 2003; "polygamous unit" has the meaning in the Tax Credits (Polygamous Marriages) Regulations 2003;";

(c) in paragraph (4)(a), for the words from "a claimant's spouse" to the end substitute "another member of the same polygamous unit";

(d) in paragraph (4)(b), for the words from "claimant's former spouse" to the end substitute "person who was formerly a member with the claimant of the same polygamous unit".

37. In regulation 3(7), (calculation of income of claimant)—

(a) in sub-paragraph (b), for "either or both" substitute "any or all";

(b) in sub-paragraph (c), for "either or both" substitute "any or all".

38. In regulation 4(1) (employment income), in the words succeeding sub-para.(k), for "either" substitute "any".

Amendments to the Tax Credits (Claims and Notifications) Regulations 2002

39. Amend the Tax Credits (Claims and Notifications) Regulations 2002 (for members of polygamous units only) as follows. 2.533

40. In regulation 2 (interpretation)—

(a) for the definition of "joint claim" substitute the following definition—

" "joint claim", means a claim under section 3(3)(aa) of the Act, as inserted by regulation 4(b) of the Tax Credits (Polygamous Marriages) Regulations 2003;";

(b) insert at the appropriate place the following definition—

" "polygamous unit" has the meaning in the Tax Credits (Polygamous Marriages) Regulations 2003;".

41. In regulation 11(2), for "both" substitute "all of the".

42. In regulation 13—

(a) in paragraph (1), for the words from "one member" to the end substitute "one or more members of a polygamous unit is to be treated as also made by the other member or members of that unit";

(b) in paragraph (2)—

(i) for "member of a married couple or an unmarried couple", substitute "or more members of a polygamous unit";

(ii) for "both members of the couple", substitute "all the members of the unit".

43. In regulation 15—

(a) in paragraph (3) for the words from "only one" to the end, substitute "one or more members of a polygamous unit die, the other member or members of the unit may proceed with the claim in the name or names of the person or persons who have died, as well as in their own name or names";

(b) in paragraph (4), for "both" (in each place it appears) substitute "all of ".

44. In regulation 16—

(a) in paragraph (1), for the words from "member of a" to the end, substitute "or more members of a polygamous unit die and the other member or members of the unit wish to make a joint claim for a tax credit";

(b) for paragraph (2), substitute—

"(2) The survivor or survivors may make and proceed with the claim in the name of the member or members who have died as well as in his or their own names.;"

(c) in paragraph (3)(a)—
  (i) for "married couple or unmarried couple", substitute "polygamous unit";
  (ii) add at the end "(or the earliest such date if more than one)".

45. In regulation 23(2), for "either member of the married couple or unmarried couple" substitute "any member of the polygamous unit".

46. In regulation .30(2), for "either" (in each place it appears) substitute "any".

47. In regulation 31(2)(a), for "either" substitute "any".

[1 **47A.** In regulation 34(3)—

(a) for "one of two joint claimants" substitute "any member of a polygamous unit"; and

(b) for "both" (in each place where it occurs) substitute "all".]

Amendments to the Tax Credits (Payment by the Board) Regulations 2002

2.534 **48.** Amend the Tax Credits (Payments by the Board) Regulations 2002 (for members of polygamous units only) as follows.

49. In regulation 2 (interpretation)—

(a) omit the definitions of "married couple" and "unmarried couple";

(b) insert at the appropriate place the following definition—
" "polygamous unit" has the meaning in the Tax Credits (Polygamous Marriages) Regulations 2003;".

50. In regulation 3—

(a) in the heading, for "couple" substitute "polygamous unit";

(b) for paragraphs (2) to (6) substitute—

"(2) There shall be established, for each particular child or qualifying young person for whom any or all of the members of the polygamous unit is or are responsible—

(a) the member of that unit who is (for the time being) identified by all the members of the unit as the main carer for that child or qualifying young person; or

(b) in default of such a member, the member of that unit who appears to the Board to be the main carer for that child or qualifying young person.

(3) The individual element of child tax credit for any child or qualifying young person shall be paid to the main carer of that child or qualifying young person.

(4) The family element of child tax credit for any polygamous unit shall be divided (pro rata) by the number of children and qualifying young persons for whom any or all of the members of that unit is or are responsible, and the proportion so attributable to each such child or qualifying young person shall be paid to the main carer of that child or qualifying young person.

(5) Any childcare element of working tax credit shall be divided (pro rata) by the number of children referred to in paragraph (2) in respect of whom relevant childcare charges are paid, and the proportion so attributable to each such child shall be paid to the main carer of that child.

(6) In this regulation—

"child" has the meaning given by the Child Tax Credit Regulations 2002;

"qualifying young person" has the meaning given by those Regulations; and

"relevant childcare charges" has the meaning given by regulation 14(1) of the Working Tax Credit (Entitlement and Maximum Rate) Regulations 2002."

Amendments to the Tax Credits (Residence) Regulations 2003

51. Amend the Tax Credits (Residence) Regulations 2003 (for members of polygamous units only) as follows. 2.535

52. In regulation 2 (Interpretation)—

(a) in the definition of "partner", for the words from "married" to the end, substitute "polygamous unit, any other member of that unit";

(b) insert at the appropriate place the following definition—" "polygamous unit" has the meaning in the Tax Credits (Polygamous Marriages) Regulations 2003;".

Amendments to the Tax Credits (Immigration) Regulations 2003

53. Amend the Tax Credits (Immigration) Regulations 2003 (for members of polygamous units only) as follows. 2.536

54. In regulation 2 (Interpretation)—

(a) for the definition of "joint claim", substitute the following definition—

"joint claim" means a claim under section 3(3)(aa) of the Act, as inserted by regulation 4(b) of the Tax Credits (Polygamous Marriages) Regulations 2003";

(b) insert at the appropriate place the following definition—

"polygamous unit" has the meaning in the Tax Credits (Polygamous Marriages) Regulations 2003;".

55. In regulation 3(2)—

(a) for the words from "married couple" to "and the other", substitute "polygamous unit is a person subject to immigration control and any other";

(b) in sub-paragraph (b), for "couple" substitute "unit".

56. In regulation 4(1) (modifications to the Tax Credits Act 2002), add at the end "(which, in the case of a claim by the members of a polygamous unit, are subject to the modifications made by regulations 4 to 21 of the Tax Credits (Polygamous Marriages) Regulations 2003)".

AMENDMENT

1. Tax Credits (Miscellaneous Amendments) Regulations 2004 (SI 2004/762), reg.19 (April 6, 2004).

Tax Credits (Provision of Information) (Functions Relating to Health) (No. 2) Regulations 2003

(SI 2003/1650)

The Commissioners of Inland Revenue, in exercise of the powers conferred upon them by sections 65(2) and 67 of, and paragraph 9 of Schedule 5 to the Tax Credits Act 2002 hereby make the following Regulations:

ARRANGEMENT OF REGULATIONS

GENERAL NOTE

2.538 These regulations supplement the Tax Credits (Provision of Information) (Functions Relating to Health) Regulations 2003 (SI 2003/731).

Citation, commencement and extent

2.539 **1.**—(1) These Regulations may be cited as the Tax Credits (Provision of Information) (Functions Relating to Health) (No. 2) Regulations 2003 and shall come into force on 17th July 2003.

(2) These Regulations do not extend to Northern Ireland.

Prescribed functions relating to health

2.540 **2.**—(1) The function specified in paragraph (2) is prescribed for the purposes of paragraph 9 of Schedule 5 to the Tax Credits Act 2002 (provision of information by the Board of Inland Revenue for health purposes).

(2) The function specified in this paragraph is the conduct, by a person providing services to the Secretary of State and the Scottish Ministers, of a survey of the mental health of persons in Great Britain who are under the age of 17 on 1st September 2003.

(3) Nothing in these Regulations limits the operation of the Tax Credits (Provision of Information Relating to Health) Regulations 2003.

Tax Credits (Provision of Information) (Function Relating to Employment and Training) Regulations 2003

(SI 2003/2041)

The Commissioners of Inland Revenue, in exercise of the powers conferred upon them by sections 65(2) and 67 of, and paragraph 5(2) of Schedule 5 to, the Tax Credits Act 2002, hereby make the following Regulations:

ARRANGEMENT OF REGULATIONS

GENERAL NOTE

These regulations, made under para. 5 of Sch. 5 to the Tax Credits Act 2002, enable information relating to tax credits, child benefit or guardian's allowance to be provided by the Board of Inland Revenue to the Secretary of State for the purposes of the operation of the Employment Retention and Advancement Scheme established under s.2 of the Employment and Training Act 1973. 2.542

Citation, commencement and extent

1.—(1) These Regulations may be cited as the Tax Credits (Provision of Information) (Function Relating to Employment and Training) Regulations 2003 and shall come into force on 29th August 2003. 2.543

(2) These Regulations do not extend to Northern Ireland.

Prescribed function relating to employment and training

2.—(1) The function specified in paragraph (2) is prescribed for the purposes of paragraph 5 of Schedule 5 to the Tax Credits Act 2002 (provision of information by the Board of Inland Revenue for employment and training purposes). 2.544

(2) The function specified in this paragraph is the operation of the Employment Retention and Advancement Scheme, that is to say the scheme for assisting persons to improve their job retention or career advancement, established by the Secretary of State under section 2 of the Employment and Training Act 1973.

Tax Credits Act 2002 (Child Tax Credit) (Transitional Provisions) Order 2003

(SI 2003/2170)

The Treasury, in exercise of the powers conferred upon them by section 62(2) of the Tax Credits Act 2002, make the following Order:

ARRANGEMENT OF ARTICLES

General Note

2.546 Section 1(3)(d) of the Tax Credits Act 2002 provides for the abolition of various component elements of the applicable amount for the purposes of income support and income-based jobseeker's allowance (namely the child allowances, family premium, disabled child premium and enhanced disability premium for a child or young person). This Order makes transitional provision in connection with the introduction of child tax credit, but only for pensioners formerly in receipt of the minimum income guarantee in income support. The Order thus applies to persons who were in receipt of income support, were aged not less than 60 and were responsible for a child, throughout the period beginning on August 22, 2003 and ending on September 28, 2003 (Art 2(1)). In such a case a person is deemed to have made a claim for child tax credit (a) on August 22, 2003 for the purpose of enabling a decision to be made by the Board of Inland Revenue on the claim and (b) on the first day of the first benefit week beginning on or after September 29, 2003 for all other purposes, e.g. as regards payment (Art. 2(2)). This Order is thus associated with the introduction of state pension credit as from October 2003.

Citation and commencement

2.547 **1.** This Order may be cited as the Tax Credits Act 2002 (Child Tax Credit) (Transitional Provisions) Order 2003 and shall come into force on 22nd August 2003.

Transitional provision

2.548 **2.**—(1) This article applies in the case of a person who throughout the period beginning on 22nd August 2003 and ending on 28th September 2003 is—

(a) in receipt of income support;
(b) aged not less than 60; and
(c) responsible for a child (within the meaning of regulation 3 of the Child Tax Credit Regulations 2002).

(2) Where this article applies to a person, he shall be treated as having made a claim for child tax credit in respect of the child for whom he is responsible as mentioned in paragraph (1)(c) of this article—

(a) on 22nd August 2003 for the purposes of enabling the Board to make an initial decision on the claim; and
(b) on the first day of the first benefit week in relation to income support beginning on or after 29th September 2003 for all other purposes.

(3) In paragraph (2) "benefit week" has the same meaning—

(a) in relation to a person in Great Britain, as it bears in regulation 2(1) of the Income Support (General) Regulations 1987; and
(b) in relation to a person in Northern Ireland, as it bears in regulation 2(1) of the Income Support (General) Regulations (Northern Ireland) 1987.

Tax Credits (Provision of Information) (Evaluation and Statistical Studies) Regulations 2003

(SI 2003/3308)

The Commissioners of Inland Revenue, in exercise of the powers conferred upon them by sections 65(2) and 67 of, and paragraph 4(2) of Schedule 5 to, the Tax Credits Act 2002 make the following Regulations:

Citation, commencement and extent

1.—(1) These Regulations may be cited as the Tax Credits (Provision of Information) (Evaluation and Statistical Studies) Regulations 2003 and shall come into force on 9th January 2004. **2.549**

(2) These Regulations do not extend to Northern Ireland.

Purposes for which information may be provided

2. The purposes of conducting evaluation and statistical studies in relation to— **2.550**

(a) the education of children and young people under the age of 17; and

(b) the provision and use of child care,

are prescribed under paragraph 4 of Schedule 5 to the Tax Credits Act 2002 (provision of information by the Board of Inland Revenue for evaluation and statistical studies).

Here "child care" means any care provided for a child whether or not of a description prescribed for any purpose under the Act.

PART III

STATUTORY SICK PAY

Statutory Sick Pay (General) Regulations 1982

(SI 1982/894) (AS AMENDED)

The Secretary of State for Social Services, in exercise of the powers conferred upon him by sections 1(3) and (4), 3(5) and (7), 4(2), 5(5), 6(1), 8(1) to (3), 17(4), 18(1), 20 and 26(1) and (3) to (5) of, paragraph 1 of Schedule 1 to, and paragraphs 2(3) and 3(2) of Schedule 2 to, the Social Security and Housing Benefits Act 1982(a) and of all other powers enabling him in that behalf, hereby makes the following regulations.

ARRANGEMENT OF REGULATIONS

Citation, commencement and interpretation

1.—(1) These regulations may be cited as the Statutory Sick Pay (General) Regulations 1982, and shall come into operation on 6th April 1983. 3.2

(2) In these regulations—

"the Act" means the Social Security and Housing Benefits Act 1982;

[[1]"the Contributions and Benefits Act" means the Social Security Contributions and Benefits Act 1992;]

[[2]"income tax month" means the period beginning on the 6th day of any calendar month and ending on the 5th day of the following calendar month;]

(3) Unless the context otherwise requires, any reference—

(a) in these regulations to a numbered section or Schedule is a reference to the section or Schedule, as the case may be, of or to the Act bearing that number;

(b) in these regulations to a numbered regulation is a reference to the regulation bearing that number in these regulations; and

(c) in any of these regulations to a numbered paragraph is a reference to the paragraph bearing that number in that regulation.

AMENDMENTS

1. Social Security (Miscellaneous Provisions) Amendment (No.2) Regulations 1992 (SI 1992/2595), reg.14 (November 16, 1992).

2. Social Security Contributions, Statutory Maternity Pay and Statutory Sick Pay (Miscellaneous Amendments) Regulations 1996 (SI 1996/777), reg.2(2) (April 6, 1996).

GENERAL NOTE

3.3 The relevant provisions in Pt I of the Social Security and Housing Benefits Act 1982 have now been replaced by Pt XII of the SSCBA 1992.

Persons deemed incapable of work

3.4 **2.**—(1) A person who is not incapable of work of which he can reasonably be expected to do under a particular contract of service may be deemed to be incapable of work of such a kind by reason of some specific disease or bodily or mental disablement for any day on which either—

(a) (i) he is under medical care in respect of a disease or disablement as aforesaid,

(ii) it is stated by a registered medical practitioner that for precautionary or convalescent reasons consequential on such disease or disablement he should abstain from work, or from work of such a kind; and

(iii) he does not work under that contract of service; or

(b) he is excluded from work, or from work of such a kind, on the certificate of a Medical Officer for Environmental Health and is under medical observation by reason of his being a carrier, or having been in contact with a case, of infectious disease.

(2) A person who at the commencement of any day is, or thereafter on that day becomes, incapable of work of such a kind by reason of some specific disease or bodily or mental disablement, and

(a) on that day, under that contract of service, does no work, or no work except during a shift which ends on that day having begun on the previous day; and

(b) does no work under that contract of service during a shift which begins on that day and ends on the next,

shall be deemed to be incapable of work of such a kind by reason of that disease or bodily or mental disablement throughout that day.

DEFINITIONS

"contract of service"—see SSCBA 1992, s.163(1).

GENERAL NOTE

Para. (1)

Regulation 2 of the SSP (General) Regulations is in virtually identical terms to the former reg.3(1) and (2) of the old Unemployment, Sickness and Invalidity Benefit Regulations 1983 (SI 1983/1598), which covered deemed sickness for the purposes of sickness benefit (see the 1994 volume of *Bonner*, p.687). The relevant case law in that context revolved around the vexed question of whether the regulation covers a pregnant claimant who is herself fit for work but is recommended to refrain from work because of the danger of contracting a disease which would threaten the life of the foetus she is carrying. Earlier cases have involved school teachers who are pregnant when there is an outbreak of Rubella in the school. 3.5

There are two reported decisions under the old law which are worthy of note. In *R(S)24/54* it was held that a precautionary absence from work was not within sub-para.(a) of the regulation because she was not under medical care in respect of the disease during a period in which she had been advised to refrain from work simply to avoid contact with the disease. That decision was rejected by the Commissioner in *R(S)1/72* where the facts were identical, except that the claimant was awaiting the outcome of tests to determine whether she was immune to Rubella and could therefore return to work. In fact, the results of those tests were not available for about five weeks owing in part to a postal strike. The Commissioner found that during the whole of that time she was under medical care in respect of the disease and was, therefore, deemed to be incapable of work and entitled to benefit. Fortunately for her, the results showed that she was immune and she was able to return to work. No question arose as to whether she would have continued to qualify for benefit if she had not been immune and had been advised to remain off work. But, the line of the Commissioner's reasoning in that case and his rejection of *R(S)24/54* rather than any attempt to distinguish it suggest that he may well have held that the claimant would remain under medical care until the danger from the infection was past.

In *R(S)4/93* the claimant was an assistant in a veterinary practice, who was potentially in danger of infection by toxoplasmosis from handling cats. She was given certificates advising her to refrain from work over a period of about six weeks. Her claim for statutory sick pay was refused by her employer and she applied to an AO for a decision on her entitlement to statutory sick pay. The Commissioner adopted the reasoning in both of the earlier cases. Thus she found that the claimant was entitled to benefit for a period of five days while awaiting the outcome of tests, which were negative, but not entitled for a further period of five weeks for which a claim had been made. The Commissioner did not specifically address the point that there had been a change in wording to the regulation since the earlier cases. The regulation now specifically refers to absence which is recommended for "precautionary" reasons. But, given that such reasons must be "consequential on such disease", meaning one for which she is "under medical care", it is probable that the new words add nothing to the interpretation.

It is, on the face of it, a rather fine distinction to hold, as in *R(S)4/93*, that the claimant is under medical care while awaiting the outcome of the tests but not under medical care once they are known. Nor is it in point to observe, as does the Commissioner in *R(S)24/54*, that the claimant is not unfit for work, only unable to work in the particular place she was employed, because the whole point of this regulation is for a claimant to be *deemed* unfit even though she may be fit. No doubt some justice is done for a claimant whose contribution record qualifies her for contribution-based jobseeker's allowance (presumably she is not to be disqualified for voluntary leaving), but where the claimant does not have such an entitlement the loss of statutory sick pay will be hard felt.

A claimant with a contribution record could also now potentially qualify for incapacity benefit because the regulations for that benefit specifically provide for a pregnant woman who has to refrain from work because of a danger to herself or her unborn child (see Incapacity for Work (General) Regulations 1995 (SI 1995/311), reg.14—see Vol.I in this series).

[1 Linking periods of incapacity for work

3.6 **2A.**—In subsection (3) of section 2 of the 1982 Act (linking periods of incapacity for work), 8 weeks shall be substituted for 2 weeks.]

AMENDMENT

1. Statutory Sick Pay (General) Amendment Regulations 1986 (SI 1986/ 477), reg.2 (April 6, 1986).

GENERAL NOTE

3.7 Section 2 of the 1982 Act, along with the other original provisions relating to statutory sick pay, was repealed by the Social Security (Consequential Provisions) Act 1992, s.3 and Sch.1. The eight-week linking rule is now to be found in SSCBA 1992, s.152(3).

Period of entitlement ending or not arising

3.8 **3.**—(1) In a case where an employee is detained in legal custody or sentenced to a term of imprisonment (except where the sentence is suspended) on a day which in relation to him falls within a period of entitlement, that period shall end with that day.

(2) A period of entitlement shall not arise in relation to a period of incapacity for work if the employee in question is in legal custody or sentenced to or undergoing a term of imprisonment (except where the sentence is suspended).

[4(2A) A period of entitlement in respect of an employee who was entitled to incapacity benefit, maternity allowance or severe disablement allowance shall not arise in relation to any day within a period of incapacity for work beginning with the first day on which paragraph 2(d) of Schedule 11 to the Contributions and Benefits Act ceases to have effect where the employee in question is a person to whom regulation 13A of the Social Security (Incapacity for Work) (General) Regulations 1995 (welfare to work beneficiary) applies.]

[1(3) A period of entitlement as between an employee and his employer shall end after 3 years if it has not otherwise ended in accordance with [3section 153(2) of the Contributions and Benefits Act] or with regulations (other than this paragraph) made under [3section 153(6) of the Contributions and Benefits Act].]

[2[3(4) Where a period of entitlement is current as between an employee and her employer and the employee—

(a) is pregnant or has been confined; and
(b) is incapable of work wholly or partly because of pregnancy or confinement on any day which falls on or after the beginning of the [54th week] before the expected week of confinement; and
(c) is not by virtue of that pregnancy or confinement entitled to statutory maternity pay under Part XII of the Contributions and Benefits Act or to maternity allowance under section 35 of that Act;

the period of entitlement shall end on that day or, if earlier, on the day she was confined.]

[3(5) Where an employee—

(a) is pregnant or has been confined; and
(b) is incapable of work wholly or partly because of pregnancy or confinement on any day which falls on or after the beginning of the [54th week] before the expected week of confinement; and
(c) is not by virtue of that pregnancy or confinement entitled to statutory maternity pay under Part XII of the Contributions and Benefits Act or to maternity allowance under section 35 of that Act;

a period of entitlement as between her and her employer shall not arise in relation to a period of incapacity for work where the first day in that period falls within 18 weeks of the beginning of the week containing the day referred to at (b) above or, if earlier, of the week in which she was confined.]

(6) In paragraphs (4) and (5), "confinement" and "confined" have the same, meanings as in [3section 171 of the Contributions and Benefits Act].]

AMENDMENT

1. Statutory Sick Pay (General) Amendment Regulations 1986 (SI 1986/477), reg.3 (April 6, 1986).
2. Statutory Sick Pay (General) Amendment (No.2) Regulations 1987 (SI 1987/868), reg.2 (June 7, 1987).
3. Social Security Maternity Benefits and Statutory Sick Pay (Amendment) Regulations 1994 (SI 1994/1367), reg.9 (June 11, 1994).
4. Social Security (Welfare to Work) Regulations 1998 (SI 1998/2231), reg.6 (October 5, 1998).
5. Social Security, Statutory Maternity Pay and Statutory Sick Pay (Miscellaneous Amendments) Regulations 2002 (SI 2002/2690), reg.13 (November 24, 2002).

DEFINITIONS

"confined"—see para.(6).
"confinement"—see *ibid.*
"employee"—see SSCBA 1992, s.163(1) and reg.16.
"employer"—see SSCBA 1992, s.163(1).
"period of entitlement"—see *ibid.*
"period of incapacity for work"—see *ibid.*
"week"—see *ibid.*

[1 Maximum entitlement to statutory sick pay in a period of entitlement

3.9 **3A.**—(1) For the purpose of determining whether an employee's maximum entitlement to statutory sick pay has been reached in a period of entitlement as between him and an employer of his, days falling within a previous period of entitlement as between the employee and any person who is or has in the past been an employer of his are, subject to paragraph (3), to be counted in the circumstances specified in paragraph (2).

(2) The circumstances specified for the purpose of paragraph (1) are—

(a) the period of entitlement as between the employee and his employer arose not more than 8 weeks after the last day in respect of which a person who is or has in the past been an employer of his was liable to make to him a payment of statutory sick pay; and either

(b) the employee has provided his employer with a statement issued in accordance with regulation 15A by a previous employer of his—

(i) on or before the seventh day after the first qualifying day in the period of entitlement; or

(ii) within such longer period as the employer may require, so however that where an employee shows good cause for delay in providing the statement, he may provide it later than the time specified in heads (i) and (ii) above but not later than the ninety-first day after the first qualifying day in the period of entitlement; or

(c) the employer has himself issued such a statement to the employee.

(3) Where an employee provides his employer with more than one statement or the employer himself issued more than one statement such as is referred to in paragraph (2), the employer shall have regard to one only of those statements and if the number of weeks specified in the statements is not the same he shall have regard to the statement which specifies the greatest number of weeks.

(4) For the purposes of paragraph (2)(b), a statement enclosed in an envelope which is properly addressed and sent by prepaid post shall be deemed to have been provided on the day which it was posted.

(5) The employer shall return the statement to the employee where—

(a) a period of entitlement does not arise as between the employee and his employer; or

(b) the employee leaves his employment with the employer within eight weeks of its commencement, and the employer is not himself required to provide the employee with a statement in accordance with regulation 15A,

and in such cases regulation 13(2) shall not apply to him.]

AMENDMENT

1. Statutory Sick Pay (General) Amendment Regulations 1986 (SI 1986/477), reg.4 (April 6, 1986).

DEFINITIONS

"employee"—see SSCBA 1992, s.163(1) and reg.16.
"employer"—see SSCBA 1992, s.163(1).

"period of entitlement"—see *ibid.*
"qualifying day"—see *ibid.*

Contract of service ended for the purpose of avoiding liability for statutory sick pay

4.—(1) The provisions of this regulation apply in any case where an employer's contract of service with an employee is brought to an end by the employer solely or mainly for the purpose of avoiding liability for statutory sick pay. 3.10

(2) Where a period of entitlement is current on the day on which the contract is brought to an end, the employer shall be liable to pay statutory sick pay to the employee until the occurrence of an event which, if the contract would have caused the period of entitlement to come to an end under section 3(2)(a), (b) or (d) or regulation 3(1) [[1]of these regulations or regulation 10(2) of the Statutory Sick Pay (Mariners, Airmen and Persons Abroad) Regulations 1982], or (if earlier) until the date on which the contract would have expired.

AMENDMENT

1. Statutory Sick Pay (Mariners, Airmen and Persons Abroad) Regulations 1982 (SI 1982/1349), reg.10(3) (April 6, 1983).

AMENDMENT

"contract of service"—see SSCBA 1992, s.163(1).
"employee"—see *ibid.* and reg.16.
"employer"—see SSCBA 1992, s.163(1).
"period of entitlement"—see *ibid.*

Qualifying days

5.—(1) In this regulation, "week" means a period of 7 consecutive days, beginning with Sunday. 3.11

(2) Where an employee and an employer of his have not agreed which day or days in any week are or were qualifying days [[1]or where in any day or days are or were such as are referred to in paragraph (3)], the qualifying day or days in that week shall be—

(a) the day or days on which it is agreed between the employer and employee that the employee is or was required to work (if not incapable) for that employer or, if it is so agreed that there is or was no such day;

(b) the Wednesday, or, if there is no such agreement between and employee as mentioned in sub-paragraph (a);

(c) every day, except that or those (if any) on which it is agreed between the employer and the employee that none of that employer's employees are or were required to work (any agreement that all day such days being ignored).

[[1](3) No effect shall be given to any agreement between an employer to treat as qualifying days—

(a) any day where the day is identified, whether expressly or reference to that or another day being a day of incapacity relation to the employee's contract of service with an employer;

(b) any day identified, whether expressly or otherwise, by period of entitlement or to a period of incapacity for work.]

AMENDMENTS

1. Statutory Sick Pay (General) Amendment Regulations 1985 (SI 1985/126), reg.2 (March 5, 1985).

DEFINITIONS

"contract of service"—see SSCBA 1992, s.163(1).
"employee"—see *ibid.* and reg.16.
"employer"—see SSCBA 1992, s.163(1).
"period of entitlement"—see *ibid.*
"period of incapacity for work"—see *ibid.*
"qualifying day": see *ibid.*
"week": see *ibid.*

GENERAL NOTE

3.12 This prescribes the manner in which qualifying days are to be determined in the absence of any effective agreement between employer on which days are to rank as such (see also SSCBA 1992, s.154). *R(SSP) 1/85* decides that "required to work" in sub-paras (a) and (c) means obliged to work under one's terms of employment, and does not embrace the situation in which the employee was merely asked to work. Thus, there the employee's normal practice of working voluntary overtime on Saturdays could not turn Saturday into a qualifying day where the contract of service merely provided for 39 hours' work on Mon–Fri. That decision (at para.10) explains how what is now SSCBA 1992, s.154 and this paragraph interrelate to set out a series of alternatives, to be applied in turn as necessary, to determine qualifying days in any particular case.

Para. (3)

This renders ineffective any agreement which, expressly or otherwise, identifies qualifying days by reference to it or another day being one of incapacity, or by reference to a period of entitlement or period of incapacity for work.

Calculation of entitlement limit

3.13 **6.**—(1) Where an employee's entitlement to statutory sick pay is calculated by reference to different weekly rates in the same period of entitlement [2. . .], the entitlement limit shall be calculated in the manner described in paragraphs (2) and (3), or, as the case may be, (4) and (5); and where a number referred to in paragraph (2)(b) or (d) or (4)(a)(ii) or (d)(ii) is not a whole number [1of thousandths, it shall be rounded up to the next thousandth].

(2) For the purpose of determining whether an employee has reached his maximum entitlement to statutory sick pay in respect of a period of entitlement there shall be calculated

(a) the amount of statutory sick pay to which the employee became entitled during the part of the period of entitlement before the change in the weekly rate;
(b) the number by which the weekly rate (before the change) must be multiplied in order to produce the amount mentioned in sub-paragraph (a);
(c) the amount of statutory sick pay to which the employee has so far become entitled during the part of the period of entitlement after the change in the weekly rate; and
(d) the number by which the weekly rate (after the change) must be multiplied in order to produce the amount mentioned in sub-paragraph (c);
(e) the sum of the amounts mentioned in sub-paragraphs (a) and (c); and
(f) the sum of the number mentioned in sub-paragraphs (b) and (d).

(3) When the sum mentioned in paragraph (2)(f) reaches [[2]28], the sum mentioned in paragraph (2)(e) reaches the entitlement limit.

(4) [[2]. . .]

(5) [[2]. . .]

AMENDMENTS

1. Statutory Sick Pay (General) Amendment Regulations 1984 (SI 1984/385), reg.2(a) (April 16, 1984).

2. Statutory Sick Pay (General) Amendment Regulations 1986 (SI 1986/477), reg.9 (April 6, 1986).

DEFINITIONS

"employee"—see SSCBA 1992, s.163(1) and reg.16.
"period of entitlement"—see SSCBA 1992, s.163(1).

Time and manner of notification of incapacity for work

7.—(1) Subject to paragraph (2), notice of any day of incapacity for work shall be given by or on behalf of an employee to his employer— 3.14
(a) in a case where the employer has decided on a time limit (not being one which requires the notice to be given earlier than [[1]. . .] the first qualifying day in the period of incapacity for work which includes that day of incapacity for work [[1]or by a specified time during that qualifying day]) and taken reasonable steps to make it known to the employee, within that time limit; and
(b) in any other case, on or before the seventh day after that day of incapacity for work.

(2) Notice of any day of incapacity for work may be given [[2]one month] later than as provided by paragraph (1) where there is good cause for giving it later [[2], or if in the particular circumstances that is not practicable, as soon as it is reasonably practicable thereafter] so however that it shall in any event be given on or before the 91st day after that day.

(3) A notice contained in a letter which is properly addressed and sent

by prepaid post shall be deemed to have been given on the day on which it was posted.

(4) Notice of any day of incapacity for work shall be given by or on behalf of an employee to his employer—

(a) in a case where the employer has decided on a manner in which it is to be given (not being a manner which imposes a requirement such as is specified in paragraph (5)) and taken reasonable steps to make it known to the employee, in that manner; and

(b) in any other case, in any manner, so however that unless otherwise agreed between the employer and employee it shall be given in writing.

(5) The requirements mentioned in paragraph (4)(a) are that notice shall be given—

(a) personally;

(b) in the form of medical evidence;

(c) more than once in every 7 days during a period of entitlement;

(d) on a document supplied by the employer; or

(e) on a printed form.

AMENDMENTS

1. Statutory Sick Pay (General) Amendment Regulations 1984 (SI 1984/385), reg.2(b) (April 16, 1984).

2. Social Security Contributions, Statutory Maternity Pay and Statutory Sick Pay (Miscellaneous Amendments) Regulations 1996 (SI 1996/777), reg.2(3) (April 6, 1996).

DEFINITIONS

"employee"—see SSCBA 1992, s.163(1) and reg.16.
"employer"—see SSCBA 1992, s.163(1).
"period of entitlement"—see *ibid.*
"period of incapacity for work"—see *ibid.*
"qualifying day"—see *ibid.*

Manner in which statutory sick pay may not be paid

3.15 **8.**—Statutory sick pay may not be paid in kind or by way of the provision of board or lodging or of services or other facilities.

Time limits for paying statutory sick pay

3.16 **9.**—(1) In this regulation, "payday" means a day on which it has been agreed, or it is the normal practice, between an employer and an employee of his, that payments by way of remuneration are to be made, or, where there is no such agreement or normal practice, the last day of a calendar month.

(2) In any case where—

(a) a decision has been made by an insurance officer, local tribunal or Commissioner in proceedings under Part I that an employee is entitled to an amount of statutory sick pay; and

(b) the time for bringing an appeal against the decision has expired and either
   (i) no such appeal has been brought; or
   (ii) such an appeal has been brought and has been finally disposed of, that amount of statutory sick pay is to be paid within the time specified in paragraph (3).

(3) Subject to paragraphs (4) and (5), the employer is required to pay the amount not later than the first pay day after—

(a) where an appeal has been brought, the day on which the employer receives notification that it has been finally disposed of;
(b) where leave to appeal has been refused and there remains no further opportunity to apply for leave, the day on which the employer receives notification of the refusal; and
(c) in any other case, the day on which the time for bringing an appeal expires.

(4) Subject to paragraph (5), where it is impracticable, in view of the employer's methods of accounting for and paying remuneration, for the requirement of payment referred to in paragraph (3) to be met by the pay day referred to in that paragraph, it shall be met not later than the next following pay day.

(5) Where the employer would not have remunerated the employee for his work on the day of incapacity for work in question (if it had not been a day of incapacity for work) as early as the pay day specified in paragraph (3) or (if it applies) paragraph (4), the requirement of payment shall be met on the first day on which the employee would have been remunerated for his work on that day.

DEFINITIONS

"employee"—see SSCBA 1992, s.163(1) and reg.16.
"employer"—see SSCBA 1992, s.163(1).

[[1] Liability of the Secretary of State for payments of statutory sick pay

9A.—(1) Notwithstanding the provisions of section 1 of the Act and subject to paragraph (4), where— 3.17

(a) an adjudicating authority has determined that an employer is liable to
(b) the time for appealing against the determination has expired; and
(c) no appeal against the determination has been lodged or leave to appeal against the determination is required and has been refused,

then for any day of incapacity for work in respect of which it was determined the employer was liable to make those payments, and for any further days of incapacity for work which fall within the same spell of incapacity for work and in respect of which the employer was liable to make payments of statutory sick pay to that employee, the liability to make payments of statutory sick pay in respect of those days shall, to the extent that payment has not been made by the employer, be that of the Secretary of State and not the employer.

(2) For the purposes of this regulation a spell of incapacity for work consists of consecutive days of incapacity for work with no day of the week disregarded.

(3) In paragraph (1) above "adjudicating authority" means, as the case may be, the Chief or other adjudication officer, a Social Security Appeal Tribunal or the Chief or any other Social Security Commissioner.

(4) This regulation shall not apply to any liability of an employer to make a payment of statutory sick pay where the day of incapacity for work in respect of which the liability arose falls within a period of entitlement which commenced before 6th April 1987.]

AMENDMENTS

1. Statutory Sick Pay (General) Amendment Regulations 1987 (SI 1987/372), reg.2 (April 6, 1987).

DEFINITIONS

"employee"—see SSCBA 1992, s.163(1) and reg.16.
"employer"—see SSCBA 1992, s.163(1).
"period of entitlement"—see *ibid.*
"week"—see *ibid.*

GENERAL NOTE

3.18 This regulation, together with regs 9B and 9C, prescribe the circumstances in which the liability to pay statutory sick pay is to be that of the Board of the Inland Revenue and not the employer. (Although the regulation still refers to the Secretary of State, those functions were transferred—along with those under regs 9B and 9C—to the Board by s.1(2) of and Sch.2 to the Social Security Contributions (Transfer of Functions, etc.) Act 1999.) The relevant circumstances are where it is determined that statutory sick pay is payable but the employer neither pays the amount due nor appeals against the decision (reg.9A) and where the employer was insolvent at the time (reg.9B). Provision is also made (reg.9C) requiring the Board to make the payments for which they are liable at weekly intervals.

[1 Insolvency of employer

3.19 **9B.**—(1) Notwithstanding the provisions of section 1 of the Act and subject to paragraph (3), any liability arising under Part I of the Act to make a payment of statutory sick pay in respect of a day of incapacity for work in relation to an employee's contract of service with his employer shall be that of the Secretary of State and not that of the employer where the employer is insolvent on that day.

(2) For the purposes of paragraph (1) an employer shall be taken to be insolvent if, and only if—

(a) in England and Wales—
   (i) he has been adjudged bankrupt or has made a composition or arrangement with his creditors;
   (ii) he had died and his estate falls to be administered in accordance with an order under section 421 of the Insolvency Act 1986; or
   (iii) where an employer is a company, a winding-up order or an administration order is made or a resolution for voluntary

winding-up is passed with respect to it, or a receiver or manager of its undertaking is duly appointed, or possession is taken by or on behalf of the holders of any debentures secured by a floating charge, or any property of the company comprised in or subject to the charge or a voluntary arrangement proposed for the purposes of Part 1 of the Insolvency Act 1986 is approved under that Part;

(b) in Scotland—

(i) an award of sequestration is made on his estate or he executes a trust deed for his creditors or enters into a composition contract;

(ii) he has died and a judicial factor appointed under section 11A of the Judicial Factors (Scotland) Act 1889 is required by that section to divide his insolvent estate among his creditors; or

(iii) where the employer is a company, a winding-up order or an administration order is made or a resolution for voluntary winding-up is passed with respect to it or a receiver of its undertaking is duly appointed or a voluntary arrangement proposed for the purposes of Part 1 of the Insolvency Act 1986 is approved under that Part.

shall not apply where the employer became insolvent before 6th April 1987.]

AMENDMENTS

1. Statutory Sick Pay (General) Amendment Regulations 1987 (SI 1987/ 372), reg.2 (April 6, 1987).

DEFINITIONS

"contract of service"—see SSCBA 1992, s.163(1).
"employee"—see *ibid.* and reg.16.
"employer"—see SSCBA 1992, s.163(1).

[1 Payments by the Secretary of State

9C.—Where the Secretary of State becomes liable in accordance with regulation 9A or 9B to make payments of statutory sick pay to a person, the first payment shall be made as soon as reasonably practicable after he becomes so liable, and payments thereafter shall be made at weekly intervals, by means of an instrument of payment [2, instrument for benefit payment] or by such other means as appears to the Secretary of State to be appropriate in the circumstances of the particular case.] 3.20

AMENDMENTS

1. Statutory Sick Pay (General) Amendment Regulations 1987 (SI 1987/372), reg.2 (April 6, 1987).
2. Social Security (Claims and Payments etc.) Amendment Regulations 1996 (SI 1996/672), reg.3 (April 4, 1996).

Persons unable to act

10.—(1) Where in the case of any employer— 3.21

(a) statutory sick pay is payable to him or he is alleged to be entitled to it;

(b) he is unable for the time being to act, and either

(i) no receiver has been appointed by the Court of Protection with power to receive statutory sick pay on his behalf; or

(ii) in Scotland, his estate is not being administered by any tutor, curator or other guardian acting or appointed in terms of law,

the Secretary of State may, upon written application to him by a person who, if a natural person, is over the age of 18, appoint that person to exercise, on behalf of the employee, any right to which he may be entitled under Part I and to deal on his behalf with any sums payable to him.

(2) Where the Secretary of State has made an appointment under paragraph (1)—

(a) he may at any time in his absolute discretion revoke it;

(b) the person appointed may resign his office after having given one month's notice in writing to the Secretary of State of his intention to do so; and

(c) the appointment shall terminate when the Secretary of State is notified that a receiver or other person to whom paragraph (1)(c) applies has been appointed.

(3) Anything required by Part I to be done by or to any employee who is unable to act may be done by or to the person appointed under this regulation to act on his behalf, and the receipt of the person so appointed shall be a good discharge to the employee's employer for any sum paid.

DEFINITIONS

"employee"—see SSCBA 1992, s.163(1) and reg.16.
"employer"—see SSCBA 1992, s.163(1).

GENERAL NOTE

3.22 The Secretary of State's functions under this regulation were transferred to the Board of the Inland Revenue by s.1(2) of and Sch.2 to the Social Security Contributions (Transfer of Functions, etc.) Act 1999.

Rounding to avoid fractional amounts

3.23 **11.**—Where any payment of statutory sick pay is made and the statutory sick pay due for the period for which the payment purports to be made includes a fraction of a penny, the payment shall be rounded up to the next whole number of pence.

Days not to be treated as, or as parts of, periods of interruption of employment

3.24 **12.**—In a case to which paragraph 3 of Schedule 2 applies, the day of incapacity for work mentioned in sub-paragraph (1)(b) of that paragraph shall not be, or form part of, a period of interruption of employment where it is a day which, by virtue of section 17(1) or (2) of the Social Security Act 1975 or any regulations made thereunder, is not to be treated as a day of incapacity for work.

Records to be maintained by employers

13.—[1(1)] Every employer shall maintain for 3 years after the end of each tax year a record, in relation to each employee of his, of— 3.25

(a) any day in that tax year which was one of 4 or more consecutive days on which, according to information supplied by or on behalf of the employee, the employee was incapable by reason of some specific disease or bodily or mental disablement of doing work which he could reasonably be expected to do under any contract of service between him and the employer, whether or not he would normally have been expected to work on that day; [2and

(b) any payment of statutory sick pay made in respect of any day recorded under sub-paragraph (a).]

[3(1A) For the purposes of paragraph (1)(b) only, the employer is not to be regarded as having made a payment of statutory sick pay where, in respect of any day recorded under paragraph (1)(a), the employee is entitled to receive, and does in fact receive, a payment or payments by way of contractual remuneration from his employer which, in aggregate, equal or exceed the amount of statutory sick pay payable in respect of that day.]

(2) [2. . .]

(3) [2. . .]

(4) [2. . .]

(5) [2. . .]

Amendments

1. Statutory Sick Pay (General) Amendment Regulations 1986 (SI 1986/477), reg.5 (April 6, 1986).

2. Social Security Contributions, Statutory Maternity Pay and Statutory Sick Pay (Miscellaneous Amendments) Regulations 1996 (SI 1996/777), reg.2(4) (April 6, 1996).

3. Statutory Sick Pay (General) Amendment Regulations 1996 (SI 1996/3042), reg.52 (April 6, 1997).

Definitions

"contract of service"—see SSCBA 1992, s.163(1).

"employee"—see *ibid.* and reg.16.

"employer"—see SSCBA 1992, s.163(1).

Provision of information in connection with determination of questions

14.—Any person claiming to be entitled to statutory sick pay, or any other person who is a party to proceedings arising under Part I, shall, if he receives notification from the Secretary of State that any information is required from him for the determination of any question arising in connection therewith, furnish that information to the Secretary of State within 10 days of receiving that notification. 3.26

GENERAL NOTE

3.27 The Secretary of State's functions under this regulation were transferred to the Board of the Inland Revenue by s.1(2) of and Sch.2 to the Social Security Contributions (Transfer of Functions, etc.) Act 1999.

Provision of information by employers to employees

3.28 **15.**—(1) [[3]Subject to paragraph (1A),] in a case which falls within paragraph (a), (b) or (c) of section 18(3) (provision of information by employers in connection with the making of claims for [[2]short term incapacity] and other benefits), the employer shall furnish to his employee, in writing on a form approved by the Secretary of State for the purpose [[3], or in a form in which it can be processed by equipment operating automatically in response to instructions given for that purpose], the information specified in paragraph (2), (3) or (4) below, respectively within the time specified in the appropriate one of those paragraphs.

[[3](1A) For the purposes of paragraph (1), where, in the particular circumstances of a case, it is not practicable for the employer to furnish the information within the specified time mentioned in paragraph (2), (3), (4)(b)(ii) or (5), he shall, not later than the first pay day within the meaning of regulation 9(1) immediately following the relevant specified time, furnish the information to his employee.]

(2) In a case which falls within paragraph (a) (no period of entitlement arising in relation to a period of incapacity for work) of section 18(3)—

(a) the information mentioned in paragraph (1) is a statement of all the reasons why, under the provisions of paragraph 1 of Schedule 1 and regulations made thereunder, a period of entitlement does not arise; and

(b) it shall be furnished not more than 7 days after the day on which the employee's employer is notified by or on behalf of the employee of the incapacity for work on the fourth day of the period of incapacity for work.

(3) In a case which falls within paragraph (b) (period of entitlement ending but period of incapacity for work continuing) of section 18(3)—

[[1](a) the information mentioned in paragraph (1) above is a statement informing the employee of

(i) the reason why the period of entitlement ended;

(ii) the date of the first day in the period of entitlement or where the employer has taken into account days falling within a previous period of entitlement as between the employee and a person who is or was an employer of his, the date of the first day in that previous period of entitlement;

(iii) the date of the last day in respect of which the employer is or was liable to make a payment of statutory sick pay to him;

(iv) the number of qualifying days falling within the last week (beginning with Sunday) in the period of entitlement in which the employer is or was liable to make to him a payment of statutory sick pay; and either

(v) where the period of entitlement ends otherwise than by virtue of section 3(2)(b) of the Act, the number of weeks (a week being 7 days beginning with Sunday) and days in respect of which the employer was liable to make a payment of statutory sick pay to him in that period of entitlement; or

(vi) where the period of entitlement ends otherwise than by virtue of section 3(2)(b) of the Act and where the employee provided the employer with a statement issued to him in accordance with regulation 15A by a person who is or was an employer of his, the number of weeks (a week being 7 days beginning with Sunday) and days in respect of which he and the previous employer were together liable to make a payment of statutory sick pay to him; and

(b) the statement shall be furnished not more than 7 days after the day on which the period of entitlement ended, or, if earlier, on the day on which it is already required to be furnished under paragraph (4).]

(4) In a case which falls within paragraph (c) (period of entitlement expected to end before period of incapacity for work ends, on certain assumptions) of section 18(3)—

[[1](a) the information mentioned in paragraph (1) above is a statement informing the employee of—

(i) the reason why the period of entitlement is expected to end;

(ii) the date of the first day in the period of entitlement or where the employer has taken into account days of incapacity for work in a previous of entitlement as between the employee and person who is or was an employer of his, the date of the first day in that previous period of entitlement;

(iii) the date of the last day in respect of which the employer is or was expected to be liable to make a payment of statutory sick pay to him;

(iv) the number of qualifying days falling within the last week (beginning with Sunday) in the period of entitlement in which the employer is or was expected to be liable to make to him a payment of statutory sick pay; and either

(v) where the period of entitlement is expected to end otherwise than by virtue of section 3(2)(b) of the Act, the number of weeks (a week being 7 days beginning with Sunday) and days in respect of which the employer will have been liable to make a payment of statutory sick pay to him in that period of entitlement; or

(vi) where the period of entitlement is expected to end otherwise than by virtue of section 3(2)(b) of the Act and where the employee provided the employer with a statement issued to him in accordance with regulation 15A by a person who is or was an employer of his, the number of weeks (a week being 7 days beginning with Sunday) and days in respect of which he and the previous employer were

(b) the statement shall be furnished—

(i) in a case where the period of entitlement is expected to end in accordance with section 3(2)(b) of the Act (maximum entitled to statutory sick pay), on or before the 42nd day before the period of entitlement is expected to end; or

(ii) in any other case, on or before the seventh day before the period of entitlement is expected to end

[3. . .].]

(5) For the purposes of section 18(3)(c)(i) (period for which the period of incapacity for work is to be assumed to continue to run) the prescribed period shall be 14 days.

Amendments

1. Statutory Sick Pay (General) Amendment Regulations 1986 (SI 1986/477), reg.6 (April 6, 1986).

2. Social Security (Incapacity Benefit) (Consequential and Transitional Amendments and Savings) Regulations 1995 (SI 1995/829), reg.15 (April 13, 1995).

3. Social Security Contributions, Statutory Maternity Pay and Statutory Sick Pay (Miscellaneous Amendments) Regulations 1996 (SI 1996/777), reg.2(5) (April 6, 1996).

Definitions

"employee"—see SSCBA 1992, s.163(1) and reg.16.
"employer"—see SSCBA 1992, s.163(1).
"period of entitlement"—see *ibid.*
"period of incapacity for work"—see *ibid.*
"prescribed"—see *ibid.*
"qualifying day"—see *ibid.*
"week"—see *ibid.*

General Note

3.29 The references to ss.3(2)(b) and 18(3) of the 1982 Act should now be read as referring to SSCBA 1992, s.153(2)(b) and SSAA 1992, s.130(3), respectively.

[1 Statements relating to the payment of statutory sick pay

3.30 **15A.**—(1) Subject to the provisions of this regulation, where—

(a) an employee is about to leave his employment with his employer, or has been employed by him in the past;

(b) the period of entitlement as between the employee and that employer will come or has come to an end within the period of 8 weeks ending with the day on which the employee's contract of service with the employer concerned expires or is brought to an end; and

[2(c) the employer is or was liable to make a payment of statutory sick pay to the employee in respect of any week within that period, and for this purpose a week includes any days rounded up to a week in accordance with paragraph (4)], [3and

(d) the employee requests one or more statements in relation to the payment of statutory sick pay,]

the employer shall provide the employee with [3one or more statements] in writing containing the information specified in paragraph (2) within 7 days of the [3employee making the request under sub-paragraph (d), or where it is not practicable, not later than his first pay day within the meaning of regulation 9(1) which would have fallen within the next income tax month immediately following that request.]

(2) The information mentioned in paragraph (1) is—
(a) the date of the first day of the period of entitlement;
(b) the number of weeks (a week being 7 days beginning with Sunday) [[2]. . .] in respect of which the employer was liable to make a payment of statutory sick pay to the employee in that period of entitlement;
(c) the date of the last day in respect of which the employer was liable to make to the employee a payment of statutory sick pay;
(d) the date the statement was made by the employer; and
(e) the full name, address and, if there is one, telephone number of the employer making the statement.

(3) For the purposes of paragraph (2)(a) and (b) above, the period of entitlement includes any previous period of entitlement relevant for the purposes of regulation 3A (maximum entitlement to statutory sick pay in a period of entitlement).

(4) For the purposes of this regulation, where the total number of days in the period of entitlement in respect of which the employer is or was liable to make the employee a payment in respect of statutory sick pay amounts in aggregate to less than a complete week or number of weeks, then the number of weeks shall be determined by disregarding the remainder where it is 3 days or less and if it is not by rounding them up to a week.

(5) Where a question arises under Part I of the 1982 Act as to or in connection with entitlement to statutory sick pay, a written statement or, as the case may be, a revised written statement containing the information specified in paragraph (2) shall be provided by the employer to the employee within 7 days of the question being determined.

(6) A question is determined for the purpose of paragraph (5) when the time for appealing from a decision of an adjudication officer, a local tribunal or a Commissioner, as the case may be, has expired or leave to appeal has been refused.

(7) [[3]. . .]

(8) An employer may, at the request of a person who is or was employed by him, provide a second copy of the statement if he is satisfied that the person making the request has a need for it.]

Amendments

1. Statutory Sick Pay (General) Amendment Regulations 1986 (SI 1986/477), reg.7 (April 6, 1986).

2. Statutory Sick Pay (General) Amendment (No.2) Regulations 1987 (SI 1987/868), reg.3 (June 7, 1987).

3. Social Security Contributions, Statutory Maternity Pay and Statutory Sick Pay (Miscellaneous Amendments) Regulations 1996 (SI 1996/777), reg.2(6) (April 6, 1996).

Definitions

"contract of service"—see SSCBA 1992, s.163(1).
"employee"—see SSCBA 1992, s.163(1) and reg.16.
"employer"—see SSCBA 1992, s.163(1).
"period of entitlement"—see *ibid.*
"week"—see *ibid.*

Meaning of "employee"

3.31 **16.**—(1) In a case where, and in so far as, a person over the age of 16 is treated as an employed earner by virtue of the Social Security (Categorisation of Earners) Regulations 1978, he shall be treated as an employee for the purposes of Part I and in a case where, and in so far as, such a person is treated otherwise than as an employed earner by virtue of those regulations, he shall not be treated as an employee for the purposes of Part I.

[1(1A) Any person who is in employed earner's employment within the meaning of the Act under a contract of apprenticeship shall be treated as an employee for the purposes of Part I.]

(2) A person who is in employed earner's employment within the meaning of the Act but whose employer—

(a) does not fulfil the conditions prescribed in regulation 119(1)(b) of the Social Security (Contributions) Regulations 1979 as to residence or presence in Great Britain, or

(b) is a person who, by reason of any international treaty to which the United Kingdom is a party or of any international convention binding the United Kingdom—

(i) is exempt from the provisions of the Act, or

(ii) is a person against whom the provisions of that Act are not enforceable,

shall not be treated as an employee for the purposes of Part I.

AMENDMENT

1. Statutory Sick Pay (Compensation of Employers) and Miscellaneous Provisions Regulations 1983 (SI 1983/376), reg.5(2) (April 6, 1983).

DEFINITIONS

"employee"—see SSCBA 1992, s.163(1) and reg.16.
"employer"—see SSCBA 1992, s.163(1).
"prescribed"—see *ibid.*

Meaning of "earnings"

3.32 **17.**—(1) [3. . .]

[4(2) For the purposes of section 163(2) of the Contributions and Benefits Act, the expression "earnings" refers to gross earnings and includes any remuneration or profit derived from a person's employment except any payment or amount which is—

(a) excluded from the computation of a person's earnings under regulation 19 or 19B of the Social Security (Contributions) Regulations 1979;

(b) a chargeable emolument under section 10A of the Social Security Contributions and Benefits Act 1992, except where, in consequence of such a chargeable emolument being excluded from earnings, a person would not be entitled to statutory sick pay.]

[1(2A) [3. . .]]

(3) For the purposes of [5section 163(2) of the Contributions and Benefits Act] the expression "earnings" includes also—

(a) any sum payable by way of maternity pay or payable by the Secretary of State in pursuance of section 40 of the Employment Protection (Consolidation) Act 1978 in respect of maternity pay;
(b) any sum which is payable by the Secretary of State by virtue of section 122(3)(a) of that Act in respect of arrears of pay and which by virtue of section 42(1) of that Act is to go towards discharging a liability to pay maternity pay;
(c) any sum payable in respect of arrears of pay in pursuance of an order for reinstatement or re-engagement under that Act;
(d) any sum payable by way of pay in pursuance of an order under that Act for the continuation of a contract of employment;
(e) any sum payable by way of remuneration in pursuance of a protective award under the Employment Protection Act 1975;
(f) any sum payable to any employee under the Temporary Short time Working Compensation Scheme administered under powers conferred by the Employment Subsidies Act 1978;
(g) any sum paid in satisfaction of any entitlement to statutory sick pay;
[[2]](h) any sum payable by way of statutory maternity pay under Part V of the Social Security Act 1986, including sums payable in accordance with regulations made under section 46(8)(b) of that Act.]
[[6]](i) any sum payable by way of statutory paternity pay, including any sums payable in accordance with regulations made under section 171ZD(3) of the Contributions and Benefits Act;
(j) any sum payable by way of statutory adoption pay, including any sums payable in accordance with regulations made under section 171ZM(3) of the Contributions and Benefits Act.]

(4) [[3]. . .]
(5) [[3]. . .]

AMENDMENTS

1. Statutory Sick Pay (Compensation of Employers) and Miscellaneous Provisions Regulations 1983 (SI 1983/376), reg.5(3) (April 6, 1983).
2. Statutory Sick Pay (General) Amendment (No.2) Regulations 1987 (SI 1987/868), reg.4 (June 7, 1987).
3. Social Security (Miscellaneous Provisions) Amendment (No.2) Regulations 1992 (SI 1992/2595), reg.15 (November 16, 1992).
4. Social Security Contributions, Statutory Maternity Pay and Statutory Sick Pay (Miscellaneous Amendments) Regulations 1999 (SI 1999/567), reg.13 (April 6, 1999).
5. Social Security, Statutory Maternity Pay and Statutory Sick Pay (Miscellaneous Amendments) Regulations 2002 (SI 2002/2690), reg.14(a) (November 24, 2002).
6. Social Security, Statutory Maternity Pay and Statutory Sick Pay (Miscellaneous Amendments) Regulations 2002 (SI 2002/2690), reg.14(b) (April 6, 2003).

DEFINITIONS

"employee"—see SSCBA 1992, s.163(1) and reg.16.

Payments to be treated or not to be treated as contractual remuneration

3.33 **18.**—For the purposes of paragraph 2(1) and (2) of Schedule 2 to the Act, those things which are included within the expression "earnings" by regulation (except paragraph (3)(g) thereof) shall be, and those things which are excluded from that expression by that regulation shall not be, treated as contractual remuneration.

Days not to be treated as, or as parts of, periods of interruption of employment

3.34 **19.**—(1) For the purposes of section 26, an employee's normal weekly earnings shall be determined in accordance with the provisions of this regulation.

(2) In this regulation—

"the critical date" means the first day of the period of entitlement in relation to which a person's normal weekly earnings fall to be determined, or, in a case to which paragraph 2(c) of Schedule 1 applies, the relevant date within the meaning of Schedule 1;

"normal pay day" means a day on which the terms of an employee's contract of service require him to be paid, or the practice in his employment is for him to be paid, if any payment is due to him; and

"day of payment" means a day on which the employee was paid.

(3) Subject to paragraph (4), the relevant period (referred to in section 26(2)) is the period between—

(a) the last normal pay day to fall before the critical date; and

(b) the last normal pay day to fall at least 8 weeks earlier than the normal pay day mentioned in sub-paragraph (a), including the normal pay day mentioned in sub-paragraph (a) but excluding that first mentioned in sub-paragraph (b).

(4) In a case where an employee has no identifiable normal pay day, paragraph (3) shall have effect as if the words "day of payment" were substituted for the words "normal pay day" in each place where they occur.

(5) In a case where an employee has normal pay days at intervals of, or approximating to one or more calendar months (including intervals of or approximating to a year) his normal weekly earnings shall be calculated by dividing his earnings in the relevant period by the number of calendar months in that period (or, if it is not a whole number, the nearest whole number), multiplying the result by 12 and dividing by 52.

(6) In a case to which paragraph (5) does not apply and the relevant period is not an exact number of weeks, the employee's normal weekly earnings shall be calculated by dividing his earnings in the relevant period by the number of days in the relevant period and multiplying the result by 7.

(7) In a case where the normal pay day mentioned in sub-paragraph (a) of paragraph (3) exists but that first mentioned in sub-paragraph (b) of that paragraph does not yet exist, the employee's normal weekly earnings shall be calculated as if the period for which all the earnings under his contract of service received by him before the critical date represented payment were the relevant period.

(8) In a case where neither of the normal pay days mentioned in paragraph (3) yet exists, the employee's normal weekly earnings shall be the remuneration to which he is entitled, in accordance with the terms of his contract of service for, as the case may be—

(a) a week's work; or
(b) a number of calendar month's work, divided by that number of months multiplied by 12 and divided by 52.

DEFINITIONS

"contract of service"—see SSCBA 1992, s.163(1).
"employee"—see SSCBA 1992, s.163(1) and reg.16.
"period of entitlement"—see *ibid.*

GENERAL NOTE

For some of the difficulties in applying this regulation, see *R(SSP) 1/89*. There, the relevant period for a school dinner lady extended from the end of one term until the last pay day before her period of incapacity began. This was 11 weeks, but as the relevant period began the day after the last pay day at the end of term it could not include the lump-sum payment that was made as a retainer throughout the vacation. Without that sum her average weekly earnings did not qualify her for statutory sick pay. 3.35

Treatment of one or more employers as one

20.—(1) In a case where the earnings paid to an employee in respect of 2 more employments are aggregated and treated as a single payment of earnings under regulation 12(1) of the Social Security (Contributions) Regulations 1979, the employers of the employee in respect of those employments shall be treated as one for all purposes of Part I. 3.36

(2) Where 2 or more employers are treated as one under the provisions of paragraph (1), liability for the statutory sick pay payable by them to the employee shall be apportioned between them in such proportions as they may agree or, in default of agreement, in the proportions which the employee's earnings from each employment bear to the amount of the aggregated earnings.

(3) [[1]Subject to paragraphs (4) and (5)] where a contract of service ("the current contract") was preceded by a contract of service entered into between the same employer and employee ("the previous contract"), and the interval between the date on which the previous contract ceased to have effect and that on which the current contract came into force was not more than 8 weeks, then, for the purposes of establishing the employee's maximum entitlement within the meaning of section 5 (limitation on entitlement to statutory sick pay in any one period of entitlement or tax year), the provisions of Part I shall not have effect as if the employer were a different employer in relation to each of those contracts of service.

[[1](4) Where a contract of service ("the current contract") was preceded by two or more contracts of service entered into between the same employer and employee ("the previous contracts") and the previous contracts—

(a) existed concurrently for at least part of their length; and
(b) the intervals between the dates on which each of the previous contracts ceased to have effect and that on which the current contract came into force was not more than 8 weeks,

then, for the purposes of establishing the employee's maximum entitlement within the meaning of section 5 the provisions of Part I shall not have effect as if the employer were a different employer in relation to the current contract and whichever of the previous contracts was the contract by virtue of which the employer had become liable to pay the greatest proportion of statutory sick pay in respect of any tax year or period of entitlement.

(5) If, in any case to which paragraph (4) applies, the same proportion of the employer's liability for statutory sick pay becomes due under each of the previous contracts, then, for the purpose of establishing the employee's maximum entitlement within the meaning of section 5, the provisions of Part I shall have effect in relation to only one of the previous contracts.]

Amendment

1. Statutory Sick Pay (Compensation of Employers) and Miscellaneous Provisions Regulations 1983 (SI 1983/376), reg.5(4) (April 6, 1983).

Definitions

"contract of service"—see SSCBA 1992, s.163(1).
"employee"—see SSCBA 1992, s.163(1) and reg.16.
"employer"—see SSCBA 1992, s.163(1).
"period of entitlement"—see *ibid.*

General Note

3.37 Specific provision is made in Statutory Sick Pay (National Health Service Employees) Regulations 1991 (SI 1991/589) in the case of NHS workers with divided contracts.

Treatment of more than one contract of service as one

3.38 **21.**—Where 2 or more contracts of service exist concurrently between one employer and one employee, they shall be treated as one for all purposes of Part I except where, by virtue of regulation 11 of the Social Security (Contributions) Regulations 1979, the earnings from those contracts of service are not aggregated for the purposes of earnings-related contributions.

Definitions

"contract of service"—see SSCBA 1992, s.163(1).
"employee"—see SSCBA 1992, s.163(1) and reg.16.
"employer"—see SSCBA 1992, s.163(1).

[1 Election to be treated as different employers not to apply to recovery of statutory sick pay

3.39 **21A.**—(1) Paragraph (2) below applies for the purposes of section 159A of the Contributions and Benefits Act (power to provide for recovery by employers of sums paid by way of statutory sick pay) and of any order made under that section.

(2) Where an employer has made 2 or more elections under regulation 3 of the Income Tax (Employments) Regulations 1993 to be treated as a different employer in respect of each of the groups of employees specified in the election, the different employers covered by each of those elections shall be treated as one employer.]

AMENDMENT

1. Statutory Sick Pay Percentage Threshold Order 1995 (Consequential) Regulations 1995 (SI 1995/513), reg.3 (April 6, 1995).

DEFINITIONS

"employee"—see SSCBA 1992, s.163(1) and reg.16.
"employer"—see SSCBA 1992, s.163(1).

[1 Offences

22. Any person who, without reasonable excuse, contravenes or fails to comply with any provision contained in regulation 9, 13, 14, 15 or 15A shall be guilty of an offence under the Social Security Administration Act 1992.] **3.40**

AMENDMENT

1. Statutory Maternity Pay (General) and Statutory Sick Pay (General) (Amendment) Regulations 2001 (SI 2001/206), reg.2 (February 23, 2001).

Statutory Sick Pay (Mariners, Airmen and Persons Abroad) Regulations 1982

(SI 1982/1349) (AS AMENDED)

The Secretary of State for Social Services, in exercise of the powers conferred upon him by sections 3(5) and (7), 22(1) and 26(1) of and paragraph 1 of Schedule 1 to the Social Security and Housing Benefits Act 1982(a) and of all other powers enabling him in that behalf, hereby makes the following regulations.

ARRANGEMENT OF REGULATIONS

Citation, commencement and interpretation

3.42 **1.**—(1) These regulations may be cited as the Statutory Sick Pay (Mariners, Airmen and Persons Abroad) Regulations 1982, and shall come into operation on 6th April 1983.

(2) In these Regulations—

"the Act" means the Social Security and Housing Benefits Act 1982;

"Part I" means Part I of the Act;

[[1]"the Contributions and Benefits Act," means the Social Security Contributions and Benefits Act 1992;

"the Contributions Regulations" means the Social Security (Contributions) Regulations 1979;]

"the General Regulations" means the Statutory Sick Pay (General) Regulations 1982;

and other expressions, unless the context otherwise requires, have the same meanings as in Part I.

(3) Unless the context otherwise requires, any reference—

(a) in these regulations to a numbered regulation is a reference to the regulation bearing that number in these regulations; and

(b) in any of these regulations to a numbered paragraph is a reference to the paragraph bearing that number in that regulation.

Amendments

1. Social Security Contributions, Statutory Maternity Pay and Statutory Sick Pay (Miscellaneous Amendments) Regulations 1996 (SI 1996/777), reg.3(2) (April 6, 1996).

General Note

3.43 These Regulations make special provision for statutory sick pay under what is now Pt XI of the SSCBA 1992 as it affects mariners, airmen, persons abroad and persons employed in operations on the Continental Shelf. Under s.163(1) of the SSCBA 1992, a person is not, as a rule, an "employee", and therefore not qualified to receive statutory sick pay, unless he or she is employed in Great Britain. Regulations 5–8 prescribe exceptions to this rule, so that certain persons who are employed in other Member States but who are subject to the legislation of the United Kingdom, certain mariners and airmen, and certain persons employed on the Continental Shelf, are "employees", though employed outside Great Britain; and so that certain limited classes of mariners and airmen are not "employees" though employed in Great Britain. Further general provision on the meaning of "employee" is made by reg.9, while reg.10 makes general provision regarding persons from abroad. Regulations 11–13, which provided for exceptions to reg.10, were repealed in 1996.

Some of the requirements of the Act and regulations made under it impose time-limits. Regulation 14 relaxes those requirements in their application to persons who are outside the United Kingdom and for that reason cannot comply with them.

It should be noted that these regulations have never been fully updated to include appropriate references to SSCBA 1992. Accordingly, all references to Part I of the Social Security and Housing Benefits Act 1982 in these regulations should be read as references to Part XI of SSCBA 1992.

Mariners—interpretation

2. In regulations 6 and 11, the expressions "British ship," "foreign-going ship" "managing owner," "mariner," "owner" and "radio officer" have the same meanings as in Case C of Part VIII of the Social Security (Contributions) Regulations 1979, and the expressions "ship" and "ship or vessel," except in regulation 6(2), include hovercraft. **3.44**

General Note

The provisions relating to Case C of Pt VIII of the Social Security (Contributions) Regulations 1979 have been re-enacted in Case C of Pt IX of the Social Security Contributions Regulations 2001 (SI 2001/1004). **3.45**

Airmen—interpretation

3. In regulations 7 and 12— **3.46**

"airman" means a person who is, or has been, employed under a contract of service either as a pilot, commander, navigator or other member of the crew of any aircraft, or in any other capacity on board any aircraft where—

(a) the employment in that other capacity is for the purposes of the aircraft or its crew or of any passengers or cargo or mails carried thereby; and

(b) the contract is entered into in the United Kingdom with a view to its performance (in whole or in part) while the aircraft is in flight, but does not include a person in so far as his employment is as a serving member of the forces;

"British aircraft" means any aircraft belonging to Her Majesty and any aircraft registered in the United Kingdom of which the owner (or managing owner if there is more than one owner) resides or has his principal place of business in Great Britain, and references to the owner of an aircraft shall, in relation to an aircraft which has been hired, be taken as referring to the person for the time being entitled as hirer to possession and control of the aircraft by virtue of the hiring or any subordinate hiring.

Definition

"contract of service"—see SSCBA 1992, s.163(1).

Continental shelf—interpretation

4. In this regulation and regulations 8 and 13— **3.47**

"designated area" means any area which may from time to time be designated by Order in Council under the Continental Shelf Act 1964 as an area within which the rights of the United Kingdom with respect to the sea-bed and subsoil and their natural resources may be exercised;

"prescribed area" means an area over which Norway or any member State (other than the United Kingdom) exercises sovereign rights for the purpose of exploring the seabed and subsoil and exploiting their natural resources, being an area outside the territorial seas of Norway or that member State [[1]or any other area which is from time to time specified under section 22(5) of the Oil and Gas (Enterprise) Act 1982];

"prescribed employment" means employment in a designated area or prescribed area in connection with [[1]any activity mentioned in section 23(2) of the Oil and Gas (Enterprise) Act 1982 in any designated area or in any prescribed area.]

AMENDMENTS

1. Social Security and Statutory Sick Pay (Oil and Gas (Enterprise) Act 1982) (Consequential) Regulations 1982 (SI 1982/1738), reg.5 (April 6, 1983).

DEFINITION

"prescribed"—see SSCBA 1992, s.163(1).

Persons in other member States—meaning of "employee"

3.48 **5.** Subject to regulations 6(2), 7(2) and 9, a person who is—

(a) gainfully employed in a member State other than the United Kingdom in such circumstances that if his employment were in Great Britain he would be an employee for the purposes of Part I or a person treated as such an employee under regulation 16 of the General Regulations; and

(b) subject to the legislation of the United Kingdom under Council Regulation (EEC) No. 1408/71;

notwithstanding that he is not employed in Great Britain, shall be treated as an employee for the purposes of Part I.

DEFINITIONS

"Pt I"—see reg.1(2).
"the General Regulations"—*ibid.*

[[1] Persons absent from Great Britain—meaning of "employee"

3.49 **5A.** Subject to regulations 5, 6(2) and 9, where a person, while absent from Great Britain for any purpose, is gainfully employed by an employer who is liable to pay in respect of him secondary Class 1 contributions under section 6 of the Contributions and Benefits Act 1992 or regulation 120 of the Contributions Regulations, he shall be treated as an employee for the purposes of Part XI of the Contributions and Benefits Act.]

AMENDMENT

1. Social Security Contributions, Statutory Maternity Pay and Statutory Sick Pay (Miscellaneous Amendments) Regulations 1996 (SI 1996/777), reg.3(3) (April 6, 1996).

DEFINITIONS

"employer"—see SSCBA 1992, s.163(1).
"the Contributions and Benefits Act"—see reg.1(2).
"the Contributions Regulations"—*ibid.*

GENERAL NOTE

The Social Security Contributions Regulations 2001 (SI 2001/1004) have nowrevoked and superseded the Social Security Contributions Regulations 1979 (SI 1979/591). Regulation 146 of the 2001 Regulations is the parallel provision to reg.120 of the 1979 Regulations. **3.50**

Mariners—meaning of "employee"

6.—(1) Subject to regulation 9, where a mariner— **3.51**

(a) is employed as such and—
   (i) the employment is on board a British ship; or
   (ii) the employment is on board a ship and the contract in respect of the employment is entered into the United Kingdom with a view to its performance (in whole or in part) while the ship or vessel is on her voyage; and
   (iii) in a case to which head (ii) applies, the person by whom the mariner's earnings are paid, or, in the case of employment as a master or member of the crewof a ship or vessel, either that person or the owner of the ship or vessel (or the managing owner if there is more than one owner) has a place of business in Great Britain; or
(b) is employed as a master, member of the crew or radio officer on board any ship or vessel, not being a mariner to whom the last preceding subparagraph applies; and
   (i) in the case of the employment being as a radio officer, if the contract under which the employment is performed is entered into in the United Kingdom, the employer or the person paying the radio officer his earnings for that employment has a place of business in Great Britain, or,
   (ii) in the case of the employment being as a master, member of the crew or radio officer, if the contract is not entered into in the United Kingdom, the employer or the person paying the earnings has his principal place of business in Great Britain,

then, unless he is a mariner to whom paragraph (2) applies, he shall, notwithstanding that he may not be employed in Great Britain, be treated as an employee for the purposes of Part I.

(2) A mariner who—

(a) is in employment (including any period of leave, other than leave for the purpose of study, accruing from the employment) as a master or member of the crew of a ship, where—

(i) the employment is on a foreign-going ship; or

(ii) the employment is partly on a foreign-going ship and partly otherwise than on such a ship, and it is a requirement of the contract of service which relates to that employment that any payment of earnings in respect of that employment is to be made during the employment on the foreign-going ship; or

(b) has been in such employment as is mentioned in sub-paragraph (a), where

(i) not more than thirteen weeks have elapsed since he was last in such employment;

(ii) he continues to be employed by the employer by whom he was employed when he was last in such employment; and

(iii) he is not employed (by that employer or any other) on terms which are inconsistent with his being able to resume such employment as is mentioned in sub-paragraph (a) after not more than thirteen weeks have elapsed since he was last in such employment;

shall, notwithstanding that he may be employed in Great Britain, not be treated as an employee for the purposes of Part I.

DEFINITIONS

"British ship"—see reg.2.
"contract of service"—see SSCBA 1992, s.163(1).
"employer"—*ibid.*
"foreign-going ship"—see reg.2.
"managing owner"—*ibid.*
"mariner"—*ibid.*
"owner"—*ibid.*
"Pt I"—see reg.1(2).
"radio officer"—see reg.2.
"ship"—*ibid.*
"ship or vessel"—*ibid.*
"week"—see SSCBA 1992, s.163(1)

Airmen—meaning of "employee"

3.52 **7.**—(1) Subject to regulation 9 and the following provisions of this regulation, where an airman is employed as such on board any aircraft, and the employer of that airman or the person paying the airman his earnings in respect of the employment (whether or not the person making the payment is acting as agent for the employer) or the person under whose directions the terms of the airman's employment and the amount of the earnings to be paid in respect thereof are determined has

(a) in the case of the aircraft being a British aircraft, a place of business in Great Britain; or

(b) in any other case, his principal place of business in Great Britain, then, notwithstanding that he may not be employed in Great Britain, he shall be treated as an employee for the purposes of Part I.

(2) Subject to the provisions of paragraph (3), an airman shall not be treated as an employee for those purposes if he is not domiciled, and has no place of residence, in Great Britain.

(3) The provisions of paragraph (2) shall have effect subject to any Order in Council giving effect to any reciprocal agreement made under section 143 of the Social Security Act 1975 (reciprocity with other countries).

DEFINITIONS

"airman"—see reg.3.
"British aircraft"—*ibid.*
"employee"—see SSCBA 1992, s.163(1).
"employer"—*ibid.*
"Pt I"—see reg.1(2).

GENERAL NOTE

Para. (3)

Section 143 of the Social Security Act 1975 has nowbeen replaced in similar terms by s.179 of the SSAA 1992. 3.53

Continental shelf—meaning of "employee"

8. Subject to regulation 9, a person in prescribed employment, notwithstanding that he may not be employed in Great Britain, shall be treated as an employee for the purposes of Part I. 3.54

DEFINITIONS

"employee"—see SSCBA 1992, s.163(1).
"Part I"—see reg.1(2).
"prescribed employment"—see reg.4.
"prescribed"—see SSCBA 1992, s.163(1).

Meaning of "employee"—general

9. No person who, by virtue of regulation 16 of the General Regulations, would not be treated as an employee for the purposes of Part I if his employment were in Great Britain, shall be treated as an employee by virtue of any of regulations 5–8. 3.55

DEFINITIONS

"employee"—see SSCBA 1992, s.163(1).
"Part I"—see reg.1(2).
"the General Regulations"—*ibid.*

[1 Persons abroad—general

10. In a case where a mariner, an airman or a continental shelf employee, respectively, within the meaning of regulation 6(1), 7 or 8, or a person who, is an employee or, is treated as an employee under regulation 5 or 5A, is incapable of work during a period of entitlement to statutory sick pay while absent from Great Britain, his entitlement to statutory sick pay shall cease only if he fails to satisfy the conditions of entitlement under Part XI of the Contributions and Benefits Act notwithstanding that his employer ceases, during the period of entitlement, to be 3.56

liable to pay, in respect of him, secondary Class 1 contributions under section 6 of the Contributions and Benefits Act or regulation 120 of the Contributions Regulations.]

AMENDMENT

1. Social Security Contributions, Statutory Maternity Pay and Statutory Sick Pay (Miscellaneous Amendments) Regulations 1996 (SI 1996/777), reg.3(4) (April 6, 1996).

DEFINITIONS

"employee"—see SSCBA 1992, s.163(1).
"employer"—*ibid.*
"period of entitlement"—*ibid.*
"the Contributions and Benefits Act"—see reg.1(2).
"the Contributions Regulations"—*ibid.*

GENERAL NOTE

3.57 See note to reg.5A.

Mariners—exception to regulation 10

3.58 **11.** [1. . .]

AMENDMENT

1. Social Security Contributions, Statutory Maternity Pay and Statutory Sick Pay (Miscellaneous Amendments) Regulations 1996 (SI 1996/777), reg.3(5) (April 6, 1996).

Airmen—exception to regulation 10

3.59 **12.** [1. . .]

AMENDMENT

1. Social Security Contributions, Statutory Maternity Pay and Statutory Sick Pay (Miscellaneous Amendments) Regulations 1996 (SI 1996/777), reg.3(6) (April 6, 1996).

Continental shelf—exception to regulation 10

3.60 **13.** [1. . .]

AMENDMENT

1. Social Security Contributions, Statutory Maternity Pay and Statutory Sick Pay (Miscellaneous Amendments) Regulations 1996 (SI 1996/777), reg.3(7) (April 6, 1996).

Time for compliance with requirements of Part I and regulations

3.61 **14.** Where—
(a) an employee is outside the United Kingdom;
(b) Part I or regulations made there under require any act to be done forthwith or on the happening of a certain event or within a specified time; and

(c) because the employee is outside the United Kingdom he or his employer cannot comply with the requirement;

the employee or the employer, as the case may be, shall be deemed to have complied with it if he performs the act as soon as reasonably practicable.

DEFINITIONS

"employee"—see SSCBA 1992, s.163(1).
"employer"—*ibid.*
"Pt I"—see reg.1(2).

Statutory Sick Pay (Medical Evidence) Regulations 1985

(SI 1985/1604) (AS AMENDED)

The Secretary of State for Social Services, in exercise of the powers conferred upon him by section 17(2A) of the Social Security and Housing Benefits Act 1982, and of all other powers enabling him in that behalf, by this instrument, which contains only provisions consequential upon section 20 of the Social Security Act 1985 and regulations made under the aforesaid section 17(2A), makes the following regulations:

ARRANGEMENT OF ARTICLES **3.62**

Citation, commencement and interpretation

1.—(1) These regulations may be cited as the Statutory Sick Pay (Medical Evidence) Regulations 1985 and shall come into operation on 6th April 1986. **3.63**

(2) In these regulations, unless the context otherwise requires

"the 1982 Act" means the Social Security and Housing Benefits Act 1982;

"signature" means, in relation to a statement given in accordance with these regulations, the name by which the person giving that statement is usually known (any name other than the surname being either in full or otherwise indicated) written by that person in his own handwriting; and "signed" shall be construed accordingly.

(3) [1. . .]

AMENDMENT

1. Social Security (Miscellaneous Provisions) Amendment Regulations 1992 (SI 1992/247), reg.6(2) (March 9, 1992).

GENERAL NOTE

3.64 These Regulations and the rules in Sch.1 prescribe the form of the statement to be issued by a doctor advising an employee that he or she should refrain from work (or need not refrain from work) for a period up to six months, or longer in certain circumstances. Regulation 2(2) provides that medical information cannot be required in respect of an employee's first seven days in any spell of incapacity for work.

Medical information

3.65 **2.**—[[1](1) Medical information required under section 17(2) of the 1982 Act relating to incapacity for work shall be provided either—

(a) in the form of a statement given by a doctor in accordance with the rules set out in Part I of Schedule 1 to these Regulations on the form set out in Part II of that Schedule; or

(b) where the doctor—

(i) has not given a statement under sub-paragraph (a) of this paragraph since the patient was examined and wishes to give such a statement but more than one day has passed since the examination; or

(ii) advises that the patient should refrain from work on the basis of a written report from another doctor, set out in Part I of Schedule 1A to these Regulations on the form set out in Part II of that Schedule; or

(c) by such other means as may be sufficient in the circumstances of any particular case.]

(2) An employee shall not be required under section 17(2) of the 1982 Act to provide medical information in respect of the first 7 days in any spell of incapacity for work; and for this purpose "spell of incapacity" means a continuous period of incapacity for work which is immediately preceded by a day on which the claimant either worked or was not incapable of work.

AMENDMENT

1. Social Security (Miscellaneous Provisions) Amendment Regulations 1992 (SI 1992/247), reg.6(3) (March 9, 1992).

SCHEDULE [[1]1] **Regulation 1(3)**

PART I

RULES

3.66 **1.** In these rules, unless the context otherwise requires

"patient" means the person in respect of whom a statement is given in accordance with these rules;
"doctor" means a registered medical practitioner not being the patient;
"2 weeks" means any period of 14 consecutive days.

2. The doctor's statement shall be in the form set out in Part II of this Schedule.

3. Where the patient is on the list of a doctor providing general medical services under the National Health Service Act 1977, or the National Health Service (Scotland) Act 1978,

[2or the list of a doctor, or a list held jointly by two or more doctors, performing personal medical services in connection with a pilot scheme under the National Health Service (Primary Care) Act 1997] and is being attended by such a doctor, the doctor's statement shall be on a form provided by the Secretary of State for the purpose and shall be signed by that doctor.

4. In any other case, the doctor's statement shall be on a form provided by the Secretary of State for the purpose and shall be signed by the doctor attending the patient.

5. Every doctor's statement shall be completed in ink or other indelible substance and shall contain the following particulars:

(a) the patient's name;
(b) the date of the examination on which the doctor's statement is based;
(c) the diagnosis of the patient's disorder in respect of which the doctor is advising the patient to refrain from work or, as the case may be, which has caused the patient's absence from work;
(d) the date on which the doctor's statement is given;
(e) the address of the doctor,

and shall bear, opposite the words "Doctor's signature", the signature of the doctor making the statement written after there have been entered the patient's name and the doctor's diagnosis.

6. Subject to rules 7 and 8 below, the diagnosis of the disorder in respect of which the doctor is advising the patient to refrain from work or, as the case may be, which has caused the patient's absence from work shall be specified as precisely as the doctor's knowledge of the patient's condition at the time of the examination permits.

7. The diagnosis may be specified less precisely where, in the doctor's opinion, a disclosure of the precise disorder would be prejudicial to the patient's well-being, or to the patient's position with his employer.

8. In the case of an initial examination by a doctor in respect of a disorder stated by the patient to have caused incapacity for work, where

(a) there are no clinical signs of that disorder, and
(b) in the doctor's opinion, the patient need not refrain from work,

instead of specifying a diagnosis "unspecified" may be entered.

9. A doctor's statement must be given on a date not later than one day after the date of the examination on which it is based, and no further doctor's statement based on the same examination shall be furnished other than a doctor's statement by way of replacement of an original which has been lost or mislaid, in which case it shall be clearly marked "duplicate".

10. Where, in the doctor's opinion, the patient will become fit to resume work on a day not later than 2 weeks after the date of the examination on which the doctor's statement is based, the doctor's statement shall specify that day.

11. Subject to rules 12 and 13 below, the doctor's statement shall specify the minimum period during which, in the doctor's opinion, the patient should, by reason of his disorder, refrain from work.

12. The period specified shall begin on the date of the examination on which the doctor's statement is based and shall not exceed 6 months unless the patient has, on the advice of a doctor, refrained from work for at least 6 months immediately preceding that date.

13. Where

(a) the patient has, on the advice of a doctor, refrained from work for at least 6 months immediately preceding the date of the examination on which the doctor's statement is based; and
(b) in the doctor's opinion, it will be necessary for the patient to refrain from work for the foreseeable future,

instead of specifying a period, the doctor may, having regard to the circumstances of the particular case, enter, after the word "until", the words "further notice".

14. The Notes set out in Part III of this Schedule shall accompany the form of doctor's statement provided by the Secretary of State.

PART II

FORM OF DOCTOR'S STATEMENT

DOCTOR'S STATEMENT

3.67 In confidence to

Mr/Mrs/Miss

....

I examined you today/yesterday and advised you that:

(a) you need not refrain from work

(b) you should refrain from work

for ....

OR until

Diagnosis of your disorder
causing absence from work ....

Doctor's remarks

Doctor's signature

Date of signing

PART III

NOTES

3.68 The following notes shall accompany the form of doctor's statement provided by the Secretary of State:

On the doctor's statement:

(1) After the words "you should refrain from work for", the period entered must not exceed 6 months unless the patient has, on the advice of a doctor, already refrained from work for a continuous period of 6 months.

(2) After the words "you should refrain from work until"

(a) if the patient is being given a date when he can return to work, the date entered should not be more than 2 weeks after the date of the examination;

(b) if the patient has already been incapable of work for at least 6 months and recovery of capacity for work in the foreseeable future is not expected, "further notice" may be entered.

AMENDMENTS

1. Social Security (Miscellaneous Provisions) Amendment Regulations 1992 (SI 1992/247), reg.6(4) (March 9, 1992).
2. National Health Service (Pilot Schemes: Miscellaneous Provisions and Consequential Amendments) Regulations 1998, reg.7 (April 1, 1998).

SCHEDULE 1A **[[1]Regulation 2(1)**

PART I

RULES

1. In these rules, unless the context otherwise requires—

"patient" means the person in respect of whom a statement is given in accordance with these rules; **3.69**
"doctor" means a registered medical practitioner not being the patient;
"special statement" means the form prescribed in Part II of this Schedule.

2. Where a doctor advises a patient to refrain from work on the basis of a written report which he has received from another doctor or where a doctor has not issued a statement since the claimant was examined and he wishes to issue a statement more than a day after the examination he shall use the special statement.
3. The special statement shall be completed in the manner described in paragraph 5 of Part I to Schedule 1.
4. Subject to rules 5 and 6 below, the diagnosis of the patient's disorder in respect of which the doctor is advising the patient to refrain from work or as the case may be, which has caused the patient's absence from work shall be specified as precisely as the doctor's knowledge of the patient's condition permits.
5. The diagnosis may be specified less precisely where in the doctor's opinion, a disclosure of the precise disorder would be prejudicial to the patient's well being, or to the patient's position with his employer.
6. In a case of a disorder stated by the patient to have caused incapacity for work, where—
(a) no clinical signs have been found of that disorder; and
(b) in the doctor's opinion, the patient need not refrain from work, "unspecified" may be entered.
7. Part B of the special statement must only be given on a date not later than one month after the date of the written report on which the special statement is based and that part shall only be used where the patient is being advised to refrain from work for a specified period of not more than one month.

[[1]PART II

3.70 FORM OF SPECIAL STATEMENT

FOR SOCIAL SECURITY AND STATUTORY SICK PAY PURPOSES ONLY

Special Statement by the Doctor

In confidence to

Mr/Mrs/Miss/Ms ....

(A) I examined you on the

following dates ....

....

....

and advised you that you should refrain from work

From .... To ....

Diagnosis of your disorder causing absence from work

....

(B) I have not examined you but, on the basis of a recent written report from—

Doctor .... (Name if known)

of

....

....

.... (Address)

I have advised you that you should refrain From work for/until

....

Doctor's remarks

Doctor's signature

Date of signing

The special circumstances in which this form may be used are described in the handbook "Medical Evidence for Social Security and Statutory Sick Pay Purposes".

AMENDMENT

1. Social Security (Miscellaneous Provisions) Amendment Regulations 1992 (SI 1992/247), reg.6(5) and Sch.2 (March 9, 1992).

Statutory Sick Pay Percentage Threshold Order 1995

(SI 1995/512)

Whereas a draft of the following Order was laid before Parliament in accordance with the provisions of section 3(3) of the Statutory Sick Pay Act 1994 and approved by resolution of each House of Parliament: 3.71

Now, therefore, the Secretary of State for Social Security, in exercise of the powers conferred by sections 159A and 175(3) and (4) of the Social Security Contributions and Benefits Act 1992 and of all other powers enabling him in that behalf, hereby makes the following Order:

Citation, commencement and interpretation

1.—(1) This Order may be cited as the Statutory Sick Pay Percentage Threshold Order 1995 and shall come into force on 6th April 1995. 3.72

(2) In this Order, unless the context otherwise requires, "income tax month" means the period beginning on the 6th day of any calendar month and ending on the 5th day of the following calendar month.

(3) A reference in this Order to a payment of statutory sick pay shall not include any such payment made in respect of a day of incapacity for work before the coming into force of this Order.

(4) Unless the context otherwise requires, any reference in this Order to a numbered article is a reference to the article bearing that number in this Order and any reference in an article to a numbered paragraph is a reference to the paragraph of that article bearing that number.

General Note

This Order makes provision for employers to recover payments of statutory sick pay where such payments amount to more than 13 per cent of their liability for Class 1 contributions payments in any income tax month. Consequently, this facility only arises where there is widespread sickness absence in a workplace. Article 2 sets out how the amount an employer may recover is to be determined. Article 3 provides for the amount determined under art.2 to be recovered by deduction from Class 1 National Insurance contributions payments. Article 4 provides for repayment by or on behalf of the Board to employers where the amount they are entitled to deduct exceeds their contributions payments. Article 5 repeals and revokes the former enactments which provided for recovery of statutory sick pay by small employers. Article 6 (not included here) makes amendments to various enactments which are consequential on the repeals and revocations in art.5. 3.73

Right of employer to recover statutory sick pay

3.74 **2.**—(1) Subject to paragraph (2) an employer is entitled to recover in accordance with articles 3 and 4 the amount, if any, by which the payments of statutory sick pay made by him in any income tax month exceed 13 per cent. of the amount of his liability for contributions payments in respect of that income tax month.

(2) For the purposes of calculating the amount an employer is entitled to recover under paragraph (1), there shall be excluded any payment of statutory sick pay which was not made—

(a) in the income tax month in which he received notice, in accordance with regulation 7 of the Statutory Sick Pay (General) Regulations 1982, of the day or days of incapacity for work to which the payment related;

(b) in a case where it would have been impracticable to make the payment in that income tax month in view of the employer's methods of accounting for and paying remuneration, in the following income tax month; or

(c) in a case where a decision had been made by an adjudication officer, social security appeal tribunal or Commissioner that the employee was entitled to that payment, within the time-limits set out in regulation 9 of those Regulations.

DEFINITION

"income tax month"—see art.1(2).

Recovery by deduction from contributions payments

3.75 **3.**—(1) An employer may recover an amount determined in accordance with article 2 in respect of any income tax month by making one or more deductions from his contributions payments for that or any following income tax month within 6 years from the end of the tax year in which he became entitled to recover that amount, except where and insofar as—

(a) that amount has been repaid to him by or on behalf of the Secretary of State under article 4; or

(b) he has made a request in writing under article 4 that that amount be repaid to him, and he has not received notification by or on behalf of the Secretary of State that the request is refused.

(2) A deduction from contributions payments made in accordance with paragraph (1) shall be disregarded for the purposes of determining whether an employer has discharged any liability of his in respect of Class 1 contributions.

DEFINITION

"income tax month"—see art.1(2).

Recovery from the Secretary of State

3.76 **4.**—(1) If the amount which an employer is or would otherwise be entitled to deduct under article 3 exceeds the amount of his contributions payments in respect of earnings paid in an income tax month, and the

Secretary of State is satisfied that that is so, then provided that the employer has requested him in writing to do so, there shall be repaid to the employer by or on behalf of the Secretary of State such amount as the employer was unable to deduct.

(2) If an employer is not liable for any contributions payments in an income tax month but would otherwise be entitled to deduct an amount under article 3, and the Secretary of State is satisfied that that is so, then provided the employer has in writing requested him to do so, that amount shall be repaid to the employer by or on behalf of the Secretary of State.

DEFINITION

"income tax month"—see art.1(2).

GENERAL NOTE

The Secretary of State's functions under this article were transferred to the Board of the Inland Revenue by s.1(2) of, and Sch.2 to, the Social Security Contributions (Transfer of Functions, etc.) Act 1999. 3.77

Repeals and revocations

5. Subject to the savings made by regulations under section 159A(4) of the Social Security Contributions and Benefits Act 1992— 3.78

(a) sections 158 and 159 of the Social Security Contributions and Benefits Act 1992 shall be repealed; and

(b) the Statutory Sick Pay (Compensation of Employers) and Miscellaneous Provisions Regulations 1983 and the Statutory Sick Pay (Small Employers' Relief) Regulations 1991 shall be revoked.

Consequential amendments

6. [*omitted*] 3.79

Statutory Sick Pay and Statutory Maternity Pay (Decisions) Regulations 1999

(SI 1999/776)

The Secretary of State for Social Security, in exercise of powers conferred by section 20(3) of the Social Security Administration Act 1992, sections 8(1)(f) and 25(3) of the Social Security Contributions (Transfer of Functions, etc.) Act 1999 and of all other powers enabling him in that behalf, with the concurrence of the Commissioners of Inland Revenue, hereby makes the following Regulations:

ARRANGEMENT OF REGULATIONS

3. Applications in connection with statutory sick pay or statutory maternity pay
4. Revocation of regulation 20 of the Social Security (Adjudication) Regulations 1995

Citation, commencement and interpretation

3.81 **1.**—(1) These Regulations may be cited as the Statutory Sick Pay and Statutory Maternity Pay (Decisions) Regulations 1999 and shall come into force on 1st April 1999.

(2) In these Regulations—

(a) "the Contributions and Benefits Act" means the Social Security Contributions and Benefits Act 1992;

(b) "employee" and "employer" have, in relation to—

(i) statutory sick pay, the meanings given by section 163(1) of the Contributions and Benefits Act;

(ii) statutory maternity pay, the meanings given by section 171(1) of the Contributions and Benefits Act.

Application for the determination of any issue arising as to, or in connection with, entitlement to statutory sick pay or statutory maternity pay

3.82 **2.**—(1) An application for the determination of any issue arising as to, or in connection with, entitlement to statutory sick pay or statutory maternity pay may be submitted to an officer of the Board by—

(a) the Secretary of State; or

(b) the employee concerned.

(2) Such an issue shall be decided by an officer of the Board only on the basis of such an application or on his own initiative.

DEFINITION

"employee"—see reg.1(2).

Applications in connection with statutory sick pay or statutory maternity pay

3.83 **3.**—(1) An application for the determination of any issue referred to in regulation 2 above shall be made only in writing, in a form approved for the purpose by the Board, or in such other manner, being in writing, as an officer of the Board may accept as sufficient in the circumstances.

(2) Where such an application is made by an employee, it shall—

(a) be delivered or sent to an office of the Board within 6 months of the earliest day in respect of which entitlement to statutory sick pay or statutory maternity pay is in issue;

(b) state the period in respect of which entitlement to statutory sick pay or statutory maternity pay is in issue; and

(c) state the grounds (if any) on which the applicant's employer has denied liability for statutory sick pay or statutory maternity pay in respect of the period specified in the application.

(*SI 1999/776, reg. 3*)

DEFINITION

"employer"—see reg.1(2).

Revocation of regulation 20 of the Social Security (Adjudication) Regulations 1995

4. Regulation 20 of the Social Security (Adjudication) Regulations 1995 is hereby revoked. **3.84**

PART IV

STATUTORY MATERNITY PAY

Statutory Maternity Pay (General) Regulations 1986

(SI 1986/1960) (as amended)

The Secretary of State for Social Services, in exercise of the powers conferred by sections 46(4), (7) and (8), 47(1), (3), (6) and (7), 48(3) and (6), 50(1), (2), (4) and (5), 51(1)(g), (k), (n) and (r) and (4), 54(1), 83(1) and 84(1) of, and paragraphs 6, 8 and 12(3) of Schedule 4 to, the Social Security Act 1986(a), and of all other powers enabling him in that behalf, by this instrument, which contains only regulations made under the sections of the Social Security Act 1986 specified above and provisions consequential upon those sections and before the end of a period of 12 months from the commencement of those sections, makes the following regulations:

ARRANGEMENT OF REGULATIONS

PART I

INTRODUCTION

PART II

ENTITLEMENT

PART III

CONTINUOUS EMPLOYMENT AND NORMAL WORKING HOURS

PART IV

GENERAL PROVISIONS

PART V

ADMINISTRATION

PART VI

PAYMENT

PART VII

OFFENCES

(SI 1986/1960, reg. 1) (as amended)

PART I

INTRODUCTION

Citation, commencement and interpretation

1.—(1) These regulations may be cited as the Statutory Maternity Pay (General) Regulations 1986 and shall come into operation in the case of regulations 1, 22 and 23 on 15th March, 1987, and in the case of the remainder of the regulations on 6th April, 1987. **4.8**

(2) In these regulations, unless the context otherwise requires—

"the 1975 Act" means the Social Security Act 1975;

"the 1978 Act" means the Employment Protection (Consolidation) Act 1978;

"the 1986 Act" means the Social Security Act 1986.

[[1]"the Contributions and Benefits Act" means the Social Security Contributions and Benefits Act 1992.]

(3) Unless the context otherwise requires, any references in these regulations to—

(a) a numbered regulation is a reference to the regulation bearing that number in these regulations and any reference in a regulation to a numbered paragraph is a reference to the paragraph of that regulation bearing that number;

(b) any provision made by or contained in an enactment or instrument shall be construed as a reference to that provision as amended or extended by any enactment or instrument and as including a reference to any provision which it re-enacts or replaces, or which may re-enact or replace it, with or without modifications.

AMENDMENT

1. Social Security (Miscellaneous Provisions) Amendment (No.2) Regulations 1992 (SI 1992/2595), reg.12 (November 16, 1992).

GENERAL NOTE

The text of these Regulations pre-dates SSCBA 1992 and was not amended at the time of the SSCBA 1992 to reflect the provisions in the 1992 Act. The Regulations remain in force, of course, by virtue of s.17(2)(b) of the Interpretation Act 1978. As a result, regulations which survive unamended from the original text refer to the SSA 1975 and SSA 1986, whilst post-1992 amendments refer to the parallel provisions in SSCBA 1992. References to the 1975 Act should therefore be read as referring to SSCBA 1992, and those to Pt V of the SSA 1986 as referring to Pt XII of the SSCBA 1992. **4.9**

PART II

ENTITLEMENT

The Maternity Pay Period

4.10 **2.**—[[2](1) Subject to paragraphs (3) to (6), where a woman gives notice to her employer of the date from which she expects his liability to pay her statutory maternity pay to begin and in conformity with that notice ceases to work for him in a week which is later than the 12th week before the expected week of confinement, then the first week in the maternity pay period shall be the week following the week in which she ceased to work, or the week immediately following the week in which she is confined, whichever is the earlier.]

(2) [[1]The maternity pay period shall be a period of [[2]26 consecutive weeks].]

(3) Where—

(a) a woman is confined before the 11th week before the expected week of confinement; or

(b) is confined after the 12th week [[1]. . .] before the expected week of confinement and the confinement occurs in a week which precedes that mentioned in a notice given to her employer as being the week she intends to give up work,

the first week in the maternity pay period [[2]shall be the week commencing on the day after the day on which she is confined.]

[[2](4) Subject to paragraph (6), where a woman is absent from work wholly or partly because of pregnancy or confinement on any day which falls on or after the beginning of the 4th week before the expected week of confinement, but not later than the week immediately following the week in which she is confined, the first week of the maternity pay period shall be the week beginning on the day following the day on which she is so absent.]

(5) [[2]. . .]

[[2](6) In a case where a woman leaves her employment at any time falling after the beginning of the 11th week before the expected week of confinement and before the start of the maternity pay period but not later than the week immediately following the week in which she is confined, the first week of the maternity pay period shall be the week after the week in which her employment ends.

(7) "week" for the purposes of a maternity pay period which falls within paragraphs (3) or (4) above means a period of 7 consecutive days.]

AMENDMENTS

1. Social Security Maternity Benefits and Statutory Sick Pay (Amendment) Regulations 1994 (SI 1994/1367), reg.2 (June 11, 1994).

2. Social Security, Statutory Maternity Pay and Statutory Sick Pay (Miscellaneous Amendments) Regulations 2002 (SI 2002/2690), reg.2 (November 24, 2002).

DEFINITION

"week"—see SSCBA 1992, s.171(1) and para.(7).

GENERAL NOTE

Since November 24, 2002, statutory maternity pay has been payable for a maximum of 26 consecutive weeks—the "maternity pay period" (para.(2)); the previous maximum was 18 weeks. The general rule for determining the start of the maternity pay period is set out in para.(1), namely the beginning of the week after the week in which the woman stops working or is confined, having given the appropriate notice to her employer. For these purposes, a week starts on Sunday (SSCBA 1992, s.171(1)). 4.11

There are then a number of further special cases detailed in paras (3)–(6). Paragraph (3) covers those situations where the woman gives birth prior to the date notified to the employer (para.(3)(a)), or before the week she notified to the employer that she intended to cease working (para.(3)(b)). In this situation the rule now is that the first week of the maternity pay period is the week commencing on the day after she is confined, excluding the general rule in the primary legislation that a week starts on a Sunday (see para.(7)). Paragraph (4) makes special provision to deal with the situation where the woman stops working because of a pregnancy-related absence in the four weeks (previously six weeks) before the expected week of confinement. In such a case, the maternity pay period commences on the day after she is absent. Finally, para.(6) covers women who leave their employment after the start of the 11th week before the expected week of confinement, but before the maternity pay period commences and not later than the week after the week of actual confinement. In such a case the first week of the maternity pay period is the week after the employment ends. This provision used to be limited to cases where the woman had been dismissed or had otherwise lost her employment without her consent.

Contract of service ended for the purpose of avoiding liability for statutory maternity pay

3.—(1) A former employer shall be liable to make payments of statutory maternity pay to any woman who was employed by him for a continuous period of at least eight weeks and whose contract of service with him was brought to an end by the former employer solely or mainly for the purpose of avoiding liability for statutory maternity pay. 4.12

(2) In order to determine the amount payable by the former employer—

(a) the woman shall be deemed for the purposes of Part V of the 1986 Act to have been employed by him from the date her employment with him ended until the end of the week immediately preceding the 14th week before the expected week of confinement on the same terms and conditions of employment as those subsisting immediately before her employment ended; and

(b) her normal weekly earnings for the period of 8 weeks immediately preceding the 14th week before the expected week of confinement shall for those purposes be calculated by reference to her normal weekly earnings for the period of 8 weeks ending with the last day in respect of which she was paid under her former contract of service.

GENERAL NOTE

4.13 This regulation, made under SSCBA 1992, s.164(8), sets out the principles governing entitlement to statutory maternity pay where an employer dismisses a woman with a view to avoiding liability to pay statutory maternity pay. In order for this provision to apply, the woman must have been continuously employed for at least eight weeks (para.(1)). Such action will also constitute an automatically unfair dismissal under Employment Rights Act 1999, s.99 and an act of sex discrimination.

Modification of entitlement provisions

4.14 **4.**—(1) [1. . .]

(2) In relation to a woman in employed earner's employment who was confined before the 14th week before the expected week of confinement [1section 164(2)(a) and (b) of the Contributions and Benefits Act] shall have effect as if for the conditions there set out, there were substituted the conditions that—

(a) she would but for her confinement have been in employed earner's employment with an employer for a continuous period of at least 26 weeks ending with the week immediately preceding the 14th week before the expected week of confinement; and

(b) her normal weekly earnings for the period of 8 weeks ending with the week immediately preceding the week of her confinement are not less than the lower earnings limit in force [1under section 5(1)(a) of the Contributions and Benefits Act] immediately before the commencement of the week of her confinement.

[1(3) In relation to a woman to whom paragraph (2) applies, section 166 of the Contributions and Benefits Act shall be modified so that subsection (2) has effect as if the reference to the period of 8 weeks immediately preceding the 14th week before the expected week of confinement was a reference to the period of 8 weeks immediately preceding the week in which her confinement occurred.]

AMENDMENTS

1. Social Security Maternity Benefits and Statutory Sick Pay (Amendment) Regulations 1994 (SI 1994/1367), reg.3 (June 11, 1994).

GENERAL NOTE

Para. (2)

4.15 If the baby is born either before or in the qualifying week, statutory maternity pay is still payable so long as the woman would have been employed for 26 weeks by the end of the qualifying week, on the assumption that the baby had not in fact been born early.

Treatment of more than one contract of service as one

4.16 **5.** Where 2 or more contracts of service exist concurrently between one employer and one employee, they shall be treated as one for the purposes of Part V of the 1986 Act, except where, by virtue of regulation 11 of the Social Security (Contributions) Regulations 1979 the earnings from those contracts of service are not aggregated for the purposes of earnings-related contributions.

[1 Prescribed rate of statutory maternity pay

6. The rate of statutory maternity pay prescribed under section 166(1)(b) of the Contributions and Benefits Act is a weekly rate of [2£102.80.] **4.17**

AMENDMENTS

1. Social Security, Statutory Maternity Pay and Statutory Sick Pay (Miscellaneous Amendments) Regulations 2002 (SI 2002/2690), reg.3 (April 6, 2003).
2. Social Security Benefits Up-rating Order 2004 (SI 2004/552), art.10 (April 4, 2004).

Liability of Secretary of State to pay Statutory Maternity Pay

7.—(1) Where— **4.18**

(a) an adjudicating authority has determined that an employer is liable to make payments of statutory maternity pay to a woman; and
(b) the time for appealing against that determination has expired; and
(c) no appeal against the determination has been lodged or leave to appeal against the determination is required and has been refused,

then for any week in respect of which the employer was liable to make payments of statutory maternity pay but did not do so, and for any subsequent weeks in the maternity pay period the liability to make those payments shall, notwithstanding section 46(3) of the 1986 Act, be that of the Secretary of State and not the employer.

(2) In paragraph (1) adjudicating authority means, as the case may be, the Chief or any other adjudication officer, a Social Security Appeal Tribunal or the Chief or any other Social Security Commissioner.

(3) Liability to make payments of statutory maternity pay shall, notwithstanding section 46(3) of the 1986 Act, be a liability of the Secretary of State and not the employer as from the week in which the employer first becomes insolvent until the end of the maternity pay period.

(4) For the purposes of paragraph (3) an employer shall be taken to be insolvent if, and only if—

(a) in England and Wales—
  (i) he has been adjudged bankrupt or has made a composition or arrangement with his creditors;
  (ii) he has died and his estate falls to be administered in accordance with an order under section 421 of the Insolvency Act 1986; or
  (iii) where an employer is a company, a winding-up order or an administration order is made or a resolution for voluntary winding-up is passed with respect to it, or a receiver or manager of its undertaking is duly appointed, or possession is taken by or on behalf of the holders of any debentures secured by a floating charge, of any property of the company

comprised in or subject to the charge or a voluntary arrangement proposed for the purposes of Part 1 of the Insolvency Act 1986 is approved under that Part;

(b) in Scotland—

(i) an award of sequestration is made on his estate or he executes a trust deed for his creditors or enters into a composition contract;

(ii) he has died and a judicial factor appointed under section 1A of the Judicial Factors (Scotland) Act 1889 is required by that section to divide his insolvent estate among his creditors; or

(iii) where the employer is a company, a winding-up order or an administration order is made or a resolution for voluntary winding-up is passed with respect to it or a receiver of its undertaking is duly appointed or a voluntary arrangement proposed for the purposes of Part 1 of the Insolvency Act 1986 is approved under that Part.

GENERAL NOTE

4.19 The functions under this regulation were transferred from the Secretary of State for Social Security to the Board of the Inland Revenue under s.1(2) of and Sch.2 to the Social Security (Transfer of Functions, etc.) Act 1999. References in this regulation to SSA 1986, s.46(3) should now be read as referring to SSCBA 1992, s.164(3).

Work after confinement

4.20 **8.**—(1) Where in the week immediately preceding the 14th week before the expected week of confinement a woman had two or more employers but one or more of them were not liable to make payments to her of statutory maternity pay ("non-liable employer"), section 47(6) of the 1986 Act shall not apply in respect of any week after the week of confinement but within the maternity pay period in which she works only for a non-liable employer.

(2) Where after her confinement a woman—

(a) works for an employer who is not liable to pay her statutory maternity pay and is not a non-liable employer, but

(b) before the end of her maternity pay period ceases to work for that employer, the person who before she commenced work was liable to make payments of statutory maternity pay to her shall, notwithstanding section 46 of the 1986 Act, not be liable to make such payments to her for any weeks in the maternity pay period after she ceases work.

GENERAL NOTE

4.21 References in this regulation to SSA 1986, ss.46 and 47(6) should now be read as referring to SSCBA 1992, ss.164 and 165(6).

No liability to pay statutory maternity pay

4.22 **9.** Notwithstanding the provisions of section 46(1) of the 1986 Act, no liability to make payments of statutory maternity pay to a woman shall arise in respect of a week within the maternity pay period for any part of which she is detained in legal custody or sentenced to a term of imprisonment (except where the sentence is suspended), or of any subsequent week within that period.

GENERAL NOTE

The reference in this regulation to SSA 1986, s.46(1) should now be read as referring to SSCBA 1992, s.164(1). 4.23

Death of woman

10. An employer shall not be liable to make payments of statutory maternity pay in respect of a woman for any week within the maternity pay period which falls after the week in which she dies. 4.24

PART III

CONTINUOUS EMPLOYMENT AND NORMAL WORKING HOURS

Continuous employment

11.—(1) Subject to the following provisions of this regulation, where in any week a woman is, for the whole part of the week,— 4.25

(a) incapable of work in consequence of sickness or injury; or
(b) absent from work on account of a temporary cessation of work; or
(c) absent from work in circumstances such that, by arrangement or custom, she is regarded as continuing in the employment of her employer for all or any purpose; or
(d) absent from work wholly or partly because of pregnancy or confinement, [2or
(e) absent from work in consequence of taking paternity leave, adoption leave or parental leave under Part 8 of the Employment Rights Act 1996,]

and returns to work for her employer after the incapacity for or absence from work, that week shall be treated for the purposes of Part V of the 1986 Act as part of a continuous period of employment with that employer, notwithstanding that no contract of service exists with that employer in respect of that week.

(2) Incapacity for work which lasts for more than 26 consecutive weeks shall not count for the purposes of paragraph (1)(a).

(3) Paragraph (1)(d) shall only apply to a woman who—

(a) has a contract of service with the same employer both before and after her confinement but not during any period of absence from work due to her confinement and the period between those contracts does not exceed 26 weeks; or
(b) returns to work in accordance with section 45(1) of the 1978 Act or in pursuance of an offer made in circumstances described in

section 56A(2) of that Act after a period of absence from work wholly or partly occasioned by pregnancy or confinement.

[[1] (3A) Where a woman who is pregnant—

(a) is an employee in an employed earner's employment in which the custom is for the employer

(i) to offer work for a fixed period of not more than 26 consecutive weeks;

(ii) to offer work for such period on 2 or more occasions in a year for periods which do not overlap; and

(iii) to offer the work available to those persons who had worked for him during the last or a recent such period, but

(b) is absent from work—

(i) wholly or partly because of the pregnancy or her confinement; or

(ii) because of incapacity arising from some specific disease or bodily or mental disablement,

then in her case paragraph (1) shall apply as if the words "and returns to work for an employer after the incapacity for or absence from work" were omitted and paragraph (4) shall not apply.]

(4) Where a woman is employed under a contract of service for part only of the week immediately preceding the 14th week before the expected week of confinement, the whole of that week shall count in computing any period of continuous employment for the purposes of Part V of the 1986 Act.

AMENDMENTS

1. Statutory Maternity Pay (General) Amendment Regulations 1990 (SI 1990/622), reg.2 (April 6, 1990).

2. Social Security, Statutory Maternity Pay and Statutory Sick Pay (Miscellaneous Amendments) Regulations 2002 (SI 2002/2690), reg.4 (April 6, 2003).

DEFINITIONS

"the 1978 Act"—see reg.1(2).

"the 1986 Act"—*ibid.*

Continuous employment and unfair dismissal

4.26 **12.**—(1) This regulation applies to a woman in relation to whose dismissal an action is commenced which consists—

(a) of the presentation by her of a complaint under section 67(1) of the 1978 Act; or

(b) of her making a claim in accordance with a dismissals procedure agreement designated by an order under section 65 of that Act; or

(c) of any action taken by a conciliation officer under section 134(3) of that Act.

(2) If in consequence of an action of the kind specified in paragraph (1) a woman is reinstated or re-engaged by her employer or by a successor or associated employer of that employer the continuity of her employment shall be preserved for the purposes of Part V of the 1986 Act

and any week which falls within the interval beginning with the effective date of termination and ending with the date of reinstatement or re-engagement, as the case may be, shall count in the computation of her period of continuous employment.

(3) In this regulation—

"successor" and "dismissals procedure agreement" have the same meanings as in section 30(3) and (4) of the Trade Union and Labour Relations Act 1974; and

"associated employer" shall be construed in accordance with section 153(4) of the 1978 Act.

DEFINITIONS

"the 1978 Act"—see reg.1(2).
"associated employer"—see para.(3).
"dismissals procedure agreement"—*ibid.*
"successor"—*ibid.*

Continuous employment and stoppages of work

13.—(1) Where for any week or part of a week a woman does no work because there is, within the meaning of section 19 of the 1975 Act a stoppage of work due to a trade dispute at her place of employment the continuity of her employment shall, subject to paragraph (2), be treated as continuing throughout the stoppage but, subject to paragraph (3), no such week shall count in the computation of her period of employment. **4.27**

(2) Subject to paragraph (3), where during the stoppage of work a woman is dismissed from her employment, the continuity of her employment shall not be treated in accordance with paragraph (1) as continuing beyond the commencement of the day she stopped work.

(3) The provisions of paragraph (1) to the extent that they provide that a week in which a stoppage of work occurred shall not count in the computation of a period of employment, and paragraph (2) shall not apply to a woman who proves that at no time did she have a direct interest in the trade dispute in question.

GENERAL NOTE

The reference in this regulation to SSA 1975, s.19 should now be read as referring to SSCBA 1992, s.27. **4.28**

Change of employer

14. A woman's employment shall, notwithstanding the change of employer, be treated as continuous employment with the second employer where— **4.29**

(a) the employer's trade or business or an undertaking (whether or not it is an undertaking established by or under an Act of Parliament) is transferred from one person to another;

(b) by or under an Act of Parliament, whether public or local and whenever passed, a contract of employment between any body corporate and the woman is modified and some other body corporate is substituted as her employer;

(c) on the death of her employer, the woman is taken into the employment of the personal representatives or trustees of the deceased;
(d) the woman is employed by partners, personal representatives or trustees and there is a change in the partners, or, as the case may be, personal representatives or trustees;
(e) the woman is taken into the employment of an employer who is, at the time she entered his employment, an associated employer of her previous employer, and for this purpose "associated employer" shall be construed in accordance with section 153(4) of the 1978 Act;
(f) on the termination of her employment with an employer she is taken into the employment of another employer and [[1]those employers are the governors of a school maintained by a local education authority and that authority].

AMENDMENT

1. Statutory Maternity Pay (General) Amendment Regulations 1990 (SI 1990/622), reg.3 (April 6, 1990).

DEFINITION

"the 1978 Act"—see reg.1(2).

Reinstatement after service with the armed forces, etc.

4.30 **15.** If a woman who is entitled to apply to her former employer under the Reserve Forces (Safeguard of Employment) Act 1985 enters the employment of that employer not later than the 6 month period mentioned in section 1(4)(b) of that Act, her previous period of employment with that employer (or if there was more than one such period, the last of those periods) and the period of employment beginning in the said period of 6 months shall be treated as continuous.

Normal working weeks

4.31 **16.**—(1) For the purposes of section 48(5) of the 1986 Act, a woman's contract of service shall be treated as not normally involving or having involved employment for less than 16 hours weekly where she is normally employed for 16 hours or more weekly.

(2) Where a woman's relations with her employer were governed for a continuous period of at least 2 years by a contract of service which normally involved employment for not less than 16 hours weekly and this period was followed by a further period, ending with the week immediately preceding the 14th week before the expected week of confinement, in which her relations with that employer were governed by a contract of service which normally involved employment for less than 16 hours, but not less than 8 hours weekly, then her contract of service shall be treated for the purpose of section 48(5) of the 1986 Act as not normally involving or having involved employment for less than 16 hours weekly.

(3) Where a woman's relations with her employer are or were governed for a continuous period of at least 2 years by a contract of service which involved—

(a) for not more than 26 weeks in that period, employment for 8 hours or more but less than 16 hours weekly; and
(b) for the whole of the remainder of that period employment for not less than 16 hours weekly, the contract of service shall be treated for the purposes of section 48(5) of the 1986 Act as not normally involving or having involved employment for less than 16 hours weekly.

GENERAL NOTE

The references in this regulation to SSA 1986, s.48(5) should now be read as referring to SSCBA 1992, ss.166(5). 4.32

[1Meaning of "week"

16A. Where a woman has been in employed earner's employment with the same employer in each of 26 consecutive weeks (but no more than 26 weeks) ending with the week immediately preceding the 14th week before the expected week of confinement then for the purpose of determining whether that employment amounts to a continuous period of at least 26 weeks, the first of those 26 weeks shall be a period commencing on the first day of her employment with the employer and ending at midnight on the first Saturday thereafter or on that day where her first day is a Saturday.] 4.33

AMENDMENT

1. Statutory Maternity Pay (General) Amendment Regulations 1990 (SI 1990/622), reg.4 (April 6, 1990).

PART IV

GENERAL PROVISIONS

Meaning of "employee"

17.—(1) In a case where, and in so far as, a woman over the age of 16 is treated as an employed earner by virtue of the Social Security (Categorisation of Earners) Regulations 1978 she shall be treated as an employee for the purposes of Part V of the 1986 Act and in a case where, and in so far as, such a woman is treated otherwise than as an employed earner by virtue of those regulations, she shall not be treated as an employee for the purposes of Part V. 4.34

(2) Any woman who is in employed earner's employment within the meaning of the 1975 Act under a contract of apprenticeship shall be treated as the employee for the purposes of Part V.

(3) A woman who is in employed earner's employment within the meaning of the 1975 Act but whose employer—
(a) does not fulfil the conditions prescribed in regulation 119(1)(b) of the Social Security (Contributions) Regulations 1979 as to residence or presence in Great Britain, or

(b) is a woman who, by reason of any international treaty to which the United Kingdom is a party of any international convention binding the United Kingdom—
  (i) is exempt from the provisions of the 1975 Act, or
  (ii) is a woman against whom the provisions of that Act are not enforceable, shall not be treated as an employee for the purposes of Part V of the 1986 Act.

Treatment of two or more employers as one

4.35 **18.**—(1) In a case where the earnings paid to a woman in respect of 2 or more employments are aggregated and treated as a single payment of earnings under regulation 12(1) of the Social Security (Contributions) Regulations 1979, the employers of the woman in respect of those employments shall be treated as one for all purposes of Part V of the 1986 Act.

(2) Where two or more employers are treated as one under the provisions of paragraph (1), liability for statutory maternity pay payable by them to a woman shall be apportioned between them in such proportions as they may agree or, in default of agreement, in the proportions which the woman's earnings from each employment bear to the amount of the aggregated earnings.

General Note

4.36 Specific provision is also made in the Statutory Maternity Pay (National Health Service Employees) Regulations 1991 (SI 1991/590) for NHS workers with divided contracts.

Payments to be treated as contractual remuneration

4.37 **19.** For the purposes of paragraph 12(1) and (2) of Schedule 4 to the 1986 Act, the payments which are to be treated as contractual remuneration are sums payable under the contract of service—
(a) by way of remuneration;
(b) for incapacity for work due to sickness or injury; and
(c) by reason of pregnancy or confinement.

Definition

"the 1986 Act"—see reg.1(2).

Meaning of "earnings"

20.—(1) [[1]. . .]

4.38 [[2](2) For the purposes of section 171(4) of the Contributions and Benefits Act, the expression "earnings" refers to gross earnings and includes any remuneration or profit derived from a woman's employment except any payment or amount which is—
(a) excluded from the computation of a person's earnings under regulation 19 or 19B of the Social Security (Contributions) Regulations 1979 (payments to be disregarded and payments to directors to be disregarded respectively);

(b) a chargeable emolument under section 10A of the Social Security Contributions and Benefits Act 1992, except where, in consequence of such a chargeable emolument being excluded from earnings, a woman would not be entitled to statutory maternity pay.]

(3) [[1]. . .]

(4) For the purposes of section [[3]section 171(4) of the Contributions and Benefits Act] the expression "earnings" includes also—

(a) any sum payable in respect of arrears of pay in pursuance of an order for reinstatement or re-engagement under the 1978 Act;

(b) any sum payable by way of pay in pursuance of an order under the 1978 Act for the continuation of a contract of employment;

(c) any sum payable by way of remuneration in pursuance of a protective award under the Employment Protection Act 1975;

(d) any sum payable by way of statutory sick pay, including sums payable in accordance with regulations made under section 1(5) of the Social Security and Housing Benefits Act 1982.

[[4](e) any sum payable by way of statutory maternity pay, including sums payable in accordance with regulations made under section 164(9)(b) of the Contributions and Benefits Act;

(f) any sum payable by way of statutory paternity pay, including sums payable in accordance with regulations made under section 171ZD(3) of the Contributions and Benefits Act;

(g) any sum payable by way of statutory adoption pay, including sums payable in accordance with regulations made under section 171ZM(3) of the Contributions and Benefits Act.]

(5) [[1]. . .]

(6) [[1]. . .]

AMENDMENTS

1. Social Security (Miscellaneous Provisions) Amendment (No.2) Regulations 1992 (SI 1992/2595), reg.13 (November 16, 1992).

2. Social Security Contributions, Statutory Maternity Pay and Statutory Sick Pay (Miscellaneous Amendments) Regulations 1999 (SI 1999/567), reg.12 (April 6, 1999).

3. Social Security, Statutory Maternity Pay and Statutory Sick Pay (Miscellaneous Amendments) Regulations 2002 (SI 2002/2690), reg.5(a) (November 24, 2002).

4. Social Security, Statutory Maternity Pay and Statutory Sick Pay (Miscellaneous Amendments) Regulations 2002 (SI 2002/2690), reg.5(b) (April 6, 2003).

DEFINITION

"the 1978 Act"—see reg.1(2).

Normal weekly earnings

21.—(1) For the purposes of [[1]Part XII of the Contributions and Benefits Act], a woman's normal weekly earnings shall be calculated in accordance with the following provisions of this regulation. **4.39**

(2) In this regulation—

"the appropriate date" means the first day of the 14th week before the expected week of confinement, or the first day in the week in which the woman is confined, whichever is the earlier. [1. . .]

"normal pay day" means a day on which the terms of a woman's contract of service require her to be paid, or the practice in her employment is for her to be paid, if any payment is due to her; and "day of payment" means a day on which the woman was paid.

(3) Subject to paragraph (4), the relevant period for the purposes of [1section 171(4) of the Contributions and Benefits Act] is the period between—

(a) the last normal pay day to fall before the appropriate date; and

(b) the last normal pay day to fall at least eight weeks earlier than the normal pay day mentioned in sub-paragraph (a), including the normal pay day mentioned in sub-paragraph (a) but excluding that first mentioned in sub-paragraph (b).

(4) In a case where a woman has no identifiable normal pay day, paragraph (3) shall have effect as if the words "day of payment" were substituted for the words "normal pay day" in each place where they occur.

(5) In a case where a woman has normal pay days at intervals of or approximating to one or more calendar months (including intervals of or approximating to a year) her normal weekly earnings shall be calculated by dividing her earnings in the relevant period by the number of calendar months in that period (or, if it is not a whole number, the nearest whole number), multiplying the result by 12 and dividing by 52.

(6) In a case to which paragraph (5) does not apply and the relevant period is not an exact number of weeks, the woman's normal weekly earnings shall be calculated by dividing her earnings in the relevant period by the number of days in the relevant period and multiplying the result by 7.

[1(7) In any case where a woman receives a back-dated pay increase which includes a sum in respect of a relevant period, normal weekly earnings shall be calculated as if such a sum was paid in that relevant period even though received after that period.]

AMENDMENTS

1. Social Security Maternity Benefits and Statutory Sick Pay (Amendment) Regulations 1994 (SI 1994/1367), reg.5 (June 11, 1994).

2. Statutory Maternity Pay (General) Amendment Regulations 1996 (SI 1996/1335), reg.2 (June 12, 1996).

[1Effect of statutory maternity pay on [2 incapacity benefit]

4.40 **21A.**—[3. . .]

AMENDMENTS

1. Statutory Maternity Pay (General) Amendment Regulations 1988 (SI 1988/532), reg.3 (April 6, 1988).

2. Social Security (Incapacity Benefit) (Consequential and Transitional Amendments and Savings) Regulations 1995 (SI 1995/829), reg.18 (April 13, 1995).

3. Social Security, Statutory Maternity Pay and Statutory Sick Pay (Miscellaneous Amendments) Regulations 2002 (SI 2002/2690), reg.6 (November 24, 2002).

[1Effect of maternity allowance on statutory maternity pay

21B. Where a woman, in any week which falls within the maternity pay period, is— 4.41

(a) in receipt of maternity allowance pursuant to the provisions of section 35(1A) of the Contributions and Benefits Act; and

(b) entitled to receive statutory maternity pay in consequence of receiving a back-dated pay increase which includes a sum in respect of the relevant period;

the employer shall only be liable to make payments of statutory maternity pay in respect of such week of an amount equal to the amount (if any) by which the rate of statutory maternity pay exceeds the rate of maternity allowance received by her in that week.]

AMENDMENT

1. Statutory Maternity Pay (General) Amendment Regulations 1996 (SI 1996/1335), reg.3 (June 12, 1996).

PART V

ADMINISTRATION

Evidence of expected week of confinement

22.—(1) A woman shall in accordance with the following provisions of this regulation, provide the person who is liable to pay her statutory maternity pay with evidence as to— 4.42

(a) the week in which the expected date of confinement occurs, and

(b) where her entitlement to statutory maternity pay depends upon the fact of her confinement, the week in which she was confined.

(2) For the purpose of paragraph (1)(b) a certificate of birth shall be sufficient evidence that the woman was confined in the week in which the birth occurred.

(3) The evidence shall be submitted to the person who will be liable to make payments of statutory maternity pay not later than the end of the third week of the maternity pay period so however that where the woman has good cause the evidence may be submitted later than that date but not later than the end of the 13th week of the maternity pay period.

(4) For the purposes of paragraph (3) evidence contained in an envelope which is properly addressed and sent by prepaid post shall be deemed to have been submitted on the day on which it was posted.

Notice of absence from work

4.43 **23.**—(1) Where a woman is confined before the beginning of the 14th week before the expected week of confinement, she shall be entitled to payments of statutory maternity pay only if—

(a) she gives notice to the person who will be liable to pay it [[2]of the date on which she was confined], and

(b) that notice is given within [[2]28 days] of the date she was confined or if in the particular circumstances that is not practicable, as soon as is reasonably practicable thereafter; and

(c) where the person so requests, the notice in writing.

(2) Where a woman is confined before the date stated in a notice provided in accordance with [[1]section 164(4) of the Contributions and Benefits Act] as being the date her absence from work is due to begin, she shall be entitled to payments of statutory maternity pay only if—

(a) she gives a further notice to the person who will be liable to pay it specifying the date she was confined and the date her absence from work [[2]. . .] began, and

(b) that further notice is given within [[2]28 days] of the date she was confined or if in the particular circumstances that is not practicable, as soon as is reasonably practicable thereafter; and

(c) where the person so requests, the notice is in writing.

(3) For the purposes of this regulation, a notice contained in an envelope which is properly addressed and sent by prepaid post shall be deemed to be given on the date on which it is posted.

[[1][[2](4) Subject to paragraph (5), section 164(4) of the Contributions and Benefits Act (statutory maternity pay entitlement and liability to pay) shall not have effect in the case of a woman who leaves her employment with the person who will be liable to pay her statutory maternity pay after the beginning of the week immediately preceding the 14th week before the expected week of confinement.]

(5) A woman who is exempted from section 164(4) of the Contributions and Benefits Act by paragraph (4) but who is confined before the 11th week before the expected week of confinement shall only be entitled to statutory maternity pay if she gives the person who will be liable to pay it notice specifying the date she was confined.]

AMENDMENTS

1. Social Security Maternity Benefits and Statutory Sick Pay (Amendment) Regulations 1994 (SI 1994/1367), reg.6 (June 11, 1994).

2. Social Security, Statutory Maternity Pay and Statutory Sick Pay (Miscellaneous Amendments) Regulations 2002 (SI 2002/2690), reg.7 (November 24, 2002).

Notification of employment after confinement

4.44 **24.** A woman who after the date of confinement but within the maternity pay period commences work in employed earner's employment with a person who is not liable to make payments of statutory maternity pay to her and is not a non-liable employer for the purposes of regulation

8(1), shall within seven days of the day she commenced work inform any person who is so liable of the date she commenced work.

Provision of information in connection with determination of questions

25. Any woman claiming to be entitled to statutory maternity pay, or any other person who is a party to proceedings arising under the 1986 Act relating to statutory maternity pay, shall, if she receives notification from the Secretary of State that any information is required from her for the determination of any question arising in connection therewith, furnish that information to the Secretary of State within 10 days of receiving that notification. **4.45**

DEFINITION

"the 1986 Act"—see reg.1(2).

GENERAL NOTE

The functions under this regulation were transferred from the Secretary of State for Social Security to the Board of the Inland Revenue under s.1(2) of and Sch.2 to the Social Security (Transfer of Functions, etc.) Act 1999. **4.46**

[[1]Provision of information relating to claims for certain other benefits

25A.—(1) Where an employer who has been given notice in accordance with [[3]section 164(4)(a) or (9)(ea) of the Contributions and Benefits Act] or regulation 23 by a woman who is or has been an employee— **4.47**

(a) decides that he has no liability to make payments of statutory maternity pay to her; or
(b) has made one or more payments of statutory maternity pay to her but decides, before the end of the maternity pay period and for a reason specified in paragraph (3), that he has no liability to make further payments to her,

then, in connection with the making of a claim by the woman for a maternity allowance or incapacity benefit, he shall furnish her with the information specified in the following provisions of this regulation.

(2) Where the employer decides he has no liability to make payments of statutory maternity pay to the woman, he shall furnish her with details of the decision and the reasons for it.

(3) Where the employer decides he has no liability to make further payments of statutory maternity pay to the woman because [[3]. . .] she has within the maternity pay period been detained in legal custody or sentenced to a term of imprisonment which was not suspended, [[3]. . .], he shall furnish her with—

(a) details of his decision and the reasons for it; and
(b) details of the last week in respect of which a liability to pay statutory maternity pay arose and the total number of weeks within the maternity pay period in which such a liability arose.

(4) The employer shall—

(a) return to the woman any maternity certificate provided by her in support of the notice referred to in paragraph (1); and

(b) comply with any requirements imposed by the preceding provisions of this regulation—

(i) in a case to which paragraph (2) applies, within 7 days of the decision being made, or, if earlier, within [[3]28 days] of the day the woman gave notice of her intended absence or of her confinement if that had occurred; or

(ii) in a case to which paragraph (3) refers, within 7 days of being notified of the woman's detention or sentence [[3]. . .].

(5) In this regulation, 'incapacity benefit' means [[2]incapacity benefit] or a severe disablement allowance.]

AMENDMENTS

1. Statutory Maternity Pay (General) Amendment Regulations 1990 (SI 1990/622), reg.7 (April 6, 1990).

2. Social Security (Incapacity Benefit) (Consequential and Transitional Amendments and Savings) Regulations 1995 (SI 1995/829), reg.18 (April 13, 1995).

3. Social Security, Statutory Maternity Pay and Statutory Sick Pay (Miscellaneous Amendments) Regulations 2002 (SI 2002/2690), reg.8 (November 24, 2002).

Records to be maintained by employers

4.48 **26.**—(1) Every employer shall maintain for 3 years after the end of the tax year in which the maternity pay period ends a record in relation to any woman who is or was an employee of his of—

(a) the date of the first day of absence from work wholly or partly because of pregnancy or confinement as notified by her and, if different, the date of the first day when such absence commenced;

(b) the weeks in that tax year in which statutory maternity pay was paid and the amount paid in each week; and

(c) any week in that tax year which was within her maternity pay period but for which no payment of statutory maternity pay was made to her and the reasons no payment was made.

(2) Except where he was not liable to make a payment of statutory maternity pay and subject to paragraphs (3) and (4), every employer shall retain for 3 years after the end of the tax year in which the maternity pay period ends any medical certificate or other evidence relating to the expected week of confinement, or as the case may be, the confinement which was provided to him by a woman who is or was an employee of his.

(3) Where an employer returns a medical certificate to an employee of his for the purpose of enabling her to make a claim for benefit under the 1975 Act, it shall be sufficient for the purposes of paragraph (2) if he retains a copy of that certificate.

(4) An employer shall not retain any certificate of birth provided to him as evidence of confinement by a woman who is or was an employee of his but shall retain a record of the date of birth.

DEFINITION

"the 1975 Act"—see reg.1(2).

PART VI

PAYMENT

Payment of statutory maternity pay

27. Payment of statutory maternity pay may be made in a like manner to payments of remuneration but shall not include payments in kind or by way of the provision of board or lodgings or of services or other facilities. **4.49**

Rounding to avoid fractional amounts

28. Where any payment of statutory maternity pay is made for any week [[1]at the earnings-related rate referred to in section 166(1) of the Contributions and Benefits Act] and the amount due for that week includes a fraction of a penny, the payment shall he rounded to the next whole number of pence. **4.50**

AMENDMENT

1. Social Security, Statutory Maternity Pay and Statutory Sick Pay (Miscellaneous Amendments) Regulations 2002 (SI 2002/2690), reg.9 (November 24, 2002).

Time when statutory maternity pay is to be paid

29.—(1) In this regulation, "payday" means a day on which it has been agreed, or it is the normal practice between an employer or former employer and a woman who is or was an employee of his, that payments by way of remuneration are to be made, or, where there is no such agreement or normal practice, the last day of a calendar month. **4.51**

(2) In any case where—

(a) a decision has been made by an adjudication officer, appeal tribunal or Commissioner in proceedings under [Social Security Administration Act 1992] as a result of which a woman is entitled to an amount of statutory maternity pay; and

(b) the time for bringing an appeal against the decision has expired and either—

(i) no such appeal has been brought; or

(ii) such an appeal has been brought and has been finally disposed of that amount of statutory maternity pay shall be paid within the time specified in paragraph (3).

(3) Subject to paragraphs (4) and (5), the employer or former employer shall pay the amount not later than the first pay day after—

(a) where an appeal has been brought, the day on which the employer or former employer receives notification that it has been finally disposed of,

(b) where leave to appeal has been refused and there remains no further opportunity to apply for leave, the day on which the employer or former employer receives notification of the refusal; and

(c) in any other case, the day on which the time for bringing an appeal expires.

(4) Subject to paragraph (5), where it is impracticable, in view of the employer's or former employer's methods of accounting for and paying remuneration, for the requirement of payment referred to in paragraph (3) to be met by the pay day referred to in that paragraph, it shall be met not later than the next following pay day.

(5) Where the employer or former employer would not have remunerated the woman for her work in the week in question as early as the pay day specified in paragraph (3) or (if it applies) paragraph (4), the requirement of payment shall be met on the first day on which the woman would have been remunerated for her work in that week.

Payments by the Secretary of State

4.52 **30.** Where the Secretary of State becomes liable in accordance with regulation 7 to make payments of statutory maternity pay to a woman, the first payment shall be made as soon as reasonably practicable after he becomes so liable, and payments thereafter shall be made at weekly intervals, by means of an instrument of payment or by such other means as appears to the Secretary of State to be appropriate in the circumstances of any particular case.

General Note

4.53 The functions under this regulation were transferred from the Secretary of State for Social Security to the Board of the Inland Revenue under s.1(2) of and Sch.2 to the Social Security (Transfer of Functions, etc.) Act 1999.

Persons unable to act

4.54 **31.**—(1) Where in the case of any woman—

(a) statutory maternity pay is payable to her or she is alleged to be entitled to it;

(b) she is unable for the time being to act;

(c) either—

(i) no receiver has been appointed by the Court of Protection with power to receive statutory maternity pay on her behalf, or

(ii) in Scotland, her estate is not being administrated by any tutor, curator or other guardian acting or appointed in terms of law,

the Secretary of State may, upon written application to him by a person who, if a natural person, is over the age of 18, appoint that person to exercise, on behalf of the woman any right to which she may be entitled under Part V of the 1986 Act and to deal on her behalf with any sums payable to her.

(2) Where the Secretary of State has made an appointment under paragraph (1)—

(a) he may at any time in his absolute discretion revoke it;
(b) the person appointed may resign his office after having given one month's notice in writing to the Secretary of State of his intention to do so; and
(c) the appointment shall terminate when the Secretary of State is notified that a receiver or other person to whom paragraph (1)(c) applies has been appointed.

(3) Anything required by Part V of the 1986 Act to be done by or to any woman who is unable to act may be done by or to the person appointed under this regulation to act on her behalf, and the receipt of the person so appointed shall be a good discharge to the woman's employer or former employer for any sum paid.

GENERAL NOTE

The functions under this regulation were transferred from the Secretary of State for Social Security to the Board of the Inland Revenue under s.1(2) of and Sch.2 to the Social Security (Transfer of Functions, etc.) Act 1999. **4.55**

PART VII

OFFENCES

[1Offences

32. Any person who, without reasonable excuse, contravenes or fails to comply with any provision contained in regulation 25, 25A, 26 or 29 shall be guilty of an offence under the Social Security Administration Act 1992.] **4.56**

AMENDMENT

1. Statutory Maternity Pay (General) and Statutory Sick Pay (General) (Amendment) Regulations 2001.

GENERAL NOTE

The penalty for such an offence is set out in s.113(3) of the SSAA 1992. **4.57**

Statutory Maternity Pay (Medical Evidence) Regulations 1987

(SI 1987/235) (as amended)

The Secretary of State for Social Services, in exercise of the powers conferred by sections 49 and 84(1) of and paragraph 6 of Schedule 4 to the Social Security Act 1986, and of all other powers enabling him in that behalf, by this instrument, which is made before the end of the period of 12 months from the **4.58** commencement of the enactments contained in the 1986 Act under which it is made, makes the following regulations:—

ARRANGEMENT OF REGULATIONS

Citation, commencement and interpretation

4.59 **1.**—(1) These regulations may be cited as the Statutory Maternity Pay (Medical Evidence) Regulations 1987 and shall come into force on 15th March 1987.

(2) In these regulations, unless the context otherwise requires—

"the Act" means the Social Security Act 1986;

"registered midwife" means a midwife who is registered as a midwife with the United Kingdom Central Council for Nursing, Midwifery and Health Visiting under the Nurses, Midwives and Health Visitors' Act 1979;

"doctor" means a registered medical practitioner;

"signature" means, in relation to any statement or certificate given in accordance with these regulations, the name by which the person giving that statement or certificate, as the case may be, is usually known (any name other than the surname being either in full or otherwise indicated) written by that person in his own handwriting; and "signed" shall be construed accordingly.

Evidence of pregnancy and confinement

4.60 **2.** The evidence as to pregnancy and the expected date of confinement which a woman is required to provide to a person who is liable to pay her statutory maternity pay shall be furnished in the form of a maternity certificate given by a doctor or by a registered midwife, not earlier than the beginning of the [[1]20th week] before the expected week of confinement, in accordance with the rules set out in Part I of the Schedule to these regulations—

(a) in the appropriate form as set out in Part II of that Schedule; or
(b) in a form substantially to the like effect with such variations as the circumstances may require.

AMENDMENT

1. Social Security (Medical Evidence) and Statutory Maternity Pay (Medical Evidence) (Amendment) Regulations 2001 (SI2001/2931), reg.3(2) (September 28, 2001).

DEFINITIONS

"doctor"—see reg.1(2).
"registered midwife"—see *ibid.*

SCHEDULE **Regulation 2**

PART I

RULES

1. In these rules any reference to a woman is a reference to the woman in respect of whom a maternity certificate is given in accordance with these rules. **4.61**

2. A maternity certificate shall be given by a doctor or registered midwife attending the woman and shall not be given by the woman herself.

3. The maternity certificate shall be on a form provided by the Secretary of State for the purpose and the wording shall be that set out in the appropriate part of the form specified in Part II of this Schedule.

4. Every maternity certificate shall be completed in ink or other indelible substance and shall contain the following particulars—

(a) the woman's name;

(b) the week in which the woman is expected to be confined or, if the maternity certificate is given after confinement, the date of that confinement and the date the confinement was expected to take place [[1]. . .];

(c) the date of the examination on which the maternity certificate is based;

(d) the date on which the maternity certificate is signed; and

(e) the address of the doctor or where the maternity certificate is signed by a [[1]registered midwife the personal identification number given to her by the United Kingdom Central Council for Nursing, Midwifery and Health Visiting ("UKCC") on her registration in Part 10 of the register maintained under section 10 of the Nurses, Midwives and Health Visitors Act 1979 and the expiry date of that registration].

and shall bear opposite the word "Signature", the signature of the person giving the maternity certificate written after there has been entered on the maternity certificate the woman's name and the expected date or, as the case may be, the date of the confinement.

5. After a maternity certificate has been given, no further maternity certificate based on the same examination shall be furnished other than a maternity certificate by way of replacement of an original which has been lost or mislaid, in which case it shall be clearly marked "duplicate".

[2PART II

FORM OF CERTIFICATE

4.62 **MATERNITY CERTIFICATE**

Please fill in this form in ink

Name of patient

Fill in this part if you are giving the certificate before the confinement.

Do not fill this in more [3 than 20 weeks] before the week the baby is expected.

I certify that I examined you on the date given below. In my opinion you can expect to have your baby in the week that includes

.... / .... / ....

Week means period of 7 days starting on a Sunday and ending on a Saturday. Fill in this part if you are giving the certificate after the confinement.

I certify that I attended you in connection with the birth which took place on .... / .... / .... when you were delivered of a child [ ] children.

In my opinion your baby was expected in the week that includes ..../ .... / ....

Date of examination ..... / ..... / ......

Date of signing .... / .... / ....

Signature

Registered midwives

Please give your UKCC Personal Identification Number and the expiry date of your registration with the UKCC.

Doctors

Please stamp your name and address here if the form has not been stamped by the [3 Health Authority] in whose medical list you are included.

AMENDMENTS

1. Social Security (Miscellaneous Provisions) Amendment Regulations 1991 (SI 1991/2284) reg.23 (November 1, 1991).

2. Social Security (Miscellaneous Provisions) Amendment Regulations 1991 (SI 1991/2284) reg.24 (November 1, 1991).

3. Social Security (Medical Evidence) and Statutory Maternity Pay (Medical Evidence) (Amendment) Regulations 2001 (SI2001/2931), reg.3(3) (September 28, 2001).

DEFINITIONS

"doctor"—see reg.1(2).
"registered midwife"—see *ibid.*
"signature"—see *ibid.*
"signed"—see *ibid.*

Statutory Maternity Pay (Persons Abroad and Mariners) Regulations 1987

(SI 1987/418) (as amended)

The Secretary of State for Social Services, in exercise of the powers conferred upon him by sections 80 and 84(1) of the Social Security Act 1986 and of all other powers enabling him in that behalf, by this instrument, which is made before the end of the period of 12 months from the commencement of the enactments under which it is made, makes the following Regulations:

ARRANGEMENT OF REGULATIONS

Citation, commencement and interpretation

1.—(1) These Regulations may be cited as the Statutory Maternity Pay (Persons Abroad and Mariners) Regulations 1987 and shall come into force on 6th April 1987. **4.64**

(2) In these Regulations, the "1986 Act" means the Social Security Act 1986;

[1"the Contributions and Benefits Act" means the Social Security Contributions and Benefits Act 1992, "the Contributions Regulations" means the Social Security (Contributions) Regulations 1979"], and the "General Regulations" means the Statutory Maternity Pay (General) Regulations 1986.

(3) Unless the context otherwise requires, any reference in these Regulations to a numbered regulation is a reference to the regulation

bearing that number in these Regulations and any reference in a regulation to a numbered paragraph is a reference to the paragraph of that regulation bearing that number.

AMENDMENT

1. Social Security Contributions, Statutory Maternity Pay and Statutory Sick Pay (Miscellaneous Amendments) Regulations 1996 (SI 1996/777), reg.4(2) (April 6, 1996).

GENERAL NOTE

4.65 These Regulations were made under the authority of what is now SSCBA 1992, s.170 and make special provision for statutory maternity pay as regards persons who are abroad or who are mariners. See also SMP (General) Regulations 1986 (SI 1986/1960), reg.17(3).

Persons in other member States—meaning of "employee"

4.66 **2.** Subject to regulation 3, a woman who is—

(a) gainfully employed in a member State other than the United Kingdom in such circumstances that if her employment were in Great Britain she would be an employee for the purposes of Part V of the 1986 Act or a woman treated as such an employee under regulation 17 of the General Regulations; and

(b) subject to the legislation of the United Kingdom under Council Regulation (EEC) No. 1408/71; notwithstanding that she is not employed in Great Britain, shall be treated as an employee for the purposes of Part V of the 1986 Act.

DEFINITIONS

"the 1986 Act"—see reg.1(2).
"the General Regulations"—see *ibid.*

[[1]Persons absent from Great Britain—meaning of "employee"

4.67 **2A.** Subject to regulations 2, 3 and 7(3), where a woman, while absent from Great Britain for any purpose, is gainfully employed by an employer who is liable to pay in respect of her secondary Class 1 contributions under section 6 of the Contributions and Benefits Act or regulation 120 of the Contributions Regulations, she shall be treated as an employee for the purposes of Part XII of the Contributions and Benefits Act.]

AMENDMENT

1. Social Security Contributions, Statutory Maternity Pay and Statutory Sick Pay (Miscellaneous Amendments) Regulations 1996 (SI 1996/777), reg.4(3) (April 6, 1996).

DEFINITIONS

"the Contributions and Benefits Act"—see reg.1(2).
"the Contributions Regulations"—see *ibid.*

Meaning of 'employee'—general

3. No woman who, by virtue of regulation 17 of the General Regulations, would be treated as not being an employee for the purposes of Part V of the 1986 Act if her employment were in Great Britain, shall be treated as an employee by virtue of these Regulations. **4.68**

DEFINITIONS

"the 1986 Act"—see reg.1(2).
"the General Regulations"—see *ibid.*

Women outside the European Community

4. [1. . .]

AMENDMENT

1. Social Security Contributions, Statutory Maternity Pay and Statutory Sick Pay (Miscellaneous Amendments) Regulations 1996 (SI 1996/777), reg.4(4) (April 6, 1996). **4.69**

Women who worked in the European Community

5.—(1) A woman who is an employee or treated as an employee under regulation 2 and who— **4.70**

(a) in the week immediately preceding the 14th week before the expected week of confinement was in employed earner's employment with an employer in Great Britain, and
(b) had in any week within the period of [126 weeks] immediately preceding that week been employed by the same employer in another member State,

shall be treated for the purposes of sections 46(2) and 48 of the 1986 Act as having been employed in employed earner's employment in those weeks in which she was so employed in the other member State.

(2) [1. . .]

AMENDMENTS

1. Social Security Contributions, Statutory Maternity Pay and Statutory Sick Pay (Miscellaneous Amendments) Regulations 1996 (SI 1996/777), reg.4(5) (April 6, 1996).

DEFINITION

"the 1986 Act"—see reg.1(2).

Time for compliance with Part V of the 1986 Act and Regulations

6. Where— **4.71**

(a) a woman is outside the United Kingdom;
(b) Part V of the 1986 Act or Regulations made under that Act or under Part III of the Social Security Act 1975 require any act to be done forthwith or on the happening of a certain event or within a specified time; and

(c) because the woman is outside the United Kingdom she or her employer cannot comply with the requirement;

the woman or the employer, as the case may be, shall be deemed to have complied with it if the act is performed as soon as reasonably practicable.

DEFINITION

"the 1986 Act"—see reg.1(2).

Mariners

4.72 **7.**—(1) In this regulation, "foreign-going ship", "home-trade ship" and "mariner" have the same meanings as in Case C of Part VIII of the Social Security (Contributions) Regulations 1979 and the expressions "ship" and "ship or vessel", except in paragraph (3), include hovercraft.

(2) Subject to regulation 3, a mariner engaged in employment on board a home-trade ship with an employer who has a place of business within the United Kingdom shall be treated as an employee for the purposes of Part V of the 1986 Act, notwithstanding that she may not be employed in Great Britain.

(3) A mariner who is engaged in employment—

(a) on a foreign-going ship; or

(b) on a home-trade ship with an employer who does not have a place of business within the United Kingdom, shall not be treated as an employee for the purposes of Part V of the 1986 Act, notwithstanding that she may have been employed in Great Britain.

DEFINITIONS

"foreign-going ship"—see para.(1).
"home-trade ship"—see *ibid.*
"mariner"—see *ibid.*
"ship"—see *ibid.*
"ship or vessel"—see *ibid.*

Continental shelf

4.73 **8.**—(1) In this regulation—

"designated area" means any area which may from time to time be designated by Order in Council under the Continental Shelf Act 1964 as an area within which the rights of the United Kingdom with respect to the seabed and subsoil and their natural resources may be exercised;

"prescribed area" means an area over which Norway or any member State (other than the United Kingdom) exercises sovereign rights for the purpose of exploring the seabed and subsoil and exploiting their natural resources, being an area outside the territorial seas of Norway or that member State or any other area which is from time to time specified under section 22(5) of the Oil and Gas (Enterprise) Act 1982;

"prescribed employment" means employment in a designated area or prescribed area in connection with any activity mentioned in section

23(2) of the Oil and Gas (Enterprise) Act 1982 in any designated area or in any prescribed area.

(2) Subject to regulation 3, a woman in prescribed employment shall be treated as an employee for the purposes of Part V of the 1986 Act notwithstanding that she may not be employed in Great Britain.

DEFINITIONS

"the 1986 Act"—see reg.1(2).
"designated area"—see para (2).
"prescribed area"—see *ibid.*
"prescribed employment"—see *ibid.*

Persons Abroad—maternity pay period not commencing or ending

9. [1. . .] 4.74

AMENDMENT

1. Social Security Contributions, Statutory Maternity Pay and Statutory Sick Pay (Miscellaneous Amendments) Regulations 1996 (SI 1996/777), reg.4(6) (April 6, 1996).

Statutory Maternity Pay (Compensation of Employers) and Miscellaneous Amendment Regulations 1994

(SI 1994/1882) (as amended)

The Secretary of State for Social Security, in exercise of powers conferred on him by sections 35(3), 167(1), (1A), (1B) and (4), 171(1) and 175(1) to (4) of the Social Security Contributions and Benefits Act 1992 and of all other powers enabling him in that behalf after agreement by the Social Security Advisory Committee that proposals in respect of regulation 9 should not be referred to it, hereby makes the following Regulations:

ARRANGEMENT OF REGULATIONS

Citation, commencement and interpretation

4.76 1.—(1) These Regulations may be cited as the Statutory Maternity Pay (Compensation of Employers) and Miscellaneous Amendment Regulations 1994 and regulations 2–7 shall have effect in relation to payments of statutory maternity pay due on or after 4th September 1994.

(2) This regulation and regulation 9 shall come into force on July 31, 1994.

(3) Regulations 2 to 8 shall come into force on 4th September 1994.

(4) In these Regulations—

[1"the Board" means the Commissioners of Inland Revenue;]

"the Contributions and Benefits Act" means the Social Security Contributions and Benefits Act 1992

"the Maternity Allowance Regulations" means the Social Security (Maternity Allowance) Regulations 1987;

[1. . .];

[1"contributions payments" has the same meaning as in section 167(8) of the Contributions and Benefits Act;]

[1"the Contributions Regulations" means the Social Security (Contributions) Regulations 2001;]

"employer" shall include a person who was previously an employer of a woman to whom a payment of statutory maternity pay was made, whether or not that person remains her employer at the date any deduction from contributions payments is made by him in accordance with regulation 5 or, as the case may be, any payment is received by him in accordance with regulation 6;

[1"the Employment Act" means the Employment Act 2002;]

"income tax month" means the period beginning on the 6th day of any calendar month and ending on the 5th day of the following calendar month;

[1. . .];

[1"income tax quarter" means, in any tax year, the period beginning on 6th April and ending on 5th July the period beginning on 6th July and ending on 5th October the period beginning on 6th October and ending on 5th January or the period beginning on 6th January and ending on 5th April;]

"qualifying day" means the first day in the week immediately preceding the 14th week before the expected week of confinement in which a woman who is or has been an employee first satisfies the conditions of entitlement to statutory maternity pay for which a deduction from a contributions payment is made by her employer in respect of a payment of statutory maternity pay made by him;

"qualifying tax year" means the tax year preceding the tax year in which the qualifying day in question falls.

[1"statutory adoption pay" means any payment under section 171ZL of the Contributions and Benefits Act;

"statutory paternity pay" means any payment under section 171ZA or 171ZB of the Contributions and Benefits Act;

"tax year" means the period of 12 months beginning on 6th April in any year;

"writing" includes writing delivered by means of electronic communications approved by directions issued by the Board pursuant to regulations made under section 132 of the Finance Act 1999;]

[[1](5) Any reference in these Regulations to the employees of any employer includes, where the context permits, a reference to his former employees.]

(6) [[1]. . .];

AMENDMENT

1. Statutory Maternity Pay (Compensation of Employers) Amendment Regulations 2003 (SI 2003/672), reg.2 (April 6, 2003). 4.77

GENERAL NOTE

These Regulations make provision for employers to be reimbursed for the cost of paying statutory maternity pay. The basic rule is that employers can recover 92 per cent of the total gross statutory maternity pay payments they make in any tax month (reg.4(a)). This is done by deducting such costs from tax payments, National Insurance contributions and other sums due to the Inland Revenue (reg.6). In certain circumstances employers may apply for advance funding from the Revenue in order to meet their statutory maternity pay liabilities (reg.5; but see reg.7A regarding overpayments of such sums). Small employers—currently defined as those whose total National Insurance contributions do not exceed £45,000 in the previous tax year (reg.2(1))—are entitled to 100 per cent of the cost of their statutory maternity pay payments (reg.4(b)) together with a further 4.5 per cent of the total statutory maternity pay paid (reg.3). This additional amount is intended to compensate small employers for the cost of employers' National Insurance contributions on statutory maternity pay.

Regulation 9 of these Regulations contained a miscellaneous amendment to reg.3(4) of the Social Security (Maternity Allowance) Regulations 1987 (SI 1987/416), which has itself subsequently been revoked, and so is not included in this volume (see Vol.I).

Meaning of "small employer"

2.—(1) Subject to the following provisions of this regulation, a small employer is an employer whose contributions payments for the qualifying tax year do not exceed [[1]£45,000]. 4.78

(2) For the purposes of this regulation, the amount of an employer's contributions payments shall be determined without regard to any deductions that may be made from them under any enactment or instrument.

(3) Where in the qualifying tax year an employer has made contributions payments in one or more, but less than 12, of the income tax months, the amount of his contributions payments for that tax year shall be estimated by adding together all of those payments, dividing the total amount by the number of those months in which he has made those payments and multiplying the resulting figure by 12.

(4) Where in the qualifying tax year an employer has made no contributions payments, but does have such payments in one or more income tax months which fall both—

(a) in the tax year in which the qualifying day falls; and
(b) before the qualifying day or, where there is more than one such day in that tax year, before the first of those days,

then the amount of his contributions payments for the qualifying tax year shall be estimated in accordance with paragraph (3) but as if the amount of the contributions payments falling in those months had fallen instead in the corresponding tax months in the qualifying tax year.

AMENDMENT

1. Statutory Maternity Pay (Compensation of Employers) Amendment Regulations 2004 (SI 2004/698), reg.2 (April 6, 2004).

DEFINITIONS

"contributions payments"—see reg.1(4).
"employer"—see *ibid.*
"qualifying day"—see *ibid.*
"qualifying tax year"—see *ibid.*

Determination of the amount of additional payment to which a small employer shall be entitled

4.79 **3.** In respect of any payment of statutory maternity pay [[1]made in the tax year commencing [[2] 6th April 2002], or in any subsequent tax year,] a small employer shall be [[3]entitled to recover an additional amount] being an amount equal to [[2]4.5 per cent.] of such payment, that percentage being the total amount of secondary Class 1 contributions estimated by the Secretary of State as to be paid in respect of statutory maternity pay by all employers in that year, expressed as a percentage of the total amount of statutory maternity pay estimated by him to be paid by all employers in that year.

AMENDMENTS

1. Statutory Maternity Pay (Compensation of Employers) Amendment Regulations 1995 (SI 1995/566), reg.2 (April 6, 1995).
2. Statutory Maternity Pay (Compensation of Employers) Amendment Regulations 2002 (SI 2002/225), reg.2 (April 6, 2002).
3. Statutory Maternity Pay (Compensation of Employers) Amendment Regulations 2003 (SI 2003/672), reg.3 (April 6, 2003).

DEFINITIONS

"employer"—see reg.1(4).
"payment of statutory maternity pay"—see *ibid.*
"small employer"—see reg.2(1).

[[1] Right of employers to prescribed amount

4.80 **4.** An employer who has made, or is liable to make, any payment of statutory maternity pay shall be entitled to recover—
(a) an amount equal to 92 per cent. of such payment; or
(b) if he is a small employer—
  (i) an amount equal to such payment; and
  (ii) an additional amount under regulation 3, in accordance with the provisions of these Regulations.]

AMENDMENT

1. Statutory Maternity Pay (Compensation of Employers) Amendment Regulations 2003 (SI 2003/672), reg.4 (April 6, 2003).

DEFINITIONS

"employer"—see reg.1(4).
"payment of statutory maternity pay"—see *ibid.*
"small employer"—see reg.2(1).

[1 Application for advance funding from the Board

5.—(1) If an employer is entitled to recover an amount determined in accordance with regulation 4 in respect of statutory maternity pay which he is required to pay to an employee or employees in any income tax month or income tax quarter and the amount exceeds the aggregate of— 4.81

(a) the total amount of tax which the employer is required to pay to the collector of taxes in respect of deductions from the emoluments of his employees in accordance with the Income Tax (Employments) Regulations 1993 for that income tax month or income tax quarter;
(b) the total amount of deductions made by the employer from the emoluments of his employees for that income tax month or income tax quarter in accordance with regulations made under section 22(5) of the Teaching and Higher Education Act 1998 or section 73B of the Education (Scotland) Act 1980 or in accordance with Article 3(5) of the Education (Student Support) (Northern Ireland) Order 1988;
(c) the total amount of contributions payments which the employer is required to pay to the collector of taxes in respect of the emoluments of his employees (whether by means of deduction or otherwise) in accordance with the Contributions Regulations for that income tax month or income tax quarter;
(d) the total amount of payments which the employer is required to pay to the collector of taxes in respect of deductions made on account of tax from payments to sub-contractors in accordance with section 559 of the Income and Corporation Taxes Act 1988 for that income tax month or income tax quarter; and
(e) the statutory paternity pay, statutory adoption pay and statutory maternity pay which the employer is required to pay to his employees in that income tax month or income tax quarter,

the employer may apply to the Board in accordance with paragraph (2) for funds ("advance funding") to pay that excess (or so much of it as remains outstanding) to the employee or employees.

(2) Where—

(a) the conditions in paragraph (1) are satisfied; or
(b) the employer considers that the conditions in paragraph (1) will be satisfied on the date of any subsequent payment of emoluments to one or more employees who are entitled to a payment of statutory maternity pay,

the employer may apply to the Board for advance funding on a form approved for that purpose by the Board.

(3) An application by an employer under paragraph (2) shall be for an amount not exceeding the amount of statutory maternity pay which the employer is entitled to recover in accordance with regulation 4 and which he is required to pay to an employee or employees for the income tax month or income tax quarter to which the payment of emoluments relates.]

AMENDMENT

1. Statutory Maternity Pay (Compensation of Employers) Amendment Regulations 2003 (SI 2003/672), reg.4 (April 6, 2003).

DEFINITIONS

"advance funding"—see para.(1).
"the Board"—see reg.1(4).
"the Contributions Regulations"—see *ibid.*
"contributions payments"—see *ibid.*
"employer"—see *ibid.*
"income tax month"—see *ibid.*
"income tax quarter"—see *ibid.*
"statutory adoption pay"—see *ibid.*
"statutory paternity pay"—see *ibid.*

[1 Deductions from payments to the Board

4.82 **6.** An employer who is entitled to recover an amount under regulation 4 may do so by making one or more deductions from the aggregate of the amounts specified in sub-paragraphs (a) to (e) of regulation 5(1), except where and insofar as—

(a) those amounts relate to earnings paid before the beginning of the income tax month or income tax quarter in which the payment of statutory maternity pay was made;
(b) those amounts are paid by him later than six years after the tax year in which the payment of statutory maternity pay was made;
(c) the employer has received advance funding from the Board in accordance with an application under regulation 5; or
(d) the employer has made a request in writing under regulation 5 that the amount which he is entitled to recover under regulation 4 be paid to him and he has not received notification by the Board that such request is refused.]

AMENDMENT

1. Statutory Maternity Pay (Compensation of Employers) Amendment Regulations 2003 (SI 2003/672), reg.4 (April 6, 2003).

DEFINITIONS

"advance funding"—reg.5(1).
"the Board"—see reg.1(4).
"employer"—see *ibid.*
"income tax month"—see *ibid.*
"income tax quarter"—see *ibid.*
"writing"—see *ibid.*

[1 Payments to employers by the Board

6A. If, in an income tax month or an income tax quarter— 4.83

(a) the total amount that the employer is entitled to deduct under regulation 6 is less than the amount which the employer is entitled to recover under regulation 4;

(b) the Board is satisfied that this is so; and

(c) the employer has so requested in writing, the Board shall pay to the employer the sum that the employer is unable to deduct under regulation 6.]

AMENDMENT

1. Statutory Maternity Pay (Compensation of Employers) Amendment Regulations 2003 (SI 2003/672), reg.4 (April 6, 2003).

DEFINITIONS

"the Board"—see reg.1(4).
"income tax month"—see *ibid.*
"income tax quarter"—see *ibid.*
"writing"—see *ibid.*

Date when certain contributions are to be treated as paid

7. Where an employer has made a deduction from a contributions payment under [1regulation 6], the date on which it is to be treated as having been paid for the purposes of [1section 167(6)] of the Contributions and Benefits Act (amount deducted to be treated as paid and received towards discharging liability in respect of Class 1 contributions) is— 4.84

(a) in a case where the deduction did not extinguish the contributions payment, the date on which the remainder of the contributions payment or, as the case may be, the first date on which any part of the remainder of the contributions payment was paid; and

(b) in a case where the deduction extinguished the contributions payment, the 14th day after the end of the income tax month during which there were paid the earnings in respect of which the contributions payment was payable.

AMENDMENT

1. Statutory Maternity Pay (Compensation of Employers) Amendment Regulations 2003 (SI 2003/672), reg.5 (April 6, 2003).

DEFINITIONS

"the Contributions and Benefits Act"—see reg.1(4).
"contributions payments"—see *ibid.*
"employer"—see *ibid.*
"income tax month"—see *ibid.*

[1 Overpayments

7A.—(1) Where advance funding has been provided to an employer in accordance with an application under regulation 5, the Board may 4.85

recover any part of it not used to pay statutory maternity pay ("the overpayment").

(2) An officer of the Board shall decide to the best of his judgement the amount of the overpayment and shall give notice in writing of his decision to the employer.

(3) A decision under paragraph (2) may be in respect of funding provided in accordance with regulation 5 for one or more income tax months or income tax quarters in a tax year—

(a) in respect of one or more classes of employees specified in a decision notice (where a notice does not name any individual employee); or

(b) in respect of one or more individual employees named in a decision notice.

(4) Subject to paragraphs (5), (6) or (7), Part 6 of the Taxes Management Act 1970 (collection and recovery) shall apply with any necessary modifications to a decision under this regulation as if the amount specified were an assessment and as if the amount set out in the notice were income tax charged on the employer.

(5) Where a decision under paragraph (2) relates to more than one employee, proceedings may be brought to recover the amount overpaid without distinguishing the sum to be repaid in respect of each employee and without specifying the employee in question.

(6) A decision to recover an amount made in accordance with this regulation shall give rise to one cause of action or matter of complaint for the purpose of proceedings under section 65, 66 or 67 of the Taxes Management Act 1970.

(7) Nothing in paragraph (5) shall prevent separate proceedings being brought for the recovery of any amount which the employer is liable to repay in respect of each employee to whom the decision relates.]

DEFINITIONS

"the Board"—see reg.1(4).
"the overpayment"—see para.(1).
"advance funding"—see reg.5(1).
"employee"—see reg.1(5).
"employer"—see reg.1(4).
"income tax month"—see *ibid.*
"income tax quarter"—see *ibid.*
"tax year"—see *ibid.*
"writing"—see *ibid.*

Revocation

4.86 **8.** The Statutory Maternity Pay (Compensation of Employers) Regulations 1987 are hereby revoked.

Statutory Maternity Pay (General) (Modification and Amendment) Regulations 2000

(SI 2000/2883)

The Secretary of State for Social Security, in exercise of the powers conferred on him by sections 164(4), (9)(e) and (10), 165(1) and (3), 171(1) and 175(1) to (4) of the Social Security Contributions and Benefits Act 1992 and of all other powers enabling him in that behalf, after agreement by the Social Security Advisory Committee that proposals to make these Regulations should not be referred to it, hereby makes the following Regulations:

ARRANGEMENT OF REGULATIONS

Citation, commencement and interpretation

1.—(1) These Regulations may be cited as the Statutory Maternity Pay (General) (Modification and Amendment) Regulations 2000 and shall come into force on 17th November 2000. 4.88

(2) In these Regulations—

"the Contributions and Benefits Act" means the Social Security Contributions and Benefits Act 1992;

"the Statutory Maternity Pay Regulations" means the Statutory Maternity Pay (General) Regulations 1986.

Modification of s.164(2)(a) of the Contributions and Benefits Act

2. Subject to regulation 4, in relation to a woman who is dismissed, or whose employment is otherwise terminated without her consent, after the beginning of the week immediately preceding the 14th week before the expected week of confinement, section 164(2)(a) of the Contributions and Benefits Act (conditions of entitlement to statutory maternity pay) shall be modified and have effect so that the words, ", wholly or partly because of pregnancy or confinement" shall not apply. 4.89

DEFINITION

"Contributions and Benefits Act"—see reg.1(2).

GENERAL NOTE

In order to qualify for statutory maternity pay, the general rule under SSCBA 1992, s.164(2)(a) is that the claimant must have been continuously employed in an employed earner's employment for 26 weeks up to the 15th week before the expected week of confinement but has then ceased to work for the employer 4.90

"wholly or partly because of pregnancy or confinement". This latter requirement caused problems for women who were dismissed for some other reason (*e.g.* redundancy). These Regulations were therefore enacted in 2000 (but with effect from 4th March 2001: reg.4) so as to extend the right to statutory maternity pay to all women, unless they left their job voluntarily.

Amendment of the Statutory Maternity Pay Regulations

4.91 **3.** . . .

GENERAL NOTE

4.92 The amendments made by reg.3 have been incorporated into the text of the Statutory Maternity Pay (General) Regulations 1986 (SI 1986/1960) in this volume.

Transitional provision

4.93 **4.** In relation to a woman whose expected week of confinement begins before 4th March 2001, the Contributions and Benefits Act and the Statutory Maternity Pay Regulations shall have effect as if these Regulations were not in force.

DEFINITIONS

"Contributions and Benefits Act"—see reg.1(2).
"Statutory Maternity Pay Regulations"—see *ibid.*

PART V

STATUTORY PATERNITY PAY AND STATUTORY ADOPTION PAY

Statutory Paternity Pay and Statutory Adoption Pay (Weekly Rates) Regulations 2002

(SI 2002/2818)

Whereas a draft of the following Regulations was laid before Parliament in accordance with section 176(1)(a) of the Social Security Contributions and Benefits Act 1992 and approved by a resolution of each House of Parliament:

Now, therefore, the Secretary of State, in exercise of the powers conferred on her by sections 171ZE(1) and 171ZN(1) of the Social Security Contributions and Benefits Act 1992 and section 5(1)(l) of the Social Security Administration Act 1992, by this instrument, which contains only provision made by virtue of sections 2, 4 and 53 of and paragraphs 8 and 11 of Schedule 7 to the Employment Act 2002 and is made before the end of the period of 6 months from the coming into force of those enactments, hereby makes the following Regulations—

ARRANGEMENT OF REGULATIONS

Citation and commencement

1.—These Regulations may be cited as the Statutory Paternity Pay and Statutory Adoption Pay (Weekly Rates) Regulations and shall come into force on 8th December 2002. 5.2

GENERAL NOTE

These Regulations specify the weekly rate of statutory paternity pay and statutory adoption pay. Statutory paternity pay is set at £75 a week where the paternity pay period began before April 6, 2003. In the current year, Statutory paternity pay is the lower of £102.80 per week or 90 per cent of the employee's normal weekly earnings where the paternity pay period starts after that date (reg.2). Statutory adoption pay is set at the lower of £102.80 per week or 90 per cent of the employee's normal weekly earnings (reg.3). Fractional amounts are rounded in accordance with reg.4. 5.3

Weekly rate of payment of statutory paternity pay

2.—(1) Where the paternity pay period begins before 6th April 2003, the weekly rate payable shall be £75. 5.4

(2) Where the paternity pay period begins on or after 6th April 2003, the weekly rate payable shall be the smaller of the following two amounts—

(a) [[1]£102.80];
(b) 90 per cent of the normal weekly earnings of the person claiming statutory paternity pay, determined in accordance with regulations 39 and 40 of the Statutory Paternity Pay and Statutory Adoption Pay (General) Regulations 2002.

AMENDMENT

1. Social Security Benefits Up-rating Order 2004 (SI 2004/552), art.11(a) (April 4, 2004).

Weekly rate of payment of statutory adoption pay

5.5 **3.** The weekly rate of payment of statutory adoption pay shall be the smaller of the following two amounts—

(a) [[1]£102.80];
(b) 90 per cent of the normal weekly earnings of the person claiming statutory adoption pay, determined in accordance with regulations 39 and 40 of the Statutory Paternity Pay and Statutory Adoption Pay (General) Regulations 2002.

AMENDMENT

1. Social Security Benefits Up-rating Order 2004 (SI 2004/552), art.11(b) (April 4, 2004).

Rounding of fractional amounts

5.6 **4.** Where any payment of statutory paternity pay is at the weekly rate specified in regulation 2(2)(b), or any payment of statutory adoption pay is at the weekly rate specified in regulation 3(b), and that amount includes a fraction of a penny, the payment shall be rounded up to the next whole number of pence.

Statutory Paternity Pay and Statutory Adoption Pay (National Health Service Employees) Regulations 2002

(SI 2002/2819)

The Secretary of State, in exercise of the powers conferred on her by virtue of sections 171ZJ(9) and (10) and 171ZS(9) and (10) of the Social Security Contributions and Benefits Act 1992 and with the concurrence of the Commissioners of Inland Revenue by this instrument, which contains only provision made by virtue of sections 2 and 4 of the Employment Act 2002 and is made before the end of the period of 6 months from the coming into force of those enactments hereby makes the following Regulations—

ARRANGEMENT OF SECTIONS

5.7 1. Citation, commencement and interpretation.
2. Treatment of more than one contract of employment as one contract.

Citation, commencement and interpretation

1.—(1) These Regulations may be cited as the Statutory Paternity Pay and Statutory Adoption Pay (National Health Service Employees) Regulations 2002 and shall come into force on 8th December 2002. 5.8

(2) In these Regulations—

"the Act" means the Social Security Contributions and Benefits Act 1992;

"the 1977 Act" means the National Health Service Act 1977;

"the 1978 Act" means the National Health Service (Scotland) Act 1978;

"the 1990 Act" means the National Health Service and Community Care Act 1990;

"the 2002 Act" means the National Health Service Reform and Health Care Professions Act 2002;

"Health Authority" means, in relation to Wales, a Health Authority established under section 8 of the 1977 Act and in relation to Scotland means a Health Board established under section 2 of the 1978 Act;

"Primary Care Trust" means a Primary Care Trust established under section 16A of the 1977 Act;

"statutory adoption pay period" means the period prescribed under section 171ZN(2) of the Act as the period in respect of which statutory adoption pay is payable to a person;

"statutory paternity pay period" means the period determined in accordance with section 171ZE(2) of the Act as the period in respect of which statutory paternity pay is payable to a person;

"Strategic Health Authority" means a Strategic Health Authority established under section 8 of the 1977 Act.

General Note

These Regulations, made under the authority of SSCBA 1992, ss.171ZJ(9) and (10) and 171ZS(9) and (10), make special provision for those NHS workers who are employed under two or more separate contracts of employment with different NHS Trusts. The regulations enable them to elect to have such contracts treated as one contract for the purposes of entitlement to statutory paternity pay and statutory adoption pay. 5.9

Treatment of more than one contract of employment as one contract

2. Where, in consequence of the establishment of one or more National Health Service Trusts under section 5 of the 1990 Act or section 12A of the 1978 Act, a person's contract of employment is treated by a scheme under section 6 of the 1990 Act or section 12B of the 1978 Act as divided so as to constitute two or more contracts, or where an order under 5.10

paragraph 23(1) of Schedule 5A to the 1977 Act provides that a person's contract is so divided, he may elect for all those contracts to be treated as one contract for the purposes of Parts 12ZA and 12ZB of the Act.

DEFINITIONS

"the Act"—see reg.1(2).
"the 1977 Act"—see *ibid.*
"the 1978 Act"—see *ibid.*
"the 1990 Act"—see *ibid.*

Notification of election

5.11 **3.** A person who makes an election under regulation 2 above shall give written notification of that election to each of his employers under the two or more contracts of employment mentioned in that regulation at least 28 days before the beginning of the statutory paternity pay period or adoption pay period or, if in the particular circumstances that is not practicable, as soon as is reasonably practicable.

DEFINITIONS

"statutory adoption pay period"—see reg.1(2).
"statutory paternity pay period"—see *ibid.*

Provision of information

5.12 **4.** A person who makes an election under regulation 2 above shall, within 28 days of giving notification of that election or, if in the particular circumstances that is not practicable, as soon as is reasonably practicable thereafter, provide each of his employers under the two or more contracts of employment mentioned in that regulation with the following information—

(a) the name and address of each of those employers;
(b) the date his employment with each of those employers commenced; and
(c) details of his normal weekly earnings during the relevant period from each employer, and for this purpose the expressions "normal weekly earnings" and "relevant period" have the same meanings as they have for the purposes of Parts 12ZA and 12ZB of the Act.

DEFINITIONS

"normal weekly earnings"—para.(c) and SSCBA 1992, ss.171ZJ(6) and 171ZS(6) and Statutory Paternity Pay and Statutory Adoption Pay (General) Regulations 2002 (SI 2002/2822), reg.40.
"relevant period"—para.(c) and SSCBA 1992, ss.171ZJ(7) and 171ZS(7) and Statutory Paternity Pay and Statutory Adoption Pay (General) Regulations 2002 (SI 2002/2822), reg.40(3).

Treatment of two or more employers as one

5.13 **5.** The employer to be regarded for the purposes of statutory paternity pay or statutory adoption pay as the employer under the one contract where two or more contracts are treated as one in accordance with regulation 2 above shall be—

(a) in the case of a person whose contract of employment is treated by a scheme under section 6 of the 1990 Act or section 12B of the 1978 Act as divided—

(i) the Health Authority or Primary Care Trust from which the person was transferred in a case where any one of the contracts of employment is with that Health Authority or Primary Care Trust; or

(ii) the first NHS trust to which a contract of employment was transferred in a case where none of the contracts of employment is with the Health Authority or Primary Care Trust; or

(b) in the case of a person whose contract of employment is divided as provided by an order under paragraph 23(1) of Schedule 5A to the 1977 Act—

(i) the Strategic Health Authority, NHS trust or Primary Care Trust from which the person was transferred, in a case where any one of the contracts of employment is with that body; or

(ii) the first Primary Care Trust to which a contract of employment was transferred in a case where none of the contracts of employment is with the body from which he was transferred.

DEFINITIONS

"the 1977 Act"—see reg.1(2).
"the 1978 Act"—see *ibid.*
"Health Authority"—see *ibid.*
"Primary Care Trust"—see *ibid.*
"Strategic Health Authority"—see *ibid.*

Time for which an election is to have effect

6. An election made under regulation 2 shall lapse at the end of the statutory paternity pay period or, as the case may be, the adoption pay period. 5.14

DEFINITIONS

"statutory adoption pay period"—see reg.1(2).
"statutory paternity pay period"—see *ibid.*

Statutory Paternity Pay and Statutory Adoption Pay (Administration) Regulations 2002

(SI 2002/2820)

The Secretary of State, in exercise of the powers conferred on her by sections 7(1), (2)(a) and (b), (4)(a), (b) and (c) and (5), 8(1) and (2)(a), (b) and (c), 10(1) and (2) and 51(1) of the Employment Act 2002 and sections 8(1)(f) and (ga) and 25 of the Social Security Contributions (Transfer of Functions, etc.) Act 1999 and with the concurrence of the Commissioners of Inland Revenue, hereby makes the following Regulations—

ARRANGEMENT OF SECTIONS

Citation and commencement

5.16 **1.** These Regulations may be cited as the Statutory Paternity Pay and Statutory Adoption Pay (Administration) Regulations 2002 and shall come into force on 8th December 2002.

GENERAL NOTE

5.17 These Regulations provide for employers to be reimbursed for the cost of making payments of statutory paternity pay and statutory adoption pay. They are therefore modelled in part on the Statutory Maternity Pay (Compensation of Employers) and Miscellaneous Amendment Regulations 1994 (SI 1994/1882). As with the regulations governing statutory maternity pay, they provide for employers to claim back 92 per cent of the total costs of their statutory paternity pay and statutory adoption pay payments, or 100 per cent in the case of small employers, with a small additional element in the latter instance (reg.3). Employers receive such monies by making deductions from income tax, National Insurance contributions and other payments that would otherwise be due to the Revenue (reg.4). There is provision for the Revenue to make a direct payment to an employer where such deductions would otherwise be insufficient (reg.6). The Board also has the power to recover overpayments from employers (reg.8).

These Regulations also require employers to maintain relevant records (reg.9) and to permit officers of the Board to inspect such records (reg.10). Furthermore, employers who decide that they have no liability to pay statutory paternity pay or statutory adoption pay to an employee or ex-employee must give any such person details of that decision and the reasons for it (reg.11). Any question relating to entitlement to statutory paternity pay or statutory adoption pay may be submitted by the employee concerned to an officer of the Board for decision (regs 12 and 13). The Board has information-gathering powers as set out in reg.14.

Interpretation

2.—(1) In these Regulations— 5.18

"adopter", in relation to a child, means a person with whom the child is matched for adoption;

"adoption leave" means leave under section 75A of the Employment Rights Act 1996;

"adoption pay period" means the period prescribed under section 171ZN(2) of the Contributions and Benefits Act as the period in respect of which statutory adoption pay is payable to a person;

"the Board" means the Commissioners of Inland Revenue;

"the Contributions and Benefits Act" means the Social Security Contributions and Benefits Act 1992;

"contributions payments" has the same meaning as in section 7 of the Employment Act;

"the Contributions Regulations" means the Social Security (Contributions) Regulations 2001;

"the Employment Act" means the Employment Act 2002;

"income tax month" means the period beginning on the 6th day of any calendar month and ending on the 5th day of the following calendar month;

"income tax quarter" means the period beginning on the 6th day of April and ending on the 5th day of July, the period beginning on the 6th day of July and ending on the 5th day of October, the period beginning on the 6th day of October and ending on the 5th day of January or the period beginning on the sixth day of January and ending on the 5th day of April;

"paternity leave" means leave under section 80A or section 80B of the Employment Rights Act 1996;

"paternity pay period" means the period determined in accordance with section 171ZE(2) of the Contributions and Benefits Act as the period in respect of which statutory paternity pay is payable to a person;

"statutory adoption pay" means any payment under section 171ZL of the Contributions and Benefits Act;

"statutory paternity pay" means any payment under section 171ZA or section 171ZB of the Contributions and Benefits Act;

"tax year" means the 12 months beginning with 6th April in any year;

"writing" includes writing delivered by means of electronic communications approved by directions issued by the Board pursuant to regulations under section 132 of the Finance Act 1999;

(2) Any reference in these Regulations to the employees of an employer includes former employees of his.

Funding of employers' liabilities to make payments of statutory paternity or statutory adoption pay

3.—(1) An employer who has made any payment of statutory paternity pay or statutory adoption pay shall be entitled— 5.19

(a) to an amount equal to 92 per cent of such payment; or

(b) if the payment qualifies for small employer's relief by virtue of section 7(3) of the Employment Act—

(i) to an amount equal to such payment; and
(ii) to an additional payment equal to the amount to which the employer would have been entitled under section 167(2)(b) of the Contributions and Benefits Act had the payment been a payment of statutory maternity pay.

(2) The employer shall be entitled in either case (a) or case (b) to apply for advance funding in respect of such payment in accordance with regulation 4, or to deduct it in accordance with regulation 5 from amounts otherwise payable by him.

DEFINITIONS

"Contributions and Benefits Act"—see reg.2(1).
"Employment Act"—see *ibid.*
"statutory adoption pay"—see *ibid.*
"statutory paternity pay"—see *ibid.*

Application for funding from the Board

5.20 **4.**—(1) If an employer is entitled to a payment determined in accordance with regulation 3 in respect of statutory paternity pay or statutory adoption pay which he is required to pay to an employee or employees for an income tax month or income tax quarter, and the payment exceeds the aggregate of—

(a) the total amount of tax which the employer is required to pay to the collector of taxes in respect of the deductions from the emoluments of his employees in accordance with the Income Tax (Employments) Regulations 1993 for the same income tax month or income tax quarter;
(b) the total amount of the deductions made by the employer from the emoluments of his employees for the same income tax month or income tax quarter in accordance with regulations under section 22(5) of the Teaching and Higher Education Act 1998 or section 73B of the Education (Scotland) Act 1980 or in accordance with article 3(5) of the Education (Student Support) (Northern Ireland) Order 1998;
(c) the total amount of contributions payments which the employer is required to pay to the collector of taxes in respect of the emoluments of his employees (whether by means of deduction or otherwise) in accordance with the Contributions Regulations for the same income tax month or income tax quarter; and
(d) the total amount of payments which the employer is required to pay to the collector of taxes in respect of the deductions made on account of tax from payments to sub-contractors in accordance with section 559 of the Income and Corporation Taxes Act 1988 for the same income tax month or income tax quarter,

the employer may apply to the Board in accordance with paragraph (2) for funds to pay the statutory paternity pay or statutory adoption pay (or so much of it as remains outstanding) to the employee or employees.

(2) Where—
(a) the condition in paragraph (1) is satisfied; or

(b) the employer considers that the condition in paragraph (1) will be satisfied on the date of any subsequent payment of emoluments to one or more employees who are entitled to payment of statutory paternity pay or statutory adoption pay,

the employer may apply to the Board for funding in a form approved for that purpose by the Board.

(3) An application by an employer under paragraph (2) shall be for an amount up to, but not exceeding, the amount of the payment to which the employer is entitled in accordance with regulation 3 in respect of statutory paternity pay and statutory adoption pay which he is required to pay to an employee or employees for the income tax month or income tax quarter to which the payment of emoluments relates.

DEFINITIONS

"the Board"—see reg.2(1).
"contributions payments"—see *ibid.*
"the Contributions Regulations"—see *ibid.*
"income tax month"—see *ibid.*
"income tax quarter"—see *ibid.*
"statutory adoption pay"—see *ibid.*
"statutory paternity pay"—see *ibid.*

Deductions from payments to the Board

5. An employer who is entitled to a payment determined in accordance with regulation 3 may recover such payment by making one or more deductions from the aggregate of the amounts specified in subparagraphs (a) to (d) of regulation 4(1) except where and in so far as— 5.21

(a) those amounts relate to earnings paid before the beginning of the income tax month or income tax quarter in which the payment of statutory paternity pay or statutory adoption pay was made;
(b) those amounts are paid by him later than six years after the end of the tax year in which the payment of statutory paternity pay or statutory adoption pay was made;
(c) the employer has received payment from the Board under regulation 4; or
(d) the employer has made a request in writing under regulation 4 that the payment to which he is entitled in accordance with regulation 3 be paid to him and he has not received notification by the Board that the request is refused.

DEFINITIONS

"the Board"—see reg.2(1).
"income tax month"—see *ibid.*
"income tax quarter"—see *ibid.*
"statutory adoption pay"—see *ibid.*
"statutory paternity pay"—see *ibid.*
"tax year"—see *ibid.*
"writing"—see *ibid.*

Payments to employers by the Board

5.22 **6.** If the total amount which an employer is or would otherwise be entitled to deduct under regulation 5 is less than the payment to which the employer is entitled in accordance with regulation 3 in an income tax month or income tax quarter, and the Board are satisfied that this is so, then provided that the employer has in writing requested them to do so, the Board shall pay the employer such amount as the employer was unable to deduct.

DEFINITIONS

"the Board"—see reg.2(1).
"income tax month"—see *ibid.*
"income tax quarter"—see *ibid.*
"writing"—see *ibid.*

Date when certain contributions are to be treated as paid

5.23 **7.** Where an employer has made a deduction from a contributions payment under regulation 5, the date on which it is to be treated as having been paid for the purposes of section 7(5) of the Employment Act (when amount deducted from contributions payment to be treated as paid and received by the Board) is—

(a) in a case where the deduction did not extinguish the contributions payment, the date on which the remainder of the contributions payment or, as the case may be, the first date on which any part of the remainder of the contributions payment was paid; and
(b) in a case where the deduction extinguished the contributions payment, the 14th day after the end of the income tax month or income tax quarter during which there were paid the earnings in respect of which the contributions payment was payable.

DEFINITIONS

"the Board"—see reg.2(1).
"contributions payments"—see *ibid.*
"Employment Act"—see *ibid.*
"income tax month"—see *ibid.*
"income tax quarter"—see *ibid.*

Overpayments

5.24 **8.**—(1) This regulation applies where funds have been provided to the employer pursuant to regulation 4 in respect of one or more employees and it appears to an officer of the Board that the employer has not used the whole or part of those funds to pay statutory paternity pay or statutory adoption pay.

(2) An officer of the Board shall decide to the best of his judgement the amount of funds provided pursuant to regulation 4 and not used to pay statutory paternity pay or statutory adoption pay and shall serve notice in writing of his decision on the employer.

(3) A decision under this regulation may cover funds provided pursuant to regulation 4—

(a) for any one income tax month or income tax quarter, or more than one income tax month or income tax quarter, in a tax year; and
(b) in respect of a class or classes of employees specified in the decision notice (without naming the individual employees), or in respect of one or more employees named in the decision notice.

(4) Subject to the following provisions of this regulation, Part 6 of the Taxes Management Act 1970 (collection and recovery) shall apply with any necessary modifications to a decision under this regulation as if it were an assessment and as if the amount of funds determined were income tax charged on the employer.

(5) Where an amount of funds determined under this regulation relates to more than one employee, proceedings may be brought for the recovery of that amount without distinguishing the amounts making up that sum which the employer is liable to repay in respect of each employee and without specifying the employee in question, and the amount determined under this regulation shall be one cause of action or one matter of complaint for the purposes of proceedings under section 65, 66 or 67 of the Taxes Management Act 1970.

(6) Nothing in paragraph (5) prevents the bringing of separate proceedings for the recovery of any amount which the employer is liable to repay in respect of each employee.

DEFINITIONS

"the Board"—see reg.2(1).
"income tax month"—see *ibid.*
"income tax quarter"—see *ibid.*
"statutory adoption pay"—see *ibid.*
"statutory paternity pay"—see *ibid.*
"tax year"—see *ibid.*
"writing"—see *ibid.*

Records to be maintained by employers

9. Every employer shall maintain for three years after the end of a tax year in which he made payments of statutory paternity pay or statutory adoption pay to any employee of his a record of— 5.25
(a) if the employee's paternity pay period or adoption pay period began in that year—
(i) the date on which that period began; and
(ii) the evidence of entitlement to statutory paternity pay or statutory adoption pay provided by the employee pursuant to regulations made under section 171ZC(3)(c) or section 171ZL(8)(c) of the Contributions and Benefits Act;
(b) the weeks in that tax year in which statutory paternity pay or statutory adoption pay was paid to the employee and the amount paid in each week; and
(c) any week in that tax year which was within the employee's paternity pay period or adoption pay period but for which no payment of statutory paternity pay or statutory adoption pay was made to him and the reason no payment was made.

DEFINITIONS

"adoption pay period"—see reg.2(1).
"the Contributions and Benefits Act"—see *ibid.*
"paternity pay period"—see *ibid.*
"statutory adoption pay"—see *ibid.*
"statutory paternity pay"—see *ibid.*
"tax year"—see *ibid.*

Inspection of employers' records

5.26 **10.**—(1) Every employer, whenever called upon to do so by any authorised officer of the Board, shall produce the documents and records specified in paragraph (2) to that officer for inspection, at such time as that officer may reasonably require, at the prescribed place.

(2) The documents and records specified in this paragraph are—

(a) all wages sheets, deductions working sheets, records kept in accordance with regulation 9 and other documents and records whatsoever relating to the calculation or payment of statutory paternity pay or statutory adoption pay to his employees in respect of the years specified by such officer; or

(b) such of those wages sheets, deductions working sheets, or other documents and records as may be specified by the authorised officer.

(3) The "prescribed place" mentioned in paragraph (1) means—

(a) such place in Great Britain as the employer and the authorised officer may agree upon; or

(b) in default of such agreement, the place in Great Britain at which the documents and records referred to in paragraph (2)(a) are normally kept; or

(c) in default of such agreement and if there is no such place as is referred to in sub-paragraph (b) above, the employer's principal place of business in Great Britain.

(4) The authorised officer may—

(a) take copies of, or make extracts from, any document or record produced to him for inspection in accordance with paragraph (1);

(b) remove any document or record so produced if it appears to him to be necessary to do so, at a reasonable time and for a reasonable period.

(5) Where any document or record is removed in accordance with paragraph (4)(b), the authorised officer shall provide—

(a) a receipt for the document or record so removed; and

(b) a copy of the document or record, free of charge, within seven days, to the person by whom it was produced or caused to be produced where the document or record is reasonably required for the proper conduct of a business.

(6) Where a lien is claimed on a document produced in accordance with paragraph (1), the removal of the document under paragraph (4)(b) shall not be regarded as breaking the lien.

(7) Where records are maintained by computer, the person required to make them available for inspection shall provide the authorised officer with all facilities necessary for obtaining information from them.

DEFINITIONS

"the Board"—see reg.2(1).
"prescribed place"—see para.(3).
"statutory adoption pay"—see reg.2(1).
"statutory paternity pay"—see *ibid.*

Provision of information relating to entitlement to statutory paternity pay or statutory adoption pay

11.—(1) Where an employer who has been given evidence of entitlement to statutory paternity pay or statutory adoption pay pursuant to regulations made under section 171ZC(3)(c) or section 171ZL(8)(c) of the Contributions and Benefits Act by a person who is or has been an employee decides that he has no liability to make payments of statutory paternity pay or statutory adoption pay to the employee, the employer shall furnish the employee with details of the decision and the reasons for it. 5.27

(2) Where an employer who has been given such evidence of entitlement to statutory adoption pay has made one or more payments of statutory adoption pay to the employee but decides, before the end of the adoption pay period, that he has no liability to make further payments to the employee because he has been detained in legal custody or sentenced to a term of imprisonment which was not suspended, the employer shall furnish the employee with—

(a) details of his decision and the reasons for it; and
(b) details of the last week in respect of which a liability to pay statutory adoption pay arose and the total number of weeks within the adoption pay period in which such a liability arose.

(3) The employer shall—

(a) return to the employee any evidence provided by him as referred to in paragraph (1) or (2); and
(b) comply with the requirements imposed by paragraph (1) within 28 days of—
   (i) in the case of entitlement to statutory paternity pay under section 171ZA(1) of the Contributions and Benefits Act, the day the employee gave notice of his intended absence or the end of the fifteenth week before the expected week of birth, whichever is the later; or
   (ii) in the case of entitlement to statutory paternity pay under section 171ZB(1) or of statutory adoption pay under section 171ZL(1) of the Contributions and Benefits Act, the end of the seven-day period that starts on the date on which the adopter is notified of having been matched with the child;
(c) comply with the requirements imposed by paragraph (2) within seven days of being notified of the employee's detention or sentence.

(4) For the purposes of paragraph (3)(b)(ii), an adopter is notified of having been matched with a child on the date on which he receives notification, under regulation 11(2) of the Adoption Agencies Regulations 1983 or regulation 12(3) of the Adoption Agencies (Scotland) Regulations 1996

that an adoption agency has decided that he would be a suitable adoptive parent for the child.

DEFINITIONS

"adopter"—see reg.2(1).
"adoption pay period"—see *ibid.*
"the Contributions and Benefits Act"—see *ibid.*
"statutory adoption pay"—see *ibid.*
"statutory paternity pay"—see *ibid.*

Application for the determination of any issue arising as to, or in connection with, entitlement to statutory paternity pay or statutory adoption pay

5.28 **12.**—(1) An application for the determination of any issue arising as to, or in connection with, entitlement to statutory paternity pay or statutory adoption pay may be submitted to an officer of the Board by the employee concerned.

(2) Such an issue shall be decided by an officer of the Board only on the basis of such an application or on his own initiative.

DEFINITIONS

"the Board"—see reg.2(1).
"statutory adoption pay"—see *ibid.*
"statutory paternity pay"—see *ibid.*

Applications in connection with statutory paternity pay or statutory adoption pay

5.29 **13.**—(1) An application for the determination of any issue referred to in regulation 12 shall be made in a form approved for the purpose by the Board.

(2) Where such an application is made by an employee, it shall—

(a) be made to an officer of the Board within six months of the earliest day in respect of which entitlement to statutory paternity pay or statutory adoption pay is in issue;
(b) state the period in respect of which entitlement to statutory paternity pay or statutory adoption pay is in issue; and
(c) state the grounds (if any) on which the applicant's employer had denied liability for statutory paternity pay or statutory adoption pay in respect of the period specified in the application.

DEFINITIONS

"the Board"—see reg.2(1).
"statutory adoption pay"—see *ibid.*
"statutory paternity pay"—see *ibid.*

Provision of information

5.30 **14.**—(1) Any person specified in paragraph (2) shall, where information or documents are reasonably required from him to ascertain whether statutory paternity pay or statutory adoption pay is or was payable, furnish that information or those documents within 30 days of receiving a notification froman officer of the Board requesting such information or documents.

(2) The requirement to provide such information or documents applies to—

(a) any person claiming to be entitled to statutory paternity pay or statutory adoption pay;
(b) any person who is, or has been, the spouse or partner of such a person as is specified in paragraph (a);
(c) any person who is, or has been, an employer of such a person as is specified in paragraph (a);
(d) any person carrying on an agency or other business for the introduction or supply to persons requiring them of persons available to do work or to perform services; and
(e) any person who is a servant or agent of any such person as is specified in paragraphs (a) to (d).

DEFINITIONS

"the Board"—see reg.2(1).
"statutory adoption pay"—see *ibid.*
"statutory paternity pay"—see *ibid.*

Statutory Paternity Pay and Statutory Adoption Pay (Persons Abroad and Mariners) Regulations 2002

(SI 2002/2821)

The Secretary of State, in exercise of the powers conferred upon her by virtue of sections 171ZI, 171ZJ(1), 171ZR and 171ZS(1) of the Social Security Contributions and Benefits Act 1992 and with the concurrence of the Treasury, by this instrument, which contains only provision made by virtue of sections 2 and 4 of the Employment Act 2002 and is made before the end of the period of 6 months from the coming into force of those enactments, hereby makes the following Regulations:

ARRANGEMENT OF REGULATIONS

7. Time for compliance with Parts XIIZA and XIIZB of the Act or regulations made under them.
8. Mariners.
9. Continental Shelf.

Citation, commencement and interpretation

5.32 **1.**—(1) These Regulations may be cited as the Statutory Paternity Pay and Statutory Adoption Pay (Persons Abroad and Mariners) Regulations 2002 and shall come into force on 8th December 2002.

(2) In these Regulations—

"the Act" means the Social Security Contributions and Benefits Act 1992;

"adopter", in relation to a child, has the same meaning as it has in the General Regulations;

"the Contributions Regulations" means the Social Security Contributions Regulations 2001;

"EEA" means European Economic Area;

"EEA Agreement" means the Agreement on the European Economic Area signed at Oporto on 2nd May 1992 as adjusted by Protocol signed at Brussels on 17th March 1993;

"EEA State" means a State which is a contracting party to the EEA Agreement;

"the General Regulations" means the Statutory Paternity Pay and Statutory Adoption Pay (General) Regulations 2002;

"statutory paternity pay (birth)" and "statutory paternity pay (adoption)" have the same meaning as they have in the General Regulations;

"week" means a period of 7 days beginning with Sunday.

(3) For the purposes of these Regulations, a person is notified of having been matched with a child for the purposes of adoption on the date on which he receives notification, under regulation 11(2) of the Adoption Agencies Regulations 1983 or regulation 12(3) of the Adoption Agencies (Scotland) Regulations 1996, that an adoption agency has decided that the person would be a suitable adoptive parent for the child, either individually or jointly with another person.

General Note

5.33 These Regulations modify Pts XIIZA and XIIZB of the SSCBA 1992, which govern statutory paternity pay and statutory adoption pay respectively, in relation to persons abroad, those who work as mariners and persons who work on the Continental Shelf.

Restriction on scope

5.34 **2.** A person who would not be treated under regulation 32 of the General Regulations as an employee for the purposes of Parts 12ZA (statutory paternity pay) and 12ZB (statutory adoption pay) of the Act if his employment were in Great Britain shall not be treated as an employee under these Regulations.

DEFINITIONS

"the Act"—see reg.1(2).
"the General Regulations"—see *ibid.*

Treatment of persons in other EEA States as employees

3. A person who is— 5.35

(a) gainfully employed in an EEA State other than the United Kingdom in such circumstances that, if his employment were in Great Britain, he would be an employee for the purposes of Parts 12ZA and 12ZB of the Act, or a person treated as such an employee under regulation 32 of the General Regulations; and

(b) subject to the legislation of the United Kingdom under Council Regulation (EEC) No. 1408/71,

notwithstanding that he is not employed in Great Britain, shall be treated as an employee for the purposes of Parts 12ZA and 12ZB of the Act.

DEFINITIONS

"the Act"—see reg.1(2).
"EEA"—see *ibid.*
"EEA State"—see *ibid.*
"the General Regulations"—see *ibid.*

Treatment of certain persons absent from Great Britain as employees

4. Subject to regulation 8(3), where a person, while absent from Great Britain for any purpose, is gainfully employed by an employer who is liable to pay secondary Class 1 contributions in respect of his employment under section 6 of the Act or regulation 146 of the Contributions Regulations, he shall be treated as an employee for the purposes of Parts 12ZA and 12ZB of the Act. 5.36

DEFINITIONS

"the Act"—see reg.1(2).
"the Contributions Regulations"—see *ibid.*

Entitlement to statutory paternity pay where person has worked in an EEA State

5.—(1) A person who is an employee or treated as an employee under regulation 3 and who— 5.37

(a) in the week immediately preceding the 14th week before the expected week of the child's birth was in employed earner's employment with an employer in Great Britain; and

(b) had in any week within the period of 26 weeks immediately preceding that week been employed by the same employer in another EEA State,

shall be treated for the purposes of section 171ZA of the Act (entitlement to statutory paternity pay (birth)) as having been employed in employed earner's employment in those weeks in which he was so employed in the other EEA State.

(2) A person who is an employee or treated as an employee under regulation 3 and who—

(a) in the week in which the adopter is notified of being matched with the child for purposes of adoption was in employed earner's employment with an employer in Great Britain; and

(b) had in any week within the period of 26 weeks immediately preceding that week been employed by the same employer in another EEA State,

shall be treated for the purposes of section 171ZB of the Act (entitlement to statutory paternity pay (adoption)) as having been employed in employed earner's employment in those weeks in which he was so employed in the other EEA State.

DEFINITIONS

"the Act"—see reg.1(2).
"adopter"—see *ibid.*
"EEA"—see *ibid.*
"EEA State"—see *ibid.*
"statutory paternity pay (adoption)"—see *ibid.*
"statutory paternity pay (birth)"—see *ibid.*
"week"—see *ibid.*

Entitlement to statutory adoption pay where person has worked in an EEA State

5.38 **6.** A person who is an employee or treated as an employee under regulation 3 and who—

(a) in the week in which he is notified that he has been matched with the child for the purposes of adoption was in employed earner's employment with an employer in Great Britain; and

(b) had in any week within the period of 26 weeks immediately preceding that week been employed by the same employer in another EEA State,

shall be treated for the purposes of section 171ZL of the Act (entitlement to statutory adoption pay) as having been employed in employed earner's employment in those weeks in which he was so employed in the other EEA State.

DEFINITIONS

"the Act"—see reg.1(2).
"EEA"—see *ibid.*
"EEA State"—see *ibid.*
"week"—see *ibid.*

Time for compliance with Parts 12ZA and 12ZB of the Act or regulations made under them

5.39 **7.** Where—

(a) a person is outside the United Kingdom;

(b) Parts 12ZA or 12ZB of the Act or regulations made under them require any act to be done forthwith or on the happening of a certain event or within a specified time; and

(c) because the person is outside the United Kingdom he or his employer cannot comply with the requirement,

the person or the employer, as the case may be, shall be deemed to have complied with it if the act is performed as soon as reasonably practicable.

DEFINITION

"the Act"—see reg.1(2)

Mariners

8.—(1) In this regulation, "foreign-going ship", "home-trade ship" and "mariner" have the same meanings as in Case C of Part 9 of the Contributions Regulations (mariners) and the expressions "ship" and "ship or vessel", except in paragraph (3), include hovercraft. **5.40**

(2) A mariner engaged in employment on board a home-trade ship with an employer who has a place of business within the United Kingdom shall be treated as an employee for the purposes of Parts 12ZA and 12ZB of the Act, notwithstanding that he may not be employed in Great Britain.

(3) A mariner who is engaged in employment—

(a) on a foreign-going ship; or

(b) on a home-trade ship with an employer who does not have a place of business within the United Kingdom,

shall not be treated as an employee for the purposes of Parts 12ZA and 12ZB of the Act, notwithstanding that he may have been employed in Great Britain.

DEFINITIONS

"the Act"—see reg.1(2).
"the Contributions Regulations"—see *ibid.*
"foreign-going ship"—see para.(1).
"home-trade ship"—see *ibid.*
"mariner"—see *ibid.*
"ship"—see *ibid.*
"ship or vessel"—see *ibid.*

Continental shelf

9.—(1) In this regulation— **5.41**

"designated area" means any area which may from time to time be designated by Order in Council under section 1(7) of the Continental Shelf Act 1964 as an area within which the rights of the United Kingdom with respect to the seabed and subsoil and their natural resources may be exercised;

"prescribed employment" means any employment (whether under a contract of service or not) in a designated area in connection with continental shelf operations, as defined in section 120(2) of the Act.

(2) A person in prescribed employment shall be treated as an employee for the purposes of Parts 12ZA and 12ZB of the Act notwithstanding that he may not be employed in Great Britain.

DEFINITIONS

"the Act"—see reg.1(2).
"designated area"—see para.(1).
"prescribed employment"—see *ibid.*

Statutory Paternity Pay and Statutory Adoption Pay (General) Regulations 2002

(SI 2002/2822)

The Secretary of State, in exercise of the powers conferred on her by sections 171ZA(2)(a), 171ZB(2)(a), 171ZC(3)(a), (c), (d), (f) and (g), 171ZD(2) and (3), 171ZE(2)(a), (b)(i), (3), (7) and (8), 171ZG(3), 171ZJ(1), (3), (4), (7) and (8), 171ZL(8)(b) to (d), (f) and (g), 171ZM(2) and (3), 171ZN(2), (5) and (6), 171ZP(6), 171ZS(1), (3), (4), (7) and (8), and 175(4) of the Social Security Contributions and Benefits Act 1992 and section 5(1)(g), (i) and (p) of the Social Security Administration Act 1992 and with the concurrence of the Commissioners of Inland Revenue in so far as such concurrence is required, by this instrument, which contains only provision made by virtue of sections 2, 4 and 53 of and paragraphs 8 and 11 of Schedule 7 to the Employment Act 2002 and is made before the end of the period of 6 months from the coming into force of those enactments, hereby makes the following Regulations—

ARRANGEMENT OF REGULATIONS

PART 1

Introduction

PART 2

Statutory paternity pay (birth)

PART 3

Statutory paternity pay (adoption)

11. Conditions of entitlement to statutory paternity pay (adoption): relationship with child and with person with whom the child is placed for adoption. **5.44**
12. Period of payment of statutory paternity pay (adoption).
13. Additional notice requirements for statutory paternity pay (adoption).
14. Qualifying period for statutory paternity pay (adoption).
15. Evidence of entitlement to statutory paternity pay (adoption).
16. Entitlement to statutory paternity pay (adoption) where there is more than one employer.

PART 4

Statutory paternity pay: provisions applicable to both statutory paternity pay (birth) and statutory paternity pay (adoption)

17. Work during a statutory paternity pay period. **5.45**
18. Cases where there is no liability to pay statutory paternity pay.
19. Statutory paternity pay and contractual remuneration.
20. Avoidance of liability for statutory paternity pay.

PART 5

Statutory adoption pay

21. Adoption pay period. **5.46**
22. Adoption pay period in cases where adoption is disrupted.
23. Additional notice requirements for statutory adoption pay.
24. Evidence of entitlement to statutory adoption pay.
25. Entitlement to statutory adoption pay where there is more than one employer.
26. Work during an adoption pay period.
27. Cases where there is no liability to pay statutory adoption pay.
28. Statutory adoption pay and contractual remuneration.
29. Termination of employment before start of adoption pay period.
30. Avoidance of liability for statutory adoption pay.

PART 6

Statutory paternity pay and statutory adoption pay: provisions applicable to both statutory paternity pay and statutory adoption pay

31. Introductory. **5.47**
32. Treatment of persons as employees.
33. Continuous employment.

PART 1

INTRODUCTION

Citation and commencement

5.48 **1.** These Regulations may be cited as the Statutory Paternity Pay and Statutory Adoption Pay (General) Regulations 2002 and shall come into force on 8th December 2002.

Interpretation

5.49 **2.**—(1) In these Regulations—

"the Act" means the Social Security Contributions and Benefits Act 1992;

"adopter", in relation to a child, means a person who has been matched with the child for adoption;

"adoption agency" has the meaning given, in relation to England and Wales, by section 1(4) of the Adoption Act 1976 and in relation to Scotland, by section 1(4) of the Adoption (Scotland) Act 1978;

"the Board" means the Commissioners of Inland Revenue;

"the Contributions Regulations" means the Social Security (Contributions) Regulations 2001;

"expected week", in relation to the birth of a child, means the week, beginning with midnight between Saturday and Sunday, in which it is expected that the child will be born;

"statutory paternity pay (adoption)" means statutory paternity pay payable in accordance with the provisions of Part 12ZA of the Act where the conditions specified in section 171ZB(2) of the Act are satisfied;

"statutory paternity pay (birth)" means statutory paternity pay payable in accordance with the provisions of Part 12ZA of the Act where the conditions specified in section 171ZA(2) of the Act are satisfied.

(2) For the purposes of these Regulations—

(a) a person is matched with a child for adoption when an adoption agency decides that that person would be a suitable adoptive parent for the child, either individually or jointly with another person; and

(b) a person is notified of having been matched with a child on the date on which he receives notification of the agency's decision, under regulation 11(2) of the Adoption Agencies Regulations 1983 or regulation 12(3) of the Adoption Agencies (Scotland) Regulations 1996.

Application

3.(1) Subject to the provisions of Part 12ZA of the Act (statutory paternity pay) and of these Regulations, there is entitlement to— 5.50

(a) statutory paternity pay (birth) in respect of children—

(i) born on or after 6th April 2003; or

(ii) whose expected week of birth begins on or after that date;

(b) statutory paternity pay (adoption) in respect of children—

(i) matched with a person who is notified of having been matched on or after 6th April 2003; or

(ii) placed for adoption on or after that date.

(2) Subject to the provisions of Part 12ZB of the Act (statutory adoption pay) and of these Regulations, there is entitlement to statutory adoption pay in respect of children—

(a) matched with a person who is notified of having been matched on or after 6th April 2003; or

(b) placed for adoption on or after that date.

DEFINITIONS

"the Act"—see reg.2(1).
"expected week"—see *ibid.*
"statutory paternity pay (adoption)"—see *ibid.*
"statutory paternity pay (birth)"—see *ibid.*

PART 2

STATUTORY PATERNITY PAY (BIRTH)

Conditions of entitlement to statutory paternity pay (birth): relationship with newborn child and child's mother

4. The conditions prescribed under section 171ZA(2)(a) of the Act are those prescribed in regulation 4(2)(b) and (c) of the Paternity and Adoption Leave Regulations 2002. 5.51

DEFINITION

"the Act"—see reg.2(1).

GENERAL NOTE

5.52 See the annotation to SSCBA 1992, s.171ZA.

Modification of entitlement conditions: early birth

5.53 **5.** Where a person does not meet the conditions specified in section 171ZA(2)(b) to (d) of the Act because the child's birth occurred earlier than the 14th week before the expected week of the birth, it shall have effect as if, for the conditions there set out, there were substituted the conditions that—

(a) the person would, but for the date on which the birth occurred, have been in employed earner's employment with an employer for a continuous period of at least 26 weeks ending with the week immediately preceding the 14th week before the expected week of the child's birth;

(b) his normal weekly earnings for the period of 8 weeks ending with the week immediately preceding the week in which the child is born are not less than the lower earnings limit in force under section 5(1)(a) of the Act immediately before the commencement of the week in which the child is born.

DEFINITIONS

"the Act"—see reg.2(1).
"expected week"—see *ibid.*

Period of payment of statutory paternity pay (birth)

5.54 **6.**—(1) Subject to paragraph (2) and regulation 8, a person entitled to statutory paternity pay (birth) may choose the statutory paternity pay period to begin on—

(a) the date on which the child is born or, where he is at work on that day, the following day;

(b) the date falling such number of days after the date on which the child is born as the person may specify;

(c) a predetermined date, specified by the person, which is later than the first day of the expected week of the child's birth.

(2) In a case where statutory paternity pay (birth) is payable in respect of a child whose expected week of birth begins before 6th April 2003, the statutory paternity pay period shall begin on a predetermined date, specified by the person entitled to such pay in a notice under section 171ZC(1) of the Act, which is at least 28 days after the date on which that notice was given, unless the person liable to pay statutory paternity pay (birth) agrees to the period beginning earlier.

(3) A person may choose for statutory paternity pay (birth) to be paid in respect of a period of a week.

(4) A choice made in accordance with paragraph (1) or (2) is not irrevocable, but where a person subsequently makes a different choice in relation to the beginning of the statutory pay period, section 171ZC(1) of the Act shall apply to it.

DEFINITIONS

"the Act"—see reg.2(1).
"expected week"—see *ibid.*
"statutory paternity pay (birth)"—see *ibid.*

Additional notice requirements for statutory paternity pay (birth)

7.—(1) Where the choice made by a person in accordance with paragraph (1) of regulation 6 and notified in accordance with section 171ZC(1) of the Act is that mentioned in sub-paragraph (a) or (b) of that paragraph, the person shall give further notice to the person liable to pay him statutory paternity pay, as soon as is reasonably practicable after the child's birth, of the date the child was born; 5.55

(2) Where the choice made by a person in accordance with paragraph (1) of regulation 6 and notified in accordance with section 171ZC(1) of the Act is that specified in sub-paragraph (c) of that paragraph, and the date of the child's birth is later than the date so specified, the person shall, if he wishes to claim statutory paternity pay (birth), give notice to the person liable to pay it, as soon as is reasonably practicable, that the period in respect of which statutory paternity pay is to be paid shall begin on a date different fromthat originally chosen by him.

(3) That date may be any date chosen in accordance with paragraph (1) of regulation 6.

DEFINITIONS

"the Act"—see reg.2(1).
"statutory paternity pay (birth)"—see *ibid.*

Qualifying period for statutory paternity pay (birth)

8. The qualifying period for the purposes of section 171ZE(2) of the Act (period within which the statutory paternity pay period must occur) is a period which begins on the date of the child's birth and ends — 5.56

(a) except in the case referred to in paragraph (b), 56 days after that date;
(b) in a case where the child is born before the first day of the expected week of its birth, 56 days after that day.

DEFINITIONS

"the Act"—see reg.2(1).
"expected week"—see *ibid.*

Evidence of entitlement to statutory paternity pay (birth)

9.—(1) A person shall provide evidence of his entitlement to statutory paternity pay (birth) by providing in writing to the person who will be liable to pay him statutory paternity pay (birth)— 5.57

(a) the information specified in paragraph (2);
(b) a declaration that he meets the conditions prescribed under section 171ZA(2)(a) of the Act and that it is not the case that statutory paternity pay (birth) is not payable to him by virtue of the provisions of section 171ZE(4) of the Act.

(2) The information referred to in paragraph (1)(a) is as follows—
(a) the name of the person claiming statutory paternity pay (birth);
(b) the expected week of the child's birth and, where the birth has already occurred, the date of birth;
(c) the date fromwhich it is expected that the liability to pay statutory paternity pay (birth) will begin;
(d) whether the period chosen in respect of which statutory paternity pay (birth) is to be payable is a week.

(3) The information and declaration referred to in paragraph (1) shall be provided at least 28 days before the date mentioned in sub-paragraph (c) of paragraph (2) or, if that is not reasonably practicable, as soon as is reasonably practicable thereafter.

(4) Where the person who will be liable to pay statutory paternity pay (birth) so requests, the person entitled to it shall inform him of the date of the child's birth within 28 days, or as soon as is reasonably practicable thereafter.

DEFINITIONS

"the Act"—see reg.2(1).
"expected week"—see *ibid.*
"statutory paternity pay (birth)"—see *ibid.*

GENERAL NOTE

5.58 The evidence of entitlement to statutory paternity pay (birth) is essentially a formof self-certification by the father or prospective father. This contrasts with the requirement to produce a medical certificate for statutory maternity pay purposes. The justification for the self-certification approach here is that it "balances the need for a light-touch procedure with the desire employers have expressed for some form of evidence to justify their payment of Statutory Paternity Pay" (*Government's Response on Simplification of Maternity leave, Paternity Leave and Adoption Leave* (DTI, 2001), para.41).

Entitlement to statutory paternity pay (birth) where there is more than one employer

5.59 **10.** Statutory paternity pay (birth) shall be payable to a person in respect of a statutory pay week during any part of which he works only for an employer—
(a) who is not liable to pay him statutory paternity pay (birth); and
(b) for whom he has worked in the week immediately preceding the 14th week before the expected week of the child's birth.

DEFINITIONS

"expected week"—see *ibid.*
"statutory paternity pay (birth)"—see *ibid.*

PART 3

STATUTORY PATERNITY PAY (ADOPTION)

Conditions of entitlement to statutory paternity pay (adoption): relationship with child and with person with whom the child is placed for adoption

11.—(1) The conditions prescribed under section 171ZB(2)(a) of the Act are that a person— 5.60

(a) is married to or the partner of a child's adopter (or in a case where there are two adopters, married to or the partner of the other adopter); and

(b) has, or expects to have, the main responsibility (apart from the responsibility of the child's adopter, or in a case where there two adopters, together with the other adopter) for the upbringing of the child.

(2) For the purposes of paragraph (1), "partner" means a person (whether of a different sex or the same sex) who lives with the adopter and the child in an enduring family relationship but is not a relative of the adopter of a kind specified in paragraph [1(2A)].

[1 (2A) The relatives of the adopter referred to in paragraph (2) are the adopter's parent, grandparent, sister, brother, aunt or uncle.]

(3) References to relationships in paragraph [1(2A)]—

(a) are to relationships of the full blood or half blood, or, in the case of an adopted person, such of those relationships as would exist but for the adoption; and

(b) include the relationship of a child with his adoptive, or former adoptive parents but do not include any other adoptive relationships.

AMENDMENT

1. Statutory Paternity Pay and Statutory Adoption Pay (Amendment) Regulations 2004 (SI 2004/488), reg.2 (April 6, 2004).

DEFINITIONS

"the Act"—see reg.2(1).
"adopter"—see *ibid.*
"partner"—see para.(2).

GENERAL NOTE

This regulation sets out the prescribed conditions for the purposes of SSCBA 1992, s.171ZB(2)(a), *i.e.* for the payment of statutory paternity pay in the case of adoption. The claimant must either be the adoptive parent's spouse or partner and expect to have the main responsibility (other than the adopter) for the child's upbringing. The definition of "partner" in para.(2) is innovative, in that it does not rely on the old "living together as husband and wife" formula. Instead, it recognises that partners may be in a heterosexual or same sex relationship. The only qualifications are that the partner lives with the adopter and the child in "an 5.61

enduring family relationship" and is not a relative of the adopter as defined in paras (2A) and (3). Guidance on the notion of "an enduring family relationship" in the context of a same-sex relationship might be sought in the decisions in *Fitzpatrick v Sterling Housing Association* [2001] A.C. 27 and *Ghaidan v Godin-Mendoza* [2004] UKHL 30; [2004] 3 WLR 113. This may be the first explicit statutory recognition in English law of parity of treatment for heterosexual and same-sex couples.

Period of payment of statutory paternity pay (adoption)

5.62 **12.**—(1) Subject to paragraph (2) and regulation 14, a person entitled to statutory paternity pay (adoption) may choose the statutory paternity pay period to begin on—

(a) the date on which the child is placed with the adopter or, where the person is at work on that day, the following day;
(b) the date falling such number of days after the date on which the child is placed with the adopter as the person may specify;
(c) a predetermined date, specified by the person, which is later than the date on which the child is expected to be placed with the adopter.

(2) In a case where statutory paternity pay (adoption) is payable in respect of a child matched with an adopter who is notified of having been matched before 6th April 2003, the statutory paternity pay period shall begin on a predetermined date, specified by the person entitled to such pay in a notice under section 171ZC(1) of the Act, which is at least 28 days after the date on which that notice was given, unless the person liable to pay statutory paternity pay (birth) agrees to the period beginning earlier.

(3) A person may choose for statutory paternity pay (adoption) to be paid in respect of a period of a week.

(4) A choice made in accordance with paragraph (1) is not irrevocable, but where a person subsequently makes a different choice in relation to the beginning of the statutory paternity pay period, section 171ZC(1) of the Act shall apply to it.

DEFINITIONS

"the Act"—see reg.2(1).
"adopter"—see *ibid.*
"statutory paternity pay (adoption)"—see *ibid.*
"statutory paternity pay (birth)"—see *ibid.*

Additional notice requirements for statutory paternity pay (adoption)

5.63 **13.**—(1) Where the choice made by a person in accordance with paragraph (1) of regulation 12 and notified in accordance with section 171ZC(1) of the Act is that mentioned in sub-paragraph (a) or (b) of that paragraph, the person shall give further notice to the person liable to pay him statutory paternity pay as soon as is reasonably practicable of the date on which the placement occurred.

(2) Where the choice made by a person in accordance with paragraph (1) of regulation 12 and notified in accordance with section 171ZC(1) of

the Act is that mentioned in sub-paragraph (c) of that paragraph, or a date is specified under paragraph (2) of that regulation, and the child is placed for adoption later than the date so specified, the person shall, if he wishes to claim statutory paternity pay (adoption), give notice to the person liable to pay it, as soon as is reasonably practicable, that the period in respect of which statutory paternity pay is to be paid shall begin on a date different from that originally chosen by him.

(3) That date may be any date chosen in accordance with paragraph (1) of regulation 12.

DEFINITIONS

"the Act"—see reg.2(1).
"statutory paternity pay (adoption)"—see *ibid.*

Qualifying period for statutory paternity pay (adoption)

14. The qualifying period for the purposes of section 171ZE(2) of the Act (period within which the statutory pay period must occur) is a period of 56 days beginning with the date of the child's placement for adoption. **5.64**

DEFINITION

"the Act"—see reg.2(1).

Evidence of entitlement for statutory paternity pay (adoption)

15.—(1) A person shall provide evidence of his entitlement to statutory paternity pay (adoption) by providing in writing to the person who will be liable to pay him statutory paternity pay (adoption)— **5.65**

(a) the information specified in paragraph (2);
(b) a declaration that he meets the conditions prescribed under section 171ZB(2)(a) of the Act and that it is not the case that statutory paternity pay (adoption) is not payable to him by virtue of the provisions of section 171ZE(4) of the Act;
(c) a declaration that he has elected to receive statutory paternity pay (adoption), and not statutory adoption pay under Part 12ZB of the Act.

(2) The information referred to in paragraph (1) is as follows—

(a) the name of the person claiming statutory paternity pay (adoption);
(b) the date on which the child is expected to be placed for adoption or, where the child has already been placed for adoption, the date of placement of the child;
(c) the date from which it is expected that the liability to pay statutory paternity pay (adoption) will begin;
(d) whether the period chosen in respect of which statutory paternity pay (adoption) is to be payable is a week;
(e) the date the adopter was notified he had been matched with the child for the purposes of adoption.

(3) The information and declarations referred to in paragraph (1) shall be provided to the person liable to pay statutory paternity pay at least 28 days before the date mentioned in sub-paragraph (c) of paragraph (2)

or, if that is not reasonably practicable, as soon as is reasonably practicable thereafter.

(4) Where the person who will be liable to pay statutory paternity pay (adoption) so requests, the person entitled to it shall inform him of the date of the child's placement within 28 days, or as soon as is reasonably practicable thereafter.

DEFINITIONS

"the Act"—see reg.2(1).
"statutory paternity pay (adoption)"—see *ibid.*

Entitlement to statutory paternity pay (adoption) where there is more than one employer

5.66 **16.** Statutory paternity pay (adoption) shall be payable to a person in respect of a statutory pay week during any part of which he works only for an employer—

(a) who is not liable to pay him statutory paternity pay (adoption); and
(b) for whom he has worked in the week in which the adopter is notified of being matched with the child.

DEFINITIONS

"adopter"—see *ibid.*
"statutory paternity pay (adoption)"—see *ibid.*

PART 4

STATUTORY PATERNITY PAY: PROVISIONS APPLICABLE TO BOTH STATUTORY PATERNITY PAY (BIRTH) AND STATUTORY PATERNITY PAY (ADOPTION)

Work during a statutory paternity pay period

5.67 **17.**—(1) Where, in a case where statutory paternity pay is being paid to a person who works during the statutory paternity pay period for an employer who is not liable to pay him statutory paternity pay and who does not fall within paragraph (b) of regulation 10 or, as the case may be, paragraph (b) of regulation 16, there shall be no liability to pay statutory paternity pay in respect of any remaining part of the statutory paternity pay period.

(2) In a case falling within paragraph (1), the person shall notify the person liable to pay statutory paternity pay within seven days of the first day during which he works during the statutory pay period.

(3) The notification mentioned in paragraph (2) shall be in writing, if the person who has been liable to pay statutory paternity pay so requests.

Cases where there is no liability to pay statutory paternity pay

5.68 **18.** There shall be no liability to pay statutory paternity pay in respect of any week—

(a) during any part of which the person entitled to it is entitled to statutory sick pay under Part 11 of the Act;
(b) following that in which the person claiming it has died; or
(c) during any part of which the person entitled to it is detained in legal custody or sentenced to a term of imprisonment (except where the sentence is suspended), or which is a subsequent week within the same statutory paternity pay period.

DEFINITION

"the Act"—see reg.2(1).

Statutory paternity pay and contractual remuneration

19. For the purposes of section 171ZG(1) and (2) of the Act, the payments which are to be treated as contractual remuneration are sums payable under a contract of service— **5.69**
(a) by way of remuneration;
(b) for incapacity for work due to sickness or injury;
(c) by reason of the birth or adoption of a child.

DEFINITION

"the Act"—see reg.2(1).

Avoidance of liability for statutory paternity pay

20.—(1) A former employer shall be liable to make payments of statutory paternity pay to a former employee in any case where the employee had been employed for a continuous period of at least 8 weeks and his contract of service was brought to an end by the former employer solely, or mainly, for the purpose of avoiding liability for statutory paternity pay. **5.70**

(2) In a case falling within paragraph (1)—
(a) the employee shall be treated as if he had been employed for a continuous period ending with the child's birth or, as the case may be, the placement of the child for adoption;
(b) his normal weekly earnings shall be calculated by reference to his normal weekly earnings for the period of 8 weeks ending with the last day in respect of which he was paid under his former contract of service.

PART 5

Statutory adoption pay

Adoption pay period

21.—(1) Subject to paragraph (2), a person entitled to statutory adoption pay may choose the adoption pay period to begin— **5.71**
(a) on the date on which the child is placed with him for adoption or, where he is at work on that day, on the following day;

(b) subject to paragraph (2), on a predetermined date, specified by him, which is no more than 14 days before the date on which the child is expected to be placed with him and no later than that date.

(2) In a case where statutory adoption pay is payable in respect of a child matched with an adopter who is notified of having been matched before 6th April 2003, the statutory adoption pay period shall begin on a predetermined date which is—

(a) on or after 6th April 2003; and

(b) no more than 14 days before the date on which the child is expected to be placed with the adopter.

(3) Subject to paragraph (4), where the choice made is that mentioned in sub-paragraph (b) of paragraph (1) or in a case where paragraph (2) applies, the adoption pay period shall, unless the employer agrees to the adoption pay period beginning earlier, begin no earlier than 28 days after notice under section 171ZL(6) of the Act has been given.

(4) Where the beginning of the adoption pay period determined in accordance with paragraph (3) is later than the date of placement, it shall be the date of placement.

(5) Subject to regulation 22, the duration of any adoption pay period shall be a continuous period of 26 weeks.

(6) A choice made under paragraph (1), or a date specified under paragraph (2), is not irrevocable, but where a person subsequently makes a different choice, section 171ZL(6) of the Act shall apply to it.

DEFINITIONS

"the Act"—see reg.2(1).
"adopter"—see *ibid.*

Adoption pay period in cases where adoption is disrupted

5.72 **22.**—(1) Where—

(a) after a child has been placed for adoption—
  (i) the child dies;
  (ii) the child is returned to the adoption agency under section 30(3) of the Adoption Act 1976 or section 30(3) of the Adoption (Scotland) Act 1978; or

(b) the adoption pay period has begun prior to the date the child has been placed for adoption, but the placement does not take place,

the adoption pay period shall terminate in accordance with the provisions of paragraph (2).

(2) The adoption pay period shall, in a case falling within paragraph (1), terminate 8 weeks after the end of the week specified in paragraph (3).

(3) The week referred to in paragraph (2) is—

(a) in a case falling within paragraph (1)(a)(i), the week during which the child dies;

(b) in a case falling within paragraph (1)(a)(ii), the week during which the child is returned;

(c) in a case falling within paragraph (1)(b), the week during which the person with whom the child was to be placed for adoption is notified that the placement will not be made.

(4) For the purposes of paragraph (3), "week" means a period of 7 days beginning with Sunday.

DEFINITION

"week"—see para.(4).

Additional notice requirements for statutory adoption pay

23.—(1) Where a person gives notice under section 171ZL(6) of the Act he shall at the same time give notice of the date on which the child is expected to be placed for adoption. 5.73

(2) Where the choice made in accordance with paragraph (1) of regulation 21 and notified in accordance with section 171ZL(6) of the Act is that mentioned in sub-paragraph (a) of that paragraph, the person shall give further notice to the person liable to pay him statutory adoption pay as soon as is reasonably practicable of the date the child is placed for adoption.

DEFINITION

"the Act"—see reg.2(1).

Evidence of entitlement to statutory adoption pay

24.—(1) A person shall provide evidence of his entitlement to statutory adoption pay by providing to the person who will be liable to pay it— 5.74

(a) the information specified in paragraph (2), in the form of one or more documents provided to him by an adoption agency, containing that information;

(b) a declaration that he has elected to receive statutory adoption pay, and not statutory paternity pay (adoption) under Part 12ZA of the Act.

(2) The information referred to in paragraph (1) is—

(a) the name and address of the adoption agency and of the person claiming payment of statutory adoption pay;

(b) the date on which the child is expected to be placed for adoption or, where the child has already been placed for adoption, the date of placement; and

(c) the date on which the person claiming payment of statutory adoption pay was informed by the adoption agency that the child would be placed for adoption with him.

(3) The information and declaration referred to in paragraph (1) shall be provided to the person liable to pay statutory adoption pay at least 28 days before the date chosen as the beginning of the adoption pay period in accordance with paragraph (1) of regulation 21, or, if that is not reasonably practicable, as soon as is reasonably practicable thereafter.

DEFINITIONS

"the Act"—see reg.2(1).
"adoption agency"—see *ibid.*
"statutory paternity pay (adoption)"—see *ibid.*

Entitlement to statutory adoption pay where there is more than one employer

5.75 **25.** Statutory adoption pay shall be payable to a person in respect of a week during any part of which he works only for an employer—

(a) who is not liable to pay him statutory adoption pay; and
(b) for whom he has worked in the week in which he is notified of being matched with the child.

Work during an adoption pay period

5.76 **26.**—(1) Where, in a case where statutory adoption pay is being paid to a person who works during the adoption pay period for an employer who is not liable to pay him statutory adoption pay and who does not fall within paragraph (b) of regulation 25, there shall be no liability to pay statutory adoption pay in respect of any remaining part of the adoption pay period.

(2) In a case falling within paragraph (1), the person shall notify the person liable to pay statutory adoption pay within 7 days of the first day during which he works during the adoption pay period.

(3) The notification contained in paragraph (2) shall be in writing if the person who has been liable to pay statutory adoption pay so requests.

Cases where there is no liability to pay statutory adoption pay

5.77 **27.**—(1) There shall be no liability to pay statutory adoption pay in respect of any week—

(a) during any part of which the person entitled to it is entitled to statutory sick pay under Part 9 of the Act;
(b) following that in which the person claiming it has died; or
(c) subject to paragraph (2), during any part of which the person entitled to it is detained in legal custody or sentenced to a term of imprisonment (except where the sentence is suspended).

(2) There shall be liability to pay statutory adoption pay in respect of any week during any part of which the person entitled to it is detained in legal custody where that person—

(a) is released subsequently without charge;
(b) is subsequently found not guilty of any offence and is released; or
(c) is convicted of an offence but does not receive a custodial sentence.

DEFINITION

"the Act"—see reg.2(1).

Statutory adoption pay and contractual remuneration

5.78 **28.** For the purposes of section 171ZP(4) and (5) of the Act, the payments which are to be treated as contractual remuneration are sums payable under a contract of service—

(a) by way of remuneration;
(b) for incapacity for work due to sickness or injury;
(c) by reason of the adoption of a child.

DEFINITION

"the Act"—see reg.2(1).

Termination of employment before start of adoption pay period

29.—(1) Where the employment of a person who satisfies the conditions of entitlement to statutory adoption pay terminates for whatever reason (including dismissal) before the adoption pay period chosen in accordance with regulation 21 has begun, the period shall begin 14 days before the expected date of placement or, where the termination occurs on, or within 14 days before, the expected date of placement, on the day immediately following the last day of his employment. **5.79**

(2) In a case falling within paragraph (1), the notice requirements set out in section 171ZL(6) of the Act and these Regulations shall not apply.

DEFINITION

"the Act"—see reg.2(1).

Avoidance of liability for statutory adoption pay

30.—(1) A former employer shall be liable to make payments of statutory adoption pay to a former employee in any case where the employee had been employed for a continuous period of at least 8 weeks and his contract of service was brought to an end by the former employer solely, or mainly, for the purpose of avoiding liability for statutory adoption pay. **5.80**

(2) In a case falling within paragraph (1)—

(a) the employee shall be treated as if he had been employed for a continuous period ending with the week in which he was notified of having been matched with the child for adoption; and

(b) his normal weekly earnings shall be calculated by reference to his normal weekly earnings for the period of 8 weeks ending with the last day in respect of which he was paid under his former contract of service.

PART 6

STATUTORY PATERNITY PAY AND STATUTORY ADOPTION PAY: PROVISIONS APPLICABLE TO BOTH STATUTORY PATERNITY PAY AND STATUTORY ADOPTION PAY

Introductory

31.—(1) Subject to paragraph (2), the provisions of regulations 32–47 below apply to statutory paternity pay payable under Part 12ZA of the Act and to statutory adoption pay payable under Part 12ZB of the Act. **5.81**

(2) The provisions of regulation 44 only apply to statutory adoption pay.

DEFINITION

"the Act"—see reg.2(1).

Treatment of persons as employees

5.82 **32.**—(1) In a case where, and in so far as, a person over the age of 16 is treated as an employed earner by virtue of the Social Security (Categorisation of Earners) Regulations 1978 he shall be treated as an employee for the purposes of Parts 12ZA and 12ZB of the Act, and in a case where, and in so far as, such a person is treated otherwise than as an employed earner by virtue of those Regulations, he shall not be treated as an employee for the purposes of Parts 12ZA and 12ZB of the Act.

(2) A person who is in employed earner's employment within the meaning of the Act under a contract of apprenticeship shall be treated as an employee for the purposes of Parts 12ZA and 12ZB of the Act.

(3) A person who is in employed earner's employment within the meaning of the Act but whose employer—

(a) does not fulfil the conditions prescribed in regulation 145(1) of the Contributions Regulations in so far as that provision relates to residence or presence in Great Britain; or

(b) is a person who, by reason of any international treaty to which the United Kingdomis a party or of any international convention binding the United Kingdom—

(i) is exempt from the provisions of the Act; or

(ii) is a person against whom the provisions of the Act are not enforceable,

shall not be treated as an employee for the purposes of Parts 12ZA and 12ZB of the Act.

DEFINITIONS

"the Act"—see reg.2(1).
"Contributions Regulations"—see *ibid.*

Continuous employment

5.83 **33.**—(1) Subject to the following provisions of this regulation, where in any week a person is, for the whole or part of the week—

(a) incapable of work in consequence of sickness or injury;

(b) absent from work on account of a temporary cessation of work;

(c) absent from work in circumstances such that, by arrangement or custom, he is regarded as continuing in the employment of his employer for all or any purposes,

and returns to work for his employer after the incapacity for or absence from work, that week shall be treated for the purposes of sections 171ZA, 171ZB and 171ZL of the Act as part of a continuous period of employment with that employer, notwithstanding that no contract of service exists with that employer in respect of that week.

(2) Incapacity for work which lasts for more than 26 consecutive weeks shall not count for the purposes of paragraph (1)(a).

(3) Where a person—

(a) is an employee in an employed earner's employment in which the custom is for the employer—
   (i) to offer work for a fixed period of not more than 26 consecutive weeks;
   (ii) to offer work for such period on two or more occasions in a year for periods which do not overlap; and
   (iii) to offer the work available to those persons who had worked for him during the last or a recent such period, but
(b) is absent from work because of incapacity arising from some specific disease or bodily or mental disablement,

then in that case paragraph (1) shall apply as if the words "and returns to work for his employer after the incapacity for or absence from work," were omitted and paragraph (4) shall not apply.

(4) Where a person is employed under a contract of service for part only of the relevant week within the meaning of subsection (3) of section 171ZL of the Act (entitlement to statutory adoption pay), the whole of that week shall count in computing a period of continuous employment for the purposes of that section.

DEFINITION

"the Act"—see reg.2(1).

Continuous employment and unfair dismissal

34.—(1) This regulation applies to a person in relation to whose dismissal an action is commenced which consists— **5.84**

(a) of the presentation by him of a complaint under section 111(1) of the Employment Rights Act 1996;
(b) of his making a claim in accordance with a dismissals procedure agreement designated by an order under section 110 of that Act; or
(c) of any action taken by a conciliation officer under section 18 of the Employment Tribunals Act 1996.

(2) If, in consequence of an action of the kind specified in paragraph (1), a person is reinstated or re-engaged by his employer or by a successor or associated employer of that employer, the continuity of his employment shall be preserved for the purposes of Part 12ZA or, as the case may be, Part 12ZB of the Act, and any week which falls within the interval beginning with the effective date of termination and ending with the date of reinstatement or re-engagement, as the case may be, shall count in the computation of his period of continuous employment.

(3) In this regulation—

"successor" and "dismissal procedures agreement" have the same meanings as in section 235 of the Employment Rights Act 1996; and

"associated employer" shall be construed in accordance with section 231 of the Employment Rights Act 1996.

DEFINITIONS

"the Act"—see reg.2(1).
"associated employer"—see para.(3).
"dismissal procedures agreement"—see *ibid.*
"successor"—see *ibid.*

Continuous employment and stoppages of work

5.85 **35.**—(1) Where, for any week or part of a week a person does not work because there is a stoppage of work due to a trade dispute within the meaning of section 35(1) of the Jobseekers Act 1995 at his place of employment, the continuity of his employment shall, subject to paragraph (2), be treated as continuing throughout the stoppage but, subject to paragraph (3), no such week shall count in the computation of his period of employment.

(2) Subject to paragraph (3), where during the stoppage of work a person is dismissed from his employment, the continuity of his employment shall not be treated in accordance with paragraph (1) as continuing beyond the commencement of the day he stopped work.

(3) The provisions of paragraph (1), to the extent that they provide that a week in which the stoppage of work occurred shall not count in the computation of a period of employment, and paragraph (2) shall not apply to a person who proves that at no time did he have a direct interest in the trade dispute in question.

Change of employer

5.86 **36.** A person's employment shall, notwithstanding a change of employer, be treated as continuous employment with the second employer where—

(a) the employer's trade or business or an undertaking (whether or not it is an undertaking established by or under an Act of Parliament) is transferred from one person to another;
(b) by or under an Act of Parliament, whether public or local and whenever passed, a contract of employment between any body corporate and the person is modified and some other body corporate is substituted as his employer;
(c) on the death of his employer, the person is taken into employment of the personal representatives or trustees of the deceased;
(d) the person is employed by partners, personal representatives or trustees and there is a change in the partners, or, as the case may be, personal representatives or trustees;
(e) the person is taken into the employment of an employer who is, at the time he entered his employment, an associated employer of his previous employer, and for this purpose "associated employer" shall be construed in accordance with section 231 of the Employment Rights Act 1996;
(f) on the termination of his employment with an employer he is taken into the employment of another employer and those employers are governors of a school maintained by a local education authority and that authority.

Reinstatement after service with the armed forces etc.

5.87 **37.** If a person who is entitled to apply to his employer under the Reserve Forces (Safeguard of Employment) Act 1985 enters the employment of that employer within the 6-month period mentioned in section 1(4)(b) of that Act, his previous period of employment with that employer (or if there was more than one such period, the last of those periods) and the period of employment beginning in that 6-month period shall be treated as continuous.

DEFINITION

"the Act"—see reg.2(1).

Treatment of two or more employers or two or more contracts of service as one

38.—(1) In a case where the earnings paid to a person in respect of two or more employments are aggregated and treated as a single payment of earnings under regulation 15(1) of the Contributions Regulations, the employers of that person in respect of those employments shall be treated as one for the purposes of Part 12ZA or, as the case may be, Part 12ZB of the Act. **5.88**

(2) Where two or more employers are treated as one under the provisions of paragraph (1), liability for statutory paternity pay or, as the case may be, statutory adoption pay, shall be apportioned between them in such proportions as they may agree or, in default of agreement, in the proportions which the person's earnings from each employment bear to the amount of the aggregated earnings.

(3) Where two or more contracts of service exist concurrently between one employer and one employee, they shall be treated as one for the purposes of Part 12ZA or, as the case may be, Part 12ZB of the Act, except where, by virtue of regulation 14 of the Contributions Regulations, the earnings from those contracts of service are not aggregated for the purposes of earnings-related contributions.

DEFINITIONS

"the Act"—see reg.2(1).
"Contributions Regulations"—see *ibid.*

Meaning of "earnings"

39.—(1) For the purposes of section 171ZJ(6) (normal weekly earnings for the purposes of Part 12ZA of the Act) and of section 171ZS(6) of the Act (normal weekly earnings for the purposes of Part 12ZB of the Act), the expression "earnings" shall be construed in accordance with the following provisions of this regulation. **5.89**

(2) The expression "earnings" refers to gross earnings and includes any remuneration or profit derived from a person's employment except any payment or amount which is—

(a) excluded from the computation of a person's earnings under regulation 25 of and Schedule 3 to, and regulation 123 of, the Contributions Regulations (payments to be disregarded) and regulation 27 of those Regulations (payments to directors to be disregarded);
(b) a chargeable emolument under section 10A of the Act, except where, in consequence of such a chargeable emolument being

excluded from earnings, a person would not be entitled to statutory paternity pay or, as the case may be, statutory adoption pay.

(3) For the avoidance of doubt, "earnings" includes—

(a) any sum payable in respect of arrears of pay in pursuance of an order for reinstatement or re-engagement under the Employment Rights Act 1996;

(b) any sum payable by way of pay in pursuance of an order made under the Employment Rights Act 1996 for the continuation of a contract of employment;

(c) any sum payable by way of remuneration in pursuance of a protective award under section 189 of the Trade Union and Labour Relations (Consolidation) Act 1992;

(d) any sum payable by way of statutory sick pay, including sums payable in accordance with regulations made under section 151(6) of the Act;

(e) any sum payable by way of statutory maternity pay;

(f) any sum payable by way of statutory paternity pay;

(g) any sum payable by way of statutory adoption pay.

DEFINITIONS

"the Act"—see reg.2(1).
"Contributions Regulations"—see *ibid.*

Normal weekly earnings

5.90 **40.**—(1) For the purposes of Part 12ZA and Part 12ZB of the Act, a person's normal weekly earnings shall be calculated in accordance with the following provisions of this regulation.

(2) In this regulation—

"the appropriate date" means—

(a) in relation to statutory paternity pay (birth), the first day of the 14th week before the expected week of the child's birth or the first day in the week in which the child is born, whichever is the earlier;

(b) in relation to statutory paternity pay (adoption) and statutory adoption pay, the first day of the week after the week in which the adopter is notified of being matched with the child for the purposes of adoption;

"normal pay day" means a day on which the terms of a person's contract of service require him to be paid, or the practice in his employment is for him to be paid, if any payment is due to him; and

"day of payment" means a day on which the person was paid.

(3) Subject to paragraph (4), the relevant period for the purposes of sections 171ZJ(6) and 171ZS(6) is the period between—

(a) the last normal pay day to fall before the appropriate date; and

(b) the last normal pay day to fall at least 8 weeks earlier than the normal pay day mentioned in sub-paragraph (a),

including the normal pay day mentioned in sub-paragraph (a) but excluding that first mentioned in sub-paragraph (b).

(4) In a case where a person has no identifiable normal pay day, paragraph (3) shall have effect as if the words "day of payment" were substituted for the words "normal pay day" in each place where they occur.

(5) In a case where a person has normal pay days at intervals of or approximating to one or more calendar months (including intervals of or approximating to a year) his normal weekly earnings shall be calculated by dividing his earnings in the relevant period by the number of calendar months in that period (or, if it is not a whole number, the nearest whole number), multiplying the result by 12 and dividing by 52.

(6) In a case to which paragraph (5) does not apply and the relevant period is not an exact number of weeks, the person's normal weekly earnings shall be calculated by dividing his earnings in the relevant period by the number of days in the relevant period and multiplying the result by 7.

(7) In any case where a person receives a back-dated pay increase which includes a sum in respect of a relevant period, normal weekly earnings shall be calculated as if such a sum was paid in that relevant period even though received after that period.

DEFINITIONS

"the Act"—see reg.2(1).
"adopter"—see *ibid.*
"the appropriate date"—see para.(2).
"day of payment"— see *ibid.*
"expected week"—see reg.2(1).
"normal pay day"—see para.(2).
"statutory paternity pay (adoption)"—see reg.2(1).
"statutory paternity pay (birth)"—see *ibid.*

Payment of statutory paternity pay and statutory adoption pay

41. Payments of statutory paternity pay and statutory adoption pay may be made in a like manner to payments of remuneration but shall not include payment in kind or by way of the provision of board or lodgings or of services or other facilities. 5.91

Time when statutory paternity pay and statutory adoption pay are to be paid

42.—(1) In this regulation, "pay day" means a day on which it has been agreed, or it is the normal practice between an employer or former employer and a person who is or was an employee of his, that payments by way of remuneration are to be made, or, where there is no such agreement or normal practice, the last day of a calendar month. 5.92

(2) In any case where—

(a) a decision has been made by an officer of the Board under section 8(1) of the Social Security Contributions (Transfer of Functions, etc.) Act 1999 as a result of which a person is entitled to an amount of statutory paternity pay or statutory adoption pay; and
(b) the time for bringing an appeal against the decision has expired and either—
  (i) no such appeal has been brought; or
  (ii) such an appeal has been brought and has been finally disposed of,

that amount of statutory paternity pay or statutory adoption pay shall be paid within the time specified in paragraph (3).

(3) Subject to paragraphs (4) and (5), the employer or former employer shall pay the amount not later than the first pay day after—

(a) where an appeal has been brought, the day on which the employer or former employer receives notification that it has been finally disposed of;

(b) where leave to appeal has been refused and there remains no further opportunity to apply for leave, the day on which the employer or former employer receives notification of the refusal; and

(c) in any other case, the day on which the time for bringing an appeal expires.

(4) Subject to paragraph (5), where it is impracticable, in view of the employer's or former employer's methods of accounting for and paying remuneration, for the requirement of payment referred to in paragraph (3) to be met by the pay day referred to in that paragraph, it shall be met not later than the next following pay day.

(5) Where the employer or former employer would not have remunerated the employee for his work in the week in question as early as the pay day specified in paragraph (3) or (if it applies) paragraph (4), the requirement of payment shall be met on the first day on which the employee would have been remunerated for his work in that week.

DEFINITIONS

"the Board"—see reg.2(1).
"pay day"—see para.(1).

Liability of the Board to pay statutory paternity pay or statutory adoption pay

5.93 **43**—(1) Where—

(a) an officer of the Board has decided that an employer is liable to make payments of statutory paternity pay or, as the case may be, statutory adoption pay to a person;

(b) the time for appealing against the decision has expired; and

(c) no appeal against the decision has been lodged or leave to appeal against the decision is required and has been refused,

then for any week in respect of which the employer was liable to make payments of statutory paternity pay or, as the case may be, statutory adoption pay but did not do so, and for any subsequent weeks in the paternity pay period or, as the case may be, adoption pay period, the liability to make those payments shall, notwithstanding sections 171ZD and 171ZM of the Act, be that of the Board and not the employer.

(2) Liability to make payments of statutory paternity pay or, as the case may be, statutory adoption pay shall, notwithstanding sections 171ZD and 171ZM of the Act, be a liability of the Board and not the employer as from the week in which the employer first becomes insolvent until the end of the paternity pay or adoption pay period.

(3) For the purposes of paragraph (2), an employer shall be taken to be insolvent if, and only if—

(a) in England and Wales—
   (i) he has been adjudged bankrupt or has made a composition or arrangement with his creditors;
   (ii) he has died and his estate falls to be administered in accordance with an order made under section 421 of the Insolvency Act 1986; or
   (iii) where an employer is a company or a limited liability partnership, a winding-up order or an administration order is made or a resolution for a voluntary winding-up is passed (or, in the case of a limited liability partnership, a determination for a voluntary winding-up has been made) with respect to it, or a receiver or a manager of its undertaking is duly appointed, or possession is taken, by or on behalf of the holders of any debentures secured by a floating charge, of any property of the company or limited liability partnership comprised in or subject to the charge, or a voluntary arrangement proposed for the purposes of Part 1 of the Insolvency Act 1986 is approved under that Part of that Act;

(b) in Scotland—
   (i) an award of sequestration is made on his estate or he executes a trust deed for his creditors or enters into a composition contract;
   (ii) he has died and a judicial factor appointed under section 11A of the Judicial Factors (Scotland) Act 1889 is required by that section to divide his insolvent estate among his creditors; or
   (iii) where the employer is a company or a limited liability partnership, a winding-up order or an administration order is made or a resolution for voluntary winding-up is passed (or, in the case of a limited liability partnership, a determination for a voluntary winding-up is made) with respect to it, or a receiver of its undertaking is duly appointed, or a voluntary arrangement proposed for the purposes of Part 1 of the Insolvency Act 1986 is approved under that Part.

DEFINITIONS

"the Act"—see reg.2(1).
"the Board"—see reg.2(1).

Liability of the Board to pay statutory adoption pay in cases of legal custody or imprisonment

44. Where— 5.94

(a) there is liability to pay statutory adoption pay in respect of a period which is subsequent to the last week falling within paragraph (1)(c) of regulation 27; or

(b) there is liability to pay statutory adoption pay during a period of detention in legal custody by virtue of the provisions of paragraph (2) of that regulation,

that liability shall, notwithstanding section 171ZM of the Act, be that of the Board and not the employer.

DEFINITIONS

"the Act"—see reg.2(1).
"the Board"—see reg.2(1).

Payments by the Board

5.95 **45.** Where the Board become liable in accordance with regulation 43 or 44 to make payments of statutory paternity pay or, as the case may be, statutory adoption pay to a person, the first payment shall be made as soon as reasonably practicable after they become so liable, and payments thereafter shall be made at weekly intervals, by means of an instrument of payment or by such other means as appears to the Board to be appropriate in the circumstance of any particular case.

DEFINITION

"the Board"—see reg.2(1).

Persons unable to act

5.96 **46.**—(1) Where in the case of any person—

(a) statutory paternity pay or, as the case may be, statutory adoption pay is payable to him or he is alleged to be entitled to it;
(b) he is unable for the time being to act; and
(c) either—
  (i) no receiver has been appointed by the Court of Protection with power to receive statutory paternity pay or, as the case may be, statutory adoption pay on his behalf; or
  (ii) in Scotland, his estate is not being administered by any tutor, curator or other guardian acting or appointed in terms of law,

the Board may, upon written application to them by a person who, if a natural person, is over the age of 18, appoint that person to exercise, on behalf of the person unable to act, any right to which he may be entitled under Part 12ZA or, as the case may be, Part 12ZB of the Act and to deal on his behalf with any sums payable to him.

(2) Where the Board have made an appointment under paragraph (1)—

(a) they may at any time in their absolute discretion revoke it;
(b) the person appointed may resign his office after having given one month's notice in writing to the Board of his intention to do so; and
(c) the appointment shall terminate when the Board are notified that a receiver or other person to whom paragraph (1)(c) applies has been appointed.

(3) Anything required by Part 12ZA or 12ZB of the Act to be done by or to any person who is unable to act may be done by or to the person appointed under this regulation to act on his behalf, and the receipt of the person so appointed shall be a good discharge to the person's employer or former employer for any sum paid.

DEFINITIONS

"the Act"—see reg.2(1).
"the Board"—see reg.2(1).

Service of notices by post

47. A notice given in accordance with the provisions of these Regulations in writing contained in an envelope which is properly addressed and sent by prepaid post shall be treated as having been given on the day on which it is posted. 5.97

Social Security Contributions and Benefits Act 1992 (Application of Parts 12ZA and 12ZB to Adoptions from Overseas) Regulations 2003

(SI 2003/499)

The Secretary of State, in exercise of the powers conferred on her by sections 171ZK and 171ZT of the Social Security Contributions and Benefits Act 1992 by this instrument, which contains only provision made by virtue of sections 2 and 4 of the Employment Act 2002 and is made before the end of the period of 6 months from the coming into force of those enactments, hereby makes the following Regulations—

Arrangement of Regulations

Citation, commencement and interpretation

1.—(1) These Regulations may be cited as the Social Security Contributions and Benefits Act 1992 (Application of Parts 12ZA and 12ZB to Adoptions from Overseas) Regulations 2003 and shall come into force, in so far as they apply powers to make regulations, on 10th March 2003, and for all other purposes on 6th April 2003. 5.99

(2) In these Regulations—

"adoption from overseas" means the adoption of a child who enters Great Britain from outside the United Kingdom in connection with or for the purposes of adoption which does not involve the placement of the child for adoption under the law of any part of the United Kingdom;

"the Act" means the Social Security Contributions and Benefits Act 1992.

General Note

These Regulations, made under provisions inserted into the SSCBA 1992 by the Employment Act 2002, apply Pts XIIZA and XIIZB of the 1992 Act, as 5.100

modified by these Regulations, to adoptions from overseas. These are adoptions of children who enter Great Britain from outside the United Kingdom in connection with or for the purposes of adoption which does not involve the placement of a child for adoption under the law of any part of the United Kingdom. The relevant adoption law requirements are set out in the Adoption (Bringing Children into the United Kingdom) Regulations 2003 (SI 2003/1173). The regulations relating to statutory paternity pay and statutory adoption pay in connection with such overseas adoptions are the Statutory Paternity Pay (Adoption) and Statutory Adoption Pay (Adoptions fromOverseas) Regulations 2003 (SI 2003/500).

Application of Part 12ZA of the Act to adoptions from overseas

5.101 **2.** Part 12ZA of the Act shall apply in relation to adoptions from overseas, with the modifications of sections 171ZB, 171ZE and 171ZJ of the Act specified in the second column of Schedule 1.

Application of Part 12ZB of the Act to adoptions from overseas

5.102 **3.** Part 12ZB of the Act shall apply in relation to adoptions from overseas, with the modifications of sections 171ZL and 171ZS of the Act specified in the second column of Schedule 2.

SCHEDULE 1 **Regulation 2**

APPLICATION OF PART 12ZA OF THE ACT TO ADOPTIONS FROM OVERSEAS

5.103

Provision	Modification
Section 171ZB(2)	[1. . .] In paragraph (a)(i), for "who is placed for adoption under the law of any part of the United Kingdom" substitute "who is adopted from overseas". In paragraph (a)(ii), for "a person with whom the child is so placed for adoption" substitute "an adopter of the child". [1In paragraph (b), omit "ending with the relevant week".] In paragraph (d), for "the day on which the child is placed for adoption" substitute "the day on which the child enters Great Britain". In paragraph (e), for "a person with whom the child is placed for adoption" substitute "an adopter of the child".
Section 171ZB(3)	[1 For subsection (3) substitute— "(3) The references in subsection (2)(c) and (d) to the relevant week are to— (a) the week in which official notification is sent to the adopter, or (b) the week at the end of which the person satisfies the condition in subsection (2)(b), whichever is the later."]
Section 171ZB(6)	For "the placement for adoption of more than one child as part of the same arrangement" substitute "the adoption from overseas of more than one child as part of the same arrangement".
Section 171ZB(7)	Omit subsection (7).
Section 171ZE(3)	In paragraph (b), for "with the date of the child's placement for adoption" substitute "with the date of the child's entry into Great Britain".

Provision	Modification
Section 171ZE(10)	For subsection (10) substitute— "(10) Where more than one child is the subject of adoption from overseas as part of the same arrangement, and the date of entry of each child is different, the reference in subsection (3)(b) to the date of the child's entry into Great Britain shall be interpreted as a reference to the date of the entry of the first child to enter Great Britain.".
Section 171ZJ(1)	In the appropriate places in the alphabetical order, insert— "adopter", in relation to a child, means a person by whom the child has been or is to be adopted;" "adoption from overseas" means the adoption of a child who enters Great Britain from outside the United Kingdom in connection with or for the purposes of adoption which does not involve the placement of the child for adoption under the law of any part of the United Kingdom, and the references to a child adopted from overseas shall be construed accordingly;" "official notification" means written notification, issued by or on behalf of the relevant domestic authority, that it is prepared to issue a certificate to the overseas authority concerned with the adoption of the child, or has issued a certificate and sent it to that authority, confirming, in either case, that the adopter is eligible to adopt and has been assessed and approved as being a suitable adoptive parent;" "relevant domestic authority" means— (a) in the case of an adopter to whom the Intercountry Adoption (Hague Convention) Regulations 2003 apply and who is habitually resident in Wales, the National Assembly of Wales; (b) in the case of an adopter to whom the Intercountry Adoption (Hague Convention) (Scotland) Regulations 2003 apply and who is habitually resident in Scotland, the Scottish Ministers; (c) in any other case, the Secretary of State.".

AMENDMENT

1. Statutory Paternity Pay and Statutory Adoption Pay (Amendment) Regulations 2004 (SI 2004/488), reg.3(2) (April 6, 2004).

SCHEDULE 2 **Regulation 3**

APPLICATION OF PART 12ZB OF THE ACT TO ADOPTIONS FROM OVERSEAS

5.104

Provision	Modification
Section 171ZL(2)	[1. . .] In paragraph (a), for "with whom a child is, or is expected to be, placed for adoption under the law of any part of the United Kingdom" substitute "who is, or is expected to be, an adopter of a child from overseas". [1In paragraph (b), omit "ending with the relevant week".]
Section 171ZL(3)	[1 For subsection (3) substitute— "(3) The reference in subsection (2)(d) to the relevant week is to— (a) the week in which official notification is sent to the adopter, or

Provision	Modification
	(b) the week at the end of which the person satisfies the condition in subsection (2)(b), whichever is the later."]
	[1. . .]
Section 171ZL(4)	In paragraph (b), for "placed for adoption with him" substitute "adopted by him".
Section 171ZL(5)	For "the placement, or expected placement, for adoption of more than one child" substitute "the adoption, or expected adoption, from overseas of more than one child".
Section 171ZS(1)	In the appropriate places in the alphabetical order, insert— ""adopter", in relation to a child, means a person by whom a child has been or is to be adopted;" "adoption from overseas" means the adoption of a child who enters Great Britain from outside the United Kingdom in connection with or for the purposes of adoption which does not involve the placement of the child for adoption under the law of any part of the United Kingdom, and the reference to an adopter from overseas shall be construed accordingly;" "official notification" means written notification, issued by or on behalf of the relevant domestic authority, that it is prepared to issue a certificate to the overseas authority concerned with the adoption of the child, or has issued a certificate and sent it to that authority, confirming, in either case, that the adopter is eligible to adopt and has been assessed and approved as being a suitable adoptive parent;" "relevant domestic authority" means— (a) in the case of an adopter to whom the Intercountry Adoption (Hague Convention) Regulations 2003 apply and who is habitually resident in Wales, the National Assembly of Wales; (b) in the case of an adopter to whom the Intercountry Adoption (Hague Convention) (Scotland) Regulations 2003 apply and who is habitually resident in Scotland, the Scottish Ministers; (c) in any other case, the Secretary of State.".

AMENDMENT

1. Statutory Paternity Pay and Statutory Adoption Pay (Amendment) Regulations 2004 (SI 2004/488), reg.3(3) (April 6, 2004).

Statutory Paternity Pay (Adoption) and Statutory Adoption Pay (Adoptions from Overseas) Regulations 2003

(SI 2003/500)

The Secretary of State, in exercise of the powers conferred on her by sections 171ZB(2)(a), 171ZC(3)(a) to (d), (f) and (g), 171ZD(2) and (3), 171ZE(2)(a), (b)(i), (3)(b), (7) and (8), 171ZG(3), 171ZJ(1), (3), (4), (7) and (8), 171ZL(8)(b) to (d), (f) and (g), 171ZM(2) and (3), 171ZN(2), (5) and (6), 171ZP(6), 171ZS(1), (3), (4), (7) and (8), and 175(4) of the Social Security

Contributions and Benefits Act 1992, section 5(1)(g), (i) and (p) of the Social Security Administration Act 1992 and with the concurrence of the Commissioners of Inland Revenue in so far as such concurrence is required, by this instrument, which contains only provision made by virtue of sections 2, 4 and 53 of and paragraphs 8 and 11 of Schedule 7 to the Employment Act 2002 and is made before the end of the period of six months from the coming into force of those enactments, hereby makes the following Regulations

ARRANGEMENT OF REGULATIONS

General

Statutory paternity pay (adoption)

Statutory adoption pay

General

Citation and commencement

5.108 **1.** These Regulations may be cited as the Statutory Paternity Pay (Adoption) and Statutory Adoption Pay (Adoptions from Overseas) Regulations 2003 and shall come into force on 6th April 2003.

GENERAL NOTE

These regulations were in force only between April 6, 2003 and May 29, 2003 (both dates included), following which they were revoked and superseded by Statutory Paternity Pay (Adoption) and Statutory Adoption Pay (Adoptions from Overseas) (No. 2) Regulations 2003 (SI 2003/1194). These latter regulations make an important typographical correction in reg. 11 and a number of other minor drafting changes.

Interpretation and scope

5.109 **2.**—(1) In these Regulations—

"the Act" means the Social Security Contributions and Benefits Act 1992;

"adopter", in relation to a child, means a person by whom the child has been or is to be adopted;

"adoption from overseas" means the adoption of a child who enters Great Britain from outside the United Kingdom in connection with or for the purposes of adoption which does not involve the placement of the child for adoption under the law of any part of the United Kingdom;

"the Application Regulations" means the Social Security Contributions and Benefits Act 1992 (Application of Parts 12ZA and 12ZB to Adoptions from Overseas) Regulations 2003;

"the Board" means the Commissioners of Inland Revenue;

"enter Great Britain" means enter Great Britain from outside the United Kingdom in connection with or for the purposes of adoption, and cognate expressions shall be construed accordingly;

"the General Regulations" means the Statutory Paternity Pay and Statutory Adoption Pay (General) Regulations 2002;

"official notification" means written notification, issued by or on behalf of the relevant domestic authority, that it is prepared to issue a certificate to the overseas authority concerned with the adoption of the child, or has issued a certificate and sent it to that authority, confirming, in either case, that the adopter is eligible to adopt, and has been assessed and approved as being a suitable adoptive parent;

"relevant domestic authority" means—

(a) in the case of an adopter to whom the Intercountry Adoption (Hague Convention) Regulations 2003 apply and who is habitually resident in Wales, the National Assembly for Wales;

(b) in the case of an adopter to whom the Intercountry Adoption (Hague Convention) (Scotland) Regulations apply and who is habitually resident in Scotland, the Scottish Ministers;

(c) in any other case, the Secretary of State;

"statutory paternity pay (adoption)" means statutory paternity pay payable in accordance with the provisions of Part 12ZA of the Act, as modified by the Application Regulations, where the conditions specified in section 171ZB(2) of the Act, as modified by the Application Regulations, are satisfied.

(2) References in these Regulations to the provisions of Parts 12ZA and 12ZB of the Act are to be construed as references to those provisions as modified by the Application Regulations.

(3) These Regulations apply to statutory paternity pay (adoption) and statutory adoption pay in respect of adoptions from overseas.

Application of the General Regulations to these Regulations

3.—(1) Subject to paragraph (2), the provisions of the General Regulations mentioned in paragraph (3) shall, in so far as they apply to statutory paternity pay (adoption) and statutory adoption pay, apply to adoptions from overseas. **5.110**

(2) Any references to the provisions of Parts 12ZA or 12ZB of the Act in the regulations of the General Regulations mentioned in paragraph (3) shall be construed as references to those provisions as modified by the Application Regulations.

(3) The provisions of the General Regulations referred to in paragraph (1) are regulations 17 to 19, 26 to 28, 31 to 39, 41 to 47 and, subject to paragraph (4), regulation 40.

(4) In the General Regulations, the provisions of regulation 40 shall apply as if—

(a) in paragraph (2)(b), for "the adopter is notified of being matched with the child for the purposes of adoption" there were substituted "the adopter receives official notification";

(b) at the end of paragraph (2), there were added "official notification" has the same meaning as in the Statutory Paternity Pay (Adoption) and Statutory Adoption Pay Adoption from Overseas) Regulations 2003".

Definitions

"the Act"—see reg.2(1).
"adopter"—see *ibid.*
"adoption from overseas"—see *ibid.*
"the Application Regulations"—see *ibid.*
"the General Regulations"—see *ibid.*
"statutory paternity pay (adoption)"—see *ibid.*

Application

4.—(1) Subject to the provisions of Part 12ZA of the Act (statutory paternity pay), the provisions of the General Regulations mentioned in paragraph (3) of regulation 3 and these Regulations, there is entitlement to statutory paternity pay (adoption) in respect of children who enter Great Britain on or after 6th April 2003. **5.111**

(2) Subject to the provisions of Part 12ZB of the Act (statutory adoption pay), the provisions of the General Regulations mentioned in paragraph (3) of regulation 3 and these Regulations, there is entitlement to statutory adoption pay in respect of children who enter Great Britain on or after 6th April 2003.

DEFINITIONS

"the Act"—see reg.2(1).
"enter Great Britain"—see *ibid.*
"the General Regulations"—see *ibid.*
"statutory paternity pay (adoption)"—see *ibid.*

Statutory paternity pay (adoption)

Conditions of entitlement to statutory paternity pay (adoption) in respect of adoptions from overseas: relationship with child and with adopter

5.112 **5.**—(1) The conditions prescribed under section 171ZB(2)(a) of the Act are that a person—

(a) is married to or the partner of a child's adopter (or in a case where there are two adopters, married to or the partner of the other adopter); and
(b) has, or expects to have, the main responsibility (apart from the responsibility of the child's adopter, or in a case where there are two adopters, together with the other adopter) for the upbringing of the child.

(2) For the purposes of paragraph (1), "partner" means a person (whether of a different sex or the same sex) who lives with the adopter and the child in an enduring family relationship but is not a relative of the adopter of a kind specified in paragraph (3).

(3) The relatives of a child's adopter referred to in the definition of "partner" in paragraph (2) are the adopter's parent, grandparent, sister, brother, aunt or uncle.

(4) References to relationships in paragraph (3)—

(a) are to relationships of the full blood or half blood or, in the case of an adopted person, such of those relationships as would exist but for the adoption; and
(b) include the relationship of a child with his adoptive, or former adoptive parents but do not include any other adoptive relationships.

DEFINITIONS

"the Act"—see reg.2(1).
"adopter"—see *ibid.*
"partner"—see para.(2).

Period of payment of statutory paternity pay (adoption) in respect of adoptions from overseas

6.—(1) Subject to notice under section 171ZC(1) of the Act, paragraph (2) and regulation 8, a person entitled to statutory paternity pay (adoption) may choose the statutory paternity pay period to begin on— 5.113

(a) the date on which the child enters Great Britain or, where the person is at work on that day, the following day;

(b) a predetermined date, specified by the person, which is later than the date on which the child enters Great Britain.

(2) In a case where statutory paternity pay (adoption) is payable in respect of a child where the adopter has received official notification before 6th April 2003, the statutory paternity pay period shall begin on a predetermined date, later than the date of entry, specified by the person entitled to such pay in a notice under section 171ZC(1) of the Act, which is at least 28 days after the date on which that notice was given, unless the person liable to pay statutory paternity pay (adoption) agrees to the omperiod beginning earlier.

(3) A person may choose for statutory paternity pay (adoption) to be paid in respect of a period of a week.

(4) A choice made in accordance with paragraph (1) or a date specified in accordance with paragraph (2) is not irrevocable, but where a person subsequently makes a different choice or specifies a different date in relation to the beginning of the statutory paternity pay period, section 171ZC(1) of the Act shall, subject to paragraph (2), apply to it.

DEFINITIONS

"the Act"—see reg.2(1).
"adopter"—see *ibid.*
"enter Great Britain"—see *ibid.*
"official notification"—see *ibid.*
"statutory paternity pay (adoption)"—see *ibid.*

Additional notice requirements for statutory paternity pay (adoption) in respect of adoptions from overseas

7.—(1) Where a person gives notice under section 171ZC(1) of the Act he shall give further notice of the following matters to the person liable to pay him statutory paternity pay (adoption)— 5.114

(a) the date on which official notification was received, within 28 days of that date, or within 28 days of his completion of 26 weeks of continuous employment with that person, whichever is the later;

(b) the date on which the child enters Great Britain, within 28 days of entry.

(2) Where the child has not entered Great Britain on the expected date, the person shall, if he wishes to claim statutory paternity pay (adoption), give notice to the person liable to pay it, as soon as is reasonably practicable, that the period in respect of which statutory paternity pay is to be paid shall begin on a date different from that originally chosen by him.

(3) That date may be any date chosen in accordance with paragraph (1) of regulation 6 or specified in accordance with paragraph (2) of that regulation.

(4) Where it becomes known to the person that the child will not enter Great Britain, he shall notify the person who would have been liable to pay statutory paternity pay (adoption), as soon as is reasonably practicable.

DEFINITIONS

"the Act"—see reg.2(1).
"enter Great Britain"—see *ibid.*
"official notification"—see *ibid.*
"statutory paternity pay (adoption)"—see *ibid.*

Qualifying period for statutory paternity pay (adoption) in respect of adoptions from overseas

5.115 **8.** The qualifying period for the purposes of section 171ZE(2) of the Act (period within which the statutory pay period must occur) is a period of 56 days beginning with the date the child enters Great Britain.

DEFINITIONS

"the Act"—see reg.2(1).
"enter Great Britain"—see *ibid.*

Evidence of entitlement for statutory paternity pay (adoption) in respect of adoptions from overseas

5.116 **9.**—(1) A person shall produce evidence of his entitlement to statutory paternity pay (adoption) in respect of adoptions from overseas by providing in writing to the person who will be liable to pay him statutory paternity pay (adoption) the declarations specified in paragraph (2) and the information specified in paragraph (3).

(2) The declarations referred to in paragraph (1) are as follows—

(a) that he meets the conditions prescribed under section 171ZB(2)(a) of the Act and that it is not the case that statutory paternity pay (adoption) is not payable to him by virtue of the provisions of section 171ZE(4) of the Act;
(b) that he has elected to receive statutory paternity pay (adoption), and not statutory adoption pay under Part 12ZB of the Act;
(c) that official notification has been received.

(3) The information referred to in paragraph (1) is as follows—

(a) the name of the person claiming statutory paternity pay (adoption);
(b) the date on which it is expected that the child will enter Great Britain or, where the child has already entered Great Britain, that date;
(c) the date from which it is expected that the liability to pay statutory paternity pay (adoption) will begin;
(d) whether the period chosen in respect of which statutory paternity pay (adoption) is to be payable is a week.

(4) The declarations mentioned in paragraph (2) and information mentioned in paragraph (3) shall be provided to the person liable to pay

statutory paternity pay (adoption) at least 28 days before the date mentioned in sub-paragraph (c) of paragraph (3) or, if that is not reasonably practicable, as soon as is reasonably practicable thereafter.

DEFINITIONS

"the Act"—see reg.2(1).
"adoption from overseas"—see *ibid.*
"enter Great Britain"—see *ibid.*
"official notification"—see *ibid.*
"statutory paternity pay (adoption)"—see *ibid.*

Entitlement to statutory paternity pay (adoption) where there is more than one employer in respect of adoptions from overseas

10. Statutory paternity pay (adoption) shall be payable to a person in respect of a statutory pay week during any part of which he works only for an employer— 5.117

(a) who is not liable to pay him statutory paternity pay (adoption); and
(b) for whom he has worked in the week in which the adopter receives official notification.

DEFINITIONS

"adopter"—see reg.2(1).
"official notification"—see *ibid.*
"statutory paternity pay (adoption)"—see *ibid.*

Avoidance of liability for statutory paternity pay (adoption) in respect of adoptions from overseas

11.—(1) A former employee shall be liable to make payments of statutory paternity pay (adoption) to a former employee in any case where the employee has been employed for a continuous period of at least 8 weeks and his contract of service was brought to an end by the former employer solely, or mainly, for the purpose of avoiding liability for statutory paternity pay (adoption). 5.118

(2) In a case falling within paragraph (1)—

(a) the employee shall be treated as if he had been employed for a continuous period ending with the day the child enters Great Britain;
(b) his normal weekly earnings shall be calculated by reference to his normal weekly earnings for the period of 8 weeks ending with the last day in respect of which he was paid under his former contract of service.

DEFINITIONS

"enter Great Britain"—see reg.2(1).
"statutory paternity pay (adoption)"—see *ibid.*

GENERAL NOTE

The first "employee" in para.(1) is a typographical error; it should, of course, read "employer". This defective drafting was not identified until the Joint Committee on Statutory Instruments published its *Seventeenth Report* (H.L. 91, 5.119

Session 2003/03). The DTI indicated to the Committee that this was a regrettable proofreading error and that the Department was "considering how best to make a correction" (*ibid.*, Appendix 1). In the end the Department decided to reissue the regulations, making this typographical correction and a number of other minor drafting changes: see Statutory Paternity Pay (Adoption) and Statutory Adoption Pay (Adoptions from Overseas) (No. 2) Regulations 2003 (SI 2003/1194).

Statutory adoption pay

Adoption pay period in respect of adoptions from overseas

5.120 **12.**—(1) Subject to notice under section 171ZL(6) of the Act and paragraph (2), a person entitled to statutory adoption pay may choose the adoption pay period to begin—

(a) on the date on which the child enters Great Britain or, where the person is at work on that day, on the following day;

(b) on a predetermined date, specified by him, which is no later than 28 days after the date the child enters Great Britain.

(2) In a case where statutory adoption pay is payable in respect of a child where the adopter has received official notification before 6th April 2003, the statutory adoption pay period shall begin on a predetermined date, later than the date of entry, specified by the person entitled to such pay in a notice under section 171ZL(6) of the Act, which is at least 28 days after the date on which that notice was given, unless the person liable to pay statutory adoption pay agrees to the period commencing earlier.

(3) Where the choice made is that mentioned in sub-paragraph (b) of paragraph (1), the adoption pay period shall, unless the employer agrees to the adoption pay period beginning earlier, begin no earlier than 28 days after notice under section 171ZL(6) of the Act has been given.

(4) Subject to regulation 13, the duration of any adoption pay period shall be a continuous period of 26 weeks.

(5) A choice made under paragraph (1), or a date specified under paragraph (2), is not irrevocable, but where a person subsequently makes a different choice or specifies a different date in relation to the beginning of the statutory adoption pay period, section 171ZL(6) of the Act shall, subject to paragraph (2), apply to it.

DEFINITIONS

"the Act"—see reg.2(1).
"enter Great Britain"—see *ibid.*
"official notification"—see *ibid.*

Adoption pay period in respect of adoptions from overseas where adoption is disrupted

5.121 **13.**—(1) Where after a child enters Great Britain the child—

(a) dies; or

(b) ceases to live with the adopter,

the adoption pay period shall terminate in accordance with the provisions of paragraph (2).

(2) The adoption pay period shall, in a case falling within paragraph (1), terminate 8 weeks after the end of the week specified in paragraph (3).

(3) The week referred to in paragraph (2) is—

(a) in a case falling within paragraph (1)(a), the week during which the child dies;

(b) in a case falling within paragraph (1)(b), the week during which the child ceases to live with the adopter.

(4) For the purposes of paragraph (3), "week" means a period of 7 days beginning with Sunday.

DEFINITIONS

"enter Great Britain"—see reg.2(1).
"week"—see para.(4).

Additional notice requirements for statutory adoption pay in respect of adoptions from overseas

14.—(1) Where a person gives notice under section 171ZL(6) of the Act he shall give further notice of the following matters to the person liable to pay himstatutory adoption pay— 5.122

(a) the date on which official notification was received, within 28 days of that date, or within 28 days of his completion of 26 weeks of continuous employment, whichever is the later;

(b) the date on which the child enters Great Britain, within 28 days of entry.

(2) Where the child has not entered Great Britain on the expected date, the person shall, if he wishes to claim statutory adoption pay, give notice to the person liable to pay it, as soon as is reasonably practicable, that the period in respect of which statutory adoption pay is to be paid shall begin on a date different from that originally chosen by him.

(3) That date may be any date chosen in accordance with paragraph (1) of regulation 12 or specified in accordance with paragraph (2) of that regulation.

(4) Where it becomes known to the adopter that the child will not enter Great Britain, he shall notify the person who would have been liable to pay statutory adoption pay as soon as is reasonably practicable.

DEFINITIONS

"the Act"—see reg.2(1).
"enter Great Britain"—see *ibid.*
"official notification"—see *ibid.*

Evidence of entitlement to statutory adoption pay in respect of adoptions from overseas

15.—(1) A person shall provide evidence of his entitlement to statutory adoption pay by providing, to the person who will be liable to pay it, a copy of the official notification and, in writing— 5.123

(a) the information specified in paragraph (2);

(b) a declaration that he has elected to receive statutory adoption pay, and not statutory paternity pay (adoption) under Part 12ZA of the Act;

(c) evidence, to be provided within 28 days of the child's entry into Great Britain, as to that date.

(2) The information referred to in paragraph (1) is—

(a) the name and address of the person claiming statutory adoption pay;

(b) the date on which it is expected that the child will enter Great Britain or, where he has already done so, that date.

(3) The information and declaration referred to in paragraph (1), other than that mentioned in sub-paragraph (c) of paragraph (1), shall be provided to the person liable to pay statutory adoption pay at least 28 days before the date chosen as the beginning of the adoption pay period in accordance with paragraph (1) of regulation 12 or specified in accordance with paragraph (2) of that regulation or, if that is not reasonably practicable, as soon as is reasonably practicable thereafter.

DEFINITIONS

"the Act"—see reg.2(1).
"enter Great Britain"—see *ibid.*
"official notification"—see *ibid.*

Entitlement to statutory adoption pay in respect of adoptions from overseas where there is more than one employer

5.124 **16.** Statutory adoption pay shall be payable to a person in respect of a week during any part of which he works only for an employer—

(a) who is not liable to pay him statutory adoption pay; and

(b) for whom he has worked in the week in which he receives official notification.

DEFINITION

"official notification"—see reg.2(1).

Termination of employment and liability to pay statutory adoption pay in respect of adoptions from overseas

5.125 **17.**—(1) Where the employment of a person who satisfies the conditions of entitlement to statutory adoption pay in respect of adoptions from overseas terminates for whatever reason (including dismissal) before the adoption pay period chosen or specified by that person in accordance with regulation 12 has begun, the period shall begin on a date chosen by that person which is at least 28 days after notice has been given and within 28 days of the date of the child's entry into Great Britain.

(2) Where the statutory adoption pay period has not commenced within a period of six months of the adopter's leaving his employer, liability to pay statutory adoption pay shall, notwithstanding section 171ZM(1) of the Act, pass to the Board.

(3) Where liability to pay statutory adoption pay has passed to the Board in accordance with paragraph (2) and the adopter, having started

employment as an employed earner, becomes entitled to statutory adoption pay by virtue of that employment, the liability of the Board shall cease and section 171ZM(1) of the Act shall apply.

DEFINITIONS

"the Act"—see reg.2(1).
"adopter"—see *ibid.*
"adoption from overseas"—see *ibid.*
"the Board"—see *ibid.*
"enter Great Britain"—see *ibid.*

Avoidance of liability for statutory adoption pay in respect of adoptions from overseas

18.—(1) A former employer shall be liable to make payments of statutory adoption pay to a former employee in any case where the employee had been employed for a continuous period of at least 8 weeks and his contract of service was brought to an end by the former employer solely, or mainly, for the purpose of avoiding liability for statutory adoption pay. 5.126

(2) In a case falling within paragraph (1)—

(a) the employee shall be treated as if he has been employed for a continuous period ending with the week in which he received official notification; and

(b) his normal weekly earnings shall be calculated by reference to his normal weekly earnings for the period of 8 weeks ending with the last day in respect of which he was paid under his former contract of service.

DEFINITION

"official notification"—see reg.2(1).

Statutory Paternity Pay (Adoption) and Statutory Adoption Pay (Adoptions from Overseas) (Administration) Regulations 2003

(SI 2003/1192)

The Secretary of State, in exercise of the powers conferred on her by section 7(1), 2(a) and (b), (4)(a), (b) and (c) and (5), 8(1) and (2)(a), (b) and (c), 10(1) and (2) and 51(1) of the Employment Act 2002 and sections 8(1)(f) and 25 of the Social Security Contributions (Transfer of Functions, etc.) Act 1999 and with the concurrence of the Commissioners of Inland Revenue, hereby makes the following Regulations:

ARRANGEMENT OF REGULATIONS

3. Application of the Statutory Paternity Pay and Statutory Adoption Pay (Administration) Regulations 2002 to adoptions from overseas.

Citation and commencement

5.128 **1.** These Regulations may be cited as the Statutory Paternity Pay (Adoption) and Statutory Adoption Pay (Adoptions from Overseas) (Administration) Regulations 2003 and shall come into force on 23rd May 2003.

GENERAL NOTE

5.129 These Regulations apply the Statutory Paternity Pay and Statutory Adoption Pay (Administration) Regulations 2002 (SI 2002/2820) to adoptions from overseas with the necessary modifications.

Interpretation

5.130 **2.** In these Regulations, "adoption from overseas" means the adoption of a child who enters Great Britain from outside the United Kingdom in connection with or for the purposes of adoption which does not involve the placement of the child for adoption under the law of any part of the United Kingdom.

Application of the Statutory Paternity Pay and Statutory Adoption Pay (Administration) Regulations 2002 to adoptions from overseas

5.131 **3.**—(1) The Statutory Paternity Pay and Statutory Adoption Pay (Administration) Regulations 2002 shall apply in the case of adoptions from overseas with the modifications set out in the following paragraphs of this regulation.

(2) In regulation 2(1) (interpretation)—

(a) in the definition of "adopter", for the words "with whom the child is matched for adoption" substitute "by whom the child has been or is to be adopted";

(b) after the definition of "income tax quarter", insert—

"official notification" means written notification, issued by or on behalf of the relevant domestic authority, that it is prepared to issue a certificate to the overseas authority concerned with the adoption of the child, or has issued a certificate and sent it to that authority, confirming, in either case, that the adopter is eligible to adopt and has been assessed and approved as being a suitable adoptive parent;";

(c) in the definition of "paternity leave", insert at the end "as modified in its application to adoptions from overseas by the Employment Rights Act 1996 (Application of Section 80B to Adoptions from Overseas) Regulations 2003"; and

(d) after the definition of "paternity pay period" insert—

"relevant domestic authority means:—

(a) in the case of an adopter to whom the Intercountry Adoption (Hague Convention) Regulations 2003 apply and who is habitually resident in Wales, the National Assembly for Wales;

(b) in the case of an adopter to whom the Intercountry Adoption (Hague Convention) (Scotland) Regulations 2003 apply and who is habitually resident in Scotland, the Scottish Ministers; and

(c) in any other case, the Secretary of State;".

(3) After regulation 2(2), insert—

"(3) References in these Regulations to provisions of Parts 12ZA and 12ZB of the Contributions and Benefits Act are to be construed as references to those provisions as modified by the Social Security Contributions and Benefits Act 1992 (Application of Parts 12ZA and 12ZB to Adoptions fromOverseas) Regulations 2003."

(4) In regulation 11(3)(b)(ii) (time within which an employer is required to give decision that he has no liability to make payments), for "the end of the seven-day period that starts on the date on which the adopter is notified of having been matched with the child" substitute "the date on which the employer's evidence was provided, or, where not all of the evidence referred to in paragraph (1) was provided on one date, the date on which the last of the evidence was provided".

(5) Omit regulation 11(4).

Statutory Paternity Pay (Adoption and Statutory Adoption Pay (Adoptions from Overseas) (Persons Abroad and Mariners) Regulations 2003

(SI 2003/1193)

The Secretary of State, in exercise of the powers conferred upon her by virtue of sections 171ZI, 171ZJ(1), 171ZR and 171ZS(1) of the Social Security Contributions and Benefits Act 1992 and with the concurrence of the Treasury, by this instrument, which contains only provision made by virtue of sections 2 and 4 of the Employment Act 2002 and is made before the end of the period of 6 months from the coming into force of those enactments, hereby makes the following Regulations:

Arrangement of Regulations

Citation and commencement

1. These Regulations may be cited as the Statutory Paternity Pay (Adoption) and Statutory Adoption Pay (Adoptions from Overseas) (Persons Abroad and Mariners) Regulations 2003 and shall come into force on 23rd May 2003. 5.133

General Note

5.134 These Regulations modify the application of the Statutory Paternity Pay and Statutory Adoption Pay (Persons Abroad and Mariners) Regulations 2002 (SI 2002/2821) as regards adoptions from overseas.

Interpretation

5.135 **2.** In these Regulations, "adoption from overseas" means the adoption of a child who enters Great Britain from outside the United Kingdom in connection with or for the purposes of adoption which does not involve the placement of the child for adoption under the law of any part of the United Kingdom.

Application of the Statutory Paternity Pay and Statutory Adoption Pay (Persons Abroad and Mariners) Regulations 2002 to adoptions from overseas

5.136 **3.**—(1) The Statutory Paternity Pay and Statutory Adoption Pay (Persons Abroad and Mariners) Regulations 2002 shall have effect in relation to adoptions from overseas with the modifications set out in the following paragraphs of this regulation.

(2) In regulation 1(2) (interpretation)—

(a) in the definition of "adopter", for "has the same meaning as it has in the General Regulations" substitute "means a person by whom the child has been or is to be adopted";

(b) after the definition of "the General Regulations", insert—

"official notification" means written notification, issued by or on behalf of the relevant domestic authority, that it is prepared to issue a certificate to the overseas authority concerned with the adoption of the child, or has issued a certificate and sent it to that authority, confirming, in either case, that the adopter is eligible to adopt and has been assessed and approved as being a suitable adoptive parent;

"relevant domestic authority" means—

(a) in the case of an adopter to whom the Intercountry Adoption (Hague Convention) Regulations 2003 apply and who is habitually resident in Wales, the National Assembly for Wales;

(b) in the case of an adopter to whom the Intercountry Adoption (Hague Convention) (Scotland) Regulations 2003 apply and who is habitually resident in Scotland, the Scottish Ministers; and

(c) in any other case, the Secretary of State;".

(c) for the definition of "statutory paternity pay (birth)" and "statutory paternity pay (adoption)" substitute—

"statutory paternity pay (adoption)" means statutory paternity pay payable in accordance with the provisions of Part 12ZA of the Act, where the conditions specified in section 171ZB(2) of the Act are satisfied;".

(3) For regulation (3), substitute—

"(3) References in these Regulations to provisions of Parts 12ZA and 12ZB of the Act are to be construed as references to those provisions as modified by the Social Security Contributions and Benefits Act 1992

(Application of Parts 12ZA and 12ZB to Adoptions from Overseas) Regulations 2003."

(4) In regulation 5(2) (entitlement to statutory paternity pay adoption))—

(a) in the first line, after "and who" insert ", in the week in which the adopter receives an official notification or completes 26 weeks' continuous employment with his employer, whichever is the later"; and

(b) in sub-paragraph (a), omit the words "in the week in which the adopter is notified of being matched with the child for the purposes of adoption".

(5) In regulation 6 (entitlement to statutory adoption pay)—

(a) in the first line, after "and who" insert ", in the week in which he receives an official notification or completes 26 weeks' continuous employment with his employer, whichever is the later"; and

(b) in paragraph (a), omit the words "in the week in which he is notified that he has been matched with the child for the purposes of adoption".

Statutory Paternity Pay (Adoption) and Statutory Adoption Pay (Adoptions from Overseas) (No.2) Regulations 2003

(SI 2003/1194)

The Secretary of State, in exercise of the powers conferred on her by sections 171ZB(2)(a), 171ZC(3)(a) to (d), (f) and (g), 171ZD(2) and (3), 171ZE(2)(a) and (b)(i), (3)(b), (7) and (8), 171ZG(3), 171ZJ(1), (3), (4), (7) and (8), 171ZL(8)(b) to (d), (f) and (g), 171ZM(2) and (3), 171ZN(2), (5) and (6), 171ZP(6), 171ZS(1), (3), (4), (7) and (8), and 175(4) of the Social Security Contributions and Benefits Act 1992, section 5(1)(g), (i) and (p) of the Social Security Administration Act 1992 and with the concurrence of the Commissioners of Inland Revenue in so far as such concurrence is required, by this instrument, which contains only provision made by virtue of sections 2, 4 and 53 and paragraphs 8 and 11 of Schedule 7 to the Employment Act 2002 and is made before the end of the period of 6 months from the coming into force of these enactments, hereby makes the following Regulations:

ARRANGEMENT OF REGULATIONS

General

Statutory paternity pay (adoption)

Statutory adoption pay

General

Citation and commencement

5.138 **1.** These Regulations may be cited as the Statutory Paternity Pay (Adoption) and Statutory Adoption Pay (Adoptions from Overseas) (No.2) Regulations 2003 and shall come into force on 30th May 2003.

General Note

5.139 These Regulations, made under provisions inserted into the SSCBA 1992 by the Employment Act 2002, make provision relating to statutory paternity pay and statutory adoption pay in respect of adoptions from overseas. They should be read together with the Social Security Contributions and Benefits Act 1992 (Application of Pts XIIZA and XIIZB to Adoptions from Overseas) Regulations 2003 (SI 2003/499), which provide for Pts XIIZA and XIIZB of the 1992 Act to have effect, with the modification prescribed in those Regulations, in relation to cases which involve adoption, but not the placement of a child for adoption under the law of any part of the United Kingdom. Regulation 19 of these (No.2)

Regulations revokes the Statutory Pay (Adoption) and Statutory Adoption Pay (Adoptions from Overseas) Regulations 2003 (SI 2003/500), which came into force on April 6, 2003 and originally made provision for paternity and adoption pay in the case of adoptions from overseas. The (No.2) Regulations are virtually in identical form to the original set. The main difference is the correction of "employee" to read "employer" in reg.11 where it first appears, but a number of other minor drafting amendments have also been made.

Interpretation and scope

2.—(1) In these Regulations— **5.140**

"the Act" means the Social Security Contributions and Benefits Act 1992;

"adopter", in relation to a child, means a person by whom the child has been or is to be adopted;

"adoption from overseas" means the adoption of a child who enters Great Britain from outside the United Kingdom in connection with or for the purposes of adoption which does not involve the placement of the child for adoption under the law of any part of the United Kingdom;

"the Application Regulations" means the Social Security Contributions and Benefits Act 1992 (Application of Parts 12ZA and 12ZB to Adoptions from Overseas) Regulations 2003;

"the Board" means the Commissioners of Inland Revenue;

"enter Great Britain" means enter Great Britain from outside the United Kingdom in connection with or for the purposes of adoption, and cognate expressions shall be construed accordingly;

"the General Regulations" means the Statutory Paternity Pay and Statutory Adoption Pay (General) Regulations 2002;

"official notification" means written notification, issued by or on behalf of the relevant domestic authority, that it is prepared to issue a certificate to the overseas authority concerned with the adoption of the child, or has issued a certificate and sent it to that authority, confirming, in either case, that the adopter is eligible to adopt, and has been assessed and approved as being a suitable adoptive parent;

"relevant domestic authority" means—

(a) in the case of an adopter to whom the Intercountry Adoption (Hague Convention) Regulations 2003 apply and who is habitually resident in Wales, the National Assembly for Wales;

(b) in the case of an adopter to whom the Intercountry Adoption (Hague Convention) (Scotland) Regulations apply and who is habitually resident in Scotland, the Scottish Ministers;

(c) in any other case, the Secretary of State;

"statutory paternity pay (adoption)" means statutory paternity pay payable in accordance with the provisions of Part 12ZA of the Act, as modified by the Application Regulations, where the conditions specified in section 171ZB(2) of the Act, as modified by the Application Regulations, are satisfied.

(2) References in these Regulations to the provisions of Parts 12ZA and 12ZB of the Act are to be construed as references to those provisions as modified by the Application Regulations.

(3) These Regulations apply to statutory paternity pay (adoption) and statutory adoption pay in respect of adoptions from overseas.

Application of the General Regulations to these Regulations

5.141 **3.**—(1) Subject to paragraph (2), the provisions of the General Regulations mentioned in paragraph (3) shall, in so far as they apply to statutory paternity pay (adoption) and statutory adoption pay, apply to adoptions from overseas.

(2) Any references to the provisions of Parts 12ZA or 12ZB of the Act in the regulations of the General Regulations mentioned in paragraph (3) shall be construed as references to those provisions as modified by the Application Regulations.

(3) The provisions of the General Regulations referred to in paragraph (1) are regulations 17 to 19, 26 to 28, 31 to 39, 41 to 47 and, subject to paragraph (4), regulation 40.

(4) In the General Regulations, the provisions of regulation 40 shall apply as if—

[1 (a) in paragraph (2)(b), for "the week in which the adopter is notified of being matched with the child for the purposes of adoption" there were substituted—

"the week in which—

(i) official notification is sent to the adopter or

(ii) the person satisfies the condition in section 171ZB(2)(b) or 171ZL(2)(b) of the Act (26 weeks' continuous employment),

whichever is the later;"]

(b) at the end of paragraph (2), there were added ""official notification" has the same meaning in the Statutory Paternity Pay (Adoption) and Statutory Adoption Pay (Adoptions from Overseas) (No.2) Regulations 2003".

AMENDMENT

1. Statutory Paternity Pay and Statutory Adoption Pay (Amendment) Regulations 2004 (SI 2004/488), reg.4 (April 6, 2004).

DEFINITIONS

"the Act—see reg.2(1).
"adopter"—see *ibid.*
"adoption from overseas"—see *ibid.*
"the Application Regulation"—see *ibid.*
"the General Regulations"—see *ibid.*
"official notification"—see *ibid.*
"statutory paternity pay (adoption)"—see *ibid.*

Application

5.142 **4.**—(1) Subject to the provisions of Part 12ZA of the Act (statutory paternity pay), the provisions of the General Regulations mentioned in paragraph (3) of regulation 3 and these Regulations, there is entitlement to statutory paternity pay (adoption) in respect of children who enter Great Britain on or after 6th April 2003.

(2) Subject to the provisions of Part 12ZB of the Act (statutory adoption pay), the provisions of the General Regulations mentioned in paragraph (3) of regulation 3 and these Regulations, there is entitlement to statutory adoption pay in respect of children who enter Great Britain on or after 6th April, 2003.

DEFINITIONS

"the Act"—see reg.2(1).
"enter Great Britain"—see *ibid.*
"the General Regulation"—see *ibid.*
"Part XIIZA"—see reg.(2).
"Pt XIIZB"—see *ibid.*
"statutory paternity pay (adoption)"—see reg.2(1).

Statutory paternity pay (adoption)

Conditions of entitlement to statutory paternity pay (adoption) in respect of adoptions from overseas: relationship with child and with adopter

5.—(1) The conditions prescribed under section 171ZB(2)(a) of the Act are that a person— 5.143

(a) is married to or the partner of a child's adopter (or in a case where there are two adopters, married to or the partner of the other adopter); and
(b) has, or expects to have, the main responsibility (apart from the responsibility of the child's adopter or, in a case where there are two adopters, together with the other adopter) for the upbringing of the child.

(2) For the purpose of paragraph (1), "partner" means a person (whether of a different sex or the same sex) who lives with the adopter and the child in an enduring family relationship but is not a relative of the adopter of a kind specified in paragraph (3).

(3) The relatives of a child's adopter referred to in the definition of "partner" in paragraph (2) are the adopter's parent, grandparent, sister, brother, aunt or uncle.

(4) References to relationships in paragraph (3)—

(a) are to relationships of the full blood or half blood or, in the case of an adopted person, such of those relationships as would exist but for the adoption; and
(b) include the relationship of a child with his adoptive, or former adoptive parents but do not include any other adoptive relationships.

DEFINITIONS

"the Act"—see reg.2(1).
"adopter"—see *ibid.*
"partner"—see para.(2).

Period of payment of statutory paternity pay (adoption) in respect of adoptions from overseas

5.144 **6.**—(1) Subject to notice under section 171ZC(1) of the Act, paragraph 92) and reg.8, a person entitled to statutory paternity pay (adoption) may choose the statutory paternity pay period to begin on—

(a) the date on which the child enters Great Britain or, where the person is at work on that day, the following day; or

(b) a pre-determined date, specified by the person, which is later than the date on which the child enters Great Britain.

(2) In a case where statutory paternity pay (adoption) is payable in respect of a child where the adopter has received official notification before 6th April 2003, the statutory paternity pay period shall begin on a predetermined date, later than the date of entry, specified by the person entitled to such pay in a notice under section 171ZC(1) of the Act, which is at least 28 days after the date on which that notice was given, unless the person liable to pay statutory paternity pay (adoption) agrees to the period beginning earlier.

(3) A person may choose for statutory paternity pay (adoption) to be paid in respect of a period of a week.

(4) A choice made in accordance with paragraph (1) is not irrevocable, but where a person subsequently makes a different choice in relation to the beginning of the statutory paternity pay period, section 171ZC(1) of the Act shall apply to it.

DEFINITIONS

"the Act"—see reg.2(1).
"adopter"—see *ibid.*
"enter Great Britain"—see *ibid.*
"official notification"—see *ibid.*
"statutory paternity pay (adoption)"—see *ibid.*

Additional notice requirements for statutory paternity pay (adoption) in respect of adoptions from overseas

5.145 **7.**—(1) Where a person gives notice under section 171ZC(1) of the Act he shall give further notice of the following matters to the person liable to pay him statutory paternity pay (adoption)—

(a) the date on which official notification was received, within 28 days of that date, or within 28 days of his completion of 26 weeks of continuous employment with that person, whichever is the later;

(b) the date on which the child enters Great Britain, within 28 days of entry.

(2) Where the child has not entered Great Britain on the expected date, the person shall, if he wishes to claim statutory paternity pay (adoption), give notice to the person liable to pay it, as soon as is reasonably practicable, that the period in respect of which statutory paternity pay is to be paid shall begin on a date different from that originally chosen by him.

(3) That date may be any date chosen in accordance with paragraph (1) of regulation 6 or specified in accordance with paragraph (2) of that regulation.

(4) Where it becomes known to that person that the child will not enter Great Britain, he shall notify the person who would have been liable to pay statutory pay (adoption), as soon as is reasonably practicable.

DEFINITIONS

"the Act"—see reg.2(1).
"enter Great Britain"—see *ibid.*
"official notification"—see *ibid.*
"statutory paternity pay (adoption)"—see *ibid.*

Qualifying period for statutory paternity pay (adoption) in respect of adoptions from overseas

8. The qualifying period for the purposes of section 171ZE(2) of the Act (period within which the statutory pay period must occur) is a period of 56 days beginning with the date the child enters Great Britain. 5.146

DEFINITIONS

"the Act"—see reg.2(1).
"enter Great Britain"—see *ibid.*

Evidence of entitlement for statutory paternity pay (adoption) in respect of adoptions from overseas

9.—(1) A person shall produce evidence of his entitlement to statutory paternity pay (adoption) in respect of adoptions from overseas by providing in writing to the person who will be liable to pay him statutory paternity pay (adoption) the declarations specified in paragraph (2) and the information specified in paragraph (3). 5.147

(2) The declarations referred to in para.(1) are as follows—

(a) that he meets the conditions prescribed under section 171ZB(2)(a) of the Act and that it is not the case that statutory paternity pay (adoption) is not payable to himby virtue of the provisions of section 171ZE(4) of the Act;
(b) that he has elected to receive statutory paternity pay (adoption), and not statutory adoption pay under Part 12ZB of the Act;
(c) that official notification has been received.

(3) The information referred to in paragraph (1) is as follows—

(a) the name of the person claiming statutory paternity pay (adoption);
(b) the date on which it is expected that the child will enter Great Britain or, where the child has already entered Great Britain, that date;
(c) the date from which it is expected that the liability to pay statutory paternity pay (adoption) will begin;
(d) whether the period chosen in respect of which statutory paternity pay (adoption) is to be payable is a week.

(4) The declarations mentioned in paragraph (2) and information mentioned in paragraph (3) shall be provided to the person liable to pay statutory paternity pay (adoption) at least 28 days before the date mentioned in sub-paragraph (c) of paragraph (3) or, if that is not reasonably practicable, as soon as is reasonably practicable thereafter.

DEFINITIONS

"the Act"—see reg.2(1).
"adoption from overseas"—see *ibid.*
"enter Great Britain"—see *ibid.*
"official notification"—see *ibid.*
"Pt XIIZB"—see reg.2(2).
"statutory paternity pay (adoption)"—see reg.2(1).

Entitlement to statutory paternity pay (adoption) where there is more than one employer in respect of adoptions from overseas

5.148 **10.** Statutory paternity pay (adoption) shall be payable to a person in respect of a statutory pay week during any part of which he works only for an employer—

(a) who is not liable to pay him statutory paternity pay (adoption); and
(b) for whom he has worked in the week in which the adopter receives official notification.

DEFINITIONS

"adopter"—see reg.2(1).
"official notification"—see *ibid.*
"statutory paternity pay (adoption)"—see *ibid.*

Avoidance of liability for statutory paternity pay (adoption) in respect of adoptions from overseas

5.149 **11.**—(1) A former employer shall be liable to make payments of statutory paternity pay (adoption) to a former employee in any case where the employee has been employed for a continuous period of at least 8 weeks and his contract of service was brought to an end by the former employer solely, or mainly, for the purpose of avoiding liability for statutory paternity pay (adoption).

(2) In a case falling within paragraph (1)—

(a) the employee shall be treated as if he had been employed for a continuous period ending with the day the child enters Great Britain;
(b) his normal weekly earnings shall be calculated by reference to his normal weekly earnings for the period of 8 weeks ending with the last day in respect of which he was paid under his former contract of service.

DEFINITIONS

"enter Great Britain"—see reg.2(1).
"statutory paternity pay (adoption)"—see *ibid.*

Statutory adoption pay

Adoption pay period in respect of adoptions from overseas

5.150 **12.**—(1) Subject to paragraph (2), a person entitled to statutory adoption pay may choose the adoption pay period to begin—

(a) on the date on which the child enters Great Britain or, where the person is at work on that day, on the following day;
(b) on the pre-determined date, specified by him, which is no later than 28 days after the date the child enters Great Britain.

(2) In a case where statutory adoption pay is payable in respect of a child where the adopter has received official notification before 6th April 2003, the statutory adoption pay period shall begin on a predetermined date, later than the date of entry, specified by the person entitled to such pay in a notice under section 171ZL(6) of the Act, which is at least 28 days after the date on which that notice was given, unless the person liable to pay statutory adoption pay agrees to the period commencing earlier.

(3) Where the choice made is that mentioned in sub-paragraph (b) of paragraph (1) or in a case where paragraph (2) applies, the adoption pay period shall, unless the employer agrees to the adoption pay period beginning earlier, begin no earlier than 28 days after notice under section 171ZL(6) of the Act has been given.

(4) Subject to regulation 13, the duration of any adoption pay period shall be a continuous period of 26 weeks.

(5) A choice made under paragraph (1), or a date specified under paragraph (2), is not irrevocable, but where a person subsequently makes a different choice or specifies a different date in relation to the beginning of the statutory adoption pay period, section 171ZL(6) of the Act shall apply to it.

DEFINITIONS

"the Act"—see reg.2(1).
"adopter"—see *ibid.*
"enter Great Britain"—see *ibid.*
"official notification"—see *ibid.*

Adoption pay period in respect of adoptions from overseas where adoption is disrupted

13.—(1) Where after a child enters Great Britain the child— 5.151
(a) dies; or
(b) ceases to live with the adopter,
the adoption pay period shall terminate in accordance with the provisions of paragraph (2).

(2) The adoption pay period shall, in a case falling within paragraph (1), terminate 8 weeks after the end of the week specified in paragraph (3).

(3) The week referred to in paragraph (2) is—
(a) in a case falling within paragraph (1)(a), the week during which the child dies;
(b) in a case falling within paragraph (1)(b), the week during which the child ceases to live with the adopter.

(4) For the purposes of paragraph (3), "week" means a period of 7 days beginning with Sunday.

DEFINITIONS

"adopter"—see reg.2(1).
"enter Great Britain"—see *ibid.*
"week"—see para.(4).

Additional notice requirements for statutory adoption pay in respect of adoptions from overseas

5.152 **14.**—(1) Where a person gives notice under section 171ZL(6) of the Act he shall give further notice of the following matters to the person liable to pay statutory adoption pay—

(a) the date on which official notification was received, within 28 days of that date, or within 28 days of his completion of 26 weeks of continuous employment, whichever is the later;
(b) the date on which the child enters Great Britain, within 28 days of entry.

(2) Where the child has not entered Great Britain on the expected date, the person shall, if he wishes to claim statutory adoption pay, give notice to the person liable to pay it, as soon as is reasonably practicable, that the period in respect of which statutory adoption pay is to be paid shall begin on a date different fromthat originally chosen by him.

(3) That date may be any date chosen in accordance with paragraph (1) of regulation 12 or specified in accordance with paragraph (2) of that regulation.

(4) Where it becomes known to the adopter that the child will not enter Great Britain, he shall notify the person who would have been liable to pay statutory adoption pay as soon as is reasonably practicable.

DEFINITIONS

"the act"—see reg.2(1).
"adopter"—see *ibid.*
"enter Great Britain"—see *ibid.*
"official notification"—see *ibid.*

Evidence of entitlement to statutory adoption pay in respect of adoptions from overseas

5.153 **15.**—(1) A person shall provide evidence of his entitlement to statutory adoption pay by providing, to the person who will be liable to pay it, a copy of the official notification and, in writing—

(a) the information specified in paragraph (2);
(b) a declaration that he has elected to receive statutory adoption pay, and not statutory paternity pay (adoption) under Part 12ZA of the Act;
(c) evidence, to be provided within 28 days of the child's entry into Great Britain, as to that date.

(2) The information referred to in paragraph (1) is—

(a) the name and address of the person claiming statutory adoption pay;
(b) the date on which it is expected that the child will enter Great Britain or, where he has already done so, the date of entry.

(3) The information and declaration referred to in paragraph (1) shall be provided to the person liable to pay statutory adoption pay at least 28 days before the date chosen as the beginning of the adoption pay period in accordance with paragraph (1) of regulation 12 or specified in accordance with paragraph (2) of that regulation or, if that is not reasonably practicable, as soon as is reasonably practicable thereafter.

DEFINITIONS

"the Act"—see reg.2(1).
"enter Great Britain"—see *ibid.*
"official notification"—see *ibid.*
"Pt XIIZA"—see reg.2(2).
"statutory paternity pay (adoption)"—see reg.2(1).

Entitlement to statutory adoption pay in respect of adoptions from overseas where there is more than one employer

16. Statutory adoption pay shall be payable to a person in respect of a week during any part of which he works for an employer— **5.154**

(a) who is not liable to pay him statutory adoption pay; and
(b) for whom he has worked in the week in which he receives official notification.

DEFINITION

"official notification"—see reg.2(1).

Termination of employment and liability to pay statutory adoption pay in respect of adoptions from overseas

17.—(1) Where the employment of a person who satisfies the conditions of entitlement to statutory adoption pay in respect of adoptions from overseas terminates for whatever reason (including dismissal) before the adoption pay period chosen or specified by that person in accordance with regulation 12 has begun, the period shall begin on a date chosen by that person which is at least 28 days after notice has been given and within 28 days of the date of the child's entry into Great Britain. **5.155**

(2) Where the statutory adoption pay period has not commenced within a period of 6 months of the adopter's leaving his employer, liability to pay statutory adoption pay shall, notwithstanding section 171ZM(1) of the Act, pass to the Board.

(3) Where liability to pay statutory adoption pay has passed to the Board in accordance with paragraph (2) and the adopter, having started employment as an employed earner, becomes entitled to statutory adoption pay by virtue of that employment, the liability of the Board shall cease and section 171ZM(1) of the Act shall apply.

DEFINITIONS

"the Act"—see reg.2(1).
"adopter"—see *ibid.*
"adoption from overseas"—see *ibid.*
"the Board"—see *ibid.*

Avoidance of liability for statutory adoption pay in respect of adoptions from overseas

5.156 **18.**—(1) A former employer shall be liable to make payments of statutory adoption pay to a former employee in any case where the employee had been employed for a continuous period of at least 8 weeks and his contract of service was brought to an end by the former employer solely, or mainly, for the purpose of avoiding liability for statutory adoption pay.

(2) In a case falling within paragraph (1)—

(a) the employee shall be treated as if he had been employed for a continuous period ending with the week in which he received official notification; and

(b) his normal weekly earnings shall be calculated by reference to his normal weekly earnings for the period of 8 weeks ending with the last day in respect of which he was paid under his former contract of service.

DEFINITIONS

"official notification"—see reg.2(1).

Revocation

5.157 **19.** The Statutory Paternity Pay (Adoption) and Statutory Adoption Pay (Adoptions from Overseas) Regulations 2003 are hereby revoked.

PART VI

INLAND REVENUE CODES OF PRACTICE AND GUIDANCE

NOTE

The Inland Revenue publishes a series of guides, leaflets and notes on all the areas within its jurisdiction. For a full lists see the Inland Revenue website at *www.inlandrevenue.gov.uk/leaflets.*

While all the guides are official publications, in the sense that they are published by the government department concerned, they have no force of law. This is emphasised by the standard warning on the cover of COP26:

> "These notes are for guidance only and reflect the position at the time of writing They do not affect any right of appeal."

Nonetheless some are particular importance as they set out Inland Revenue standard procedures for dealing with areas within official discretion. The list below is of those most important to tax credits practice. Those in bold are included in this volume.

TC600 and notes	The claim form and accompanying explanations
WTC2	Child tax credit and working tax credit – a guide
WTC3	**Tax Credit penalties. How tax credit examinations are settled**
WTC4	Tax Credit penalties. How tax credit enquiries are settled *(This is very similar to WTC 3 save that it deals with subsequent enquiries rather than initial examinations)*
WTC/AP	Child tax credit and working tax credit: how to appeal against a tax credit decision or award
COP23	**Code of Practice 23: Child tax credit and working tax credit: Local Office Examinations**
COP26	**Code of Practice 26: What happens if we have paid you too much tax credit. A code of practice setting our how it will deal with overpaid tax credit**
COP27	Child tax credit and working tax credit: Local Office Enquiries *(This is very similar to COP23 save that it deals with subsequent enquiries rather than initial examinations)*

LEAFLET WTC 3

TAX CREDIT PENALTIES

HOW TAX CREDIT EXAMINATIONS ARE SETTLED

Introduction

The Government is committed to supporting families and tackling child poverty through the child tax credit, and making work pay through the working tax credit. As part of this support, it is important that people receive what they are entitled to. 6.1

Sometimes people may receive more than they are entitled to – through innocent error on their part or by the Revenue or where a claimant deliberately claims too much. The Inland Revenue has a duty to ensure that the claims process is as simple as possible, and allows genuine claimants to receive the right amount of tax credit at the right time.

To check that you have been awarded the right amount, we may need to ask you for some more information. This will help us to understand your circumstances and look at your claim in full. We want to make sure that you do not receive too little tax credit or too much. Either way, we will tell you if we find something wrong. We will then discuss with you how best to put things right. If your award is too low, we shall change it to the right amount. And if the extra information indicates that you may have made an incorrect claim, we shall talk to you about this so that we can help you correct it. We shall explain what we believe is wrong, and how that affects your claim. Once we have agreed the correct claim you will need to repay any overpayment of tax credits. We will discuss with you how best to arrange this. We call this process an "examination" of your claim.

In some cases, people fail to tell us about information which affects their claim, deliberately give us incorrect information, or do not take enough care in completing their claim. In these cases the person may need to pay a penalty. We shall explain why that is so.

There are three reasons that penalties may be charged: These are if

- we find deliberate or negligent errors in the claim or the information you have given to us, or
- you fail to tell us of changes in your circumstances when you should do, or
- you fail to supply information or evidence we ask for.

Why have you sent me this leaflet?

We have sent you this leaflet because 6.2

- you have asked us to, or

- our examination of your claim now suggests that you may have to pay a penalty.

If we have been examining your claim you will already have been contacted by us to explain what happens during the examination. We will also have asked you for some more information. This will help us to understand your circumstances and look at your claim in full. We remind you what happens during an examination, here.

We also want you to be aware of

- why we would like you to co-operate with our examination
- the penalties you may have to pay, and
- your rights of appeal against those penalties and our decisions.

What if I claim as part of couple?

6.3 If you made a joint claim for tax credits with your partner, then we will send them a copy of this leaflet too. You are each responsible for the information you provide in your claim.

Any penalty will be chargeable only on the partner whose error or failure means that a penalty is due, unless we believe that the other partner must reasonably have known that the statement made or the information supplied was incorrect.

If both partners must reasonably have known that the statement made or the information supplied was incorrect then any penalty will normally be charged on the couple. So wherever this booklet mentions the amount of a maximum penalty it means the maximum that can be charged, whether to an individual claimant or to a couple. Normally the actual penalty will be much less, as we explain later in this leaflet (on page [761]).

What if I have special needs?

6.4 If you have any special needs, for example related to a disability, we will help you as much as we can. If it would be helpful to meet to discuss any errors in your claim to tax credits, but your disability means it is difficult for you to travel to us, then we can visit you at home or your place of employment if you ask us to.

Please explain your needs to the person who has written to you (their details are on any letter they have sent) or phone your local Inland Revenue Enquiry Centre and ask to speak to the Customer Services Manager. Office phone numbers are in your local phone book under 'Inland Revenue' and at ***www.inlandrevenue.gov.uk/local***.

If you phone, please have any letter we have sent you handy, as we may need to ask you for some details from it.

During the examination

Can I have help to deal with your examination?

6.5 We will assist you where we can but you may find it helpful or reassuring to get independent advice. This might be from a voluntary sector worker (such as Citizens Advice), an accountant or other professional adviser, or a friend or relative.

If you want us to deal with someone else on your behalf then you need to tell us in writing. Your letter should include your full name, address, postcode and any tax credit reference number you have.

If you have made a joint claim for tax credits, and you want us to discuss matters that are relevant to both of you with someone else, both you and your partner must sign the letter.

If you don't send us a letter, another person can still phone us on your behalf, as long as

- we are satisfied that you are with them at the time, and
- you confirm that you are happy for us to speak to them.

For couples, both of you must confirm that you are happy for us to speak to them, if you want us to discuss matters which are relevant to both of you.

Do I have to co-operate with your examination?

We would welcome your co-operation in establishing your entitlement to tax credits. The extent to which you co-operate and provide us with information is entirely a matter for you to decide. It may be a good idea to get independent advice on this. 6.6

We will make notes of all meetings, and copies of these notes will be given to you or your adviser if you ask for them.

Our examination may show that an offence has been committed for which you may have to pay a penalty. This leaflet sets out how we work out any penalty.

In calculating the amount of the penalty, we will take into account the extent to which you have been helpful and have freely and fully volunteered any information about income or circumstances which were omitted or incorrectly stated.

What should I do now?

When we ask you for information you should reply as quickly as you can. 6.7
If you need extra time, then let us know how much and why. You should tell us straight away if

- you have difficulty getting the information we need and we will discuss with you how to get it
- you think the information we have asked for is not relevant to our examination
- you believe you have already given us the information.

We will give you a reasonable amount of time to give us information or evidence that we need. As such, it is important that you let us know if you are unable to send us what we have asked for. Otherwise, you could be charged penalties.

In calculating any penalty where you made incorrect statements or have given us incorrect information or evidence, we will take into account the extent to which you

- have been helpful, and
- have freely and fully volunteered information about income or circumstances which you omitted or incorrectly stated.

What happens when you have all the information?

6.8 When you have given us all the information we work out and agree any change in your tax credits award and any overpayment or underpayment.

Before we work out your tax credit award, we may ask if you have given us full and complete details of your circumstances. So, we will ask you to sign a 'certificate of full disclosure'. You should consider carefully the statements and information you've given us before you sign it.

We want you to be sure that you have told us about anything that may affect the amount of your tax credits award.

We get information from various sources at different times, including details of

- full-time and part-time earnings from employers
- pensions you receive
- self-employment
- rents you pay or receive
- interest you pay or receive
- dividends you receive
- income from trusts
- amounts paid to child carers
- other claims to tax credits.

We consider such information together with what you have stated in your claim or during the examination. We want to avoid having to examine your claim again. If a later examination reveals an irregularity that you had not made us aware of during an earlier examination then a further or higher penalty is likely to be charged.

Once we have agreed the right amount of your tax credit award and the amount overpaid to you we will explain any penalty we may charge you.

Do I have to pay interest?

6.9 If we overpaid you tax credits because deliberately or without taking reasonable care

- you made an incorrect statement, or
- you gave us incorrect information or evidence

we may ask you to pay interest on the overpayment, and pay back the overpayment itself.

We don't charge interest on any tax credits we overpay because of a failure to notify a change of circumstances.

You have the right to appeal against our decision to charge you interest on an overpayment (see **'Can I appeal?'** on page [765]).

Interest may also be payable if you are late in paying any penalty we have charged. You have no right of appeal against this interest charge.

Penalties - introduction

We hope that few people will deliberately or negligently make errors in their tax credit claims, or fail to provide information at the right time. But if that does happen the claimant may need to pay a penalty. Here, we tell you: 6.10

- when a penalty may be charged,
- the maximum penalty that we may charge,
- the factors we take into account in working out the penalty.

In practice, where you need to pay these penalties they will usually be much less than the maximum.

Penalties if I choose not to co-operate?

If you don't let us have the information we've requested within the time we specify, then we can refer your case to an appeals tribunal. They can impose **a penalty of up to £300.** 6.11

If you still don't give us the information, we can charge you **a further penalty of up to £60 for each day that you fail to do so.**

These are the maximum penalties for not supplying information. In practice, where we charge these penalties they will usually be much less.

If you fail to give us the information we've asked for, **we may decide to end or amend your payment of tax credits.**

You can appeal against

- both of the penalties mentioned above, and
- our decision to end or amend the payment of tax credits.

We do not treat your use of your rights of appeal as non-co-operation. If you choose to appeal it will not affect the amount of penalty that we may charge.

For more information see **Can I appeal?** on page [765].

Penalties because of errors in my claim or the information I give you?

We can charge you penalties when you have 6.12

- deliberately made an incorrect statement, or you did not take reasonable care in completing the claim form
- either deliberately, or because you did not take reasonable care, given incorrect information about your circumstances or in response to our questions

The penalty can be up to **£3,000**. In practice, where we charge penalties, they will usually be much less than this maximum amount.

When working out this penalty, we will take into account

- the extent to which you voluntarily told us about anything that was wrong
- your help in bringing our examination to an end
- the seriousness of your errors or omissions, and
- whether you have previously made an incorrect claim, given incorrect information, or failed to provide information.

If you filled in the claim form with the guidance we sent you, but this guidance was incorrect and was the cause of the error, then we consider you to have taken reasonable care. **You will not be liable to a penalty or interest charge for this error.**

If we tell you that a penalty is due, you have the right to appeal against our decision. For more information see **Can I appeal?** on page [765].

Penalties for not telling us of a change in circumstances?

6.13 We can also charge you penalties if you did not tell us **within three months** about certain changes in your circumstances, which would affect the amount of your award.

The changes in circumstances you need to tell us about are

- your weekly child care costs go down to nil or by at least £10 a week for four weeks in a row
- you start, or stop, being a partner in a couple
- you or your partner leave the UK permanently, or go abroad for more than 8 weeks (12 weeks if you remain abroad because you are ill or because a family member is ill or has died).

The maximum penalty we can charge you for failing to tell us about one of these changes within 3 months is **£300**. In practice, where we charge this penalty it will usually be much less than this maximum amount.

When working out this penalty, we will take into account

- the seriousness of your failure, and
- whether you have previously failed to tell us about changes in your circumstances, which you should have told us about.

You can appeal against the decision to charge this penalty. For more information see **Can I appeal?** on page [765].

This penalty is due even if the failure

- was not deliberate, or
- was not because you failed to take reasonable care.

But, we will not charge the penalty if you had a reasonable excuse (a valid reason) for not telling us about your change of circumstances.

What is a reasonable excuse?

A reasonable excuse is something that stops you from telling us about the change in your circumstances. 6.14

We consider each case on its own facts. For example, if you had a serious illness immediately before the deadline, and from that date to the time you told us of the change, the illness stopped you from dealing with your affairs. We would regard that as a reasonable excuse.

If you have suffered a coma, major heart attack, stroke or any other serious mental or life-threatening illness, we would regard that as a reasonable excuse.

Where an illness involves a lengthy stay in hospital or convalescence, we would normally expect you to arrange to tell us of a change of circumstances in time.

We do not regard 'being too busy' as a reasonable excuse.

It is important that you tell us if you think you have a reasonable excuse. It helps if you do this as soon as possible.

Summary table of Penalty and Interest Charges

6.15

Situation	*Penalty*	*Interest payable on Overpaid Credits*
Failure to supply information	Maximum £300	No
Continued failure to supply information	Maximum £60 per day	No
Fraudulently or negligently providing incorrect information in claim or in response to request	Maximum £3000	Yes
Failure to notify change of circumstances	Maximum £300	No

Notes:

- In practice the penalties charged will usually be much less than the maximum amount
- Interest is payable on penalties that are paid late.

The end of the examination

What happens at the end of the examination?

Normally, by the time our examination of your claim has ended we will have agreed with you 6.16

- the amount of any tax credits overpaid or underpaid
- how you should repay any overpayment, and
- any change to the amount of your tax credits award.

We will tell you if we believe a penalty is payable either in a meeting or in a letter. You or your adviser (if you have one) can give your side of things. We will then tell you the amount of the penalty that we think is due.

It is important that you tell us about any facts which you think might affect our decision to charge a penalty, or the amount of that penalty. This includes anything you think we have not given enough attention to. We will then consider the effect this has on the amount of penalty we had in mind, and comment on any figure that you have suggested. As a result, we might be able to reach an agreement either straightaway or after a few days.

Also, if we have not already done so, we will tell you the amount of interest we could charge you.

What if my claim is correct, or you don't charge interest and penalties?

6.17 If there is nothing wrong with your claim or we are satisfied that

- any error was not made deliberately, or
- you took reasonable care despite making an error, or
- you had a reasonable excuse for not notifying a change of circumstances

then we will not charge interest or a penalty, and will close the examination.

What if the examination shows you have underpaid me?

6.18 We will increase the amount of your payment to pay you the correct amount so that you receive your full entitlement for the year.

Can I claim compensation for my costs arising from the examination?

If an underpayment has arisen as a result of a mistake or unreasonable delay by us then we will pay back reasonable costs that are a direct result of our mistake or unreasonable delay. In some circumstances we will pay compensation for distress. Our code of practice called "Putting things right — how to complain" (COP1) gives further details.

What happens after we agree the penalties chargeable?

6.19 At the end of an examination, you will normally only have to pay any penalty straightaway.

Where possible, we will collect any overpaid tax credits by adjusting the tax credits you receive for the rest of the year. If, at the end of the tax year, there is still an overpayment, we will ask you to repay it.

If we find that you should not have received any tax credits, we will ask you to pay it all back. We will tell you how much you must repay and whether any interest is payable. We will then add this to any penalties and ask you to pay one sum.

We will explain that we do not normally take formal action to charge penalties or interest. Instead we normally ask someone to offer to pay any penalties or interest (and any overpaid tax credits that you should repay straightaway). If you are prepared to make such an offer, we will

- suggest an amount that we would accept (the amount of any penalty will be what we have already explained as being appropriate), and
- a date that you should pay it by.

We will ask you to send us a formal letter offering to pay the agreed sum by a specific date. If we are happy, we will then send you a letter accepting your offer.

This exchange of letters forms a legally binding agreement (or contract) between us and binds us both by its terms. If you keep to the terms of the agreement, then we will too. In accepting your offer, we cannot take formal penalty action by issuing charge notices formally determining the amount of the penalty.

If you offer us a different sum that we cannot accept, we will tell you in writing why we are not happy. We will ask you to make a revised offer.

When we send you the acceptance letter, we will include a payslip showing where to send your payment. If you pay under the terms of the agreement, that will be an end to the matter. If not, we may charge you interest for late payment. And we could take court action to recover the whole amount due under the terms of the binding agreement.

What if I cannot pay?

If you agree with the amount you should pay, but cannot pay it all straightaway, you can ask to pay by instalments. If we agree, we will expect you to make as large a down payment as you can and to pay the rest, including additional interest, by agreed instalments as quickly as possible. 6.20

If you could pay at the time we reached our agreement but your circumstances change and you find that you cannot pay the agreed instalments, you should tell us as soon as possible.

What if I do not make an offer?

If you do not want to make an offer or you make one that we cannot accept, we will formally issue legal notices charging the penalty, and any interest. 6.21

You can appeal against these notices. See **Can I Appeal?** [below].

If you do not appeal against these notices then you will have to pay the penalties and the interest, as well as any overpaid tax credits.

Making an appeal

Can I appeal?

You have a right to appeal against the decision 6.22

- when you make a claim and we decide not to award tax credits
- when you make a claim and you disagree with the amount of tax credit award

- when you tell us about a change of circumstances and we decide not to increase your tax credit award
- whenever we decide to amend or end your tax credit award
- when we or an independent tribunal decides to impose a penalty
- when we decide to charge interest on an overpayment.

You have **30 days** from the date shown on the decision notice, to make your appeal **in writing**.

You can find out more about appeals by reading our leaflet WTC/AP 'How to appeal against a tax credit decision or award', available on our website at *www.inlandrevenue.gov.uk* or from any Inland Revenue Enquiry Centre. Or, if you prefer, we will explain to you how to make an appeal.

What happens after I have appealed?

6.23 We will try, wherever possible, to reach agreement with you about the amount of tax credits you are entitled to and about penalties and interest we believe are appropriate.

If we reach agreement with you on the amount of award, penalty or interest, we will send you a letter setting out the details of the agreement. If this agreement affects the decision we have already made, we will send you a notice of our new decision. If you change your mind about our agreement, you must write to us **within 30 days**. Otherwise the agreement stands.

You do not have to reach an agreement with us, and you can ask for advice at any time.

If we cannot reach agreement, we will send your appeal, along with an explanation of the law and facts we used to make our decision, to the Appeals Service. An appeals tribunal will then hear your appeal. Both the Appeals Service and the appeals tribunal are completely independent of the Inland Revenue.

The tribunal may decide on an appeal against:

- the award – the amount of that award
- the penalty – the amount, which may be less or more than the amount we've set out
- the interest – whether interest is chargeable

We may use the information or documents that you gave us during the examination in any appeal proceedings.

Can I still negotiate after formal action has started?

6.24 Yes. If you want to make an offer to pay you can reopen negotiations with us at any time before we finish the formal penalty action.

General Note

The text of WTC4, "Tax credit penalties: how tax credit enquiries are settled" is essentially the same as WTC3. The final part of the text, "further information", has not been included. This version was published on 31 March 2004, as was WTC4.

CODE OF PRACTICE 23

CHILD TAX CREDIT AND WORKING TAX CREDIT LOCAL OFFICE EXAMINATIONS

Any special needs

If you have any special needs, for example related to a disability, we will help you as much as we can. If it would be helpful to meet to discuss any errors in your claim to tax credits, but your disability means it is difficult for you to travel to us, then we can visit you at home or your place of employment if you ask us to. 6.25

Please explain your needs to the person who has written to you (their details are on any letter they have sent) or phone your local Inland Revenue Enquiry Centre and ask to speak to the Customer Services Manager. Office phone numbers are in your local phone book under 'Inland Revenue' and at *www.inlandrevenue.gov.uk/local.*

If you phone, please have any letter we have sent you handy, as we may need to ask you for some details from it.

Why are you sending me this booklet?

We are sending you this booklet because we have written to you to say we are examining your claim, and we want to tell you what you can expect, and what your rights and obligations are. If you have made a claim as a member of a couple, we write to you both separately, and send you both separate copies of this booklet. 6.26

This Code of Practice tells you how our local offices will carry out these examinations. It gives you a chance to understand the process and ask us any questions. It promises you fair treatment under the law and in accordance with our service commitment to you. There is a copy of the service commitment at the back of this booklet, which explains the rules that we will follow and your rights and responsibilities in particular situations.

What do you mean by "examining" my claim?

During the year, we pay you tax credits in a provisional amount, based on your income for an earlier year. After the end of the year, when you have told us what your actual income was for the year, we will adjust the amount of tax credits you were due for the year based on your actual income. We examine claims during the year so we can ensure that the payments we are making match your circumstances and income. 6.27

We are examining your claim to make sure you are receiving the correct amount of tax credits, and that the circumstances and the income you have told us about are correct. We will ask you questions about any points that we need to clear up, so that we can put right any mistakes as soon as possible.

The questions we will ask you during our examination will normally be about your circumstances, and we will consider the circumstances you reported in your claim and any changes you have, or should have, told us about. We may also check that you have reported your income correctly, or that any estimate you provide of your current year's income is realistic. As the income you are asked to put on your tax credits claim is based on your income for tax purposes, we will not ask you detailed questions about the basis on which you have calculated your income.

What is the difference between an examination and an enquiry?

6.28 We carry out examinations during the year, while we are paying you tax credits on a provisional basis. We carry out enquiries after the end of the year, when you have reported your income and circumstances for the year just gone, to ensure that the amount of tax credits we have paid you is correct. If we need to make enquiries after the end of the year, we will write to you again and send you a copy of our Code of Practice on Enquiries.

If we have examined your claim during the year, it does not mean that we will enquire into your entitlement after the end of the year. But if we do need to ask you questions about your entitlement after the end of the year, we can enquire into it whether or not we examined your claim during the year.

Why have you decided to examine my claim?

6.29 We carry out a wide range of checks on all claims, including

- looking at the information in the claim form
- comparing it with information from other sources.

If you have been awarded tax credits in respect of childcare charges you are paying, we may also check the details with your childcare providers. We carry out checks with providers by telephone and in writing.

After all these checks, if we think your claim may be incorrect, that you have incorrectly reported a change of circumstances, or that you have not told us about changes in your circumstances when you should have done, we will examine your claim in more detail.

When will you examine my claim?

6.30 We examine some claims before we have started to make payments, and others after payments have begun. Sometimes we will examine a claim both before and after we have started to make payments.

We will write to you, and send you this booklet, whenever we are examining your claim, whether it is before or after we have started paying you. We may occasionally need to examine your claim more than once after we have started paying you. But we will only do this if you provide new information (for example, about a change in your circumstances), or we receive further information which we need to ask you about.

We can start an examination at any time during the year to which it relates. If we have already begun to pay you tax credits, we cannot start to examine your claim after the end of the year to which it relates. If you send in your claim after the end of the year, we can start an examination before we begin making payments, but we cannot start an examination once we have made a payment of tax credits.

Once we start an examination into your claim we will bring it to an end as soon as we have received all the information we need to make a decision about your entitlement. We may occasionally need to continue examining your claim after the end of the year to which it relates.

Do I have to co-operate with your examination?

We would welcome your co-operation in establishing your entitlement to tax credits. The extent to which you co-operate and provide us with information is entirely a matter for you to decide. It may be a good idea to get independent advice on this. (Please see **Can I have help to deal with with your examination** below.) 6.31

We will make notes of all meetings, and copies of these notes will be given to you or your adviser if you ask for them.

Our examination may show that an offence has been committed for which you may have to pay a penalty, which is worked out as described in leaflet WTC3 "Tax Credit Penalties: How tax credit examinations are settled".

In calculating the amount of the penalty, we will take into account the extent to which you have been helpful and have freely and fully volunteered any information about income or circumstances which were omitted or incorrectly stated. You can find further information about penalties on page [775].

Can I have help to deal with your examination?

If you prefer, we will deal with someone else on your behalf. This might be an accountant, tax adviser or other professional adviser, a voluntary sector adviser (such as a Citizens' Advice Bureau), or a friend or relative. If you want us to write to them or to discuss your affairs with them over the telephone, we will need a short letter, signed by you, which confirms that you have authorised us to do so. The letter should include your full name, address, postcode and any tax credit reference number you have. If you have claimed tax credits as a couple and you want us to discuss matters which are relevant to both of you with someone else, the letter will need to be signed by both you and your partner. 6.32

If we do not have such a letter from you, another person may still phone one of our contact centres on your behalf, as long as we are satisfied that you are present with them at the time and you confirm that you are happy for us to speak to them. For couples, we will need both you and your partner to confirm that you are happy for us to speak to someone else on your behalf if you want us to discuss matters which are relevant to both of you.

You will always remain personally responsible for the information provided by another person on your behalf and for paying back overpaid tax credit. If we cannot make any progress with your adviser regarding outstanding information we will contact you directly. We will also continue to send you copies of important documents as well.

What do I have to do if you ask for information?

6.33 You should respond as promptly as you can when we ask for information. This will help to keep your time and costs, and ours, to a minimum.

Where we need to ask further questions, we will make it clear what it is that we need to know and why. We may need to see documents such as bank statements or household bills. Once again we will tell you why we are asking for them and exactly what it is that we need to see. If you have made a claim as a member of a couple, we will normally ask both of you for the information, though we will sometimes ask only one of you to provide it.

We will try to

- take up as little of your time as possible by asking early on in our examination for everything we need to know
- avoid asking for information in a piecemeal way, but this is not always possible as one question may lead to another.

Time limits

6.34 We will give you a reasonable amount of time to let us have the information — normally 30 days, but we will be flexible about this. You should tell us if you think we have not given you enough time, say how much longer you need and why. We will let you have more time if this seems reasonable. If we cannot agree we will give you our reasons.

You should tell us straight away if

- you have difficulty getting the information we need and we will discuss with you how you might get hold of it
- you think it is not relevant to our examination.

We will consider the reasons carefully, and if we still think we need the information we will explain why.

Formal powers

6.35 It is vital that you contact us if you cannot send the information we have asked for as, after the time limit is up, we can use our statutory powers to obtain it. If it gets to this stage we will first

- explain our statutory powers and how we intend to use them
- inform you of any possible penalties that might arise if you do not let us have the information we have asked for
- tell you about your right to appeal to an independent appeals tribunal.

Our leaflets WTC3 "Tax Credit Penalties: How tax credit examinations are settled" and WTC/AP "How to appeal against a tax credit decision or award" contain more information on penalties and on appeals.

Returning documents

Any documents you have sent to us will be returned to you as soon as possible. If you need them before that, you may ask us to return them. You should tell us what you need, and when you think you will be able to return them to us. We will then either 6.36

- send them to you, with the understanding that you will send them back to us complete and undamaged, or
- if we cannot return the original documents we will send a copy out, free of charge and within seven days of receiving your request, if possible.

Will you obtain information from anyone else?

As part of an examination it may be necessary for us to contact an employer or childcare provider to confirm information relevant to your claim. If so, the contact will always be in writing or by telephone, and we will tell you in advance what we intend to do. 6.37

What happens if you ask for a meeting?

We may ask to meet you and any other appropriate person, including your spouse or partner, to find out more about your claim. You can also ask your adviser or helper to attend the meeting. 6.38

You do not have to come to meetings but they give you the chance to explain any points you think we may not have understood, and to ask questions. You can ask for a meeting at any time during our examination.

Place and time

We may suggest that a meeting takes place at 6.39

- your home, or
- our offices.

You should tell us if the place we have suggested is not convenient for you, or if you have any special needs, for example, wheelchair access or an interpreter. We will always try to agree with you in advance where and when the meeting will take place. Meetings normally take place in office hours, but if this is difficult for you, you should tell us, and we will try to meet you at another time.

In exceptional circumstances we may need to visit you at your home without prior agreement. We will only do this if we have repeatedly tried, and failed, to contact you in writing and by telephone. If we do call on you unannounced you can refuse to answer our questions immediately. Then we will try to arrange another time to visit you, or for you to call at our offices. We will never visit you at your place of work without agreeing the visit with you in advance.

If we visit you at your home, we will show you our official identification. Even if you have agreed that we should meet at your home, you do not have to answer our questions there and then if you prefer not to do so. You should tell us if this is the case, and we will try to arrange another meeting, or will put our questions in writing.

Answering our questions

6.40 These meetings are a very important part of the examination process, so if you are not sure of an answer, or cannot remember, say so. If you believe an answer you gave may not be correct then let us know straight away.

Bringing documents

6.41 When you come to a meeting please make sure that you, or the person helping you, bring with you any papers or documents (such as bank statements or household bills) that you may need to answer our questions about your claim. If you are unsure what you may need you can ask us.

Taking notes

6.42 We will take notes of any meetings we have with you and let you have a copy as soon as possible afterwards. We may ask you to sign these, to show that they cover what was talked about. You can comment on these notes and tell us about anything you disagree with. You do not have to sign them or comment on them, but a signed record could be useful if we cannot reach agreement and have to ask the independent appeals tribunal to decide matters.

You or the person helping you can also take notes during the meeting.

Can I stop your examination?

6.43 You do not have the right to ask us to stop examining your claim. We will bring our examination to end as soon as we believe we have all the information we need to make a decision. You have the right to appeal against that decision.

If you consider we are not treating you fairly, you can make a complaint. The section headed **Complaints** [omitted — see general note] explains how you can make a complaint.

Will you stop my payments while you examine my claim?

6.44 If we examine your claim before we start making payments, we will begin to make any payments due as soon as we have finished our examination.

If we examine your claim after we have begun to make payments, we will not normally make any change to the amount we pay until we have finished our examination. But we may need to amend your award, and reduce or stop your payments, before our examination is complete if you have not provided the information we need. If we do this, you will have the right of appeal against our decision.

How will I know when you have finished your examination?

6.45 We will always write to you to tell you that we have finished examining your claim. If we have not yet made you an award of tax credits, we will make a decision on your claim. If we have already started to make payments of tax credits, we may make a new decision on your claim. You will have the right of appeal against these decisions.

What happens if you find nothing wrong during your examination?

If we have all the information we need and find nothing wrong, we will tell you and let you know that we have finished our examination. If we examined your claim before we started making payments, we will begin to make any payments due. 6.46

What happens if I have not received enough tax credit?

During our examination we may find that there is a mistake in your claim, and that you are entitled to more tax credit than you have been awarded. If so, we will revise your award to show the correct amount of tax credit. Any increases to your award due to a change of circumstances which you did not tell us about can only be backdated to three months prior to the date on which we found out about the change. 6.47

What happens if you find something wrong?

If we find something wrong in your claim we will

- suggest changes we think are reasonable in the light of all the information we have 6.48
- try to agree with you any changes that are needed
- explain how we arrive at the changes we suggest (for example, if you have calculated your childcare charges incorrectly, we will explain how you ought to have calculated them).

If you do not understand the changes we suggest you should let us know. If you do not agree with the changes, and we make a decision based on them, you will have the right of appeal against that decision.

Where we have not yet made an award of tax credit

We will make an award in a different amount to that claimed based on what we believe are your correct income and circumstances, or no award at all. You will have the right of appeal against our decision. 6.49

Where you have received more tax credit than you should

If we think you are being paid too much tax credit, we will amend your award. This could mean 6.50

- reducing the amount we are paying you from then on, so that we pay you the right amount of tax credit for the year, or
- not paying you any more tax credit for the rest of the year, if we have already paid you as much as, or more than, you are entitled to.

You will have the right of appeal against our amendment.

If we find during our examination that you should not have received any tax credit at all, we will stop your award of that credit. We will ask you to pay back all the payments of tax credit we have made.

Our Code of Practice on Overpayments (COP26 – What happens if we have paid you too much tax credit?) explains what will happen if we have paid you too much tax credit. It is available on our website or from Inland Revenue Enquiry Offices.

Contracts

6.51 Where our examination shows that a penalty or interest may be chargeable (see the sections **Do I have to pay penalties?** on page [775], and **Do I have to pay interest?** on page [776]), we will try to agree matters through a contract between us. A contract is an exchange of letters, where you offer to pay us any tax credits, penalties or interest you owe, and we formally accept your offer. Before asking you to enter into a contract, we will talk to you and your adviser or helper, if you have one, and give you our leaflet WTC3 "Tax Credit Penalties: How tax credit examinations are settled".

Can I appeal?

6.52 You have a right of appeal against decisions we make. You can appeal against our decision in any of the following circumstances

- when you make a claim and we decide not to make an award of tax credits
- when you make a claim and you disagree with the amount of tax credits we award
- when you tell us about of change of circumstances and we decide not to increase your award of tax credits
- whenever we decide to amend your award of tax credits or to end the award
- when we or an independent tribunal decide to impose a penalty
- when we decide to charge interest on an overpayment.

You have 30 days from the date shown on the notice we will send you to make your appeal in writing.

You can find out more about appeals by reading our leaflet WTC/AP "How to appeal against a tax credit decision or award" available on our website or from any Inland Revenue Enquiry Centre. Or if you prefer we will explain to you how to go about the appeals procedures.

What happens after I have appealed?

6.53 We will try, wherever possible, to reach an agreement with you about the amount of tax credits you are entitled to. If we reach agreement with you we will send you a letter setting out the details of the agreement. If this agreement affects the decision we have already made, we will send you a notice of our new decision. If you change your mind about our agreement, you must write to us within 30 days, otherwise the agreement stands.

You are under no obligation to agree with us, and you can seek advice at any time before saying you agree. If we cannot reach an agreement, we will send your appeal, along with an explanation of the law and facts we used to make our decision, to the Appeals Service. Your appeal will then be heard by an appeals tribunal. Both the Appeals Service and the appeals tribunal are completely independent of the Inland Revenue.

Our leaflet WTC/AP "How to appeal against a tax credit decision or award" contains more information about the independent appeals tribunal, and explains what you can expect if they hear your appeal.

Do I have to pay penalties?

You may have to pay penalties if during our examination 6.54

- we find something wrong with your claim
- you provide us with incorrect information

and we consider that you have been fraudulent or negligent. The maximum penalty we can charge you for making an incorrect claim or giving us incorrect information is £3000.

We can only seek penalties for incorrect claims or information if the error was due to negligence or fraud. If you commit a deliberate act of fraud you may be prosecuted. You may have been negligent even if you did not intend to over-claim tax credits. Before signing and submitting your claim, you should have taken care to ensure that all entries were correct. If you did not do so, this may amount to negligence.

You may also have to pay penalties if you delay in telling us about the following changes in your circumstances:

- your average weekly childcare costs decrease to nil, or by at least £10 per week, for four consecutive weeks
- you become, or cease to be, a member of a couple
- you or your partner leave the UK permanently, or go abroad for more than eight weeks (12 weeks if you remain abroad because you are ill or because a member of your family is ill or has died).

We cannot charge you a penalty in respect of any other changes in your circumstances or income which you did not tell us about.

The maximum penalty we can charge you for failing to tell us about one of these changes is £300. You should let us know if you think you have a reasonable excuse for not telling us in good time about any of these changes. You can find more information about "reasonable excuse" in our leaflet WTC3 "Tax Credit Penalties: How tax credit examinations are settled".

You may also have to pay penalties if you do not send us information we ask for when we are examining your claim. We can ask the independent appeals tribunal to decide an appropriate initial penalty, up to £300. If you still do not provide the information, we may decide to charge further penalties of up to £60 a day until you do send it.

You have the right of appeal against any decision to charge a penalty, whether it has been made by the independent appeals tribunal or by us.

These are the maximum amounts of penalties we can charge, and we do not charge the maximum in every case. When we calculate the amount of any penalty we think you should pay, we will take into account

- the extent to which you voluntarily disclosed anything that was wrong
- your help in bringing our examination to an end
- the seriousness of your errors or omissions
- whether you have previously made an incorrect claim, provided incorrect information, failed to provide information, or failed to tell us about changes in your circumstances.

If, during our examination, we think that you may have to pay a penalty, we will give you a copy of our leaflet WTC3 "Tax Credits Penalties: How tax credit examinations are settled". This leaflet explains how we work out penalties and reach settlements.

You should tell us about any matters you think are relevant when we are working out any penalty that may be charged.

We will try to reach an agreement by contract (see the paragraph headed "**Contracts**" on page [774] of this leaflet) if we are charging you penalties. If we cannot reach an agreement, we may formally decide the amount of penalty we think is appropriate. If we do this, you will have the right of appeal against our decision (see the section headed **Can I Appeal?** on page [774] of this leaflet).

Do I have to pay interest?

6.55 If we have carried out an examination into your tax credit claim and find that we have paid you too much tax credit, you may be asked to pay interest on the overpayment as well as paying back the overpayment itself. But we can only ask you to pay back interest if the overpayment arose because of your negligence or fraud. You have the right of appeal against our decision to charge you interest on an overpayment.

Interest is also payable if you are late in paying any penalty we have charged.

We may include interest in any contract settlement we reach, rather than charging it separately.

What happens at the end of your examination?

6.56 When our examination has shown something is wrong we will

- explain what it is
- tell you how to get things right for the future.

If our examination shows your claim was incorrect, you provided incorrect information, or failed to tell us in time about a change in your circumstances which you should have notified within three months, we may ask you to sign a Certificate of Full Disclosure confirming that you have now told us about everything that may affect your entitlement to tax credits. We ask you to sign this certificate so that we have your written assurance that you have disclosed all the facts that may be relevant to our examination.

We will not ask you to sign a Certificate of Full Disclosure if

- we found nothing wrong, or
- your tax credits award was increased as a result of our examination, rather than reduced.

If you sign a Certificate of Full Disclosure you know to be false, and we find this out at a later stage, we will take this into account when deciding what further action we need to take. So you should consider the certificate carefully before signing it, to ensure you understand the implications.

General Note

The text of COP27, "Local office enquiries", is essentially the same as COP 23. This text (and that of COP 27) was issued on March 31, 2004. The final part of the text ("Your rights under out service commitment to you") has not been included. See COP1, "Putting things right—how to complain" (not reproduced in this volume) for full details. **6.57**

CODE OF PRACTICE 26

WHAT HAPPENS IF WE HAVE PAID YOU TOO MUCH TAX CREDIT?

This leaflet explains what happens if we have paid you too much tax credit and how to pay it back

How we work out your tax credit

Your tax credit award for the tax year 2003–04 (the year 6 April 2003 to 5 April 2004) is based on your circumstances during that year. Your initial award is based on your income for the tax year 2001–02. Your entitlement to tax credit for 2003–04 will be decided finally when your income for that year is known. Your final tax credit will be based on 6.58

- your 2003–04 income, if that is lower than 2001–02's, **or**
- your 2001–02 income, if your 2003–04 income has risen but not by more than £2,500, **or**
- your 2003–04 income less £2,500, if your 2003–04 income has risen by more than £2,500. For example, if the rise were £3,000, your 2003–04 tax credit would only take £500 of the increase into account.

We do this so that we provide extra support if your income falls but also allow room for your income to rise before it affects your tax credits.

Once we have made a tax credit award, it can be adjusted if things have changed. We adjust awards

- during the tax year, if you tell us about a change in your circumstances or we need to correct the information your award is based on. We also adjust your award if you tell us that your income in 2003–04 is likely to be different from 2001–02's income. And we adjust awards to put right the amount we are paying you, so that we do not pay you too much tax credit for the year
- at the end of the year, when we have all the information about your circumstances and income and can make our final decision about your entitlement to tax credits for the year.

When we adjust an award, we may find that we have not paid you enough tax credit. If we do, we will pay out the extra straightaway in a single payment. We may also find that we have paid you too much tax credit. If we have, you will normally be expected to pay it back.

This Code of Practice explains what will happen if we find that you have been paid too much tax credit and how you will be expected to pay it back. It also explains what we will do if an overpayment is the result of a mistake on our part or paying back what you owe would cause you and your family hardship.

Adjusting awards during the year

6.59 During the tax year, we may find that we need to adjust your payments to avoid paying you too much tax credit over the year. This might be because

- there was a delay before we knew about, or processed, a change in your circumstances that reduced your award, or
- you tell us that you expect your income for 2003–04 to be higher than the income on which we have based your award, or
- your award was not based on the right information or you have been paid the wrong amount for your circumstances and income.

If we find out during the year that we have been paying you too much tax credit, we will normally

- reduce the amount we are paying you from then on, so that we pay you the right amount of tax credit for the year, or
- not pay you any more tax credit for the rest of the year, if we have already paid you as much as, or more than, you are entitled to. If we have already paid you more than you are entitled to, we may also ask you to pay back the extra after the end of the year, once all the relevant information about your income and circumstances is available.

If we adjust your payments during the year, you should contact us if they are reduced to a level that causes you hardship or if you think a possible overpayment should not be recovered. We will then, depending on the size of your award, make additional payments to bring your tax credits back to a higher level. We will set those payments taking into account the maximum amounts by which we would reduce your award for the following year if we were collecting an overpayment from it. These additional payments will mean that you have an overpayment at the end of the year.

Stopping awards

6.60 If we find during the year that you were not entitled to a tax credit at all, we will stop your award of that credit. You will be expected to pay back all the payments of that tax credit we have made.

Finalising awards at the end of the year

6.61 After the end of the year, once all the information about your income and circumstances is available, we will compare your tax credit entitlement with what we have paid you.

We will write to you about your claim and ask you to confirm that we have a correct and complete picture of your circumstances during the year and to tell us your income (or an estimate of your income) for the year.

Once we have that information, we will send you a notice about your final tax credit entitlement for the year just ended. If we have paid you too much tax credit, we will usually expect you to pay it back. In the notice finalising your award for the year, we will tell you the amount you have been overpaid and explain why it arose. We will also tell you how we expect you to pay it back. If we have paid you too little tax credit, we will pay out the extra as a single payment.

There are several reasons why we might find at the end of the year that you have been paid too much tax credit. For example

- if we did not know about a change of circumstances that reduced your entitlement
- if your income rose by more than £2,500 in tax year 2003–04, compared with your 2001–02 income, and we did not know about it,

or

- if you told us about a change in your income during the year but your actual income is different from what you expected.

If we identify an overpayment when we finalise your tax credit award, we can ask you to pay it back by one of the following methods

- reducing your tax credit award for the current year
- adjusting your PAYE code to collect the amount overpaid by increasing the tax you pay on your earnings. This will apply for overpayments relating to 2004–05 and later years. For overpayments from the tax year 2003–04, you can pay back the amount overpaid in 12 monthly instalments
- making a payment to us direct, due **within 30 days**. But for overpayments arising in 2003–04, you will be able to pay in 12 monthly instalments if you wish.

Where we can, we will ask you to pay back overpaid tax credit from the previous year by taking the money from a tax credit award you are entitled to for the current year. Depending on the size of your award, we will not take more than a certain percentage of your tax credits for the next year to pay off what you owe us.

The maximum amounts by which we would reduce your award are

- 10% for claimants receiving the maximum award
- 100% for claimants receiving only the family element of Child Tax Credit
- 25% for all other claimants.

If we ask you to pay back a tax credit overpayment direct because you have no continuing tax credit award, we will write to you setting out the amount you owe. We will also send you a payslip telling you what to do if you want to pay over 12 months.

Appealing against the amount due

If you disagree with our decision during the year that you are entitled to less tax credit, or that you were not entitled to a tax credit at all, you can **6.62** appeal against it. You can also appeal if you disagree with our decision about your tax credit entitlement after the end of the year.

You can only appeal about our decisions on your entitlement. If you accept that our decision about your entitlement is right, but object to our decision about recovering an overpayment, you should get in touch with us straightaway to discuss this.

You have **30 days** from the date shown on the notice of our decision in which to appeal. You can make an appeal after that if you had a reasonable excuse for not meeting the time limit. If you only realised that you needed to appeal once you had received a detailed calculation from us, we would regard that as a reasonable excuse. You should make any appeal to

Tax Credit Office
Preston
PR1 0SB.

In Northern Ireland, please make any appeal to

Tax Credit Office
Dorchester House
52–58 Great Victoria Street
Belfast
BT2 7WF.

If you want more information about how to make an appeal, please ask for our leaflet WTC/AP 'How to appeal against a tax credit decision or award'.

Couples

6.63 Tax credits can be claimed by

- individuals
- married couples who are living together, or
- a man and a woman who are living together as husband and wife.

For couples, you and your partner must claim tax credits jointly. You both take responsibility for the information in the claim and for changes you tell us about. If you have been paid too much tax credit, all the information above about how we recover overpayments still applies. In addition, however, because you make a joint claim, we can ask either of you to pay us back the amount we have overpaid you.

Where we can, we will recover an overpayment by reducing a continuing tax credit award to you and your partner. If we have to ask you to pay direct, our first step will be to ask you jointly to pay us the money. For 2003–04 overpayments identified at the year end, you can pay in instalments over 12 months if you wish.

At a later date, after looking at the facts in individual cases, we may also ask

- the partners in a couple to pay us different amounts of the overpayment, or
- one partner to pay us the whole of the amount.

But we would only do this if, in an individual case, there were a difference between the partners' ability to pay. And, in law, both partners would remain liable to pay the full amount unless we sent out new notices saying otherwise. Different payment methods could apply to each of the partners.

In a case in which a couple had broken up and owed money in relation to tax credits before the break-up, we would look at each case on its facts and take into account the circumstances, income and expenses of each of the former partners in reaching a decision.

When might we not recover an overpayment?

We may decide that you should not be asked to pay back all or part of an overpayment, if 6.64

- you were paid too much because of a mistake by us and it was reasonable to think your award was right, or
- it would cause hardship to you or your family if you had to pay the tax credit back. We may also accept payment over a longer period of time in a case of this kind.

Overpayments if we have made a mistake

If we find that, because we have made a mistake, we have not paid you all the tax credit you are entitled to, we will pay you the extra tax credit in a single sum straightaway. 6.65

We will not ask you to pay back an overpayment if it arose because we made a mistake and you could reasonably have thought your award was right. This would include cases where we instructed your employer to pay you the wrong amount of Working Tax Credit, provided you could reasonably think you were being paid the right amount.

Some mistakes by us that lead to overpaid tax credit may happen because you gave us some information and we did not act upon it. If you tell us about a change, you can expect to get a revised award notice from us within a few days. But if you tell us something and we do not act upon it **within a month**, and you could reasonably think your tax credit award was correct, we would not ask you to pay back the additional tax credit you were paid.

It would have to be reasonable to think that your tax credit award was correct. For example, if we were paying you tax credits on the basis of the wrong number of children, that is the sort of thing we would expect you to spot on your award notice and tell us about. And we would also expect you to tell us if your employer was paying you more tax credit than your award notice said you were entitled to.

In deciding whether it was reasonable to think your award was correct, we will consider all the circumstances of your case.

We will take the same approach where the mistake that led to the overpayment was made by another Government Department.

2003–04 adjustments

6.66 If we have adjusted your tax credit payments to avoid overpaying you for 2003–04, and you think we should not have made the adjustment because the overpayment was our mistake, you should contact the Tax Credit Office or Helpline. We will consider whether to make additional payments to you to correct the position.

Cases where payment would cause hardship

6.67 After considering the facts in individual cases, we may decide not to collect all or part of an overpayment of tax credit, or to allow you more time to pay, if payment would cause you and your family hardship.

What factors we will take into account

6.68 We will look sympathetically at your proposals for paying us what you owe but we must take account of all the circumstances before we make a decision. We may need to talk to you before we make a decision and may ask for more information.

When we consider whether it would cause you and your family hardship if we tried to recover an overpayment, or whether we should agree to you paying back the amount over a period of time, we will take account of

- your current and future income and essential living expenses
- your savings, investments and other assets which you could use over the short to medium term to make the payments - these might make it more appropriate to delay payment than not ask for payment at all
- your other liabilities, for example, repayments of your mortgage, rent or rent arrears, overpayments of social security benefits or other debts
- whether you are due to make other payments to us, and how paying the current debt over a period of time might affect them
- how long it will take you to pay back the overpayment
- your previous payment history with us
- whether paying what you owe us would result in you not being able to afford essential services, such as gas, electricity or water, immediately or over time, because you would not be able to continue paying those bills if you were paying back your debt to us
- whether you have a child or children under five or a chronically ill or disabled person in the family whose health could be affected by your paying back the debt, even over an extended period
- any other factors which are relevant.

If you have difficulty making a payment when it is due

If you are due to make a payment to us but do not expect to be able to make it when it is due, you should tell us immediately. Contact the Helpline at the number shown on your end of year notice, notice to pay or reminder. 6.69

When you contact us, we will ask

- for the reference number shown on the latest correspondence from us and any other information we need to identify the right tax credit bill
- how much you can pay on the date the payment is due, and
- when you will be able to pay the rest.

Your local Citizens Advice Bureau or other local advice centre, or your accountant or tax adviser, can help you to work out what level of payment you could reasonably afford.

If you do not keep to a payment arrangement with us without telling us, we will have to pursue what you have not paid in the same way as any other debt, taking legal proceedings to recover the debt if necessary.

If you miss making a payment to us

If you miss the date for making a payment to us, we will get in touch to remind you and give you the chance to pay before we take further action. 6.70

If you still do not pay what you owe, we will contact you again. This may be by letter or by telephone. If we have been unable to get in touch with you, we may try to contact you by visiting you at your home or, if you are self-employed, at your business premises. We may ask you to call at our offices. You can call at a local office convenient for you, for example, close to your home or work.

We will deal promptly with letters from you or from anyone acting for you and will normally reply **within 28 days**. If we cannot reply quickly, for instance because of the amount or complexity of the material you have sent us, or because we have to involve another office, we will let you know the reason for the delay and say when you can expect a response.

If we visit you, we will show you identification to prove who we are.

What we will do if you continue not to pay

Our action will depend upon the circumstances and, in particular, the amount you owe, your previous payment history, your financial circumstances and the extent to which you have kept us informed. 6.71

If we cannot agree a payment arrangement with you or you have not replied to our requests, we will, as a last resort, take steps to enforce payment. Any enforcement action may involve legal costs, which you have to pay. We will always try to get in touch with you before we do this.

Who will we talk to about your tax credit affairs?

Confidentiality

6.72 You have the right to the same degree of confidentiality about tax credit repayment matters as you have about all other aspects of your tax credit affairs.

If you visit our offices, you can, if you wish, discuss your affairs in a private room where you cannot be overheard.

Representation by someone else

6.73 If you prefer, we will deal with someone else on your behalf. This might be a voluntary sector adviser (such as a Citizens Advice Bureau), your accountant or other professional adviser or a friend or relative.

If you want us to write to them or to discuss your affairs with them over the telephone, we will need written authority from you on a form 64–8 or a short (signed) letter, to confirm that we can do so. The letter, signed by you, should include your full name, address, postcode and any tax credit reference number you have. If you have claimed tax credits as a couple and you want us to discuss matters relevant to both of you with someone else, we will need written authority from both you and your partner.

If we do not already have authority from you, another person may still phone one of our contact centres on your behalf, as long as we are satisfied that you are present with them at the time and you confirm that you are happy for us to speak to them. For couples, we will need both you and your partner to confirm that you are happy for us to speak to someone else on your behalf if you want us to discuss matters that are relevant to both of you.

You will always remain personally responsible for the information provided by another person on your behalf and for paying back overpaid tax credit, and, if we cannot make any progress with them, we will contact you directly. We will also continue to send you copies of important documents as well, unless an appointee is acting for you.

Keeping you informed

6.74 You can ask us at any time to explain your rights, or why we have taken a particular action, or what you are obliged to do under the law in any given situation. Our leaflet IR141 'Open Government' also gives more information about this.

How to complain

6.75 If you have a complaint and matters are not resolved to your satisfaction so that you want to take things further, please tell us. You can contact us by

- phone on **0151 966 1151**
- fax on **01772 239067**, or
- writing to

Tax Credit Office
Preston
PR1 0SB.

For more information about how to make a complaint, or taking cases to the Adjudicator or the Ombudsman, please see our leaflet COP1 "Putting things right. How to complain."

GENERAL NOTE

This leaflet was issued in December 2003. The final part of the leaflet, "Further information" has not been included. 6.76

INDEX